Students, please read this page carefully. Sign it and, for campus
your professor or teaching assistant the first week of classes. For distance learning
students, please sign it, make a PDF, and send it as an email attachment to your professor
the first week of class.

FMS 300: Television and Cultural Studies
Code of Academic Integrity

You are expected to turn in original work for this course. Quotations or ideas
paraphrased from other work must be properly cited. Taking credit for another's ideas or
writing is plagiarism, which is a serious violation of the University's Code of Academic
Integrity (http://www.asu.edu/studentaffairs/studentlife/srr/index.htm)

In the "Student Academic Integrity Manual," ASU define "plagiarism [as] using
another's words, ideas, materials, or work without properly acknowledging and
documenting the source. Students are responsible for knowing the rules governing the
use of another's work or materials and for acknowledging and documenting the source
appropriately."

Academic dishonesty, including inappropriate collaboration, will not be tolerated. There
are severe sanctions for cheating, plagiarizing, and any other form of dishonesty.

Your signature indicates your understanding of ASU's Code of Academic Integrity and
definition regarding plagiarism.

_____   _____

Name   Date

Film and Media Studies
PO BOX 870402
Tempe, AZ 85287-0402

film.asu.edu
(480) 965-6747
(480) 965-9110 fax

COLLEGE of LIBERAL ARTS & SCIENCES

ARIZONA STATE UNIVERSITY

Dear Student,

Welcome to your custom textbook! This book represents a unique opportunity for the faculty in Film and Media Studies (FMS) at Arizona State University (ASU) to tailor material to your specific course and to offer it to you at an affordable price. Although designed to support FMS 300: Television and Cultural Studies, at ASU, we have designed this book to appeal to courses that cover this topic at other universities across the country.

Film and Media Studies professors have taken great care and attention in selecting the most relevant and contemporary readings for each book. Rather than trying to fit a given course around a general text, we have instead planned each textbook so that the chosen readings pertain to specific course lessons. This way, all the learning material for your FMS course, including screenings, lectures, clips, and interactive features, dovetails precisely with your readings.

To flexibly serve all of our students, we have designed the textbook to be used both in-class and online. This is particularly important to our students as the program accrues an ever-larger online profile. We have dozens of online classes either existing or in development to support an online undergraduate major and online graduate MAS programs. We also serve students in other film and media programs across the country and around the world.

Film and Media Studies at ASU has devised this textbook as a way to keep the cost manageable for students. We have been able to assemble a wealth of material in each book; material that acquired independently might have necessitated that the student buy a number of books. The comprehensive nature of our selected readings allows students to buy one reasonably priced book only. Film and Media Studies also gives students the option of purchasing the eBook version of this textbook compared to the paperback, further reducing costs and protecting the environment at the same time.

The faculty hopes that you are as excited about the material as we are. Because FMS has chosen articles and book chapters that we find most interesting and applicable, these books are a joy for us to teach. We hope that you take the same pleasure in reading and studying them as we did in putting them together.

Feel free to contact us at filminfo@asu.edu. To learn more about our program and online offerings, please visit our website at www.film.asu.edu.

Sincerely,

Daniel Bernardi, PhD
Director

U.S. Television and Cultural Studies

Bambi Haggins, Editor
Arizona State University

Custom Publishing

New York   Boston   San Francisco
London   Toronto   Sydney   Tokyo   Singapore   Madrid
Mexico City   Munich   Paris   Cape Town   Hong Kong   Montreal

Pearson
Custom Publishing
is a division of

www.pearsonhighered.com

ISBN 10: 0-558-31619-0
ISBN 13: 978-0-558-31619-8

Copyright Acknowledgments

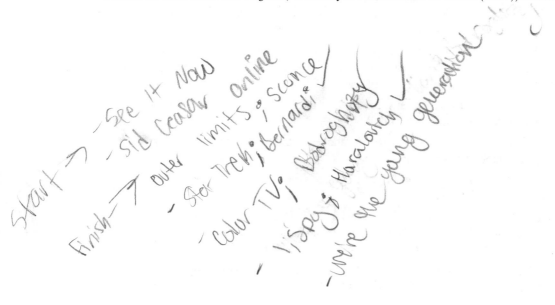

Contents

PART I

*In the Beginning:
Televisualizing the
American Dream*

Television: Boon or Bane?

Jack Gould

Television, according to "the promotional genii of Radio Row," will revolutionize education and entertainment, and automatically "enrich our culture beyond our fondest dreams." But Mr. Gould, Radio Editor of the New York Times, *points out that television can be a menace of frightening proportions to American culture. Like aural broadcasting, television is apt to become subservient to the selling of merchandise. Irritating advertising and innocuous programs may force themselves on us in a startling new dimension. Seeing in this situation a challenge to community leaders, the author specifically notes the responsibility of educators to contribute more than snobbish criticism to the development of the new medium.*

Some years ago, Elmer Rice, the playwright, enthralled a Town Hall audience in New York by asserting, "I've been saying for twenty years the theatre was dead." Knowing Elmer, theatre folk accepted his redundancy with quiet good humor, the Sardi luncheon set good-manneredly keeping their titters to a minimum.

In television, however, life is different. Any number of self-anointed prophets have been insisting for twenty years that television was alive and in the stillness of executive luncheon clubs atop mid-Manhattan skyscrapers there have been fervent "Amens." In periodic waves—the latest in the wake of the televising of the Louis-Conn waltz contest at Yankee stadium—the promotional genii of Radio Row have pulled out all stops and modestly predicted that our way of entertainment, our way of information, and our way of education are to be revolutionized by the elusive electron.

Without pause for breath or thought, the eager pamphleteers then continue to the inevitable conclusion that ipso facto television will be good for that entertainment, information and education. The mere addition of the sense of sight to the sense of hearing in the nation's homesteads, aver they, automatically will enrich our culture beyond our fondest dreams.

For television's own good, it is time to call a halt to this nonsense. Such talk confuses the idealistic potential of television with the practical probability of what television will bring. And on the latter basis it is no exaggeration to maintain that television represents right now more of a menace to American culture than it does a conceivable boon.

Fundamentally, the prevalent willingness to accept television's future without searching question is to disregard the great lesson of recent years. This is the fact that a scientific discovery is as nothing compared with what men will do with it, how they will use it. The advent of atomic energy was a turning point in civilization; yet what keeps the world awake at nights is not the bomb itself, but how it can be made to serve—and not destroy—us. In television, however, the bulk of thinking has taken, through carelessness or premeditated intention, a contrary course. It has been preoccupied with the marvel of sending pictures through the air and not with what kind of pictures would be sent.

What television presents in its truly vital and critical phase—management—is not a "new" industry at all, but rather an extension of an old one—radio. The radio broadcasters and radio equipment manufacturers are in the majority among applicants for television stations. As of old, the National Broadcasting Company and the Columbia Broadcasting System are jockeying for a dominant position, with the other chains hopeful of sharing what crumbs are left. On the sidelines, with the country's best-known talent in pocket, are several motion picture concerns, waiting to see whether television will fall on its face or whether they should try to absorb it.

Radio's Chain of Control

With radio people in television's saddle, it becomes pertinent to examine briefly and realistically, for a change, the sinister chain down which actual control of a radio station runs. On paper and under the law, the people own the air, without which there can be no radio or television. They in turn delegate it to Congress. Congress has authorized the Federal Communications Commission to allot the space in the air. The FCC licenses a person as a broadcaster. The broadcaster sells time to a sponsor. The sponsor engages an advertising agency to prepare a program. The agency hopes that the program will sell goods.

In other words, what we hear is actually decided by persons whom the public does not know and has never heard of—the agency executive. In newspapers and magazines, which understandably see no reason to give free advertising space regularly to products or sponsors, radio shows are popularly spoken of as an "NBC program" or a "CBS show," and indeed the chains for promotional reasons have done nothing to discourage the practice. But in actual fact, what we hear primarily are shows conceived and prepared by Young and Rubicam; J. Walter Thompson; Foote, Cone and Belding, etc. The network today by most accurate definition is a "time broker" and only incidentally and half-heartedly for the most part—when there is unsold or "sustaining" time to be filled—a creative force.

In this writer's opinion, the advertising fraternity has perhaps carried an unreasonable share of the recent criticism directed against excessive commercialism on the air. Again, it is a question of confusing the fact with the reason for it. Granted that the "L.S.M.F.T." routine is objectionable on the Jack Benny show, the reason for it is that NBC hasn't stopped it. It can if it wants to.

With their sights fixed on one main objective—the sale of merchandise—it is foolhardy to expect the advertising agencies to resist the laws of human nature and not do their utmost to achieve that sale. If the *Saturday Evening Post* permitted an advertisement to be inserted midway in its lead article of the week, the advertiser would be foolish not to grab it. If the whole story could be conceived to aid the product—have the heroines always say they took Lux baths and not just baths—what advertiser could resist the chance? That is exactly what has happened in radio.

An understanding of what the contemporary program sponsor is seeking to accomplish explains why that program so often may be antithetical to the best interests of entertainment and education. No sponsor seriously attempts to justify the interruption of a dramatic performance or an important news broadcast for commercial advertising as either good radio or good listening. But he does and has justified the middle commercial as being good advertising and good for his business. In the honest words of the late George Washington Hill, president of the American Tobacco Company, the sponsor is not in the business of entertaining the public, but of selling his merchandise.

Television and Economic Pressure

This recitation of the entrenched position of the advertiser in the entertainment and cultural phase of broadcasting is not intended to rake over old coals only recently reignited by the Federal Communications Commission report on program balance, but rather as the only possible means of introducing one's self to television.

For television by its very nature, if the laissez faire of radio is passively accepted, will prove not a brake on subservience to the dollar bill, but rather an impetus of almost incalculable and alarming potential. The expense of television can scarcely be imagined, if all those wonderful predictions made for it are to be realized. The task of presenting even a few hours of television weekly, not to say a full schedule comparable to today's radio, will run into untold millions of dollars. Whether projected by film or "live" actors, there is the problem of costumes, settings, lighting, and rehearsing wholly unknown to radio, and the unions have made it clear that they do not intend to miss out on this new gravy train. The real estate needs for television studio space will be immense. Equipment requirements, including relaying facilities, will be exceptionally costly, particularly at first.

Unlike radio, which started on a financial shoe string and in twenty-five years burgeoned forth as a multi-million dollar industry, television has required and will continue to require for several years a very substantial capital investment. Some experts have estimated conservatively that a new television broadcaster had best be prepared to lose $250,000 annually for the next five years, with the chance then that his equipment may be seriously out of date if not hopelessly obsolescent.

As can be seen, the television broadcaster is going to be under severe economic pressure to keep his head above water and this truism already has resulted in two obvious results: (a) television will be possible only for those with very substantial resources, and (b) there will be every incentive to cut corners in regard to preserving the medium's integrity if badly-needed income is thereby obtained.

Irritation in a New Dimension

Already television has started down radio's path. The advertising agencies have been invited by the two major chains, CBS and NBC, to continue their activities in program preparation, and the results have been exactly what might have been expected. The emphasis again is on the selling function and not on television for itself.

This manifestation already has provided the cartoonists a field day, but what the cartoonists may not appreciate is that it is no joke actually to sit through many of television's commercials. A glass company offered a playlet which had a foursome sitting at the dinner table. As each course progressed, the diners dwelt at length on the merits of the different type of glassware on the table, with particular emphasis on the patented "lip."

After just finishing your own dinner, watch if you will, the preparation of a batch of macaroni garnished by superlatives from the announcer. Amuse yourself witnessing how easily this soap washes out dainties. Or eavesdrop on mine hero of the drawing room comedy commenting on the delicious such-and-such coffee being served and then resuming the play's *bon mots*. Those are but indications from which one may draw his own conclusions when he realizes that patent medicines are among the most advertised products on the air.

In short, what television promises is the irritation, the insistence, and repetition of today's radio advertising in a new dimension. No longer will it be just heard, but it will become truly alive before our own eyes! Mr. Heatter will not talk of that hair tonic; he will rub it into his scalp so that we can all see how it's done night after night. Will Helen Hayes switch from "Victoria Regina" to a kind word for "my sponsor" and then back to Lawrence Housemann's work?

The Dangers of Commercialism

Grim as these evident probabilities may be, the greater danger lies in the fact that commercialism already threatens to undermine television as a positive social force in the community. As the record of radio has so vividly demonstrated, the understandably cautious approach of the advertiser, ever anxious not to offend, is wholly incompatible with a vigorous, articulate and progressive medium.

The great weakness of radio today is that the key figure is the least recognized. He is the writer, the man who, radio could remember, provides the funny lines which make the comedian and the breathless beauty of phrase which makes a Cornell or a Bergman shine anew. If he is not liberated from an agency's shackles of timidity, the added expanse of a visible stage will prove only an embarrassment and a handicap. Unless those who would run television undergo an intellectual purging from within, the video art's accomplishment will be only to compound with sight the innocuity of today.

The tragedy of television is that thus far it is just being allowed to drift into being without serious thought as to where it should go or what it should do. Internal strife over technical matters already has torn the industry asunder; and before it has even really started, a dog-eat-dog philosophy prevails. There has been no serious discussion on standards of taste, no consideration of how much advertising copy can be tolerated within a given period without jeopardizing television, no appreciation of the fact that the coming of television provides a propitious moment for the radio man to "save face" and recapture his soul, to assume the leadership which his license from the government implies.

Television's leaders in carefully prepared handouts made a great to-do over broadcasting pictures of the first United Nations sessions in New York, but scarcely noticed was the fact that the same men largely refused to oust a soap opera on a radio chain so that millions could partake of the historic moment when Gromyko first walked out. The public service opportunities of television are lavishly extolled to all who will listen, but those who would perform it cannot quite bring themselves to disturb radio's evening schedule so that they can do that job properly.

If the truth be said, more than a few radio men envision television as a way out of the stagnation which has paralyzed aural broadcasting. It is a bright star on the horizon, providing a tactful escape from facing reality, from recognizing that a deeper and wider use rather than abuse of the airwaves, whether they carry sound or sight, is clearly necessary. That they would thus cynically sacrifice a medium which could provide untold enlightenment for society is beside the point.

The Challenge to Educators

But if the prospective television broadcaster seems ill prepared for the tremendous responsibility which soon will be his, so, too, are those who would most regret his failure—the community leader, the clergy, and, particularly, the educator. For there is no more shameful page in American culture than that those who could best aid and further broadcasting have for the most part deliberately ignored it or only kibitzed on the side.

Countless numbers of the nation's colleges from time to time have prepared painstaking brochures dissecting radio, and professors as a class are among broadcasting's more articulate critics; yet, by and large, education has refused to participate in radio. When radio began, education did not understand it and resigned without a fight to commercial interests coveting the few available wave lengths. When education did take to the air, it was generally a colossal bore because the ivory tower was not left behind but brought into the studio.

In recent years, the Federal Communications Commission has undergone a major change of heart and has purposely broadened the opportunities for educational institutions to assume their logical function ideally suited to their capabilities. Yet while the howl goes on about Radio Row's inadequacies, they themselves have sought a distressingly low number of frequency modulation permits and but a handful of television applications.

The educator must stop playing the role of the snob in so far as radio and television are concerned if he would not have his classroom efforts negated by insidious and subtle commercial forces hostile to the culture to which he has dedicated his life. If radio's Corwinesque pretense at literature disturbs the English teacher, is not the English teacher's default in radio in part responsible?

Television affords a golden opportunity for the educational institution. The development of the art from the creative standpoint has to all intents and purposes barely started, and the school is not automatically at the disadvantage which prevails if it now goes into radio. What the school may lack in expensive equipment it can more than equal in the direly needed imagination and progressiveness which it should not be afraid to offer.

Financing, indeed, may be a very real problem, but a television station certainly should be at least considered on the same favorable basis as a new building or another survey on radio's influence on American behavior. In many cases television may be integrated with a wide variety of courses—the sciences, the theatre, public opinion, psychology, debating, current events—and, indeed, it should be.

Conclusions

At all events, television must have what radio has not—an alert, articulate, and critical audience which can make its influence felt. The present conspiracy of silence attendant to television's birth is an ill omen for its future. All those engaged in the arts, sciences, and politics must show a greater awareness of what television will mean if it serves them, and they do not serve it. If we want it to be, television can be a blessing such as rarely comes to mankind. If we are uninterested or indifferent to it—as we are now—it can be a veritable menace of frightening proportions.

The Meaning of Memory: Family, Class, and Ethnicity in Early Network Television Programs

George Lipsitz

Almost every Friday night between 1949 and 1956, millions of Americans watched Rosemary Rice turn the pages of an old photograph album. With music from Edvard Grieg's "Holverg Suite" playing in the background, and with pictures of turn-of-the-century San Francisco displayed on the album pages, Rice assumed the identity of her television character, Katrin Hansen, on the CBS network program *Mama*. She told the audience about her memories of her girlhood, her family's house on Steiner Street, and her experiences there with her big brother Nels, her little sister Dagmar, her Papa, and her Mama— "most of all," she said, "when I remember that San Francisco of so long ago, I remember Mama" (Meehan and Ropes 1954).

Katrin Hansen's memories of her Norwegian immigrant working-class family had powerful appeal for viewers in the early years of commercial network broadcasting. *Mama* established itself as one of CBS' most popular programs during its first season on the air, and it retained high ratings for the duration of its prime time run (Mitz 1983:458). The show's popularity coincided with that of other situation comedies based on ethnic working-class family life—*The Goldbergs*, depicting the experiences of Jews in the Bronx; *Amos 'n Andy*, blacks in Harlem; *The Honeymooners* and *Hey Jeannie*, Irish working-class families in Brooklyn; *Life with Luigi*, Italian immigrants in Chicago; and *Life of Riley*, working-class migrants to Los Angeles during and after World War II.[1]

The presence of this subgenre of ethnic, working-class situation comedies on television network schedules seems to run contrary to the commercial and artistic properties of the medium. Television delivers audiences to advertisers by glorifying consumption, not only during commercial breaks but in the programs themselves (Barnouw 1979). The relative economic deprivation of ethnic working-class households would seem to provide an inappropriate setting for the display and promotion of commodities as desired by the networks and their commercial sponsors. Furthermore, the mass audience required to repay the expense of network programming encourages the depiction of a homogenized mass society, not the particularities and peculiarities of working-class communities. As an artistic medium, television's capacity for simultaneity conveys a sense of living in an infinitely renewable present—a quality inimical to the sense of history permeating shows about working-class life. Yet whether set in the distant past like *Mama*, or located in the contemporaneous present, the subgenre of ethnic working-class situation comedies in early network television evoked concrete historical associations and memories in their audiences (Boorstin 1973:392–397).

Anomalous to the commercial and artistic properties of television, these programs also ran counter to the dominant social trends in the era in which they were made. They presented ethnic families in working-class urban neighborhoods at the precise historical moment when a rising standard

8

TABLE I

Program	Ethnicity	Occupations	Location	Dwelling
Mama	Norwegian	Carpenter	San Francisco	house
The Goldbergs	Jewish	Tailor/Small Business	Bronx/Long Island	apartment/house
Amos 'n Andy	Black	Cab Driver/Hustler	Harlem	apartment
The Honeymooners	Irish	Bus Driver/Sewer Worker	Brooklyn	apartment
Life with Luigi	Italian	Shopkeeper	Chicago	apartment
Life of Riley	Irish	Machinist	Los Angeles	duplex/cottage
Hey Jeannie	Scottish/Irish	Cab Driver	Brooklyn	apartment

of living, urban renewal, and suburbanization contributed to declines in ethnic and class identity.[2] They showed working-class families struggling for material satisfaction and advancement under conditions far removed from the *embourgeoisement* of the working-class celebrated in popular literature about the postwar era. They displayed value conflicts about family identity, consumer spending, ethnicity, class, and gender roles that would appear to be disruptive and dysfunctional within a communications medium primarily devoted to stimulating commodity purchases (see Table 1).

The dissonance between ethnic working-class situation comedies and their artistic, commercial, and historical surroundings might be explained by the persistence of artistic clichés and the conservatism of the entertainment business. Though four of these seven television programs previously existed as radio serials, radio popularity did not guarantee adaptation to television: many successful radio series never made that transition, and television networks actually made more profit from productions specially created for the new medium (Allen 1985:126, 164; de Cordova 1985). Even when radio programs did become television shows, they underwent significant changes in plot and premise. Television versions of urban ethnic working-class situation comedies placed more emphasis on nuclear families and less on extended kinship relations and ethnicity than did their radio predecessors.[3] Those changes reflect more than the differences between television and radio as media: they illuminate as well significant transformations in U.S. society during the 1950s, and they underscore the important role played by television in explaining and legitimizing those transitions to a mass audience.

More than their shared history in radio or their reliance on common theatrical traditions from vaudeville and ethnic theater unites the subgenre of urban ethnic working-class situation comedies. Through indirect but powerful demonstration, all of these shows arbitrated complex tensions caused by economic and social change in postwar America. They evoked the experiences of the past to lend legitimacy to the dominant ideology of the present. In the process they served important social and cultural functions, not just in returning profits to investors or attracting audiences for advertisers, but most significantly as a means of ideological legitimation for a fundamental revolution in economic, social, and cultural life.

The Meaning of Memory

In the midst of extraordinary social change, television became the most important discursive medium in American culture. As such, it was charged with special responsibilities for making new economic and social relations credible and legitimate to audiences haunted by ghosts from the past. Urban ethnic working-class situation comedies provided one means of addressing the anxieties and contradictions emanating from the clash between the consumer present of the 1950s and collective social memory about the 1930s and 1940s.

The consumer consciousness emerging from economic and social change in postwar America conflicted with the lessons of historical experience for many middle- and working-class American families. The Great Depression of the 1930s had not only damaged the economy, it also undercut the political and cultural legitimacy of American capitalism. Herbert Hoover had been a national hero in the 1920s, with his credo of "rugged individualism" forming the basis for a widely shared cultural ideal. But the depression discredited Hoover's philosophy and made him a symbol of yesterday's blasted hopes to millions of Americans. In the 1930s, cultural ideals based on mutuality and collectivity eclipsed the previous decade's "rugged individualism" and helped propel massive union organizing drives, anti-eviction movements, and general strikes. President Roosevelt's New Deal attempted to harness and co-opt that grass roots mass activity in an attempt to restore social order and recapture credibility and legitimacy for the capitalist system (Romasco 1965). The social welfare legislation of the "Second New Deal" in 1935 went far beyond any measures previously favored by Roosevelt and most of his advisors, but radical action proved necessary for the Administration to contain the upsurge of activism that characterized the decade. Even in the private sector, industrial corporations made more concessions to workers than naked power realities necessitated because they feared the political consequences of mass disillusionment with the system (Berger 1982).

World War II ended the depression and brought prosperity, but it did so on a basis even more collective than the New Deal of the 1930s. Government intervention in the wartime economy reached unprecedented levels, bringing material reward and shared purpose to a generation raised on the deprivation and sacrifice of the depression. In the postwar years, the largest and most disruptive strike wave in American history won major improvements in the standard of living for the average worker, both through wage increases and through government commitments to insure full employment, decent housing, and expanded educational opportunities. Grass roots militancy and working-class direct action wrested concessions from a reluctant government and business elite—mostly because the public at large viewed workers' demands as more legitimate than the desires of capital (Lipsitz 1981).

Yet the collective nature of working-class mass activity in the postwar era posed severe problems for capital. In sympathy strikes and secondary boycotts, workers placed the interests of their class ahead of their own individual material aspirations. Strikes over safety and job control far outnumbered wage strikes, revealing aspirations to control the process of production that conflicted with capitalist labor-management relations. Mass demonstrations demanding government employment and housing programs indicated a collective political response to problems previously adjudicated on a personal level. Radical challenges to the authority of capital (like the 1946 United Auto Workers' strike demand that wage increases come out of corporate profits rather than from price hikes passed on to consumers), demonstrated a social responsibility and a commitment toward redistributing wealth, rare in the history of American labor (Lipsitz 1981:47–50).

Capital attempted to regain the initiative in the postwar years by making qualified concessions to working-class pressures for redistribution of wealth and power. Rather than paying wage increases out of corporate profits, business leaders instead worked to expand the economy through increases in government spending, foreign trade, and consumer debt. Such expansion could meet the demands of workers and consumers without undermining capital's dominant role in the economy. On the presumption that "a rising tide lifts all boats," business leaders sought to connect working-class aspirations for a better life to policies that insured a commensurate rise in corporate profits, thereby leaving the distribution of wealth unaffected. Federal defense spending, highway construction programs, and home loan policies expanded the economy at home in a manner conducive to the interests of capital, while the Truman Doctrine and Marshall Plan provided models for enhanced access to foreign markets and raw materials for American corporations. The Taft-Hartley Act of 1947 banned the class-conscious collective activities most threatening to capital (mass strikes, sympathy strikes, secondary boycotts); the leaders of labor, government, and business accepted as necessity the practice of paying wage hikes for organized workers out of the pockets of consumers and unorganized workers, in the form of higher prices (Lipsitz 1981).

Commercial network television played an important role in this emerging economy, functioning as a significant object of consumer purchases as well as an important marketing medium. Sales of sets jumped from three million during the entire decade of the 1940s to over five million *a year* during the 1950s (*TV Facts* 1980:141). But television's most important economic function came from its role as an instrument of legitimation for transformations in values initiated by the new economic imperatives of postwar America. For Americans to accept the new world of 1950s' consumerism, they had to make a break with the past. The depression years had helped generate fears about installment buying and excessive materialism, while the new Deal and wartime mobilization had provoked suspicions about individual acquisitiveness and upward mobility. Depression era and wartime scarcities of consumer goods had led workers to internalize discipline and frugality while nurturing networks of mutual support through family, ethnic, and class associations. Government policies after the war encouraged an atomized acquisitive consumerism at odds with the lessons of the past. At the same time, federal home loan policies stimulated migrations to the suburbs from traditional, urban ethnic working-class neighborhoods. The entry of television into the American home disrupted previous patterns of family life and encouraged fragmentation of the family into separate segments of the consumer market.[4] The priority of consumerism in the economy at large and on television may have seemed organic and unplanned, but conscious policy decisions by officials from both private and public sectors shaped the contours of the consumer economy and television's role within it.

Commercial Television and Economic Change

Government policies during and after World War II shaped the basic contours of home television as an advertising medium. Government-sponsored research and development during the war perfected the technology of home television while federal tax policies solidified its economic base. The government allowed corporations to deduct the cost of advertising from their taxable incomes during the war, despite the fact that rationing and defense production left business with few products to market. Consequently, manufacturers kept the names of their products before the public while lowering their tax obligations on high wartime profits. Their advertising expenditures supplied radio networks and advertising agencies with the capital reserves and business infrastructure that enabled them to dominate the television industry in the postwar era. After the war, federal antitrust action against the motion picture studios broke up the "network" system in movies, while the FCC sanctioned the network system in television. In addition, FCC decisions to allocate stations on the narrow VHF band, to grant the networks ownership and operation rights over stations in prime markets, and to place a freeze on the licensing of new stations during the important years between 1948 and 1952 all combined to guarantee that advertising-oriented programming based on the model of radio would triumph over theater TV, educational TV, or any other form (Boddy 1985; Allen 1983). Government decisions, not market forces, established the dominance of commercial television, but these decisions reflected a view of the American economy and its needs which had become so well accepted at the top levels of business and government that it had virtually become the official state economic policy.

Fearing both renewed depression and awakened militancy among workers, influential corporate and business leaders considered increases in consumer spending—increases of 30% to 50%— to be necessary to perpetuate prosperity in the postwar era (Lipsitz 1981:46, 120–121). Defense spending for the Cold War and Korean Conflict had complemented an aggressive trade policy to improve the state of the economy, but it appeared that the key to an expanding economy rested in increased consumer spending fueled by an expansion of credit (Moore and Klein 1967; Jezer 1982). Here too, government policies led the way, especially with regard to stimulating credit purchases of homes and automobiles. During World War II, the marginal tax rate for most wage earners jumped from 4% to 25%, making the home ownership deduction more desirable. Federal housing loan policies favored construction of new single family detached suburban housing over renovation or construction of central city multifamily units. Debt-encumbered home ownership in accord with these policies stimulated construction of 30 million new housing units in just twenty years, bringing the percentage of home-owning Americans from below 40% in 1940 to more than 60% by 1960. Mortgage policies encouraging long term debt and low down payments freed capital for other consumer purchases, while government highway building policies undermined mass transit systems and contributed to increased demand for automobiles (Hartman 1982:165–168). Partly as a result of these policies, consumer spending on private cars averaged $7.5 billion per year in the 1930s and 1940s, but grew to $22 billion per year in 1950 and almost $30 billion by 1955 (Mollenkopf 1983:111).

For the first time in U.S. history, middle-class and working-class families could routinely expect to own homes or buy new cars every few years. Between 1946 and 1965 residential mortgage debt rose three times as fast as the gross national product and disposable income. Mortgage debt accounted for just under 18% of disposable income in 1946, but it grew to almost 55% by 1965 (Stone 1983:122). In order to insure eventual payment of current debts, the economy had to generate tremendous expansion and growth, further stimulating the need to increase consumer spending. Manufacturers had to find new ways of motivating consumers to buy ever increasing amounts of commodities, and television provided an important means of accomplishing that end.

Television advertised individual products, but it also provided a relentless flow of information and persuasion that placed acts of consumption at the core of everyday life. The physical fragmentation of suburban growth and declines in motion picture attendance created an audience more likely to stay at home and receive entertainment there than ever before. But television also provided a locus redefining American ethnic, class, and family identities into consumer identities. In order to accomplish this task effectively, television programs had to address some of the psychic, moral, and political obstacles to consumption among the public at large.

The television and advertising industries knew that they had to overcome these obstacles. Marketing expert and motivational specialist Ernest Dichter stated that "one of the basic problems of this prosperity is to give people that sanction and justification to enjoy it and to demonstrate that the hedonistic approach to life is a moral one, not an immoral one" (Jezer 1982:127). Dichter went on to note the many barriers that inhibited consumer acceptance of unrestrained hedonism, and he called on advertisers "to train the average citizen to accept growth of his country and its economy as *his* growth rather than as a strange and frightening event" (Dichter 1960:210). One method of encouraging that acceptance, according to Dichter, consisted of identifying new products and styles of consumption with traditional, historically sanctioned practices and behavior. He noted that such an approach held particular relevance in addressing consumers who had only recently acquired the means to spend freely and who might harbor a lingering conservatism based on their previous experiences (Dichter 1960:209).

Insecurities and anxieties among consumers compelled network television to address the complex legacies of the 1930s and 1940s in order to promote consumption in the 1950s. In the middle of its appeals to change the world in the present through purchase of the appropriate commodities, commercial network television in its early years also presented programs rooted in the historical experiences and aspirations of diverse working-class traditions. From the evocations of the depression era that permeated the world of *The Honeymooners*, to the recycled minstrel show stereotypes of *Amos 'n Andy*, from the textured layers of immigrant experience underpinning the drama and charm of *The Goldbergs* and *Mama*, to the reenactment of immigration in contemporaneous circumstances in *Life of Riley, Life with Luigi,* and *Hey Jeannie*, the medium of the infinitely renewable present turned to past traditions and practices in order to explain and legitimate fundamentally new social relations in the present.

Family Formation and the Economy—The Television View

Advertisers incorporated their messages into urban ethnic working-class comedies through indirect and direct means. Tensions developed in the programs often found indirect resolution in commercials. Thus Jeannie MacClennan's search for an American sweetheart in one episode of *Hey Jeannie* set up commercials proclaiming the abilities of Drene shampoo to keep one prepared to accept last minute dates and of Crest toothpaste to produce an attractive smile (*Hey Jeannie:* "The Rock and Roll Kid"). Conversations about shopping for new furniture in an episode of *The Goldbergs* directed viewers' attention to furnishings in the Goldberg home provided for the show by Macy's department store in exchange for a commercial acknowledgement (*The Goldbergs:* "The In-laws").

But the content of the shows themselves offered even more direct emphasis on consumer spending. In one episode of *The Goldbergs*, Molly expresses disapproval of her future daughter-in-law's plan to buy a washing machine on the installment plan. "I know Papa and me never bought anything unless we had the money to pay for it," she intones with logic familiar to a generation with memories of the Great Depression. Her son, Sammy, confronts this "deviance" by saying, "Listen, Ma, almost everybody in this country lives above their means—and everybody enjoys it." Doubtful at first, Molly eventually learns from her children and announces her conversion to the legitimacy of installment buying by proposing that the family buy two cars so as to "live above our means—the American way" (*The Goldbergs:* "The In-laws"). In a subsequent episode, Molly's daughter, Rosalie, assumes the role of ideological tutor to her mother. When planning a move out of their Bronx apartment to a new house in the suburbs, Molly ruminates about where to place her furniture in the new home. "You don't mean we're going to take all this junk with us into a brand new house?" asks an exasperated Rosalie. With traditionalist sentiment Molly answers, "Junk? My furniture's junk? My furniture that I lived with and loved for twenty years is junk?" But in the end she accepts Rosalie's argument—even selling off all her old furniture to help meet the down payment on the new house, and deciding to buy new furniture on the installment plan (*The Goldbergs:* "Moving Day").

Chester A. Riley confronts similar choices about family and commodities in *The Life of Riley*. His wife complains that he only takes her out to the neighborhood bowling alley and restaurant, not to "interesting places." Riley searches for ways to impress her and discovers from a friend that a waiter at the fancy Club Morambo will let them eat first and pay later, at a dollar a week plus ten percent interest. "Ain't that dishonest?" asks Riley. "No, it's usury," his friend replies. Riley does not borrow the money, but he impresses his wife anyway by taking the family out to dinner on the proceeds of a prize that he received for being the one-thousandth customer in a local flower shop. Though we eventually learn that Peg Riley only wanted attention, not an expensive meal, the happy ending of the episode hinges totally on Riley's prestige, restored when he demonstrates his ability to provide a luxury outing for the family (*Life of Riley:* R228).

The same episode of *The Life of Riley* reveals another consumerist element common to this subgenre. When Riley protests that he lacks the money needed to fulfill Peg's desires, she answers that he would have plenty if he didn't spend so much on "needless gadgets." His shortage of cash becomes a personal failing caused by incompetent behavior as a consumer. Nowhere do we hear about the size of his paycheck, relations between his union and his employer, or, for that matter, the relationship between the value of his labor and the wages paid to him by the Stevenson Aircraft Company. Like Uncle David in *The Goldbergs*—who buys a statue of Hamlet shaking hands with Shakespeare and an elk's tooth with the Gettysburg address carved on it—Riley's comic character stems in part from a flaw which in theory could be attributed to the entire consumer economy: a preoccupation with "needless gadgets." By contrast, Peg Riley's desire for an evening out is portrayed as reasonable and modest—as reparation due her for the inevitable tedium of housework. The solution to her unhappiness, of course, comes from an evening out rather than from a change in her own work circumstances. Even within the home, television elevates consumption over production; production is assumed to be a constant—only consumption can be varied. But more than enjoyment is at stake: unless Riley can provide her with the desired night on the town, he will fail in his obligations as a husband (*Life of Riley:* R228; *The Goldbergs:* "Bad Companions").

A similar theme provides the crisis in an episode of *Mama*. Dagmar, the youngest child, "innocently" expresses envy of a friend whose father received a promotion and consequently put up new wallpaper in his house. "Why doesn't Papa get promoted?" Dagmar chirps, "Everyone else does." When Mama explains that a carpenter makes less money than other fathers, Dagmar asks if it wouldn't be smarter for Papa to work in a bank. Overhearing this dialogue, Papa decides to accept his boss' offer to promote him to foreman, even though he knows it will ruin his friendships with the other workers. The logic of the episode instructs us that fathers will lose their standing if they disappoint their families' desires for new commodities (*Mama:* "Mama and the Carpenter"). Shows exploring tensions between family obligations and commodity purchases routinely assert that money cannot *buy* love, but they seem less clear about whether one can trade material wealth for affection. Even the usually self-absorbed Kingfish on *Amos 'n Andy* gives in to his nephew Stanley's wish for "a birthday party with lots of expensive presents," while Jeannie MacClennan's search for romance suffers a setback when a prospective suitor sees her shabby apartment with its antiquated furniture (*Amos 'n Andy*: "Andy the Godfather"; *Hey Jeannie*: "The Rock and Roll Kid"). On *The Goldbergs*, a young woman is forbidden to marry the man she loves because, her mother says, "I didn't raise my daughter to be a butcher's wife" (*The Goldbergs*: "Die Fledermaus"); and Alice Kramden in *The Honeymooners* can always gain the upper hand in arguments with her husband by pointing to his inadequacies as a provider. In each of these programs, consumer choices close the ruptures in personal relations, enabling the episode to reach narrative and ideological closure.

One episode of *Mama* typifies the confusion between consumer purchases and family happiness pervading urban ethnic working-class situation comedies in early network television. "Mama's Birthday," broadcast in 1954, delineated the tensions between family loyalty and consumer desire endemic to modern capitalist society. The show begins with Mama teaching Katrin to make Norwegian potato balls, the kind she used long ago to "catch" Papa. Unimpressed by this accomplishment, Katrin changes the subject and asks Mama what she wants for her upcoming birthday. In an answer that locates Mama within the gender roles of the 1950s she replies, "Well, I think a fine new job for your Papa. You and Dagmar to marry nice young men and have a lot of wonderful children—just like I have. And Nels, well, Nels to become president of the United States" (Meehan and Ropes 1954). In one sentence Mama has summed up the dominant culture's version of legitimate female expectations: success at work for her husband, marriage and childrearing for her daughters, the presidency for her son—and nothing for herself.

But we learn that Mama does have some needs, although we do not hear it from her lips. Her sister, Jenny, asks Mama to attend a fashion show, but Mama cannot leave the house because she has to cook a roast for a guest whom Papa has invited to dinner. Jenny comments that Mama never seems to get out of the kitchen, adding that "it's a disgrace when a woman can't call her soul her own," and "it's a shame that a married woman can't have some time to herself." The complaint is a valid one, and we can imagine how it might have resonated for women in the 1950s. The increased availability of household appliances and the use of synthetic fibers and commercially processed food should have decreased the amount of time women spent in housework, but surveys showed that homemakers spent the same number of hours per week (51 to 56) doing housework as they had done in the 1920s. Advertising and marketing strategies undermined the potential of technological changes by upgrading standards fo cleanliness in the home and expanding desires for more varied wardrobes and menus for the average family (Hartmann 1982: 168). In that context, Aunt Jenny would have been justified in launching into a tirade about the division of labor within the Hansen household or about the possibilities for cooperative housework, but network television specializes in a less social and more commodified dialogue about problems like housework: Aunt Jenny suggests that her sister's family buy her a "fireless cooker"—a cast iron stove—for her birthday. "They're wonderful," she tells them in language borrowed from the rhetoric of advertising. "You just put your dinner inside them, close 'em up, and go where you please. When you come back your dinner is all cooked" (Meehan and Ropes 1954). Papa protests that Mama likes to cook on her woodburning stove, but Jenny dismisses that objection with an insinuation about his motive, when she replies, "Well, I suppose it *would* cost a little more than you could afford, Hansen" (Meehan and Ropes 1954).

By identifying a commodity as the solution to Mama's problem, Aunt Jenny unites the inner voice of Mama with the outer voice of the sponsors of television programs. Mama's utility as an icon of maternal selflessness would be compromised if she asked for the stove herself, but Aunt Jenny's role in suggesting the gift removes that taint of selfishness while adding the authority of an outside expert. Aunt Jenny's suggestion of hypocrisy in Papa's reluctance to buy the stove encourages the audience to resent him for not making enough money and even to see his poverty as a form of selfishness—denying his wife the comforts due her. In reality, we know that Aunt Jenny's advice probably contains the usual distortions of advertising claims, that even if the fireless cooker enabled Mama to go where she pleased while dinner cooked, it would bring with it different kinds of tasks and escalating demands. But in the fantasy world of television, such considerations do not intervene. Prodded by their aunt, the Hansen children go shopping and purchase the fireless cooker from a storekeeper who calls the product "the new Emancipation Proclamation—setting housewives free from their old kitchen range" (Meehan and Ropes 1954). Our exposure to advertising hyperbole should not lead us to miss the analogy here: housework is compared to slavery, and the commercial product takes on the aura of Abraham Lincoln. The shopkeeper's appeal convinces the children to pool their resources and buy the stove for Mama. But we soon learn that Papa plans to make a fireless cooker for Mama with his tools. When Mama discovers Papa's intentions she persuades the children to buy her another gift. Even Papa admits that his stove will not be as efficient as the one made in a factory, but Mama nobly affirms that she will like his better because he made it himself. The children use their money to buy dishes for Mama, and Katrin remembers the episode as Mama's happiest birthday ever (Meehan and Ropes 1954).

The stated resolution of "Mama's Birthday" favors traditional values. Mama prefers to protect Papa's feelings rather than having a better stove, and the product built by a family member has more value than one sold as a commodity. Yet the entire development of the plot leads in the opposite direction. The "fireless cooker" is the star of the episode, setting in motion all the other characters, and it has unquestioned value even in the face of Jenny's meddlesome brashness, Papa's insensitivity, and Mama's old-fashioned ideals. Buying a product is unchallenged as the true means of changing the unpleasant realities or low status of women's work in the home.

This resolution of the conflict between consumer desires and family roles reflected television's social role as mediator between the family and the economy. Surveys of set ownership showed no pronounced stratification by class, but a clear correlation between family size and television purchases: households with three to five people were most likely to own television sets, while those with only one person were least likely to own them. (Swanson and Jones 1951). The television industry recognized and promoted its privileged place within families in advertisements like the one in the *New York Times* in 1950 that proclaimed, "Youngsters today need television for their morale as much as they need fresh air and sunshine for their health" (Wolfenstein 1951). Like previous communications media, television sets occupied honored places in family living rooms, and helped structure family time; unlike other previous communications media, they displayed available commodities in a way that transformed all their entertainment into a glorified shopping catalogue.

Publicity about television programs stressed the interconnections between family and economy as well. Viewers took the portrayals of motherhood on these shows so seriously that when Peggy Wood of *Mama* appeared on the *Garry Moore Show* and asked for questions from the audience, women asked for advice about raising their families, as if she were actually Mama, rather than an actress playing that role (*TV Guide* 1954:11). The *Ladies Home Journal* printed an article containing "Mama's Recipes," featuring photographs of Peggy Wood, while Gertrude Berg wrote an article as Molly Goldberg for *TV Guide* that contained her recipes for borscht and blintzes. "Your meal should suit the mood of your husband," Berg explained. "If he's nervous give him a heavy meal. If he's happy a salad will do" (*Ladies Home Journal* 1956:130–131; *TV Guide* 1953A:7). Actors on the shows also ignored the contradictions between their on-stage and off-stage roles. Actress Marjorie Reynolds told *TV Guide* that she enjoyed playing Mrs. Chester A. Riley, because "I've done just about everything in films from westerns to no-voice musicals, and now with the Riley show, I'm back in the kitchen. Where every wife belongs" (*TV Guide* 1953B:17).

The focus on the family in early network television situation comedies involved a special emphasis on mothers. Images of long-suffering but loving mothers pervaded these programs and publicity about them. Ostensibly representations of "tradition," these images actually spoke to a radical rupture with the past: the establishment of the isolated nuclear family of the 1950s with its attendant changes in family gender roles. The wartime economic mobilization that ended the depression stimulated an extraordinary period of family formation that was in sharp contrast to the experience of preceding decades. Americans married more frequently, formed families at a younger age, and had more children in the 1940s than they had in the 1920s and 1930s (Hartmann 1982:164–165). The combination of permissive recommendations for childrearing and social changes attendant to increases in consumer spending isolated mothers as never before. Work previously shared with extended kinship and neighbor networks now had to be done by machines, at home in isolation. Childrearing took up more time and responsibility, but inflation and expanded consumer desires encouraged women to work outside the home for pay. When the conflicting demands of permissivism created guilt and feelings of inadequacy, outside authorities—from child psychologists to television programs—stood ready to provide "therapeutic" images of desired maternal behavior.

While placing special burdens on women, changes in family identity in the postwar era transformed the roles of all family members. As psychoanalyst Joel Kovel demonstrates, the decomposition of extended kinship networks made the nuclear family the center of the personal world, "a location of desire and intimacy not previously conceptualized" (Kovel 1978:13–14). Kovel argues that participation in civil society can keep individuals from sliding back into total narcissism, but that separation of family from society in modern capitalism blocks access to the public realm. The family becomes the locus of all social demands, lauded all the more in theory as its traditional social function disappears in practice. The family appears to be private and voluntary, yet its isolation from neighborhood and class networks leave it subject to extraordinary regulation and manipulation by outside authorities like psychologists and advertisers. The family appears to be the repository of mutuality and affection, but commodity society has truncated its traditional functions into the egoism of possession. The family appears to maintain the privileges and authority of patriarchy, but "like a house nibbled by termites," the outwardly strong appearance of patriarchy masks a collapsing infrastructure no longer capable of wielding authority in an increasingly administered and institutionalized society. According to Kovel, the demise of the traditional family creates a need for authority that becomes filled by the "administrative mode"—the structure of domination that offers commodities as the key to solving personal problems (Kovel 1978:13–14). Sociologist Nancy Chodorow draws a similar formulation in her observation that "the decline of the oedipal father creates an orientation to external authority and behavioral obedience" (Chodorow 1978:189). Chodorow also points out that the idealization of masculinity inherent in the "distant father" role in the nuclear family gives ideological priority to men, while channeling rebellion and resentment against the power wielded by the accessible and proximate mother. Kovel and Chodorow both stress that these patterns are neither natural nor inevitable: they emerge in concrete social circumstances where the nuclear family serves as the main base of support for consumer society (Chodorow 1978:181; Kovel 1978:19).

Commercial network television emerged as the primary discursive medium in American society at the precise historical moment that the isolated nuclear family and its concerns eclipsed previous ethnic, class, and political forces as the crucible of personal identity. Television programs both reflected and shaped that translation, defining the good life in family-centric, asocial, and commodity-oriented ways. As Todd Gitlin argues, "What is hegemonic in consumer capitalist ideology is precisely the notion that happiness, or liberty, or equality, or fraternity can be affirmed through existing private commodity forms, under the benign protective eye of the national security state" (Newcomb 1978). Yet the denigration of public issues and the resulting overemphasis on the home contained contradictions of their own. If the harmonious and mutually supportive family of the past granted moral legitimacy to the consumer dilemmas of urban, ethnic working-class families, the tensions of the modern nuclear household revealed the emerging nuclear family to be a contested terrain of competing needs and desires.

The structural tensions basic to the "father absent-mother present" gender roles of the nuclear family identified by Chodorow pervaded television portrayals of urban ethnic working-class life in the 1950s. Peg Riley, Alice Kramden, and Sapphire Stevens heroically endure their husbands' failures to deliver on promises of wealth and upward mobility, and they earn the sympathy of the audience by compensating for the incompetent social performance of their spouses. Yet their nagging insistence on practical reason also marks them as "shrews," out to undercut male authority. Male insensitivity to female needs forms the focal point of humor and sardonic commentary—as in the episode of *The Life of Riley* where Riley can't understand Peg's complaints about staying home all the time. "I can't figure her out," he tells his son. "She's got a home to clean, meals to cook, dishes to wash, you two kids to look after, floors to scrub—what more does she want?" (*Life of Riley*: R228). Few shows displayed hostility between husbands and wives as openly as *The Honeymooners*. (Even the title functioned as bitter irony.) When Alice employs sarcasm in response to Ralph's "get rich quick" schemes and his neglect of her needs, Ralph invariably clenches his fist and says, "one of these days, Alice, one of these days, pow! right in the kisser!" Coupled with his threats to send her "to the moon," the intimation of wife-beating remains a recurring "comic" premise in the show. Jackie Gleason told one interviewer that he thought many husbands felt the way Ralph did about their wives. And an article in *TV Guide* quoted an unnamed "famous" psychiatrist who contended that the program's popularity rested on male perceptions that women had too much power, and on female perceptions that male immaturity demonstrated the superiority of women (*TV Guide* 1955:14). *The Honeymooners* might end with a humbled Ralph Kramden telling Alice, "Baby, you're the greatest," but the show clearly "worked" because tensions between men and women spoke to the experiences and fears of the audience (see Table 2).

Structural tensions within families, women betrayed by irresponsible and incompetent husbands, and men chafing under the domination of their wives: hardly an ideal portrait of family life. These depictions reflected the fissures in a fundamentally new form of family, a form which increasingly dominated the world of television viewers. One might expect commercial television programs to ignore the problems of the nuclear family, but the industry's imperial ambition—the desire to have all households watching at all times—encouraged exploitation of the real problems confronting viewers. Censorship ruled out treatment of many subjects, but family tensions offered legitimate and fertile ground for television programs. Individuals cut off from previous forms of self-definition and assaulted by media images encouraging narcissistic anxieties had insatiable needs to survey the terrain of family problems, to seek relief from current tensions and assurance of the legitimacy of current social relations. In order to create subjects receptive to the appeals of advertisers and to achieve ideological and narrative closure for their own stories, the creators of television programs had to touch on real issues, albeit in truncated and idealized form. While they unfailingly offered only individual and codified solutions to those problems, the mere act of exposing the contradictions of the nuclear family created the structural potential for oppositional readings. Representation of generational and gender tensions undercut the legitimating authority of the televised traditional working-class family by demonstrating the chasm between memories of yesterday and the realities of today. If the programs remained true to the past, they lost their relevance to current tensions. Yet when they successfully addressed contemporary problems, they forfeited the legitimacy offered by the past and made it easier for their viewers to escape the pull of parochialism and paternal authority embedded in the traditional family form. This clash between the legitimizing promise of urban ethnic working-class shows and their propensity for exposing the shortcomings of both past and present social relations went beyond their treatment of family issues and extended as well to matters of work, class, and ethnicity.

TABLE 2

Program	Star's Gender	Children	Father or Male Lead	Mother or Female Lead	Extended Family
Mama	Female	Three	Distant but warm	Competent	Relatives/neighbors
The Goldbergs	Female	Two	Distant but warm	Competent	Relatives/neighbors
Amos 'n Andy	Male	None	Irresponsible	Hostile	Lodge brothers/ in-laws
The Honeymooners	Male	None	Irresponsible	Hostile	Neighbors
Life with Luigi	Male	None	Irresponsible	Warm	Neighbors
Life of Riley	Male	Two	Incompetent	Warm	Neighbors
Hey Jeannie	Female	None	Irresponsible	Competent	Neighbors/boarder

Work, Class, and Ethnicity

In addition to consumer issues, the changing nature of working-class identity also influenced the collective memory of viewers of ethnic urban working-class situation comedies in the 1950s. The decade of the 1940s not only witnessed an unprecedented transformation in the nature of the American family, but it also saw an extraordinary social upheaval among workers, which labor historian Stanley Aronowitz has characterized as "incipient class formation" (Aronowitz 1983). War mobilization reindustrialized the sagging U.S. economy, but also reconstituted the working class. Migrations to defense production centers and breakthroughs by women and blacks in securing industrial employment changed the composition of the work force. Traditional parochial loyalties waned as mass production and full employment created new work groups on the shop floor and new working-class communities outside the factory gates. Mass strikes and demonstrations united workers from diverse backgrounds into a polity capable of sustained collective action. Of course, racism and sexism remained pervasive on both institutional and grass roots levels, but the mass activity of the postwar era represented the stirrings of a class consciousness previously unknown in a proletariat deeply divided by ethnicity, race, and gender. By the 1950s, expanded consumer opportunities, suburbanization, and access to education offered positive inducements away from that class consciousness, while anti-Communism, purges, and restrictions on rank and file activism acted negatively to undercut trade unions as crucibles of class consciousness. Yet retentions of the incipient class formation of the 1940s percolated throughout the urban ethnic working-class situation comedies of the 1950s.

Jeannie Carson, the star of *Hey Jeannie*, began her career in show business by singing to Welsh miners as they came out of the pits. Appropriately enough, her U.S. television series adopted a working class locale—the home of Al Murray, a Brooklyn cab driver, and his sister Liz (*TV Guide* 1956:17). The setting imposed certain structural directions on the program's humor—directions that gave voice to sharp class resentments. One episode concerns Al Murray's efforts to hide his cab in a neighbor's garage so that he can take the day off from work to see his beloved Dodgers play baseball at Ebbetts Field. Sensing Murray's dereliction of duty, the cab company president delivers a self-righteous harangue about the evils of such behavior to his secretary. Pontificating about the social responsibilities of a taxicab company, "a public utility," he asks his secretary if she knows what happens when one of his cabs is not operating. "No, what?" she inquires. "It cuts into my profits," he responds. (*Hey Jeannie:* "Jeannie The Cabdriver"). Humor based on such hypocrisy by employers has a long history in working-class culture, but it is rarely the subject of mass media comedy. As the episode continues, the boss' secretary (in an act of solidarity) calls Liz and Jeannie to warn them that the boss is out on the streets looking for Al's cab. Jeannie takes the taxi out of the garage to prevent Al's boss from finding it there, but accustomed to driving in her native Scotland, she drives on the left side of the street and gets stopped by a police officer. The policeman discovers that she is an immigrant and lets her off with a warning, remembering his own days as a newly arrived immigrant from Ireland. The resolution of the show finds Jeannie getting to the ballpark in time to get Al back to the cab where his boss finds him and apologizes for even suspecting his employee of misconduct. The episode vibrates with class consciousness, from the many acts of solidarity that get Al off the hook to the final victory over the boss—a victory gained by turning work time into play time, and getting away with it. That kind of collective activity in pursuit of common goals appears frequently in the urban ethnic working-class situation comedies of the 1950s, in incidents ranging from a rent strike by tenants in *The Goldbergs* to community protest against destruction of a favorite neighborhood tree in *Life With Luigi* (*The Goldbergs:* "The Rent Strike"; *Life with Luigi:* "The Power Line").

Even though the workplace rarely appears in television comedies about working-class life, when it does provide a focus for comic or dramatic tensions, it also seethes with class resentments. On one episode of *Mama*, Lars Hansen tells another worker that he prefers working for Mr. Jenkins to working for Mr. Kingsley because "Mr. Jenkins doesn't lose his temper so much." Mr. Kingsley also demands speed-ups from the men and tries to pressure Papa into making the other workers produce at a faster pace (*Mama:* "Mama and the Carpenter"). In this episode, the workplace appears as a place where workers with common interests experience fragmentation. Even after Jake Goldberg graduates from his job as a tailor to become owner of a small dressmaking firm, work prevents him from enjoying life. Business pressures take him away from his family and prevent him from developing recreational interests. When Molly's Uncle David starts playing pool, Jake confides that he never learned to play because "pool is a game that requires leisure." However, his business sense causes him to lean over the table, touch it, and murmur with admiration, "nice quality felt, though" (*The Goldbergs:* "Bad Companions"). Jake's work brings in a bigger financial reward than Al Murray's cab driving or Lars Hansen's carpentry, but it still compels him to trade the precious minutes and hours of his life for commodities that he hardly has time to enjoy. Work as a noble end in itself is almost entirely absent from these shows. No work ethic or pride in labor motivates these workers. In fact, Ed Norton's pride in his job as a sewer worker provides a recurrent comic premise in *The Honeymooners*. The object of work in these programs consists of material reward to enhance one's family status or to obtain some leisure time commodity.

Work not only appears infrequently in 1950s comedies about working-class life, but blue-collar labor often appears as a stigma—a condition that retards the acquisition of desired goods. But even demeaning portrayals of working-class people contain contradictions, allowing for negotiated or oppositional readings. Advertisers and network officials pointed to Chester A. Riley's "magnificent stupidity" as the key to the big ratings garnered by *The Life of Riley*, but that "stupidity" sometimes masked other qualities. At a fancy dinner where the Rileys are clearly out of place, they meet a blue blood named Cecil Spencer Kendrick III. "You mean there's two more of you inside?" Riley asks. The audience laughter at his gaffe comes in part from resentment against the antidemocratic pretensions of Kendrick and his associates (*Life of Riley:* R228). Similarly, when Riley's neighbor, Jim Gillis, tries to impress him with tales about the fancy food at an expensive restaurant, Riley gets Gillis to admit that crepes suzette are nothing more than "pancakes soaked in kerosene and then set on fire" (*Life of Riley:* R228). That sense of the unintentional insight also propels the malaprop-laden humor of Molly Goldberg. Who could dispute her self-sacrificing virtue when Molly vows to save money by getting old furniture: "I don't care how old, even antique furniture would be fine"? She complains that her cousin has been gone for two weeks and that she hasn't seen "hide nor seek of him," and she warns her uncle that she will give him only one word of advice, and that word is "be sure" (*The Goldbergs:* "Is There a Doctor in the House?"; *The Goldbergs:* "Boogie Comes Home"). When Molly says that "patience is a vulture," or that "it never rains until it pours," her misstatements carry wisdom (*The Goldbergs:* "Moving Day"; *The Goldbergs:* "Is There a Doctor in the House?").

Resentments about work, refusals to acknowledge the legitimacy of the upper classes, and creative word play abound in these programs, transmitting the texture of decades of working-class experience. Similarly, comedy about fraternal orders and ethnic lodges appear in television shows of the 1950s as a reflection of real historical experience. In history, fraternal orders and mutual aid societies comprised essential resources for working-class immigrants, often providing insurance, burial expenses, recreational facilities, and adult education at a time when the state accepted none of those responsibilities. In the urban ethnic working-class situation comedies of the early 1950s, the fraternal lodge appears as an archaic and anachronistic institution, a remnant of the past at odds with the needs of the family. Lars Hansen brings home officials of the Sons of Norway for dinner, thereby creating more work for Mama.[5] Chester A. Riley wastes his time and money on the Brooklyn Patriots of Los Angeles, an organization set up to revere the world he left behind when he moved his family west. The Mystic Knights of the Sea provide Kingfish with a theater of operations for bilking his "brothers" out of their money, and for indulging his inflated sense of self-importance. The Royal Order of Raccoons keep Ralph Kramden from spending time with Alice, and they divert his paycheck away from the family budget toward lodge dues. In one show Alice asks Ralph what benefit she derives from his lodge activities. He proudly informs her that his membership entitles both of them to free burial in the Raccoon National Cemetery in Bismark, North Dakota. With appropriate sarcasm, Alice replies that the prospect of burial in North Dakota makes her wonder why she should go on living (*The Honeymooners:* "The Loud Speaker").

In organic popular memory, lodges retained legitimacy as sources of mutuality and friendship. But in an age when suburban tract housing replaced the ethnic neighborhood, when the state took on welfare functions previously carried out by voluntary associations, and when the home sphere became increasingly isolated from the community around it, the lodge hall became a premise for comic ridicule. In television programs, the interests of the family took precedence over those of the fraternal lodge, and a binary opposition between the two seemed inevitable. Yet the very inclusion of lodges in these programs demonstrates the power of the past in the discourse of the present. Television programs validated the atomized nuclear family at the expense of the extended kinship and class relations manifested in the fraternal order. When successful, these shows undercut the ability of the past to provide legitimacy for contemporary social relations. When unsuccessful, these shows called attention to the possibility of other forms of community and culture than those that dominated the present.

Cultural specificity about working-class life provided credibility for early network television programs, but at the same time created problems for advertisers. Erik Barnouw points out that sponsors hardly relished the prospect of shows situated in lower-class environments—like the enormously successful teleplay, *Marty*—because "Sponsors were meanwhile trying to 'upgrade' the consumer and persuade him to 'move up to a Chrysler,' and 'live better electrically' in a suburban home, with help from 'a friend at Chase Manhattan.' The sponsors preferred beautiful people in mouth-watering decor to convey what it meant to climb the socioeconomic ladder. The commercials looked out of place in Bronx settings" (Barnouw 1979:106). When advertisers coasted on the borrowed legitimacy of working-class history to lend sincerity and authenticity to their appeals to buy coffee and soap, they also ran the risk of exposing contradictions between the past and present. Author Kathryn Forbes, who wrote the book on which *Mama* was based, complained that the television Hansen family had too much wealth to present accurately the circumstances she had written about. Forbes's book portrays the Hansen family with four children in a house shared with relatives and boarders; on television they have three children in a house to themselves. In the Forbes book, Mama represents a traditional mother raising independent daughters—using her traditional cooking skills to make social connections that allow Katrin to pursue an untraditional career as a writer. On television, tradition reigns as Mama instructs Katrin about cooking to help her land a husband, and Katrin becomes a secretary rather than a writer. Other shows made similar adaptations to the ideological norms of the 1950s. On radio and for most of their years on television, the Goldbergs lived in a multifamily Bronx dwelling where neighbors and relatives blended together to form an extended community. By the time the television show reached its last year of production in 1955–56, the Goldbergs moved to a suburban house in a Long Island subdivision where physical and emotional distances constituted the norm. The radio version of *Amos 'n Andy* began to neglect the solid family man and independent businessman Amos as early as the 1940s; but the television show which began in 1951 pushed Amos even farther into the background in order to zero in on the marital problems and home life of the shiftless and irresponsible Kingfish. In each of these shows, television versions tended to accentuate the dilemmas of atomized nuclear families and to downplay the dramas emanating from extended class and ethnic associations.

The working class depicted in urban ethnic working-class situation comedies of the 1950s bore only a superficial resemblance to the historical American working class. Stripped of essential elements of ethnic and class identity, interpreted through perspectives most relevant to a consumer middle class, and pictured in isolation from the social connections that gave purpose and meaning to working-class lives, the televised working-class family summoned up only the vaguest contours of its historical counterpart. Even in comparison to depictions of class in other forms of communication, like folklore, theater, music, literature, or radio, television presented a dessicated and eviscerated version of working-class life. Yet the legitimizing functions served by locating programs in working-class environments caused some attempts at authenticity that brought sedimented class tensions to the surface. While the producers of these television shows hardly intended to direct viewers' attentions toward real ethnic and class conflicts, the social location of the writers and actors most knowledgeable about working-class life served to make some of these programs focal points for social issues. When producers took on working-class settings as a form of local color, they burdened themselves with the contradictions of the communities that provided the color, as evidenced by public controversies over *The Goldbergs* and *Amos 'n Andy*.

Part of the convincing authenticity of *The Goldbergs* came from actors and writers who developed their skills within the Yiddish theater and the culture that supported it. An organic part of that culture included political activists, including Communists, socialists, and antifascists whose concerns found expression in a variety of community activities including theater. Philip Loeb, who played Jake Goldberg, became the center of controversy when an anti-Communist right-wing publication accused him of subversive connections arising from his appearance at antifascist rallies and his having signed a petition calling for the admission of Negroes into professional baseball. Nervous sponsors and advertising representatives, afraid of threatened boycotts by the anti-Communists, dropped their support of the show and demanded that its producer and star, Gertrude Berg, fire Loeb. At first she refused, pointing out that Loeb had never been a Communist, but ultimately Berg gave in to the pressure and fired her co-star in order to keep her show on the air. Sponsors resumed their support after Loeb left the program in 1952, and *The Goldbergs* ran for four more years. Loeb received a $45,000 settlement in exchange for dropping any legal actions against the show, but he never worked again as an actor because producers viewed him as "controversial." In 1956, Loeb committed suicide (Barnouw 1982: 126; Jezer 1982:193–194; Kanfer 1973:154; *New Republic* 1952A:8, 1952B:22). Similarly, Mady Christians played Mama in the Broadway play *I Remember Mama*, but could not play that role on television; anti-Communist pressure groups questioned her loyalty because she had worked on behalf of refugees from fascism in the 1930s and 1940s with individuals accused of subversion. Blacklisted from her profession, Christians sank into a severe depression that friends felt sapped her strength and made her unable to overcome health problems that led to her death in 1951. Leob and Christians dismayed advertisers, not because of their political views, but because their presence provoked political controversy and interfered with the illusions created by their programs of a world without politics. Like the real Goldbergs and Hansens in American history, Philip Loeb and Mady Christians lived in a world where ethnicity connected them to complicated political issues. The controversy over their views and the public attention directed toward them threatened to unmask the world of *Mama* and *The Goldbergs* as a created artifact—depriving it of legitimating power.

Amos 'n Andy contained similar, but more culturally explosive, connections. Stereotyped and demeaning portrayals of black people have long constituted an obsessive theme in American theater, and for that matter, in American life. Historian Nathan Irvin Huggins points out that the minstrel show stereotypes enabled white society at the turn of the 20th century to attribute to black people the characteristics that it feared most in itself. At a time when industrialization demanded a revolutionary transformation in behavior that compelled Americans to accept Victorian standards about thrift, sobriety, abstinence, and restraint, the minstrel show emerged to present laziness, greed, gluttony, and licentiousness as traits singularly associated with black people. These images worked to legitimate the emerging Victorian code by associating opposition to the dominant ideology with the despised culture of Afro-Americans. The minstrel show "Negro" presented white society with a representation of the natural self at odds with the normative self of industrial culture. Uninhibited behavior could be savored by the ego during the minstrel performance, but overruled afterwards by the superego. The viewer could release tension by pointing to the minstrel show "darkie" and saying "It's him, not me." But the viewer came back, again and again. The desire to subjugate and degrade black people had political and economic imperatives of its own, but emotional and psychic reinforcement for that exploitation came from the ways in which racist stereotypes enabled whites to accept the suppression of their natural selves.

The centrality of racist images to white culture presented peculiar problems for Afro-Americans. Entry into white society meant entry into its values, and those values included hatred of blacks. In order to participate in the white world, blacks had to make concessions to white America's fantasy images. As Huggins notes, black people found it dangerous to step out of character, either on or off stage. The great black vaudeville entertainer Bert Williams demonstrated the absurd contradictions of this process; he donned blackface makeup to perform on stage—a black man imitating white men imitating black men. Williams's artistic genius and stubborn self-respect led him to inject subtle elements of social criticism into his act, but for most spectators, he merely reinforced their a priori conclusions about the stage Negro (Huggins 1978).

The black cast of *Amos 'n Andy* came out of the theatrical traditions that spawned Williams, and they perpetuated many of his contradictions. As a successful radio program, the all-black world of *Amos 'n Andy* had been performed mostly by its white creators (Freeman Gosden and Charles Correll). With the move to television, Gosden and Correll hired an all-black cast, but they nonetheless faced protests from community groups. The National Association for the Advancement of Colored People and black actor James Edwards campaigned to have the program taken off the air because they felt that it made the only televised presentation of Afro-American life an insulting one. The NAACP complained in federal court that black citizens routinely suffered abuse from whites addressing them as "Amos" or "Andy," and that the program defamed black professionals by presenting them as liars and cheats. In response, black actors employed on the program and a few black intellectuals defended *Amos 'n Andy* as a harmless satire and an important vehicle for bringing much needed exposure to black actors (Cripps 1983; Macdonald 1983:27–28; *Newsweek* 1951:56).

Placed in historical context, *Amos 'n Andy* did for the values of the 1950s what the minstrel show accomplished for previous generations. Everything considered precious but contested in white society—like the family or the work ethic—became violated in the world of Kingfish. Ambition and upward mobility drew ridicule when pursued by blacks. In a society nurtured on Horatio Alger stories about rising from rags to riches, this lampooning of a black man's aspirations could function to release tensions about the fear of failure. It could redirect hostility away from the elite toward those on the bottom of society. When Kingfish pretends to be educated and uses grandiose language, the audience can howl derisively at his pretensions, but the same audience could glow with warm recognition when Mama Hansen uses her broken English to express her dreams for her son to grow up to be president. Ambition viewed as worthy and realistic for the Hansens becomes a symbol of weak character on the part of the Kingfish.

Consistent with the values of the 1950s as mediated through popular culture, family responsibilities—or neglect of them—define Kingfish even more than does his work. The glorification of motherhood pervading psychological and popular literature of the 1950s becomes comedy in *Amos 'n Andy*. Wives named for precious stones (Ruby and Sapphire) appear anything but precious, and "Mama" in this show appears as a nagging harpy screaming at the cowering—and emasculated—black man. Kingfish shares Ralph Kramden's dreams of overnight success, but his transgressions against bourgeois morality are more serious. Kingfish has no job, his late night revelries and lascivious grins hint at marital infidelity, and he resorts to criminal behavior to avoid what he calls "the horrors of employment."[6] He betrays his family and cheats his lodge brothers (and by implication the "brothers" of his race) with no remorse. But his most serious flaws stem from his neglect of the proper roles of husband and father. In one episode, Kingfish's late night excursions cause his wife, Sapphire, to leave home and live with her mother. Kingfish misses her and orders one of his lackeys to find out where she has gone. When the report comes back that Sapphire has been seen entering an obstetrician's office, Kingfish assumes that he is about to become a father. In reality, Sapphire has simply taken a job as the doctor's receptionist, but the misunderstanding leads Kingfish to tell Amos how much fun he plans to have as a father. When Amos warns him that fatherhood involves serious responsibilities, Kingfish replies, "What you mean serious? All you gotta do is keep 'em filled up wid milk an' pablum and keep chuckin' em under de chin" (*Amos 'n Andy:* "Kingfish Has a Baby"). Kingfish's ignorance plays out the worst fears of people in a society with a burgeoning obsession with family. By representing the possibility of incompetent parenting, Kingfish provides the audience with a sense of superiority, but one that can be maintained only by embracing parental responsibilities. Lest we miss the point of the show, when Kingfish and his friend Andy go to a clinic for prospective fathers, where they learn to bathe a baby by practicing with a doll, Kingfish lets his slip under the water and "drown" (*Amos 'n Andy:* "Kingfish Has a Baby").

Black protest made *Amos 'n Andy* a much debated phenomenon, unmasking the calculation that went into its creation. In the context of the 1950s, when migration to industrial cities created greater concentrations of black political and economic power, these protests could not be dismissed casually by advertisers or the networks. Blatz Beer decided to drop its sponsorship of *Amos 'n Andy* in 1954, knocking the show off prime time schedules and into syndication until 1966, when another wave of protests made it untenable even in reruns. As the program most thoroughly grounded in ideologically charged historical material, *Amos 'n Andy* lent itself most easily to critical historical interpretation and action, a capacity at odds with the interests of advertisers. But like shows rooted in white working-class histories, structural contradictions in black working-class life also held open the possibility for oppositional readings of the program's content. Black activist and author Julius Lester recalls his own formative experiences with *Amos 'n Andy* in his autobiography in a way that provides the quintessential act of reinterpreting hierarchically prepared and distributed mass culture. Ruminating on the seeming paradox of a home life that installed black pride into him but that also encouraged him to listen to the antics of the Kingfish, Lester recalls that

> In the character of Kingfish, the creators of Amos and Andy may have thought
> they were ridiculing blacks as lazy, shiftless, scheming and conniving, but to us
> Kingfish was a paradigm of virtue, an alternative to the work ethic. Kingfish lived:
> Amos made a living. It did not matter that my parents lived by and indoctrinated
> me with the Puritan work ethic, Kingfish had a joie de vivre no white person could
> poison, and we knew that whites ridiculed us because they were incapable of such
> elan, I was proud to belong to the same race as Kingfish. [1976:14]

Whether through the careful decoding exemplified by Julius Lester, or through the politicization of *Amos 'n Andy* by mass protest, audience response to the program in some cases focused on the show's artifice and distortions of history. As was the case with *The Goldbergs*, the traditions needed to provide legitimacy for advertising messages surrounding *Amos 'n Andy* contained sedimented contestation that undermined their effectiveness, and instead provoked negotiated or oppositional readings. Dominant ideology triumphed on television in the 1950s, just as it did in political life, but historically grounded opposition remained possible and necessary for at least part of the audience.

The realism that made urban ethnic working-class situation comedies convincing conduits for consumer ideology also compelled them to present alienations and aspirations subversive to the legitimacy of consumer capitalism. As Antonio Gramsci insists, ideological hegemony stems from the ability of those in power to make their own interests appear to be synonymous with the interests of society at large. But appeals for legitimacy always take place within concrete historical circumstances, in contested societies with competing interests. In a consumer capitalist economy where unmet needs and individual isolation provide the impetus for commodity desires, legitimation is always incomplete. Even while establishing dominance, those in power must borrow from the ideas, actions, and experiences of the past, all of which contain a potential for informing a radical critique of the present.

Dialogue, Negotiation, and Legitimation: Method and Theory

Recent scholarship in literary criticism, cultural studies, and sociology offers investigative methods and theoretical frameworks essential to understanding the historical dialogue about family, class, and ethnicity in early network television. The literary criticism of and "dialogic imagination" proposed by Mikhail Bahktin demonstrates how all texts inherit part of the historical consciousness of their authors and audiences (Newcomb 1984:37–41). Cultural studies theorist Stuart Hall notes that commercial mass media seek legitimacy with the audiences by effectively representing diverse aspects of social life, including memories of past experiences, current contradictions, and potential sources of division and opposition (Hall 1979). Sociologist Jürgen Habermas observes that contemporary capitalist culture destroys the very motivations that it needs to function effectively, such as the work ethic or the willingness to defer gratification. Consequently, capitalist societies draw upon the borrowed legitimacy of cultural values and beliefs from the past, like religion or the patriarchal family, in order to provide the appearance of moral grounding for contemporary forces inimical to the interests of tradition (Habermas 1975). Taken collectively, these approaches to culture provide a useful context for understanding the persistence of seemingly outdated and dysfunctional elements in early network television.

Bakhtin's analysis of text construction argues that communication does not begin in the present with a speaker or story; but rather that both speech and narrative come from a social matrix that is, at least in part, historical. Each speaker enters a dialogue already in progress; every work of art contains within it past, present, and future struggles over culture and power. Terms and forms of communication from the past not only make current discourse comprehensible and legitimate, but they also imbed within the present a collective historical experience rich with contradictions. The producers of early network television worked in a new medium, but they addressed an audience acclimated to specific forms of comedy and drama that reflected, however indirectly, the real texture of past struggles and present hopes.[7]

Structural unities underlie the seemingly divergent stories of different ethnic, working-class situation comedies. Viewers rarely saw Ralph Kramden's bus or Jake Goldberg's dressmaking shop, but the cameras introduced them to every detail of furnishing in the Kramden and Goldberg households. Difficulties encountered in the aircraft factory assembly line by Chester A. Riley or at the construction site by Lars Hansen paled in significance in contrast to the dilemmas of consumption faced in the Riley and Hansen families. The texture and tone of *Life with Luigi* and *Amos 'n Andy* came from the ethnic worlds they depicted, but the plots of those shows dealt with the aspirations of individuals as if ethnic rivalries and discrimination did not exist. Instead, ethnics attain a false unity through consumption of commodities: Jeannie MacClennan learns to "be an American" by dressing fashionably and wearing the right makeup; Luigi Basco hopes to prove himself a worthy candidate for citizenship by opening a checking account and purchasing an insurance policy; Molly Goldberg overcomes her fears of installment buying and vows to live above her means—which she describes as "the American way" (*Hey Jeannie:* "The Rock and Roll Kid"; *Life with Luigi:* "The Insurance Policy"; *The Goldbergs:* "The In-laws"). Comedies in this subgenre are clearly cases where, as Stuart Hall points out, the commercial mass media tend to direct popular consciousness toward consumption and away from production. They present social actions and experiences as atomized individual events in order to fragment groups into isolated consumers, and they resolve the tensions confronting their audiences by binding them together in false unities and collectivities defined for the convenience of capital accumulation (Hall 1979).

But Hall also shows that the imperial aspirations of the mass media, their imperative to attract as large an audience as possible, lead to a disclosure of contradictions that allows cultural consumers to fashion oppositional or negotiated readings of mass culture. In order to make their dramas compelling and their narrative resolutions dynamic, the media also reflect the plurality of consumer experiences. A system that seeks to enlist everyone in the role of consumer must appear to be addressing all possible circumstances: a system that proclaims consensus and unanimity must acknowledge and explain obvious differences within the polity, if for no other reason than to co-opt or trivialize potential opposition. Television and other forms of commercial electronic media so effectively recapitulate the ideology of the "historical bloc" in which they operate that they touch on all aspects of social life—even its antagonistic contradictions (Hall 1979). While the media serve to displace, fragment, and atomize real experiences, they also generate and circulate a critical dialogue as an unintended consequence of their efforts to expose the inventory of social practice.

Of course, mere disclosure of opposition does not guarantee emancipatory practice: ruling elites routinely call attention to "deviant" subcultures in order to draw a clear distinction between permitted and forbidden behavior. In urban ethnic working-class situation comedies in the 1950s, "deviant" traits—like Kingfish's aversion to work in *Amos 'n Andy* and Lars Hansen's lack of ambition in *Mama*—taught object lessons about the perils of unconventional behavior. Yet the operative premises and enduring tensions of each of these shows revolved around the "otherness" of the lead characters. The "old-world" attitudes of newly arrived immigrants in *Hey Jeannie* and *Life with Luigi* or the proletarian cultural innocence manifested in *The Life of Riley* or *The Honeymooners* led to comedic clashes that exposed the inadequacies and deficiencies of those on the margins of society.

But at the same time, these clashes counterposed the conformity and materialism of the mainstream to the narratively privileged moral superiority of those with connections to the past. Traditional values and beliefs prevented protagonists in these shows from achieving success and happiness as defined by society, but those values and beliefs also facilitated a critical distance from the false premises of the present. As Gertrude Berg noted in explaining the popularity of her character Molly Goldberg, Molly "lived in the world of today but kept many of the values of yesterday" (Berg 1961:167).

The narrative sequence that framed every episode of *Mama* demonstrates the centrality of this dialogue between the past and present in early network television programs. As soon as Katrin Hansen introduced the show with the words "I remember Mama," a male narrator announced, "Yes, here's Mama, brought to you by Maxwell House Coffee." The camera then panned away from the photograph album to show Mama (played by Peggy Wood) making coffee for the Hansen family in their turn-of-the-century kitchen. The authority of the male narrator's voice established a connection between the continuity of family experience and the sponsor's product, between warm memories of the past and Mama in the kitchen making coffee. In this progression, the product becomes a member of the Hansen family, while tradition and emotional support become commodities to be secured through the purchase of Maxwell House coffee. The sponsor's introduction announced ownership of the television show, but it also laid claim to the moral authority and warmth generated by the concept of motherhood itself.[8]

Katrin Hansen's retrospective narrative and the pictures from the family album reassured viewers by depicting events that had already happened in the emotionally secure confines of the audience's collective childhood. This false authenticity encouraged viewers to think of the program as the kind of history that might be created in their own homes. A CBS press release during the program's first broadcast season proclaimed, "On 'Mama' we try to give the impression that nobody is acting," and went on to claim success for that effort, quoting an unnamed viewer's contention that the show depicted a real family because "nobody but members of a real family could talk like that" (Nelson 1949). Free from the real history of ethnic, class, and gender experience, the history presented on *Mama* located its action within the personal spheres of family and consumer choices. Within these areas, realism could be put to the service of commodity purchases, as when the narrator followed his opening introduction with a discourse about how Mama in her day "had none of the conveniences of today's modern products" like Minute Rice, Jello, or instant coffee (*Mama*: "T. R.'s New Home"). Thus the morally sanctioned traditions of hearth and home could be put to the service of products that revolutionized those very traditions—all in keeping with Ernest Dichter's advice to his fellow advertising executives: "Do not assert that the new product breaks with traditional values, but on the contrary, that it fulfills its traditional functions better than any of its predecessors" (Dichter 1960:209).

Every episode of *Mama* began and ended with Mama making coffee in the kitchen—but to very different effect. The opening sequence, with the announcer's statement about Maxwell House coffee, validates commodities; the ending sequence, however, validates both moralities and commodities. There Katrin, in the kitchen or as a voice-over, summarizes the meaning of that week's story for the audience by relating the lesson that she learned from it. Invariably these lessons belonged to the sphere of old-fashioned values, elevating human creations over commodities and privileging commitment to others over concern with self. In these lessons, the audience discovered that the toys Papa made with his hands meant more to the children than the fancy ones they saw in stores, or that loyalty to family and friends brought more rewards than upward mobility. These resolutions often directly contradicted the narratives that preceded them: after twenty-five minutes of struggle for happiness through commodity acquisition, the characters engaged in a one-minute homily about the superiority of moral goals over material ones. Then, with the high moral ground established, a voice-over by the announcer reminded viewers of the wonderful products that the sponsor of *Mama* had to offer.

The complicated dialogue in the opening and closing segments of *Mama* illumines the complex role played by historical referents in early network television. The past that brought credibility and reassurance to family dramas also contained the potential for undermining the commodified social relations of the present. The Hansen family interested advertisers because audiences identified their story as part of a precious collective memory resonating with the actual experiences and lessons of the past. The Hansens could not be credible representatives of that past if they appeared to live among the plethora of consumer goods that dominated the commercials, or if they appeared uncritical of the consumer world of the present that made such a sharp break with the values of the past. Yet the Hansen family had little value to advertisers unless their experiences sanctioned pursuit of commodities in the present. The creators of the program—like those engaged in production of the other urban ethnic working-class comedies on television—resolved this potential contradiction by putting the borrowed moral capital of the past at the service of the values of the present. They acknowledged the critique of materialism and upward mobility sedimented within the experiences of working-class families, but they demonstrated over and over again how wise choices enabled consumers to have both moral and material rewards. By positing the nuclear family as a transhistorical "natural" locus for the arbitration of consumer desires, television portrayed the value crises of the 1950s as eternal and recurrent. By collapsing the distinction between family as consumer unit and family as part of neighborhood, ethnic, and class networks, television programs in the early 1950s connected the most personal and intimate needs of individuals to commodity purchases. They implied that the past sanctioned rather than contradicted the ever-increasing orientation toward shopping as the cornerstone of social life, an orientation that characterized media discourse in the postwar era.

The reliance on the past to sanction controversial changes in present behavior forms the core of Jürgen Habermas's analysis of contemporary capitalism's "legitimation crisis." According to Habermas, the consumer consciousness required by modern capitalism revolves around "civil and familial-vocational privatism"—a syndrome that elevates private consumer decisions over social relations and public responsibility (Habermas 1975:71–75). Individuals see families as centers of consumption and leisure, while they regard employment as primarily a means of engaging in status competition. Instead of the rooted independence demanded by traditional family and community life, contemporary capitalist society encourages an atomized dependence on outside authorities—advertisers, self-help experts, and psychiatric, educational, and political authorities. Clearly useful for purposes of capital accumulation, this process undermines traditional motivations for work, patriotism, and personal relations, causing real crises in social relations. In addition, the infantile narcissism nurtured by this consumer consciousness encourages a search for validation from outside authorities—for communication which assures people that the impoverishment of work, family, and public life characteristic of late capitalism constitutes a legitimate and necessary part of progress toward a better life as defined by opportunities for more acquisition and more status.

For Habermas, the mass media play a crucial role in legitimation, but they do so imperfectly. The new forms of family and vocational consciousness cannot be justified on their own, but can be validated by invoking the moral authority of past forms of family and work identity. Thus the "work ethic" is summoned to justify a system based on commodified leisure, while mutual love and affection are called on to sanction families that exist primarily as consumer units. The social relations of the past are used to legitimate a system that in reality works to destroy the world that created those relations in the first place. Consequently, the invocation of the past in the service of the present is a precarious undertaking. Tradition used to legitimate untraditional behavior may instead call attention to the disparity between the past and the present; collective popular memory may see the manipulative use of tradition by advertisers as a conscious strategy, as an attempt to create artifacts that conflict with actual memory and experiences. As Habermas cautions, "traditions can retain legitimizing force only as long as they are not torn out of interpretive systems that guarantee continuity and identity" (Habermas 1975:71).

Habermas provides us with a framework capable of explaining both the presence of historical elements in early network television shows and their limitations. In conjunction with Bakhtin's emphasis on dialogue and Hall's delineation of negotiation, Habermas's analysis explains how portrayals of traditional, ethnic, working-class families might have been essential for legitimizing social forces that undermined the very values that made those families respected icons in popular consciousness. At the same time, Habermas directs our attention to the fundamental instability of this legitimation process, to the ways in which audiences might come to see manipulative uses of the past as prepared and created artifacts at war with the lessons of history as preserved in collective popular memory.

After 1958, network television eliminated urban ethnic working-class programs from the schedule. Marc Daniels, who directed *The Goldbergs*, recalls that a changing society less tied to class and ethnicity demanded different kinds of entertainment, and certainly the emergence of ethnically neutral, middle-class situation comedies between 1958 and 1970 lends credence to that view (Daniels 1984). The entry of major film studios into television production in the mid 1950s also had an impact, since the working-class shows tended to be produced by small companies like Hal Roach Studios. Major studio involvement in television production increased the proportion of action/adventure shows with production values ill-suited to the realism of urban ethnic working-class programs. In action and adventure shows, no embarassing retentions of class consciousness compromised the sponsors' messages, and no social associations with ethnic life brought up disturbing issues that made them susceptible to protests and boycotts.

One might conclude that television and American society had no need for urban ethnic working-class programs after 1958 because tensions between consumerist pressures and historical memories had been resolved. But the reappearance of race, class, and ethnicity in the situation comedies of the 1970s like *All in the Family, Chico and the Man*, and *Sanford and Son* testifies to the ongoing relevance of such tensions as existed in the 1950s to subsequent mass media dialogue. The programs of the 1970s reprised both aspects of the 1950s shows—legitimation through representation of the texture of working-class life, and commodification of all human relationships, especially within families. Like their predecessors, urban ethnic working-class shows of the 1970s mixed their commercial and consumerist messages with visions of connection to others that transcended the limits of civil and familial vocational privatism. They held open possibilities for transcending the parochialisms of traditional ethnicity and for challenging the patriarchal assumptions of both extended and nuclear families. The same communications apparatus that presented consumerism as the heir to the moral legacy of the working-class past also legitimized aspirations for happiness and community too grand to be satisfied by the lame realities of the commodity-centered world.[9]

In the early 1950s, an advertising instrument under the control of powerful monopolists established itself as the central discursive medium in American culture. With its penetration of the family and its incessant propaganda for commodity purchases, television helped erode the social base for challenges to authority manifest in the mass political activity among American workers in the 1940s. Yet television did not so much insure the supremacy of new values as it transformed the terms of social contestation. As mass culture gained in importance as an instrument of legitimation, oppositional messages filtered into even hierarchically controlled media constructions like network television programs. The internal contradictions of capitalism fueled this process by generating anxieties in need of legitimation, and by turning for legitimation to the very beliefs and practices most threatened by emerging social relations. Thus every victory for the ideology of civil and familial vocational privatism can also constitute a defeat. Every search for legitimacy can end in the dilution of legitimacy by unmasking media messages as prepared and fabricated ideological artifices. Even successful legitimation fails to a degree because the new social relations destroy their own source of legitimacy.

This is not to assume that the final outcome of television's ideological imperatives must be emancipatory. Inculcation of narcissistic desire coupled with destruction of traditional sources of moral restraint might well suit the needs of capital and produce a population eager for fascist authority. But structural conditions exist for an alternative future. As Joel Kovel argues, "The point is not that people desire the administrative mode, it is rather that administration protects them against the desires they can not stand, while it serves out, in the form of diluted rationalization, a hint of the desire and power lost to them" (Kovel 1978:19). The separation of individuals from political and community life, combined with the destruction of cultural traditions that previously gave direction and purpose to individuals, might make status competition and "possession" of a secure family role all that much more attractive. Certainly the neo-conservatism of the 1980s seems to hinge upon "protecting" the family from the increasing barbarism of society, and upon shifting the blame for the social disintegration caused by civil and familial vocational privatism onto the opposition movements formed to combat it.[10] But the sleight of hand inherent in the neo-conservative position allows for other possibilities. Reconnection to history and to motivational structures rooted within it is both desirable and possible. More than ever before, communication and criticism can help determine whether people accept the commodity-mediated desires that turn others into instruments and objects, or whether they build affirmative communities in dialogue with the needs and desires of others. By identifying the historical reality behind the construction of television texts in the early 1950s, we demystify their "organic" character and reveal their implications as created artifacts. We uncover sedimented critiques from the past and potential forms of opposition for the present.

The historical specificity of early network television programs led their creators into dangerous ideological terrain. By examining them as part of our own history, we learn about both the world we have lost and the one we have yet to gain. Fredric Jameson claims that "history is what hurts, what sets inexorable limits to individual as well as collective praxis" (Jameson 1981:102). But the unfinished dialogue of history can also be what helps, what takes us back into the past in order to break its hold on the present. By addressing the hurt, and finding out how it came to be, we begin to grasp ways of understanding the past, and ending the pain.

Notes

Acknowledgments: I wish to thank Nick Browne, Gary Burns, Robert Deming, Tom Dumm, Michael Fischer, Jib Fowles, Mary Beth Haralovich, Susan Hartmann, Connie Labelle, Elizabeth Long, Barbara Tomlinson, and Brian Winston for their comments and criticisms on previous drafts of this article.

1. Stuart Ewen condemns these shows as hostile to immigrant life and imposing consumerism on it in his *Captains of Consciousness* (1976:208–210). Marty Jezer takes a more favorable view in *The Dark Ages* (1982:191–194).

2. Of course, class, ethnicity, and race remained important, but their relationship to individual identity changed radically at this time. The bureaucratization of trade unions and xenophobic anti-Communism also contributed to declines in ethnic and class consciousness.

3. See the discussion in this article of *Mama, The Goldbergs*, and *Amos 'n Andy*.

4. Neilsen ratings demonstrate television's view of the family as separate market segments to be addressed independently. For an analysis of the industry's view of children as a special market, see Patricia J. Bence (1985), "Analysis and History of Typology and Forms of Children's Network Programming from 1950 to 1980."

5. The *Mama* show relied on the Bay Ridge, Brooklyn chapter of the Sons of Norway for advice on authentic Norwegian folk customs and stories, according to Dick Van Patten and Ralph Nelson, in remarks made at the Museum of Broadcasting, New York City, on December 17, 1985.

6. The depiction of Kingfish's refusal to work had especially vicious connotations in an era where the crisis in black unemployment reached unprecedented depths.

7. For a discussion of the role of media borrowing from earlier forms see Daniel Czitrom (1983).

8. This is not to single out *Mama* as an especially commercial program. In fact, its advertisers allowed the show to run with no middle commercial, using only the opening and closing commercial sequences. Yet other shows incorporated commercial messages into dramatic program-like segments, especially *The Goldbergs* and *Life with Luigi*.

9. For an excellent discussion of 1970s television see the forthcoming book by Ella Taylor, *All in the Work-Family*.

10. Protection of the family represents an old social theme for conservatives and a traditional device for creating dramatic tension. But never before have they been as thoroughly unified as

dramatic and political themes and never before have they dominated conservative thought as they have in the last decade.

References Cited

Allen, Jeanne
    1983   The Social Matrix of Television: Invention in the United States. *In* Regarding Television. E. Ann Kaplan, ed. Pp. 109–119. Los Angeles: University Publications of America.

Allen, Robert
    1985   Speaking of Soap Operas. Chapel Hill: University of North Carolina Press.

Amos 'n Andy
    1951   Kingfish Has a Baby. Theater Art Library. University of California, Los Angeles.
    1953   Andy, The Godfather. Academy of Television Arts Collection. T 15645. University of California, Los Angeles.

Aronowitz, Stanley
    1983   Working Class Hero. New York: Pilgrim.

Barnouw, Erik
    1979   The Sponsor. New York: Oxford University Press.
    1982   Tube of Plenty. New York: Oxford University Press.

Bence, Patricia J.
    1985   Analysis and History of Typology and Forms of Children's Network Programming from 1950 to 1980. Paper presented at the Society for Cinema Studies Meetings. New York City. June 12.

Berg, Gertrude
    1961   Molly and Me. New York: McGraw Hill.

Berger, Henry
    1982   Social Protest in St. Louis. Paper presented at a Committee for the Humanities Forum. St. Louis, Missouri. March 12.

Boddy, William
    1985   The Studios Move Into Prime Time: Hollywood and the Television Industry in the 1950s. Cinema Journal 12(4):23–37.

Boorstin, Daniel
    1973   The Americans: The Democratic Experience. New York: Vintage Press.

Chodorow, Nancy
    1978   Reproduction of Mothering. Berkeley: University of California Press.

Cripps, Thomas
    1983   The Amos 'n Andy Controversy. *In* American History and American Television. John O'Connor, ed. Pp. 33–54. New York: Ungar.

Czitrom, Daniel
    1983   Media and the American Mind. Chapel Hill: University of North Carolina Press.

Daniels, Marc
    1984   Presentation at the Director's Guild of America. July 11, Los Angeles, California.

de Cordova, Richard
    1985   The Transition from Radio to Television. Unpublished paper presented at the Society for Cinema Studies Meetings. June 12, New York.

Dichter, Ernest

    1960   The Strategy of Desire. Garden City: Doubleday.

Ewen, Stuart

    1976   Captains of Consciousness: Advertising and the Social Roots of the Consumer Culture. New York: McGraw Hill Book Company.

Goldbergs, The

    1949   The Rent Strike. Museum of Broadcasting, New York.

    1955   Moving Day. Academy of Television Arts Collection. 35F341. University of California, Los Angeles.

    1955   The In-Laws. Academy of Television Arts Collection. F3218. University of California, Los Angeles.

    1955   Bad Companions. Academy of Television Arts Collection. F3219 University of California, Los Angeles.

    1955   Boogie Comes Home. Academy of Television Arts Collection. F3220. University of California, Los Angeles.

    1955   Die Fledermaus. Academy of Television Arts Collection. F3222. University of California, Los Angeles.

    1955   Is There A Doctor in the House? Academy of Television Arts Collection. F3225. University of California, Los Angeles.

Habermas, Jürgen

    1975   Legitimation Crisis. Boston: Beacon Press.

Hall, Stuart

    1979   Culture. The Media and the "Ideological Effect." *In* Mass Communication and Society. James Curran, Michael Gurevitch, and Janet Woollacott, eds. Beverly Hills: Sage Publications.

Hartmann, Susan

    1982   The Home Front and Beyond. Boston: Twayne.

Hey Jeannie

    1956   The Rock and Roll Kid. Academy of Television Arts Collection. University of California, Los Angeles.

    1956   Jeannie the Cab Driver. Academy of Television Arts Collection. University of California, Los Angeles.

Honeymooners, The

    1956   The Loud Speaker. Academy of Television Arts Collection. VT451. University of California, Los Angeles.

Huggins, Nathan

    1978   Harlem Rennaisance. New York: Oxford University Press.

Jameson, Frederic

    1981   The Political Unconscious: Narrative as a Socially Symbolic Act. Ithaca: Cornell University Press.

Jezer, Marty

    1982   The Dark Ages. Boston: South End.

Kanfer, Stefan

    1973   A Journal of the Plague Years. New York: Atheneum Books.

Kovel, Joel

    1978   Rationalization and the Family. Telos 37:5–21.

Ladies Home Journal

    1956   September. Pp. 130–131.

Lester, Julius

    1976   All is Well. New York: W. Morrow.

Life of Riley

    1953   Academy of Television Arts Collection. R228. University of California, Los Angeles.

Life with Luigi

    1952   The Insurance Policy. Script 2. Norman Tokar Papers. Special Collections Room. Doheny Library. University of Southern California, Los Angeles, California.

    1952   The Power Line. Script 10. Norman Tokar Papers. Special Collections Room. Doheny Library. University of Southern California, Los Angeles, California.

Lipsitz, George

    1981   Class and Culture in Cold War America: A Rainbow at Midnight. New York: Praeger.

Macdonald, J. Fred

    1983   Blacks and White TV. Chicago: Nelson Hall.

Mama

    1953   Mama and the Carpenter. Academy of Television Arts Collection. VT517. University of California, Los Angeles.

Meehan, Elizabeth and Bradford Ropes

    1954   Mama's Birthday. Theater Arts Collection. University Research Library. University of California, Los Angeles.

Mitz, Rick

    1983   The Great TV Sitcom Book. New York: Perigree.

Mollenkopf, John

    1983   The Contested City. Princeton: Princeton University Press.

Moore, Geoffrey, and Phillip Klein

    1967   The Quality of Consumer Installment Credit. Washington, D.C.: National Bureau of Economic Research.

Nelson, Ralph

    1949   Press Release. Ralph Nelson Collection. Number 875. Box 44. Special Collections. University Research Library. University of California, Los Angeles.

New Republic

    1952a   January 21. P. 8.

    1952b   February 18. P. 22.

Newcomb, Horace

    1978   TV: The Critical View. New York: Oxford University Press.

    1984   On the Dialogic Aspects of Mass Communications. Critical Studies in Mass Communications 1:34–50.

Newsweek

    1951   July 9. P. 56.

Romasco, Albert U.

    1965   The Poverty of Abundance. New York: Oxford University Press.

Stone, Michael

    1983   Housing the Economic Crisis. *In* America's Housing Crisis: What Is to be Done? Chester Hartman, ed. Pp. 99–150. London and New York: Routledge and Kegan Paul.

Swanson, Charles E., and Robert L. Jones

    1951   Television Ownership and its Correlates. Journal of Applied Psychology 35:352–357.

Taylor, Ella

    In Press   All in the Work-Family. Berkeley: University of California Press.

TV Facts

    1980   New York: Facts on File.

TV Guide

    1953a   August 7. P. 7.

    1953b   November 2. P. 17.

    1954   May 7. P. 11.

    1955   October 1. P. 14.

    1956   December 29. P. 17.

Wolfenstein, Martha

    1951   The Emergence of Fun Morality. Journal of Social Issues 7(4):15–25.

Amos 'n' Andy *and the Debate Over American Racial Integration*

Thomas Cripps

By 1948, the American popular press, the ruling Democratic Party, and even the most conservative of entertainment media, the movies, had signaled to their constituencies that the touchy issue of racial integration would move to the center of American attention. At the same time, Afro-Americans, especially the growing middle class, swelled the ranks of activist organizations dedicated not merely to older, ambiguous goals of "fair play" and "equality of opportunity," but to full participation in the main social and economic activities of American life.

The Columbia Broadcasting System, like most American broadcasters, had often behaved as though blacks did not exist. But as post-World War II racial activism grew into a genuine social movement, CBS acted with more than its usual indifference by announcing its plans to produce a television version of its twenty-year old radio program, *Amos 'n' Andy*. A comic anachronism that depended for its humor on stereotypical racial traits, the new television program provided the occasion for blacks to debate, both with CBS and among themselves, the precise nature of racial prejudice.

At stake was the right to a nationwide monopoly of broadcasting facilities through which the image of Afro-Americans was to be presented to an enormous American audience. On one side was a complex, increasingly political black bourgeoisie; on the other a highly visible weekly comedy that depicted blacks as feckless, verbally crippled, ineptly conniving parvenus with hearts of gold.

More than any other point of contention, the misrepresentation of the black middle class set black activists on edge. For decades, black intellectuals ranging from racial nationalists to assimilationists had looked to this class for leadership. Whether rooted in the antebellum free Negro community, in the sturdy Southerners who had graduated from Booker T. Washington's Tuskegee Institute, or in the urban Northerners who formed "the talented tenth" symbolized by the black philosopher, W. E. B. DuBois, this class had distinguished itself from the mass of blacks. Churched, stably employed, affiliated with an intricate network of clubs and fraternal orders, the middle class found in *Amos 'n' Andy* a polar opposite that demeaned aspiration, burlesqued the complex distinctions that marked black social classes, and presented to a national white audience an image of maddening oversimplicity.[1]

As early as 1931 black educator Nannie Burroughs spoke for the middle class when she complained of broadcasters who characterized blacks as a uniformly "ignorant, shouting, fighting, rowdy element," a contention summed up by John H. Law, a part-time actor: "The Negro intelligentsia dislikes the lump into one social group." By 1951, the year *Amos 'n' Andy* reached the television screen, these sentiments had been solidified into a movement led by the National Association for the Advancement of Colored People, which had already attained considerable success in changing the black image in Hollywood movies. Among the dissenters were Hollywood blacks who viewed the NAACP as a threat. As one of them, Ernestin Wade, put it, "Agitation from officials of Negro organizations in the past jeopardized the progress of Negro shows."[2]

Amos 'n' Andy, till then a blessedly invisible and therefore relatively innocuous comedy, had come to television in 1951 after more than twenty years on radio. On radio it had never aroused the single-minded wrath that seemed to mark the black response to the television version. For every critic who had complained, another could be found who saw merit in the show. As early as 1932, a survey of black students and "adult leaders" revealed a spectrum of opinion ranging from enjoyment to "marked resentment and emphatic disapproval," a finding later confirmed by a Chicago Urban League study reported in the black *Los Angeles Sentinel*. Another early critic, Bishop W. J. Walls, when he attacked the show emphasized not its substance but the uses to which it was put—"a commercialization of primitive weakness." Later, at the height of the NAACP campaign against the show, some of the nation's prestigious black newspapers expressed similar ambivalence toward the TV series.[3] To this day, despite persistent hostility toward the show, black collectors, scholars, and fans divide on the question of the racism in *Amos 'n' Andy*.[4]

Why did black activists devote so much time, energy, and expense to snuffing out *Amos 'n' Andy* if they knew as well as its makers and sponsors that the black community split in its opinion of the show and its impact? The answer is to be found in the rise of the black bourgeoisie to postwar political awareness and its recent success in influencing the racial content of motion pictures. Wartime propaganda had hinted at an enhancement of postwar black status; NAACP memberships had risen tenfold during the 1940s; CBS's announcement of the proposed series came in 1948, less than a year before the release of Harry S. Truman's Civil Rights Commission report, which had called for a "year of rededication" to American ideals of social justice; and, beginning in 1949, Hollywood dramatized these social changes in a cycle of "message movies."[5] In this social mood, CBS's decision to broadcast a television version of *Amos 'n' Andy* seemed a regressive flaunting of lily-white power in the faces of a formerly vulnerable minority. Moreover, CBS stood alone in its programming preferences, if we may credit a report written by the agent of Hugh Wiley, a writer of black Southern local-color stories. Wiley's agent explained a dry spell that began in 1947 as follows: "Stories dealing with the negro character are, unfortunately impossible to sell," not merely because *Amos 'n' Andy* preempted the field but because of "extreme pressure" from blacks.[6]

Wiley's man had hit on the central difference between postwar and prewar black America—the national "pressure" that black middle-class Americans were capable of mounting against the networks. It was *their* taste, sensibility, and identity that CBS violated in its narrow depiction of blacks as urban riffraff, tricksters, Falstaffs, and snarling matriarchs marked by naive cunning, languid manners, and drawling malapropisms.

Before the war the NAACP had been a mere shadow of its postwar bulk, and black protest had been limited to empty protests over racial epithets and a few bids for ownership of low-wattage stations. Broad-casters, therefore, had done little to cultivate black listeners, and blacks had appeared on the air only in local broadcasts of religious music, prime-time guests shots by musicians, and a few servile roles in situation comedies and soap operas. As a social scientist put it, the black performer "introduces the humor, the clowning, and also enables the middle-class housewife to smile in a sort of superior, patronizing way."[7] At their best, radio programs occasionally included "on a 'sustaining' or unsponsored basis" the Hampton Institute Choir, Paul Robeson, Ethel Waters, and bits of jazz and vaudeville. Years passed between dramas such as CBS's *John Henry* (1932) and WMCA's made-for-New York show, *A Harlem Family* (1935).[8] The narrowest, most stereotyped black roles were reserved for the huge prime-time audiences who saw blacks only as obstreperous maids and valets in popular situation comedies. One of the best, *The Jack Benny Show*, played limitless variations on the relationship between a parsimonious employer and his irreverent, bumptious valet, Rochester (Eddie Anderson).[9]

Before World War II, blacks had felt powerless to act against this white monopoly of access to broadcasting, but the war helped shake the foundations of the social order, at the least in the form of necessitarian gestures toward enlisting blacks in a national effort, and at the most in the form of hints and promises of a better life after the war. Black journalists exploited the situation by demanding a "Double V"—a simultaneous victory over foreign fascism and domestic racism—thereby linking American war aims to black social goals.[10]

The broadcasters responded to the heat of the moment with dozens of shows, among them Roi Ottley's *New World a 'Comin'*; Wendell Willkie's *Open Letter on Race Hatred*, following the Detroit riot of 1943; Kate Smith's guest shot on *We the People* (1945), in which she urged an end to racism, not "at a conference table in Geneva" but in "your own home," a plea that drew twenty thousand requests for transcripts; a black doctor and a black soldier in the soap operas *Our Gal Sunday* and *The Romance of Helen Trent*; CBS's black situation comedy, *Blueberry Hill*; and scattered dramas written by leftists such as Norman Corwin. Together they eroded the monopoly held by the comic servants in *Fibber McGee and Molly, The Great Gildersleeve*, and their epigones.[11]

After the war, the liberal mood became, said Walter White of the NAACP, a "rising wind" of social change. New shows that reflected the times included ABC's *Jackie Robinson Show*, which ranged from sports to social issues; WDAS's (Philadelphia) prize winning *Bon Bon Show*; and CBS's production of Katherine Dunham's *The Story of a Drum*.[12]

Typical of these programs was Richard Durham's self-proclaimed "rebellious, biting, scornful, angry, cocky" *Destination Freedom* (1948–1950), a series of 105 historical sketches produced at WMAQ (Chicago). Durham, a writer for *Ebony* and the *Chicago Defender*, introduced listeners to black history through such characters as abolitionist Harriet Tubman, rebels Denmark Vesey and Toussaint L'Ouverture, and a number of modern activists.[13]

Coincident with the trend of programming, black organizations took up fresh strategies: giving awards, prodding sponsors, enlisting the support of foundations, and joining in cooperative ventures. Sometimes they actually sponsored programs such as the Urban League's production of Erik Barnouw's *The Story They'll Never Print*, a drama about an unemployed black veteran that was chosen for Joseph Liss's book, *Radio's Bess Plays*.[14]

Within the industry itself, researchers began to identify a heretofore untargeted audience of prosperous black listeners. WLIB, Harlem's station, for example, reported a "vast Negro market potential" of billions of dollars, a population then bursting into Greater New York, a college enrollment that had risen by 1000 percent, and an unemployment rate of only 4 percent. The trade magazine *Sponsor* confirmed the boom in black wealth in a story on "the forgotten 15,000,000" black consumers. *Ebony*, a glossy magazine that catered to this new class, ventured a linkage between black wealth, political power, and the coming medium of television. Pointing to evidence that blacks outpurchased whites in the pursuit of consumer goods, *Ebony* characterized sponsor-dominated television as "an amazing new weapon which can be all-powerful in blasting America's bigots."[15] With each new exposure of the prospective black audience, the broadcasters increased their repertoire of gestures from mere slanted programming to appointing Jackie Robinson a vice-president of WNBC. Among the performers, no less than nine groups campaigned for improved black opportunity in broadcasting.[16]

Coincident with this rising black presence, commercial television emerged as a visual medium that had only just become profitable after nearly two decades of technical development. As early as 1939, Julius Adams of the *Amsterdam News* had anticipated black attitudes toward the new medium and even toward *Amos 'n' Andy*. Because television seemed unconstrained by a racist tradition and not yet dominated by entrenched whites, Adams touted it as "Our New Hope." As to *Amos 'n' Andy*, Adams argued that although blacks had tolerated it during its invisible radio period, "it would be suicide to put a show like this on television."[17] By 1950, *Variety* agreed with Adams on the basis of a wave of black performers who had broken into TV: "Negro Talent Coming into Own on TV Without Using Stereotypes: A Sure Sign That Television Is Free of Racial Barriers."[18]

Indeed, in the three years between 1950 and 1952, the life span of the *Amos 'n' Andy* show, network executives embarked on "a new policy of cultivating the Negro audience"—at least according to the trade papers. When NBC hired a public relations firm to direct a series of seminars intended to lead toward "a more realistic treatment of the Negro on the air and the hiring of more Negro personnel." *Variety* characterized it as part of a "movement." In fact there was something to the story; all manner of memoranda passed among the topmost broadcasting executives, urging cooperation with the Urban League, "integration without identification" in casting radio shows, more black material, and "the creation of new program ideas designed to realize" these new goals.[19] But at lower levels executives complained of wooden, unresponsive black auditions, or claimed that "there are certain positions where you feel it might not be advisable to use Negroes," such as those who face the public.[20]

For a brief moment during the same period, a black production company broke the white monopoly on filmmaking for television. The All America company—a creature of William D. Alexander, a some-time funtionary in a black college and in the Office of War Information; Claude A. Barnett, president of the Associated Negro Press; and Emmanuel Glucksman, a white producer of B movies—made a deal with Chesterfield Cigarettes to combine stock shots from their own inventory and other sources with topical news film of black celebrities.[21] Unfortunately, ambition outstripped execution, and this idea—which had been pressed by black entrepreneurs for more than thirty years— ended up in syndication in small markets and profitless dates in Southern grind houses. Glucksman, who hated the rough-and-tumble of location shooting, settled for "talking heads" in claustrophobic office settings, stills, fabricated events, canned ceremonies such as sorority inductions, honorary degrees, Ralph Bunche laying a wreath on Gandhi's tomb, and a black family in Queens enmeshed in its symbols of, as the voice-over said, "gracious living," all of them punctuated by shots of Barnett plugging "our cigarette." *Variety* sniffed at the pioneering effort as "little more than a lot of name-dropping with pictures" fit only for the "southern markets" that eventually bought them at bargain prices.[22]

Into this world of newly felt, newly flexed, black middle-class consciousness, activism, and wealth descended *Amos 'n' Andy*, complete with baggy pants, plug hats, foul cigars, pushy wives, misfired schemes, and mangled grammar. Organized blacks were shocked, not so much at what they saw, but at the timing of its release in the year of liberal "rededication," at a cresting of black political consciousness. Indeed, at first it was not even altogether clear that Freeman Gosden and Charles Correll, the two white originators of the radio series, would decide to abandon blackface in favor of using black actors. In any case, organized blacks reckoned that no good could result from a genre of visual humor that made fun of the black bourgeoisie.[23]

From the moment the story broke in 1948, when the *Los Angeles Sentinel* reported that the *Amos 'n' Andy* radio show had begun integrating blacks into its cast, a confrontation between the NAACP and CBS seemed inevitable. And yet it should be seen that ambiguity clouded the issue. On one hand, organized middle-class blacks winced at the thought of their collective image resting in the charge of two white men whose adult life had been devoted to week after week of creating a nationwide running gag about blacks. On the other hand, blacks in show business pointed to increased opportunities for actors to be generated by the show. On the side of the NAACP, James Hicks of the *Amsterdam News* refused CBS advertising and complained that the show "stinks"; speaking for the actors, Billy Rowe of the *Pittsburgh Courier* labeled the NAACP group "pinks."[24]

With blacks unable to marshal a united front, CBS assembled a production team composed of two executives; Gosden and Correll; director Charles Barton; the veteran vaudevillian, Flournoy Miller, as consultant on racial matters; and a corps of black actors composed of new recruits as well as Johnny Lee and Ernestine Wade from the radio show. They began shooting at the Hal Roach Studio. The decision to record the show in film was a pioneering strategy founded upon hoped-for profits in syndication.[25] Their creature enjoyed a national premiere on June 28, 1951, impervious to the ineffectual black pressure against the show.

At this point CBS seemed to have won the day. Blatz Beer proved to be an eager sponsor. The Roach studio, working with an uncommonly high budget of $40,000, gave *Amos 'n' Andy* a showmanlike gloss: In Charles Barton, a veteran director of Abbott and Costello farces at Universal, they possessed an early master of television style with its cadenced sequences of medium close-ups and two-shots that quickly became conventions of situation comedies. Fortunately for CBS, Barton proved not a good journeyman director but an amiable, sentimental buffer between the originators of the show and the black staff, one of whom remembered Gosden as "an old Southern hardcore general" who tried to "make us mouth *their* words . . . to imitate *them*." For Barton the company was "the greatest family you ever saw," while one of the black actors agreed that "there was a lot of tension . . . because our director, Charlie Barton, was so human and considerate." CBS shrewdly played this angle in its press releases, which minimized the racial basis of the shows while emphasizing the "warm feelings" shared by the members of the company.[26]

The product of their labors played on similar sentiments. Putting aside the racial material that grated upon the sensibilities of organized blacks, from the premiere onward the shows presented happy people with small problems that were solved each evening by restoring equilibrium to some momentarily ruffled situation. The winsome characters were models for the next generation of television heroes—neutral, bland, goodhearted. Amos (Alvin Childress) was an island of sanity in a sea of manic connivance; Andy (Spencer Williams), a mixture of innocence and eye-winking worldliness; and Kingfish (Tim Moore), the potentate of a gimcrack lodge and a fabricator of rickety schemes. The women displayed a similar range of sense and eccentricity: even-tempered Amos had a wife to match; flirtatious Andy, a string of shallow disappointments; and Kingfish, a shrew who was the equal of his own comic pushiness. The supporting characters, all played by veterans such as Johnny Lee, Nick Stewart, Jester Hairston, and the Randolph sisters, represented various extremes of virtue and vice that provided a frame for the principals. As the show matured, the malleable characters grew away from some of the premises of the radio show in ways that allowed Kingfish to serve as a pejorative model beside which the others seemed saner, wiser, less avaricious, and therefore more humane, decent folk. In this way, the dignity of Afro-America seemed less at risk, and the race of the characters seemed to matter less than it had in radio.

Predictably, the first round of criticism of the show focused on the fringe characters and on Kingfish, whose malapropisms, feckless scheming, and anachronistic costumes and manners seemed a caricature of black middle-class aspiration. Even *Variety*, usually a defender of show business, complained of "the molasses-tempered janitor who is a throwback to the Stepin Fetchit era," and called for a toning down of exaggerated manners and stereotypes and a shifting of focus from burlesque to sympathy for the plight of the race. Led by the NAACP, the black middle class challenged what they took to be a parody of their historical struggle for social mobility in a hostile society.[27]

At first, the NAACP protest, which *Variety* played on page one, began with letters of complaint to the sponsor—Schenley Distilleries, the parent company of Blatz Beer—only hours after the premiere. In a few days the protest spread to various white liberal groups such as the American Jewish Committee, which proposed a team of consultants that included black psychologist Kenneth Clark of City College of New York and political scientist Robert MacIver of Columbia. The team was to draft an "unobjectionable" substitute program similar to the "loveable [and] admirable" *The Goldbergs* and other ethnic shows that had avoided alienating ethnic activists.

With many shows already "in the can," the network pointed out that the slightest changes would take weeks to reach television screens. Nevertheless, through the summer of 1951, the activists pressed on by means of outraged press releases, a rousing resolution at the NAACP convention in Atlanta, and nominal support from a small cluster of allies such as the United Auto Workers—and yet with scant results save for isolated gestures such as the decision of WTMJ-TV (Milwaukee) to drop the show.[28]

The snag in the NAACP campaign was not in its tactics but in the fact that the issue rested upon the ability of the organized black middle class to translate its own resentments into a collective black will to act. Instead of this intended outcome, however, the campaign exposed an undercurrent of dissension in black circles. Newspaper columnists, actors with deeply felt loyalties to show business, and television viewers compromised the NAACP's claims to solidarity, thereby softening the drive for dignified portrayals of the black bourgeoisie. As Billy Rowe of the *Pittsburgh Courier* pointed out, if black audiences wished "to look at people of their own color, performing for people of every color," this desire was in itself an aspect of racial integration that doomed the NAACP to "fighting a losing battle."[29]

Indeed, Rowe had hit upon the vulnerable center of NAACP demands. Walter White of the NAACP, in attacking the white monopoly on American broadcasting, depicted this nettlesome fact *only* in terms of its slandering the middle class. By focusing on *Amos 'n' Andy's* caricature of the middle class as indecorous, prone to use "street slang," and no more than a nest of "quacks and thieves [and] slippery cowards, ignorant of their profession," White appeared to concede that the CBS show had been accurate in its depiction of the black lower classes.[30]

With few exceptions, the black newspapers took a position in the middle between the NAACP and CBS, either because they reflected their readers or because they hesitated to offend the broadcasters and advertisers from whom they derived revenue. Occasionally, a paper played both angles, blasting the show as "disgusting" while also running CBS press releases. On the extremes were the *Amsterdam News*, which refused advertising for *Amos 'n' Andy*, and Billy Rowe of the *Courier*, who touted the show as "the greatest television show on earth."[31]

Actors heatedly denied the NAACP's charge that *Amos 'n' Andy* smeared the middle class. Clarence Muse, for example, spoke for black Hollywood when he praised the show as an "artistic triumph" that played upon "real Negroes you and I know." In a swipe at the NAACP he announced, "I have switched to Blatz Beer." One of the most senior members of the cast and a former director of feature films, Spencer Williams, also asserted the case for verisimilitude in opposition to the NAACP. Of one scene he asked rhetorically: "Now there's a situation that could happen in any home with any race of people, isn't that right?" Yet the actors' main concern was not so much art or social messages, but with their own version of striving for integration—job opportunities in Hollywood. One of their guilds, the Coordinating Council of Negro Performers, threatened to picket the New York NAACP to make their point. Individual dissenters kept their counsel. "I knew it was wrong," said Nick Stewart years later, but "I went along with it."[32]

As the split in black opinion became evident, broadcasters, advertisers, and white journalists joined in a collective expression of astonishment at the inflexibility of the NAACP position. Indeed, one ad executive felt "nonplussed" because Blatz's advertising agency drew such vigorous fire while "making a frank bid for Negro trade . . . [through] a policy of integration in hiring . . . [and] taking pains to assure the show's complete acceptance." The advertising tradepapers agreed, *Printer's Ink* predicting that the show would "be with us for a long, long time," while *Advertising Age* reported that "most Negroes in this area do not go along with the NAACP." In general, the white press probably believed, with Harriet Van Horn of the *New York World Telegram and Sun*, that the NAACP was "a trifle touchy."[33]

The central issue in the debate never came into focus. Both sides assumed that they were in essential agreement on the future of blacks in American life—a benignly liberal drift toward an eventually painless, fully integrated place in the American social order. Indeed, in its primitive stages the genre of television situation comedy tended to promote, ratify, and reinforce this bland, center-left vision of the future by depicting American society as a self-correcting system that was responsive to demands for "fair play."

Television producers had quickly invented a formula that expressed their sentiments as they applied to various ethnic groups—the Jews in *The Goldbergs*, Nordics in *I Remember Mama* (a novel, a drama, and a movie before its TV debut), and the Italians in *Luigi* (a "thoroughly moral character . . . [and] not a one-sided stereotype," according to *Variety*), *Papa Cellini*, and *Bonino*, the latter starring Ezio Pinza of the Metropolitan Opera. All of them shared a pool of interchangeable parts: an extended family, crotchety but warmly sentimental old folks, happy problems happily resolved in twenty-eight minutes of air time, and a division of characters into an older generation encrusted with cultural survivals from the old country and a younger group of super-Americans who had assimilated the virtues of the new land.[34]

Unfortunately, *Amos 'n' Andy* was asked to perform similar service for an ethnic group whose history included slavery, discrimination, and exclusion from the opportunity for easy assimilation implied in the gently comic plots of the European ethnic shows. Thus their traits of eccentric manners, dialect, and other cultural baggage were perceived not as vestiges of a national culture but as the mocking of racial subculture that was an aberration of white American culture. Moreover, the black middle class that spoke against *Amos 'n' Andy* perceived itself as having successfully struggled to overcome the cultural bondage that the characters in the show seemed looked into. In fact, within the shows this point was given emphasis in that the central figures, Andy and Kingfish, spoke in rural dialects, wore slightly off-center-clothing such as derbies and flashy suits, and behaved with exaggerated, hat-in-hand diffidence and cunning obsequiousness, while only the minor figures—the clerks and functionaries—were allowed the crisp Yankee accents and officious surroundings that marked them as middle-class successes. Thus, the NAACP activists were correct in their resentments, especially in view of the fact that the American broadcasting system allowed them no adversarial voice on the air.

At the same time, the writers engaged to write the television version—Bob Ross, Bob Mosher, Joe Connelly, Jay Sommers, Paul West, Dave Schwartz, and others—took pains to depict most of the supporting characters with a neat, pristine middle-class politesse. The actors—Jeni LeGon, Napoleon Simpson, and others—reinforced the writers' intentions with self-confident, solid bits of business; well-spoken, modulated voices; and a firm sense of place as though they had been born in paneled offices. The set decorators followed the same line of thought. Exteriors—even an alley through which a white thief had escaped—were clean and devoid of trash. In the kitchens were full refrigerators, four-burner stoves, matching china; on the walls were the stock symbols of middle-brow culture—Barbizon landscapes, Van Gogh's *Bridge at Arles*, and Kingfish's favorite painting, Hals's *The Laughing Cavalier*; scattered about their parlors were the candy dishes and books of a typical middle-class room.

In the scripts, the writers left the blocking, shot selection, movement and business, and other fragments of characterization entirely to the director and the actors on the set. Thus the development of specific details of character were placed in the hands of the actors—an important factor to black viewers who might get derivative pleasure from seeing Sam McDaniel, or some other actor forced by Hollywood circumstance into a lifetime of demeaning roles, play a straight role, uncluttered by heavy-handed dialect. Finally, in the few shows in which a heavy criminal appeared, he was sure to be played by Anthony Warde or some other white denizen of B movies.[35]

The ambience of the sets was matched by the equally bourgeois motivations of the characters. While it is true that neither of the two principals succeeded at their erratic careers, their failure never resulted from want of striving. The premise of the episode entitled "Jewel Store Robbery," for example, is that Kingfish and Andy ruefully reminisce about wasted opportunity. "Sapphire was right, Andy," says Kingfish. "I done wasted my entire life. Me who had such a brilliant record in school." Often at moments like these, the supporting characters appear as contrasts against which to measure the principals. In this show, Roy Glenn appears as a sleek, imposingly dressed, basso-voiced success. The comic plot turns on the humiliating fact that Kingfish's circumstances have forced his wife, Sapphire, to hire out as Glenn's maid. At the denouement Amos hammers home the point in a brief exchange with Andy:

> *I feel kinda sorry for the Kingfish. But you know, you can't much blame the King-*
> *fish for wantin' the folks down in Marietta to think he's a bigshot up here. It's*
> *just human nature for everybody to want somebody to think they is important.*
> *I guess that's what keeps a lot of us going in life.*

Moreover, the attention of the viewer is never allowed to stray from the plot and the characters into current events along the racial front. White characters, for instance, are never allowed to refer to race or even to notice that the principals are black. In one show in which a gang of white counterfeiters appear, they have a private opportunity to discuss the blacks but identify them only as "those two birds upstairs."[36]

The plots reinforced the message put forth by the set decorations and characterizations. In "Happy Stevens," for example, Kingfish and Sapphire, cranky and backbiting from a marriage gone stale, seek help from "the happy Harringtons," two white talk show hosts. But in the end, they not only learn that they can live with themselves, unpropped by the "cultured, charming chitchat" advocated by their radio counselors, but also that the station prefers them to the white Harringtons. In

"Kingfish's Secretary" the situation is used not so much to depict some small victory but rather to show how Kingfish has matured beyond his origins in Marietta. The dramatic contrast is provided by a Southern woman who has come north in answer to a matrimonial advertisement. The country woman suffers from comparision with the chic secretaries, primly dressed neighbors, well-stocked Harlem stores, and flippant dialogue of Harlem. Kingfish and Andy, with their slurred diction, outdated clothes, and perpetual suspension in midcareer between golden opportunities, suggest that although they are no longer bumpkins like the woman from the South, they are also still marching toward some form of bourgeois success. "That must be the scrubwoman," says Kingfish as he casually compares her with his own evolving parvenu style of life.[37]

Of all the shows, the most well known and affecting was a Christmas story that *Variety* described as "an almost classic bit." A simple story of a child's dream fulfilled at Christmastime, it provided a showcase for Andy to display his most deeply felt sentiments while seeking work that would allow him to buy a brown-skinned, talking doll for Arabella, Amos's precocious daughter. Andy's laying of the gift under the Christmas tree inspires Amos to compose a bedtime story in the form of a sentimental exegesis of the Lord's Prayer as it plays on the radio in the background, set to the music of Albert Hay Malotte.

As though challenging the NAACP, every incident, character, and set contributed to a touching domestic drama that was anything but an exploitation of black life. Indeed, the most persistently nettling quality of the program in the minds of black activists was not in the substance of plot or character but mainly in the survival of a stylized Negro dialect. Nevertheless, it often seemed balanced or disarmed by the middle-class accents that marked many of the shows. Thus, when Arabella asks crisply, "Wouldn't it be wonderful to have a white Christmas?" Andy replies with a favorite uncle's devotion, "Them's the best kind." Whatever Andy's small crimes against the language, he is treated with deferential respect by the janitor, who calls him *"Mistub* Andy." And if Andy professes that poverty is "rebarrassin'," or uses some other comic neologism, the preponderance of supporting characters speak in Yankee accents appropriate to the setting. A coolly professional nurse; a department store executive played by Napoleon Simpson, a veteran of Hollywood jungle movies; a floorwalker played by Milton Woods, a star in "race movies"; and a string of winsome kids who sit on Andy's lap as he plays the store's Santa Claus all speak in radio-announcer American.

In the end, Andy has played out a perfect bourgeois scenario: he has focused on a goal, worked for wages to accomplish it, deferred his own gratification, and ceremonially presented the fruits of his labors in a socially correct call on Arabella's parents. And he has accomplished all this at considerable psychic cost to himself in that he chose not to present Kingfish with a gift and had been insulted for it.

Every setting, prop, and gesture reaffirmed the form and substance of middle-class life. When Andy calls, Amos and his wife are enjoying a Christmas Eve pause in front of their tree. At the sound of the doorbell, Amos puts on a dark jacket, straightens his tie, and receives his old friend with a formal handshake. The rooms are jammed with the same icons of conventionality that have dressed the sets of all the programs in the series.

As though to confirm the theological sources of Andy's selfless behavior, the last scene is devoted entirely to Amos's interpretation of the Lord's Prayer. Up to this moment, every two-shot close-up of the characters has been in conventional television style—a succession of fixed, eye-level shots of "talking heads," intercut with reaction shots edited for easy continuity. Here, however Barton lowers the camera angle, tilting up on Arabella's bed, a setup broken by cutaways that tilt down on the recumbent and reverent girl. The sequence asserts Amos's fatherly authority and gives him an imposing presence through which to give a line-by-line exegesis of the prayer—which plays, *sotto voce*, on the radio. Amos's resonant expression of humanity's need for a deity, and his evoking of a natural order in which mankind may live with a hope for community, harmony, and brotherhood ends with a shot of falling snow, seen through the window from Arabella's point of view.[38]

Over the seventy-odd weeks of production, these softly decent characters and homilies balanced the shambling presence of Kingfish, thereby blunting the case of the NAACP. *Variety*, which frequently spoke for show business and for liberalism, used the Christmas show as a swipe at what it considered off-target militance. "Despite the hassle over civil rights currently engulfing the nation in this Presidential election year, *Amos 'n' Andy* isn't going to influence any viewer one way or the other," declared the trade paper. "If anything, the series shrewdly brings out some of the best characteristics of the Negro." Indeed, even though the cast was solidly black in almost every show, *Variety* inferred a subtle integrationist message that logically followed from "the great value of showing a Negro family living normal lives in normal surroundings sharing the emotional and religious experience of all people."[39]

Gradually the NAACP saw its image as defender of the oppressed take on an unaccustomed ambiguity as a pressure group whose "touchiness" in attacking the "most liberal" of the networks ruined the careers of black actors and polarized black opinion. Apart from the younger generation of black Hollywood, which shared the dismay of the NAACP at "the harm" done by *Amos 'n' Andy*, countless black actors and loyal listeners felt put upon by "outsiders" and, according to actress Lillian Randolph, "various white groups" who used the NAACP as a weapon to "eliminate the Negro actors [and] put [me] out of business."[40] Musician Lionel Hampton, the most conservative of black performers, set forth this economic line in its broadest social terms: "I look upon the new 'Amos 'n' Andy' television show as an opening wedge toward greater opportunities and bigger things for scores of our capable artists who haven't been able to get a break in video until this new Blatz-CBS show started." Blatz released the results of a poll that supported the performers against the NAACP, claiming that 77 percent of black New Yorkers liked the show. In 1952, Estelle Edmerson, a young graduate student, surveyed the actors and confirmed a deep vein of resentment at the NAACP pressure on their livelihoods, a strong sense of accomplishment, and gratitude toward the sponsor and network. They felt grateful for "a toe in the door" (Willie Best) and to be able "to eat three times a day" (Roy Glenn); they refused to "see anything objectionable" on the air (Eddie Anderson); they complained of organized blacks that "we, as a race, are too sensitive" (Johnny Lee); and they praised "the baby entertainment medium, television, [that] has accepted the Negro entertainer" (Cab Calloway). Ruby Dandridge extended Calloway's opinion by pointing to CBS's hiring of Flournoy Miller, whom "they ask for opinions when in doubt as to the insults to the Negro people." Whites such as Ed Sullivan also testified "that TV as a medium was made to order for Negro performers." Dissenters—most of them trained actors such as James Edwards, Juano Hernandez, and Frank Silvera—insisted on "the harm" done to liberalism by the show.[41]

In the end, the ambiguities both in the content of *Amos 'n' Andy* and in the splintered black response to it undercut the NAACP campaign to remove the show from the air. This is not to cast the organization as a lone figure in hopeless cause. By August 1951 the National Urban League had opened its own letter-writing campaign, which also attracted several white liberal groups. But intellectuals such as George Norford, drama critic of the *Amsterdam News*, and G. James Fleming, a political scientist from the Virgin Islands and an *Amsterdam News* reporter, began to hope to divert the attention of blacks toward a demand for "an open communications system" rather than the divisive question of whether or not *Amos 'n' Andy* excluded or burlesqued black bourgeois behavior. Indeed, the NAACP itself by 1954 turned its attention to studying the black broadcasting marketplace, ways to develop a "National Negro Broadcasting Council," and eventually a means of producing "network-calibre, quality programming" for independent Negro-appeal stations. One enthusiastic advocate told Walter White of the NAACP that radio—if not television—was "potentially the greatest instrument of progress that has ever been available to a minority race," a source of "cultural self-expression on a mass scale." and a source of jobs and income.[42]

Nevertheless, in the short run the NAACP had failed to cast *Amos 'n' Andy* as an enemy of the entire black world. Instead, the show had been characterized as a slander against only the black middle class. Thus, instead of fulfilling a *Chicago Defender* prediction that the "disgusting" revival of "stereotyping" would "be crushed . . . by the frontal assault of an enlightened and protesting people," the campaign merely sputtered out. Blatz's decision to withdraw from sponsorship at the end of the 1953 season was depicted in the trades not as a defeat at the hands of the NAACP, but as a quest for a higher-class image accomplished by picking up the prestigious *Four Star Playhouse*.[43] The show survived in syndication, often earning solid ratings and audience shares. Far into the 1960s *Amos 'n'*

Andy played as a "strip," or daily program, usually in fringe time but occasionally in prime.[44] In the large markets such as New York, heavyweight sponsors like Trans-World Airways bought the time slots. And when it finally expired in major markets it played on in small-time Southern metropolitan areas, remembered not as a vanquished enemy, but almost as a martyr—"one of the alltime major casualties of the radio-to-video transition," according to *Variety*.[45]

Why had the NAACP engaged in what seemed like a fruitless enterprise that split blacks and alienated white liberals? What had been gained by the playing out of the episode? The answers are not entirely clear, but they lie in the shifting goals and rising hopes of the postwar black leadership. World War II had enlarged black goals to include the possibility of eventual full integration into American life at the precise moment of a boom in memberships in black activist organizations. Simultaneously, *Amos 'n' Andy* arrived in full view of the television audience, complete with symbolic baggage from an older time in black history and broadcasting history. Solidly rooted in a segregated world, by its existence, even on television, it seemed to cast doubt over black social goals and to mock the newly powerful, organized black middle class. The virtues of black aspiration and success were simply too deeply imbedded in the fabric of the programs to invite appreciation by organized black activists—even though evidence suggests a faithful audience of black viewers.

Notes

1. Black middle-class values are taken up in David G. Nielson, *Black Ethos* (Westport, Conn., 1980), and August Meier, *Negro Thought in the Age of Booker T. Washington, 1885–1915* (Ann Arbor, Mich., 1965).

2. The quotations are from Estelle Edmerson, "A Descriptive Study of the American Negro in United States Professional Radio, 1922–1953" (Master's thesis. University of California-Los Angeles, 1954). pp. 115, 87, 94. NAACP activities are recorded in that organization's files in the Library of Congress.

3. H. B. Alexander, "Negro Opinion Regarding *Amos 'n' Andy*," *Sociology and Social Research* 16 (March 1932): 345–354, Bishop J. Walls, "What About Amos 'n' Andy?" *Abbott's Monthly*, December 1930, pp. 38–40. 72, the latter in James Weldon Johnson Memorial Collection, Beineke Library, Yale; *Los Angeles Sentinel*, 18 March 1948.

4. The Enoch Pratt Free Library of Baltimore reported that especially among "older" patrons demand was so heavy "you could hardly get hold of" some tapes. (telephone interviews with Florence Connor and Carolyn Houck, Pratt Library). Also available in Afro-American Studies Program, University of Maryland. College Park, Md., the director of which, Al-Tony Gilmore, is writing a book on *Amos 'n' Andy*. See also James Wolcott, "Holy Mack'ell: Amos 'n' Andy Videotapes Are Hot Items on the Nostalgia Market," *Esquire*, January 1981, pp. 11–12.

5. President's Committee on Civil Rights, *To Secure These Rights* (Washington, D. C., 1947). A good essay and bibliography on the period is Richard Polenberg, *One Nation Divisible: Class, Race and Ethnicity in the United States Since 1938* (New York, 1980). chap. 3, p. 330.

6. David Freeman, Jaffe Agency, to Hugh Wiley, 26 March 1953; 21 April 1952, Wiley Papers, Bancroft Library, Berkely, Calif.

7. L. S. Cottsell quoted in Paul F. Lazarsfeld, *Radio and the Printed Page* (New York, 1940), pp. 56–57, and in Edmerson, "Negro in Radio," p. 195.

8. J. Fred MacDonald. "Stride Toward Freedom—Blacks in Radio Programming," paper loaned by author, pp. 7–14, later a chapter in his *Don't Touch That Dial!* (Chicago, 1980).

9. Sample of Benny-Anderson dialogue in MacDonald, "Stride Toward Freedom." p. 11a. Black ambivalence toward Rochester can be seen in Edmerson. "Negro in Radio." pp. 185–187 (newspapers and *The Negro Yearbook* cited), and in Anderson himself, telephone interview between Anderson and Cripps, June 1970, in which he claimed never to have crossed boundaries of had taste nor depicted unreal characters.

10. See *Pittsburgh Courier*, 4 March 1942, for an example. A rich literature includes John B. Kirby, *Black Americans in the Roosevelt Era: Liberalism and Race* (Knoxville, Tenn., 1980).

11. For a sample of reviews of local and prime time network programs see *Variety*, 7 October 1942, p. 26; 11 March 1942, pp. 18, 35; 13 May 1942, pp. 32–33; 20 May 1942, p. 36; 10 Febraury 1943, p. 30; 17 February 1943. p. 28; 3 March 1943. p. 33; 8 April 1942. p. 30; 13 March 1944, p. 53; 3 May 1944, p. 1; 22 March 1944, p. 3; 16 February 1944, p. 43; see also MacDonald, "Stride Toward Freedom." pp. 25–33.

12. *Sponsor*, December, 1949, p. 44, on Robinson, cited in Edmerson, "Negro in Radio," pp. 12. 45; synopsis of *Story of a Drum*, CBS 15 February 1946, in Katherine Dunham Collection, Box 7, Morris Library, Southern Illinois University, Carbondale, Ill.

13. Docments from *Destination Freedom* Collection, Institute for Popular Culture Studies, Northeastern Illinois University, cited in J. Fred MacDonald, "Radio's Black Heritage: *Destination Freedom*, 1948–1960," *Phylon* 39 (March 1978): 66–73.

14. Edmerson, "Negro in Radio," p. 165, and conversations between Barnouw and Cripps, 1975–1976. Edmerson's informants, pp. 350–359, cited sponsors who feared pejorative associations with blacks ("nigger flour") and "a mixed reception from Negroes themselves." Thus civil rights groups inquired into broadcasting as a weapon. Ann Tanneyhill of the National Urban League, for example, argued: "I do hope we will be able to move into the fields of motion pictures and radio in 1948. We 'scooped' other race relations agencies on the comic book but I fear they will beat us to the draw on motion pictures and radio." *Morning for Jimmy* file, NUI. Records, Library of Congress.

15. "The Forgoten 15,000,000," *Sponsor*, October 1949, pp. 24–25, 54–55; Edmerson, "Negro in Radio," pp. 350–354; "Selling the Negro Marker," cover story in *Tide*, 20 July 1951, in NAACP Records; "Can TV Crack America's Color Line? *Ebony*, May 1951, p. 58. *Ebony* from 1948 through 1952 gave heavy coverage to television as though believing its own assertion that "television has supplied ten-league boots to the Negro in his fight to win what the Constitution of this country guarantees."

16. *Variety*, 9 January 1952, p. 32; 3 September 1952, p. 26;6 February 1951, p. 31; 11 January 1950, p. 28 (in which George S. Schuyler's talk show is seen as "in line with a new policy of cultivating the Negro audience").

17. *Amsterdam News* (New York City), 12 August 1939.

18. *Variety*, 3 May 1950, pp. 30, 40.

19. On programming, see *Variety*, 8 February 1950, p. 58; 19 April 1950, p. 24; "Television," *Ebony*, June 1950, pp. 22–25; *Variety*, 11 January 1951, p. 28; 10 September 1952, p. 30; 22 October 1952, p. 27; 26 November 1952, p. 30. On policies of executives, *Variety*, 8 November 1950, p. 26; 17 January 1951, p. 26; 18 July 1951, p. 1.

20. Edith Tedesca, CBS personnel, quoted in Edmerson. "Negro in Radio," p. 103.

21. Glucksman-Barnett correspondence in Barnett Papers, Chicago Historical Society, NUL interceded for blacks seeking entry into broadcasting, as in placing lyricist Joe Lutcher as a prospective writer of Camel cigarette commercials, thereby providing another crack in the white monopoly. Wesley R. Brazier to Guichard Parris, 5 December 1952, Series 5, Los Angeles 1944–61 file, box 42, NUL Records.

22. Reels are scattered among Clark College, Atlanta; Library of Congress; and Kit Parket, Carmel, Calif.; Glucksman to Barnett, 25 August 1954; *Variety*, 11 August 1954, p. 41.

23. *Amos 'n' Andy* began in 1929 on Chicago radio, moving eventually to network broadcasting, recordings, two RKO films in 1930, and animated cartoons (cartoon in Library of Congress, films on KDKA-TV, (Pittsburgh); *Variety*, 9 October 1930, p. 31; 20 August 1930, p. 4; 8 October 1930, p. 22. See also Norman Kagan, "Amos 'n' Andy: Twenty Years Late, or Two Decades Early?" *Journal of Popular Culture* 6 (Summer 1972); 71–75.

24. Quoted in Kagan, "Amos 'n' Andy," pp. 71–75.

25. *Los Angeles Sentinel*, 18 March 1948; *Variety*, 1 February 1950; 28 April 1948, p. 1; 4 October 1950, p. 30; 5 November 1950, p. 1, the latter for a report of the national post-prime time sneak preview.

26. Interviews, June 1970 and the summers of 1976 and 1977, between the author and Nick Stewart, Bill Walker, Ernest Anderson, Jester Hairston, Alvin Childress, Sig Mickelson, and Charles Barton.

27. *Variety* 4 October 1950, p. 30; C. L. Dellums to Walter White, 6 December 1950, NAACP Records.

28. *Ebony*, May 1951, p. 21; *Variety*, 4 October 1950, p. 30; *Color*, clipping; Dellums to White, 6 December 1950; Lindsay II. White et al. to Lewis S. Rosenstiel, Schenley Distillers, copy, 27 June 1951 (all but *Ebony* and *Variety* in "*Amos 'n' Andy*" file, NAACP Records).

29. *Pittsburgh Courier*, 7 July 1951; *Variety*, 4 July 1951, p. 1; Walter White to Committee, copy, 10 July 1951; White, memorandum for file, 11 July 1951, and on 10 July 1951 marked "not to be given out," in NAACP Records. The committee included the topmost rank of the national NAACP, along with Ralph Bunche, journalists Norman Cousins and Lewis Gannett, Louis T. Wright, Channing Tobias of the YMCA, and Algernon Black of the National Council of Churches.

30. *New York Times*, 22 September 1951; Walter White to "subscribing newspapers," copy, 12 July 1951; Gloster B. Current to "NAACP branches and state conferences," copy, 16 July 1951; NAACP press release, "Why the Amos 'n' Andy TV Show Should Be Taken Off the Air," 15 August 1951; press release, "New Protests Mark 4th Week . . . 26 July 1951"; Ardie A. Halyard, Milwaukee Branch, to Current, 27 July 1951, NAACP Records.

31. Walter White to newspapers, 2 August 1951; White to Billy Rowe, 27 July 1951, NAACP Records, in which White argued that the shows affected society to the point of causing a riot, and demanded proof of Rowe's linkage of the NAACP with the Communist Party.

32. For the mixed black response see *Chicago Defender*, 23 June 1951 (Fred O'Neal): 7, 14, 28 July 1951; 18 August 1951 (CCNP); *Variety* 28 January 1953, p. 1 (NBC defense), 24 June 1953, p. 1 (sponsors); *Defender*, 29 September 1951 (UAW); 25 August, 18 August 1952 (anti-NAACP actors); 8 September 1951 (Negro Masons' split); 29 September 1951 (clerical protest); *Variety*, 8 August 1951, p. 1 (statements by Lester Walton and Noble Sissle); *Negro Achievement* 9 (November 1952), p. 40, latter in Johnson Collection, Beineke Library, Yale.

33. W. Richard Bruner, "Amos 'n' Andy Hassle Won't Stop TV Show," *Printer's Ink: Advertising Age*, 13 August 1951; Arnold M. Rose, "TV Bumps into the Negro Problems" *Printers' Ink*, 2 July 1951, p. 36; Walter White, "Negro Leader Looks at TV Race Problem," *Printer's Ink*, 24 August 1951, p. 31; *New York World Telegram and Sun*, 27 July 1951; *Interracial Review*, September 1951; *New Leader* 15 October 1951; Gosden and Correll quoted in *Advertising Age*, 13 August 1951; Harold Doman and Thelma Eastman, draft petition on "integration," 31 July 1951; Lindsay II. White and James E. Allen, NAACP, copy, to Lewis S. Rosenstiel, Schenley, 27 June 1951; Walter White to newspapers, copy, 2 August 1951, all in NAACP Records.

34. *Variety*, 23 August: 1950, p. 28, 24 September 1952, p. 30 (*Luigi*); 1 October 1952, p. 101 (*Cellini*); 16 September 1953, p. 31 (*Bonino*); Walter White memorandum, 10 July 1951, recounting the rule of Edward J. Lukas, American Jewish Committee, in influencing the content of the *The Goldbergs*, NAACP Records.

35. "Happy Stevens," "The Kingfish's Secretary," and "The Rare Coin" in Enoch Pratt Free Library; scripts in Library of Congress and in Special Collections, UCl.A.

36. "The Jewel Store Robbery," in Pratt Library, script in Library of Congress.

37. Source as in note 35.

38. "The Christmas Show," viewed through the courtesy of Professor Al-Tony Gilmore, chairman, Afro-American Studies. University of Maryland, College Park, Md.

39. *Variety*, 31 December 1952, p. 18.

40. Edmerson, "Negro in Radio," pp. 89, 117, 126–129, 192, 391–393, 396, 403.

41. Hampton quoted, *Pittsburgh Courier*, 4 August 1951, in Edmerson, "Negro in Radio," p. 391; Blatz sample in *California Eagle*, 23 August 1951, also in Edmerson, p. 193. Her other interviews derived from pages cited in note 40.

42. Interview between George Norford and the author, 29 October 1970, in which Norford recalled a tension between feeling that the shows were "funny as hell" and his opposition to network exclusivity that denied blacks access to the air; conversations with Professor Emeritus G. James Fleming of Morgan State University, especially one on 31 October 1975. On the NUL campaign, see Ann Tanneyhill, NUL, to Frank Stanton, CBS, 10 August 1951; Tanneyhill to Bill Chase, 10 August 1951; Tanneyhill to Lewis S. Rosenstiel, 10 August 1951, Series 7, Box 1, NUL Records. On the NAACP's inquiry into a "National Negro Broadcasting Council" and some form of "network-calibre" programming for blacks, see Harry Novik, WLIB, to Walter White, 10 January 1951; 7 July 1954; and David D. Osborn et al. to White, [July 1954], 19 pp., in NAACP Records.

43. *Chicago Defender*, 7, 14, 28 July 1951; *Variety*, 18, June 1952, p. 28 (Blatz's withdrawal); 11 March 1953, p. 25 (*Four Star* and also the outsized "nut" of *Amos 'n' Andy*); *Variety*, 8 August 1951, (a page-one story on the threats of Lester Walton, a veteran black drama critic, and Noble Sissle, a famous bandleader, to picket NAACP offices as a means of dramatizing black opposition).

44. In the decade following the suspension of production, *Amos 'n' Andy* remained a staple of the syndication market, generally in a pattern of good solid ratings in southern states and through the West to Bakersfield, and in smaller markets. Thus in the same summer week in 1955, it finished first among syndicated shows in Little Rock but ninth in Washington. Where it was possible to measure, it seemed to play equally well in northern towns such as Evansville and southern towns like Shreveport, but also in large markets where heavy black populations resided such as Detroit. One week in 1956, it was number one in New Orleans with a rating of more than 50 and an audience share of more than 80, while one month later in New York, in keeping with its pattern of flopping in large markets, it finished tenth with a rating of 7.5, against *Looney Tunes*. This trend also included less clearly measurable traits, among them the possibility that when *Amos 'n' Andy* was opposed by programs that were slanted toward children, the adults in the family overrode the tastes of the young. In Shreveport in the summer of 1961, for example, *Huckleberry Hound* finished fourth with a rating of 16 as against the 22 posted by *Amos 'n' Andy*. Gradually, through the early 1960s, even though the same viewing patterns persisted, the size of the figures tailed off. Ratings consistently fell below 20, even in southern and small-town markets, and even in towns such as Dayton, Bakersfield. Atlanta, Charlotte, and New Orleans the show regularly finished ninth or tenth in the local race for hegemony in syndication. Sample made by Alma Taliaferro Cripps and Paul Hagan Cripps for the years 1954–1963.

45. *Variety* continued to cover the story even as the combative elements of it diminished. See 2 July 1952, p. 24; 31 December 1952, p. 18; 13 May 1953, pp. 38–39; 16 September 1953, p. 21; 3 June 1953, p. 25; 13 January 1954, p. 25. For postmortems in addition to the *Esquire* article cited in note 4, see "The Case of the Missing Roast Beef," *Ebony*, April 1958, p. 143; "Requiem for the Kingfish." Ebony, July 1959, pp. 57–64; Edward T. Clayton, "The Tragedy of Amos 'n' Andy," *Ebony*, October 1961, pp. 66–73 (which reported that "no other Negro show has been able to find a national sponsor"); and Thomas Cripps, "The Films of Spencer Williams," *Black American Literature Forum* 12 (Winter 1978): 128–134.

The Spectacularization of Everyday Life: Recycling Hollywood Stars and Fans in Early Television Variety Shows

Denise Mann

Many advertisements took their place alongside other mass diversions—the amusement park, the slick-paper romance, the movies. None demanded to be taken literally or even all that seriously; yet all promised intense "real life" to their clientele, and all implicitly defined "real life" as something outside the individual's everyday experience.

Jackson Lears[1]

At the turn of the century in America, the burgeoning field of mass amusement institutionalized the promise that "real life" was just around the corner. Hollywood, with its charged overpresence of stars, glitter and glamor, went on to institutionalize the idea that "real life" was to be found in the movie theater. Studio publicity departments singled out female fans, in particular, for their devoted attention to Hollywood stars and product tie-ins through fan magazines and mass circulation magazines.[2]

Hollywood Stars and Female Fans

The privileged relationship between the motion picture industry and the female fan at the turn of the century has been charted in several social histories as well as in theoretical studies such as Miriam Hansen's recent analysis of the Valentino case and its relationship to female viewer habits.[3] Little attention has been given to the transformation that takes place in this impassioned relationship some thirty years later once Hollywood stars and stories are received in the mundane circumstances of women's everyday lives—the domestic setting of television. The transfer of Hollywood stars to the home via television during the transitional period from 1946 to 1956 shifts the viewing context not just from a public, community event to a private, isolated experience, but also restructures the spectator's fantasy engagement with the movies. This change constitutes a radical transformation in the social imaginary that had previously bound Hollywood stars to their fans. Television representations of the Hollywood star as well as radio's representations before them, reflect a decay in aura[4] once they have been transferred to the new broadcast media.

This study focuses on the television comedy variety show and musical variety show which featured guest stars from Hollywood. These formats represent two arenas of nostalgic return, not only to earlier entertainment traditions (to vaudeville, burlesque, minstrel, etc.), but to strategies adopted by Hollywood films and by their publicity departments to engage women as the most devoted audience of Hollywood stars. The fan and mass-circulation magazines surrounding Hollywood and its star system marked women spectators as an economically and socially viable group—one which the broadcast industry sought to incorporate as an audience for its own mass-media forms.[5]

The Hollywood star offered a potent connection with the fascination of Hollywood cinema—invoking not only the cinema's "cult of subjectivity" but also the star's association with a charged "otherness"; alternatively, the Hollywood star's association with consumer excesses and ostentatious behavior ran counter to fifties ideals of homogeneity and equal opportunity for all.[6] The Hollywood studio publicity departments in previous decades had devised various techniques to negotiate the contrasts in lifestyle and appearance between the Hollywood star and the average working-class or middle-class woman. Contradictory representations of women in the films themselves—as glamorous "screen sirens" and average housewives or working women—do not begin in the postwar period but can be traced to an earlier period. For instance, Mary Ann Doane discusses this phenomenon in the woman's films of the forties using the example of Bette Davis as the twin sisters in *A Stolen Life*.[7] She notes that these oppositional roles are recapitulated in the advertiser's address to female audiences which claim "Every Woman Plays a Double Role . . . [as] Secretary and Siren. . . ." In addition, Jane Gaines's analysis of the forties "pin-up" demonstrates how easily this standardized icon of eroticism was adapted to conform to the more conventional female social roles of wife and mother.[8]

While these studies indicate that contradictory representations of women exist prior to the period under examination, television substantially alters the spectator's relation to these conflicting beauty ideals and social roles for women. In particular, the television variety show helped arbitrate the contrasts in lifestyle between the Hollywood screen siren and the average woman by bringing the performative aspects of vaudeville (its direct address and mugging for the camera) into conflict with the cinema's "illusionist" conventions, challenging as well, the passivity inherent in the cinema's representation of the woman in her object-like-ness.

Early television variety shows adopted a complex set of narrative strategies to produce a "marriage of spectacle and intimacy."[9] This integration of opposing tendencies is based, on the one hand, on television's self-conscious attempts to duplicate vaudeville, burlesque and Broadway theater, entertainment forms which took place in communities bound by ethnic and class alliances.[10] On the other hand, TV variety shows retained ties to the "intimacy" of the classical Hollywood cinema in narrative skits which took place in domestic settings (and which reproduced the illusion of centered subjectivity); this continuity was produced in part by borrowing stylistic elements from the cinema (e.g., close-ups to convey interiority and point-of-view editing).

Recycling the Movie Star as Individual

For working-class and middle-class women of postwar America, the home no longer constituted a sanctuary from the forces of consumer culture—despite efforts of popular culture to convey the contrary through nostalgic references to the past; for instance, Serafina Bathrick's analysis of nostalgic family-musicals from the forties demonstrates how these films cultivated a female audience of consumer allies by translating the more traditional values of home and family to contemporary products of the culture industry.[11] National advertising, network corporations and their bureaucratic agencies had penetrated the daily lives of the family at home with their magazine and radio commercial messages by the 1930s. These and related advertising and network corporate structures were responsible for relaying Hollywood stars and stories to female fans via television—institutions whose presence was foregrounded by means of the various mediating figures of network announcer, product announcer and, in the case of the variety show, the TV show host. The illusion of "centeredness" which the classical codes had insured, mobilizing individual desire through elaborate fantasy scenarios, had been substituted in the television setting by a complex organization composed of anonymous institutions which "made it possible" for these stars to appear on television.

This changed circumstance of spectatorship meant a decentered relation between star and fan. In turn, this decenteredness altered the previous terms of the bond, throwing into jeopardy the apparent "autonomy" and "individualism" of the media celebrity. Richard de Cordova's work on the early manifestations of the star system has demonstrated how star discourses work to suggest the marks of enunciation, contradicting Metz's claim that the classical Hollywood film effaces this discursive register.[12] The emphasis on the performative activities of movie stars coupled with a studio star system which promotes the illusion of "individualism" surrounding its stars through its publicity and press releases, makes these performers appear to subsume the category of enunciative address.

This institutionalization of the cult of the individual by the studio star system and studio publicity departments underwent a series of decisive changes in the postwar period. In the midst of the CBS talent raids in 1948, the broadcast star was legally reconfigured to adapt to the new capital gains tax structure.[13] Star names were reconstituted as "property" to be administered primarily by the celebrity rather than by the studio or network. These highly publicized negotiations over star properties in popular press and trade discourses regulated knowledge of these celebrities[14]—emphasizing their status as property over their status as private persons.[15] In the fifties, Hollywood actors began renegotiating their contracts as well, setting up independent companies and demanding control over their image, their roles, and their own advertising and publicity, even in those instances when they made studio films.[16] Ironically, even though motion picture actors were taking charge of their own image, this radically undermined their status as individuals—an image that studio publicity departments began carefully monitoring as early as 1909.[17]

During this transitional period, one means of reengaging the public's imaginary relation to movie stars on television was to enact a nostalgic return to their earlier careers and to the popular discourses surrounding these stars. For instance, there were prime-time variety shows and family sitcoms which targeted the whole family and featured the regular appearance of movie stars as guests. Programs such as *I Love Lucy, The Jack Benny Show* and *The Martha Raye Show* contained narratives which reworked the middle-class housewife's relationship to these celebrated figures from Hollywood by foregrounding the position of the female fan. In addition, in the mid-fifties, a series of "tributes to Hollywood" emerged. One of the first of these appeared in 1952 when Ed Sullivan saluted the career of producer Samuel Goldwyn. This was followed by several movie tie-ins produced by the studios which provided ten to fifteen minute "trailers" of recent Hollywood releases, including *MGM Parade, Warner Brothers Presents* and 20th Century–Fox's *Front Row Center* (for General Electric) as well as Disney's *Disneyland* and *The Mickey Mouse Club*. In addition, Paramount Pictures's interest in York Productions, which it jointly owned with Dean Martin and Jerry Lewis, resulted in *The Colgate Sunday Hour* and *The Colgate Comedy*. The latter show followed Ed Sullivan's lead in "saluting" new feature pictures through talent tie-ups.

These movie talent tie-ins on television proliferated into publicity campaigns, talent promotional tours and sundry merchandising activities which resulted in an almost seamless penetration of Hollywood's consumer appeals into the interstices of the family's everyday life.[18] Daniel Boorstin characterized this tendency in postwar America as television's capacity to create a bond among viewers which constitutes a false community of consumers: "never before had so many individuals been so dependent on material goods for their identity."[19] This community of consumer citizens produced a radical break from the individual spectator's personal past and the community's shared historical past. One of the ways in which television variety shows and other products of fifties culture industry helped negotiate entry into the modern era for middle-class viewers was by adapting the now devalued Hollywood "cult of subjectivity" to more longstanding traditions and values from the past—in particular by wedding the fifties version of the "nineteenth-century True Woman and the twentieth-century movie star."[20]

For instance, *Look* magazine featured a fashion article on the "back button" dress which conflates the fifties nostalgia for the past with the vogue for leveling class differences between stars and fans. This complex advertising strategy is accomplished by featuring movie star Charlton Heston helping his wife, Lydia Clarke, into a "recycled" fashion concept—the back button dress.[21] By conveying the idea that women are helpless, the fashion feature does not just sell women on a "new" style, but reinforces cultural stereotypes of the "True Woman" and the caretaker husband, and promotes the institution of marriage as well: these dresses require "a husband's helping hand" to allow the woman to get dressed in the morning. The article notes the ironies of this fashion design for "America's 14 million unmarried women," but celebrates nonetheless, this "impractical throw-back to the 19th century. . . ." The writer notes the contradictions for modern women who "breathed a sigh of relief with the passing of the unwieldy back-laced corset . . . but now, down their backs (find) not only buttons, but snaps, hooks and slide fasteners to harness the girls again and put a high premium on a man—personal maids being even harder to come by."[22] The feature encourages fashion-conscious modern women to take up these impractical designs by conflating the traditional values of home and marriage with the image of the Hollywood star as domestic homebody. Charlton Heston's function is thereby split between that of husband and "auratic star"—between attending to the "homey" task of helping his wife get dressed in the morning, *and* introducing "romantic" fantasy associations into an otherwise banal activity.

Recycling Middle-Aged Stars on TV

In a 1955 article, "Old Film Stars Never Die—Just Keep B.O. Rolling Along," *Variety* states that the box office draw of current stars doesn't match that of stars nurtured under the star system of previous decades.[23] The article claims that "audiences today apparently are much slower to 'make' a star . . . [hence] the studios are competing energetically for men and women who played their first lead parts in the middle 30s." *Variety*'s list of durable "glam personalities" includes Clark Gable, Bette Davis, John Wayne, Betty Grable, Spencer Tracy, Ginger Rogers. . . ." According to *Variety*, the only newcomers who command the same box office stature as these older stars are Marilyn Monroe and Marlon Brando. The disadvantages of relying on the older stars, of course, is "that the passage of years is beginning to whittle away at the appeal of the stars of yesteryear."

Variety's comments reiterate the popular view that the old stars and the old Hollywood represented a "glamour" and "extravagance" that was no longer valid in 1950s America—except, that is, through nostalgic recyclings of the star's previous persona in new formats. Popular culture forms which recycled stars in this way include, for instance, the "self-reflexive" musicals of the fifties (Fred Astaire in *Bandwagon*, Judy Garland in *A Star is Born*); middle-class magazine photo essays featuring star biographies which chart the career of the star in pictures; advertising for contemporary beauty and fashion ideals associated with Hollywood stars; and variety shows "saluting" the stars and their careers.

The success of each of these popular culture strategies depended on their ability to trigger the audience's memory of details from the star's personal life and screen persona. Much of early television programming, then, consisted of "simulations" of popular culture traditions from the past. Many of these fragments of past performances emerged out of ethnic theater—leisure practices which took place in communities defined by ethnic, class and gender specificities; however, once these forms were transposed to television, they were stripped of any previous associations with the community. These nostalgic images from the past appeared on early television shows in an abstracted, fragmented form, borrowing elements from vaudeville and burlesque; taking scenes from already self-reflexive Hollywood stories (e.g., Gloria Swanson's spoof on her role in *Sunset Boulevard* on *The Texaco Star Theater*); or in caricatures of famous performers from the past (e.g. Milton Berle's drag impersonation of Carmen Miranda).[24] This postmodernist impulse—the creation of a new television spectacle out of the fragments and reworkings of the original spectacular, public event—invoked "simulated" emotions and produced a synthetic sense of community, united by its shared memory of previous media contexts. This is nowhere more evident than in early television variety shows which restaged Hollywood stories and recycled stars. Hollywood's penetration into the television industry provided a means of spectacularizing the everyday. By evoking memories of intensely felt emotions and an opulent world that existed outside the home, these programs provided a much needed antidote to the homogenizing tendencies of so much of the popular culture imagery of the postwar period. One movie producer summed up popular assumptions about the differences between Hollywood stars and TV stars: "TV can give them stories about frustrated butchers and homely aunts . . . but we can take an audience into Vesuvius or plunk them headfirst into the China Sea."[25]

The movies in postwar America promoted themselves by holding onto their associations with aristocratic behavior and conspicuous consumption. Television variety shows featuring Hollywood stars as guests were capitalizing on the lingering appeal of these idols of consumption. On the other hand, these same TV shows contained skits which made Hollywood stars appear as intruding figures, threatening the positive values and associations of domesticity and family life maintained by the television star, week after week.[26] According to Jane Gaines, audiences were more likely to direct their bitterness and envy toward Hollywood stars during the Depression, or in war-torn America "because they were visible and identifiable whereas institutions are anonymous."[27] A brief examination of popular discourses on Hollywood stars reveals strategies which may have helped audiences negotiate their contradictory responses to Hollywood stars during the period of vast social and economic upheaval that followed WWII. Many of these same techniques are taken up by the TV variety show.

Hollywood/Television: A Period of Consolidation

According to Roland Marchand, in postwar America the popular press conveyed an image of average Americans as being more affluent, having more leisure time and more opportunity to improve their standard of living.[28] But in point of fact, only those in the very top income bracket were noticeably affected by the postwar boom.[29] The 1950s saw a 26% rise in average income with credit and installment buying providing more possibility for more families to duplicate the portrait of the affluent suburban family being promoted by advertisers. But most lower-to-middle-class families had to struggle to meet this ideal image.

In response to perceived changes in the public's attitude toward these idols of consumption in an era which valued equality of opportunity, in 1956 *Look* featured an article called "Hollywood Revisited: A Psychological X-Ray of the Movie Colony Today—its Manners, its Conflicts, its Morals—Where Television, Wide-screen and Middle-age Have Forever Changed the Life and Work of the Glamorous."[30] Charting the lives of Hollywood stars in 1956, the article proclaims: "they are less carefree, less reckless, less extravagant. Today it's chic to be simple."[31] The article is meant to demonstrate how "toned down" Hollywood stars have become, and yet photos of the stars convey the opposite impression. One shows Susan Hayward wearing an "odd getup" consisting of harem pants, halter top and what look like police boots, an outfit designed to "beguile the blasé." Another features Sonja Henie's flamboyant arrival at a party at Ciros. She wears a sequined trapeze artist costume and rides a baby elephant. The article conveys the ambivalence fifties fans felt toward Hollywood, their dissatisfaction with its class pretensions and also their ongoing fascination with its sensual excesses. This provided women at home with an imaginary link to a charged "real life" outside their everyday life in the domestic sphere.

On the other hand, the animosity expressed in this article toward Hollywood stars' aristocratic sensibilities can be traced to the forties, when studio publicity efforts downplayed certain stars in order to militate against what the studios perceived as reader hostility toward the stars' "upper class" lifestyles. For instance, in her analysis of fan magazines in the forties, Jane Gaines says Lana Turner was brought down to earth in a report which told readers that "she returned her rented sable to the furrier after every party . . . [while] Joan Crawford was described as a homebody who preferred listening to Bing Crosby or Dinah Shore to listening to opera."[32] Radio (and later television) stars such as Bing Crosby and Dinah Shore came to embody the "down to earth" qualities favored by the popular press in the postwar period. Studio press releases began to emphasize those qualities which made movie stars appear to be "homebodies." By deemphasizing class distinctions, representations of Hollywood stars in fan and mass circulation magazines during the forties and increasingly during the fifties served a therapeutic function, helping the housewife or working woman overcome feelings of powerlessness and the inability to rise above her current social role or class standing.[33]

Postwar Fashion and Beauty Ideals for the Average Housewife

By the 1950s, popular ideals regarding women's bodies and clothes were in transition. *Look* and *Life* began featuring articles on fashion and body types that emphasized comfort and uniformity in contrast to Hollywood's often unwieldy and extravagant designs. For instance, when Gregory Peck and 20th Century-Fox star, Maris Pavan, appeared in *The Man in the Gray Flannel Suit, Look* carried a series of ads and fashion spreads which showed the stars sporting ubiquitous gray flannel suits.[34] "Gray flannel is in the limelight from Hollywood to the Eastern suburbs," *Look* claims. "Whether a girl is a movie star, advertising executive or housewife, gray flannel's appeal to her is limitless." To convey this "classless, ageless fashion," *Look* features a suburban wife meeting her husband in gray flannel slacks (by Evan-Picone) at the Pelham, N. Y. railroad station in a photograph which is not only larger, but dominant on the page, placed above the photo of the movie stars wearing gray flannel.[35] Another example promoted by *Look* magazine is the "strapless apron [which] shows your shoulders."[36] The caption explains that "it goes on in a jiffy over strapless dresses—and still keeps you looking beautifully bare." For fashions that extend "classlessness" in the opposite direction, *Look* magazine in 1948 offers ranch clothes that take clothing previously designed for the "hard-working" ranch life to the "vacation-minded" American from Portland, Maine, to Portland, Oregon.[37]

As these features suggest, postwar fashion tastes reflect a composite of opposing ideals—a conflation of the star's wardrobe with that of the average suburban housewife, or alternatively, the conflation of working man's clothes with the middle-class leisure set. The "leveling" effect of these outfits is overdetermined in the fashion feature on gray flannel suits which explains: for the "huckster," gray flannel conveys "sincerity," and for the average woman it conveys "slickness."[38] While this ad expresses the mistrust and skepticism which underlines the public's reading of visual images and consumer appeals in the media, it also produces a compensatory image of social relations in postwar America.

The superficial appearance of equal opportunity for all underlying these complex popular culture strategies—their purportedly neutral goal of "classlessness"—can in point of fact be seen to reinforce an ideology of political indifference which diffuses whatever class consciousness had been prompted by studio releases foregrounding class distinctions between the stars and their fans in the thirties and forties. In her analysis of fan magazines, Jane Gaines indicated the extent of this class awareness which prompted readers to express anger toward press releases which tried to downplay the celebrity's obvious advantages over their working-class counterparts.[39] A series of ads for Auto-Lite Spark Plugs which appeared in *Look* magazine in 1948 epitomize this superficial homogenizing process. These ads emphasize the crossover between movie stars and average housewives by featuring "lookalikes." In one of these ads, a housewife from Brooklyn, N. Y., who "looks so much like Miss [Dorothy] Lamour that strangers frequently ask her for her autograph on the street . . ." is pictured side by side with a photograph of the "real" Dorothy Lamour. The ad asks the reader to guess which is the movie star.[40]

In the same year, *Look* offers a feature asking average citizens "How has having a movie star's name affected you?" Average men and women with stars' names are interviewed—including a beautician named Anne Sheridan, a cafeteria helper named Esther Williams, and a truck driver named Harold Lloyd.[41] Photos of the average citizen are produced, but none are provided of the stars to whom they are compared. If the reader had been allowed to scrutinize one photograph next to the other, it would have introduced an uncomfortable "class awareness," reminding the reader of the material discrepancies dividing the two groups. The subtlety of this rhetorical strategy serves two ends: it preserves the auratic qualities of the stars (by invoking in the reader memories of some previous experience of a fantasy engagement with a favorite star as the movies, or in a fan magazine); secondly, it neutralizes any evidence of the material class distinctions separating stars and fans. This double-edged strategy plays an important role in the development of early television variety programming which introduced Hollywood stars into their shows. By dividing the auratic from the class-defined characteristics of the Hollywood star, early television programs were able to exercise any lingering associations of Hollywood stars with aristocratic behavior.

TV Stars: Frustrated Butchers, Homely Aunts and Obsessive Fans

The previous discussion indicates that popular attitudes toward Hollywood stars were in a process of transition in postwar America, Visual representations of TV stars as ordinary individuals—frustrated butchers and homely aunts—can be seen as a compensatory gesture designed to counteract the celebrity's status as either upper class, or as corporate property. However, a brief look at the popular discourse on television stars and radio stars before them reveals them reveals the contradictions which were exposed in trying to portray these "corporate salesman" as authentic individuals. For instance, *Look* magazine's 1949 spread on Arthur Godfrey lauded him for his "honest, plain common-sense approach."[42] In the following month, several viewers wrote letters to the editor expressing their mixed feelings about Godfrey's supposed sincerity.[43] These readers challenged the popular press' image of Godfrey as natural and spontaneous, pointing out his ultimate responsibility to sponsors. For Instance, reader R.L. Morrisey notes: "this guy Godfrey has the formula, all right. He slouches down in an easy chair, takes off his tie, rolls up his sleeves and convinces 40,000,000 radio listeners that he's just like good ol' Uncle Fred. Like Uncle Fred, he spins salty yarns and leads the group singing. But unlike Uncle Fred, Godfrey's payoff is of strictly big business proportions. . . ."[44]

This letter and others like it evoke the contradictions attending reception of radio's purportedly authentic stars. On the other hand, despite the unmistakable hostility of this letter, Morrisey closes by conceding that Godfrey satisfies a "social need" for the majority of viewers. This therapeutic mode points to the conflicting needs which media celebrities satisfied in postwar America. Morrisey concludes: "More power to Godfrey . . . because he's a daily tonic to so many people."[45]

In the early thirties Jack Benny's radio show produced a separation of star functions by displacing the role of the "glamorous star" onto his Hollywood guest stars, making Benny himself their dupe or fool. (This separation was already in place in his vaudeville persona—his ironic presentation of himself as an arrogant, pretentious concert violinist who plays the violin badly.) In his radio and television programs Benny undermined his own status as star by pitting himself against glamorous movie stars like Marilyn Monroe, Claudette Colbert or Ronald Colman. By coveting their Oscars, their film roles, and their co-stars, he was openly acknowledging his "difference" from the Hollywood star, a difference which audiences no doubt recognized when they compared themselves to Hollywood stars. By contrasting the TV stars to their Hollywood counterparts, the believability and trustworthiness of the former were reinforced. This split in function attributed to each set of stars—the broadcast vs. the Hollywood—provided a means of rechanneling the libidinal attachment fans felt for Hollywood stars, and at the same time encouraged women to empathize with TV stars as sincere product salespersons.

One of the rhetorical strategies used in variety show skits to integrate these two arenas was to nest one audience/text relation within the other: in other words, the Hollywood star/fan relation was framed in the context of the broadcast star/audience relation. This narratological structure is apparent when Marilyn Monroe makes her first television appearance on Benny's show. Benny holds the position both of movie star fan *and* TV star/host. As TV star/host, Benny introduces Marilyn Monroe as his guest star. However, once he steps into character in the skit that follows, he maintains his character role of movie star fan and he also plays himself—Jack Benny, the TV star.

In the skit, his imaginary relation to the auratic star is constructed *in her absence:* he imagines that he is pursuing Marilyn Monroe; in fact, he is pursuing an ordinary-looking woman. Like Benny's character, this woman is imaginatively tied to Hollywood's romantic fantasies—she reads a

Hollywood fan magazine. When Benny confuses her with Marilyn Monroe, she adapts herself immediately to the fantasy scenario. In contrast, once he realizes she's not Marilyn Monroe, he pulls away. She testily reminds him that he's not Errol Flynn either. The exchange is symptomatic of the contrast in popular attitudes toward Hollywood vs. TV stars. In addition, the skit characterizes popular assumptions about female spectators—that they have a more active imaginary—allowing them to participate more fully in the Hollywood romance scenario. But, it is suggestive that in this instance the male TV star is being put in the "feminized" position of the fan.

This strategy informs other comedy variety shows which place the TV star in the powerless, "feminized" role of the movie star fan. These rhetorical strategies can be seen as a way of arbitrating the contrasts between the movie star and the home audience via the TV star. Benny's power and autonomy vanish once he adopts the "feminized" position of the adoring fan in the narrative skit. It returns once he reappears on stage as the star of his own show and speaks to the audience in "direct address." These changing power dynamics are the result of shifting rhetorical positionings rather than some essentially "female" characteristic of desire. By having TV stars (both male and female) function in this intermediary role of "feminized" spectator (conforming to popular assumptions about female fans), these TV variety shows may have helped produce alternative and multiple positions of identification and so helped mediate the public's receptivity to Hollywood stars. However, this case requires further exploration.

The TV Star/Host as Authentic Individual

After the skit, Benny comes out on stage to thank Fox Studios for allowing him to "dream" about Marilyn Monroe on his show. The irony implicit in Benny's statement is that while the sponsor has made a contractual agreement with the studio to have one of its stars appear on television, what has in fact been purchased is the imaginary affect or aura linking Hollywood stars to their fans. This imaginary relation is the result of the star's pictures, publicity and fan materials—synthesizing aspects of the actor's public and private life. As a result, stars like Marilyn Monroe appear out of place in the overtly commercial context of television, unless that presentation is negotiated—in this case by the split roles of the TV star as star/host and fan. When Marilyn does finally appear on stage at the end of the show, plugging her recent film, wearing a glamorous evening gown and adopting her often photographed "open mouthed smile," her Hollywood star persona remains intact. Her appearance on Benny's show functions much like the traditional product testimonial for shampoo and other beauty products—an accepted formula for linking the female star's image to consumer products while at the same time providing promotional tie-ins to the star's recent pictures.[46]

The Hollywood star persona from the past projected a cohesive portrait of an individual—a synthesis of the various elements of the star's career and home-life, all engineered by the studio publicity department. Even overt product tie-ins had to refer the viewer to the star's glamorous persona. In contrast, the radio and television host's star persona is radically split between his or her function as autonomous individual and as corporate spokesperson. In order to systematize the heterogeneity underlying this "direct address" to the audience, Benny, along with Ed Wynn and several other performers, began incorporating an ironic perspective into their speech. The radio star could reengage listener trust by calling attention to the commercial structure of the television address. For instance, in 1931, Benny began substituting his opening line, "Hello, again" with "Jello, again."[47] In addition, Benny expresses the irony of trying his "direct sell" techniques on audiences who were immune to sales pitches: "Gee, I thought I did that pretty well for a new salesman. I suppose nobody will drink it [Canada Dry] now."[48] Irony allows the radio host to expose the materiality underlying his or her speech—its commercial context in the sponsored program. By giving viewers the impression that advertisers and their stars had placed all their cards on the table, viewer skepticism was partially circumvented.[49]

Benny's ironic speech may have distanced him in part from the advertising context, however, it produced a tenuous "individuality" against the overbearing commodification of his broadcast star persona. The instability of the TV star image as a coherent originator of the TV show's enunciative address is further complicated once that position is held by a woman in view of the spectator's memory of the patriarchal bias underlying the Hollywood cinema and its typical portrayal of women as spectacle of a male gaze.

The Everyday Female TV Star vs. The Glamorous Hollywood Star

Alongside the development described above, the TV star's "divided" and hence unstable position of enunciative address, is another set of discourses about female TV stars and female product announcers. These emphasize their "naturalness" in contrast to Hollywood's elaborate machinery for deception. A 1954 article, "Claws Out!—Glamor Girls vs. TV Actresses," graphically outlines the opposition by stating that Hollywood stars are the product of Hollywood's massive publicity techniques, their glamour the result of Hollywood's extensive costume, makeup and lighting.[50] Television advertisers perpetuated this image of the TV star's naturalness in their appeals to women. *Television Magazine*, for instance, advised advertisers not to use overly glamorous stars to advertise their products because women don't like to see a glamorous woman washing dishes or scrubbing floors.[51] When asked about Kate Smith selling products on the air, a viewer says "... I don't see how Kate Smith would have too much time to use a sewing machine. And ... I don't think she herself puts it [floor wax] on or knows anything about it." When asked if that bothered her, the viewer said: "No, I just don't think about it because I love to hear Kate Smith talk and sing, she's a wonderful woman."[52] These advertising claims reinforced the view that mass media images of housewives were "natural" and images of glamorous Hollywood stars were unnatural. These popular assumptions intervene in the spectator's reception of Hollywood stars on television variety programming in the early period.

Martha Raye—Recasting The Movie Star as Television Star

These contradictory attitudes toward female media celebrities in the postwar period frame the following discussion of *The Martha Raye Show*. Martha Raye's address to women at home—as herself (presumed to be an authentic individual) and as a product spokesperson (for Hazel Bishop cosmetics)—is complicated by her previous Hollywood persona. The remainder of this study is devoted to the Martha Raye case in view of the relationship between her film and television roles. Her contradictory representations of femininity from films made in the thirties and forties figure significantly into relevision's negotiated portraits of feminine ideals for the postwar period.

From 1936–1938 Raye appeared in a series of Paramount films playing various "trouble-prone secretaries" and "boy-mad coeds."[53] In 1938 Paramount decided to change her image as slapstick comedienne and feature her in a series of glamour girl roles, including *Give Me a Sailor* (1938) in which she won not only a legs contest against Betty Grable but the leading man as well. This was followed by several other films which adapted Raye's image to suit more conventional standards of feminine behavior and beauty from the forties. The contradictions inherent in Raye's movie career are restaged in her 1950s television show. Opposing representations of women are structurally woven into the variety format. The program alternated between staged spectacles featuring Raye in elaborate gowns and glamorous lighting and narrative skits in which Raye plays average working-class and middle-class women.

Raye's suitability for sincere product testimonials was jeopardized by the instability of her image. For instance, *The Martha Raye Show* opened with Raye demonstrating Hazel Bishop cosmetics while "mugging" in front of the camera, mocking traditional cosmetic ads which used glamorous models or movie stars. The second and third ads in the program returned to a more conventional ad structure (and notably excluded Raye). These ads took place in Hollywood, a shift in location that did not in fact take place but was indicated by an announcer and by showing filmed scenes of familiar Hollywood locales. These techniques were designed to transform the "live" New York stage into Hollywood for the benefit of the home audience. Lesser known female stars were brought onto the stage to demonstrate the glamorizing effects of these cosmetics. Despite these efforts to reproduce the typical association of Hollywood and glamour (a standard technique borrowed from magazine advertising), Hazel Bishop spokesperson, Raymond Spector, repeatedly voiced his dissatisfaction with his company's sponsorship of Raye's show and eventually dropped the show in the 1955 season.[54]

This shift in locations—from filmed sequences to the television stage—has other implications beyond the advertiser's cooption of Hollywood's glamour for product demonstrations. Spatial continuity between TV's "live" sets and filmed exteriors appear in other portions of the "live" variety show and demonstrate television's debt to classical Hollywood conventions on a number of fronts. Typically, these two "spaces" are brought together by means of conventions borrowed from classical Hollywood films; for instance, in an episode which shows Martha leaving her apartment and entering the street, the transfer from the staged, domestic setting to the filmed exterior is produced by having her neighbor look out the apartment window and wave to Martha below. The second (filmed) shot shows Martha looking back up from the street. The sequence perpetuates this alternation of staged and filmed views, culminating in an automobile crash (which is simulated by intercutting filmed long-shots of Martha, driving her antiquated car in busy city streets, and close-ups of Martha inside the car, shot on a stage). When Martha collides with a Rolls Royce belonging to a glamorous Hollywood starlet, the sequence that follows highlights the striking contrast between Martha and the movie star. This is conveyed by returning to a "staged" version of the street scene and by shooting the scene in a frontal long-shot: Martha's austere clothes and old car are juxtaposed to the glamorous movie star's furs, jewels and Rolls Royce. The overt class dimensions of this scene are commingled with questions of preferred beauty standards for women. The sequence overtly parodies the convention of the male gaze at the female-as-object: several male bystanders "reconstruct" the accident in favor of the glamorous movie star, pretending not to see Martha, focusing their attention instead on the starlet. On the other hand, the audience is able to see both women side by side, as well as the inequity of the social dynamics at play, and is encouraged, thereby, to empathize with Martha.

These reconstructed views, depending on the audience's familiarity with Hollywood conventions—the object/glance structure in this case—would *not* be enacted for the studio audience. In order to overcome this lapse in the variety show's "marriage of spectacle and intimacy," large monitors were placed above the stage for the benefit of the studio audience.[55] This addition of a frame or screen to the "live" television event undermines statements made by critics of the period who criticized TV for enacting a simple return to vaudeville and other forms of ethnic theater.[56] TV producers may have been responding in part to these critics when they adapted these theatrical stage traditions by incorporating alternative forms of representation. In particular, the presence of a screen, necessary to mediate the studio audience's reading of the "live" theatrical event, reveals the extent to which variety shows abstracted elements from these earlier forms of stage entertainment and adapted them to contemporary rastes by incorporating conventions inherited from the classical Hollywood film.

TV Retraces the Past: Adapting Hollywood Conventions to Postwar Ideals—The Case of Martha Raye

In previous sections I examined strategies taken up by the popular press both to preserve the star's auratic properties and efface the troubling question of class underlying the star/fan relation through visual representations which leveled material differences separating these two social groups. To this set of contingencies, *The Martha Raye Show* contributes yet another dimension—the need to adapt her unstable femininity to contemporary ideals of domesticity and feminine behavior. Her TV variety show made use of a complex series of narrative strategies to realign contemporary social roles for women with representations of women institutionalized by the Hollywood cinema. As described above, several episodes of *The Martha Raye Show* undermine the Hollywood convention of the male gaze at the female-as-object as men avert their eyes from Martha and stare at attractive

Hollywood starlets. These scenes are invariably shot in television's predominantly-used frontal long-shot and *not* according to the Hollywood convention of the object/glance structure which tends to naturalize gendered hierarchies. In these instances, using theatrical staging helped negotiate viewers' responses to Raye's unstable image: female spectators were more likely to align themselves with Raye's social circumstances rather than identify with the glamorous Hollywood starlet if allowed to scrutinize the material discrepancies between the two women in the tableau shot. The shot reveals class dimensions which had been effaced in the example cited earlier—*Look*'s editorial feature, "How Has Having a Star's Name Affected You?" Rather than suppress the class dimensions of the movie star/female fan relation, *The Martha Raye Show* produces hyperbolic versions of this power relation. Martha Raye's guest stars appeared variously as a king, a movie mogul, a director, a famous celebrity (Liberace), a millionaire son of a corporate president, and an advertising executive. In each case, Raye plays an "average girl." (She is identified as such by newspaper headlines, radio announcers and an advertising accountant). Raye plays a maid, a waitress, a manicurist.

In most episodes of *The Martha Raye Show*, Raye plays the role of the female fan in love with her Hollywood guest stars. Mary Ann Doane has described several Hollywood melodramas, such as *Stella Dallas* and *The Spiral Staircase*, which also incorporate scenes of female viewers at the movies.[57] These women are typically portrayed as victims in narrative trajectories which make the cinematic apparatus appear "to be mobilized against the woman."[58] By fixing her as object of another's gaze, she loses the capacity to see and hence to act on her desires. In contrast, the television variety show's representation of female fans produces a different result. While Raye is often "caught" by the gaze of the camera, her status as object-of-the-look is undermined when she stares back, mugging for the camera. In addition, her aggressive pursuit of her male guest stars from Hollywood overturns the Hollywood trope of the powerless woman "caught" by the male gaze. Raye and other "average-looking" female fans who appear on the show tend to stare at, chase and throw themselves at Raye's male guest stars. *The Martha Raye Show*, then, reframes the TV spectator's role—making it into a more complex, contradictory engagement on several fronts: first, by subverting Hollywood's representation of the woman as erotic spectacle of the male gaze; second, by challenging the one-sidedness and passivity of the object/glance structure; and finally, by challenging preconceptions about the acceptable limits of female expressions of desire.

On those occasions when other "average" women appear on *The Martha Raye Show* alongside Raye, she mediates between these women and the Hollywood star (just as she mediates between the home audience and the guest star). In one case, Martha appears on stage with Gordon McRae to negotiate the exchange between him and his fan club. In another episode, Raye is the only woman who is *not* in love with Cesaroni (Cesar Romero parodying Liberace, a fifties sex symbol). The latter show opens in a flashback to Martha being tried by a courtroom full of angry, vengeful female fans for having disfigured their beloved object of desire. (Raye accidentally knocked out his teeth, ruining his "perfect smile.") These episodes provide unflattering portraits of female fans, producing an imperceptible negotiation for viewers at home—one which encourages them to change the imaginary bond between themselves and their favorite Hollywood star. Invariably, these scenes invite viewers to dissociate themselves from empathetic identification by breaking down the Hollywood convention of the "fourth wall." By having the voice-over announcer speak directly to Raye or to the fans who in turn state into the camera, the possibility of identification with these women is complicated.

The typical skit in *The Martha Raye Show* encourages the home viewer to observe critically Martha's one-sided love affair with her rich and famous Hollywood guest star. (The male movie star always has ulterior motives for seducing Martha which are revealed to the audience but not to Martha.) For instance, in one skit, Douglas Fairbanks, Jr. plays a corporate executive in charge of the Fizzo Soft Drink account. He is searching for the perfect woman to advertise his product. He conducts his search by compiling a composite photograph from "the best parts" of seven beautiful women; the final portrait results, ironically, in a photograph of Martha Raye's face. This hyperbolic parody of advertisers' objectification and commercialization of the female image produces contradictory readings. The scene denounces the advertiser's objectification of the female image; however, when Martha eagerly takes up the position of the new Fizzo Girl, the criticism is diffused. The home audience is encouraged to identify with Martha's newly-won position of power and fame as a media star, despite the fact that she plays only a "pitchgirl."

The latter skit reinforces a contemporary trend in the popular press surrounding television—one which encourages women at home to identify with "pitchgirls" who look like housewives.[59] This viewpoint is maintained by having the Fizzo agency receive thousands of letters from female spectators reassuring them that they prefer product spokespersons to be "average" women like Raye rather than glamorous stars. By encouraging women at home to identify with media celebrities whose lives mirror their own, a new form of celebrity worship is invoked and a new form of cultural hegemony is validated—one which constructs women as "consumer allies" by aligning the values of home and family with popular media representations of celebrities. On the other hand, Raye's slapstick performances undermine these same ideals of domesticity and femininity; Raye "washes" the piano with a squeegee and serves cake to her future in-laws using her hands. Once again, her mugging for the camera challenges the stability and passivity invoked in Hollywood representations of women-as-objects. During her performance as the Fizzo Girl she becomes drunk and unruly, making a mockery of the fifties popular ideal of the happy housewife as product spokesperson.

In these episodes, the dominant values of domesticity and femininity are thrown back into a state of flux. The variety show's veneer of ironic self-awareness waylays viewer skepticism. But, by undermining the stability of the woman's image (her object-like-ness in the Hollywood object/glance structure), it also induces an arena of liminality between the old and new sets of values, between the gendered power relations typically associated with the classical Hollywood film (a set of assumptions which inevitably lead one back to Mulvey) and the as yet unformulated power relations being set forth in television's address to women.

The Martha Raye Show challenges the naturalization of gendered power relations learned from the typical Hollywood text in part by exposing conventions such as the object/glance structure. These television shows function as oppositional texts to the extent that they respond to perceived changes in the values and attitudes of the public in the midst of a period of vast social and economic change. *The Martha Raye Show* tends to intercede in conventional narrative trajectories of identification (such as that produced in *Now Voyager*, for instance, which encourages viewers to identify with the homely girl only insofar as she learns how to adopt forties standards of feminine beauty by the end of the film). This is accomplished in *The Martha Raye Show* by introducing alternative views of femininity—in particular, by incorporating negotiated (i.e., oppositional, carnivalesque, slapstick) portraits of the middle-class housewife from fifties popular culture. Ultimately, these compensatory images of femininity from the fifties can be seen to serve a conservative function by helping the home viewer arbitrate the contrast between the Hollywood glamour girl and their own lives.

Another means by which the variety show responded to conflicting representations of female behavior and female desire was by offering alternative conceptual frameworks from which to derive pleasure from the typical Hollywood romance scenario. For instance, when Fairbanks seduces Martha in his apartment, the scene is a parodic inversion of a Hollywood love scene. As Raye sits on the sofa, the lights dim, the music goes up and the bar emerges from the wall, but, in spite of her awareness of the "mechanics" underlying his seduction, Raye falls in love with Fairbanks anyway. The female audience at home, although perhaps aware of the deception inherent in the seduction, is encouraged to identify with Raye's romantic conquest of Fairbanks.

Raye's internal state of mind is conveyed by the changes in lighting and the shift to soft focus. The scene therefore retains a certain continuity with classical Hollywood conventions used to express interiority and encourage identification. On the other hand, Martha's excessive mugging for the camera calls attention to the overly present technology: stage hands appear from behind pictures hanging on the wall, throwing blossoms and squirting perfume on Martha to signify her euphoric state. The audience's focus is split between acknowledging the artificiality of the romantic scenario (the result of technology's intrusion into the domestic setting) and being imaginatively tied to Raye through identification with her interior state of mind. These structural oppositions are welded together in away that goes beyond Hollywood's typical forms of "self-reflexivity" in backstage musicals which take place in a theatrical setting (as in Gene Kelly's seduction of Debbie Reynolds on the studio lot in *Singin' in the Rain*). These early TV texts refer to a spectator "outside" of the staged scene, challenging thereby, the narrow fictional world of the typical Hollywood film—a strategy designed to make the viewer feel like a participant in the construction of the televised scene.[60]

Because they expose techniques by which Hollywood engages its audience, it is tempting to assign these television texts a subversive or critical role. The television variety show encourages oppositional readings by structurally opposing diverse representational practices (alternating between vaudeville's direct address and proscenium space and the Hollywood film's close-up, closed fiction, and framed view). On the other hand, these oppositional practices can be seen as consistent with rhetorical strategies initiated in the radio period—techniques designed to divert viewer skepticism by exposing the corporate structure and commercial logic underlying the production of these imaginary scenarios. These strategies can be seen to perpetuate the radio star's ironic perspective (described earlier in terms of Jack Benny and Arthur Godfrey). Only now the irony has penetrated the entire fabric of the variety show structure by means of a systematic deconstruction of Hollywood codes responsible for making women passive participants in a libidinally charged, imaginary relationship with Hollywood's stars.

The variety show host, by mediating the Hollywood star/fan relation *for* the television audience, provided the foundation upon which the Hollywood/network interaction was built in the years to come.[61] Previously, female fans at the movies, who were engaged in an unspoken social contract with Hollywood stars, were encouraged to suppress their awareness of the institutionalized mechanisms underlying that relationship. But female spectators of television variety shows were encouraged to reengage in fantasy relationships with Hollywood stars, knowing all the while that they were corporate-produced, commercially-sponsored, consumer-dependent romances.

Conclusion

The variety show contributed to the negotiation of Hollywood's participation in television and to the public's receptiveness to its stars. The "presentational mode" of the variety show abstracted elements from vaudeville's theatrical setting to provide a space in which to transpose the auratic qualities of the Hollywood star to the new mundane setting of the family living room. However, once the transfer of the glamorous into the everyday had been negotiated (preserving women's imaginary relationship to Hollywood's stars and fantasy scenarios), this popular format began to wane by the late fifties. Its restaging of Hollywood's stars and stories pointed up the schizophrenic underside of the Hollywood star/fan relation—its commercial logic and corporate structure.

On the other hand, during this transitional period of negotiation between the two industries, TV's recycled images of Hollywood glamour and glitter encouraged women at home to access the imaginary fantasy world and self-contained moments of pleasure which average women could achieve as fans sitting in front of their TV sets in their own homes. By foregrounding the power relations organizing the Hollywood star/fan encounter (through techniques of ironic reversal and parody of classical Hollywood conventions) viewers were asked to recognize the practical limits of these imaginary scenarios—pleasurable fantasies which could *not* be extended to women's actual social circumstances. Ultimately these television tributes to Hollywood served both the interests of the network hegemony and consumer culture by diverting viewer skepticism away from the anonymous corporate institutions and reasserting media celebrities as the focal point of the public's combined hostility and admiration.

NOTES

1. T.J. Jackson Lears, "From Salvation to Self-Realization: Advertising and the Therapeutic Roots of Consumer Culture, 1880–1930," in *The Culture of Consumption: Critical Essays*

in American History, 1880–1980, ed. Richard Wightman Fox and T. J. Jackson Lears (New York: Pantheon Books, 1983), pp. 1–38.

2. Charles Eckert, "The Carole Lombard in Macy's Window," *Quarterly Review of Film Studies* 3:1 (Winter 1978), pp. 1–22; Maria La Place, "Bette Davis and the Ideal of Consumption," *Wide Angle* 6:4 (1985), pp. 34–43; Jane Gaines, "The Popular icon as Commodity and Sign: The Circulation of Betty Grable, 1941–55." Diss. Northwestern University, 1982.

3. Judith Mayne, "Immigrants and Spectators," *Wide Angle* 5:2 (1982), pp. 32–41; Elizabeth Ewen, *Immigrant Women in the Land of Dollars: Life and Culture on the Lower East Side, 1890–1925* (New York: Monthly Review Press, 1985); Miriam Hansen, "Pleasure, Ambivalence, Identification: Valentino and Female Spectatorship," *Cinema Journal* 25:4 (Summer 1986), pp. 6–32.

4. Walter Benjamin, "The Work of Art in the Age of Mechanical Reproduction," in *Illuminations.* Reprinted from the French, 1936; ed. Hannah Arendt (New York: Schocken, 1969), pp. 217–352. In adapting Benjamin's concept to the Hollywood star, I depart slightly from its original meaning—used to describe mass produced products of the culture industry which have lost their uniqueness and claims to autonomy. The changed status of Hollywood stars in the postwar era is a function of popular discourses regulating knowledge of these individuals. These discourses emphasize the stars as institutional products and deemphasize their status as private persons. John Viera details the modern day legal ramifications of this change—which require legal protections for individual claims on such abstract "properties" as celebrity names and images, both during the individual's lifetime and posthumously in "The Law of Star Images, Media Images and Personal Images: Personality as Property." Diss. University of Southern California, 1985.

5. "The Audience—A Profile of TV Owners, Their Habits and Preferences," *Television Magazine* (November 1953), pp. 19–21. According to this survey, "the highest number of women before the TV receiver [in 1953] is earned by comedy variety shows, with quiz-audience participation, drama and musical variety close behind."

6. Mary Ann Doane, *The Desire to Desire: The Woman's Film of the 1940s* (Bloomington & Indianapolis: Indiana University Press, 1987), p. 26. Doane discusses the ramifications of this association of Hollywood stars and consumerism for women: "the glamour, sheen and fascination attached to the movie screen seemed most appropriate for the marketing of a certain feminine self-image."

7. Mary Ann Doane, p. 29.

8. Jane Gaines, p. 16.

9. Sylvester "Pat" Weaver, cited in Judine Mayerle, "The Development of the Television Variety Show as a Major Program Genre at the National Broadcasting Company: 1946–1956." Diss. Northwestern University, 1983, p. 217.

10. Judine Mayerle discusses this continuity in great detail; for example, she notes: "In order to have as much of an old-time vaudeville flavor as possible, NBC/Kudner/Texaco considered renting a vaudeville house and broadcasting the show from there. . . ." p. 87.

11. For a complete discussion of this phenomenon, see Serafina Kent Bathrick, "The True Woman and the Family-Film: The Industrial Production of Memory." Diss. University of Wisconsin-Madison, 1981.

12. Richard deCordova, "The Emergence of the Star System in America: An Examination of the Institutional and ideological Function of the Star: 1907–1922." Diss. University of California, Los Angeles, 1986, p. 120.

13. Robert Metz, *CBS: Reflections in a Bloodshot Eye* (Chicago: Playboy Press, 1975), pp. 137–145; Irving A. Fein, *Jack Benny: An Intimate Biography* (New York: G. P. Putnam's Sons, 1976), pp. 121–124. Also see Arthur Frank Wertheim, *Radio Comedy* (New York: Oxford University Press, 1979).

14. Richard deCordova. My use of this concept follows from deCordova's analysis of the early star system using an historical methodology informed by Foucault.

15. "Talent Agents: Have They Won Control over TV Costs?" *Sponsor* 9:1 (January 24, 1955), pp. 35–37, 116, 119–120. "Should You Hire Your Competitor's Star?" *Sponsor* 7:1 (June 15, 1953), pp. 32–33, 82. "Tips on Using Your Film Show Talent in Ads," *Sponsor* 7:1 (June 15, 1953), p. 36. "Five Ways to Promote Your Program," *Sponsor* 6:2 (October 20, 1952), pp. 40–41, 64–72.

16. "Stars Now Experts on Ads, Too," *Variety* 200 (October 12, 1955), p. 5.

17. Richard deCordova, pp. 116–17.

18. Charles Sinclair, "Should Hollywood Get it for Free?" *Sponsor* 9:2 (August 8, 1955), p. 102. Every kind of plug imaginable has been used to boost the new Disneyland amusement park. As one ABC TV official in New York network headquarters likes to paraphrase Churchill: "Never have so many people made so little objection to so much selling."

19. Daniel Boorstin cited in Marty Jezer, *The Dark Ages: Life in the United States* 1945–1960 (Boston: South End Press, 1982), p. 133.

20. Serafina Bathrick, p. 5. Bathrick's analysis demonstrates how nostalgic family-musicals sought ". . . to remake and so to naturalize the history of the relationship between the nineteenth century True Woman and the twentieth century movie star." I have extrapolated from her analysis a model for analyzing how other fifties products of the culture industry made this transition into the postwar era.

21. Marjorie Schlesinger Deane, "The Dress That Needs a Man," *Look* 20 (February 7, 1956), pp. 80, 82–85.

22. Marjorie Schlesinger Deane, p. 80. The pages of *Look* in the fifties have numerous references to recycled "old-fashioned fashions;" for instance "a return of 'buckles, buttons and bows to modern shoes, and the 1956 version of the hobble-skirt as briskly modern.'" *Look* 20 (July 24, 1956), pp. 58–59.

23. Fred Hift, "Old Film Stars Never Die—Just Keep B.O. Rolling Along," *Variety* 200 (September 7, 1955), p. 7. Also see "Is TV a Haven for Hollywood Has-Beens?" *TV Guide* 2:3 (August 21–27, 1954), p. 22.

24. Arthur Frank Wertheim, "The Rise and Fall of Milton Berle," *American History/American Television: Interpreting the Video Pass*, ed. John E. O'Connor (New York: Frederick Ungar Publishing Co., 1983), pp. 55–78. Wertheim argues that Berle's ethnically derived vaudeville humor was no longer responsive to changing tastes in view of the altered demographics of the audience—from urban metropolitan areas, expanding in 1952–1954 to small town and rural regions with the addition of coaxial cable and national hookup. Various strategies taken up by *The Martha Raye Show* and *The Buick-Berle Show* in the mid-fifties reflect this process of adaptation to a program format stripped of its association with an ethnic and class-defined community.

25. Leo Rosten, "Hollywood Revisited: A Psychological X-Ray of the Movie Colony Today—its Manners, its Conflicts, its Morals—Where Television, Wide-screen and Middle-age Have Forever Changed the Life and Work of the Glamorous," *Look* 20 (January 10, 1956), pp. 17–30.

26. "How Can Prominent TV Entertainers Best Avoid a 'Boom and Bust' in Their Popularity on Video?" *Sponsor* 9:1 (June 27, 1955), pp. 54–55. Charles B. Ripin says: ". . . material taken from real life situations . . . [allows] the audience to project itself into the skit and participate with the entertainer." "Sid Caesar has recently shown an appreciation of this thinking by inserting his 'family type' sketches." Lefebvre, cited in Bathrick (p. 4), remarks that everyday life "evades the grip of form," and "cludes all attempts at institutionalization," However, as Bathrick demonstrates, the family-musical [and by extension, the television variety show] are culture industry products which make female audiences believe they have participated in the construction of the film's spectacle of everyday life.

27. Jane Gaines, p. 475. Gaines's remarks refer to the thirties and forties but may be seen as true of the fifties as well.

28. Roland Marchand, "Visions of Classlessness, Quests for Dominion: American Popular Culture, 1945–1960" in *Reshaping America: Society and Institutions, 1945–1960*, eds. Robert H. Bremner and Gary W. Reichard (Columbus, Ohio University Press, 1982), pp. 163–192.

29. Richard Parker cited in Marchand, p. 170.

30. Leo Rosten, pp. 17–28.

31. Leo Rosten, p. 21.

32. Jane Gaines, p. 471.

33. In a four page photo essay on Gregory Peck with his new wife at home, he is described as a star who "disdains the noisy trappings of 'star stuff.' " Stanley Gordon, "Tall, dark and dignified . . . Gregory Peck," *Look* 20 (July 24, 1956), p. 82; another article says Gable, "unlike other stars . . . likes to hang around and talk with 'lower echelons.' " Joe McCarthy, "Clark Gable: How He Became King of Hollywood," *Look* 19 (November 1, 1955), p. 104.

34. "The Girl in the Gray Flannel Suit," *Look* 20 (April 3, 1956), pp. 59–61; Ad for *The Man in the Gray Flannel Suit, Look* 20 (April 3, 1956), p. 83.

35. *Look* 20 (April 13, 1956), p. 61.

36. "*Look's* Strapless Apron Shows Your Shoulders," *Look* 12 (March 2, 1948), p. 49.

37. "Ranch Clothes Craze," *Look* 12 (March 2, 1948), pp. 55–56.

38. *Look* 20 (April 3, 1956), p. 59.

39. Jane Gaines, p. 443. Gaines has demonstrated the type of class backlash that occurred in the forties; for instance, when working class women objected to the unlikely press depiction of Lana Turner as ". . . a lonely, almost friendless beauty. . . ." In another case, a black college girl wrote to Bette Davis in a question and answer feature of *Photoplay-Movie Mirror Magazine*. She told Davis that she felt she shared with the stars the ability to make a success of herself, although she admits that "it is a little more difficult for her than for a white girl." Davis's response effaced the race issue altogether by saying "God helps those who help themselves" (p. 420).

40. Auto-Lite Spark Plugs ad. "Which is *Really* Dorothy Lamour?" *Look* 12 (March 30, 1948), p. 15.

41. "How Has Having a Movie Star's Name Affected You?" *Look* 12 (March 16, 1948), pp. 14, 16.

42. Jonathan Kilbourne, "America's Man Godfrey," *Look* 13 (February 1, 1949), pp. 28–29, 32.

43. "Letters and Pictures: Whose Man Godfrey Is He, Anyhow?" *Look* 13 (March 4, 1949), p. 8. The public's mistrust of Godfrey culminates when Godfrey publicly fires Julia La Rosa for his "loss of humility." Fans and critics question his actions in a series of editorials, articles and interviews; see for instance, Bob Stahl, "Godfrey Snaps Back at 'Untruths,' " *TV Guide* 2:28 (July 7–14, 1954), pp. 13–14.

44. *Look* 13 (March 4, 1949), p. 8.

45. *Look* 13 (March 4, 1949), p. 8.

46. Atwan, R., D. McQuade and J. Wright, *Edsels, Luckies, and Frigidaires: Advertising the American Way* (New York, Dell, 1979), p. 312. "Familiar movie formula of planting guest stars in exchange for movie credits has been brought to a new high polish on tv, as in Marilyn Monroe's visit to CBS TV's 'Person to Person,' " *Sponsor* 9: 2 (August 8, 1955), p. 33.

47. Wertheim, *Radio Comedy* (New York: Oxford University Press, 1979), p. 141.

48. Wertheim, p. 141.

49. ". . . the effective use of humor and ridicule involving the sponsor and his product can actually enhance the value of the testimonial." "Pitfalls in Commercial Techniques," *Television Magazine* 10 (November 1953), p. 36.

50. "Claws Out! Movie Glamor Girls vs. TV Actresses," *TV Guide* 2:11 (March 12–18, 1954), pp. 5–7. "Hollywood bigwigs are backed by tremendous glamor buildup that TV players can only envy."

51. Joseph C. Franklin and G. Maxwell Ule, "Is Your Brand Showing?" *Television Magazine* 10 (July 1953), p. 24. "Housewives don't want to see anything that's not so. . . . Now we all know how to wash dishes, and if we're looking at television and we see somebody come on, she's got diamonds on her hands, she's all dressed up, and she's in the height of fasion—you know, a model."

52. Joseph C. Franklin and G. Maxwell Ule, "Who Speaks for You?" *Television Magazine* 10 (September 1953), pp. 49–50.

53. Tom O'Malley, "Raucous Raye: Martha's Clicking Again Without Hollywood's Glamor Treatment," *TV Guide* 2:3 (January 15–21, 1954), pp. 15–17. James Robert Parish and William T. Leonard, *The Funsters* (New Rochelle: Arlington House Publishers, 1979), pp. 519–527.

54. "Why I'm Through with Big TV Shows," *Sponsor* 9:1 (May 2, 1955), pp. 31–32, 93–95. Raymond Spector, head of both Hazel Bishop, Inc., and the Raymond Spector Agency, says: "He is not renewing the spectaculars or NBC TV's *The Martha Raye Show*. He states that he is not interested in Martha Raye's high ratings but the question of "intensity of viewing . . . [i.e.,] whether the loyalty and affection which a star generates flows over to the commercials" (p. 94). Spector favors "sentimental and heavily emotional" melodramatic over spectacular shows; for instance, he prefers *This is Your Life*, a program which engages members of the studio audience in tearful reunions with individuals from their past.

55. Sylvester "Pat" Weaver cited in Judine Mayerle, p. 217.

56. "Fred Allen Speaks Out on Television," *Television Magazine* 6 (December 1949), p. 27. "Everything is for the eye these days—'Life,' 'Look,' the picture business. Nothing is for the mind . . . Berle isn't doing anything for television. He's photographing a vaudeville act."

57. Doane, p. 37.

58. Doane, p. 37.

59. "They've Got Sales Appeal: In TV It's No Longer a Man's World," *TV Guide* 1:35 (November 27—December 3, 1953), pp. 10–11. "Dorothy Collins' Success Key: Listen for Opportunity's Knock," *TV Guide* 1:3 (April 17–23, 1953), pp. 16–19.

60. See for instance, "I'm on Your Side: Ken Murray Finds it Safer to String Along with the Audience," *TV Guide* 1:10 (June 5–12, 1954), pp. 16–18. "I become the liaison between the show and the audience. . . . I represent you, the audience. For example, I'll just stand at one end of the stage and look at the girls performing. If they tell a bum joke I'll turn and shrug: 'They're pretty bad, but what can I do. You see, I'm on your side.'"

61. "Glamor that sells merchandise is the television order of the day. That's why Gloria Swanson was selected mistress of ceremonies of the *Crown Theater* series of telefilms. . . ." *TV Guide* 1:8 (May 22–28, 1954), pp. 10–12. During the mid-fifties with the "rise of the telefilm," the smooth penetration of movie stars into television is institutionalized.

Live Television: Program Formats and Critical Hierarchies

William Boddy

Aesthetic distinctions offered by television critics in the early 1950s were often argued on essentialist grounds. Gilbert Seldes's 1952 *Writing for Television* was typical: "On the controversy on the merits of live and filmed television programs, it is possible to hold that one is better or cheaper or more effective than the other, but it is not possible to maintain that they are identical. Common experience tells us that two things produced by different means, under different material and psychological conditions, will probably not be the same."[1]

According to many early writers on television, the essential technological feature of television versus the motion picture was the electronic medium's capacity to convey a simultaneous distant performance visually. In this regard, the medium was a unique synthesis of the immediacy of the live theatrical performance, the space-conquering powers of radio, and the visual strategies of the motion picture. In 1956, Jack Gould wrote of live television: "Alone of the mass media, it removes from an audience's consciousness the factors of time and distance. . . . Live television . . . bridges the gap instantly and unites the individual at home with the event afar. The viewer has a chance to be in two places at once. Physically, he may be at his own hearthside but intellectually, and above all, emotionally, he is at the cameraman's side." The critical feature of live television, according to Gould, is that "both the player in the studios and the audience at home have an intrinsic awareness of being in each other's presence." Seldes described this metaphysic of presence in live television: "The essence of television techniques is their contribution to the sense of immediacy. . . . The tension that suffuses the atmosphere of a live production is a special thing to which audiences respond; they feel that what they see and hear is happening in the present and therefore more real than anything taken and cut and dried which has the feel of the past."[2]

The opposition between film's "feel of the past" and the immediacy of live television created different putative audience paradigms for film and live programs, in which viewers of a live performance were seen as more highly involved than those of film programs. Gould argued in his 1952 article. "A Plea for Live Video," that film programs on television "lack that intangible sense of depth and trueness which the wizardry of science did impart to 'live' TV. . . . The lasting magic of television is that it employs a mechanical means to achieve an unmechanical end." The potential linking of technological immediacy to more metaphysical notions of authenticity, depth, and truth reached an apotheosis in Gould's 1956 essay, where he excoriated "the ridiculous conceit of film perfectionists who think they can be better than life itself. . . . In their blind pursuit of artificial perfectionism, the TV film producers compromise the one vital element that endows the home screen with its own intangible excitement: humanness. Their error is to try to tinker with reality, to improve upon it to a point where it is no longer real. In so doing, they break the link between human and human. The viewer loses his sense of being a partner and instead becomes a spectator. It is the difference between being with somebody and looking at somebody."[3]

The linking of a technological essentialism in the service of a implicit liberal humanism can also be seen in a 1952 text by Edward Barry Roberts, script editor for "Armstrong Circle Theatre": "More than prose, more than the stage, more than motion pictures—oh, so much more than radio—television, with its immediacy, gets to the heart of the matter, to the essence of the character, to the depicting of the human being who is *there*, as if under a microscope, for our private contemplation, for our approval, our rejection, our love, our hate, our bond of brotherhood recognized." Television script editor Ann Howard Bailey in 1953 described the unique capabilities of the television camera for dramatic storytelling and concluded: "As the television writer learns to look within himself and those around him for the eternal and infinitely variable human conflicts, he will learn how the television camera can serve as the scalpel with which to lay bear the human heart and spirit."[4]

If the metaphysics of presence was one element of the ontology of television argued by early television critics, another was the medium's practical situation of production and reception. William I. Kaufman and Robert S. Colodzin argued in 1950: "Unlike both the movies and the theatre, television does not play to the mass audience . . . it plays to a group of perhaps five or six people at a time." The intimacy of the viewing group had implications for television dramaturgy, directing techniques, and performance style. Kaufman and Colodzin explained that "Emphasis must be on quick character development, on revealing close-ups which make the lift of an eyebrow or the flash of a smile more important than the sweep of an army. Dialogue must be carefully written and sincere in tone because of the intimacy of the audience and the actors and the constant scrutiny of the main characters of the play by an audience which is practically 'on top of the performers.'"[5]

Writer Donald Curtis elaborated on the special demands on the television performer in a 1952 essay: "The actor in television must visualize the conditions under which his performance is being viewed. He is coming into a home and joining an intimate family group which averages from two to six persons. There is no place for acting here. He must 'be' what he represents. . . . The television camera goes inside of an actor's mind and soul, and sends the receiving set exactly what it sees there."[6]

Broadcast critic Charles Slepmann in 1950 saw in television drama the development of a new performance style, "not, as in the film, predominantly physical, but psychological—both sight and sound serving to give overt support to the covert expression of the mind." In an introduction to a collection of television plays, William Bluem observed that "In some ways TV is the penultimate technological extension of the naturalistic drama and its rejection of romantic superficiality in favor of the inner revelation of human character. The entire theatrical movement towards realism in acting and staging seems to culminate upon the small screen, where it can work out its own absolutes of form and style."[7]

Like the prescriptions on performance style in television, commentary on television staging and direction found a rationale for theatrical naturalism in the concrete production and viewing circumstances of the medium. As Seldes explained, "Every television program is in a sense an invasion; you turn on your television set and someone comes into your living room, and you tune in one station or another according to whom you want in your room at any particular moment."[8]

The early literature on television production constantly emphasized the necessity for naturalist performances, frequent close-ups, and simplified, naturalistic staging. A 1945 CBS publication explained that "because viewers express a natural wish to 'get a good look' at a character, producers should whenever possible use close-ups to introduce all characters on a program." In a 1946 article in *Television*, ABC executive Harvey Marlowe argued that television drama had no need for elaborate sets and that 80 percent of the typical television play would be shot in close-up. In 1950, Kaufman and Colodzin advised would-be television playwrights that "[a] good television script must be simple to produce," with sets that are "few and inexpensive." The cast "should be limited to a small number of characters," and "[s]pecial effects should be avoided in instances where simpler methods would be just as dramatic." An example of a rigorous application of the reductive design of television's theatrical naturalism was Albert McCleery's "Cameo Theatre," in which a small cast sat on stools on an arena stage without scenery, costumes, or props. In his *Best Television Plays 1950–51*, Kaufman called the McCleery program "pure television."[9]

For the TV playwright as well, the special properties of the television medium seemed to support a new kind of dramatic realism. Paddy Chayefsky wrote in 1955 that "lyrical writing, impressionistic writing and abstract and expressionistic writing are appalling in television whereas they might be gauged exciting in the theatre." In his contribution to the 1952 anthology, *How to Write and Direct for Television*, Chayefsky elaborated:

> *In television, there is practically nothing too subtle or delicate that you cannot examine with your camera. The camera allows us a degree of intimacy that can never be achieved on stage. Realism in the theatre is a stylized business; what one achieves is really the effect of realism. In television, you can be literally and freely real. The scenes can be played as if the actors were unaware of their audience. The dialogue can sound as if it had been wiretapped. . . . The writer has a whole new, untouched area of drama in which to poke about. He can write about the simplest things, the smallest incidents, as long as they have dramatic significance.*[10]

Television's ability to bring intimate details of a performance to its audience, along with the practical constraints of staging live television drama, also led the critics to suggest the most appropriate forms of dramatic structure for the medium. For Erik Barnouw, the structural principles of early live drama on television meant that "The structure of these plays related to circumstances under which they were produced." As a result there emerged "plays of tight structure, attacking a story close to its climax—very different from the loose, multi-scene structure of film."[11]

Barnouw's juxtaposition of the dramatic structures of film and television was widely echoed in the early television literature. The same distinction was often cast in terms which opposed the drama of character to the drama of plot. Edward Barry Roberts argued in 1952, for example, that "the new playwriting inescapably is founded on character. . . . The most successful 'live' television plays, therefore, would seem to be those which do not have much plot." Another script editor advised would-be television writers in 1953: "Live TV is limited in scope: that is, it cannot depend upon broad panorama, colossal montages, or the thrill of the hunt or chase to help the limping script. Literally, the 'words are the thing,' and in nine out of ten TV shows, the climax depends upon what the characters say rather than what they do."[12]

Seldes argued that television's technological immediacy gave the medium an "overwhelming feel of reality": "The result is that television can render character supremely well and it is not theoretical or idealistic but very practical to say that it should not abandon its prime quality." Seldes wrote that until 1952, television drama seemed to be following the theatrical model of a drama of character over one of plot, but warned that "This may not always be true of television drama because *the conditions in which television is received make it a prime medium for communicating character*, but as a lot of TV drama is being made in Hollywood by people in the Hollywood tradition, the struggle for character drama may be a bitter one." Like the essentialist rationale for naturalism in staging and acting in television, Seldes's defense of character drama derived from the technological and phenomenological premises of the medium: the casual environment and attitude of viewers at home detracted from the effectiveness of complicated plot structures, he argued.

Beyond the criteria of live versus film and character versus plot, critics also placed the unique teleplay of the anthology series above works in the continuing series and dramatic serial. Seldes called the sixty-minute original teleplay in an anthology series the "top of the prestige pyramid of all television drama." The critic identified in the sixty-minute original teleplay "something like a new dramatic form . . . slowly emerging," and in a 1956 look at the first ten years of television programming Seldes found "the most honorable accomplishments of television . . . in the hour-long play. . . ."[13]

The thirty-minute program was consistently compared unfavorably to the hour-long dramatic program on television. In 1955, Don Sharpe of Four Star Productions compared the thirty-minute and sixty-minute programs in an article in *Television* and concluded that "The half-hour dramatization is primarily a stunt and frequently a trick." For Sharpe, "The viewer of the hour program is satisfied to sit and wait for something to happen, as he would in the legitimate theatre." But on the other hand, argued Sharpe, "unless a thirty-minute show develops an almost immediate impact . . . there is a good chance that many viewers will switch channels or take the pooch for a stroll." Vance Bourjaily wrote in *Harper's* that "the half-hour show is too brief, and it is interrupted by a commercial too soon after it begins, to be anything but a hook, a gimmick, and a resolution." Jack Gould argued that "the half-hour program with the middle commercial inevitably puts a premium on the contrived plot and on action for its own sake. . . . there can be almost no characterization and the emphasis is more on stereotypes than on real people."[14]

In sum, most prominent television critics of the early 1950s denigrated the program forms and dramatic values they associated with Hollywood in favor of those they linked with the New York-based television networks. The opposition is nowhere more stark than in the critical perception of the differing roles for the television writer in the two contexts. Like the critical debates over the aesthetic proclivities of the two media, the image of the writer was colored by long-standing cultural attitudes toward the motion picture industry. In the context of pre-auteurist American film criticism, individual contributions by writers or directors in the Hollywood studio system tended to be devalued by sociological or belletrist accounts of Hollywood as a monolithic dream factory where faceless contract writers toiled in confining genres at the whim of autocratic and philistine moguls. The image of the serious writer in Hollywood in mid-century American literature and popular criticism was that of a figure compromising or renouncing the autonomy and artistic possibilities available in other literary forms. These general cultural attitudes toward the writer in Hollywood played an important part in setting a tone for the debates over television program forms in the 1950s.

Broadcast writer and critic Goodman Ace in a 1952 article, "The Forgotten Men of TV," characterized the expectations of writers in Hollywood telefilms by citing an unattributed quotation from Lucille Ball regarding the writers' contribution to "I Love Lucy": "We never see them. We never discuss anything with them. After two readings we get on our feet and throw the scripts away." A 1954 article, "Writer Is a Dirty Word," described Ace's trip to Hollywood, where, he wrote, "for the most part, television writers, especially comedy writers, are considered a necessary but evil part of the TV set-up."[15]

The employment situation and critical reputation of the writer in live television drama were very different, although it took some time before the TV writer earned the prominence associated with most accounts of television's Golden Age. An article in the premier issue of *Television* in 1944, for example, lamented that "The program end of television has been an arid wasteland, almost devoid of imagination, showmanship, and (what is equally important) any indications of a knowledge of the nature of television. . . . The big bottleneck will be in good writers and directors, artists and executives with imagination and showmanship who understand their medium." In May 1947 an article in the magazine was still complaining: "Capable actors are available, good original scripts are not. . . . Perhaps it would be better for television to forego dramatic production unless top scripts are available, for television will only suffer in comparison to other media when mediocre productions are staged."[16]

The manager of NBC's Script Department wrote in 1948: "Television's primary need is for material, and the one who provides that material in a suitable form may be said to be one of the most important, if not *the* most important, person in the television picture—the writer." Charles Underhill, head of CBS television programming, in 1950 wrote succinctly of the television programmer: "Greatest need: material. Solution: uncover young writers, woo Hollywood and Broadway writers." *Variety* concluded that the development of writing talent suited "specifically for TV looms as the most necessary ingredient for programming in 1950."[17]

Seldes described the new market for television scripts: "For writers, the turning point in television came somewhere in the early spring of 1951." The number of Writers Guild of America members reported working in television grew from 45 in February 1951 to 110 by the end of that year. In 1952, Edward Barry Roberts, an NBC script editor, wrote: "The centers of production are swarming with would-be television writers. The competition is killing, although paradoxically there aren't enough really good writers to supply the demand. . . . Yet it is only through good writing that television will grow, and fulfill its potential destiny as the most fascinating and the most important means ever known of communicating information, entertainment and education. . . . We are all waiting hopefully and impatiently for the television artist-playwrights to appear."[18]

The title "artist-playwright" attached to the work of the writer in live television drama suggests the importance and prestige frequently associated with the new craft. In a June 1952 episode of the ABC public-affairs program "Horizons," entitled "The Future of Television Drama," producer Alex Segal argued that "I think TV eventually, if given time to develop, if not rushed, and if not sidetracked, will do the wonderful thing we always wished for, that of bringing the legitimate theatre into the home in its final stage." Most TV critics and many of the other creative personnel in television saw the writer at the center of television drama. In 1952, Herbert Spencer Sussan, a CBS producer-director called the writer "truly the creative artist" in television and described the work of the TV director as "akin to the director of a symphony orchestra, fusing many elements into harmonious unity." Chayefsky later recalled how the prestige associated with TV writing could ignite the career of a young writer of live drama of the mid-1950s: "Right at that time, it was a writer's medium. Think of all those shows that were done in New York—'Philco,' 'Studio One,' 'Kraft Television Theatre,' 'Robert Montgomery Presents,' 'U.S. Steel Hour'—all those other weekly half-hour shows, perfect for writers. If you could come in at the right time and do something that caught on, it was the beginning of a career." Indeed, the best known writers of television drama—Paddy Chayefsky, Rod Serling, Reginald Rose, Horton Foote, Robert Alan Aurthur—came not from established careers in the motion picture industry but achieved first public notice through their work in television.[19]

The prominence and prestige accorded to writers in live television drama—TV's new artist-playwrights—were often contrasted with the plight of writers working in feature films and filmed television. In 1957, Serling compared the role of the writer in live and filmed television:

> *Probably most fundamental in any discussion of the differences between live and filmed television is the attitude reserved for their creators. It is rare in Hollywood that a filmed show will make anything but a perfunctory reference to its author. Hollywood television took a leaf out of the notebook of the motion pictures and shoved its authors into a professional Siberia. The writer of the filmed television play was never and is not now an identifiable name in terms of the audience.*
>
> *This is in sharp contrast to the New York live television writer who has been granted an identity, an importance and a respect second only to the legitimate playwright. For this reason, it is rare that a "live" playwright will write for filmed shows, despite that fact that, in the long run, the half-hour film may bring him almost ten times the total price of the live script.[20]*

Writers of live television drama often maintained a significant degree of control over their material. Television writer Ernest Kinoy looked back at the position of the television writer in the mid-1950s:

> *The general practice in live television of this time was to accept the notion of the writer as the original instigator-creator of a particular play. . . . This was picked up from Broadway, where the author is considered the man who has produced the work, who has done the thing which is going to be presented. Therefore, you would, in most cases, continue with it in a relatively respected position, along through the rehearsals to the final presentation on the air. And your opinion was sought and listened to with varying degrees of attention. But as a pattern, the writer was considered to belong with his property until it was finally presented.[21]*

In addition to a measure of control from the completed script through the production process, the live television writer was accorded a position by critics and the public closer to that of the legitimate playwright than the Hollywood contract-writer. Gore Vidal, who wrote seventy television plays over a two-year period in the mid-1950s, recalled a few years later: "If you did a good show on 'Philco,' you would walk down the street the next morning and hear people talking about your play." In an interview in the *New York Times* in 1956, thirty-one-year-old Serling pointed to television's appeal to a writer interested in social commentary: "I think that of all the entertainment media, TV lends itself most beautifully to presenting a controversy. You can just take a part of the problem, and, using just a small number of people, get your point across."[22]

Serling is perhaps the best example of a young writer who achieved prominence through a series of live drama scripts in the mid-1950s. His first major teleplay, "Patterns," was hailed by the *New York Times* as "one of the high points in the television medium's evolution," and was repeated in live performance on "Kraft Television Theatre," the first time a live drama was restaged for the medium. Within two weeks after the airing of "Patterns," Serling told an interviewer: "I received twenty-three firm offers for television writing assignments. I received three motion picture offers for screenplay assignments. I had fourteen requests for interviews from leading magazines and newspapers. I had two offers of lunch from Broadway producers. I had two offers to discuss novels with publishers."[23]

Serling won a Peabody Award in 1956 and Emmy awards for his television plays in 1955, 1956, and 1957. *Vogue* magazine described the writer in 1957 as a "revved-up, good-looking playwright of thirty-two," and *Cosmopolitan* profiled Serling in 1958 as the most conspicuous member of "a new class of millionaire writers in America." Serling's sudden success and visibility in the popular press was only one indication of the cultural position of the television writer and the original television play in the era of live drama. New York television critic John Crosby wrote in a 1973 recollection:

> *Does TV generate that kind of excitement any more? Certainly not over the author of a TV play. In the 1950s everyone was interested in TV—the educated and the featherbrains alike. It was new and we were very innocent. . . . I remember walking into "21," a fairly sophisticated beanery, one day in the 1950s and finding the whole restaurant buzzing with talk about another Rod Serling play, "Requiem for a Heavyweight". . . . The important thing was that "Requiem" set the whole town talking in much the same way Al Jolson used to do when he'd walk out on the stage of the Winter Garden and knock 'em dead in the 1920s. Television was the medium of the moment and it attracted all the brilliant young kids. . . . [24]*

The TV writer, then, stood at the center of the artistic promise of live television drama, and many playwrights became widely reported commentators on the medium and its programming in the rest of the decade. For many television critics in the 1950s, the television playwright symbolized the medium's commitment to the live format and to the dramatic forms to which they were fiercely attached. The rising debate within the industry and in the popular press over the role of the television writer in the 1950s therefore becomes one marker of a shift in general cultural attitudes toward the medium. Television writers were at once the objects of, and often acute commentators upon, the enormous changes in commercial television in the second half of the 1950s.

Notes

1. Gilbert Seldes, *Writing for Television* (New York: Doubleday, 1952). p. 30.

2. Jack Gould, "'Live' TV vs. 'Canned,'" *New York Times Magazine*, February 5, 1956, p. 27; Seldes, *Writing for Television*, p. 32.

3. Jack Gould, "A Plea for Live Video," *New York Times*, December 7, 1952; Gould, "'Live' TV," p. 34.

4. Edward Barry Roberts, "Writing for Television," in *The Best Television Plays, 1950–1951*, ed. William I. Kaufman (New York: Hastings House, 1952), p. 286, emphasis in original; Ann Howard Bailey, "Writing the TV Dramatic Show," in Irving Settel and Norman Glenn, *Television Advertising and Production Handbook* (New York: Thomas Y. Crowell, 1953), p. 226.

5. William I. Kaufman and Robert Colodzin, *Your Career in Television* (New York: Merlin Press, 1950), p. 62.

6. Donald Curtis, "The Actor in Television," in *The Best Television Plays, 1950–1951*, ed. Kaufman, pp. 319–20.

7. Charles Slepmann, *Radio, Television and Society* (New York: Oxford University Press, 1950), p. 357; William Bluem and Roger Manvell, eds., *TV: The Creative Experience: A Survey of Anglo-American Progress* (New York: Hastings House, 1967), p. 17.

8. Seldes, *Writing for Television*, p. 79. Seldes continued: "In a dramatic program you are inviting a group of people to live a portion of their lives with you. The closer their lives come to the tenor of the lives of yourself and your friends, the more the invasion has taken on the nature of a visit; the characters must be with you without reservation and without pressure, so that in the end you can move from your living room into their lives."

9. Columbia Broadcasting System, *Television Audience Research* (New York: Columbia Broadcasting System, 1945), p. 7; Harvey Marlowe, "Drama's Place in Television," *Television*, March 1946, p. 17; Kaufman and Colodzin, *Your Career in Television*, p. 61; Kaufman, ed., *The Best Television Plays, 1950–1951*, p. 263.

10. Paddy Chayefsky, "Good Theatre in Television," ibid., p. 45.

11. Erik Barnouw, *The History of Broadcasting in the United States*, vol. 3: *The Image Empire* (New York: Oxford University Press, 1970), p. 31.

12. Roberts, "Writing for Television," pp. 296–97; Baily, "Writing the TV Dramatic Show," p. 214.

13. Seldes, *Writing for Television*, 1952, pp. 105, 138, 148, 151, 152, emphasis in original; Gilbert Seldes, "A Clinical Analysis of TV," *New York Times Magazine*, November 23, 1954, p. 55.

14. Don Sharpe, "TV Film: Will Economics Stifle Creativity?," *Television*, April 1955, p. 30; Vance Bourjaily, "The Lost Art of Writing for Television," *Harper's*, October 1959, p. 152; Jack Gould, "Half-Act Drama," *New York Times*, February 10, 1952, sec. 2, p. 13.

15. Goodman Ace, *The Book of Little Knowledge: More Than You Want to Know About Television* (New York: Simon and Schuster, 1955), pp. 8, 18.

16. "Programming," *Television*, Spring 1944, p. 21; "Programming," *Television*, May 1947, p. 31.

17. Richard P. McDongh, "Television Writing Problems." In *Television Production Problems*, ed. John F. Royal (New York: McGraw-Hill, 1948), p. 28; "The Programmers," *Television*, February 1950, p. 14; "Video's '50 Accent on Writing," *Variety*, December 21, 1949, p. 27.

18. Seldes, *Writing for Television*, p. 9; Milton MacKaye, "The Big Brawl: Hollywood vs. Television," *The Saturday Evening Post*, January 26, 1952, Part 2, p. 119; Roberts, "Writing for Television," p. 300.

19. Alex Segal, "The Future of Television Drama," "Horizons," June 6, 1952, collection of the Museum of Broadcasting, New York; Herbert Spencer Sussan, "The Voice Behind the Cameras," in *The Best Television Plays, 1950–1951*, ed. Kaufman, p. 302; Max Wilk, *The Golden Age of Television: Notes from the Survivors* (New York: Delacorte, 1976), p. 132.

20. Rod Serling. "TV in the Flesh vs. TV in the Can," *New York Times Magazine*, November 24, 1957, pp. 52, 54.

21. U.S. Federal Communications Commission, Office of Network Study, *Second Interim Report: Television Program Procurement, Part II* (Washington, D.C.: U.S. Government Printing Office, 1965), p. 630.

22. Ibid., p. 626; Vidal went on: "It was a strange feeling . . . you have this audience, and writers—at least my kind of writer—wants as large an audience as he can possibly get, to do as much damage as they can to the things they think stand in want of correction to society." Rod Serling, interview with J. P. Shanley, *New York Times*, April 22, 1956, sec. 2, p. 13.

23. The original reaction to "Patterns," its restaging, and play's effect on Serling's career are discussed in J. P. Shanley, "Notes on 'Patterns' and a Familiar Face," *New York Times*, February 6, 1955, sec. 2, p. 15. Rod Serling, *Patterns* (New York: Simon and Schuster, 1957), p. 30.

24. "People Are Talking About," *Vogue*, April 1, 1957, p. 138; T. F. James, "The Millionaire Class of Young Writers," *Comopolitan*, August 1958, p. 40; John Crosby, "It Was New and We Were Very Innocent," *TV Guide*, September 22, 1973, p. 6.

See It Now: *A Legend Reassessed*

Daniel J. Leab

"**B**anal," "meretricious," "mediocre," "a vast wasteland"—these phrases are but some of the many negative judgments passed on the general runs of American commercial television programming since the end of World War II. With startling unanimity a surprising number of disparate critics have attacked the great mass of such programming—which, according to one understandably concerned viewer, "now constitutes a major source of behavior . . . for the American people."[1]

These same critics, however, have had a very different reaction to the series *See It Now*, both during its heyday in the mid-1950s and since then. Moreover, this positive response does not arise just because these critics have a tendency (in the words of one concerned viewer) "to disdain the world of television [as] popular culture." They have found *See It Now* better, have argued that its producers had "the simplicity of mind and the sweep of imagination to understand what television can do best in the news field," and "have maintained that it must be numbered among television's "hours of greatness."[2]

What was *See It Now*? There are many answers to that question. A simple (and certainly not incorrect) answer is to describe it as does one current guide to American TV as "the prototype of the in-depth quality television documentary." A veteran network news executive has aptly characterized *See It Now* as a "brilliant" example of "informational programming." A media historian has perceptively lauded the series for "its recognition of television's intrinsic characteristics of intimacy and immediacy in presentation" and for its "probing controversial treatment of . . . events and conditions of our existence." A media critic probably summed up its characteristics best when, in reviewing the history of *See It Now*, he noted that the series examined important subjects "sensibly, critically, fearlessly . . . employed the best of pictures with powerful prose [and] called on the top experts who could add information or opinion."[3]

Such a complex effort did not, like Athena, spring full-grown from the head of Zeus. *See It Now*, throughout its history, was very much the product of the intense and unceasing efforts of a dedicated, hardworking group of people, headed by the series' creators and coproducers, Edward R. Murrow and Fred W. Friendly. The better known of the two men was, is, and probably always will be Murrow. To state that is not to slight Friendly but simply to accept a fact pointed out in 1959 by a newspaper correspondent dealing with their efforts at CBS (the Columbia Broadcasting System): "Murrow's . . . personal prestige overshadows the network and every other figure at the network. A documentary turned out by the team of Murrow . . . and Friendly is, in the public mind, not a CBS documentary or a Murrow-Friendly documentary. It is a Murrow program." And Murrow's prestige and reputation have not diminished over the years. On the contrary, he has become even more respected and revered. In 1975, on the tenth anniversary of Murrow's death, Sir Hugh Greene (then director of the British Broadcasting Corporation) called him "the patron saint of the broadcasting profession." Murrow, as one history of CBS News puts it, "has become the stuff of legend, a figure of Olympian stature."[4]

That legendary stature was hard won. Born in 1908, in modest circumstances, Murrow was graduated from Washington State College in the Depression year 1930. After stints with student and education organizations, he joined CBS in 1935 as director of talks, a low-level job whose main responsibility was to secure important figures for various broadcasts over the fledgling network. Two years later CBS sent him overseas as its European director, then a relatively humble job. As Murrow's biographer points out, he was sent overseas as "an arranger of talks and musical events," not as a correspondent. Adapting to the changing circumstances caused by World War II, however, he did a superb job for the network. By war's end in 1945, he had played a significant role in transforming CBS's one-man European show (himself) into a highly professional, outstanding news operation staffed by correspondents imbued with his zeal and dedication. "Murrow's boys," as they inevitably came to be known, for decades served as the backbone of CBS news and public affairs programming.[5]

His accomplishments as an administrator notwithstanding, Murrow made his public mark as a broadcaster. The rush of Nazi aggression gave him the opportunity. When Hitler marched into Austria in 1938, Murrow—then in Poland—chartered a twenty-four passenger German airliner for himself, flew to Vienna, and broadcast from there and subsequently from London about what had befallen Austria. His broadcasts to the United States during the next months, as diplomatic crisis followed diplomatic crisis and then after hostilities commenced in September 1939, had what has been described as "the special quality of excellence."[6]

As Friendly noted years later: "Whether speaking from the rooftops of London during the Blitz [the massive German air raids on London in 1940–1941] or on a bombing raid over Berlin or from [the concentration camp] Buchenwald on the day it was liberated, Murrow became one of the most identifiable and trusted voices of the war." Although not trained as a print journalist, he had a way with words; his peers were, as one said, "keenly aware of his excellence as a reporter." And these verbal abilities were coupled with a superb and dramatic sense of delivery as well as with a breadth and humanity of thought. Murrow, as one scholar has perceptively and correctly indicated, "in effect sought to become the radio listener's surrogate, speaking in terms he could understand or developing images he could sympathize with." The poet Archibald MacLeish, in discussing Murrow's Blitz broadcasts, said that he "burned the city of London in our houses and we felt that flame . . . [he] laid the dead of London at our doors." Indeed, some of these broadcasts have been described as "metallic poetry."[7]

Morever, Murrow had no hesitation about making his views known. He did not believe in objectivity for its own sake. He saw no value in balancing Hitler evenly against Churchill. Murrow, as one observer has said, compared "artificial fairness . . . with balancing the views of Jesus Christ with those of Judas Iscariot." The broadcaster, as his wife once stated, was a "sufferer," and his wartime broadcasts reflected that aspect of his character, but they also reflected something more—what William Paley (the long-time CBS head and for a while a close personal friend of Murrow) recalls as "some higher mission that overrode his inherent gloom." One of Murrow's boys, Charles Collingwood, has asserted that Murrow's broadcast career was influenced by his belief "that we lived in a perfectible world."[8]

Murrow returned to the United States in 1946 an extremely popular figure and a vice-president of CBS (in charge of news and public affairs). Like many of his peers in the media business, and like many other Americans in general, he hoped the media that "had helped defeat external enemies would now be useful in fighting subtler battles against injustice and ignorance." But within a few years the euphoric idealism of the postwar months had given way to a rancid climate of fear as the cold war fastened its grip on American society. Already in 1947, before McCarthyism had become rampant in the media, a disquieted Murrow—obviously uncomfortable as a network executive—resigned his administrative position to return to broadcasting full time. He was happy to do so: "The administrative end has ridden me like a piano on my back." And truth be known, the essentially shy and private Murrow had not done well as a CBS executive.[9]

It was at this time that Murrow met Friendly. Born Ferdinand Wachenheimer in 1915, Friendly grew up in petit-bourgeois circumstances in Providence, Rhode Island. In the mid-1930s, after finishing his education, he entered radio work in Providence, changing his name to Fred Friendly (the surname is a family name of his mother's side of the family). He had some success in Providence, especially with a program series of dramatized biographies of important historical figures, such as Edison and Marconi. Known as *Footprints in the Sands of Time*, the series was later bought from Friendly by a recording company.[10]

World War II was for Friendly—in his own words—"a relatively soft war." After being inducted in 1941, he was involved in the development of a panel competition, "Sergeant Quiz," used for testing GIs on knowledge acquired in basic training. He traveled for the army's Information and Education Section, setting up the quiz at various camps and lecturing to soldiers about the war's background. In 1943 he became overseas correspondent for the *CBI Roundup*, the army daily for the China-Burma-India theater of operations (a sort of Asian equivalent of *Stars and Stripes*). Friendly reported from all over the world on such events as the D-Day landings in France and the atomic bombings of Hiroshima and Nagasaki. After the war he spent the next few years, as one history puts it, "making the rounds of networks and agencies trying to sell program ideas." He sold to the National Broadcasting System in 1948 a panel quiz show called *Who Said That?* It was well received, with one influential media critic calling the program "one of the happier of recent inspirations in radio."[11]

Most commentary about Murrow verges on hagiography, and I could find little serious writing about him or his efforts that did not incline to the adulatory. There is no such unanimity of opinion about Friendly. There is general agreement about his "enormous energy," "superb technical skills," "superior taste." He has been dubbed affectionately by his colleagues "Big Moose," and has been less warmly styled "Brilliant Monster." A man of great passion, Friendly has been known to be extravagant in praise of his associates; he also, when dissatisfied, expressed his displeasure in no uncertain ways—shouting loudly and at times abusively, and even flying "into tantrums" now and then. The story is probably apocryphal, but it is reported that once he "picked up a table and threw it at the head of a young assistant." But this passion, inspired by very high standards, also enabled him to do things that supposedly couldn't be done. Fellow producers, who were not particularly enamored of him, remember Friendly as "a gutsy guy" and as someone who "went ahead and did what everybody who knew better knew you couldn't do. He broke the rules." In so doing Friendly made basic, lasting contributions to the art of TV documentary. As for *See It Now*, a close observer of its operations recounted at the time that "Friendly's vitality . . . permeates the offices. . . . Murrow is held in awe."[12]

Such distinctions aside—and the different personalities of the men account for them as much as anything—their collaboration was close and effective (years later a veteran of the series emphasized that it "*was* Fred Friendly as much as it was Ed Murrow"). As in any joint creative relationship involving people of intelligence, passion, and energy, there were occasional tensions between Murrow and Friendly, but nothing lasting or serious. Murrow's biographer has found only "a sole major occasion" in their long association when Friendly was seriously reproached by his associate, and that was when their active collaboration had been over for some years. In the main, they worked extremely well in tandem, especially given the divergent backgrounds of the two men. The working marriage of their great, if diverse, skills produced enviable offspring both before and after *See It Now*.[13]

The collaboration began with production of a record album, *I Can Hear It Now*, "the history of an era spoken by the men who made it and narrated by Edward R. Murrow." This forty-five minute "scrapbook in sound" began with Will Rogers discussing the Depression in 1932 and ended with General Douglas MacArthur accepting the surrender of the Japanese aboard the battleship *Missouri* in 1945. Chance played a role in the making of this album and the birth of the Murrow-Friendly team. Facilities were available because the musicians' union had for the moment banned its members from playing recording sessions, and as Friendly recalls, CBS "wanted material to keep the idle recording facilities busy."[14]

I Can Hear It Now, released toward the end of 1949, was a phenomenal success both critically and commercially. It won many awards including the Newspaper Guild Page One Award for its "stirring presentation of contemporary history." Selling approximately 250,000 copies within a year of its release, *I Can Hear It Now* was, by all accounts, "the first non-musical album to be a financial success." Murrow and Friendly collaborated on other such records over the next few years (including an

I Can Hear It Now for the years 1945–1949, which was released in 1950, and a collection of Winston Churchill's speeches).[15]

The Murrow-Friendly partnership then put together for broadcast over the CBS radio network a weekly program, *Hear It Now,* which made its debut toward the end of 1950. Described as a "document for the era," "a new magazine of the air," "a current history set forth in the voice of the people who make it," *Hear It Now* was produced with verve, imagination, and intelligence. The hour-long program did well in the ratings and was a critical success (the prestigous Peabody Award was but one of several it earned). Designed to deal both with important and not-so-important issues and events of the week past, *Hear It Now* was kaleidoscopic in content. Thus the first show included commentary on the war in Korea from the perspective of Marine recruits, Carl Sandburg reading poetry, and Thomas Dewey and Bernard Baruch discussing the state of the economy.[16]

See It Now initially was a half-hour television version of the Murrow-Friendly radio series. It premiered Sunday afternoon, November 18, 1951, on the CBS-TV network. During the 1951–1952 season, *See It Now* was presented from 3:30 to 4:00 in the afternoon, thus making it part of what Murrow aptly called "that intellectual ghetto" of Sunday afternoon programming. *See It Now* inched its way to the fringes of prime time during the 1952–1953 season, when it was presented Sundays between 6:30 and 7:00 in the evening. The series had a regular half-hour slot on Tuesday night at 10:30 during the 1953–1954 and 1954–1955 seasons. Thereafter, until July 1958, when the program went off the air, *See It Now* was an irregularly scheduled program presented about eight times a season, usually for an hour but occasionally for ninety minutes. At this point, jaundiced spectators dubbed the series "See It Now and Then."[17]

The first telecast in 1951 utilized a familiar magazine-style format, one that would define the series for its first two seasons. It included Murrow talking either live or on film with CBS correspondents about purported atrocities taking place during the Korean War and about United Nations efforts toward achieving disarmament; the telecast also included a very moving filmed visit in Korea with Fox Company's Second Platoon, United States 19th Infantry, a visit that emphasized the men rather than hardware of issues. This segment caught the soldiers (to use a critic's description) "as they ate and slept and gambled and groused and joked, catching the tedium of warfare, the waiting, the humor of an essentially unhumorous profession."[18]

For all the pungency of this segment, *See It Now,* as one media historian correctly points out, "in content . . . made a cautious start." And the format remained cautious for some time. Murrow and Friendly dealt and quite well (winning various prestigious awards) with a potpourri of topics, none really controversial. One student has described the bulk of the subjects covered during the 1951–1952 and 1952–1953 TV seasons as "current events of interest to the nation as a whole . . . such as speeches of national significance, disasters, and international happenings" as well as features "which added more of a note of sheer entertainment." These topics—whose treatment in each case seldom exceeded ten minutes—included floods in the United States and England, Winston Churchill speaking at a British political rally, a visit to a West Virginia coal mine, an interview with historian Arnold Toynbee, and a trip on the Orient Express. Some topics were dealt with live; more were filmed (as would be true throughout the history of the series); all were held together by Murrow's incisive and urbane commentary. At the time Murrow told an interviewer that "we try to handle stories differently from the way they were presented earlier," but he also declared, in response to the many critical garlands gathered by *See It Now* during its first two broadcast seasons, that "everyone yelled genius. . . . We only did the obvious." And these early *See It Now* programs, although they ran somewhat longer, differed little in concept or style from the traditional movie newsreel.[19]

From the start Murrow and Friendly seem to have been clearly aware of what TV could do. The first *See It Now* program presented a startling innovation, one that highlighted the potential of the medium. Making use of the just-developed coast-to-coast broadcasting facilities (a combination of coaxial cable and microwave relay), Murrow sat on a swivel chair before two TV monitors that could be viewed by his live audience and called on Camera One to "bring in the Atlantic Ocean." Then he called for a picture of the Pacific Ocean on the other monitor, and these live pictures of the oceans were followed by simultaneous live views of the Brooklyn and Golden Gate bridges and the New York and San Francisco skylines. A gimmick? Yes. But an extraordinarily effective gimmick, for, as Murrow told his audience, the telecast allowed "a man sitting in his living room . . . for *the first time* to look at two oceans at once."[20]

Such mechanical wizardry aside, Murrow and Friendly well understood, as the newsman told their viewers that night, that "this is an old team trying to learn a new trade." It took time to do that; it also took an understanding of the need to change *See It Now's* format, so that often the bulk of the half-hour broadcast time would be devoted to one subject, and it took a willingness to incorporate in various programs what Friendly has succinctly described as "the missing ingredients . . . conviction, controversy, and a point of view." By the beginning of the 1953–1954 season the *See It Now* team (not only Murrow and Friendly, but also the staff they had put together) had learned the new trade and were willing to put their new learning to use.[21]

During this season and the next, *See It Now* hit its stride, dealing with a wide range of subjects: programs were devoted to Senator Joe McCarthy, the New York Philharmonic, the Las Vegas boom, the fight against polio, and the "Stockmobile" (a Merrill, Lynch office on wheels that serviced various Massachusetts towns). The majority of the programs were not controversial muckraking exercises; many were pleasant, entertaining visual essays (such as *A Visit to Flat Rock—Carl Sandburg*, in which the poet talked about Lincoln, Ty Cobb, "bad poetry," and goat's milk and goober peas). Some shows were obviously better than others, yet almost none lacked interest. But it was a transformed *See It Now's* treatment of McCarthyism and other provocative subjects such as the relationship between cigarette smoking and lung cancer that helped to make television an indispensable medium. So said Erik Barnouw, claiming that "few people now dared to be without a television set."[22]

When Murrow and Friendly zeroed in on a subject, they did so in an innovative manner that differed considerably from previous documentary filmmakers and from contemporary TV practice. They were interested neither in the "innocent eye" of a Robert Flaherty nor in "the poetic propaganda" of a John Grierson—to mention just two of the dozens of modern documentary. Nor were Murrow and Friendly interested in evenhanded, objective analysis—despite protestations to the contrary. (Murrow at one point stated on the air that "this program [*See It Now*] is not a place where personal opinion should be mixed up with ascertainable fact. We shall do our best . . . to resist the temptation to use this microphone as a privileged platform from which to advocate action.") For both Murrow and Friendly, however, the temptation often proved too great. As C. M. Hammond, Jr., perceptively points out, they "did for documentary what the progenitors of earlier linkups between film and news failed to do; namely, they reported not only what was happening, but also *what was wrong with what was happening.*" Murrow and Friendly had a sense of justice, and they believed that where injustice existed, "then proper attention must be paid via public exposure to redressing or eliminating" such injustice. For them, as they said, television was an "entirely new weapon in journalism."[23]

This weapon was first unsheathed the evening of October 20, 1953, with the airing of *The Case of Lt. Milo Radulovich A0589839*. This program dealt with a twenty-six year-old University of Michigan student who lost his Air Force Reserve commission and was separated from the service as a security risk. As the articulate and attractive Radulovich explained on camera:

> *The Air Force does not question my loyalty in the least. . . . They have presented*
> *me with allegations . . . to the effect that my sister and dad . . . have read what we*
> *now called subversive newspapers, and that my sister and father's activities are*
> *questionable . . . Against me, the actual charge . . . is that I had maintained a close*
> *and continuing relationship with my dad and my sister over the years.*

Radulovich was not discharged for being disloyal; he was discharged because the Air Force considered him a potential security risk if he continued associating with his father and sister.[24]

No matter how absurd the charges against Radulovich may now seem, it took courage for Murrow and Friendly to deal with such a subject in the chilling political and social climate of the early 1950s. At that time in the United States to invoke the Fifth Amendment before a congressional committee investigating subversion was considered tantamount to an admission of guilt. In at least one community it meant being denied a license to sell secondhand furniture. Professional wrestlers who wished to perform in the state of Indiana were required to take a loyalty oath. So too were CBS employees, including Murrow and Friendly, when the network decided to appease those who because of its less than rabidly patriotic news orientation had dubbed CBS the "Communist Broadcasting System." The early 1950s were, as journalist Fred Cook asserts, a "time of national paranoia . . . in which millions of average Americans looked fearfully over their shoulders wondering whether *they* would be tapped next to explain themselves."[25]

However the period has been labeled, be it the Age of Fear or the Era of Anxiety, a key figure was the junior senator from Wisconsin, Joseph R. McCarthy, who gained notoriety as a recklessly zealous, indefatigable hunter of Communists and subversives in American public and private life. One problem with the senator's zealousness was that it was tempered only rarely with sound judgment and that just about everybody who disagreed with him could be designated "subversive." The senator gave his name to the era, and "McCarthyism" has become part of the American language. But it must be remembered that the process McCarthy symbolized ("personal attacks on individuals by means of widely publicized indiscriminate allegations esp. on the basis of unsubstantiated charges") had begun in post-World War II America, before he gained prominence, and unfortunately continued well into the decade, even after McCarthy's powers waned in the mid-1950s. What one historian has dubbed "The Great Fear" had many aspects; nonetheless "the key notion was guilt by association." And, in effect, it was that with which Radulovich was being charged by the Air Force, on the basis of evidence presented by witnesses he could not confront.[26]

See It Now's treatment of the Radulovich case is a first-rate example of advocacy reporting and a good indication of how the Friendly-Murrow team dealt with controversial subjects. The program opened with a subdued statement by Murrow that set the tone for what followed:

> *Good evening. A few weeks ago there occurred a few obscure notices in the newspaper about a Lt. Milo Radulovich, a lieutenant in the Air Force Reserve, and also something about Air Force regulation 35-62. That is a regulation which states that a man may be regarded as a security risk if he has close and continuing association with Communists or people believed to have Communist sympathies. Lt. Radulovich was asked to resign. He declined. A Board was called and heard his case. At the end it was recommended that he be severed from the Air Force, although it was also stated that there was no question whatever as to Lt. Radulovich's loyalty. We propose to examine insofar as we can, the case of Lt. Radulovich.*[27]

Murrow referred to Radulovich as "no special hero—no martyr" and allowed him to explain eloquently that the basis for the Air Force's concern was the relationship with his father and sister. There followed statements from various people in Dexter, Michigan, where Radulovich lived, all of whom supported him. His lawyer, the town marshal, the proprietor of a local dry-cleaning establishment, a former mayor, a gas-station owner, the commander of the local American Legion post— some of these people did not know Radulovich personally, but in effect all served as character witnesses, as they expressed disagreement with the Air Force's policy and actions. The lawyer declared that in more than thirty years of practice he had "never witnessed such a farce and travesty." The Legionnaire said he would not know Radulovich "if he came down the middle of the street," but he felt that was "beside the point." He believed that if the people "purging" this man "get away with it, they are entitled to do it to anybody. You or me or anybody else . . . then we all had better head for cover." Each of these people was filmed in what are known as "shoulder shots," that is, just the head and shoulders visible. All were filmed in a manner that emphasized the serious, positive tenor of their remarks. The TV camera, as is well known, can play tricks, making a subject seem honest and straightforward or quite the reverse. Radulovich's supporters were filmed in such a way as to underline their remarks, not to undercut them.[28]

The program then turned to the cause of Radulovich's problem—his father, John, and his sister, Margaret. A United Auto Workers local officer and co-worker with the father asserted that the union "don't want any part" of the Communists, but "I would never classify John Radulovich as subversive in any way, shape, or form." In introducing the father, Murrow pointed out that John Radulovich "denied subscribing to the *Daily Worker* and said he subscribed to the Serbian language newspaper, which was pro-Tito, because he liked their Christmas calendars." The father, in a touching sequence, read in a thick accent a letter he had written to the president asking for "justice for my boy." The sister made a short statement in which she did not commit herself politically in any way, except to assert, "My political beliefs are my own private affair." There was no probing of the sister, who indicated that she felt that her brother was "being forced to undergo a strain for a very unjust cause."[29]

The filmed portion of the program ended with responses by Milo Radulovich and his wife, Nancy, to questions asked by *See It Now* staffer Joseph Wershba. They were filmed in their modest but comfortable living room, which, as one critic said, exuded "the atmosphere of the average American home." Nancy Radulovich said she did not "regret anything. . . . I wouldn't want him to take it lying down. If he did, he would be admitting to something we aren't guilty of." Milo Radulovich asked "if I am being judged on my relatives, are my children going to be asked to denounce me?" And he again asserted that he did not believe that "this procedure that I have been subjected to by the Air Force is in that democratic tradition."[30]

What Friendly has described as the "tail piece"—the last few minutes in the program—were given over to Murrow's stirring and thought-provoking live commentary. He read from parts of the transcript of the hearing, demonstrating its essential unfairness (e.g., the evidence was in a closed envelope that could not be examined by Radulovich or by his attorney). Murrow said:

> *We are unable to judge the claims against the Lieutenant's father or sister because neither we, nor you, nor they, nor the lieutenant, nor the lawyers know precisely what was contained in that manila envelope. Was it hearsay, rumor, gossip, slander, or was it hard ascertainable fact that could be backed by creditable witnesses. We do not know.*
>
> *. . . Security officers will tell you that a man who had a sister in Warsaw, for example, might be entirely loyal, but would be subjected to pressure as a result of threats that might be made against his sister. . . . They contend that a man who has a sister in the Communist Party in this country might be subjected to the same kind of pressure, but here again no evidence was adduced to prove that Radulovich's sister is a member of the party and the case against his father was certainly not made.*
>
> *We believe that "the son shall not bear the iniquity of the father," even though that iniquity be proved; and in this case it was not. But we believe, too, that this case illustrates the urgent need for the Armed Forces to communicate more fully than they have so far done, the procedures and regulations to be followed in attempting to protect the national security and the rights of the individual at the same time. Whatever happens in the whole area of the relationship between the individual and the state, we will do it ourselves. . . . And it seems to Fred Friendly and myself . . . that that is a subject that should be argued about endlessly.[31]*

The response to this program was remarkable. Friendly recalls that the reaction was "more than Ed had hoped for" and that CBS received "hundreds of phone calls, most of them favorable, but some bitter denunciations of Murrow and CBS." The mail response, according to a contemporary report, "rather surprised the staff." Approximately eight thousand letters were received, with the bias about 100 to 1 in favor of Radulovich. Media historian Erik Barnouw reports that "a few newspaper columnists denounced the program, but there were many paeans of praise." Typical were the hosannahs offered by *New York Times* staffer Jack Gould, then perhaps the nation's most influential media critic, who called the Radulovich program "a long step forward in television journalism." Years later CBS head William Paley nostalgically wrote of the program's "impact," but Friendly remembers that he "never heard a word from company executives about the Radulovich broadcast other than about the mail count." Perhaps the most gratifying response came from the Air Force. Five weeks after the broadcast of the Radulovich program the secretary of the Air Force appeared on *See It Now* and announced that he had "decided . . . it is consistent with the interests of the national security to retain Lt. Radulovich in the United States Air Force Reserve. . . . The question . . . raised as to security has thus been resolved in Lt. Radulovich's favor." *See It Now* cannot take sole credit for this decision, but its airing of Radulovich's plight did result in the necessary "public exposure," and did alert the nation's media, an essential portion of which took up the case.[32]

The putting together of the Radulovich program was typical of the way *See It Now* worked, even though the routine did vary from subject to subject. A story about Radulovich caught Murrow's eye in one of the various out-of-town newspapers that he regularly perused. He clipped it and asked Friendly to follow up. At other times the initiative would come from Friendly; both agreed that seldom could "an idea's organization . . . be actually attributed to either one of them specifically." Murrow at one time said that many of the program's topics were chosen "on anticipatory news judgment."[33]

To check out the Radulovich story a staff member, Joseph Wershba, was sent to Michigan. The story seemed to be a promising enough feature for him to request a camera crew, and one was sent. Altogether about five hours of film was shot, even though less than twenty-five minutes was used. Such a ratio of footage shot or compiled to film used was not unusual; for the McCarthy program the staff put together over fifteen times as much footage as was finally utilized. Filming the interviews was, on the whole, a standard procedure. As described by a staff cameraman at the time:

> *. . . Two cameras are used, both . . . start off at the same time. The first . . . takes a closeup picture of the person being interviewed. The . . . other takes a long shot—or a picture encompassing possibly both interviewer and interviewee with some of the surrounding scene. . . . This second camera films approximately 3 minutes and stops. As the first camera begins to run out of film, the second takes over shooting closeups while the first reloads. When reloaded, the first camera resumes the closeup filming. . . . Cameras are always trained on the person being interviewed throughout the interview period. . . . After the interview, pictures are taken of the interviewer repeating the questions as if he were actually asking them . . . for the first time. . . . Extra pictures are taken . . . for the sake of visual variety and editing purposes.*

Most scenes, whether interviews or not, were shot several times from different angles and in different ways (close-ups, medium shots, long views, etc.).[34]

Once shot, the film was rushed to New York City, where Friendly would assign segments of the program being prepared to various staff members. Often the footage would just keep coming in, and there would be constant reevaluation and reediting. "The circumstances under which *See It Now* was assembled . . . and telecast" were, as Barnouw accurately points out, "primitive." Friendly recalls that for the Radulovich program

> *the film shot in Dexter, Michigan, was developed and printed in a laboratory on Ninth Avenue. The screening and editing were done at the Fifth Avenue facilities near Forth Fifth Street. The Murrow off-camera narration was recorded in a studio near his office, piped over to the mixing facility on Fifth Avenue and thence would be sent by telephone circuit to . . . Master Control at Grand Central.*[35]

Often the results that came out of this semiorganized chaos, as with the Radulovich program, were splendid, but there could unfortunately also be stumbles. Staff member Palmer Williams recalled that the first program of the 1954–1955 season (which dealt with Berlin's role in the cold war) was the "biggest stumble" because of a lack of cohesion as the film "poured in."[36]

See It Now was produced in what Friendly describes as "a pressure cooker atmosphere." To keep the series topical, especially while it still was a half hour, a program often had to be put together on very short notice. The Radulovich program, from conception to broadcast, was put together in less than three weeks. The lack of sophisticated technology (*See It Now* did not, for example, have the benefit of "live on tape," or minicameras, or computer-assisted editing) meant that often the ninety-six hours prior to broadcast time were extremely hectic. Friendly believes much of the success of the series was due to the willingness of the staff to put in long hours under almost impossible conditions: "We had a hardy bunch of guys who were a band of brothers under Ed."[37]

For the Radulovich program, like many others, the final editing work began on the Friday before the Tuesday night broadcast. Editing continued through the weekend, and on Monday work went on around the clock and through the night. Murrow, whose final commentary usually was live, looked at the editing on Monday but was still concerned with writing a strong conclusion to the program. Because the Radulovich program had not been finalized by late Tuesday afternoon (a not unusual occurrence), it was impossible to put together a composite print (*See It Now* was what was then called a "three-track production"—the picture was printed on one track, the sound printed on another, and on the third Murrow's narration was recorded; the three tracks had to be synchronized—put "in sync"). When the show ran weekly, it was not always possible to make up a composite print of the whole program. The Radulovich program did not even have a complete run-through prior to air time, but it had very much impressed staff who had seen just parts of it. Friendly recalls that *See It Now's* on-the-air director, Don Hewitt, "told the crew he'd murder someone if we lost 'sync' that night, as we had a few weeks ago."[38]

Just before the Radulovich program went on the air Murrow told Friendly, "Things will never be the same around here after tonight." And he was right: the implications of the broadcast were inescapable. It was quite clear, as media historian Barnouw points out, that *See It Now* "was not merely probing the judicial processes of the Air Force and Pentagon—a quixotic venture few broadcasters would have undertaken at this time—but was examining the whole syndrome of McCarthyism with its secret denunciations and guilt by association." This program was followed by others that dealt with McCarthyism—one program concerned the denial of an Indianapolis public auditorium to the American Civil Liberties Union for an organizational meeting in that city. Making use of splendid editing, *See It Now*, through vivid if not always fair intercutting, in effect created a debate between what was said at the ACLU meeting—which was held in a church hall—and an American Legion assembly called to denounce the ACLU meeting. Murrow forwent his usual tail piece and gave the last word to Father Victor L. Goosens, pastor of St. Mary's Roman Catholic Church, who had made the church's social center available to the ACLU.

> *When the climate is such that so many people are so quick to . . . ignore the law and to deny to others the right to peaceful assembly and free speech—then somebody certainly has to take a stand. . . . And it's up to us . . . to lead the way, because we know that . . . the American freedoms . . . are all based upon the rights which God has given us. And if the church and religion do not uphold those basic principles which come from God, then who will?[39]*

Having taken on the "ism," Murrow and Friendly, in the colorful but accurate words of a media critic, now "decided to lunge for the heart of the beast." Since the spring of 1953 the *See It Now* staff had collected a film record of Senator McCarthy in action. A considerable amount of footage had been amassed, but a kind of equivocation delayed use of this material. Each week the staff would update the material, and each week, as Murrow's biographer reports, "Friendly would consult [with his partner] and then say 'No, let's hold for another week.'" Finally, Murrow and Friendly decided that the time was ripe for such a program, and it was scheduled for March 9, 1954.[40]

Unhappy comments on the tenor of the times in which this broadcast was scheduled are evidenced by the fact that Murrow had come to believe his telephone was being tapped and that Friendly felt it was necessary for the unit putting the McCarthy program together to meet and discuss their personal lives and backgrounds. As Friendly put it candidly to his partner (and perhaps not unreasonably in the context of the 1950s), "It would not be fair to CBS to enter into this battle if we had an Achilles heel." Murrow agreed. The unit was called together; they discussed (as Friendly remembers) not only the quality of the program, but also the question of whether there was "anything in their own backgrounds that would give the Senator a club to beat us with, because if the broadcast was successful, he and his supporters would certainly be looking for one."[41]

Whether or not the program could be judged a success depended on the political beliefs of the viewer and the critics, but the program certainly achieved its purpose—which, as a contemporary critic saw it, was "to show McCarthy as Murrow and Friendly believed him to be." The "report on Senator Joseph R. McCarthy told mainly in his own words and pictures" remains understandably the most famous of all the *See It Now* broadcasts—not the most typical, not the best in terms of style or format by any means, and certainly not the most objective. Murrow and Friendly believed it really important to show Senator McCarthy in action browbeating witnesses at congressional committee hearings, contradicting himself without any regard to truth, resorting to innuendo and slander, playing the bully. And this they did.[42]

Viewers could see and hear McCarthy assert, "Those who wear the label 'Democrat' wear it with the stain of a historic betrayal . . . twenty years of treason"; refer to that party's 1952 presidential candidate as "Alger, I mean Adlai" Stevenson (a reference to Alger Hiss, who had been convicted of perjury but really had been tried for his 1930s associations); place himself above the nation's chief executive and promise "to continue to call them as I see them regardless of who happens to be President." And how did Senator McCarthy see them? According to *See It Now* his vision was bleak: "When the shouting and the tumult dies the American people and the President shall realize that this unprecedented mud-slinging against my Committee by the extreme left-wing elements of the press and radio were caused solely because another Fifth Amendment Communist was finally dug out of the dark recesses and exposed to the public view."[43]

See It Now included footage from what was referred to as "a sample investigation" with commentary by Murrow on the senator's statements. The witness was Reed Harris, an employee of the United States Information Agency, who had been suspended from Columbia University some twenty years earlier and then had accepted legal counsel provided by the ACLU. The footage showed Senator McCarthy at his "browbeating worst," as this excerpt from the program demonstrates:

McCarthy: The question is did the Civil Liberties Union supply you with an attorney?
Harris: They did supply an attorney.
McCarthy: The answer is yes?
Harris: The answer is yes.
McCarthy: You know the Civil Liberties Union has been listed as a front for and doing the work of the Communist Party.
Harris: Mr. Chairman, this was 1932.
McCarthy: I know it was 1932. Do you know they since have been listed as front for and doing the work of the Communist Party?
Harris: I do not know they have been listed so, sir.
McCarthy: You don't know they have been so listed?
Harris: I have heard that mentioned or read that mentioned. . . .
Murrow: The Reed Harris hearing demonstrated some of the Senator's techniques. Twice he said that the American Civil Liberties Union was listed as a subversive front. The Attorney General's list does not and never has listed the ACLU as subversive, nor does the FBI or any other government agency.

Overall this *See It Now* program portrayed Senator McCarthy in what one writer recently cogently described as "his full, foul glory. . . . remorelessly revealing his shabby practices and demeanor."[44]

On camera, Murrow cannot be said to have paid even lip service to objectivity. His comments may not have been fair, but they were sincere, and he left no doubt that intense conviction motivated him. The usually urbane and cool Murrow seemed strained, concerned, moved. Indeed, Joe Wershba remembers that "for the first and last time," prior to the airing of a program, Murrow "made an ideological preachment" to the staff. And Murrow's eloquent summation at the end of the program had just the right touch. Turning to the camera, he said:

> *No one familiar with the history of this country can deny that congressional committees are useful . . . but the line between investigation and persecution is a very fine one and the junior Senator from Wisconsin has stepped over it repeatedly. . . .*
>
> *This is no time for men who oppose Senator McCarthy's methods to keep silent, or for those who approve. We can deny our heritage and our history, but we cannot escape responsibility for the result. There is no way for a citizen of the republic to abdicate his responsibilities. As a nation we have come into our full inheritance at a tender age. We proclaim ourselves—as indeed—we are—the defenders of freedom, what's left of it, but we cannot defend freedom abroad by deserting it at home. The actions of the junior Senator from Wisconsin have caused alarm and dismay amongst our allies abroad and given considerable comfort to our enemies, and whose fault is that? Not really his. He didn't create the situation of fear; he merely exploited it, and rather successfully. Cassius was right: "The fault, dear Brutus, is not in our stars but in ourselves."*[45]

Viewer response to the McCarthy program was extraordinary. A CBS spokesman said it was "the largest spontaneous response" the network had ever experienced. More than twelve thousand telegrams and telephone calls had been received within forty-eight hours of the broadcast. Murrow's biographer notes that although the newscaster received "some hostile comment . . . the general reaction was not only favorable but highly approving." Within two weeks, reported a writer at the time, "some 22,000 letters had been received and sorted, of which all but approximately 2,500 were pro-Murrow." According to this count the radio was 9 to 1 in favor of Murrow, except for California where the response was 8 to 3. Friendly later estimated that between seventy-five and a hundred thousand wrote, telegraphed, or telephoned in response to the program: "We never really knew the exact count." He also reported that even after McCarthy, taking advantage of *See It Now*'s offer to respond on the air, presented a filmed half-hour rebuttal that strongly attacked Murrow, the mail "continued to run in Murrow's favor . . . but the ratio did drop down to . . . two to one." An unfortunate side effect was that there were threats against Murrow's eight-year-old son Casey, and that (as Friendly writes) "for years afterward some one always met Casey at school and escorted him home."[46]

The critical response to the McCarthy program was, in the main, quite flattering, except for McCarthy's media partisans, who responded as might be expected: One suggested that *See It Now* should be retitled "See It My Way," and a Hearst newspaper columnist referred to the broadcast as a "hate McCarthy telecast" by a "pompous portsider." Praise for the McCarthy program was widespread. A *New Yorker* magazine writer dubbed the program "an extraordinary feat of journalism." A trade journal rhapsodized that "no greater feat of journalistic enterprise has occurred in modern times." Jack Gould's enthusiasm for the broadcast was so great that he began his comments by asserting, "Last week may be remembered as the week that broadcasting recaptured its soul."[47]

Gould's enthusiasm for the broadcast, however, was tempered by a fear of its implications, a fear that concerned a number of persons then and still remains a worry for most observers of the electronic media (especially given the growth of its impact and power since then). Gould commented:

> *It is difficult to see how Mr. Murrow could have done other than he did without abandoning his and television's journalistic integrity . . . but what was frightening about Mr. Murrow's broadcast . . . was . . . what if the camera and microphone should fall into the hands of a reckless and demagogic commentator.*

Gilbert Seldes, an eminent, veteran commentator on the arts, also pondered that point both then and later. He considered the program on McCarthy "noteworthy," indeed "the most important single broadcast in television" to that time, and yet he felt "in the long run it is more important to use our communications system properly than to destroy McCarthy." Moreover, the senator's reply, argued Seldes, demonstrated the "emptiness" of the equal time formula; Seldes said he had no love for

McCarthy, but the situation seemed akin to one in which "a man clubbed another and then passed him the stick knowing full well he could not use it effectively."[48]

It seems to me obvious that the *See It Now* program on Senator McCarthy was neither fair nor objective. Nor could it be, given the temper of the men who created it. Murrow's tone in constantly describing McCarthy as "the junior Senator from Wisconsin" was clearly meant to be pejorative and obviously reflected the broadcaster's distaste for the politician and what he stood for. A significant portion of the program consisted of McCarthy's statements (be they half-truths, distortions, or what have you) being corrected by an overserious Murrow. As one McCarthy biographer points out, "The editing portrayed Joe [McCarthy] . . . belching, picking his nose, contradicting himself, giggling at his own vulgar humor." A substantial portion of the program's footage depicting the senator stacked the deck against him visually. As one critic summed up the choice of footage: "It showed the Senator at his worst, or least coherent."[49]

The issues raised by this particular program remain crucial. There were and are those who feel, to use one historian's words, "that treatment of McCarthy was no crueler than McCarthy's treatment of numerous innocent witnesses before his committee." And there are those, like Gould and Seldes, who worry about the misuse of the media. Perhaps the questions raised are not answerable except from an individual point of view. What is clear—as one scholar pointed out a decade later—is that with this broadcast *See It Now* had turned "from making film *tell* something to making it *will* something."[50]

Just as there has been a divided response to the content of this particular program, so there has been a twofold response to the impact of *See It Now's* treatment of Senator McCarthy. A few year later Seldes argued that *See It Now* had carried the war aggressively into McCarthy's territory, and that "it was plain that the McCarthy who appeared a few weeks later" at the Senate hearings inquiring into his strange and strained relationships with the U.S. Army "had already suffered a tactical defeat and was aware of it." TV producer Fred Freed years later recalled the liberating effect of the program and how *See It Now's* action helped him and others at least to begin to combat McCarthyism, which had resulted in widespread blacklisting in the media industry: "Most of the time most of us just submitted to the pressure. We wouldn't admit it then, and it's painful to admit now. With *See It Now* that began to change. . . . Murrow stood up to him. Then others in the industry began to." A McCarthy biographer writing years later believes that the program damaged McCarthy, that it "had done what so many of the great news media had so long refrained from doing . . . laid bare the soul and techniques of a demagogue."[51]

See It Now had waited a long time to attack McCarthy. And there were and are those who felt it waited too long to join the small, stalwart band who had been willing to combat the senator (such as Eric Sevareid, a colleague of Murrow and Friendly at CBS, who had by 1952 already broadcast over radio several negative analyses of McCarthy, and in one commentary had unflatteringly likened him to an incompetent character in *Winnie-the-Pooh*). Typical is the recent study which maintains that Murrow's courage was "cautious," and that the "most remarkable thing about the program was that it was late" in attacking McCarthy. In the mid-1970s Jack Gould recalled that Murrow himself at the time said, "We're bringing up the rear." But I think the latter comment is more a matter of Murrow understatement than anything else. Given the low level of courage displayed in general by network broadcasting executives, the fears that kept most controversy of *any* kind off the airwaves, and the hesitant history of the industry in dealing with such matters as blacklisting, one should not in retrospect slight the efforts of Murrow and Friendly. They may have been late in taking on the senator, but at the time they confronted the "ism" with the Radulovich program it was not yet clear which way the wind would finally blow. And even if there was a delay in confronting the senator, that delay did not diminish the impact the broadcast had at the time, an impact upon which almost all contemporary commentators agree. What was important was not that Senator McCarthy was being exposed as a "tricky operator," but that attention was being drawn to the situation by a man of "Murrow's stature" with a "vast television pulpit." Murrow probably summed up the situation best a few years later when he declared, "The time was right. . . . We did it fairly well. . . . There was a great conspiracy of silence at the time; when there is such a conspiracy and somebody makes a loud noise it attracts all the attention."[52]

It may be that Murrow is right when he avers that the program received "too much credit," but it is a sad footnote and a fascinating commentary on the recent writing of American history that while journalists and media types dealing with the period mention this *See It Now* program (whatever their approach to it), the works penned by professional historians do not. They usually touch on the televising of the Army-McCarthy hearings without taking into account the following: only the then relatively insignificant American Broadcasting Company network and the tiny Dumont network carried the hearings live during the day (reaching fewer than seventy-five stations). Moreover, ABC carried the hearings only as far as Denver. The National Broadcasting Company did carry the hearings to the West Coast for a few days but then, as an angry Seldes points out, "announcing that *there was not enough public interest to justify the expense,* contented itself with copious excerpts from the hearings shown late in the evening." Interestingly enough, CBS did not carry the hearings at all except for some clips shown on news programs late at night.[53]

While finishing up the McCarthy program Friendly had said to Murrow, "This is going to be a tough one to do." And Murrow replied, "They're all going to be tough after this." Some years later Friendly, commenting on this conversation and the subsequent history of *See It Now,* declared, "We have been swimming upstream ever since." The swim might have been easier if *See It Now* had pulled its punches and concentrated on innocuous subjects, but while the series did some lighthearted programs, it also continued to do programs that caused controversy. And as Friendly later wrote: "The attitude at CBS was 'Why does Murrow have to save the world every week?' "[54]

An unfortunate byproduct of the continuing controversy was the decision of the Aluminum Corporation of American (Alcoa), which had sponsored *See It Now* since its third program in 1951, to terminate that support at the end of the 1954–1955 season. The relationship between Alcoa and *See It Now* had been a good one; as Murrow said at the time, "I have a wonderful arrangement with my sponsor. They make aluminum and I make films." Alcoa's decision to sponsor *See It Now* had grown out of a desire to influence not a mass audience but specifically the kind that watched programs such as *See It Now.* TV was not a mass medium in the early 1950s—the cost of sets limited most viewers to what Friendly has described as "an up-scale elitist audience, one that a company would want to influence." And this audience Alcoa reached through *See It Now.* The company withstood heavy pressure over the years resulting from this sponsorship, but the company's priorities were changing: competition in the aluminum industry was steadily increasing, the company had decided to plunge into the consumer market and not just sell wholesale—institutional advertising no longer seemed pertinent. But the decisive factor was probably the question of controversy, which could affect its sales on every level. As Friendly recounts: "Alcoa salesman had difficulty explaining why this company felt it necessary to sponsor programs against McCarthy . . . and 'for socialized medicine'— which is what some doctors thought our program on the Salk vaccine advocated."[55]

Alcoa never interfered with *See It Now.* As John Fleming, Alcoa's corporate liaison with the series, put it, "When you hire an editor you let him alone to work as he sees best." Nor did CBS interfere with *See It Now,* which operated with an autonomy akin to the "independence granted a columnist such as Walter Lippman or Arthur Krock" (to use Friendly's words). This freedom from corporate supervision owed much to Murrow's prestige, determination, and intimate relationship with William Paley, to whom Murrow had direct access.[56]

See It Now's continuing provocative stance seems to have undermined Murrow's status at CBS and to have led to the decisions to have the program irregularly scheduled and finally canceled. Indeed, how far that erosion had gone is indicated by the dramatic confrontation between Murrow and Paley over the end of *See It Now.* During the course of a long, heated argument Murrow angrily asked Paley, "Bill, are you going to destroy all this? Don't you want an instrument like the *See It Now* organization, which you have poured so much money into for so long, to continue?" And Paley replied, "Yes, but I don't want this constant stomach ache every time you do a controversial subject."[57]

The relationship between *See It Now*'s producers and their corporate superiors at CBS had never been an easy one. Paley had graciously called Murrow the morning of the McCarthy broadcast and said, "I'll be with you tonight, Ed, and I'll be with you tomorrow as well." Although it was clear at the time that Murrow and Friendly had Paley's approval, "with the advantage of hindsight it becomes apparent" (as one writer has noted) "that they did not have the official support of CBS as a corporation." Thus, for a number of their controversial broadcasts (including the Radulovich and McCarthy broadcasts), Murrow and Friendly found it necessary to pay out of their personal funds for *New York Times* advertisements announcing the programs, announcements that did not carry the CBS logo.[58]

See It Now's provocativeness upset and alienated Paley, but it was the changes in television broadcasting in the United States as much as the lack of corporate support within CBS that doomed the series. It was during the early and mid-1950s that television went national, with programs being aired coast to coast. Moreover, there was during these years, as one media study points out, "a fantastic growth pattern. . . . from 6 percent penetration of American homes by television in 1949 to 76 percent in 1956." And the year before, *The $64,000 Question* had debuted in June in the time slot just prior to *See It Now*, had achieved smash ratings almost instantaneously, and had started the quiz show boom.[59]

What Friendly and others in the industry called "opportunity costs" now came strongly into play. *See It Now*, according to Murrow's biographer, "had always been a sore spot with the company's accountants despite its prestige." It might often cost more than $100,000 to produce an individual program, and in the early days of *See It Now* Alcoa paid only $23,000 toward the cost of the program and an additional $34,000 for the air time. By 1955 Alcoa was paying $55,000 for the air time, but Revlon—the sponsor of the much-cheaper-to-produce *$64,000 Question*—was paying $80,000 for its half hour. On seeing the first *$64,000 Question* show, a wary, concerned Murrow, already aware of the problems *See It Now* faced at CBS, turned to Friendly and asked, "Any bets on how long we'll keep this time period now?"[60]

The answer was not long in coming, and by the 1957–1958 season *See It Now* had returned to the intellectual ghetto of late Sunday afternoons. And then it was terminated. The economics of the situation as well as internal politics at CBS had resulted in what Friendly later called "The Strange Death of *See It Now*." What one critic has described as "consensus TV" now reigned. The axing of the series disturbed Murrow and Friendly. The latter later recalled, "When the end came Ed and I were very, *very* bitter."[61]

It has become fashionable in recent years to disparage the Murrow-Friendly collaboration, to downplay its impact, to downgrade Friendly, to deprecate Murrow for "working both sides of the street" (a reference to his efforts with *Person to Person*, the highly successful TV show which, in effect, made into an art nondemanding celebrity interviewing on television). It seems to me that these criticisms are at best quibbles. *See It Now*, in my opinion, is TV documentary at its best. The series admittedly had some clinkers; not everything it dealt with was vital; mistakes were made—but withal *See It Now* never compromised its integrity, and as with the Radulovich and McCarthy programs the series took an unpopular but necessary stand. In an extremely challenging and important speech to a 1958 convention of radio and television news directors, Murrow declared that he "did not advocate that we turn television into a 27-inch wailing wall," but he would "just like to see it reflect occasionally the hard, unyielding realities of the world in which we live." And that *See It Now* did, and did quite well.[62]

See It Now has spawned many imitations, but in my opinion none have lived up to the original. *60 Minutes* has lasted longer, has achieved greater commercial and ratings success, has managed to become an integral part of CBS. Certainly the *See It Now* presence is felt on that show; in 1981 its executive producer (Don Hewitt), managing editor (Palmer Williams), and one of its more distinguished producers (Joseph Wershba) were *See It Now* alumni, as were staffers such as cameraman Bill McClure. But peruse the recently published "complete text of 114 stories . . . of Season XII of *60 Minutes*," and you will be disappointed. The treatments lack depth and fire, the exposés are mostly of the obvious or of relatively powerless individuals, the subjects are a not-overdistinguished mishmash. *60 Minutes*, as one critic has pointed out, is "a feature magazine, designed for relaxed viewing."[63]

Relaxation was not the aim of the producers of *See It Now*, and the series did not relax viewers—it enraged them, it informed them, it convinced them. As TV documentary, *See It Now* does not seem to me ever to have been equaled. There are programs that have been slicker, but none more seminal for the form. Speaking to an English audience, Murrow once said, "There is . . . no substitute for the man who has at least a mild fire in his belly and is able to pierce that screen with his own conviction." That *See It Now* did, and did well—not always with every program, but certainly with great consistency and intelligence. The hardware has improved immeasurably since the 1950s, but *See It Now* still remains a superb model for anyone interested in the TV documentary.[64]

Notes

1. Michael J. Arlen, *The View from Highway I* (New York: Farrar, Strauss & Giroux, 1976), pp. 3, 5; John Crosby, *Out of the Blue* (New York: Simon & Schuster, 1952), p. 284; Newton M. Minow, *Equal Time: The Private Broadcaster and the Public Interest*, edited by Laurence Laurent (New York: Atheneum, 1964), p. 52 (Minow's description of television programming unfortunately generally still holds true. He told his audience, the approximately 3000 delegates to the annual convention of the National Association of Broadcasters, "You will see a procession of game shows, violence, audience participation shows, formula comedies about totally unbelievable families, blood and thunder, mayhem, violence, sadism, murder, Western badmen, Western goodmen, private eyes, gangsters, more violence and cartoons. And, endlessly, commercials—many screaming, cajoling, and offending"); Michael Novak, "Television Shapes the Soul," in *Television: The Critical View*, edited by Horace Newcomb (New York: Oxford University Press, 1979), 2nd ed. p. 308.

2. Novak, "Television Shapes," p. 315; Arlen, *Highway 1*, p. 51; Crosby, *Out of the Blue*, p. 237; Minow, *Equal Time*, p 308.

3. Tim Brooks and Earle Marsh, *The Complete Directory to Prime Time Network TV Shows: 1946–Present* (New York: Ballantine Books, 1979), p. 53; William Small, *To Kill a Messenger: Television News and the Real World* (New York: Hastings House, 1970), pp. 18–19; A. William Bluem, *Documentary in American Television* (New York: Hastings House, 1965), pp. 99–100; John Crosby, "The Demise of 'See It Now,' " *New York Herald Tribune*, 11 July 1958.

4. Helen Dudar, "A Post Portrait: Ed Murrow," *New York Post*, 1 March 1959; Sir Hugh Greene in "Good Night and Good Luck" (1975 BBC-TV Production), distributed by Instructional Media Services, Washington State University; Gary Paul Gates, *Air Time: The Inside Story of CBS News* (New York: Harper & Row, 1978), p. 13. How much Murrow still remains a touchstone in his profession is demonstrated by Dan Rather's reminiscences. He recalls that the phrase "I think you have it in you to be another Ed Murrow" gets "vastly overworked" but still "it sings." And he found that in the mid-1970s, a decade and a half after Murrow left CBS, "it was astonishing how often" Murrow's name and work "came up" during program discussions at *CBS Reports*. Dan Rather with Mickey Hershkowitz, *The Camera Never Blinks: Adventures of a TV Journalist* (New York: William Morrow, 1977), pp. 160, 295. There is a splendid capsule profile of Murrow in William Manchester, *The Glory and the Dream: A Narrative History of America, 1932–1972* (Boston: Little, Brown, 1974), pp. 513–516. There is a somewhat more tough-minded but waspish assessment of Murrow in David Culbert's *News for Everyman: Radio and Foreign Affairs in Nineteen-Thirties America* (Westport, Conn: Greenwood Press, 1976, pp. 179–196.

5. Alexander Kendrick, *Prime Time: The Life of Edward R. Murrow* (Boston: Little, Brown, 1969), p. 139.

6. David Halberstam, *The Powers That Be* (New York: Knopf, 1979), p. 39.

7. Fred W. Friendly, *Due to Circumstances Beyond Our Control . . .* (New York: Random House, 1967), p. xvi; Edward R. Murrow, *This Is London* (New York: Simon & Schuster, 1941), from the introduction by Elmer Davis, p. viii; Lawrence S. Rudner, "Born to a New Craft: Edward R. Murrow, 1938–1940," *Journal of Popular Culture* 15 (1981): 101; Archibald MacLeish, "To Ed Murrow, Reporter," *Journal of Home Economics* 34 (1942): 361. There is a splendid two-record selection of Murrow's wartime broadcasts available: Fred W. Friendly et al., eds., *Edward R. Murrow: A Reporter Remembers*, vol. 1, "The War Years" (Columbia Records 02L 332).

8. Les Brown, *The New York Times Encyclopedia of Television* (New York: Times Books, 1977), p. 288; Janet Murrow quoted in Halberstam, *Powers That Be*, p. 44; William Paley, *As It Happened: A Memoir* (Garden City, N.Y.: Doubleday, 1979), p. 151; "TV News Past and Present: A Conversation with Charles Collingwood" (broadcast over WNYC-TV, New York City, 27 September 1982).

9. Robert Lewis Shayon, "Murrow's Lost Fight," *Saturday Review of Literature*, 22 May 1965, p. 94; "Murrow at the Mike," *Newsweek*, 28 July 1947, p. 56.

10. *Current Biography, 1957*, pp. 196–197. Friendly insists that his middle name was Friendly and not Freundlich at the time he switched the names and that the family name had been changed much earlier (Friendly interview with the author, October 29, 1981). On the wall above his desk in his Columbia University office is a large picture from the turn of the century of a relative's store in Eugene, Oregon; on the plate glass window of the store is the word "Friendly."

11. Friendly, *Circumstances*, p. xvii; Murray Yaeger, "An Analysis of Edward R. Murrow's 'See It Now' Television Program" (Ph.D. diss., University of Iowa, 1956), p. 35; John Crosby quoted in *Current Biography*, p. 197.

12. Paley, *Memoir*, p. 299; Halberstam, *The Powers That Be*, p. 135; Robert Metz, *Reflections in a Bloodshot Eye* (Chicago: Playboy Press, 1975), p. 279; Gates, *Air Time*, pp. 106, 108; Arthur Barron quoted in Arthur Rosenthal, *The New Documentary in Action: A Casebook in Film-making* (Berkeley & Los Angeles: University of California Press, 1971), p. 145; Fred Freed quoted in David Yellin, *Special: Fred Freed and the Television Documentary* (New York: Macmillian), 1973, p. 20; Yaeger, "Analysis," pp. 36–37. Harvey Swados has penned a splendid profile of Friendly that attempts to assess and analyze the contradictory tendencies evident in the man: "Fred Friendly's Vision," in *Radical at Large: American Essays* (London: Rupert Hart-Davis, 1968), pp. 129–141.

13. Joseph Wershba, "Murrow vs. McCarthy: See it Now," *New York Times Magazine*, 4 March 1979, p. 22; Kendrick, *Prime Time*, p. 508. It is worth mentioning that Friendly's comments about Murrow in an oral history interview are quite respectful (Fred W. Friendly interview, Oral History Project, Columbia University, *passim*). Perhaps the best comments by Friendly about Murrow are to be found in "Good Night and Good Luck," when he tells the BBC interviewer, "Ed Murrow was no God. He was a great journalist and a great human being. . . . He made his mistakes like all the rest of us do."

14. Edward R. Murrow and Fred W. Friendly, *I Can Hear It Now* (Columbia m1495); Friendly, *Circumstances*, p. xviii. Despite the many imitations since then, the quality, style, and intelligence governing the making of this record and its successors have kept them from being cliché or old hat. To realize the superiority of *I Can Hear It Now* one need only compare it to one of its imitative competitors such as *Hark! The Years* (Capitol s282), which was narrated by Fredric March in a frenetic manner and punctuated by shrill music.

15. Quoted in Yaeger, "Analysis," p. 48; Kendrick, *Prime Time*, p. 317. There is an excellent, illuminating review of the first *I Can Hear It Now* album in Crosby, *Out of the Blue*, pp. 237–239.

16. Kendrick, *Prime Time*, p. 329; Yaeger, "Analysis," p. 48.

17. Edward R. Murrow, "What's Wrong with TV?" *Reader's Digest*, February 1959, p. 55; Manchester, *Narrative History*, p. 516.

18. Crosby, *Out of the Blue*, p. 249.

19. Erik Barnouw, *A History of Broadcasting in the United States*, vol. 3, *The Image Empire* (New York: Oxford University Press, 1970), p. 45; Yaeger, "Analysis," p. 49; *New York Times*, 4 May 1952, p. 2:1; James L. Baughman, "*See It Now* and Television's Golden Age," *Journal of Popular Culture* 15(1981):108. There is an interesting selection of *See It Now* transcripts in the Edward R. Murrow papers, Edwin Ginn Library, Fletcher School of Law and Diplomacy, Tufts University, Medford, Mass.; these papers have been microfilmed and are available from the Microfilming Corporation of America. There is also a limited selection of *See It Now* transcripts at the Billy Rose Theater Collection of the Performing Arts Research Center, New York Public Library at Lincoln Center, New York City (hereafter referred to as the Billy Rose Collection, NYPL). See also Edward R. Murrow and Fred W. Friendly, *See It Now: A Selection in Text and Pictures* (New York: Simon & Schuster, 1955).

20. Murrow quoted in Crosby, *Out of the Blue*, p. 247 (emphasis mine).

21. Murrow and Friendly, *Selection*, p. xi; Friendly, *Circumstances*, p. 3.

22. Barnouw. *Image Empire*, p. 54.

23. Murrow quoted in Yaeger, "Analysis," p. 57; Charles Montgomery Hammond, Jr., *The Image Decade: Television Documentary, 1965–1975* (New York: Hastings House, 1981), p. 40; Murrow and Friendly, *Selection*, p. xi.

24. Murrow and Friendly, *Selection*, pp. 31–32. *See It Now* (23 November 1952) had briefly touched on a similar issue when it dealt with the case of Harrison, N.Y., high-school officials who refused use of the school auditorium to persons who did not sign a loyalty oath.

25. David Caute, *The Great Fear: The Anti-Communist Purge under Truman and Eisenhower* (New York: Simon & Schuster, 1978), p. 22; Metz, *Reflections*, p. 282; Fred Cook, *The Nightmare Decade: The Life and Times of Senator Joe McCarthy* (New York: Random House, 1941), p. 3.

26. *McCarthyism*, edited by Thomas C. Reeves (Hinsdale, Ill.: Dryden Press, 1973), p. 2; *Webster's Third New International Dictionary*, 1961; Caute, *Great Fear*, p. 18.

27. Murrow and Friendly, *Selection*, pp. 31–32.

28. Ibid., pp. 32, 33. I was able to screen several *See It Now* Programs, including this one, through the generosity of Fred Friendly.

29. Ibid., pp. 36, 38.

30. Yaeger, "Analysis," p. 133.

31. Friendly, *Circumstances*, p. 13; Murrow and Friendly, *Selection*, pp. 39–41.

32. Friendly in "Good Night and Good Luck"; Friendly, *Circumstances*, pp. 16–17: "Eyes of Conscience: See It Now," *Newsweek*, 7 December 1953, p. 65; Erik Barnouw, *Tube of Plenty: The Evolution of American Television* (New York: Oxford University Press, 1975), p. 177; *New York Times*, 25 October, 1953, p. 2:13; Paley, *Memoir*, p. 283; Murrow and Friendly, *Selection*, p. 43.

33. Yaeger, "Analysis," p. 95; Murrow quoted in Yaeger.

34. Leo Rossi quoted in Yaeger, "Analysis," pp. 157–158.

35. Barnouw, *Tube of Plenty*, p. 175; Friendly, *Circumstances*, p. 12.

36. Williams quoted in Yaeger, "Analysis," p. 65.

37. Friendly, *Circumstances*, p. 12; Friendly in "Good Night and Good Luck."

38. Friendly, *Circumstances*, p. 14.

39. Ibid., pp. 3–4; Barnouw, *Tube of Plenty*, p. 175; Murrow and Friendly, *Selection*, p. 53.

40. Laurence Bergren, *Look Now, Pay Later: The Rise of Network Broadcasting* (Garden City, N.Y.: Doubleday, 1980), p. 186; Kendrick, *Prime Time*, p. 97. An interesting side note is pointed out by David Oshinsky in a recent biography of McCarthy (*A Conspiracy So Immense: The World of Joe McCarthy* [New York: The Free Press, 1983]). On the same day the *See It Now* show was broadcast, Senator Ralph Flanders (R-Vt.) made a speech critical of McCarthy and "this speech

was only the beginning" (p. 397), culminating in his proposal in July of a resolution to censure McCarthy.

41. Friendly *Circumstances*, pp. 32–33; Friendly, Oral History Project, Columbia University, p. 18.

42. Yaeger, "Analysis," p. 29.

43. Transcript, Billy Rose Collection, NYPL, *passim*. It was also published in *Top TV Shows of the Year*, edited by Irving Settel (New York: Hastings House, 1955), pp. 61–71.

44. Transcript, Billy Rose Collection, NYPL, p. 10; Cook, *Nightmare Decade*, p. 446; Bergren, p. 187.

45. Wershba, "Murrow vs. McCarthy," p. 22; transcript, Billy Rose Collection, NYPL, p. 16.

46. *New York Times*, 11 March 1954; Kendrick, *Prime Time*, p. 54; Yaeger, "Analysis," p. 174; Friendly, *Circumstances*, pp. 43, 52, 58.

47. Quoted in Jack Gould, "TV and McCarthy," *New York Times*, 14 March 1954, p. 2:11; Jack O'Brian, quoted in Friendly, p. 13 (typical of the smear efforts directed against *See It Now* was Pan American Association, New York Inc., *What You Don't See in "See It Now"* [New York: Pan American Anti-Communist Association of New York, 1957], a pamphlet that among other things accused Murrow of having "favorably publicized Left . . . causes and . . . slandered anti-Communists" [p. 2], and of having repeatedly "shown his bias in favor of Left-wingers [p. 3]); Philip Hamburger, "Man from Wisconsin," *The New Yorker*, 20 March 1954, p. 71; "Radio, TV Takes the Stage in New McCarthy Tempest," *Broadcasting*, 15 March 1954, p. 31; Gould, "TV and McCarthy."

48. Gould, "TV and McCarthy"; Gilbert Seldes, *The Public Arts* (New York: Simon & Schuster, 1956), pp. 217, 226; Seldes, "Murrow, McCarthy and the Empty Formula," *Saturday Review of Literature*, 24 April 1954, p. 26. For a similar view even more forcefully expressed by someone who also opposed McCarthy see John Cogley, "The Murrow Show," *Commonweal*, 16 March 1954, pp. 163–164.

49. Thomas C. Reeves, *The Life and Times of Joe McCarthy* (New York: Stein and Day, 1982), p. 564; Baughman, "Golden Age," p. 108.

50. George Gordon, *The Communications Revolution: A History of the Mass Media in the United States* (New York: Hastings House, 1977), p. 271; Bluem, *Documentary*, p. 98.

51. Seldes, *Public Arts*, p. 20; Freed quoted in Yellin, p. 51; Cook, *Nightmare Decade*, p. 497.

52. Eric Sevareid, *In One Ear* (New York: Knopf, 1952), pp. 207–208; Edwin R. Bayley, *McCarthy and the Press* (Madison, University of Wisconsin Press, 1981), pp. 193, 195 (Gould reminiscence of Murrow statement); Harry Castleman and Walter J. Podrazik, *Watching TV: Four Decades of American Television* (New York: McGraw Hill, 1982), p. 88; Murrow quoted in Dudar, "Post Portrait," 27 February 1959. The most interesting account of the Army-McCarthy hearings is Michael Straight, *Trial by Television* (Boston: Beacon Press, 1954), who maintains that "those who watched learned for themselves what they would not have learned any other way" (p. 3).

53. Seldes, *Public Arts*, p. 235. A look through the following surveys of American history, chosen at random—John M. Blum et al., *The National Experience* (New York: Harcourt Brace Jovanovich, 1981), vol. 2; David Burner et al., *The American PEOPLE* (St. James, N.Y.: Revisionary Press, 1980), vol. 2; Harry J. Carman et al., *A History of the American People—Since 1865* (New York: Knopf, 1967); Carl Degler, *Out of Our Past: The Forces That Shaped Modern America*, rev. ed. (New York: Harper & Row, 1970); Carl Degler et al., *The Democratic Experience: Civil War to the Present*, 5th ed. (Glenview, Ill.: Scott Foresman, 1981): Charles M. Dollar, ed., *America: Changing Times—Since 1865* (New York: John Wiley, 1979); John A. Garraty, *The American Nation*, 4th ed. (New York: Harper & Row, 1979), vol. 2; Ray Ginger, *People on the Move: A United States History* (Boston: Allyn & Bacon, 1975); Rebecca Brooks Gruver, *An American History: From 1865 to the Present* (Reading, Mass.: Addison-Wesley, 1981); Samuel Eliot Morison, *The Growth of the Republic*, 6th ed. (New York: Oxford University Press, 1969),

vol. 2; Edwin Rosenzenc and Thomas Bender, *The Making of American Society—Since 1865*, 2nd ed. (New York: Knopf, 1978); Irwin Unger, *These United States: Questions of Our Past* (Boston: Little, Brown, 1978)—shows that none of these widely used books mention the McCarthy program, that four (Burner, Degler, Degler et al., and Ginger) don't mention the televising of the hearings. Three of these textbooks mention Murrow: Blum in passing, and Dollar and Ungar for his broadcasts from Europe. A survey of the following textbooks dealing with twentieth-century U.S. history as well as those dealing with more recent events reveals equally sparse coverage. See: Oscar Barck, Jr., and Nelson M. Blake, *Since 1900*, 5th ed. (New York: Macmillan, 1974); Frank Freidel, *America in the Twentieth Century*, 4th ed. (New York: Knopf, 1976); Walter LeFeber and Richard Polenberg, *The American Century: A History of the United States Since the 1890s*, 2nd ed. (New York: John Wiley, 1979); William Leuchtenburg et al., *The Unfinished Century: America Since 1890* (Boston: Little, Brown, 1973); Arthur Link and William B. Catton, *American Epoch: A History of the United States Since 1900*, 4th ed. (New York: Knopf, 1974); Forest MacDonald, *The Torch Is Passed: The United States in the 20th Century* (Reading, Mass.: Addison-Wesley, 1968); David Shannon, *Twentieth Century America*, 3rd ed. (Chicago: Rand McNally, 1974); Paul Conkin and David Burner, *A History of Recent America* (New York: Thomas Y. Crowell, 1974); Norman A. Graebner, *The Age of Global Power: The United States Since 1939* (New York: John Wiley, 1979); Eric F. Goldman, *The Crucial Decade—and After* (New York: Knopf, 1975); Robert D. Marcus, *A Brief History of the United States Since 1945* (New York: St. Martin's Press, 1975); William Leuchtenburg and the editors of *Life, The Great Age of Change* (New York: Time Inc., 1964); Lawrence S. Wittner, *Cold War America: From Hiroshima to Watergate* (New York: Praeger, 1974). All mention the televising of the Army-McCarthy hearings (albeit Marcus has them of the wrong McCarthy hearings), but only three (Conkin, Goldman, and Wittner) mention the McCarthy program of *See It Now*, and one of these unfortunately places it after the hearings.

54. Dudar, February 27, 1959; Friendly, *Circumstances*, p. 69.

55. Murrow quoted in Kathy Pedell, "This Is Murrow . . . ," *TV Guide: The First 25 Years*, compiled and edited by Jay S. Harris in association with the editors of *TV Guide* (New York: Simon & Schuster, 1978), p. 28 (the Pedell article originally ran in 1955); Friendly, *Circumstances*, p. 75; Friendly interview, 29 October 1981.

56. Fleming quoted in Yaeger, "Analysis," p. 56; Friendly, *Circumstances*, p. 9. Some questions have been raised about the extent of this autonomy. Helen Dudar, dealing with the scheduling of the McCarthy program "without the knowledge of . . . CBS brass," asserted that "some observers" thought that was "as plausible as the idea of . . . a rocket team launching an Atlas Missile without notifying the Pentagon." (Dudar, February 27, 1959.)

57. Friendly, *Circumstances*, p. 92. This essay does not have the space to deal with the complex relationship between Paley and Murrow during the latter's last years. Murrow died of lung cancer in 1965. Suffice it to say that despite such acid-etched portraits as that penned by Halberstam ("And so on the occasion of the death of Edward R. Murrow, William S. Paley who had done so much to make him and almost as much to break him, and who wanted to be sure that the company got credit for Murrow, went on the air to say that he personally would miss Ed Murrow, as would everyone else at CBS," *The Powers That Be*, p. 154), there also seems to have been a less dark side. Murrow's biographer comments on Paley's interest in the ailing Murrow during the latter's last months and Paley's suggestion that "even if inactive Murrow could serve as a consultant to CBS, telling it 'what was wrong' " (Kendrick, *Prime Time*, p. 508). Paley, of course, has his own view: "Murrow would not have been Murrow nor I myself if we had not had differences of opinion during our long professional and personal relationship. These differences and their meaning have been distorted by careless writers who interpret disputes as estrangements" (Paley, *Memoir*, p. 297).

58. Paley quoted in Kendrick, *Prime Time*, p. 59; Bergreen, *Look Now*, p. 186.

59. William H. Read, *America's Mass Media Merchants* (Baltimore & London: Johns Hopkins University Press, 1976), p. 67.

60. Edward Jay Epstein, *News from Nowhere: Television and the News* (New York: Random House, 1973), p. 90; Kendrick, *Prime Time*, p. 339; Murrow quoted in Metz, *Reflections*, p. 204. There are some interesting comments on the economics of CBS News at the time in James L. Baughman's "The Strange Death of 'CBS Reports' Revisited," *Historical Journal of Film, Radio, and Television* 2(1982):29–30.

61. Friendly, *Circumstances*, p. 68; Richard Elman, "United States: Consensus TV," *Censorship* 2 (Autumn 1966):42–45; Robert Higgins, "Did You Know THIS Was Going On?" *TV Guide*, 19 February 1966, p. 11

62. *In Search of Light: The Broadcasts of Edward R. Murrow 1938–1961*, edited with an introduction by Edward Bliss, Jr. (New York: Knopf, 1967), p. 363.

63. *60 Minutes Verbatim* (New York: Arno Press/CBS News, 1980), p. ii; Andrew Hacker, "Exposing People for Fun and Profit," *Fortune, 7* September 1981, p. 124.

64. *Variety*, 28 October 1959, p. 2.

Disneyland

Christopher Anderson

The month of October 1954 marked a watershed for television production in Hollywood. Alongside those marginal movie industry figures who had labored to wring profits from television production during the late 1940s and early 1950s, there appeared a new breed of established producers attracted by television's explosive growth following the end of the FCC's station application freeze in 1952.[1] Early in the month, Columbia Pictures became the first major studio to produce episodic TV series when its TV subsidiary, Screen Gems, debuted *Father Knows Best* on CBS and *The Adventures of Rin Tin Tin* on ABC. Within three days in late October, two of the film industry's top independent producers, David O. Selznick and Walt Disney, joined the migration to prime time. Selznick, producer of *Gone With the Wind* (1939), made Hollywood's most auspicious debut with a program broadcast simultaneously on all four existing networks, a two-hour spectacular titled *Light's Diamond Jubilee*. Selznick was soon joined by fellow independent producer Walt Disney, whose premiere television series, *Disneyland*, entered ABC's regular Wednesday-night schedule on the twenty-seventh of October. Disney had forged a reputation as the cinema's maestro of family entertainment; now his *Disneyland* series promised to deliver what *Time* described as "the true touch of enchantment" to American homes.[2] Unlike their predecessors in television, these were established members of the movie industry who diversified into TV production without leaving movies behind. The first to link production for the two media, these producers sparked the full-scale integration of movie and TV production in Hollywood during the second half of the 1950s.

As the recipient of nearly two dozen Academy Awards for his studio's cartoon animation, Walt Disney was one of Hollywood's most acclaimed independent producers and certainly, along with Selznick, the most celebrated Hollywood producer to enter television by 1954. Disney possessed the independent producer's belief in television as an alternative to the movie industry's restrictive studio system, but his conception of television's role in a new Hollywood was more sweeping than that of colleagues who saw the electronic medium as nothing more than a new market for traditional film production. Unlike virtually every other telefilm producer in Hollywood, Disney harbored no illusions about dominating TV production; his modest production plans initially encompassed only the *Disneyland* series. Still, Disney was the first Hollywood executive during the 1950s to envision a future built on television's technical achievements—the scope of its signal, the access it provided to the American home. For Disney network television arrived as an invitation to reinvent the movie business, to explore horizons beyond the realm of filmmaking.

Disney later admitted that he was "never much interested" in radio, but television, with its ability to display the visual appeal of Disney products, was another matter entirely. The studio aired its first television program on NBC during December 1950. Sponsored by Coca-Cola, "One Hour in Wonderland" was set in a Disney Christmas party and featured excerpts promoting the studio's upcoming theatrical release, *Alice in Wonderland* (1951). In 1951 Disney produced its second hour-long program for NBC, a special sponsored by Johnson and Johnson. Disney's subsequent plans for a television series started with a seemingly outlandish demand: To obtain the first Disney TV series, a network would have to purchase the series and agree to invest at least $500,000 for a one-third share in the studio's most ambitious project, the Disneyland amusement park planned for construction in suburban Los Angeles. NBC and CBS balked at these terms, but ABC, mired in third place, decided to accept.[3] In uniting the TV program and the amusement park under a single name, Disney made one of the most influential commercial decisions in post-war American culture. Expanding upon the lucrative character merchandising market that the studio had joined in the early 1930s, Disney now planned to create an all-encompassing consumer environment that he described as "total merchandising." Products aimed at baby boom families and stamped with the Disney imprint—movies, amusement park rides, books, comic books, clothing, toys, TV programs, and more—would weave a vast, commercial web, a tangle of advertising and entertainment in which each Disney product—from the movie *Snow White* to a ride on Disneyland's Matterhorn—promoted all Disney products. And television was the beacon that would draw the American public to the domain of Disney. "We wanted to start off running," Walt later recalled. "The investment was going to be too big to wait for a slow buildup. We needed terrific initial impact and television seemed the answer."[4]

Television served a crucial role in Disney's plans for creating an economic and cultural phenomenon that exceeded the boundaries of any single communications medium. By raising capital through the ABC investment and raising consciousness through its depiction of the park's construction, television's figurative representation of Disneyland actually called the amusement park into existence, making it possible for the first time to unite the disparate realms of the Disney empire. With the home as its primary site of exhibition, television gave Disney unparalleled access to a family audience that he already had cultivated more effectively than any Hollywood producer in the studio era. As a result of the post-war baby boom, Disney's target audience of children between the ages of five and fourteen grew from 22 million in 1940 to 35 million in 1960.[5] Television provided the surest route to this lucrative market.

As a text, the *Disneyland* television program also marked a rite of passage for the Disney studio. Its broadcast signaled the studio's transition from the pre-war culture of motion pictures to a post-war culture in which Disney's movies were subsumed into an increasingly integrated leisure market that also included television, recorded music, theme parks, tourism, and consumer merchandise. By depicting the new amusement park as another of Walt's fantasies brought to life by the skilled craftsmen at the Disney studio, the *Disneyland* TV program gave a recognizable symbolic form to Disney's elaborate economic transformation, mediating it for the American public by defining it as another of the Disney studio's marvels. It is only a slight exaggeration, therefore, to claim that Disney mounted an entertainment empire on the cornerstone of this first television series.

Unlike many who groped for a response to the dramatic changes that swept the movie industry following World War II, Walt Disney and his brother Roy answered uncertainty with a calculated plan for diversification. Biographer Richard Schickel has suggested that the Disneys addressed the unstable post-war conditions more aggressively than other Hollywood leaders because their company had suffered misfortunes during the early 1940s, when virtually everyone else in Hollywood had prospered. During the late 1930s, Disney had stood for a moment at the pinnacle of the movie industry. Although an independent producer who worked outside the security of the major studios, Disney took extraordinary financial risks that ultimately paid off in the critical and financial success of *Snow White* (1937), which trailed only Selznick's *Gone With The Wind* as one of the two most profitable Hollywood movies of the 1930s.[6] But Disney's good fortunes lasted only briefly. Following *Snow White*, Disney nearly buried his studio beneath ambitious plans for expansion. With box-office disappointments like the costly animated feature *Fantasia* (1940), the closing of foreign markets due to the war, and over-investment in new studio facilities, Disney faced burdensome corporate debts that weighed even more heavily once banks shut off credit to the studio in 1940. Disney raised funds reluctantly by offering stock to the public, but only government contracts to produce educational cartoons kept the studio active during the war. "The only good thing about the situation," according to Schickel, "was that the problems that were later to plague the rest of the industry had been met by Disney at a time when the government could help out and when the general buoyancy of the industry could at least keep him afloat. The result, of course, was a head start in gathering know-how to meet the crisis that was coming—a head start in planning for diversification first of the company's motion picture products, then of its overall activities."[7]

Plagued by adversity during the 1940s, Walt and Roy Disney entered the 1950s with a plan to transform the Disney studio from an independent producer of feature films and cartoon short-subjects into a diversified leisure and entertainment corporation. Instead of retrenching, as others had, the Disneys fortified their company through a careful process of diversification. Beginning in 1953, the company implemented a series of changes designed to redefine its role in Hollywood. Disney established its own theatrical distribution subsidiary, Buena Vista, in order to end its reliance on major studio distribution. The studio also ceased production on its by-then unprofitable cartoon short subjects, cut back on expensive animated features, and began to concentrate on nature documentaries and live-action movies following the success of *Treasure Island* (1950) and *Robin Hood* (1952).[8] Blue-prints for Disneyland and ideas about television production took shape during this period of corporate transition.

As Disney's schemes for expansion pointed toward television, the ABC-TV network eagerly cultivated ties with the motion picture industry.[9] Hollywood-produced television series became the cornerstone in ABC's plans for differentiating itself from NBC and CBS. As the third-place network, ABC elected to build its audience in direct opposition to the established networks. While the other networks routed their established stars or experimented with expensive spectaculars and the possibility of attracting viewers with unique video events, ABC remained committed to the traditional strategy of programming familiar weekly series that defined television viewing as a consistent feature in the family's domestic routine. Robert Weitman, the network's vice-president in charge of programming, emphasized the importance of habitual viewing in ABC's programming strategies. "The answer seems to be in established patterns of viewing," he explained. "People are annoyed when their favorite show is pre-empted, even for a super-special spectacular." Leonard Goldenson, who had spent decades in the business of movie distribution and exhibition, recognized the similarities between television viewing and the experience of moviegoing during the studio era. "The real strength and vitality of television," he claimed, "is in your regular week-in and week-out programs. The strength of motion pictures was always the habit of going to motion pictures on a regular basis, and that habit was, in part, taken away from motion pictures by television."[10] ABC's programming strategy was built on the belief that television's fundamental appeal was less its ability to deliver exotic events, than its promise of a familiar cultural experience.

As a result, ABC's regularly scheduled series would serve as the basis for network counter-programming, the principal tactic in the network's assault on CBS and NBC. Rather than compete against an established series or live event with a program of similar appeal, ABC hoped to offer alternative programming in order to attract segments of the audience not being served by the other networks. The network would construct and project a specific identity by treating its schedule as the expression of a unique relation to the broadcast audience. "Whatever the audience is not watching at any given time makes for new possibilities," Goldenson noted. "We are not trying to take away audiences from CBS and NBC. . . . We are trying to carve our own network character, to create new audiences."[11] This tactic was based on a related aspect of ABC's programming philosophy—its attention to audience demographics. Governed by the belief that "a network can't be all things to all people," ABC chose to target "the youthful families" with children, a section of the audience whose numbers had increased rapidly since World War II. "We're after a specific audience," claimed Goldenson, "the young housewife—one cut above the teenager—with two to four kids, who has to buy the clothing, the food, the soaps, the home remedies." As this statement implies, ABC chose to align itself with small-ticket advertisers, those selling the type of products that young families might be more likely to need and afford. Goldenson justified ABC's entire programming strategy when he remarked, "We're in the Woolworth's business, not in Tiffany's. Last year Tiffany made only $30,000."[12]

Anxious to acquire Hollywood programming that appealed to a family audience, ABC gambled on Disney by committing $2 million for a fifty-two-week series (with a seven-year renewal option) and by purchasing a 35 percent share in the park for $500,000. Without even a prospective format to present to advertisers, ABC invoked the Disney reputation alone to sell the program under a joint-sponsorship package to American Motors, the American Dairy Association, and Derby Food. Sponsorship of the season's twenty original episodes was sold at $65,000 per episode, and the network time was billed to advertisers at $70,000 per hour. During the late 1950s, when ABC's ratings and advertising revenue finally approached the levels of NBC and CBS, Leonard Goldenson consistently referred to the Disney deal as the network's "turning point." Indeed, *Disneyland* attracted nearly half of ABC's advertising billings during 1954, the final year during which the network operated at a loss.[13]

Although Walt Disney repeatedly assured the press that the *Disneyland* TV series would stand on its own terms as entertainment, the program served mainly to publicize Disney products. *Disneyland*'s identification of the amusement part and the TV series was confirmed during the first episode when Walt informed viewers that "Disneyland the place and Disneyland the show are all the same." Both the series and the park were divided into four familiar movie industry genres: Fantasyland (animated cartoons), Adventureland (exotic action-adventure), Frontierland (Westerns), and Tomorrowland (science-fiction). Introduced by Walt himself, each week's episode represented one of the park's imaginary lands through a compilation of sequences drawn from the studio's cartoon short-subjects, nature documentaries, animated and live-action features, or short films produced as outright promotions for Disney movies about to enter theatrical release. *Disneyland*'s format and pervasive self-promotion were unprecedented for television, but it had roots in the popular radio programs broadcast from Hollywood during the 1930s and 1940s. Hosted by actors, directors, or celebrity journalists, programs like *Hollywood Hotel* and *Lux Radio Theatre* offered musical performances or dramatizations of studio feature films, but their strongest lure was the glimpse they provided into the culture of Hollywood. Through informal chats with performers and other members of the industry, these radio programs perpetuated an image of Hollywood glamour while promoting recent studio releases.[14] Disney simply adapted this format for television. As the master of ceremonies, he turned himself into a media celebrity, much as director Cecil B. DeMille earlier had ridden *Lux Radio Theatre* to national fame.[15]

The actual production of *Disneyland* required a minimal financial investment by the Disney studio. At a time when the typical network series featured thirty-nine new episodes each season, Disney's contract with ABC called for only twenty original episodes, with each of them repeated once, and twelve broadcast a third time during the summer. Instead of producing twenty episodes of new television programming each season, Disney viewed the deal as an opportunity to capitalize on the studio's library of films dating back to the debut of Mickey Mouse in the late 1920s. The wisdom of this format, as Richard Schickel has noted, "was that it allowed the studio to participate in TV without surrendering control of its precious film library."[16] Long after many of the major studios had sold the TV rights to their films, the Disneys boasted that they still owned every film they ever made. Although it is not generally remembered, during the first three years of *Disneyland*, the studio produced only one narrative film made expressly for the series—the three-part "Davy Crockett" serial that took the nation by storm during that first season.[17] More typically, the *Disneyland* TV series introduced a new generation of children to the studio's storehouse of cartoons.

Even with a program that consisted largely of recycled material, the studio admitted that it would not turn a profit from its first year in television. There were production costs in preparing the theatrical product for broadcast (editing compilation episodes or filming Walt's introductory appearances) and in producing its limited amount of original programming. But these costs generally were defrayed throughout the studio's various operations. The three hour-long episodes of the "Davy Crockett" series, for instance, cost $600,000—more than three times the industry standard for telefilm production—and yet, during that year alone, the cost was spread over two separate network broadcasts and a theatrical release. By employing up to 80 percent of the studio's production staff, the television operation also enabled the Disney studio to meet the expense of remaining at full productivity. In addition, all costs not covered by the network's payments were charged to the studio's promotion budget—another indication of the program's primary purpose.[18]

Nearly one-third of each *Disneyland* episode was devoted directly to studio promotion, but the entire series blurred any distinction between publicity and entertainment. Indeed, *Disneyland* capitalized on the unspoken recognition that commercial broadcasting had made it virtually impossible to distinguish between entertainment and advertising. One episode, "Operation Undersea," provided a behind-the-scenes glimpse at the making of *20,000 Leagues Under the Sea* (1954) just one week before Disney released the film to theaters.[19] This episode was later followed by, "Monsters of the Deep," a nature documentary that provided another opportunity to plug the studio's most recent theatrical release. An episode titled, "A Story of Dogs," preceded the release of *Lady and the Tramp* (1955), Disney's second major feature distributed to theaters during the initial TV season.

Viewers didn't mind that *Disneyland* was simply a new form of Hollywood ballyhoo, because Disney framed the program within an educational discourse, reassuring viewers that they inhabited a position of privileged knowledge that was available only through television. Amidst paternalistic fears over the pernicious influence of television, comic books, and other forms of mass culture, Disney's middle-brow didacticism was disarming. In each episode, *Disneyland* rewarded its viewers with an encyclopedic array of general information borrowed loosely from the fields of history, science, and anthropology, while also sharing more specialized knowledge about the history of the Disney studio and its filmmaking procedures. Through this specialized knowledge about the Disney studio, the *Disneyland* TV series defined a particular relationship between television and movies, one in which television served an inchoate critical function by providing commentary on Disney movies. Though produced by the studio itself, *Disneyland* nevertheless contained elements of a critical discourse on the cinema. It educated viewers to perceive continuities among Disney films, to analyze certain aspects of the production process, and to recognize the studio's body of work as a unified product of Walt's authorial vision.

Disneyland's most obvious strategy for educating viewers was its use of behind-the-scenes footage from the Disney studio. The first episode introduced the Disney studio through images of Kirk Douglas playing with his sons on the studio lot, James Mason fighting a man-made hurricane on the stage of *20,000 Leagues Under the Sea*, animators sketching models, and musicians recording the score for a cartoon. By representing the studio as an active, self-contained creative community bustling with activity, these scenes evoke impressions of studio-era Hollywood while masking the fact that historical conditions had rendered those very images obsolete. Disney also used behind-the-scenes footage to demonstrate the elaborate process of filmmaking, particularly the intricacies of animation. Although one might think that a filmmaker like Disney would be afraid of ruining the mystery of animation by revealing how its effects are achieved, Richard Schickel has observed that "Disney always enjoyed showing people around his studio and explaining to them exactly how the exotic process of creating an animated film proceeded." In fact, Disney originally planned for the amusement park to be located at the studio, with demonstrations of the filmmaking process as one of its major attractions.[20] In one feature film, *The Reluctant Dragon* (1941), Disney displayed the animation process by allowing Robert Benchley to lead moviegoers on a tour of the Disney studio. But this was a one-shot experiment that couldn't be repeated in other movies without becoming a distracting gimmick. Following in the tradition of the earlier Hollywood radio shows, therefore, Disney defined television as a companion medium to the cinema, an informational medium that could be used to reveal the process of filmmaking—since that impulse could not be indulged in the movies themselves. While Disney movies were presented as seamless narratives, television gave Disney the license to expose their seams.

Disney's willingness to display the process of filmmaking suggests that reflexivity in itself is not a radical impulse. More a disciple of Barnum than Brecht, Disney had no intention of distancing his audience from the illusion in his movies. Instead, he appealed to the audience's fascination with cinematic trickery. Disney exhibited what historian Neil Harris describes as an "American vernacular tradition" perhaps best exemplified by P. T. Barnum. Barnum's showmanship depended on his recognition that the public delights both in being fooled by a hoax and in discovering the mechanisms that make the hoax successful. Through his fanciful exhibitions, Barnum encouraged "an aesthetic of the operational, a delight in observing process and examining for literal truth."[21] Far from being hoodwinked by Barnum's artifice, the audiences that witnessed his exhibitions took pleasure in uncovering the process by which these hoaxes were perpetrated.

Inheriting Barnum's sense of showmanship, Disney developed his own "operational aesthetic" through television, enhancing his audience's pleasure—and anticipation—by offering precious glimpses of the filmmaking process. Of course, Disney's depiction of the production process was selective; it ignored the economics of filmmaking in favor of focusing on the studio's technical accomplishments. *Disneyland* never explored such issues as labor relations at the Disney studio or the economics of merchandising that sent the largest share of profits into Walt's pockets. Instead, in what has become a cliché of "behind-the-scenes" reporting on filmmaking, *Disneyland* treated each movie as a problem to be solved by the ingenuity of Disney craftsmen. This created a secondary narrative that accompanied the movie into theaters, a story of craftsmen overcoming obstacles to produce a masterful illusion. With this strategy, viewers were given an incentive to see the completed movie, because the movie itself provided the resolution to the story of the filmmaking process as depicted on *Disneyland*.

The program also educated viewers through its attention to Disney studio history. The determination to recycle the Disney library shaped the series during its early seasons, making *Disneyland* an electronic museum devoted to the studio's artistic achievements. Before the arrival of television, Hollywood's history was virtually inaccessible to the general public, available only sporadically through the unpredictable re-release of studio features and short subjects. Movies themselves may have been preserved in studio vaults, but for moviegoers accustomed to an ever-changing program at local theaters, the Hollywood cinema during the studio era was much like live television—an ephemeral cultural experience in which each text inevitably dissolved into memory, swept away in the endless flow of serial production. Although much of television in the mid-1950s traded on the immediacy of live broadcast, the sale of motion pictures to broadcasters meant that television also became the unofficial archive of the American cinema, in which Hollywood's past surfaced in bits and pieces, like fragments of a dream. One of the pleasures of *Disneyland* was the chance it offered to halt the flow of mass culture by remembering relics from the Disney vaults.

Although *Disneyland* may have struck a nostalgic chord for older viewers, the program's presentation of studio history was less sentimental than reverential. Cartoons nearly forgotten were resurrected with a solemnity normally reserved for the most venerable works of art. This attitude is apparent from the first episode when Walt announces that the end of each episode will be reserved for Mickey Mouse. After leading the viewer through an elaborate description of the proposed amusement park and other studio activities, Disney stands behind a lectern and turns the pages of a massive bound volume, an illustrated chronicle of Mickey's adventures. In spite of the flurry of changes at the studio, he explains, one should not lose sight of an eternal truth: "It all started with Mickey. . . . The story of Mickey is the story of Disneyland." As he continues, the scene segues into Mickey's first appearance in the cartoon "Plane Crazy," and then dissolves to one of his most famous appearances, as the Sorcerer's Apprentice in *Fantasia*. The tone of the scene—Disney's scholarly disposition, the sight of Mickey's history contained in a stately book—implies that the Disney studio's products are not the disposable commodities of pop culture, but artifacts worthy of remembrance. Walt's role as narrator is to reactivate forgotten cartoons in the public's cultural memory by demonstrating their canonical status within the artistic history of the Disney studio. As an electronic museum, *Disneyland* invoked the cultural memory of its audience mainly to publicize new Disney products. In spite of its commercial motives, however, the series also made it possible to conceive of Hollywood as having a history worthy of consideration.

"Monsters of the Deep," a typical episode from the first season of *Disneyland*, demonstrates the strategies for situating new Disney movies in the context of the studio's history and production practices. The episode introduces Walt in his studio's research department. Wearing a dark tweed jacket and surrounded by books and charts, he appears professorial. Inspired by knowledge, yet free from scholastic pretension, he is television's image of an intellectual, kindly and inviting. Speaking directly to the camera, he leads the viewer through a discussion of dinosaurs, using illustrations from enormous books to punctuate his presentation. This lecture seems motivated only by Disney's inquisitive character until the Disney sales pitch gradually seeps in. "We told the story of dinosaurs large and small in *Fantasia*," Disney reminds viewers as the screen dissolves to images from the animated feature. As Disney explains the habitat, feeding patterns, and behavior of dinosaurs, the footage from *Fantasia* becomes recontextualized, as though it were a segment from a nature documentary, a reminder that even Disney's most fantastic films have educational value. Disney segues into a report on sea monsters, asking whether giant squids have existed among the mysteries of the ocean, tracing the enigma through debates over the veracity of historical accounts. This query provides a transition to a discussion of the problems involved in creating a plausible giant squid for the Disney feature, *20,000 Leagues Under the Sea*. From the research department, the scene dissolves to a studio soundstage where star Kirk Douglas performs a song from the movie and then guides the television viewer through a behind-the-scenes glimpse of the special effects used to stage the movie's spectacular battle sequence featuring a giant squid. Afterwards, Disney draws a line of continuity through the studio's present and past accomplishments by introducing viewers to an extended sequence from the studio's most famous scene of undersea adventure, Pinocchio's escape from the whale, Monstro, in the 1940 feature, *Pinocchio*. Even the last two sequences, so clearly intended to advertise Disney products, carry the promise of edification as they define a limited and specialized knowledge—the Disney canon, the production of Disney movies—that is directed toward enhancing the experience of *20,000 Leagues Under the Sea*.

Because the *Disneyland* TV series delivered viewers like no program in ABC history, even the program's advertisers didn't mind subsidizing Disney's opportunity for self-promotion. *Disneyland* concluded the season as the first ABC program ever to appear among the year's ten highest-rated series. It was viewed weekly in nearly 40 percent of the nation's 26 million TV households.[22] The trade magazine, *Sponsor*, applauded Disney's skill at blending entertainment and salesmanship, quoting an unnamed ABC executive who quipped, "Never before have so many people made so little objection to so much selling."[23] Through its Emmy awards, the television industry affirmed its approval of Disney's venture, nominating Walt as TV's "Most Outstanding New Personality" and honoring "Operation Underseas"—an episode about the making of *20,000 Leagues Under the Sea*—as TV's Best Documentary.[24]

For the movie industry, the most telling detail in the entire Disney phenomenon was the surprising performance of the studio's feature films. By releasing its features through its own distribution company, Buena Vista, and by timing the release dates to coincide with simultaneous promotion on the television program, Disney emerged as the top-grossing independent production company of 1955. Undoubtedly aided by its exposure on the TV series, *20,000 Leagues Under the Sea* grossed $8 million when it finally played in movie theaters—the largest sum ever reached by a Disney movie on its initial release. It finished the year as Hollywood's fourth highest-grossing movie and became the first Disney movie ever to crack the list of twenty all-time top-grossing films. In addition, Disney's new animated feature, *Lady and the Tramp*, pulled in $6.5 million—the highest figure for any of Disney's animated films since *Snow White*. Even its first feature-length True-Life Adventure, *The Vanishing Prairie* (1955), grossed a respectable $1.8 million.[25]

The most startling evidence of TV's marketing potential came from the studio's experience with Davy Crockett. Disney edited together the "Davy Crockett" episodes that already had aired twice on TV and released them as a feature film during the summer of 1955. *Davy Crockett: King of the Wild Frontier* may have been a typical "program oater," as *Variety* claimed, but it earned another $2 million at the box office because it had been transformed by television into a national phenomenon.[26] The accompanying Crockett merchandising craze gathered steam throughout the year, ultimately surpassing the Hopalong Cassidy boom of the early 1950s. By mid-1955, as "The Ballad of Davy Crockett" climbed the pop music charts, Crockett products—including jeans, pistols, powder horns, lunch boxes, the ubiquitous coonskin caps, and much more—accounted for nearly 10 percent of all consumer purchases for children, with sales figures for Crockett merchandise estimated to exceed $100 million by the end of the year.[27] Disney's apparent golden touch during 1954 and 1955 demonstrated to Hollywood that the studio had tapped into a rich promotional vein by integrating its various activities around television and the family audience.

The *Disneyland* TV program's most significant accomplishment, however, was the fanatical interest it generated in the Disneyland amusement park. Without the growth of national network television and the access it provided to the American family, Disney would not have gambled on the park. "I saw that if I was ever going to have my park," he explained, "here, at last, was a way to tell millions of people about it—with TV."[28] Disney needed television not simply to publicize the park, but to position it properly as a new type of suburban amusement, a bourgeois park designed to provide edifying adventures for baby-boom families instead of cheap thrills for the urban masses. To distinguish his park from such decaying relics as Luna Park at Coney Island, Disney assured the public that any amusement experienced in his park would be tempered by middle-class educational values. Disneyland wouldn't be another park trading in the temporal gratifications of the flesh, but a popular monument to human knowledge, a "permanent world's fair" built around familiar Disney characters and a number of unifying social goals, including educating the public about history and science.[29] The park was inextricably linked to television, because TV enabled Disney to redefine the traditional amusement park as a "theme park." With the assistance of the *Disneyland* TV series, Disney brought discipline to the unruly pleasures of the amusement park, organizing them around the unifying theme of Disney's authorial vision. By invoking cultural memories of Disney films, the TV series encouraged an impulse to re-experience texts that became one of the theme park's central attractions.

Just as it hooked American television viewers with the serialized story of Davy Crockett, the *Disneyland* TV series also bound up its audience in the ongoing story of what came to be mythologized as "Walt's dream." The seriality of *Disneyland*—and its direct relationship to the creation and continued development of the park—was crucial to the program's success. Before Disney, prime-time series were episodic; narrative conflicts were introduced and resolved in the course of a single episode. Open-ended serials were confined to daytime's soap opera genre. Disney certainly wasn't concerned about issues of TV narrative, but the *Disneyland* series demonstrated an incipient understanding of the appeal of serial narrative for network television. The success of the three-part "Davy Crockett" serial was attributable at least in part to its ability to engage viewers in an ongoing narrative. Similarly, with Walt as on-screen narrator, the *Disneyland* series, in effect, narrated the construction of Disney's amusement park, making the project a matter of continued concern for the show's viewers by creating a story out of the construction process and certifying it as the crowning achievement of an American entrepreneurial genius in a league with Thomas Edison and Henry Ford.

No less than three entire episodes, and portions of others, were devoted to the process of conceiving, building, and inaugurating the park. As the climax of the construction process, viewers witnessed the park's opening ceremonies on July 17, 1955, in a live, two-hour broadcast hosted by Art Linkletter, Robert Cummings, and Ronald Reagan. It was only appropriate that the first amusement park created by television should be introduced in a ceremony designed explicitly for television as a media event.[30] The first season of *Disneyland* was a unique type of television text, an open-ended series in which the episodes built toward a final resolution, staged as a television spectacular. By constructing a story around the events of the park's development, and by creating an analogy between the TV program and the park, the Disney organization provided a narrative framework for the experience of Disneyland.

The series represented the transition front the movie studio to the theme park by treating the park as the studio's most ambitious production. In the first episode, "The Disneyland Story," Walt introduces viewers to the park as an idea, shifting constantly between a huge map of the park, a scale-model replica, and stock footage that invokes each of the park's imaginary lands. The first season of *Disneyland*, he explains, will enable viewers "to see and share with us the experience of building this dream into a reality." The second construction episode, "A Progress Report," initiates the journey from the studio to the park as Walt takes a helicopter flight from his office to the new location. This episode also begins the process of identifying Disneyland with the culture of the automobile and the superhighway. Although the transition to the construction site could be managed by a straight cut or a dissolve, the helicopter flight instead laboriously tracks the highway that a typical traveler would follow to reach the park. With Walt providing commentary, the flight depicts both a literal and figurative passage from Hollywood to Disneyland, tracing a path from the Disney studio in Burbank, over the heart of Hollywood, down the Hollywood Freeway, connecting to the Santa Ana Freeway, and finally reaching the Disneyland exit in Anaheim—"a spot chosen by traffic experts as the most accessible spot in Southern California." Once at the construction site, the labor of construction is depicted through fast-motion photography. Accompanied by ragtime music, the scurrying workers driving bulldozers, digging ditches, and planting trees seem like animated figures; their labor takes on a cartoonish quality. In keeping with the tradition of the program's behind-the-scenes footage, Walt pauses to demonstrate how the technical feat of time-lapse photography works, but never addresses the actual labor of the workers whose activities are represented.

The third episode picks up the construction after the park's major structures have been built, as the various rides and special effects are being installed. Again, the series demonstrates how these devices, such as authentic-looking mechanical crocodiles, were designed and created at the Disney studio. This episode establishes a continuity between motion picture production and the creation of the park, demonstrating studio activities that have been reoriented to service the park. The underwater monorail employed to move the submarine in *20,000 Leagues Under the Sea* has become the basis for the Disneyland monorail train: the stage where Davy Crockett recently fought the battle of the Alamo is now the site of construction for the park's authentic Mississippi River steamboat; the sculptors and technicians who created the squid in *20,000 Leagues Under the Sea* are now making a mechanical zoo for the park. Once these devices are loaded onto trucks, they are transported to the park. As voice-over commentary reviews the route, viewers again follow the highway from the studio to the park, making the journey at ground level this time.

Television made the entire Disney operation more enticing by fashioning it as a narrative experience which the family TV audience could enhance—and actually perform—by visiting the park. Here again Disney shrewdly perceived television's ability to link diverse cultural practices that intersected in the domestic sphere of the home. In effect, Walt identified the program with the park in order to create an inhabitable text, one that would never be complete for a television-viewing family until they had taken full advantage of the postwar boom in automobile travel and tourism to make a pilgrimage to the park itself. A trip to Disneyland—using the conceptual map provided by the program—offered the family viewer a chance to perform in the Disneyland narrative, to provide unity and closure through personal experience, to witness the "aura" to which television's reproductive apparatus only could allude.

In a sense, Disney succeeded by exploiting the quest for authentic experience that has become central to the culture of modernity. In fact, tourism, as Dean MacCannell suggests, is based on the modern quest for authenticity, the belief that authentic experience exists somewhere outside the realm of daily experience in industrial society.[31] While Walter Benjamin predicted that mass reproduction would diminish the aura surrounding works of art, Disney seems to have recognized that the mass media instead only intensify the desire for authenticity by invoking a sublime, unmediated experience that is forever absent, just beyond the grasp of a hand reaching for the television dial. As a tourist attraction, Disneyland became the destination of an exotic journey anchored firmly by the family home, which served not only as the origin and terminus of the journey, but also as the site of the television set that would confirm the social meaning of the vacation experience. A father visiting the park expressed something of this sentiment. "Disneyland may be just another damned amusement park," he explained, "but to my kids it's the Taj Mahal, Niagara Falls, Sherwood Forest, and Davy Crockett all rolled into one. After years of sitting in front of the television set, the youngsters are sure it's a fairyland before they ever get there."[32] Television defined Disneyland as a national amusement park, not a park of local or regional interest like previous amusement parks, but a destination for a nation of television viewers. In the first six months alone, one million paying customers passed through the gates at Disneyland; 43 percent arrived from out of state. After the first full year of operation the park had grossed $10 million, one-third of the company's revenue for the year, and more than any Disney feature had ever grossed during its initial release.[33]

Disney's integration of television into the studio's expansive marketing schemes identified television as a worthy investment for Hollywood's major studios. Events leading up to Disney's debut may have suggested to executives of the major studios that they reconsider television production, but only Columbia, through its Screen Gems subsidiary, had acted decisively before Disney's triumph during the 1954–55 TV season. Disney's video success made it apparent that television had become the dominant national advertising medium by the mid-1950s. Providing a channel to an ever-expanding family audience, television could become the most effective marketing tool ever imagined by the movie industry. By following Disney's example and forming alliances with television networks, rather than with advertisers, the studios could ensure their access to the medium without surrendering autonomy to television's traditionally powerful sponsors.

Disney expanded his role in television during Fall 1955 with the premiere of *The Mickey Mouse Club* in ABC's weekday afternoon schedule. With this new program and the ongoing *Disneyland* series, Disney continued to use television mainly as an opportunity for studio publicity. Besides producing a sequel to "Davy Crockett," for instance, Disney created no original programming for *Disneyland* until the 1957–58 season. Disney's concept of "total merchandising" continued to shape the type of text that his company produced for television. Whereas traditional notions of textuality assume that a text is singular, unified, and autonomous, with a structure that draws the viewer inward, Disney's television texts were, from the outset, fragmented, propelled by a centrifugal force that guided the viewer away from the immediate textual experience toward a more pervasive sense of textuality, one that encouraged the consumption of further Disney texts, further Disney products, further Disney experiences. *Disneyland* drew the attention of viewers to the TV text only to disperse it outward, toward Disney products.[34]

Television made possible Disney's vision of "total merchandising" because it gave him the ability to integrate apparently isolated segments of the national commercial culture that developed after the war. In this sense, the entire Disneyland phenomenon may have been the first harbinger of Max Horkheimer and Theodor Adorno's prediction for the apotheosis of the television age, the moment when "the thinly veiled identity of all industrial culture products can come triumphantly out into the open, derisively fulfilling the Wagnerian dream of the *Gesamtkunstwerk*—the fusion of all the arts in one work."[35] By offering the first glimpse of a new Hollywood—in which television profitably obscured conventional distinctions among the media—Disney provided the impulse for the major studios to enter television and a blueprint for the future development of the media industries.

Notes

1. For an account of the post-1952 boom in new television stations, television advertising revenue, and television set ownership, see J. Fred MacDonald, *One Nation Under Television: The Rise and Decline of Network TV* (New York: Pantheon, 1990), 59–62.

2. "This Week in Review," *Time*, 8 November 1954, 95.

3. Katherine and Richard Greene, *The Man Behind the Magic: The Story of Walt Disney* (New York: Viking, 1991), 119; Frank Orme, "Disney: 'How Old Is a Child?' " *Television* (December 1954): 37; "Disney 'Not Yet Ready' for TV," *Variety* (23 May 1951): 5; "Disney's 7-Year ABC-TV Deal," *Variety* (21 February 1954): 41.

4. "The Wide World of Walt Disney," *Newsweek* (31 December 1962): 49–51: "The Mouse That Turned to Gold," *Business Week* (9 July 1955): 74. The origins of Disney's character merchandising are described in "The Mighty Mouse," *Time* (25 October 1948): 96–98. For a more detailed discussion of the Disney corporation's use of character merchandising in relation to other TV products of the early 1950s, see "He'll Double as a Top-Notch Salesman," *Business Week* (21 March 1953): 43–44.

5. John McDonald, "Now the Bankers Come to Disney," *Fortune* (May 1966): 141.

6. During its initial release release, *Snow White* grossed $8 million and became the first movie to exceed $5 million at the box-office. *Gone With the Wind* grossed over $20 million in its first year of release. Richard Schickel, *The Disney Version* (New York: Simon and Schuster, 1968), 229; Ronald Haver, *David O. Selznick's Hollywood* (New York: Bonanza Books, 1980), 309.

7. Schickel, *The Disney Version*, 28.

8. McDonald, "Now the Bankers Come to Disney," 141, 224; Schickel, *The Disney Version*, 308–16; "Disney's Live-Action Profits," *Business Week* (24 July 1965): 78.

9. For a more detailed description of the history of ABC-TV's relations with the motion picture industry during this period, see Christopher Anderson, *Hollywood TV* (Austin: University of Texas Press, 1994).

10. "The Spectaculars: An Interim Report," *Sponsor* (15 November 1954): 31; "Twenty-Five Years Wiser About Show Business, Goldenson Finds TV the Biggest Star," *Broadcasting* (14 July 1958): 84.

11. Herman Land, "ABC: An Evaluation," *Television Magazine* (December 1957): 94.

12. Ibid., 93; "The abc of ABC," 17; "The TV Fan Who Runs a Network," *Sponsor* (15 June 1957): 45. It should be noted that ABC did not possess demographic ratings that would have enabled the network to determine the success of its programming strategy.

13. "Peaches and Cream at ABC-TV," *Variety*, 16 June 1954, 25; "The abc of ABC," 17; Klan, "ABC-Paramount Moves In," 242; Albert R. Kroeger, "Miracle Worker of West 66th Street," *Television* (February 1961): 66; "Corporate Health, Gains in Radio-TV Theme of AB-UPT Stockholders Meeting," *Broadcasting-Telecasting* (21 May 1956): 64; Frank Orme, "TV's Most Important Show," *Television* (June 1955): 32.

14. See Michele Hilmes, *Hollywood and Broadcasting: From Radio to Cuble* (Champaign: University of Illinois Press, 1990), pp. 63–72; 78–112.

15. Walt also recognized that the Disney empire needed an identifiable author to crystallize the company's identity for the public, to "personify the product," as *Business Week* once noted. The naming of an author became an issue within the company as far back as the 1920s, when Walt convinced Roy to change the name of the company they had co-founded from Disney Brothers Productions to Walt Disney Productions. Consequently, as the studio expanded in 1953, Walt began to assume a more public persona, hosting the TV program and identifying himself with all things Disney, while diminishing Roy's identity. In 1953—against Roy's opposition—Walt formed Retlaw Enterprises (Walter spelled backwards), a private company which completely controlled merchandising rights to the name Walt Disney. In return for licensing the name to Walt Disney Productions, Retlaw received 5 percent of the income from all corporate merchandise. Since the Disney name was imprinted on everything associated with the company, Retlaw immediately generated enormous wealth for Walt. See John Taylor, *Storming the Magic Kingdom: Wall Street, the Raiders, and the Battle for Disney* (New York: Alfred A. Knopf, 1987), 7, 10.

16. Schickel, *The Disney Version*, 20.

17. "Disneyland Repeats Getting Bigger Audiences Than First Time Around," *Variety* (20 April 1955): 32. A complete filmography of Disney television programs through 1967 appears in Leonard Maltin, *The Disney Films*, second edition (New York: Crown Publishers, 1984), 321–26. For an examination of the Disneyland-inspired Davy Crockett phenomenon that swept through American culture beginning in 1954, see Margaret Jane King, *The Davy Crockett Craze: A Case Study in Popular Culture* (Unpublished Ph.D. Dissertation, University of Hawaii, 1976).

18. Orme, "How Old Is a Child?" 37, 72.

19. Critics within both the movie and television industries sarcastically referred to this episode as "The Long, Long Trailer," after the Lucille Ball-Desi Arnez film of the same title. See "A Wonderful World: Growing Impact of the Disney Art," *Newsweek* (18 April 1955): 62–63.

20. Schickel, *Disney Version*, 152; "Tinker Bell, Mary Poppins, Cold Cash," *Newsweek* (12 July 1965): 74.

21. Neil Harris, *Humbug: The Art of P. T. Barnum* (Chicago: University of Chicago Press, 1973), 79.

22. Tim Brooks and Earle Marsh, *The Complete Directory to Prime Time Network TV Shows*, Third Edition (New York: Ballantine Books, 1985), 1031. *Disneyland* remained among the top fifteen programs through 1957, and then fell from the top twenty until it shifted to NBC—and color broadcasts—in 1961.

23. Charles Sinclair, "Should Hollywood get it for free?" *Sponsor* (8 August 1955); 102.

24. Maltin, *The Disney Films*, 315.

25. "Disney Parlays Romp Home," *Variety* (30 November 1955): 3; "All-Time Top Grossing Films," *Variety* (4 January 1956): 84. At the time, *20,000 Leagues Under the Sea* was the nineteenth highest-grossing film of all time.

26. Ibid.

27. "The Wild Frontier," *Time* (23 May 1955): 92. Unfortunately for Disney, the studio could not control licensing of Crockett products, because it did not possess exclusive rights to the name or character of Davy Crockett. Since the mid-nineteenth century companies had used the Crockett name on products from chewing tobacco to whiskey. The Disney studio never again made this mistake. See also "U.S. Again Subdued by Davy." *Life* (25 April 1955): 27; "Mr. Crockett is a Dead Shot As a Salesman." *New York Times*, 1 June 1955, 38.

28. Schickel, *The Disney Version*, 313.

29. "Father Goose," *Time* (27 December 1954): 42; "Tinker Bell, Mary Poppins, Cold Cash," 74.

30. For an account of the opening ceremonies, see Bob Chandler, "Disneyland As 2-Headed Child of TV & Hollywood Shoots for $18 Mil B.O.," *Variety* (20 July 1955): 2. Chandler observes that the inauguration of Disneyland marked the "integration and interdependence of all phases of show biz."

31. Dean MacCannell, *The Tourist: A New Theory of the Leisure Class* (New York: Schocken Books, 1976), 159.

32. "How To Make a Buck," *Time* (29 July 1957): 76.

33. Ibid., Schickel, *The Disney Version*, 316.

34. Michele Hilmes describes the use of this strategy in the Hollywood-produced radio program, *Lux Radio Theater*. See Hilmes, *Hollywood and Broadcasting*, 108–10.

35. Max Horkheimer and Theodor W. Adomo, *Dialectic of Enlightenment* (New York: Continuum, 1987), 124.

PART II

Redeeming The "Wasteland": Television & Social Change

the "outer limits" of oblivion

Jeffrey Sconce

In a medium already renowned for its intrusive presence in the American home, few television shows have featured opening credit sequences as calculatedly invasive as that of *The Outer Limits*. A narrational entity known only as the "control voice" opened each week's episode with these unnerving words of assurance:

> *There is nothing wrong with your television set.*
> *Do not attempt to adjust the picture.*
> *We are controlling transmission.*
> *We will control the horizontal.*
> *We will control the vertical.*
> *We can change the focus to a soft blur, or sharpen it to crystal clarity.*

On screen, the control voice demonstrated its power by taking command of the picture tube to program a display of warbling sine waves, vertical rolls, and other forms of electronic choreography. Having now completely gained possession of the family console, the control voice issued its final command and warning:

> *For the next hour, sit quietly, and we will control all that you see and hear. You are about to participate in a great adventure. You are about to experience the awe and mystery that reaches from the inner mind to* The Outer Limits.

At this cue, the theme music would swell for the opening credits, after which the control voice would relinquish command, at least momentarily, to the "true" masters of the screen—the commercial advertisers. At the end of each week's episode, the control voice would make one last announcement, coming back to "return control" of the television to its temporarily dispossessed owner.

Debuting in the fall of 1963 on ABC's Monday night schedule, *The Outer Limits* was never a major commercial success. While the program rated as high as the top twenty shortly after its premiere, a scaled-down and less lavish version of the show continually faced the prospects of cancellation during its second season, a fate to which it finally fell victim when ABC replaced the series in January of 1965 with *The King Family*. During its brief run on Monday and then Saturday nights, *The Outer Limits* served first as ABC's lead-in to *Wagon Train* and then to *The Lawrence Welk Show*. During its second season, the program found itself the loser in head to head competition with such formidable cultural icons as Flipper, Jackie Gleason, and Mr. Magoo. Less than a triumph in terms of its network run, the series lasted only a season and a half to compile a meager total of forty-eight episodes. Like many other television science fiction series, *The Outer Limits* has subsequently grown in stature and legend to become somewhat of a cult classic, and is now often compared and conflated in popular memory with Rod Serling's *The Twilight Zone*. But when the individual episodes are sorted out, clear differences emerge between the two series. What perhaps most distinguishes *The Outer Limits* from Serling's more prolific and widely syndicated show is *The Outer Limits'* consistently bleak tone, both thematically and stylistically, as well as its emphasis on relentlessly pessimistic social commentary. Even in the midst of a tale of the apocalypse, *The Twilight Zone* would at least occasionally crack a sinister smile.[1] Not so *The Outer Limits*. Debuting in the months immediately preceding the assassination of President Kennedy and vanishing at the threshold of the nation's growing civil unrest at mid-decade, *The Outer Limits* presented a signature moment of unmitigated doom on American television, often suggesting that the sciences, technologies, and citizens of "the new frontier" were on a collision course with oblivion.

Significantly, the original title planned for the series had been *Please Stand By*, the familiar invocation of panicked broadcasters when confronting social or technological disaster. This interruption in the routinized flow of commercial broadcasting always makes viewers take pause as they consider the possibility of an impending catastrophe. Such alarm was especially pronounced during the Cold War years, when the intrusion of a network "special report" could signify imminent nuclear annihilation. Debuting in the still palpable wake of the Cuban Missile Crisis, *The Outer Limits'* invasive credit sequence exemplified the program's larger textual solution to a persistent challenge in adapting the horror genre to television. As the most "domestic" of entertainment media, television has always posed difficulties in accommodating horror, a genre objectionable not only to watchful parents but also to squeamish advertisers. From the beginning of network programming, science fiction and horror programs such as NBC's *Lights Out* and CBS's *Suspense* were consistently under attack for broadcasting material thought to be too disturbing for the family living room. *The Outer Limits* also became a target of such controversy, and on occasion provided ABC with headaches in standards and practices and affiliate clearance. But what made the series more threatening than a simple "monster show," and yet somewhat immune to standard forms of network censorship, was its unique strategy for maximizing television's intrinsic potential for horror. Ingeniously, *The Outer Limits* framed its tales of monsters, aliens, and mad scientists by casting television itself as a medium of the void, suggesting that its transmissions might expose the viewer to a horrifying oblivion. Exploiting a longstanding fascination in American culture with the potentially supernatural qualities of all electronic media, *The Outer Limits* transformed television's "window on the world" into a window on the "otherworldy," and threatened to exile the viewer to this vast "electronic nowhere" that seemed to lurk behind the otherwise celebrated technologies of "the new frontier."

This essay examines the rather obsessive centrality of cathode-ray "oblivions" in *The Outer Limits*, analyzing the series' visions of the void in relation to the decade's primary site for domestic and technological interaction—the television set. "Oblivion" was the only truly recurring monster in this anthology program, and it took a variety of forms over the forty-eight episode run of the series. Regardless of its shape or dimension, however, oblivion in *The Outer Limits* was almost always mediated by some form of paranormal electronic technology and centered most immediately on the American family, a scenario that offered repeated parables about the audience's own relationship to their TV set, and the set's relationship, in turn, to a vast electronic "nowhere." Whether faced with new beings, mysterious powers, or strange technologies, the characters in these stories (and the viewer at home) had to struggle against uncanny and frequently electronic forces that threatened not just to kill them, but to dissolve them into nothingness.

Of course, even as vast and seemingly boundless a concept as "oblivion" exists within some degree of historical specificity. Surveying the ubiquity of this trope across the run of the series, one is left with the question as to why this particular invocation of televisual nothingness should have such resonance within this historical period. Answers to such complex representational questions must remain imprecise, but three looming and often interrelated "oblivions" of the New Frontier era would seem to be key in producing these electronically mediated visions of the void—the infinite depths of outer space, the emotional "limbo" of suburban domesticity, and the specter of absolute nuclear annihilation. Both in the social reality of the audience and the science fictional "unreality" of the series, television figured as the crucial bridge between these realms as the pivotal technology in the New Frontier's melding of space, science, and suburbia. In this respect, *The Outer Limits* can be considered within the same cultural moment described by Lynn Spigel as informing the "fantastic family sitcom," a cycle of programs she identifies as engaging in a parody of the narrative and social conventions of domestic comedy. Spigel argues that the fantastic sitcom, like much of the popular culture of this era, developed in response to a series of disappointments in American life during the

1950s, chief among these being the homogenizing conformity demanded by suburban living and the seeming vulnerability of American technology in the wake of Sputnik. "[T]his historical conjuncture of disappointments provided the impetus for a new utopian future—one based on the rhetoric of Kennedy's New Frontier and fortified with the discourse of science and technology."[2] As with the supernatural science fiction sitcoms discussed by Spigel (*Bewitched, I Dream of Jeannie*, and *My Favorite Martian*), *The Outer Limits* also exploited the era's emerging fascination with space and science to interrogate the bland "ideology of domesticity" cultivated during the Eisenhower years. But while *The Outer Limits* shared the same cultural project of the fantastic sitcom in reexamining American family life, differences in terms of genre (horror rather than comedy) and format (anthology drama rather than episodic series) often pushed *The Outer Limits* into territory that was far more disturbing and apocalyptic. Unencumbered by the burden of continuing characters and a consistent "situation," *The Outer Limits* had the occasional license to destroy the centerpiece of both postwar life and episodic television, the nuclear family. From episode to episode, there was the persistent subtext that America's intense investment in space, science, and domesticity masked an immense abyss, an anomic nothingness lurking at the core of the nation's identity. While acknowledging the "awe and mystery" of new territories of scientific exploration, *The Outer Limits* also suggested that America might find the "New Frontier" itself to be a terrifying vacuum, an annihilating and discorporative void accessed through television.

The intersection of the series' highly self-reflexive commentary on television as a system beyond human control and its continuing narrative preoccupation with electronic technology as a gateway to oblivion suggests that television remained, even a decade after its introduction into the American home, a somewhat unsettling and alien technology. As a medium of powerful instantaneousness, television displayed a perilously immediate relationship to public danger and disaster, exerting an ambiguous and unknown "control" over the American family. Following a decade of both fascination and disillusionment with the new medium, *The Outer Limits* narrativized the increasingly endemic critiques leveled at television as a potentially threatening technological zone within domestic space. In this respect, the series elaborated the rhetoric of television's many detractors who already considered the medium to be its own form of "oblivion," one that in extreme cases could deliver families into an even more remote and terrifying "vast wasteland" than the one envisioned by FCC Chair Newton Minow. The format of the series implied that the viewer was also vulnerable to such assimilation simply by watching TV, thereby exploiting the medium's potential for terror to the fullest. A viewer who watches a horror film at a theater, after all, can return to the safety of their home and put the experience behind them. The very premise of the *The Outer Limits*, on the other hand, allowed that fear to linger with the viewer. The intervention and presence of the "control voice" suggested that even after the program was over and the receiver was turned off, the television set itself still loomed as a gateway to oblivion simply by sitting inert and watchful in the living room. And this, perhaps, is what made the show too unsettling for its own historical moment and yet such a success in the years following its cancellation. For the first generation to grow up with TV sets lurking in their living rooms, *The Outer Limits* combines the pleasures of horror and nostalgia. It remains the only show to evoke so explicitly the dual sense of fascination and fear that attended the early years of television, a time when the TV set became the most ubiquitous, obsequious, and yet imperious of technologies to occupy domestic space and childhood memory.

monsters in the static

Stories of "haunted" televisions had circulated throughout the decade preceding the premiere of *The Outer Limits*, and were already a stock part of American folklore. On December 11th of 1953, readers of *The New York Times* met a family from Long Island that had been forced to "punish" their decidedly paranormal TV set for scaring the children with visions of a soul lost in the electronic nowhere. As Jerome E. Travers and his three children were watching "Ding Dong School," the face of an unknown woman mysteriously appeared on the screen and would not vanish, even when the set was turned-off and unplugged. "The balky set," which "previously had behaved itself," according to the *Times*, "had its face turned to the wall . . . for gross misbehavior in frightening little children."[3] The haunted television finally gave up the ghost, so to speak, a day later, but not before scores of newspapermen, magazine writers, and TV engineers had a chance to observe the phenomenon. Visitors to the Travers' home also included Francey Lane, a singer from the Morey Amsterdam show that had preceded "Ding Dong School" on the day of the initial haunting. Lane was thought to be the face behind the image frozen on the screen, and her agent apparently felt it would make for good publicity to have the singer meet her ghostly cathode double.[4]

Even before television, the theme of the electronic "nowhere" in telecommunications had a long history in pulp magazines, dimestore paperbacks, and B movies. Radio, telephony, and telegraphy had each inspired tales of uncanny, haunted, and otherwise alien media, ranging from stories of phone calls from the dead to aspirations of contacting other planets through the wonders of wireless. Such tales, in turn, had their roots in the Spiritualist movement of the nineteenth century. The Spiritualists had looked to the electromagnetic telegraph as both an inspiration and a model of explanation for their belief in the "spiritual telegraph," an otherworldly telecommunications device they believed to have been fashioned in the afterlife by such figures as Socrates and Benjamin Franklin. In this earliest cultural conflation of electrical science, telecommunications technology, and parapsychology, the vast "electronic nowhere" was thought to be a peaceful and benevolent haven that housed electrically charged souls.[5]

In *The Outer Limits* and other tales of television's "electronic nowhere," however, these beneficent images of an electronic heaven became instead visions of terrifying isolation, rendering the comforting notion of the afterlife into the more ominous realm of an electromagnetic void. Appropriately, the close association of broadcasting and oblivion in *The Outer Limits* began with the program's pilot. In "The Galaxy Being," which also served as the series premiere on September 16th of 1963, an inventor scans the airwaves with a powerful transceiving device that draws energy from a nearby radio station. He captures strange signals, "three-dimensional static," that transform on a viewscreen into the image of an alien. When the inventor leaves the radio station that evening, an accident teleports the alien to earth via the transmitted signal, where as a three-dimensional electronic being, he quickly becomes the prey of local authorities. Cornered by his attackers, the alien destroys the radio tower as a demonstration of his power, and then warns the encroaching mob. "There are powers in the universe beyond anything you know," he says. "There is much you have to learn. . . . Go to your homes. Go and give thought to the mysteries of the universe." The crowd disperses while the inventor and the alien return in peace to the radio station. But the alien laments that he cannot return to his home planet because he has broken a law forbidding contact with other worlds. Exiled from home and only an electronic phantom on earth, the alien consigns himself to oblivion. "End of transmission," he says as he reduces the transmitter power that first brought him to earth, turning the dial until at last he completely vanishes.

This poignant tale was a fit debut for a series that would continue to explore the relationship among electronic transmission, physical discorporation, and social alienation. As a story of an alien being contacted and then teleported through the "three-dimensional static" of an intergalactic television set, "The Galaxy Being" dramatized decades of cultural speculation that wireless might be used to contact other planets, especially Venus and Mars.[6] Centered squarely in the rhetoric of the New Frontier, "The Galaxy Being" developed this familiar premise into a more disturbing tale of electronic existentialism. "You must explore. You must reach out," says the alien, echoing the words of NASA officials and its patron administration. But while advocating interstellar exploration, this episode also played on the suspense and fear encouraged by news broadcasts as NASA launched Alan Shepard, John Glenn, and other astronauts into the great void of outer space. By simultaneously maximizing the drama of these launches while mediating the home viewer's entry into outer space, television became not only the preferred medium for witnessing the space race, but also a seemingly privileged means of anxious access to space itself. With the Galaxy Being "tuning" himself out of existence, this debut episode cultivated such anxiety by portraying outer space and television's electronic space as a common limbo where one might be "transmitted" into nothingness.

Such themes continued in the second episode of *The Outer Limits*, "The Borderland." In this episode, experiments with high-powered electrical fields reveal the possibility of an alternate dimension. During an experiment to contact a wealthy man's dead son, a malfunction disrupts the equipment and blows the breakers, trapping a scientist in an eerie electrical netherworld that exists between the dimensions of life and death. Unable to navigate through this limbo realm, the man cries out helplessly to his wife as he describes the terrifying nothingness that engulfs him. The viewer sees him as a figure thrashing behind a wall of static, as if trapped within the viewer's own television set. In the end, the scientist is saved, but not before the wealthy patron of the experiment leaps through the wall of static in search of his son, only to be forever lost in the other electrical dimension.

With their mutual fixation on electronic transmission as a bridge between worlds, both "The Galaxy Being" and "The Borderland" exploited to the fullest *The Outer Limits*' simulation of an intercepted paranormal transmission, suggesting the possibility of alternate life forms and dimensions lurking in the familiar realm of televisual static. TV transmission in general, even in its more mundane forms, was a topic of much public interest in the early 1960s, as "ultra high frequency" radio signals and orbiting space capsules both tested "the outer limits" of the atmosphere. Beyond the usual articles advising husbands how to take to the rooftops to improve reception, the popular press also gave wide coverage to the decade's emerging forms of signal transmission, including UHF and color TV.[7] Most influential in associating television transmission with outer space was the 1962 launch of "Telstar," the American satellite that first made possible live television broadcasts across the ocean. As with a host of other international media that preceded it, Telstar inspired a series of utopian predictions concerning telecommunications and world peace that portrayed the space-traveling television signal as a world ambassador.[8] A symbol of the earth united through the heavens, the launching of Telstar strengthened an already strong cultural association between television and outer space, and reinvigorated television's status as an extraordinary and fantastic technology.

In the paranormal imagination, however, television transmission presented more a terrifying electronic "nothingness" than an avenue of political utopia, especially when these signals were imagined traveling through the lonely infinitude of outer space. Where does the Galaxy Being go when he turns off the transmitter? What exactly is this strange electromagnetic limbo between life and death represented in "The Borderlands"? In the paranormal broadcast signal encountered with television, the phenomenon of transmission is not so much a link to other worlds as an uncanny, alternate dimension in and of itself, a limbo realm not unlike the vast expanses of outer space that television so frequently depicted during the decade. This is the horror facing the Galaxy Being, the scientists in "The Borderlands," countless other characters on *The Outer Limits*, and even the viewer at home. Television does not threaten to transport them "elsewhere," but succeeds in assimilating them, at least temporarily, into its own "nowhere." Television thus threatened to consume its subjects, if not into the actual vacuum of outer space, then into its own logics and fictions that existed in an etherial space which, nevertheless, could often feel more real, more "live" than the everyday material environment of the viewer's home.

One of the more interesting antecedents of *The Outer Limits*' fascination with television, space, and oblivion comes from the otherwise mundane pages of *TV Guide*. In a piece dubbed "Television's Biggest Mystery," the magazine shared with its readers the enigma of KLEE, a station once based in Houston, Texas.

> At 3:30 pm. British Summer Time, September 14, 1953, Charles W. Brafley of London picked up the call letters KLEE-TV on his television set. Later that month and several times since, they have been seen by engineers at Atlantic Electronics, Ltd., Lancaster, England. . . . The call letters KLEE-TV have not been transmitted since July, 1950, when the Houston station changed its letters to KPRC-TV. . . . A check of the world's television stations confirms the fact that there is not now and never has been another KLEE-TV.[9]

neve

In this fantastic scenario, KLEE's signal has somehow become "lost" in what should have been the nanosecond separating transmission and reception, an infinitesimal moment in time transformed into an apparently infinite limbo. Combining anxieties over agency with the mysteries of physics, the KLEE story posited an electrical form of consciousness at the center of this riddle, one not unlike the Galaxy Being or the interdimensional scientist of *The Outer Limits*. Temporarily forgotten, the KLEE enigma returned when the vagabond station was spotted once again, this time on the TV set of Mrs. Rosella Rose of Milwaukee, Wisconsin, sometime in February of 1962, a full twelve years after the Houston station had abandoned the KLEE station card.[10] In this updated version, KLEE's mysterious signal now carried more than just a station identification, allowing a glimpse into an alternate universe on the other side of the television screen. Mrs. Rose reported briefly seeing the image of an unknown man and woman arguing on a balcony. "The picture faded out then and the KLEE flashed on again," reported Mrs. Rose, "and here's the really strange part—superimposed over the KLEE, which was still on, the word 'HELP' flashed on, off, and on again. The screen then went black."[11] This captive's cry for help suggests that television could serve, not only as a realm of oblivion, but also as a seemingly sentient gatekeeper or cruelly malevolent jailer. This installment in the KLEE story thus makes manifest an anxiety common to all other televisual tales of the electronic nowhere. It provokes the fear that viewers too might one day find themselves trapped within the television set, whisked away by this most domestic of technologies into an electronic netherworld.

The KLEE mystery and *The Outer Limits* stories that followed it, be they based on "true" incidents or long-standing legends, are unsettling for the same reasons that the telegraph of 1848 must have seemed so utterly fantastic. The fleeting and inexplicable transmissions of KLEE, the Galaxy Being, and the "borderlands" are eerie in that they are symptomatic of a general loss of "self-presence" felt socially in electronic communications as a whole. As readers thumbed through their weekly copies of *TV Guide*, the KLEE mystery reminded them that "live" messages and "living" messengers were no longer coterminous, and that consciousness itself could exist in seeming independence from either a sender or a receiver. Similarly, *The Outer Limits* alluded to the existence of an invisible and perhaps imperious empire in the ether. And while the Spiritualists found this dissolution and reconstitution of consciousness via electronic media to be a promising mode of spiritual contact, even a utopian key to solving all of the material world's problems, the wandering consciousness in these tales suggests that by the time of television, signals once under human command seemed either out of control, or even worse, under the control of increasingly sinister forces. By the early 1960s, the once wondrous "otherworld" of electronic telecommunications had become a vast reservoir of cultural anxiety, presenting a localized fear about television itself, certainly, but also a more general unease over the increasingly atomized world television had helped to create. The great electronic nowhere, in other words, no longer represented a gathering of souls, but presented instead their atomization and dispersal across infinity.[12]

But abduction and assimilation by television's electromagnetic nowhere was not the only anxiety expressed in these tales. As a story of television's "distant sight," KLEE also fascinates because it suggests a certain "vision on the air," positing an electrical omniscience associated with television broadcasting as an invisible blanket covering the earth. Even if the television cannot actually assimilate us, there remains the disturbing thought that, just as we can potentially peer into other worlds through the television, these other worlds may be peering into our own living room. Such anxieties must have been particularly acute in the early 1960s as both the United States and Soviet Union launched satellites into the stratosphere for the explicit purpose of surveying the world below to the smallest detail. In an age of growing satellite saturation in the sky and absolute set penetration in the home, the spatiotemporal enigmas of TV transmission provided a sinister variation on a cultural anxiety dating back to the earliest days of television. Spigel notes that early discourses on television often expressed "a larger obsession with privacy, an obsession that was typically expressed through the rhetorical figure of the window, the border between inside and outside worlds."[13] In its more benevolent form, the "window" of television activated the medium's marvelous "aesthetics of presence," showcasing the medium's ability to transport the viewer "live" to localities around the world. Within this growing complex of surveillance technologies and political tensions, however, television was also the most plausible agent to serve as a "window on the home." Period accounts of television often pondered the seemingly inevitable reversibility of the watcher and the watched presented by all telecommunications technology. Of Telstar, for example, Arthur C. Clarke waxed poetically that "no dictator can build a wall high enough to stop its citizens' listening to the voices from the stars." And yet he also conceded that the launching of such communications satellites would eventually make "absolute privacy impossible."[14] In the mad political and scientific race to colonize, communicate, and survey from the sky, who could know exactly what capacities Telstar, Comsat, and their Soviet counterparts actually had or to what uses these secret technologies might eventually be put?

Surveillance technology has long been a fixture of science fiction, of course, and *The Outer Limits* made frequent use of this device. One episode in particular, however, forged a most explicit relationship between advanced television technology, outer space, and seemingly paranormal forms of surveillance, again playing on public anxieties about television as an electronic eye in the home. "O.B.I.T." (1963) told the story of a highly advanced video monitoring system in use at an American military base, a device that allows its operator to monitor secretly the actions of any individual on or near the compound. An investigating senator sets out to learn more about the machine, the Outer Band Individuated Teletracer, or O.B.I.T. as it is known for short. He is told that each person generates his or her own distinct electronic signal, and that the O.B.I.T. machine has the ability to tune in these frequencies anywhere within a range of a few hundred miles. In a dramatic courtroom finale, a general appears on the stand to insist that a "monster" lurks the base and haunts the O.B.I.T. screen. Surveying the courtroom with O.B.I.T. reveals a sinister computer technician to be the monster, an alien from another world whose human disguise can only be uncloaked by this mysterious form of television. The creature boasts that it has brought the O.B.I.T. technology to earth in order to demoralize, divide, and conquer the planet by instilling fear and suspicion through the entire population. "The machines are everywhere," he says to the stunned humans, "and they'll demoralize you, break your spirit, create such rifts and tensions in your society that no one will be able to repair them!" A less than subtle reworking of Orwell with a touch of HUAC paranoia added for good measure, "O.B.I.T." nevertheless concretized a suspicion no doubt held by many during this period. If television can be seen anywhere and everywhere at once, then why could it not potentially "see" anywhere and everywhere as well? The device of the "Individuated Teletracer" expanded the fear of surveillance beyond the actual apparatus of the home television set by appealing to the existence of this larger electromagnetic blanket enveloping the earth, a realm where each person unknowingly sent off electrical signals that could be intercepted and monitored on "alien" TV sets. The story of "O.B.I.T" may have seemed outlandish, but no more so than a *Life* magazine article from 1964 reporting on a device called T.E.S.T., or the "Tanner Electronic Survey Tabulator." *Life* described T.E.S.T. as a "spooky little truck" that patrolled suburban streets, "its innards. . .crammed full of fancy electronic equipment that can and does silently violate the sanctuary of those lighted living rooms to determine 1) whether the occupants are watching their television sets, and if so, 2) on what channel."[15] The inventor of T.E.S.T. predicted his device would revolutionize the imprecise science of "ratings" by covertly monitoring televisions and families in the home, whether they chose to be monitored or not. If a mere panel truck could accomplish such a feat, then it was reasonable to suppose that high-tech satellites could watch over entire nations, cities, and neighborhoods, perhaps even telecasting private images from the home to any number of sinister agencies, be they governmental or extra-terrestrial.

The "control voice's" closing narration to the "O.B.I.T." episode reminded viewers that Americans were their own worst enemies in terms of such suspicion. Exploiting the insatiable American desire to know the secrets of both outer space and the family next door, the aliens are confident that this nation of atomized, isolated, and alienated citizens can easily be brought to its knees. A fragmented and distrustful society connected only through the dull glow of its televisions screens is no match for this seductive technology of alien surveillance, one that allows these estranged citizens to spy on one another's personal traumas and family secrets. In these particularly paranoid transmissions from *The Outer Limits*, television threatened to expose another mammoth void structuring American consciousness in the early 1960s—the suffocating emotional oblivion to be found within the American home.

domestic asylum

As many social historians have noted, the nuclear family emerged as the primary social unit in American postwar society. In a coordinated effort to encourage commodity consumption, stimulate housing starts, and repopulate the nation, a variety of forces in postwar America coalesced to renew faith in family life and to reinvent its meanings in new mass-produced consumer suburbs. But this reorientation of American social life was not without profound consequences. In flight from the nation's urban centers and severed from a whole nexus of earlier community relations, the nuclear families of white suburbia suddenly stood in self-imposed isolation as their own primary network of personal identity and social support. Within the increasingly isolated family, the middle-class mother became the abandoned keeper of the household. This shift in social identity from the community to the family restructured many Americans' engagement with both the social world and the family circle, and provided each member of the family with a new social role to internalize and obey.[16]

Throughout the 1950s and into the 1960s, television developed a highly codified series of narrative conventions to represent this emerging suburban ideal, constructing a middle-class utopia of labor-saving appliances, manicured lawns, and spacious architecture, all designed to showcase the white suburban housewife as the ultimate symbol of material success and domestic bliss. Within this ordered space, postwar wives traded one form of "freedom" for another: exiled from the workplace and public life, they were "liberated" within the home through a series of consumer goods. As Mary Beth Haralovich notes, housewives were "promised psychic and social satisfaction for being contained within the private space of the home; and in exchange for being targeted, measured, and analyzed for the marketing and design of consumer products, [they were] promised leisure and freedom from house-work."[17] Even with its newly purchased array of "emancipating" ovens, irons, and washing machines, however, the suburban home and the rigid social order it presupposed could be a prison at times, especially for women, but also for men who became caught up in the "rat race" of consuming for status. Yet, as Elaine Tyler May observes in her study of postwar families, there was little incentive to change the decade's often oppressive domestic regime. "Forging an independent life outside of marriage carried enormous risks of emotional and economic bankruptcy, along with social ostracism," observes May. "As these couples sealed the psychological boundaries around the family, they also sealed their fates within it."[18]

At times, however, this sealing of "psychological boundaries" around the family could produce not only a general sense of disaffection, but clinical diagnoses of psychosis and possible institutionalization. A study of schizophrenia in the early 1950s, for example, revealed that married women were far more likely to suffer schizophrenic episodes than married men, and noted that a common stage in the "breakdown" of schizophrenic housewives was "the increasing isolation of the wife from family and social relationships, her more-or-less progressive detachment from participation in social reality."[19] Discussing this study some twenty-five years later, Carol Warren notes that "the problems in everyday living experienced by these women—loneliness, isolation, and the stress of the housewife role—were reflections of the conventional structure of marriage and the family in the 1950s. But they were also psychiatric symptoms."[20] Warren goes so far as to argue that the individual "psychopathologies" of these women were in fact socially symbolic prisons, and she describes the "delusions and hallucinations" experienced by these schizophrenic women as "metaphors for their social place."[21] One woman, for example, "saw herself as having been hypnotized by her husband and her doctors, as punished for her offenses by [electro-shock therapy], and as the victim of a master conspiracy to rob her of control of her own life."[22] Another subject in the study heard voices that accused her of not properly caring for her children, a condition that worsened to the point that she eventually set fire to her own home.[23]

Glorifying the virtues of the privatized family and bound more to narrative than social conventions, television's domestic sitcom had no language with which to engage the potential mental disintegration of Mayfield, Springfield, and the other well-scrubbed communities of televisionland. And though the fantastic sitcom often played on the temporary illusion of suburban schizophrenia (talking horses, Martian uncles, maternal automobiles, etc.), it was *The Outer Limits* that presented the most expansive textual space in which to expose and explore this suburban psychopathology. Often presented in tandem with the vacuum of space and the vast "electronic nowhere" of television was *The Outer Limits'* equally terrifying portrait of a more claustrophobic "emotional nowhere." In these domestic visions of oblivion, husbands and wives found themselves trapped, either metaphorically or quite literally, within the suffocating confines of the American home, often to the point of madness. *The Outer Limits* frequently portrayed the American home as a "domestic asylum," cultivating the ambiguity between the dominant conception of the household as a cozy "refuge" from the real world and a more critical view of the home as a place of the insane. As explored in *The Outer Limits*, the "domestic asylum" of the American suburbs was a zone of torpor and constraint, an emotional void every bit as alienating as the electronic oblivion to be found in television.

Frequently presenting an explicit critique of the idealized portrait of the American family, *The Outer Limits* often explored the "delusions and hallucinations" that might befall a June Cleaver, Margaret Anderson, or Donna Stone once the camera was turned off. In "The Bellaro Shield" (1964), for example, a "deviant" housewife is driven insane by a literalized metaphor of her domestic confinement. Passed over for promotion in his father's company, a scientist forgets to deactivate a new laser technology he has been developing. Its beam intercepts an alien who is transported, much like the Galaxy Being before him, into the scientist's home.[24] When the scientist's socially ambitious wife, Judith, discovers that her husband has "captured" an alien, she is sure this scientific triumph will convince her father-in-law to make her husband chairman. Even more enticing, the alien carries with him a small device in his hand that allows him to activate an impenetrable shield, one that can be expanded to any dimension. Judith realizes this technology would revolutionize the defense industry and make her husband's company the most powerful in the world, so she arranges for the father to return to see an amazing demonstration of his son's "new invention." She then steals the technology from the alien, striking the creature in the back of the head and prying the device from his hand. When the father arrives, Judith demonstrates the wondrous new technology that she credits her husband for pioneering. Clicking the device, she activates the "Bellaro Shield," which she has named after both her husband and father-in-law. After demonstrating that the shield can withstand bullets and even laser fire, however, she discovers that she cannot deactivate the force field. She is trapped within its glass-like walls and is quickly running out of air. In the end, the alien regains consciousness, returns to the lab, and deactivates the shield before he expires. But the experience of entrapment has been too much for Judith. She continues to flail away at the now phantom shield. She has gone completely mad and is convinced that she is still imprisoned within it and will be forever.

"The Bellaro Shield" is a rich and conflicted text in what it says about the relationship of marriage, gendered ambition, and domestic asylum in the early 1960s. On the one hand, Judith is clearly "punished" for having disrupted her prescribed role as the passive homemaker. She is depicted early in the text as a suburban Lady MacBeth, aggressively pursuing her husband's corporate career even when he will not. For this alone, she might be considered demented in the social context of postwar suburbia, where such ambition could easily be categorized as "crazy."[25] On the other hand, while portraying the harsh penalty of gender deviance. "The Bellaro Shield" also evokes the potential terror of domestic isolation through an exaggerated technological metaphor of the overly restrictive household. The Bellaro Shield, a device named (appropriately enough) after the patriarchal forces that contain her in the home on a daily basis, presents an intense and focused field of power that threatens to imprison Judith forever. In this respect, one can not help but be struck by how the shield itself, as a box-like, glass prison within the home, stands as a metaphor for television. After activating the shield, Judith finds herself at the center of domestic space trapped behind suffocating panes of glass. The others look on in horror. Closeups of the entombed housewife present the illusion that Judith is actually pressing against the glass of the viewer's home screen. This dynamic image of a woman flailing behind glass walls, at first real and then imaginary, is a dense and multivalent emblem that merges the period's visions of electronic and domestic oblivion. Women such as Judith were trapped by television in two ways, physically removed from the world and isolated within the home by this imperious domestic technology, while also trapped within its constricting conventions of representation. If the suburban home was truly a "domestic asylum," then television was the household's watchful warden, enforcing the housewife's solitary confinement while also instructing her in the desired behaviors for suburban assimilation. As a televised housewife, Judith is perched between these electronic and domestic voids, trapped within a prison of brick and mortar on the one hand and of light and electricity on the other.

"The Bellaro Shield" aligns *The Outer Limits* with a larger cycle of period science fiction centering on mass society critiques of television, women, and the home. Keith Laumer's short story, "The Walls," first published in *Amazing Stories* in 1963, tells a similar tale of a "domestic asylum" with a housewife in the not-too-distant future slowly driven to madness by her husband's desire for an ever more constricting television system in the home. The story begins with Harry replacing the couple's conventional TV set with a "full-wall," a system that features a screen taking up an entire wall of the living room. Soon, Harry proudly adds a second "full-wall" unit adjacent to the first, transforming half of the living room into a giant TV screen. At this point, Flora's fate becomes inevitable. A third full-wall unit is installed and then a fourth until finally the entire apartment is pervaded by an omnidirectional spectacle so strong that the room's doors and corners can no longer be perceived. The saturation of sound and image proves to be too much, causing Flora to panic one day while Harry is still away at work. Just before fainting; she deactivates the system. When she wakes up, she finds herself alone in the apartment surrounded, like Judith Bellaro, by four glass walls that now recede as mirrors into infinity. Also like Judith, she "misreads" her domestic situation through a video induced psychosis.

> *But how strange. The walls of the cell block were transparent now; she could see all the other apartments, stretching away to every side. She nodded; it was as she thought. They were all as barren and featureless as her own. . . . They all had four Fullwalls. And the other women—the other wives, shut up like her in these small, mean cells; they were all aging, and sick, and faded, starved for fresh air and sunshine. She nodded again, and the woman in the next apartment nodded in sympathy. All the women were nodding; they all agreed—poor things. . . . She stood in the center of the room, not screaming now, only sobbing silently. In the four glass walls that enclosed her, she stood alone. There was no point in calling any longer.*[26]

With their common themes of a lost reality within the home, these tales merge the electronic oblivion of television and the emotional oblivion of the home, not by pulling the victimized spectator into the television apparatus itself, but by having the void of television expand, both materially and symbolically, to become a totalizing and wholly simulated realm of electronic incarceration, one that concretizes a lonely emotional void already silently in place in the home. In this respect, both the Bellaro Shield and the full-wall system are manifestations of the emotional walls that already separate husband and wife in these tales, and which no doubt divided many actual suburban homes of the decade.

As bleak as this vision of marriage and domesticity may be, it was eclipsed by a 1964 episode of *The Outer Limits* entitled "The Guests." In this particularly hallucinatory tale, a young drifter (prominently coded as an independent bachelor who drives a convertible, wears a leather jacket, and dons sporty sunglasses) promises an injured man that he will go to a nearby house for help. He makes his way to a gloomy, gothic-looking house at the top of the hill and soon finds himself surrounded by a most peculiar "family," one that consists of an elderly married couple, an aspiring movie actress, and a young woman named Tess. "The Drifter," as this family calls him for most of the episode, has been lured into this domestic trap by an alien creature in the attic. The alien uses those in the house as subjects of an experiment, probing their minds for information on human emotions. When the drifter tries to flee, he discovers that all the doors and windows are sealed. A romance slowly develops between the drifter and Tess, and after a time, she confesses finally that there is a way to escape the "prisonhouse." Each person has an individual "exit door" through which they may leave. The drifter begs Tess to escape with him, but she says she cannot leave the house. Vowing his undying love, the drifter says he will spend eternity with Tess in the house. But she will not allow this fate to befall him. She dashes out of her personal exit door and promptly dematerializes, leaving behind only a locket. "There is nothing for me out there either, Tess," says the drifter as he turns despairingly to go back into the house. But the alien is done with the experiment. The drifter has revealed to him the "missing emotion" in his study of earthlings—love. The alien lets the drifter go and then destroys the house with the other occupants still trapped inside.

Much like "The Bellaro Shield," "The Guests" conducts a rather conflicted examination of love, marriage, and domesticity. Though the episode presents romantic love as the key for resolving the entire narrative, it does this only after portraying marriage and domestic life as little better than a waking death. The elderly wife in the house refers to their existence as a "dreamy nothingness," and when asked why she stays in the home replies, "A wife's duty is to share her husband's life sentence." She implies too that the drifter might also decide to "plunk right down here and dream a life. And live a dream." In the end, the drifter is willing to "settle down" with Tess and continue their vigil in the suffocating, dark, gray, Victorian house, but Tess "frees" him by sacrificing herself. Usually the prized object of display within the home, the housewife in this case becomes a vortex of stasis that threatens to draw the young bachelor forever into the domestic void.

Expanding the static borders of the "domestic asylum" to include an entire suburban neighborhood, a final and in many ways summarily emblematic episode of *The Outer Limits* is worth examining for its complex vision of "oblivion" as a melding of space, suburbia, and the American family. In "A Feasibility Study," a 1964 episode written by series creator Joseph Stefano, an alien space craft removes and then "telecasts," atom by atom, a six-block suburban neighborhood from Beverly Hills to the planet Luminous ("It works very much like your television transmission," says an alien later in the episode when explaining the process to a bewildered human). In the morning, residents of this community wake and prepare for the day unaware that their homes are now light years away from earth, having been telecast across the galaxy by an alien transmitter. Eventually, the humans learn that they are part of a "feasibility study" to see if humans can survive on Luminous to work as slaves. The Luminoids, as this race is called, have become literally petrified by an airborne virus so that they can no longer move. Slowly aging into rock-like creatures, they need a mobile species to do the more menial chores of running the planet. The humans also discover that they too can become infected with the petrifying virus should they actually touch a Luminoid. In the episode's climax, the human community gathers at the church to discuss their fate. Having come into direct contact with the Luminoids, an infected husband and wife stumble into the church already bearing signs of their imminent petrifaction. After a passionate plea by one of their neighbors, the community decides to trick the Luminoids into thinking that humans are also vulnerable to the airborne form of the virus and are therefore unsuitable to work on the planet. In order to save the human race back on earth from the fate of intergalactic slavery, the entire suburban community lines up to infect themselves by touching the already diseased husband and wife.

Explicitly an allegory about the horrors of slavery (albeit an ironic racial reversal where white suburbanites find themselves dispossessed, segregated, and in eventual solidarity), "A Feasibility Study" is equally remarkable for what it implicitly suggests about the incarcerating dimensions of suburbia in the early 1960s. The story concludes with a heroic and uplifting sacrifice, but this resolution does little to address the depressing portrait of suburban isolation and domestic alienation depicted in the previous hour. At the opening of the story, for example, the narrative's central couple is on the verge of separating. After a year of marriage, the wife complains that she can no longer tolerate her husband's demands that she give up her career interests and remain in the house. As the alien plot unfolds, this couple gradually falls back in love and eventually leads the sacrifice made by the entire community. This is an uplifting ending, perhaps, both in terms of combating intergalactic slavery and rekindling romantic love. But there is still something rather sinister about a story that begins with an oppressed wife packing to leave her husband and then ends with the same wife acquiescing as she is turned into a rock. Similarly, the image of an entire suburban neighborhood marooned on a remote planet and hurtling forever through the void of space makes for an eerie yet apropos commentary on the state of suburbia in the 1960s. For this community of suburban exiles, lost in the stars, yet permanently confined to a six-block patch of land, the decision to become infected by the petrifying virus may represent a brave sacrifice, but there is also the more nihilistic subtext that this final act of community is more of a suicide pact than a collective form of resistance.

"the world is unstable and may collide and blow up"

As these episodes demonstrate, *The Outer Limits*, like the fantastic sitcom, frequently drew attention to the conventionality of domestic life. Also like the fantastic sitcom, the series even reaffirmed on occasion romantic love and heterosexual marriage as the ideal resolution to certain textual and social problems. But its reliance on a separate set of narrative conventions and a profoundly different sense of the "fantastic" often placed the family, not as a site of (temporarily) renegotiated social roles, but as a source of violent disruption and a target of imminent extinction. Spigel notes that the fantastic sitcom operated through a logic of "displacement and distortion," employing "safety valves" that "diffused the 'trouble' in the text."[27] Compared to these sitcoms, the "fantastic" elements of *The Outer Limits*—its weird aliens and strange technologies—worked not so much to displace and distort anxieties about American life, but instead to *intensify* these anxieties by presenting the family with a series of apocalyptic crises that challenged the solvency and legitimacy of this social institution.

Perhaps no oblivion of the early 1960s was as palpable as that of nuclear annihilation, another void continually rehearsed both by *The Outer Limits* and television in general. "The Premonition" (1965), airing a week before the show's final exile from network airwaves, opens with a testpilot pushing record speeds in an experimental aircraft high above the desert. Below, his wife drives their daughter to the military base's day school. After the jet descends out of control and makes a crash landing, the pilot emerges to find that the entire world is frozen in time. Out on the desert plains, a coyote chasing a rabbit stands as a still tableau, as do birds hanging in the air around him. Seeing his unconscious wife still behind the wheel of her car, he revives her, and she too quickly remarks that time seems to be standing still. Together, they return to the base and find everyone absolutely frozen in place. In their struggles, they meet the "limbo being," a man who long ago also entered this "black oblivion" of frozen time. "I am what you are," he says, "trapped in this limbo-world between the present and the future." In perhaps the series' most vivid account of oblivion, he describes the hell that awaits them should they not escape. "Time will pass you by, and leave you where I am now, in the forever now, black motionless vold . . . no light . . . no sun . . . no stars . . . no time . . . eternal nothing . . . no hunger . . . no thirst . . . only endless existence. And the worst of it? You can't die." The pilot and his wife also discover that their daughter will be killed immediately once time is unfrozen, as her tricycle stands only feet away from a runaway truck. Working together, they finally devise a plan to both save their daughter and reemerge from the realm of the "limbo being." Once this is accomplished, they remember nothing of their experience outside of normal time. Nevertheless, they rush to the airbase with a strange premonition that their daughter might be in trouble. But they find her happy and at play, no longer endangered by the truck.

With its images of figures locked in time, the episode's lingering shots of frozen coyotes, static birds, and motionless human figures in the desert recall the unnerving imagery of the government's atomic tests at Yucca Flats in the mid-1950s, and by implication, the frozen moment of horror preceding the nuclear obliteration of Hiroshima and Nagasaki. In the Yucca Flats detonation, as is well known, the government built an entire town on the desert plains of New Mexico. "Survival City," as this outpost was called, featured a population of department store mannequins who occupied a row of houses on "Doomsday Drive." The entire experiment was staged as a high profile media event, with CBS and NBC sharing the production costs in the hopes of capturing a vividly personal and highly rated encounter with the A-bomb. In a perverse attempt to "humanize" the story, reporters even went so far as to "Interview" a family of these clothing-store dummies, the "Darlings," as they sat posed for destruction. "With the help of Kit Kinne, Foods Editor of the *Home* show," observed *Newsweek* in the midst of the bomb's pre-blast publicity blitz, "American housewives inspected the Darlings' cupboards and iceboxes and speculated on the effects of the blast on such items as baby food, dish-washers, and children's nightgowns."[28] Such "survival" coverage in the mid and late 1950s helped precipitate the national mania for fallout shelter construction in the early 1960s, a campaign that once again placed the American home most palpably at the center of an impending oblivion. Civil defense literature evoked images of the suburban neighborhood as a final and lonely frontier. Faced with the prospect of nuclear annihilation, block after block of suburban families would be trapped, not just in their homes, but in the even more tomb-like concrete shelters in their basements and backyards. In the midst of such nuclear oblivion, their only link to the outside world or to the neighbors next door would come through an even more remote and disembodied form of television: the Emergency Broadcasting System.

The Yucca Flat nuclear test experienced delays to the point that the networks abandoned their extensive, in-depth coverage of the event.[29] Nevertheless, cameras were there to record the devastation as the bomb decimated "Survival City," the Darlings, and its other mute and motionless residents. These eerie images of post-blast mannequins scattered across the desert were exhibited on a number of television programs and made it in still form to the pages of *Life*, where all of America could scrutinize at their own leisure their possible fate in the nuclear age.[30] With its images of the static desert, "The Premonition" rehearsed this sense of nervous anticipation experienced before any big blast, be it a desert test or an imminent enemy launch. Vulnerable and helpless, the young married protagonists struggle, like so many other Americans of the period, to save their child from the seemingly inevitable destruction that awaits her. Lost in this eternal moment of anticipatory dread, their only contact is with the "limbo being," a creature who himself is a specter of the atomic blast. Wearing shredded clothing and deathly afraid of fire, the "limbo being" is filmed throughout the episode as a reverse negative. A black-and-white inversion of the world around him, the "limbo being" wanders as a glowing, irradiated creature doomed to "the forever now, the black motionless void."

As with so many other episodes of *The Outer Limits*, however, "The Premonition" ultimately returned the viewer back to images of the reigning space age. Test pilots, of course, were major cultural heroes of the time, seen as braving death to lay the groundwork for the eventual colonization of space. Breaking through a "new frontier" of speed, the pilot and his wife, like Shepard, Glenn, and the families of all other astronauts to follow, stand at the precipice of the greatest oblivion of all—the timeless and depthless expanses of outer space. In this respect, the televised volley of rocket launches in the late 1950s and early 1960s not only made Americans more aware of their technological competition with the Soviets, but also produced a new understanding of the earth and its rather humble place in the vastness of the universe. Like the Copernican revolution centuries earlier, NASA's frenzied launching of monkeys and men into the black void of space could not help but tangibly remind an already nervous world that it was very insignificant, incredibly vulnerable, and ultimately quite alone in the galaxy. "The growing preoccupation with outer space is one of the features of our present civilization," observed a psychiatrist writing in 1960. "It is not surprising that it should enter into the manifestations of certain neurotic symptoms."[31] Presenting a number of case studies in such neurosis, this psychiatrist discusses the plight of a thirty-three-year-old man who would no doubt feel quite at home in the world of *The Outer Limits*, a subject who felt "unsafe" because, as he put it, "'the earth is a ball spinning round and I am on it.'" The psychiatrist comments:

> He became completely incapacitated and had to be admitted to [the] hospital with the fear "of going to disappear in outer space." He felt that his feet were on the ground and that the sky was above and he had to keep reminding himself that the force of gravity was keeping him down—"otherwise I would float Into space."... Phrases which commonly occurred included: "It's space that's getting me—the curvature of the globe makes everything insecure." "We are surrounded by a hostile environment—if I think about it I want to run for cover."... His home was described as "a little small house on the globe and all the space above—and that is insecure."[32]

Another patient reported a more specific fear of satellites and space stations, while still another admitted both fear and fascination with space programs on television. Describing her attraction/repulsion for these shows, she complained, "It's a nuisance when you are interested in things and they frighten you."[33] Living in the age of humanity's first tentative journeys into outer space gave her a general sense of anxiety over "peculiar things happening in the universe."[34] Her biggest fear was that "the world is unstable and may collide and blow up." "She became worried," notes the psychiatrist, "'about all the collisions there might be up in outer space because of all of this indiscriminate sending up of satellites.' She felt, 'there is no planning and it might affect the natural order of things.'"[35]

The Outer Limits, of course, exacerbated such fears and did indeed suggest that earthling science could easily result in instability and disaster, as slow-witted humans ventured into a realm in which they had no business interfering. At the disembodied mercy of the "control voice," the audience could do nothing better but watch, powerless to intervene as any number of cosmic catastrophes befell the earth. Although viewers never actually see outer space in "The Premonition," it is space technology that opens this time rift, unlocking a hellish limbo that concretizes the terrifyingly abstract infinity of outer space by mapping it temporally onto the everyday world. Replicating the vast spatio-temporal rhythms of the heavens, the frozen air base becomes an expansive void where humans remain separated, like stars and planets, by unimaginable gulfs of time and space. From this realm of suspended animation, the "black oblivion" of the limbo being, the parents must watch helplessly as their daughter "speeds" at an uncannily slow pace toward her death in front of the runaway truck, her temporally and spatially dislocated tricycle as distant, imperiled, and helpless as the most remote Mercury capsule.

In a particularly vivid account of the impending oblivion of the early 1960s, this episode thus united two very different borders along the New Frontier: the infinitesimal yet potentially cataclysmic intricacies of the atom and the infinite expanses of outer space. Both the atom and outer space challenged Americans to imagine a fantastic terrain mapped by courageous scientists, powered by mysterious orbital mechanics, and somehow accessed through the equally mystifying workings of the television set. Between the spinning stars, planets, and galaxies of the universe existed a void beyond human imagination, a "final frontier" on a scale so vast as to be terrifying. Within the whirling protons and electrons of the atom, meanwhile, existed a power beyond human imagination, a destructive force so devastating that it was almost incomprehensible. In between these two perilous borders of "new frontier" science stood the American family, plagued by their own often unstable dynamics and woefully unprotected from these other forces by their feeble suburban homes. Vulnerable and withdrawn, they could nevertheless witness the continuing exploration of these often terrifying realms through their television sets.

All ends well in "The Premonition," as the encroachment of oblivion remains just that, a premonition. But even so, this episode demonstrates once again how frequently and often quite explicitly *The Outer Limits* disrupted the medium's characteristically self-congratulatory monologue on both the American family and the prospects of unlimited progress in American science and technology. *The Outer Limits* was remarkable, if for no other reason, by virtue of this consistent opposition to the new public celebration of the family, science, and technology that dominated the early 1960s. Playing on topical fears and anxieties that posed often tangible threats to the family during this period, *The Outer Limits* repeatedly sided with the alien's often cataclysmic critiques of the homogenizing inertia bred in American suburbia and the technological hubris bred in American laboratories. The series consistently implied that destruction and chaos lurked behind the gleaming facades of the new social and scientific order represented by television, and suggested that television itself, as a technology of cascading electrons, radioactive waves, invisible frequencies, distant transmissions, and other "strange" sciences was a direct conduit for the domestic and electronic oblivions occupying the public mind in the early part of the decade: Invading the home as a broadcast emanating from these more alienating encampments along the New Frontier, *The Outer Limits* confirmed that television was indeed an oblivion of sorts, or at the very least an eerie electronic presence hovering over a number of potential "vast wastelands" in 1960s America.

Notes

1. This humor is perhaps epitomized in the famous episode "Time Enough at Last," which featured Burgess Meredith as an overworked clerk and nervous bookworm who finds himself the sole survivor of a nuclear holocaust. He finds the library is still standing, and, with unlimited time to read, he sets out to enjoy the classics of literature, only to break his special prescription reading glasses.

2. Lynn Spigel, "From Domestic Space to Outer Space: The 1960s Fantastic Family Sit-Com," in *Close Encounters: Film, Feminism, and Science-Fiction*, ed. by Elizabeth Lyon, Constance Penley and Lynn Spigel (Minneapolis: University of Minnesota Press, 1991), 209.

3. "Haunted TV is Punished: Set with Face that Won't Go Away Must Stare at the Wall," *The New York Times*, 11 December 1953, 33.

4. "Face on TV set Goes, Mystery Lingers On." *The New York Times*, 12 December 1953, 16. See also *Television Digest*, 12 December 1953, 11.

5. For a more complete account of this history, see Jeffrey Sconce, *Television Ghosts: A Cultural History of Electronic Presence in Telecommunications Technology* (Durham: Duke University Press, forthcoming).

6. During the 1910s and 1920s, serious debate took place within the scientific community over the prospects of contacting Mars and other worlds via wireless transmissions. Some scientists even explored the possibility of creating a "universal" code language with which to engage the Martians once the radio link was established. See H.W. and C. Wells Nieman, "What Shall We Say to Mars? A System for Opening Communication Despite the Absence of any Common Basis in Language," *Scientific American*, 20 March 1920, 312. For many years, intergalactic communication was seen to be a fantastic yet most logical application of radio technology (a legacy that continues today in NASA's SETI program). NASA's SETI program (Search for Extra-Terrestrial Intelligence) involves using radio telescopes to monitor the universe for intelligent radio transmissions.

7. The FCC's decision to require "click-stop" tuning in all American-made television sets combined with the Industry's vigorous promotion of color TV made both UHF and color topics of public anticipation and discussion in the early sixties. In their own way, UHF and color presented new "dimensions" in broadcasting, an association encouraged by accounts of radio astronomers and commercial broadcasters battling for control over these bandwidths and frequencies. See D.S. Greenberg, "Radio Astronomy: TV's Rush for UHF Threatens Use of Channel," *Science*, 1 February 1963, 393; and D. S. Greenberg, "Radio Astronomy: FCC Proposes Compromise to Share Frequencies with UHF Broadcasters," *Science*, 12 April 1963, 164.

8. One commentator on Telstar wrote, "To get to know each other on a worldwide scale is the human race's most urgent need today; and this is where Telstar can help us." He continued, "It can make it possible for each section of the human race to become familiar with every other section's way of living: and, once this mutual familiarity is established, there is some hope that we may all become aware of the common humanity underlying the differences in our local manners and customs." See Arnold J. Toynbee, "A Message for Mankind from Telstar," *The New York Times Magazine*, 12 August 1962, 31. Also see Michael Curtin's essay in this volume.

9. "TV's Biggest Mystery," *TV Guide*, 30 April 1964, 23.

10. Curtis Fuller, "KLEE . . . Still Calling." *Fate*, April 1964, 39.

11. Fuller, 40.

12. *The Outer Limits* was undoubtedly the medium's most vocal commentator on its own powers of discorporation and alienation. But so dominant was this theme that even within the narrative universe of *Star Trek*, the most utopian of all television's explorations into space, one episode featured a disembodied Captain Kirk dissolved and abandoned in the translucent energy stream of the transporter. Having been transformed into an other-dimensional ghost by this now most familiar technology for the discorporation and "telecasting" of human

beings, Kirk's electronic body floats eerily across the mirrors, halls, and viewscreens of the Enterprise until his eventual rescue and reconstitution, a cogent reminder that even in the twenty-fourth century, television transmission would remain the most immediate gateway to the terrifying voids of the universe. See "The Tholian Web" episode, *Star Trek* (NBC). The discorporation, teleportation, and telecasting of matter were also central devices in science-fiction cinema of the 1950s and 1960s, most notably in *The Fly* (20th Century-Fox, 1958).

13. Lynn Spigel, *Make Room for TV* (Chicago: University of Chicago Press, 1992), 117.

14. Telstar, Telstar—Burning Bright," *Life*, 3 August 1962, 4.

15. "A Watch Truck is Watching You," *Life*, 25 September 1964.

16. Within the period, many psychologists explicitly defined the family in such disciplinary terms as "a process of reciprocal roles perceived, expected, and performed by family members." According to this model, the "happiness" of any given family was "assumed to be reflected in the extent to which roles are accepted and shared among its members." See A. R. Mangus, "Family Impacts on Mental Health," *Marriage and Family Living* (August 1957): 261.

17. Mary Beth Haralovich, "Sit-coms and Suburbs: Positioning the 1950s Homemaker," in *Private Screenings: Television and the Female Consumer*, ed. by Lynn Spigel and Denise Mann (Minneapolis: University of Minnesota Press, 1992), 111.

18. Elaine Tyler May, *Homeward Bound: American Families in the Cold War Era* (New York: Basic Books, 1988), 36.

19. Harold Sampson, Sheldon L. Messinger, and Robert Towne, *Schizophrenic Women: Studies in Marital Crisis* (New York: Atherton Press, 1964), 21, 128.

20. Carol A. B. Warren, *Madwives: Schizophrenic Women in the 1950s* (New Brunswick: Rutgers University Press, 1991), 58.

21. Warren, 58.

22. Warren, 58.

23. Sampson, et al., 158.

24. Preceding this broadcast, an article entitled "TV Transmission on Laser Beam Demonstrated by North American" appeared in *Aviation Weekly*, 18 March 1963, 83.

25. Psychological studies of the period argued that a married woman's sense of self-worth was most often bound to their "feminine" role of housekeeper and careprovider. See Robert S. Weiss and Nancy Morse Samelson, "Social Roles of American Women: Their Contribution to a Sense of Usefulness and Importance," *Marriage and Family Living* (November 1958): 358–366.

26. Keith Laumer, "The Walls," in *Nine by Laumer* (New York: Doubleday, 1967), 67–69.

27. Spigel, "From Domestic Space to Outer Space," 214.

28. "It Better Be Good," *Newsweek*, 9 May 1955, 84.

29. "Mouse at Yucca Flat: Televising Atomic Bomb Test," *Newsweek*, 16 May 1955, 63.

30. See "Victims at Yucca Flats: Mannequins," *Life*, 16 May 1955, 58; and "Close-up to the Blast," *Life*, 30 May 1955, 39–42.

31. R. J. Kerry, "Phobia of Outer Space," *Journal of Mental Science*, Vol. 106. (1960): 1386.

32. Kerry, *Phobia of Outer Space*, 1386.

33. Kerry, *Phobia of Outer Space*, 1386.

34. Kerry, *Phobia of Outer Space*, 1386.

35. Kerry, *Phobia of Outer Space*, 1386.

I Spy's *"Living Postcards"*
The Geo-Politics of Civil Rights

Mary Beth Haralovich

The network and producer Sheldon Leonard have, with more guts than ordinary observers could imagine, cast Negro comedian Bill Cosby in a feature role, then turned about in the premiere . . . and racked another ethnic group, the Chinese. . . . But the Chinese commies are bound to be the new heavies of pulp fiction.
—review of I Spy's *first episode,* Variety, *22 September 1965*

I Spy (NBC, 1965–68) represents the first visible result of civil rights pressures on the television industry.[1] An hour-long weekly drama, *I Spy* served up racial integration with a team of U.S. intelligence agents (Robert Culp as Kelly Robinson and Bill Cosby as Alexander Scott) who travel the world undercover as a professional tennis player and his trainer. *I Spy*'s cultural significance lies not only in its embrace of racial integration through cast and characters but also in its representation of the value of civil rights for the U.S. position in the Cold War. In their dealings with Communists and Soviet agents, *I Spy*'s agents use advances in civil rights as a weapon in the Cold War, asserting progress in U.S. race relations and defending against charges that the United States is a racist country.

I Spy's foreign locations add dimension and spectacle to television spy fiction. In their travels, the spies enact the global politics of the Cold War. But as tourists, they enjoy the sights and sounds of other countries, embrace cultural if not political difference, and celebrate humanist similarities. As a travelogue, *I Spy* uses color cinematography and locations to provide a form of what Cynthia Enloe calls "living postcards . . . natives in their exotic environment." Even as it reveals the terrain of the Cold War, *I Spy* demonstrates the case and pleasures of foreign travel, including "sex tourism," the sexual availability of local women for the white male tourist.[2]

Television historians have applauded *I Spy*'s efforts at racial equality, which they credit to a series design that allowed a black character most of the flexibility and opportunities afforded white characters. In *Blacks and White TV*, J. Fred MacDonald argues that because "It affected the history of blacks in American television, the most crucial series in the latter half of the 1960s was *I Spy*." MacDonald appreciates the "bold decision" to cast an integrated partnership, one that "broke the color line as had no series in TV history," providing opportunities for other African American performers as well as for Cosby. Historians Allen Woll and Randall Miller welcome "a sympathetic, realistic black character in a lead role," and Eric Barnouw values the "feeling of equality and warm friendship" revealed in the performances. MacDonald applauds *I Spy* for providing audiences with the "educational experience [of seeing] an Afro-American hero operating constructively abroad in the service of the United States." He takes pleasure in Cosby/Scott's very presence in European locations and finds that Scott was "able to feel and express emotions historically forbidden to black characters in mainstream entertainment media . . . [including] physical expressions of inter-racial romance." In "Tele-visual Representation and the Claims of 'The Black Experience,' " Phillip Brian Harper discusses

Cosby's "belief in the unique contributions that the show could make to improved U.S. race relations and his sense of solidarity with other blacks involved in the civil rights struggle."[3]

Despite the attempted equality of the partners, *I Spy* opens with a credits sequence dominated by Robinson/Culp. A tennis player in silhouette swings his racket as names of world cities move by, ending with "USA" (In red, white, and blue).[4] The racket becomes a gun as the tennis player becomes a crouched man in a suit. He shoots offscreen three times. The exploding bullets become the series name: *I Spy*. This title dissolves to a cool and collected Robinson/Culp, wearing a suit and tie. He uses a lighter to ignite a cigarette and then a bomb, which he casually losses offscreen. After the explosion, his eyes look down from the top of a split screen onto a series of scenes taken primarily from the episode to come. Aside from his name above the title—and depending on the episode—Scott/Cosby might make only one appearance in the credits sequence. However, as if to underscore the integrated partnership, the credits of *I Spy*'s first episode pair Scott/Cosby with Robinson/Culp in various action scenes. One shot is a close-up of two hands—one black and one white—each pointing a gun in the same direction.

Like other TV spies of the period, Robinson is derived from James Bond, by 1965 a staple of spy fiction.[4] Scott, however, has a more complex etiology that attempts to explain how an African American came to occupy his position. *The Cold War File*, a compendium of spy fiction, describes Robinson as "a major contender at Wimbledon . . . a romantic and an adventurer . . . equally proficient in the arts of seduction and assassination." *The Cold War File* describes Scott's up-by-the-bootstraps super achievements: despite "racial barriers and an impoverished childhood," Scott became a college football star, champion tennis player, graduate of Temple University (as is Cosby), Rhodes scholar, and fluent in eleven languages.[5] Repressing the pointed race commentary of 1960s social issue comedians such as Lenny Bruce and Dick Gregory, Scott's character design takes on attributes of two heroic figures—Moe Berg (the multilingual athlete-spy of World War II) and Arthur Ashe (the African American tennis champion who won the first U.S. Open in 1968).[6]

Although exhibition tennis and espionage are motivations for setting the series in foreign lands, *I Spy*'s travelogue is also a register of its verisimilitude as spy fiction. Foreign countries are contested territory in the Cold War, and they are also accessible sites for tourism. *I Spy*'s esplonage is visually grounded in NBC's first prime-time season of color programming in 1965.[7] The action takes place against the vistas and skylines of foreign locations. The spies often function as tour guides, particularly in Mexico, which is presented as our friendly neighbor to the south, a haven for U.S. spies on vacation.

I Spy is one among many films and TV shows connected with 1960s espionage culture, but its recombination of spy fiction and travelogue makes it different from the others. Although *I Spy*'s spies can be suave and witty, the series engages the 1960s world of esplonage not through parody but through realism. In *Get Smart* (NBC, 1965–69; CBS 1969–70), *Mission: Impossible* (CBS, 1966–73; ABC, 1988–90), *The Man from U.N.C.L.E.* (NBC, 1964–68), and *The Avengers* (ABC, 1966–69), agents typically take on one specific mission at a time to fight fantastic or ambiguous Soviet bioc villains. *I Spy*'s agents are deployed worldwide to observe and interfere with Communist activities. Robinson and Scott behave in many ways like "real" CIA agents—as they have been described in intelligence histories.[8]" They do not reveal their actual identities to civilians, but other spies know them to be spies—and vice versa. Not reliant on gimmicks or gunplay, Robinson and Scott often work without weapons and try to convince people of the wisdom of rejecting Communism.[9]

One source of *I Spy*'s verisimilitude and ideological positioning in the 1960s is public awareness of intelligence and its role in state security. In the early 1960s, there were several highly visible Cold War incidents—the missile gap, the U-2 spy mission, the Cuban missile crisis. In addition, the period has been described as the "Cult of the Defector" for the way defections were announced in "government-sponsored press conference[s]." Although such public events raised questions about the autonomy of the CIA and the legality of its actions, esplonage remained central to the U.S. struggle with the Soviet bloc for world domination. Barnouw suggests that 1960s TV spy fiction may have contributed to "public acceptance of a foreign policy based on good guy/bad guy premises [and] clandestine warfare" and helped Americans get used to the covert actions of the CIA.[10] *I Spy* adopts the

Cold War attitude prevalent in the CIA and State Department of the time: that Communism is pernicious and pervasive, that Communists are dupes who follow Party-line directions from Moscow.

Although *I Spy* was produced in the mid-1960s—in the wake of the 1963 March on Washington, Freedom Summer, and the Civil Rights Act of 1964—one can look at the series (and at civil rights law) as a solution to the State Department's public relations problems of the 1950s. In her study of U.S. race relations and foreign policy during the Cold War, Mary Dudziak shows how race discrimination became "a critical cultural and ideological weak point" for U.S. foreign policy during the 1950s.

> *Voting rights abuses, lynchings, school segregation, and antimiscegenation laws were discussed at length in newspapers around the world, and the international media continually questioned whether race discrimination made American democracy a hypocrisy. How can democracy be attractive to Third World countries when the U.S. abuses its citizens of color? This situation was exacerbated by "African Americans [such as entertainer Josephine Baker, actor-singer Paul Robeson, and writer W. E. B. DuBois who] criticized race discrimination in the United States before an International audience."*[11]

I Spy resembles an official response to the U.S. Cold War predicament of the 1950s. At a time when both the Cold War and civil rights are hot, *I Spy* reassures audiences that U.S. intelligence is working to protect U.S. interests abroad, and it affirms the value of civil rights for the United States by showing an integrated partnership that is friendly, color-blind, and pairiotic. Travelling the world, Robinson and Scott represent racial harmony both in their relationship and in dialogue with Communists. Robinson and Scott occupy the discursive role the State Department searched for in the 1950s: African Americans who would travel overseas and say "the right thing" about race relations in the United States. Dudziak notes, "Patriots were supposed to close ranks" when overseas. One could be critical in the United States but, "when sent abroad [one should] emphasize racial progress in the United States and argue that persons of color had nothing to gain from communism."[12] Emerging from an environment that compressed civil rights activism and Cold War vigilance, *I Spy* presented analogues to 1950s black activists such as Baker and Robeson.

The first episode of *I Spy* pointedly announces the series's stance on civil rights and the Cold War. Written by Robert Culp, whose personal commitment to racial integration was important to the series.[13] "So Long, Patrick Henry" (first season, 1965) deals with an African American Olympic medalist who defects to the People's Republic of China for $250,000 in a Swiss bank account (more than he would earn as a professional athlete in the United States at the time). Suspecting that the defector may be unhappy with his situation, the U.S. government assigns Robinson and Scott to determine whether he wants to return to the United States.

As with the public parade of actual defectors, the athlete and his Chinese handlers appear together in several press conferences. When they announce his defection, the athlete rejects a speech prepared by the Chinese ("Who wrote this thing, huh?") to credit himself with his successful rise in spite of racism ("I'm the best, see, because I worked like a slave—if you'll pardon the expression—to get that way"). At the press conference that concludes the episode, the athlete denounces Chinese attempts to control the Afro-Asian games (described by Mr. Tsung, the main Chinese heavy, as a means for China to "be firmly entrenched in Africa"). The athlete leaves the press conference to a standing ovation from the assembled group of Africans and Asians after he states: "They'll poison it for you. . . . So have your games, but you do it yourselves. I'll help you if I can, but right now I just want to go home."[14]

Robinson and Scott's contact with the defector is an opportunity for the agents to explain—to the defector and thus to the viewing audience—current race conditions in the United States and the need for commitment to racial integration. Throughout, Robinson and Scott visually express their disgust with the defector. In a key conversation in a bar, Scott explains the dual struggle for International and domestic civil rights. The United States is "trying to make the law of the land stick, holding the world together with one hand and trying to clean their own house with the other—yeah, something no country's ever done before in the history of the world." Scott declares, "The whole world is trying to keep bloody fools like you from selling themselves back into slavery." The word "slavery" gets the defector's attention.

Yet *I Spy* is not a didactic tract. The series also presents its messages through hip banter between Robinson and Scott.[15] In this episode's epilogue, a summary joke merges integration espionage, and sex tourism. A bellboy whom Scott enlists to help the agents refers to himself as "007." Scott wants to reward the bellboy by taking him to "an English movie" about "the adventures of 007." When Robinson resists, Scott implores, "Don't knock the competition. . . . You may learn something. Not only does he get the women, but he gets them painted all the different colors of the rainbow. It's called widescreen integration." Open discussion of race relations is important to *I Spy*. In addition to dialogue and narrative logic, *I Spy* relies on visual confirmation of racial equality in the way Robinson and Scott exercise their partnership, living and working together.

In "Tonia" (second season, 1967), Robinson and Scott again confront a black American who has been duped by Communists, this time in Italy. Scott figures centrally—as an African American, as a heterosexual lover, and as a patriot.[16] "Tonia" takes place in Rome, where anti-U.S. actions are widespread: Uncle Sam hangs in effigy from a building; a bartender at the U.S. Officers' Club reports to a Communist cell leader; Communists look at Robinson and Scott with distaste; the hammer-and-sickle graces a street poster; other street posters announce demonstrations against the war in Vietnam; a Communist cell leader attempts to destroy Robinson and Scott's integrated partnership.[17]

The daughter of a black USO performer, Tonia is an American who moved to Italy when she was a child. Now involved with the Communist Party, she confronts Scott about racism and poverty in the United States. As Tonia and Scott walk through a side street in Rome, they pass children playing in cardboard boxes. Scott remarks, "Apart from the fact that it's Italy, it's no different from my old neighborhood" in Philadelphia. Tonia counters this humanist observation ("Americans think that poor people are morally inferior") and accuses the United States of "ruthless exploitation of racial minorities." Scott offers a good-natured reply, one that deflects discussion of race relations with wry recitations of Marxist theory: "I see. And capitalist warmongers and their Wall Street lackeys." Their ideological difference is a motif of the episode. Scott accuses Tonia of living in a "political dream world" and of spouting "cliches" and "assumptions." She charges him with being an "agent of American militarism." When Scott asks her to go on a picnic, Tonia prefers that their meeting be a "seminar, a discussion period."

But Tonia makes one remark that hits home. She reproaches Scott for being Robinson's servant, for "carrying the white man's rackets." Unable to reveal his actual identity as a U.S. agent and Robinson's partner. Scott is disturbed by this accusation. Later, Scott complains to Robinson ("People think I'm your servant") as, dressed in format attire en route to the officers' club, the two men leave their hotel room. Robinson is at once sympathetic ("She's been brought up on propaganda") and a good-natured Joker ("You get a good salary and every other Sunday off"). Although their spy partnership cannot be publicly spoken of, Robinson and Scott's joint destination, easy camaraderie, similar formal wear, and shared sleeping quarters visually underscore their equality.

In "Tonia," both the Soviets and the Americans justify their counter-espionage strategies. Blair, a representative of the U.S. State Department, wants Scott to "go after that girl," since "Washington has been on my back for weeks to make contact among these extreme left-wingers." The United States is "dying for information" about leftist activities in Rome ("how well are they organized, what are their immediate plans") to avoid disturbances such as the "riot last month at a NATO base [in which] three people [were] killed . . . any excuse for a good noisy anti-American demonstration." Blair explains that young people are duped by Communists: "The direction comes from [the Party]. Regardless of what these kids say, they are not independent."

On the other side of the Cold War, Zugman, the Communist cell leader, explains to Tonia the need to break up the Robinson-Scott partnership. They are "doubly effective. Not only are they engaged in espionage, but their mere presence is always a source of constant propaganda." Zugman shows Tonia newspaper clippings—photos of Robinson and Scott together in cities around the world: Tokyo, Hong Kong, Acapulco, Mexico City, Rome. Robinson and Scott are "the very picture of harmony, equality, racial equality. They destroy one of our most important propaganda points." Zugman rips a photo of Robinson and Scott in half to illustrate the effect he wants from Tonia—to create jealousy in order to "set them at each other's throats." Tonia refuses and Zugman kills her, setting up Robinson as the murderer.

The episode concludes by establishing a parallel romantic effectiveness between Robinson and Scott in that both have enticed Communist women to the West. Zugman had once been a high-level agent in Latin America but lost his position when his daughter defected to the United States. Robinson denies accountability: "She thought she was in love with a tennis player [but] she was in love with freedom." Like Robinson, Scott wooed a woman to freedom, as Tonia came to believe in him. In the epilogue, Scott continues to reach out to people of color. Strolling down a street in Rome, the agents see a young black girl sitting on a stoop. Scott gives the girl two gelatos saying, "mia sorella" (my sister). In "Tonia" and "Goodbye, Patrick Henry," Scott's interactions with black characters suggest an essential bond through through race.

In *I Spy's* Mexico episodes, race is not as politically inflected as it is in Europe or Asia. Mexico is not contested territory in the Cold War but our friendly neighbor to the south. Although Soviet agents travel easily in Mexico, Communism does not have the pernicious presence it can have in Europe or Asia. In Mexico, spies from both sides find respite from espionage life. *I Spy's* Mexico episodes typically begin with Robinson and Scott on vacation—relaxing, shopping, fishing, enjoying the attractions of city and country, including (for the white agent) the sexuality of local women.

I Spy uses sounds and images to articulate Mexico as a beautiful, comfortable, and exotic site for tourism. "Return to Glory" (first season, 1966) illustrates how *I Spy* combines the Mexican travelogue with geopolitics, weaving tourism with intelligence gathering. Robinson and Scott are assigned to evaluate a Latin American general living in exile in Mexico. Deposed by revolutionary forces, the general plans to launch an invasion to regain his country. Robinson and Scott are in Taxco (shopping for a silver chafing dish for Scott's mother) when they are contacted by a Mexican national who is a U.S. agent working undercover (In serape and sombrero) as a street photographer. Robinson and Scott are ordered to contact the general and recommend action to the United States, but they are told to take no position because "the State Department cannot officially be involved . . . in military adventures . . . especially if they are frivolous." At the same time that the United States was building its forces in Vietnam, *I Spy* adopts a familiar government discourse of disavowal: the United States is aware of international actions but does not become involved in them.

I Spy positions characters in a mise-en-scène and sound calculated to reveal indigenous musical arts of Mexico. In a club with several performance spaces, Robinson and Scott meet the general's wife and adviser (whose past service includes working for the French at Dien Blen Phu and Algiers—"all losers," Scott observes pessimistically). As they talk, the group moves from room to room, pausing to witness Indian acrobats, a drummer, a mariachi band. Later, the agents encounter street musicians who dance and play before an appreciative crowd. *I Spy* typically shows Robinson and Scott in long shot, leisurely driving along roads that display the vistas of the Mexican countryside.

The agents often have a native guide—a woman or a boy whom Robinson has charmed—who explains Mexican history and customs. These conversations are a significant motif in *I Spy's* Mexican episodes. The series is didactic in its explanations of customs and its assertions of commonalities between the peoples of the United States and Mexico. Although they can draw on stereotypes, these conversations are an effort to celebrate Mexican culture and to appreciate cultural differences between the United States and Mexico.

"Happy Birthday . . . Everybody" (third season, 1968) opens with Robinson and Scott at a site overlooking Guanajuato. They enjoy the view and identify the site as a monument to the Mexican Revolution. Rosie (this episode's guide and Robinson's sex interest) tells Robinson that bargaining with vendors is expected when shopping in Mexico. As Robinson buys a toy from a boy for three pesos (down from five), he explains that one peso is worth 20 cents. Later, at the historic Teatro Juarez, a long take tracks with strolling mariachis into a town square where Robinson regales a group of rapt children with the story of "mama burro, papa burro, and baby burro" as Rosie translates.

"Bet Me a Dollar" (first season, 1966) uses a wager to motivate tours of Mexico City and the countryside. The episode opens with generic signifiers of Latin America: a flamenco guitarist and dancer. Robinson intervenes as two men beat up a third against a wall scrawled with "Viva El Presidente" graffiti.[18] In the scuffle, Robinson is scratched by a knife infected with anthrax. Unaware of the impending danger from his wound, Robinson and Scott alleviate their boredom between missions by playing "hide-and-seek"—Robinson takes a 24-hour headstart and Scott tries to find him. The chase passes through diverse places that illustrate the range of Mexican life accessible to tourists: a river boat fiesta in Xochimilco; in Mexico City, the grounds of the university with its Diego Rivera mural; a bus ride to the country. Rustic spectacle—a collage with a religious shrine, a peasant driving a burro-drawn cart along a country road—converges with the modern world, illustrated here by a village pharmacy where a young woman welcomes the chance to speak English. The *I Spy* Mexican travelogues depict Mexico as a synthesis of rural and modern life.

Enloe observes that "tourism [is a] motor for global integration . . . drawing previously 'remote' societies into the International system, usually on unequal terms."[19] To a degree this is the case in *I Spy*, in which emulating the greater economic privilege of the United States is assumed to be a natural and attractive goal for Mexico. In "Bet Me a Dollar," Robinson enlists Ramon, a boy who earns money shining shoes, to help him elude Scott. Introducing Ramon to credit cards ("very progressive, no?") and expense accounts, Robinson interpellates Ramon into modern corporate business practices, situating the man (the U.S. present) and the boy (Mexico's future) in what Dean MacCannell describes as "mutual complicity . . . the interaction between the postmodern tourist and the ex-primitive."[20] However, the episode avoids making an easy distinction between modern urban progress and rural underdevelopment. When Robinson needs emergency medical aid, for example; a villager provides alternative medicine—herbs that effectively reduce his fever and save his life.

In the Mexico episodes, *I Spy* appreciates cultural differences, suppresses politics, and naturalizes a humanistic unity between the peoples of the United States and Mexico. The fight that begins "Bet Me a Dollar" takes place in front of political graffiti. Lest a causal connection be drawn between bacterial warfare and presidential politics, a Mexican doctor explains that the fight was caused by "machismo—who is the better man." Robinson understands: "We call it the same thing." At the university, Ramon confidently points to an optimistic future through education, explaining that "there are many students here ready to serve Mexico." Mexico's Left, which might have played a narrative role the way Italy's did in "Tonia," is repressed in favor of tourism and humanism.[21]

The Mexico episodes often have little directly to do with the Cold War, and the Mexican people are not implicated in a Communist conspiracy for world domination. Instead, Mexico provides an opportunity for *I Spy* to assert friendly relations and cultural similarity with a foreign country situated at the U.S. border. Yet, Soviet presence in the Mexico episodes is a reminder of the Cold War in Latin America and Cuba. However, instead of emphasizing Cold War vigilance in Mexico, *I Spy* presents a collegial fraternity between Soviet and U.S. spies. This relationship lowers the international stakes: even as they work against each other on opposite sides, the spies share mutual understanding and respect. Mexico is a haven from the stresses of espionage work for the Soviet agents as much as it is for the Americans.

In "A Day Called 4 Jaguar" (first season, 1966), a Soviet air force officer (Dimitri, a "people's hero" who wears the Order of Lenin) finds refuge from a goodwill tour of Latin America by hiding out in a remote Mexican village that retains Aztec rituals. This episode introduces Mexico's Aztec past through the living history museum of the village. The interpretation of Aztec culture is delivered through both the Soviet and American tourist-spies. Scott reads from a book about Mexico, describing Quetzalcoatl and his place in Aztec lore—twice, as if it were too complex to understand one time through. He works to pronounce the god's name correctly.

Dimitri hears a physical resemblance to Quetzalcoatl, a "bearded blue-eyed man." A student of anthropology and Aztec culture before his military service, Dimitri is attracted to the village for its "timelessness and innocence, purity." He explains that the villagers know that he is not actually Quetzalcoatl, but they use him as a reminder of Aztec life. The villagers serve meals ("cooked in this exact manner for 2,000 years") and prepare baths (Scott squirms in the hot tub as comic relief while

Robinson negotiates with Dimitri). However, the U.S. spies observe that the Aztec villagers do not live completely in the past. As Robinson and Scott pass a man working with an acetylene torch, they comment on the "ancient and modern mix" and "overlapping cultures." The Aztec villagers have no dialogue and express themselves only through their actions. Aztec identity is defined by the U.S. and Soviet tourist-agents, who merge anthropological observations with nostalgia for a bucolic past.

Unlike the Aztec villagers, other rural Mexicans in the episode vocally resent and resist the U.S. presence in Mexico. In *I Spy*, economic difference tends to be suppressed, but occasionally tensions emerge from the imperialist advantages that make Mexico available for U.S. tourism. As Scott and Robinson search for Dimitri in villages, they offer money ("$15 . . . $20 . . . name your own price") for guides into the jungle. In one village, Robinson and Scott are surrounded by threatening male peasants: "You Americans come here waving your dollars and we, like hungry dogs, are expected to do tricks for that. What do you know of a man's pride, his honor? No man in this village will accept your insulting offer." Although *I Spy* episodes regularly include opportunities for the agents to counter anti-U.S. sentiments, here their only response is to flee from these peasants, whose animosity is grounded in the unequal economic and political relationship between the United States and Mexico.

Robinson is the lead signifier of the pleasures and freedoms of U.S. economic and patriarchal imperialism: he is a guide to the benefits of corporate capitalism and to sex tourism; he is the hip white American male tourist, free to travel and free to engage in sexual relations with native women. As Enloe explains, "[The] male tourist . . . is freed from standards of behavior imposed by respectable women back home. . . . Local women are welcoming and available in their femininity."[22] Part of Robinson's attractiveness is the assumption that he holds an income that can contribute to personal and local economies. *I Spy* adopts a well-known argument about tourism: "There is no difference between [the locals] and Europeans, with the single exception that the Europeans have money and [the locals] don't."[23]

In "Happy Birthday . . . Everybody," Rosie wants Robinson to buy her things; "I want one" (a pinata). "Can I have this?" (a primitive statue). "I want it" (a huge vase). When Robinson resists, saying that the vase is too large for her apartment, Rosie replies, "It was big enough for you wasn't it? And you're taller." Although Rosie is probably not a prostitute and does not appear impoverished, Enloe observes that "sex tourism requires Third World women to be economically desperate enough to enter prostitution."[24] Part of the attraction of the white male tourist is that he is backed with first world capital.

On one level, *I Spy* offers a world that is apparently "color blind" in that the agents travel without anyone (except Communists) noticing that Scott is black or that the partnership is interracial. However, the spies are not equal in terms of their sexual activity. Although their mission benefits from the attractiveness of both men to women,[25] *I Spy* tends to suppress the black man's sexuality. Although some television historians claim that Scott had equal access to romance, in *I Spy* sex tourism is more available for the white man. Robinson is presented as irresistible to women: he is a sexually available and attractive American version of James Bond. Women ogle Robinson as he walks by. In "Bet Me a Dollar," two women compete over the quality of the repair to Robinson's pants, torn in the knife fight ("I could do it better." "No, you couldn't."), and a nurse asks him for a date. "A Day Called 4 Jaguar" opens with Robinson and a Mexican woman making out among lush foliage.

Although he has his share of body display and shirtless screentime, Scott's sexuality is marginalized relative to Robinson's. "Bet Me a Dollar" ends in Acapulco, where Robinson enjoys a backrub from a Mexican woman while Scott sits under an umbrella with the boy, Ramon. In "A Day Called 4 Jaguar," Robinson banters with a woman from a synchronized swim team while Scott comically flaps around in goggles and swim fins. In "It's All Done with Mirrors" (first season, 1966), Scott quietly steps aside and waits for his more adventuresome partner to return from a tryst. In all of these examples, the black male tourist-spy functions as a sidekick to the more sexually active white male tourist-spy.

Richard Dyer observes in *White*. "The point of seeing the racing of whites is to dislodge them/us from the position of power, with all the inequities, oppression, privileges and sufferings in its train, dislodging them/us by undercutting the authority with which they/we speak and act in and on the

127

world." Despite inequalities in the actions available to Robinson and to Scott, *I Spy* boldly sustained an argument for racial equality for three seasons on prime-time television. Its discourses on domestic civil rights and geopolitics echo those offered by John F. Kennedy in his inaugural address on January 20, 1961:

> *[We are] unwilling to witness or permit the slow undoing of those human rights to which this Nation has always been committed, and to which we are committed today at home and around the world. . . . Let every nation know . . . that we shall pay any price, bear any burden, meet any hardship, support any friend, oppose any foe, in order to assure the survival and the success of liberty.*

Each week, *I Spy* dramatized this effort to create harmony between two seemingly incongruous goals: social justice and global hegemony. Through its interracial partners and its insistence that state security is enhanced by racial equality, *I Spy* affirms the value of civil rights for the United States, at home and overseas.[24]

Notes

1. Advocacy groups had pressured U.S. television to improve its representation of blacks since the early 1950s when *Amos 'n' Andy* (cas, 1951–53) was on the air, but it was not until the widespread civil rights activism of the 1960s that the television industry responded. See Kathrya C. Montgomery, *Target Prime Time: Advocacy Groups and the Struggle over Entertainment Television* (New York: Oxford University Press, 1989). Although they credit civil rights activism for influencing the networks, Woll and Miller also recognize that 1960s television advertising practices allowed African Americans to become identified as a demographic group with disposable income. See Allen L. Woll and Randall M. Miller, *Ethnic and Racial Images in American Film and Television: Historical Essays and Bibliography* (New York: Garland Publishing, 1987), 72–77.

2. Cynthia Enloe, *Bananas, Beaches, and Bases: Making Feminist Sense of International Politics* (Berkeley: University of California Press, 1989). 26, 35–40. Enloe derives the term "living postcards" from world's fair displays of other cultures.

    From the start, Sheldon Leonard's conception of the series integrated the travelogue: "The spy genre would yield opportunities for action and adventure and would give us the mobility I wanted. It could take us into obscure, picturesque corners of the world" (Leonard, *And the Show Goes On: Broadway and Hollywood Adventures* [New York: Limelight Editions, 1995], 144).

3. J. Fred MacDonald, *Blacks and White TV: Afro-Americans in Television since 1948* (Chicago: Nelson-Hall Publishers, 1983), 109–12: Woll and Miller, *Ethnic and Racial Images in American Film and Television*, 72; Eric Barnouw, *Tube of Plenty: The Evolution of American Television*, 2d rev. ed. (New York: Oxford University Press, 1990), 370–72. Cosby crossed over into white-dominated television as guest host for *The Tonight Show* and host of a television documentary about African American history (Woll and Miller, *Ethnic and Racial Images in American Film and Television*, 77). Phillip Brian Harper, "Televisual Representation and the Claims of 'the Black Experience.'" *Living Color: Race and Television in the United States*, ed. Sasha Torres (Durham: Duke University Press, 1998), 67–68. Despite reports of Interracial romances (see ibid., 77), Scott was usually reserved for African American women characters such as those played by Barbara McNair in "Night Train to Madrid" (second season, 1967) or Lesiey Uggams in "Tonia."

4. Several people have told me that they remember *I Spy* opening with the silhouettes of two men holding tennis rackets that became guns. However, available videotapes of *I Spy* present only one man in silhouette.

5. Andy East, *The Cold War File* (Metuchen, N.J.: Scarecrow Press, 1983), 299–300. For a discussion of James Bond's cultural location, including his transformation from book to film, see

Tony Bennett and Janet Woollacott, *Bond and Beyond: The Political Career of a Popular Hero* (New York: Methuen, 1987).

6. I am grateful to Tim Anderson for telling me about Moe Berg. See Nicholas Dawidoff, *The Catcher Was a Spy: The Mysterious Life of Moe Berg* (New York: Pantheon, 1994). The Olympic games have long been caught up in international affairs, and this theme is developed in *I Spy's* first episode, discussed in this essay.

Exhibition tennis forms part of the verisimilitude of *I Spy*, as does the increasing visibility of tennis champions of color. In *Off the Court*, Arthur Ashe deliberates on race and tennis: how the class status of tennis makes it difficult for nonwhites to become tennis players; how Ashe coped with being the "first black" to win tennis competitions; the awareness of race among Third World tennis players (described by Pancho Segura as "brown bodies"); the blackpower salute from the winners' platform at the 1968 Olympics in Mexico City. See Arthur Ashe with Neil Amdur, *Off the Court* (New York: New American Library, 1981). For a history of tennis, see United States Lawn Tennis Association, *Official Encyclopedia of Tennis* (New York: Harper and Row, 1972), 1–68.

For examples of 1960s political comedy, see Frank Kofsky, *Lenny Bruce: The Comedian as Social Critic and Secular Moralist* (New York, Monad Press, 1974); and Dick Gregory, *From the Back of the Bus* (New York: E. P. Dutton, 1962).

7. By the mid-1960s, television was well on the way to a complete conversion to color. The major manufacturer in the TV Industry, RCA, joined its broadcast partner, NBC, to open the television market to color. See Brad Chisholm, "Red, Blue, and Lots of Green: The Impact of Color Television on Feature Film Production," in *Hollywood in the Age of Television*, ed. Tino Balio (Boston: Unwin Hyman, 1990), 227.

Despite a production budget that invested in foreign locations as well as color, *I Spy* had to overcome equipment problems before it hit its stride as a travelogue. *Variety's* review of the first episode was critical: "The location work in Hong Kong was a dishevelled patchwork." Indeed, Leonard describes the difficulties the crew encountered with rental equipment in Hong Kong (Leonard, *And the Show Goes On*, 148–49). Yet, transporting production equipment was extremely expensive. Leonard credits *I Spy* cinematographer Fouad Said with designing the solution: the Cinemobile, a location van outfitted with compact production gear and small enough to be loaded into a cargo plane (ibid., 153–55).

Variety was more pleased with the quality of *I Spy's* second-season opener: "Producer Sheldon Leonard has learned to gain maximum production values from exteriors [in Palm Springs]." At the beginning of *I Spy's* third season, *Variety* glowed that *I Spy* holds the "distinction as one of video's better travelogs . . . even on the smallscreen those 35mm vistas panned beautifully in color" (reviews of *I Spy* in *Variety*, 22 September 1965, 21 September 1966, 13 September 1967).

Shooting on location also supplied grist for *I Spy's* publicity (see Sheldon Leonard, "Having a wonderful time—except, of course, for that typhoon and a few other mishaps." *TV Guide*, 24 July, 1965, 6–9; Dick Hobson, "The Ptomaine in Spain Came Mainly on the Plane," *TV Guide*, 25 March 1967, 15–18).

I Spy's location work also circumvented unions and "Model T techniques" in Hollywood. *TV Guide* reported that Said practiced techniques so "incendiary . . . that for many years his own union barred him from shooting in the U.S. It feared that, were his practices to be adopted, whole complexes of studios, soundstages and backlots would be obsolete overnight; vast inventories of archaic cameras, lights, arcs, generators, dollies and microphones would be relegated to the junkpiles; and armies of super-annuated technicians would be mercifully released to retirement" (Dick Hobson, "Little Fou's Big Revolution," *TV Guide*, 23 March 1968, 22–27).

I Spy was not the first Sheldon Leonard television show to use foreign locations. Producer Leonard took *Make Room for Daddy/The Danny Thomas Show* (ABC, 1953–57; CBS 1957–65) to England, Ireland, France, and Italy "to get it away from the confines of Stage Five and open it up." He found the creative challenges of "working on foreign locations immensely stimulating" (see Leonard, *And the Show Goes On*, 97–98). The *I Spy* chapters of Leonard's autobiography are replete with anecdotes about shooting on location in Asia, Europe, and Mexico.

8. James Der Derian's poststructuralist analysis of international relations describes the "collective alienation" in which countries become "dependent on a common diplomatic culture as well as a collective estrangement" from other state systems, in the "modern panopilcism" of espionage, Robinson and Scott are HUMINT—human intelligence operatives. Although still important to state security, HUMINT "lacks the ubiquity, resolution, and pantoscopic power of the technical intelligence system" (TECHINT, COMINT, ELINT, RADINT, TELINT, PHOTOINT) (Der Derian, *Antidiplomacy: Spies, Terror, Speed, and War* [Cambridge, Mass.: Blackwell, 1992], 30–31).

    For insider descriptions of espionage work see Jock Haswell, *Spies and Spymasters: A Concise History of Intelligence* (London: Thames and Hudson, 1977); Joachim Joesten, *They Call it Intelligence: Spies and Spy Techniques since World War II* (New York: Abelard-Schuman, 1963); Sir Kenneth Strong, *Men of Intelligence: A Study of the Roles and Decisions of Chiefs of Intelligence from World War I to the Present Day* (London: Cassell, 1970); Nigel West, *Games of Intelligence: The Classified Conflict of International Espionage* (London: Weidenfeld and Nicolson, 1989).

    Allen Dulles, the first director of the CIA, who served until the Bay of Pigs failure, "saw the whole world as an area of conflict, in which the prime duty of an intelligence service was to provide its government with warning of hostile or provocative acts wherever they might occur. . . . [Dulles believed that] a close-knit and coordinated intelligence community, constantly on the alert, should be able to report accurately and quickly on developments in any part of the globe" (Strong, *Men of Intelligence*, 128). Indeed, one can ponder the role television journalists might have played in Cold War espionage and the verisimilitude of *I Spy*. In *I Spy*'s first episode, the end credits thank NBC's Far Eastern news staff for their cooperation.

9. *I Spy* does not set up a simple opposition between Communism and democracy. "It's All Done with Mirrors" (first season, 1966) ends with some cynicism about Cold War alliances and U.S. state power. Dr. Zoltan Karolyl is a Soviet brainwashing expert ("hate me . . . love me . . . obey me") who has set up a laboratory in Acapulco to create "a universe of pain" from which Robinson will "do anything, believe anything, to escape." Karolyl attempts to condition Robinson to kill Scott in public and thereby embarrass the United States. In a finale set against the ocean harbors of Acapulco, Scott relies on his three-year friendship with Robinson to break Karolyl's conditioning. Unlike the Soviet agent in "A Day 4 Jaguar," who killed his lifelong friend out of loyalty to the state, Robinson withstands the urge to assassinate Scott. Captured, Karolyl defects to the United States ("I am corrupt") and asks to continue his brainwashing experiments for the United States in Mexico. Robinson mutters that the United States will probably take the offer and then assign Robinson and Scott to be Karolyl's bodyguards. Although Robinson and Scott are certainly loyal to the United States, they occasionally express a weariness about government authority and the exigencies of spywork.

10. Barnouw, *Tube of Plenty*, 367: Joesten, *They Call it Intelligence*, 226; see also intelligence histories cited above.

11. Dudziak argues that "the Soviet Union increased its use of race in anti-American propaganda; by 1949. American race relations were a 'principle Soviet propaganda theme.'" With race discrimination giving a propaganda advantage to the Soviet bloc, the U.S. government "came to realize that if [it] wished to save Third World countries for democracy, [it] would have to improve the image of American race relations" (Dudziak, "Josephine Baker, Racial Protest, and the Cold War," *Journal of American History*, 81, no. 2 [September 1994]: 543–46).

12. Ibid., 568. She explains that Baker, Robeson, and DuBois "angered [U.S.] government officials" who "attempt[ed] to counter the influence of such critics . . . by sending speakers around the world who would say the right things about American race relations. The 'right thing' was: yes, there are racial problems in the United States, but it was through democratic processes

(not communism) that optimal social change for African Americans would occur" (ibid., 546). An exemplar of this position was New York Representative and "staunch civil rights advocate [Adam Clayton] Powell [who] refused to criticize the United States before a foreign audience" (ibid., 557). As Herman Gray observes. "For all of their limits and contradictions, commercial network television's representations of blackness are socially and culturally rooted someplace and are in dialogue with very real issues" (Gray, *Watching Race: Television and the Struggle for "Blackness"* [Minneapolis: University of Minnesota Press, 1995], 55).

13. See Dick Hobson, "He bears witness to his beliefs," *TV Guide*, 15 January 1966, 10–12. In this story, Cosby comments, "We don't have any race jokes in the scripts. Even in real life, race jokes would be embarrassing to Bobby and embarrassing to me."

14. In the 1960s, the People's Republic of China organized the Games of the New Emerging Forces (GANEFA) during the debate over whether Taiwan or China would be the official Chinese representative to the Olympics (see Jonathan Kolatch, *Sports, Politics, and Ideology in China* [New York: Jonathan David Publishers, 1972]). Awam Amkpa, Phebe Chao, and Roger Sorkin have all shared with me anecdotal accounts of the China-Africa relationship during this period. In the late 1960s, the People's Republic of China built stadia and theaters across Africa as gifts of friendship.

15. Culp came to *I Spy* as an experienced television lead actor: Cosby came from stand-up comedy (including three record albums and a Grammy) with television exposure mostly on *The Tonight Show* (NBC, 1954–) (MacDonald, *Blacks and White TV*, 100; and Robert de Ronos, "The Spy Who Came in for the Gold," *TV Guide*, 23 October 1965, 17). De Roos explains that Culp and Cosby developed "a language of their own." The combination of Culp's 1960s hipster word play and Cosby's facility with stand-up contributed to the verbal style of the show, what *Variety* described as "good voice overlap form, though this hits gets a bit strained after a time" (review of *I Spy*, *Variety*, 13 September 1967). Leonard found that the banter became a problem: "It's easy to be amused by a witty ad lib and to overlook the damage it's doing to the structure of the tale you're telling. . . . What had started as harmless interjections became increasingly intrusive ad-libs, often inconsistent with the story line" (see Leonard, *And the Show Goes On*, 171–73).

16. Scott/Cosby appears in nearly every scene in the credits sequence of this episode.

17. This strategy appears in other *I Spy* episodes. See discussion of "It's All Done with Mirrors" in note 9. Considering the series's Cold War attitude, it is interesting to note that Leonard attempted to coproduce *I Spy* "stories that emphasized the benefits of cooperation between the great powers" with the Soviet Union. Negotiations broke down when Leonard determined that it would take more than twice the time to film an episode in the Soviet Union (Leonard, *And the Show Goes On*, 193–95).

18. *I Spy* often uses posters and graffiti to identify a country and its politics.

19. Enloe, *Bananas, Beaches, and Bases*, 31.

20. Dean MacCannell, *Empty Meeting Grounds: The Tourist Papers* (New York: Routledge, 1992), 30.

21. Mexico has long had an open door for travel by Soviets. Filmmaker Sergei Eisenstein traveled and worked in Mexico in the early 1930s. Guidebooks direct tourists to the house in Coyoacan, near Mexico City, where Leon Trotsky was assassinated in 1940. For a survey of Cold War struggles over Latin America see George Black, *The Good Neighbor: How the United States Wrote the History of Central America and the Caribbean* (New York: Pantheon, 1988). For discussion of the 1968 student rebellion in Mexico City see James M. Goodsell, "Mexico: Why the Students Rioted," *Essays on the Student Movement*, ed. Patrick Gleeson (Columbus, Ohio: Charles E. Merrill, 1970), 91–99.

22. Enloe, *Bananas, Beaches, and Bases*, 28, 32.

23. MacCannell, *Empty Meeting Grounds*, 41.

24. Enloe, *Bananas, Beaches, and Bases*, 36.

25 Although the sexually available agent is part of the pleasure of spy fiction, MacCannell argues that the unattached agent is also important to maintaining the security of the state: "Heterosexual arrangements . . . disrupt the individual's attachment to 'higher' orders of organization: for example, the gang, the state, the corporation. . . . A man who can be entirely satisfied by the love and companionship of a woman is lost to the state" (MacCannell, *Empty Meeting Grounds*, 60).

"Happy Birthday . . . Everybody" illustrates this point. An explosives expert has escaped from prison and seeks to kill the U.S. agent who "red dogged" him. The agent, now retired, lives peacefully with his young American wife and their son outside Guanajuato. The criminal places explosives in a piñata, intending to blow up the family during the boy's birthday party. The agent's age and his devotion to family separate him from effective action, compelling Robinson and Scott to watch over the family's safety.

26 Richard Dyer, *White* (London: Routledge, 1997), 2.

"Is This What You Mean by Color TV?"
Race, Gender, and Contested Meanings in NBC's Julia

Aniko Bodroghkozy

America in 1968: Police clash with the militant Black Panthers while one of the group's leaders, Huey Newton, is sentenced for murder; civil rights leader Martin Luther King is assassinated in Tennessee, sparking violent uprisings and riots in the nation's black ghettos; the massive Poor People's Campaign, a mobilization of indigent blacks and whites, sets up a tent city on the Mall in Washington, D.C.; at Cornell University, armed black students sporting bandoliers take over the administration building and demand a black studies program.[1] In the midst of all these events—events that many Americans saw as a revolutionary or at least an insurrectionary situation among the black population—NBC introduced the first situation comedy to feature an African-American in the starring role since *Amos 'n' Andy* and *Beulah* went off the air in the early 1950s.[2] *Julia*, created by writer-producer Hal Kanter, a Hollywood liberal Democrat who campaigned actively for Eugene McCarthy, starred Diahann Carroll as a middle-class, widowed nurse trying to bring up her six-year-old-son, Corey. After the death of her husband in a helicopter crash in Vietnam, Julia and Corey move to an integrated apartment complex, and she finds work in an aerospace industry clinic.

NBC executives did not expect the show to succeed.[3] They scheduled it opposite the hugely successful *Red Skelton Show*, where it was expected to die a noble, dignified death, having demonstrated the network's desire to break the prime-time color bar. Unexpectedly, the show garnered high ratings and lasted a respectable three years.

Despite its success, or perhaps because of it, *Julia* was a very controversial program. Beginning in popular magazine articles written before the first episode even aired and continuing more recently in historical surveys of the portrayals of blacks on American television, critics have castigated *Julia* for being extraordinarily out of touch with and silent on the realities of African-American life in the late 1960s. While large numbers of blacks lived in exploding ghettos, Julia and Corey Baker lived a luxury lifestyle impossible on a nurse's salary. While hostility and racial tensions brewed, and the Kerner Commission Report on Civil Disorders described an America fast becoming two nations separate and unequal, tolerance and colorblindness prevailed on *Julia*.

The show came in for heavy criticism most recently in J. Fred Mac-Donald's *Blacks and White TV: Afro-Americans in Television Since 1948*. MacDonald describes *Julia* as a "comfortable image of black success . . . in stark juxtaposition to the images seen on local and national newscasts."[4] The show, according to MacDonald, refused to be topical; when dealing with racial issues at all, it did so only in one-liners. He also describes black and white discomfort with the show, claiming that the series was a sell-out intended to assuage white consciences and a "saccharine projection of the 'good life' to be achieved by those blacks who did not riot, who acted properly, and worked within the system."[5]

MacDonald's text-based criticism of *Julia* would appear to be quite justified. However, there was a whole range of politically charged meanings attributed to the program during its network run that critics like MacDonald haven't discussed. What critics of the program have ignored are the diverse and often conflicted ways in which both the producers and viewers of *Julia* struggled to make sense of the show in the context of the racial unrest and rebellions erupting throughout American society. Historically situated in a period of civil dislocations when massive numbers of black Americans were attempting, both peacefully and not so peacefully, to redefine their place within the sociopolitical landscape, *Julia* functioned as a symptomatic text—symptomatic of the racial tensions and reconfigurations of its time.

The extent to which *Julia* functioned as a site of social tension is particularly evident in the viewer response mail and script revisions in the files of producer Hal Kanter, and it is also apparent in critical articles written for the popular press at the time.[6] These documents allow us to begin to reconstruct the contentious dialogue that took place among audiences, magazine critics, and the show's producer and writers. They also provide clues to how such conflicts materialized in the program narrative itself. A key feature of this dialogue was a discursive struggle over what it meant to be black and what it meant to be white at the close of the 1960s. Black viewers, white viewers, and critics all made sense of the program in notably different ways. Although a struggle over racial representation was the overt issue, their responses to the program also occasionally exhibited a nascent, if conflicted, attempt to speak about gender and the representation of women.

Producing Difference

The script files in the Hal Kanter papers show quite clearly how Kanter and his production team struggled to construct images of African-Americans in the context of the civil rights movement. Particularly revealing is the file for a 1968 episode entitled "Take My Hand, I'm a Stranger in the Third Grade," which contains the initial six-page outline (the first working out of the episode's storyline) and a thirty-six-page first draft script (the first fleshing out of the story in dialogue form) written by Ben Gershman and Gene Boland, the latter one of the series' four black writers.[7]

The story revolved around Corey's friend Bedelia Sanford, a black schoolmate who tried to win his affection by stealing toys for him. In the original storyline, Julia confronted Bedelia's mother, who lived in a slum with numerous children. She flared up at Julia's expressions of sympathy for her situation, calling Julia "one of those uppitty [*sic*] high-class Colored ladies who thinks she's somebody because she went to college and has a profession. Well, says Mrs. S., she's got a profession too—she's on welfare." Hal Kanter underlined that final line and wrote in the margin next to it: "NO, SIRS!"

In the first draft script, Mrs. Sanford had suddenly metamorphosed into an upper-class black woman whose preoccupation with money-making pulled her away from attending to her daughter. When Julia accused her of trying to buy Bedelia's love, Mrs. Sanford accused Julia of "always tearing down our own." She called Julia a mediocre Negro who had attained all the status she would ever have. Julia retorted, "[B]ut that Gauguin print and that Botticelli and your *white maid* all rolled together isn't going to change the fact that you are a failure as a mother."

The adjustment of the Sanfords' economic status upward indicates that Kanter and his writers were uncertain and anxious about their depiction of black Americans. The characters were either demeaning ghetto stereotypes or they were upper-class "white Negroes," a term used by critics to describe Julia. The stereotypical images of African-American life that most whites had previously taken for granted had, by the late sixties, become, at least to *Julia*'s creators, problematic constructs. As predominantly white creators of black characters, Kanter and his writing team wanted to avoid racist representations but appeared stumped in their attempt to come up with something that wasn't merely a binary opposition. The repertoire of black images was inadequate and there was no new repertoire on which to draw.

While racial depiction and definition functioned as a highly politicized dilemma for the producers of *Julia*, the question of gender representation was another matter. One might expect that a program dealing with a working woman's attempts to raise her child alone would open a space for questioning sexual inequality. If scenes from the series' first episode and pilot are any indication, this appears not to have been the case. While racist depictions of blacks were being questioned, sexist portrayals of women were not. The show and its creators seemed as blithely unconscious in their portrayal of women as they were self-conscious in their portrayal of blacks.

The first episode of the series, "The Interview," written by Hal Kanter and aired September 24, 1968, includes the following scene between Julia and her future boss, Dr. Chegley.[8] Julia had just entered Chegley's office to be interviewed for a nurse's position. Chegley had his back to Julia as she entered. He looked at an X-ray and, without looking at her, asked her to identify it. She replied that it was a chest X-ray. He then turned to face her and the following dialogue ensued:

> CHEGLEY: You have a healthy looking chest. . . . I believe you're here to beg me for a job.
>
> JULIA: I'm here at your invitation, Doctor, to be interviewed for a position as a nurse. I don't beg for anything.
>
> CHEGLEY: I'll keep that in mind, Walk around.
>
> JULIA: Beg your pardon?
>
> CHEGLEY: You just said you don't beg for anything.
>
> JULIA: That's just a figure of speech.
>
> CHEGLEY: I'm interested in your figure without the speech. Move. Let me see if you can walk.
>
> JULIA: I can. [*Walking*] I come from a long line of pedestrians.
>
> CHEGLEY: Turn around. [*As she does*] You have a very well-formed fantail. [*As she reacts*] That's Navy terminology. I spent thirty years in uniform. [*Then*] Do you wear a girdle?
>
> JULIA: No, sir.
>
> CHEGLEY: I do. I have a bad back, Now you can sit down.

The pilot, "Mama's Man," also written by Kanter, contains a similar scene.[9] Julia was being interviewed by a manager at Aerospace Industries, Mr. Colton, who became very flustered when he saw Julia. He told her that all her qualifications were in order, but that she was not what he expected. Julia asked whether she should have been younger or older, or, "Should I have written at the top of that application—in big, bold, black letters, 'I'm a Negro?!' " Cohon told her that had nothing to do with it. The problem was that she was too pretty. "When we employ nurses far less attractive than you, we find that we lose many man-hours. Malingerers, would-be Romeos, that sort of thing. In your case, you might provoke a complete work stoppage."

In contemporary terms these two scenes display examples of the most egregious sexism and sexual harassment. However, when the episodes aired, the women's liberation movement, which dates its public birth to the Miss America pageant protest on September 7, 1968, was not yet a part of public consciousness. *Julia*'s creators thus did not yet have to contend with the oppositional voices of the women's movement. On the other hand, the producers were quite concerned with the highly visible civil rights and black power movements, and were well aware of the fact that representations of racial discrimination and harassment were now socially and politically unacceptable. The scenes from these two episodes of *Julia* reveal a self-conscious understanding of that unacceptability; however, anxiety about that situation resulted in a displacement. Discrimination and harassment were shifted from racism onto sexism. Both job interview scenes needed to relieve the anxiety created over Julia's difference. The writers could not allow her racial difference to function as an appropriate reason for the denial of a job or for demeaning banter, but there were no such political taboos in relation to her sexual difference.

Conflicted Reception

The conflicted production process can indicate some of the ways in which *Julia* worked through social and political anxieties in American culture in the late 1960s. However, the interpretive strategies brought to bear upon the text both by critics and by viewers are even more significant because they can show us how these tensions and conflicts were dealt with by different social groups within American society at the time.

Recent work in cultural studies has demonstrated that meanings are not entirely determined by the text or by its producers. As Stuart Hall's "encoding-decoding" model has shown, readers of a text are active agents and need not accept the meanings constructed by a text's producers. Readers can oppose or negotiate with the meanings that the text promotes as the correct or preferred interpretation.[10] By examining how audiences interpreted *Julia*, we can see how the crisis in race relations grew as people attempted to come to grips with the meanings of racial difference in the face of militant challenges by a black oppositional movement.

By juxtaposing the interpretive strategies and discourses mobilized by critics writing in the popular press and by viewers writing to Kanter or to the network, we can examine how privileged cultural elites interpreted the show as well as how television viewers constructed meanings often at odds with those of the critics. The viewer mail (some 151 letters and postcards) filed in the Hal Kanter papers provides a particularly rich case study of how *Julia*'s audiences attempted to make sense of the program and how they grappled with racial difference and social change through their engagement with the show. At times, the statements in the letters echo those in the popular press; more frequently, both the reading strategies and the debates are different. Many of the letters have carbon copy responses from Kanter attached, setting up a fascinating, often contentious dialogue. But what is most compelling about the letters is the way they reveal the remarkably conflicted, diverse, and contradictory responses among audience members.

These letters, the majority of which came from married women, should not be seen as representative of the larger audience's responses to the program.[11] Letter writers tend to be a particularly motivated group of television viewers. There is no way to determine whether the sentiments that crop up over and over again in the letters were wide-spread among viewers who did not write to the producers. Thus my analysis of these letters is not an attempt to quantify the *Julia* audience or to use the documents as a representative sample. While neither the letter writers nor the critics in the popular press were representative of the audience as a whole, their readings were symptomatic of struggles over racial definition. Perhaps, then, the best way to work with these documents is to see them as traces, clues, parts of a larger whole to which we have no access. Indeed, like all histories of audience reception, this one presents partial knowledge, pieces of the past that we must interpret in a qualified manner.[12]

One trend that became evident almost immediately among the favorable letters written by white viewers was a marked self-consciousness about racial self-identification: "I am white, but I enjoy watching 'Julia.'"[13] "Our whole family from great grandmother down to my five year old, loved it. We just happen to be caucasian." "As a 'white middle class Jewish' teacher, may I say that it is finally a pleasure to turn on the T.V. and see contemporary issues treated with honesty, humor, and sensitivity."[14]

One way in which to account for the self-consciousness of many letter writers identifying themselves as whites was that the novelty of a black-centered program raised questions about traditional and previously unexamined definitions of racial identity and difference. One mother of two boys in Ohio struggled with this very issue in her letter:

> *Being a white person I hope this program helps all of us to understand each other.
> Maybe if my children watch this program they will also see the good side of Negro
> people [rather] than all the bad side they see on the news programs such as riots,
> sit-ins, etc. I know this program will help my two sons so when they grow up they
> won't be so prejudice[sic].*

While the woman made some problematic distinctions between good black people and bad black people, there was an attempt to grapple with racial difference. Definitions of what it meant to be white had suddenly become an uncertain terrain. The crisis in race relations signified by "riots, sit-ins, etc." made the black population visible, and the depiction of African-Americans had ceased to be a stable field. As representations of black people had become an arena of contested meanings, so too had self-representations of whites become uncertain. One manifestation of that uncertainty was self-consciousness. In the aftermath of the civil rights movement and in the midst of black power sentiment, the question of what it now meant to be white in America was an issue that needed working through.

Another way to think about race was, perhaps paradoxically, to deny difference. A letter from a rather idealistic fifteen-year-old girl in Annandale, Virginia, affirmed, "Your new series has told me that at least SOME people have an idea of a peaceful and loving existence. So what if their skin pigmentation is different and their philosophies are a bit different than ours *they are still people*." Another woman from Manhattan Beach, California, who described her race as Caucasian and her ancestry as Mexican, wrote, "I love the show. Keep up the good work. This way the world will realize that the Negro is just like everyone else, with feelings and habits as the Whites have." A mother of twins in Highland Park, New Jersey, observed, "And it's immensely valuable to the many non-Negroes who just don't know any Negroes, or don't know that all people mostly behave like people."

Perhaps these viewers engaged in a denial of the "otherness" of black people in an attempt to reduce white anxiety about racial difference. By affirming that blacks were "just people" and just like everyone else, these viewers defined "everyone else" as white. White was the norm from which the Other deviated. In their sincere attempts to negotiate changing representations of race, these viewers denied that blacks historically had not fit the constructed norm of the white middle-class social formation. In this move, the viewers were, of course, assisted by the program itself. The show's theme music was a generic sit-com jingle lacking any nod to the rich traditions of African-American musical forms. Julia's apartment, while nicely appointed, and with a framed photo of her dead hero husband prominently displayed, was also completely generic. Unlike a comparable but more recent black family sitcom, *The Cosby Show*, with its lavish townhouse decorated with African-American artworks, Julia's home contained no culturally specific touches. Diahann Carroll's speech was also completely uninflected, on the one hand differentiating her from her prime-time predecessors such as *Amos 'n' Andy* and *Beulah*, but on the other hand evacuating as much ethnic and cultural difference as possible. For viewers picking up on the interpretive clues provided by the show, black people were "just people" to the extent that they conformed to an unexamined white norm of representation.

While this denial of difference may have been typical, it was by no means the dominant interpretive strategy employed by viewers who wrote letters. In fact, many viewers were clearly struggling with the problem of representation, both of blacks and of whites. The criticism leveled by many viewers—that the show was unrealistic and was not "telling it like it is"—reveals a struggle over how reality should be defined.

The refrain "tell it like it is" became a recurring theme in debates about *Julia*, both in the popular press and among the viewer letters. In a rather scathing review, *Time* magazine criticized the show for not portraying how black people really lived: "She [Julia] would not recognize a ghetto if she stumbled into it, and she is, in every respect save color, a figure in a white milieu."[15] Robert Lewis Shayon, the TV-radio critic for *Saturday Review*, was also particularly concerned with *Julia*'s deficiencies in representing this notion of a black reality. In the first of three articles on the series, he, like the *Time* reviewer, castigated the program for turning a blind eye to the realities of black life in the ghettos. For Shayon, the reality of the black experience was what was documented in the Kerner Commission report: "Negro youth, 'hustling in the jungle' of their 'crime-ridden, violence-prone, and poverty-stricken world'—that's the real problem, according to the commission report."[16] The world of *Julia*, on the other hand, was a fantasy because it did not focus on the problems of black youth (which for Shayon meant young black males) and because it did not take place in a ghetto environment. The unconsciously racist notion that the black experience was essentially a ghetto experience remained unexamined in these popular press accounts.

This attempt to define a singular, totalized "Negro reality" became a point of dispute in Shayon's follow-up columns on May 25 and July 20, 1968. Shayon received a letter in response to his first column from M.S. Rukeyser, Jr., NBC's vice president for press and publicity. He also received a letter from Dan Jenkins, an executive at the public relations firm handling television programming for General Foods, one of *Julia*'s main sponsors. Shayon juxtaposed the responses of these men to an interview given by Hal Kanter, which affirmed that the show would tell the truth, show it like it is. Shayon noted that Jenkins appeared to hold a contradictory view:

> *Jenkins, the publicity agent, wrote: "It is not, and never has been the function of a commercial series to 'show it as it is, baby.' On those rare occasions when the medium has taken a stab at limning the unhappy reality of what goes on in much of the world (e.g.,* East Side, West Side*), the public has quickly tuned out.*[17]

Shayon went on to quote from Rukeyser's letter: "We have no real quarrel with your [Shayon's] subjective judgment on the degree of lavishness of Julia's apartment, wardrobe, and way of life. There has been controversy within our own group about this."[18] Shayon also quoted from another interview with Kanter, who seemed to step back from his earlier stance. By "showing 'it like it is,' [Kanter] was talking not of ghetto life, but of 'humorous aspects of discrimination . . . properly handled . . . without rancor, without inflammation, and withal telling their attempts to enjoy the American dream.' "[19] In his article of July 20, 1968, Shayon added Diahann Carroll's response, quoting from an Associated Press story about the controversy generated by Shayon's initial article: "We're dealing with an entertainment medium. . . . *Julia* is a drama-comedy; it isn't politically oriented. Because I am black that doesn't mean I have to deal with problems of all black people."[20]

By bringing together the sentiments of the show's creator and its network, sponsor, and star, the Shayon pieces revealed just how conflicted the production process for *Julia* was. There was no consensus on what "telling it like it is" meant. Rukeyser's letter openly admitted to controversy over how Julia and her world should be depicted. Shayon's series of articles opened up for examination the problem of representation. If black identity had become a shifting field in the wake of the crisis in race relations, then "telling it like it is" would be impossible. Shayon thought he knew how *Julia* should tell it, but his articles indicated that in 1968 the program's creators were far less certain.

Unlike the critics, viewers generally did not want to relocate Julia and Corey to a ghetto. Instead, viewers who criticized the show for not "telling it like it is" were more concerned with the presentation of black characters than they were with the upscale setting. A male viewer in Chicago wrote:

> *On another point which bears remarks is the unwillingness to allow the program to be "black." I do not object to white people being in the cast. What I do object to is selecting the black cast from people (black people) who are so white oriented that everybody has a white mentality, that is, their expressions are all that of white people. Choose some people whose expressions and manners are unquestionably black. The baby-sitter was, for example, so white cultured that you would have thought she was caucasian except for the color of her skin.*

Hal Kanter's reply to this letter indicated how contested this issue was: "We all make mistakes, don't we, Mr. Banks? Please try to forgive me for mine in the spirit of universality and brotherhood we are attempting to foster."

Mr. Banks's letter revealed an uncertainty over how to portray black people. Kanter's testy reply indicated that despite his rhetoric of brotherhood (and sameness), this was a problem that plagued the show's creators—a problem already evident in the script development for "Take My Hand." How would one represent "unquestionably black" expressions and manner? The representation of "black" was defined by Mr. Banks negatively by what it was not: it was not white. The dilemma of what "black" signified outside a cultural system in which "white" was the norm was still left open to question.[21]

Other viewers, also uncomfortable with the unrealistic quality of the program, pointed out more problems in the representation of blacks. A woman in Berkeley, California, observed:

> *Your show is in a position to dispell [sic] so many misconceptions about Black people & their relationships to whites. I am just one of many who are so very disappointed in the outcome of such a promising show.*
>
> *Please, help to destroy the misconceptions—not reinforce them! Stop making Miss Carroll super-Negro and stop having blacks call themselves "colored"*

and make your characters less self-conscious and tell that "babysitter" to quit overacting.

This concern with representing blacks as "Super Negro" was also voiced in the popular press. In a *TV Guide* article in December 1968, Diahann Carroll was quoted saying:

> *With black people right now, we are all terribly bigger than life and more wonderful than life and smarter and better—because we're still proving. . . . For a hundred years we have been prevented from seeing accurate images of ourselves and we're all overconcerned and overreacting. The needs of the white writer go to the superhuman being. At the moment, we're presenting the white Negro. And he has very little Negro-ness.*[22]

These references to the "Super Negro" or the "white Negro" indicated an unmasking of an ideologically bankrupt representational system unable to come to terms with a representation of blacks that was independent of white as the defining term. The self-consciousness to which Diahann Carroll and the letter writer alluded was similar to the self-consciousness of other viewers who felt a need to identify themselves by race. Racial identity and its representation may have become an uncertain and contested field as "black" and "white" became unhinged from their previous definitions, but they were still imbricated within a white representational system.

This problem of racial definition was raised by other viewers who objected to blacks being differentiated and defined at the expense of white characters. Many viewers, particularly white housewives, took exception to the juxtaposing of Julia to her white neighbor, Mrs. Waggedorn. One mother of a four-year-old in Philadelphia said she would not watch the program anymore "as I believe you are protraying [sic] the white mother to be some kind of stupid idiot.—The colored boy & mother are sharp as tacks which is fine but why must the other family be portrayed as being dumb, dumb, dumb." Another "white suburban mother of four" in Fort Worthington, Pennsylvania, complained that Mrs. Waggedorn was a "dumb bunny" while Julia was a "candidate for 'Mother of the Year.'" A third letter from a "quite typical New England housewife and mother of three" in Hyde Park, Massachusetts, stated:

> *If Diahann Carroll were to play the roll [sic] of the neighborly housewife, and vice verser [sic], the black people of this country would be screaming "Prejudice." Why must Julia be pictured so glamorously dressed, living in such a luxurious apartment, dining off of the finest china while her white neighbor is made to appear sloppy, has rollers in her hair. . . .*
>
> *If your show is to improve the image of the negro woman, great! But— please don't accomplish this at the expense of the white housewife.*

The reading strategy these viewers brought to the text was one of polarization. They saw a form of reverse discrimination. Explicit in their letters was an anxiety over the representation of race, black versus white. Implicit, however, was a nascent critique of the representation of gender. All three of these letter writers self-consciously defined themselves by occupation: white housewives and mothers. In the depiction of Mrs. Waggedorn, they saw a stereotypical representation of themselves and were quite aware that they were being demeaned as women.

The positions articulated by these women to a certain extent mirror concerns raised in a number of women's magazines. Articles written about the series, or more specifically the series' star, Diahann Carroll, focused not on questions of race but rather on questions of motherhood. An article in *Ladies' Home Journal* written by the widow of slain civil rights activist Medgar Evers, while not ignoring the question of race representation, emphasized a theme of female bonding between Mrs. Evers and Diahann Carroll, two black women forced to raise children on their own.[23] A *Good Housekeeping* article completely evacuated the issue of race, dealing only with dilemmas Diahann Carroll faced attempting to raise her daughter while pursuing a career.[24]

Thus, while questions of race representation were highly politicized both in the popular press and among viewers, questions about the representation of gender and motherhood were rendered entirely apolitical in both articles in the women's magazines. Instead, the issues were personalized: they were Diahann Carroll's problems or Mrs. Medgar Evers's problems, but they were not discussed as social problems. Similarly, the white housewives who objected to the portrayal of Mrs. Waggedorn had no political discourse through which to articulate their anger at an offensive female stereotype. Both the women's magazine writers and the housewives seemed aware that there was something problematic about the gender-based positions of mothers and housewives within the social order. However, they lacked the means to shift their analysis of the problem from the personal to the social. One could argue that the women's movement, still in its infancy in the late 1960s, provided such an analysis, at least for middle-class white women who formed the main constituency for the emergent women's liberation movement. Just as the black oppositional movement revealed that the position of African-Americans within the social landscape was politically, economically, and socially circumscribed and required political solutions, so the emergence of the women's movement revealed a similar set of concerns about the position of women. However, such an analysis, widely available in relation to race, was not yet accessible to a general female audience.[25]

The viewer response letters examined so far attempted, either by denying difference or by trying to grapple with it, to engage with the program in order to think through ways in which to rework race relations. While many of the letters exhibited unexamined racist discourses, the racism seemed unintended and unconscious, a manifestation of the shifting ground. *Julia*, as a text that worked hard to evacuate politically charged representations and potentially disturbing discourses of racial oppression, would appear to be an unlikely candidate for overtly racist attacks. However, a surprisingly large number of the letters in the Hal Kanter papers reveal an enormous amount of unmediated anxiety felt by some viewers about changes being wrought in the wake of the civil rights and black oppositional movements.

Concerns that reappeared in these letters tended to focus on a discomfort with seeing increasing numbers of African-Americans on television, fears that traditional racial hierarchies were being eradicated, and anxieties about interracial sexuality. While *Julia* never dealt with issues of miscegenation or intermarriage, many of these viewers read them into the program anyway. Some of these viewers may have done so because, unlike the black mammy figures traditionally predominant in the mass media, Julia conformed to white ideals of beauty. That her white male bosses were shown recognizing her sexuality may have provided the cues some viewers needed to construct scenarios such as the one provided by an anonymous viewer from Los Angeles:

> What are you trying to do by making "Julia." No racial problems—she is playing opposite a white, she is suppose [sic] to live in an all white apt house. It's racial because you will have it so Nolan [Dr. Chegley, Julia's boss] will fall in love with her and have to make her over—repulsive—You had better write a part for a big black boy so he can mess with a white girl or they will get mad.

Anxiety over social change and transformations in race relations erupted here in a full-blown fear of interracial sexuality. For this viewer, integration created a moral panic whereby the sudden visibility of blacks in "white society" could only mean that "big black boys" wanted to mess with white girls.

Other viewers, less obsessed with questions of miscegenation, exhibited fears about integration by expressing anger at television as an institution. They blamed television for creating social strife and causing blacks to forget their proper place. One anonymous viewer from Houston, Texas, who signed her or his comments "the silent majority," wrote:

> Living in Texas all my life I have always lived around the negroes and they used to be really fine people until the T.V. set came out & ruined the whole world! Not only have you poor white trash taken advantage of them & ruined their chances now you have ruined the college set. You are good at getting people when they are most vulnerable and changing their entire thinking!

These letters indicate how besieged some people were feeling in the midst of the turmoil of the late 1960s. In Julia, some viewers may have seen the "new Negro" as one who threatened their racially hierarchized universe. All the anxiety-reducing mechanisms employed by the program's creators to defuse notions of difference merely exacerbated anxiety for these viewers. They did not need to see explicit interracial sexuality dealt with on the television screen to see miscegenation as the logical (and inevitable) outcome of the erasure of racial difference. Such letters show the ideological extremes viewers could go to in their meaning-making endeavors. Julia as a text certainly did not encourage these interpretations. But since meanings are neither entirely determined not controlled by the text and since viewers are active agents in the process of constructing their own meanings, we can see how disturbing the process can be. Cultural studies theorists analyzing oppositional reading strategies have generally focused on how such viewers position themselves against dominant ideology. By implication such reading positions are often seen as positive evidence of cultural struggle against the constraining policies, perspectives, and practices of the ruling social order or "power bloc."[26] However, as these letters show, an oppositional reading strategy need not be a liberatory or progressive strategy.

Another issue that seemed to bother the hostile viewers was the mere presence of blacks on television. Blacks were slowly becoming more visible as supporting players in such popular programs as I Spy. The Mod Squad, Hogan's Heroes, and Daktari. Blacks were also occasionally being featured in commercial advertisements by 1967. But in the summer of 1968, the networks, at the urging of the Kerner Commission, outdid themselves offering an unprecedented number of news documentaries on the state of black America, including CBS's acclaimed Of Black America, a seven-part series hosted by Bill Cosby.[27] For some viewers this was clearly too much: "We have had so much color shoved down our throats on special programs this summer its [sic] enough to make a person sick," wrote one viewer from Toronto. An anonymous viewer from Eufaula, Oklahoma, wrote, "After the riots and [the] network filled 'Black American' shows all summer, white people aren't feeling to [sic] kindly toward colored people shows. You are ahead of the time on this one." Yet another anonymous viewer from Red Bluff, California, asserted, "I will not buy the product sponsoring this show or any show with a nigger in it. I believe I can speak for millions of real americans [sic]. I will write the sponsors of these shows. I am tired of niggers in my living room." A third anonymous viewer from Bethpage, Long Island, asked, "Is this what you mean by color T.V. ugh. Click!!" Moreover, many of these people made no distinction between documentary representations of civil strife and the fictional world of Julia. Since both in some way concerned black people, Julia was really no different from the news specials about ghetto riots.

In the end, the reason it is useful to consider these disturbing and offensive letters is because of what they can tell us about the polysemic nature of reception. Julia was heavily criticized for constructing a "white Negro," for playing it safe in order not to scare off white viewers, for sugarcoating its racial messages. While all of that may be true, the show's "whiteness," middle-classness, and inoffensiveness did not defuse its threat to entrenched racist positions. This threat was also made evident by the fact that many of the hostile letters carried no return address. Unlike other viewers who wrote letters, both favorable and unfavorable, these letter writers were not interested in opening up a dialogue with the show's producers. The anonymity both shielded their besieged positions and revealed that such positions were no longer easily defensible.

While the majority of letters in the Hal Kanter papers appear to be from white viewers, there are a significant number of letters from viewers who identified themselves as black.[28] Some of these letters share minor similarities with some of the responses from white viewers. For the most part, however, the reading strategies differ markedly. Jacqueline Bobo, drawing on the work of David Morley and Stuart Hall, has discussed the importance of "cultural competencies," or cultural codes, in order to make sense of how black women made their own meanings of The Color Purple.[29] As David Morley has stated:

> What is needed here is an approach which links differential interpretations back
> into the socio-economic structures of society, showing how members of different

groups and classes sharing different "cultural codes" will interpret a given message differently, not just at the personal idiosyncratic level, but in a way "systematically related" to their socio-economic position.[30]

Bobo shifts the emphasis from social and economic structures to those of race in order to determine what codes black women employed when interpreting the film. This model can also help us understand the unique ways in which black viewers of *Julia* made sense of the program.

One crucial distinction between black and white viewers was that many of the black viewers displayed a participatory quality in their engagement with the program. They tended to erase boundaries between themselves and the text. Many letter writers asked if they could write episodes or play parts on the show. An eleven-year-old boy from the Bronx wrote:

> *I am a Negro and I am almost in the same position as Corey. . . . Your show really tells how an average black or Negro person lives.*
> *I like your show so much that if you ever have a part to fill I would be glad to fill it for you.[31]*

A teenage girl from Buffalo wanted to create a new character for the show: Julia's teenage sister. She proceeded to describe what the sister's characteristics would be and how she would like to play the part. A female teacher from Los Angeles wrote:

> *The thought occurred to me that* Julia *may be in need of a close friend on your television show—and/or Corey Baker may need a* good first grade teacher (me). . . . *I am not a militant but a* very proud Negro.[32]

The viewers who wanted to write episodes generally made their offer at the end of the letter after having detailed what they considered wrong with the show. Other viewers wanted to get together with Kanter personally to discuss the matter. One young woman from Detroit, studying mass media at college, suggested a meeting with Kanter: "Perhaps I can give you a better idea of what the Black people really want to see and what the white person really *needs* to see."[33]

While white viewers offered criticisms of the program, only the black viewers took it upon themselves to offer their assistance in improving the show. Their participatory relationship to the text indicated a far more active attempt at making the show meaningful. For the black viewers the struggle over representation was between the actual program as created by white producers and a potential, but more authentic, program to be created by the black viewers. By acting in and writing for the show, they became producers of meaning, rather than mere recipients of meaning constructed by whites. Asserting the values of their cultural codes, they attempted to bring their own knowledge to the text. The positive engagement evidenced by these viewers arose from an articulation of self-affirming representation.

Ebony, a mass-circulation magazine targeted at a primarily middle-class black readership, also tried to find racially-affirming representations in the program. Unlike other popular press accounts, *Ebony* took pains to emphasize the show's positive aspects while acknowledging its shortcomings. Pointing to *Julia*'s four black scriptwriters, the article indicated that the show would provide new opportunities for African-Americans in the television industry.[34] *Ebony* appeared to support the program specifically because the magazine saw that blacks were assisting (even if in a limited way) in its production.

One of the main areas of concern for many black viewers was whether the representation of blacks was realistic or whether the program portrayed a white world for white viewers. The denial of difference that numerous white viewers applauded was challenged by many, although not all, black viewers. A black woman from Los Angeles wrote:

> *Your show is geared to the white audience with no knowledge of the realness of normal Negro people.*
> *Your work is good for an all white program—but something is much missing from your character—Julia is unreal.*

> *To repeat again—Julia is no Negro woman I know & I'm Negro with many*
> *friends in situations such as hers.*

Kanter replied somewhat sarcastically: "I'm glad you think our work is 'good for an all white program.' I'll pass your praise along to our black writer and black actors."

While some of the white viewers, who had self-consciously identified themselves by race, appeared to think *Julia* was addressed primarily to a black audience, this black viewer had the opposite impression. The black audience was evacuated by a text that denied the "realness" of black identity. The mass-media student quoted above made a similar observation:

> *The show does not portray the life of the typical probing Black woman, it is rather*
> *a story of a white widow with a Black face. Even though she does possess the*
> *physical appearance of a Black woman (minus expensive clothing, plush apart-*
> *ment, etc.) she lacks that certain touch of reality.*

The problem of realism was again a manifestation of a crisis in representation, a crisis in how to define black identity and who would be authorized to do so. In his reply to the student, Kanter acknowledged the problem, stating, "I have considered its [your letter's] content and have come to the conclusion you may be right."

Those white viewers who agreed that the show was unrealistic and that Julia was a "white Negro" were more likely to do reality checks with other white characters with whom they could identify, such as Mrs. Waggedorn. Black viewers who found the show unrealistic and who found Julia to be a "white Negro" had difficulty identifying with any of the characters. The woman with many friends in Julia's situation searched the text in vain looking for confirmation of her identity as a black woman. Unlike the black women Jacqueline Bobo studied who found positive, progressive, and affirming meanings about black womanhood in *The Color Purple*, this particular woman found nothing in *Julia*. The text did not speak to her experiences. It did not construct a reading position from which she could use her cultural codes and find useful meanings. On the contrary, her experience as a black woman, along with those of her friends, blocked any possibility of finding a place for herself within the text. The strategy of breaking down textual boundaries and inserting oneself into the program by offering to write episodes or play a role may have functioned to avert this problem. It may have given some black viewers a mechanism by which to place themselves within the program and assert their own identities as African-Americans.

The other major arena of concern for black viewers, as well as for some white critics, was the depiction of the black family. This issue is a difficult one for feminist theory. The reading strategies employed by black viewers of *Julia* present a problematic situation since, from a (white) feminist perspective, it would be difficult to see their readings as empowering for women. Only one of the viewers who commented on the portrayal of the black family took an anti-patriarchal position. The other black viewers (all of whom were women) criticized the show for not having a strong male head of the family.

The one woman who did not take the creators of *Julia* to task for omitting a strong patriarch was herself reacting to *Saturday Review* critic Shayon's remarks that *Julia* was perpetuating the "castration theme in the history of the American Negro male."[35] Offering her services as a writer of short stories and plays, the viewer went on to provide the following observations:

> *No one ever let the Negro woman have her say even the middle class one. No one*
> *really knows how hard it is for the Negro woman when her man walks out on her*
> *leaving her with four or five babies.*

Another woman from Chicago offered an analysis more representative of black viewers:

> *I don't think any more of you for excluding the black man from this series than*
> *I think of the "original" slave owners who first broke up the black family!*
> *You white men have never given the black man anything but a hard time.*

> *If you really want to do some good you'll marry "Julia" to a strong black man before the coming TV season is over and take her from that white doctor's office and put her in the home as a housewife where she belongs!*
>
> *Otherwise a lot of black women—like me, who love, respect, and honor their black husbands will exclude "Julia" from our TV viewing just as you have excluded our black male from your show!*

A married woman from Brooklyn who signed herself "An Ex-Black Viewer" wrote:

> *After viewing the season premiere of "Julia," I, as a black woman find myself outraged. Is this program what you call a portrayal of a typical Negro family (which is, incidentally, fatherless?) If so, you are only using another means to brainwash the black people who, unfortunately, may view your program weekly.*

The problems associated with the show's portrayal of black family life were also discussed in black academic circles. In an article on blacks in American television that appeared in *The Black Scholar* in 1974, Marilyn Diane Fife strongly attacked *Julia* for ignoring black men. By making the central character a widowed black woman, the program neatly sidestepped the critical issue of black men and their position within African-American culture, as well as their position within American society. Fife observed:

> *Traditionally the black female has accommodated more to the white power structure. The real social problems of blacks have always turned around the black man's inability to have dignity, and the power and respect of his family. "Julia" disregards all this by turning the only black male roles into potential suitors, not actual male figures involved in the overall series.[36]*

Fife thus suggested that the focus on a female black lead rendered the series safer, less likely to grapple with issues that might upset white viewers.

White feminists may be particularly uneasy with such analyses since they seem to affirm the very conditions of patriarchal family structures that they have challenged. However, for black women, this critique of patriarchy has ignored questions of racism that are seen as crucial to an understanding of the situation of black women. The historically different positions occupied by black and (middle-class) white women within the social order should alert us to the problems of grafting feminist perspectives developed within a white middle-class milieu onto the experiences of black women. However, this necessity of acknowledging difference seems to render problematic the mobilization of much feminist theory to apply to anything but the experiences of white women. Given this dilemma, I (along with other feminists) would suggest that feminist theory needs to respond to the specific historical situations of different women living in patriarchal systems.[37]

Indeed, a more historically grounded examination of the unique experiences of black women within family structures can help explain the responses of these women to *Julia*. As Angela Davis and Jacqueline Jones have pointed out in their histories of black women, the life of a housewife within a patriarchal familial structure was quite uncommon for black women. For these women, work generally meant exploitative labor for whites that took black women away from their own families and communities.[38] Unlike middle-class white women, who may have seen work outside the home as potentially liberating, the history of work for black women had no such emancipatory connotations. The viewer who wanted Julia taken out of the white doctor's office was thus making sense of Julia's labor from within this larger history of black women's work. That Julia resorted to leaving Corey locked up alone in their apartment while she went off to her job interview may have had deeper meanings for black women who historically had been forced to leave their children to fend for themselves while they cared for the children of either white owners or white employers.

Another way in which to examine the perspectives of these black women is to situate them in relation to dominant ideas about the black family that were in circulation at the time. It is likely that these discourses would have been familiar to educated, professional, middle-class members of the African-American community. Many of the black letter writers identified themselves by profession—teachers, nurses, students—and tended to write grammatically and stylistically sophisticated letters. This leads me to assume that they were most likely middle-class viewers. The dominant perspective on the black family, with which these viewers were likely to be familiar, was an intensely misogynistic view of a destructive "black matriarchy."

This thesis was first put forth by the influential African-American sociologist E. Franklin Frazier, who began writing about the black family in the 1930s. He attributed a matriarchal character to black familial structure and found its source in the dislocation and stresses of slavery and discrimination. While this familial structure remained strong within the black community after emancipation, Frazier contended that matriarchal formations predominated in mostly lower-class, impoverished urban and rural families. Rather than give much credit to the strength and resiliency of black women, Frazier saw their power within the family as a sign of dysfunction. Those families who managed to achieve middle-class or upper-middle-class status assumed patriarchal characteristics mirroring white families, thus assimilating more successfully into the American norm. Frazier felt that blacks had been unable to retain their African cultural heritage when ripped away from their homeland by slave traders. He therefore felt blacks needed to adopt the familial arrangements dominant in their new homeland in order to survive as a people. Thus the two-parent nuclear family with a strong male head, a structure Frazier saw in upwardly mobile black families, was desirable.[39]

Frazier, like many of the white viewers of *Julia* who attempted to deny difference, did not see any problems with this white norm. Patriarchy seemed to work in constructing successful families if we view the white middle-class model as normative. But Frazier, like most theorists of the black family, was concerned primarily with the black male and was thus rather blind to the position of the female in familial structures, whether black or white.

Frazier's perspective can help us understand why the familial structure in *Julia* was considered so problematic for many black viewers as well as for numerous critics who may also have been familiar with this thesis. On the one hand, the Baker family seemed the epitome of an upwardly mobile black family. Julia, as a nurse, was a professional who had joined the middle class. She and Corey, living in an integrated apartment building with white neighbors, appeared to be completely assimilated into white society. On the other hand, this assimilated, middle-class black family had no male head. Like lower-class and ghettoized black families, a woman took sole responsibility for running the family. The black family depicted in *Julia* thus threatened the dichotomized model Frazier had described. The Bakers collapsed the distinctions between the upwardly mobile middle-class family predicated on patriarchy and the impoverished and dysfunctional lower-class family predicated on matriarchy.

The Moynihan Report was even more influential in distributing ideas about the black family in the 1960s.[40] Produced by the Department of Labor in 1965 (around the time of the Watts uprising), the report described black families caught within a "tangle of pathology." One characteristic of this so-called pathology was the supposed preponderance of female-headed black households in comparison to white households. Echoing the misogynist stance of Frazier, Moynihan felt this situation had grave consequences for African-Americans as a people:

> *In essence, the Negro community has been forced into a matriarchal structure*
> *which, because it is so out of line with the rest of the American society, seriously*
> *regards the progress of the group as a whole, and imposes a crushing burden on*
> *the Negro male and, in consequence, on a great many Negro women as well.[41]*

The report was denounced by many in the black community who felt that it put as much, if not more, of the blame on the black family structure as it did on white racism and discrimination in order to explain the dire situation of many blacks in American society.[42] While some scholars attempted to trace matriarchal or matrilinear familial structures back to black cultural ancestry in West Africa, few in the 1960s were championing female-dominated families within scholarly or popular discourses.

Within this cultural climate, where so much attention was being focused on the apparently pathological and destructive quality of female-headed black households, *Julia* was a likely target for criticism from black viewers. As an unattached, independent woman, Julia could be seen as a threatening figure, yet another strong matriarch perpetuating in the ???realm of popular culture a familial model menacing African-American social life. It is unfortunate that the emergent women's movement, which would most likely embrace a figure such as Julia precisely because she was independent and career-oriented, would find it impossible to speak to the unique oppressions of black women. The perniciousness of the black matriarchy myth remained unexposed.[43]

The readings provided by viewer letters and popular press critics should indicate that there was no one preferred, dominant, or definitive set of meanings attached to *Julia*. Different viewers brought their socially, culturally, racially, and historically determined interpretive strategies to bear upon the program. And because of the historically specific moment of *Julia*'s appearance, a moment of racial strife when previously unquestioned categories of racial identity and definition no longer held firm, the program itself was as conflicted as the interpretations of it. Even Kanter at times acquiesced to the dissenting views of his audience.

By looking at *Julia* as a symptomatic text—symptomatic of the crisis in race relations and its concomitant representations—we can see how a document of popular culture can serve as a piece of historical evidence, embodying within itself tensions working their way through American society at a particular moment. The social and political turmoil of the 1960s manifested itself within a multitude of institutions and sectors of American civil society. Even television, saddled with the moniker "the vast wasteland" for its vapid and blithely apolitical programming in the 1960s, could not escape the turmoil. *Julia* straddled the vacuous "wasteland" and the more socially relevant programming inaugurated at CBS with *All in the Family* in 1970.[44] Despite flirting with relevance, Julia tended to slide toward innocuous cuteness. However, when we shift our attention away from the program and onto its audiences, we find contentious and sometimes highly politicized responses. By concentrating on reception, we can thus begin to chart the dynamics of historical and social change. In the process, American television in the 1960s starts to look less and less like a vast wasteland.

Notes

I would like to extend my thanks to Lynn Spigel, John Fiske, Charlotte Brunsdon, David Morley, Julie D'Acci, the graduate students of the Telecommunications section of the Communications Arts Department, University of Wisconsin-Madison, and David Aaron for their suggestions and comments on various drafts of this paper.

1. David Caute, *The Year of the Barricades: A Journey Through 1968* (New York: Harper & Row, 1988).

2. *Amos 'n' Andy* remained in syndication until 1966. NBC attempted a short-lived variety show with Nat King Cole in 1957.

3. Les Brown, *Television: The Business Behind the Box* (New York: Harcourt Brace Jovanovich, 1971), pp. 78–79.

4. J. Fred MacDonald, *Blacks and White TV: Afro-Americans in Television since 1948* (Chicago: Nelson-Hall Publishers, 1983), p. 116.

5. MacDonald, p. 117. *Julia* was also criticized by the U.S. Commission on Civil Rights in its influential publication *Window Dressing on the Set: Women and Minorities in Television* (Washington, D.C.: U.S. Commission on Civil Rights, August 1977).

6. The Hal Kanter papers are located at the Wisconsin Center Historical Archives, State Historical Society, Madison, Wisconsin. The Kanter papers contain primarily final draft scripts for all the *Julia* episodes; Kanter's personal correspondence, production materials for the series, and ratings information; and a large selection of viewer letters. Most of the letters to which I will be referring later in this paper are filed in folders labeled "fan letters, favorable" and "fan letters, unfavorable." Some viewer letters are also scattered among Kanter's correspondence folders.

7. This script is located in the Hal Kanter papers, Box 18.

8. This script is filed in the Hal Kanter papers, Box 19.

9. This script is filed in the Hal Kanter papers, Box 18.

10. Stuart Hall, "Encoding/Decoding," *Culture, Media, Language*, ed. Hall et al. (London: Hutchinson, 1980), pp. 128–138.

11. Sixty-one of the letters came from married women and twenty-three from single women or those whose marital status was unidentifiable. Thirty-three letters came from men. The rest were either unidentifiable by gender or from children and young people. The preponderance of women viewers is mirrored in ratings materials located in a ratings folder in Hal Kanter papers, Box 18. A breakdown of the *Julia* audience for a two-week period ending Sept. 28, 1969, showed that women between the ages of 18 and 49 formed the largest bulk of the audience, followed by female teens. Men between the ages of 18 and 49 formed the smallest share of the audience.

12. Carlo Ginzburg, "Morelli, Freud and Sherlock Holmes Clues and Scientific Method," *History Workshop 9* (Spring 1980), pp. 5–36. Ginzburg argues that for historians a conjectural approach (the analysis of clues) "holds the potential for understanding society. In a social structure of ever-increasing complexity like that of advanced capitalism, befogged by ideological murk, any claim to systematic knowledge appears as a flight of foolish fancy. To acknowledge this is not to abandon the idea of totality. On the contrary; the existence of deep connection which explains superficial phenomena can be confirmed when it is acknowledged that direct knowledge of such a connection is impossible. Reality is opaque; but there are certain points—clues, signs—which allow us to decipher it" (p. 27).

13. All of the following viewer letters, unless marked otherwise, are in the Hal Kanter papers, Box 18.

14. The writers of these letters are, respectively, a male viewer from DuBois, Pennsylvania, a female viewer from Colton, California, and a female viewer from New York City.

15. "Wonderful World of Color," *Time* (December 13, 1968), p. 70.

16. Robert Lewis Shayon, "'Julia': Breakthrough or Letdown," *Saturday Review* (April 20, 1968), p. 49.

17. Robert Lewis Shayon, "'Julia' Symposium: An Opportunity Lost," *Saturday Review* (May 25, 1968), p. 36.

18. Shayon, "'Julia' Symposium," p. 36.

19. Shayon, "'Julia' Symposium," p. 36.

20. Robert Lewis Shayon, "'Julia': A Political Relevance?" *Saturday Review* (July 20, 1968), p. 37.

21. For an examination of white as norm see Richard Dyer's "White," *Screen* 29:4 (Autumn 1988), pp. 44–64. Dyer observes, "In the realm of categories, black is always marked as a colour . . . and is always particularising; whereas white is not anything really, not an identity, not a particularising quality, because it is everything—white is no colour because it is all colours" (p. 45).

22. Richard Warren Lewis, "The Importance of Being Julia," *TV Guide* (December 14, 1968), p. 26.

23. Mrs. Medgar Evers, "A Tale of Two Julias," *Ladies' Home Journal* (May 1970), pp. 60–65.

24. "Diahann Carroll's Juggling Act," *Good Housekeeping* (May 1969), pp. 38–51.

25. Betty Friedan's groundbreaking text of second-wave feminism, *The Feminine Mystique* (New York: Dell, 1963), analyzed the discontented housewife stories that began to crop up in women's magazines in the early 1960s. Despite her enormously influential work, Friedan's analysis did not appear to affect the type of stories published in magazines such as *Ladies' Home Journal*. The blindness of this particular magazine to the emergent women's liberation movement was made plain in March, 1970, when over a hundred feminists occupied the magazine's offices demanding sweeping editorial and policy changes. See Alice Echols, *Daring to Be*

Bad: Radical Feminism in America 1967–1975 (Minneapolis: University of Minnesota Press, 1989), pp. 195–197.

26. See, for instance, John Fiske, *Television Culture* (London & New York; Methuen, 1987) and *Understanding Popular Culture* (Boston: Unwin Hyman, 1989).

27. MacDonald, pp. 138–139.

28. Thirteen women, one man, and three children or young people identified themselves as black. There was also a group of thirteen letters from an inner-city grade school writing class. From the tone of the letters, I suspect the class was predominantly made up of black children.

29. Jacqueline Bobo, "*The Color Purple:* Black Women as Cultural Readers," *Female Spectators: Looking at Film and Television*, ed. E. Deidre Pribram (London & New York: Verso, 1988), pp. 90–109.

30. David Morley, *The Nationwide Audience* (Chapel Hill & London: University of North Carolina Press, 1985), p. 14.

31. This letter is located in the Hal Kanter papers, Box 1, among Kanter's general correspondence. A significant number of letters from self-identifying black viewers can be found in this general correspondence rather than in the fan letter files.

32. Hal Kanter papers, Box 1.

33. Hal Kanter papers, Box 1.

34. *Ebony* (November 1968), pp. 56–58.

35. *Saturday Review* (April 20, 1968), p. 49.

36. Marilyn Diane Fife, "Black Images in American TV: The First Two Decades," *The Black Scholar* (November 1974), pp. 13–14.

37. For an overview of this debate see Linda Gordon, "On Difference," *Genders* (forthcoming).

38. See Angela Y. Davis, *Women, Race & Class* (New York: Vintage Books, 1981), and Jacqueline Jones, *Labor of Love, Labor of Sorrow: Black Women, Work and the Family, From Slavery to the Present* (New York: Vintage Books, 1985).

39. See E. Franklin Frazier, *The Family: Its Function and Destiny* (New York: Harper & Row, 1959), and his classic statement on black families, *The Negro Family in the United States* (Chicago: University of Chicago Press, 1939). For a good introduction to the various debates about the black family in the 1960s and early 1970s see *Black Matriarchy: Myth or Reality*, ed. John H. Bracey, Jr., August Meier, and Elliott Rudwick (Belmont, Calif.: Wadsworth, 1971).

40. Daniel P. Moynihan, *The Negro Family: The Case for National Action* (Washington, D.C.: U.S. Department of Labor, Office of Planning and Research, March 1965).

41. Moynihan in Bracey, Meier, and Rudwick, p. 140.

42. See, for instance, noted black sociologist Andrew Billingsley's book *Black Families in White America* (Englewood Cliffs, N.J.: Prentice-Hall, Inc., 1968), pp. 199–202.

43. Black feminists have more recently begun to explode this myth. For a critique of Frazier, Moynihan, and other discourses on the black family, see Bonnie Thornton Dill, "The Dialectics of Black Womanhood," in *Feminism and Methodology*, ed. Sandra Harding (Bloomington and Indianapolis: Indiana University Press, 1984), pp. 97–108.

44. Todd Gitlin discusses the "turn toward relevance" in network programming in the wake of the social movements of the 1960s in his book, *Inside Prime Time* (New York: Pantheon Books, 1983), pp. 203–220.

Star Trek *in the 1960s: Liberal-Humanism and the Production of Race*

Daniel Bernardi

The approach expresses the "message" basic to the series: We must learn to live together or most certainly we will soon all die together. Although Star Trek had to entertain or go off the air, we believed our format was unique enough to allow us to challenge and stimulate the audience. Making Star Trek happen was a bonecrusher, and unless it also "said something" and we challenged our viewers to think and react, then it wasn't worth all we had put into the show.

—*Gene Roddenberry (Whitfield 112)*

Superior ability breeds superior ambition.

—*Spock, "Space Seed"*

In "A Journey to Babel" (1967), the crew of the U.S.S. Enterprise, the flagship of the United Federation of Planets, is charged with bringing delegates from different worlds to an interstellar conference at Babel, the code name for the planet that is their destination. In this episode of *Star Trek,* the audience is treated to a variety of extraterrestrials, sentient beings casually labelled alien "races" by members of the Enterprise crew. Like the animals of Noah's ark, the aliens are prominently shown in pairs. They wear distinct garb and have multicolored coiffeurs. We see Vulcans, with their fiendishly pointed ears and eyebrows. There are gold-skinned small people and blue-skinned, antennae-bearing Andorians. There are a couple of Tellarites with pig-like faces, their noses turned up like snouts. We even see glimpses of two African-American actors dressed in nomadic apparel, apparently the delegates from a black world. The title and narrative of the episode explicitly draws upon the biblical story of the Tower of Babel in which, according to the Old Testament, the descendants of Noah attempted to unite the "scattered" peoples of the world by building a tower that could reach to heaven and God Himself. Not unlike the biblical story, the Enterprise's journey to Babel, its mission to unite scattered races, is marred by the confusion of tongues—in this case, by peculiar-looking aliens with conflicting, disruptive, and sometimes violent motivations.

In the secondary storyline to "A Journey to Babel," the character of Spock (Leonard Nimoy), the Enterprise's Science Officer, is defined and complicated. We find out that his childhood was fraught with prejudice: "neither Human nor Vulcan," his human mother (Jane Wyatt) explains. Spock is a "half-breed." We also find out that Spock's father, Sarek (Mark Lenard), is unhappy with his son's enlistment in the mostly human Federation of Planets. The two have not spoken in years. As the episode progresses, this storyline intensifies as Sarek becomes deathly ill and requires a blood transfusion from his son. Because of both an injury to Captain Kirk (William Shatner) inflicted by an Orion spy intent on sabotaging the mission to Babel and a threat posed by a mysterious vessel tracking the starship, it becomes necessary for the Vulcan Science Officer to take command of the Enterprise. As a consequence, he refuses to save his father's life. His first duty is to the ship and its mission. Spock is a loyal "half-breed."

As the episode comes to a close, the main and secondary storylines merge neatly in a "happy ending." In order to help Spock save his father, Kirk overcomes the intense pain of the knife wound and miraculously resumes his command of the ship. He mounts a heroic defense against the now-attacking vessel. This frees Spock to donate his green blood, once "purified" of its human elements, to his ailing father. In a medium shot, we actually see the green blood of Spock pour through the tubes that lead to his father—a clear signifier of his innate difference. Thus, not only is the enemy plot thwarted by Captain Kirk, but Spock and Sarek both survive, literally much closer to each other than they were before. Narrative resolution is achieved with the Enterprise and crew still en route to Babel, the optimistic trek for a more harmonious universe available for future episodes.

There are perhaps more famous *Star Trek* episodes that represent and narrativize racial difference and conflict, such as "Let That Be Your Last Battlefield," which features half-black and half-white humanoids who battle and attempt to kill each other because they are oppositely colored. Nevertheless, "A Journey to Babel" reveals in obvious and perhaps less than obvious ways many of the functions of race that run throughout the entire Star Trek series. First, it keeps the cast of color, notably the black delegates and Uhura (Nichelle Nichols), the Swahili Communications Officer, in the background—visible but not essential. Sulu (George Takei), the Japanese-American Helmsman, is not in this episode. Second, through the allegory of Babel, the episode foregrounds the diversity of the galaxy, and some of the ways in which that diversity causes conflict and hinders universal harmony. Star Trek is renowned for imagining an egalitarian Earth—absent of racism, sexism, and capitalism—that exists in a hostile galaxy overcrowded with uncivilized and violent alien worlds. Third, through the character of Spock, the episode draws upon the tension and conflict caused by being a "half-breed." Star Trek is also renowned for addressing the experiences and ideologies of physiognomic and cultural difference via science-fiction metaphors like aliens. Finally, the resolution of the episode, its return to narrative stasis, leaves both the hope and struggle for universal peace intact. James T. Kirk, the white captain who is at least allegorically linked to the biblical Noah, can continue to humanize the universe.

This essay aims to uncover and critique the relationship between the meaning of race and the liberal-humanist project in *Star Trek*. While there are no doubt many factors informing this relationship, I want to concentrate on the activities of institutions and decision-makers responsible for the making of the series.[1] This includes NBC, the network on which the series aired, Gene Roddenberry, the creator and executive producer, as well as various writers, directors, and actors. These "authors," I hope to show, were consciously and thus intentionally involved in a liberal-humanist project very much mindful of such 1960s experiences as the civil rights movement, the anti-war movement, and the Cold War. A value and belief system that espouses political equality and social egalitarianism, liberal-humanism emphasizes individual worth and freedom, racial and gender equality, and the importance of secular human values. It suggests that humans, with their rational minds, can comprehend all problems—earthly or galactic—by systematic action from within established institutions such as a united federation of states and paradigms such as liberal democracy. Progress for the liberal-humanist discourse of the 1960s, the zeitgeist of the decade, and certainly for the makers of Star Trek, is determined by the extent to which the government, in this case the United Federation of Planets, and the people, in this case the crew of the U.S.S. Enterprise, serve to expand liberty and civility to all people and, as the case may be, to all aliens.

Contrary to what is commonly said about this science-fiction series, I will argue that Star Trek's liberal-humanist project is exceedingly inconsistent and at times disturbingly contradictory, often participating in and facilitating racist practice in attempting to imagine what Gene Roddenberry called "infinite diversity in infinite combinations." The varied and contradictory aspects of the series are perhaps ultimately due to what cultural studies scholar David Theo Goldberg recognizes as the historic paradox of liberalism: "The more ideologically hegemonic liberal values seem and the more open to difference liberal modernity declares itself, the more dismissive of difference it becomes and the more closed it seeks to make the circle of acceptability" (6-7). This paradox informs the activities—the writing, directing, and network gatekeeping—of the decision-makers responsible for the making of *Star Trek*.

Before beginning my analysis, it is perhaps important to stress that, in analyzing the project of key decision-makers, I do not mean to imply that they simply pour their ideology into a Star Trek container that is then guzzled whole by a passive audience. I am not suggesting that the meaning of *Star Trek* texts is singularly or even dominantly caused by institutions such as networks and individuals such as creative decision-makers. In my view, the relationship between the intent to imbed ideology in a text and the ideology of a text is never direct or without contradiction. A dialogical understanding of television authorship as well as a dialectical understanding of ideology resists such reductive and deterministic explanations.

I agree with semioticians such as Mikhail Bakhtin and Roland Barthes that texts are polysemic, or intertextual and dialogical, and that the reader is ultimately the site of signification: "a text," Barthes writes, "is made of multiple writings, drawn from many cultures and entering into mutual relations of dialogue, parody, contestation, but there is one place where this multiplicity is focused and that place is the reader" (148). Texts are more complex, made of multiple "writings," than simple reflections of authorial intent. Moreover, readers are a psychologically active and socially complex group that bring their own identities and histories, their own values and protocols for interpretation, to texts. Indeed, audiences are far too heterogeneous and complex to be duped into complete or unconscious interpellation; for that matter, the unconscious is too enigmatic and Hollywood far too dysfunctional to produce a uniform ideology.

Yet I also recognize that entertainment institutions and decision-makers, network executive and craftspeople, do imbed and attempt to fix meaning. And this agency has a significant impact on the broadcast texts themselves. As cultural studies scholars Tony Bennett and Janet Woollacott point out:

> the deliberations, calculations and policies which actually inform the making of
> a film (or television series) have a direct and discernible bearing on the processes
> through which ideologies are worked over and transformed into a specific filmic
> form. (202)

For instance, if the character of Spock and the storyline that reveals his complexity had been cut from "A Journey to Babel," then the duality of Spock, his half-breed condition, would not be a space for signification. Moreover, while we cannot ascertain all the possible readings of episodes like "A Journey to Babel," we can say with confidence that it would have been different had the decision-makers relied upon Native-American myths instead of Judeo-Christian ones. Indeed, the Judeo-Christian allegories in episodes like "A Journey to Babel," as intertextual references which are nonetheless intentional, guide our readings of *Star Trek*'s imaginary universe as a diverse, overcrowded, and dangerous place. In their attempts to effect signification and fix meaning, television authors both limit and enable reading probabilities. They both facilitate and set boundaries to meaning-production.

It is precisely for this reason that scholars interested in analyzing and coming to terms with the meaning of race in film and television ought to consider more fully the production process and thus the institutions and individuals responsible for helping to make race in American popular culture meaningful.

The Practice of Liberal-Humanism. The articulation of race in *Star Trek*—from its casting of actors to its metaphors and allegories—was uncommon in network television of the 1960s. The meaning of race in the 1950s and early 1960s was dominated by a segregationist tone, a separate but unequal trajectory. Television was what television historian J. Fred McDonald called "white." This is evident in the network programming of the period, which was governed by an overt policy of exclusion and segregation. When African-Americans and Native Americans were represented in such series as Amos 'N Andy (1951–1953) and The Lone Ranger (1949–1957), they were characterized as either shiftless and unintelligent or as obedient servants to white men. Representations of Asian and Latino Americans were almost non-existent, although they received similar treatment when present. A case in point is Sammee Tong in Bachelor Father (1957–1962), an Asian "house boy" who spoke, walked, and expressed himself in stereotypical ways.

The dominant meaning of race in the 1950s and early 1960s was openly and massively contested in the mid to late 1960s. Civil rights advocates such as Martin Luther King, Jr., Malcolm X, the American-Indian and anti-war movements, among others, struggled to push the meaning of race toward a more egalitarian ideal. As sociologists Michael Omi and Howard Winant have shown, during the 1960s new conceptions of racial identity and its meaning, new modes of political organization and confrontation, and new definitions of the state's role in promoting and achieving "equality" were explored, debated, and fought on the battlegrounds of politics. (95)

The civil rights movement had its successes, including the 1964 Civil Rights Act, the 1965 Voting Rights Act, and the 1968 Fair Housing Act.

The mid-to-late 1960s was also a time when the National Aeronautics and Space Administration (NASA), the United States government agency responsible for space exploration and the development of space technology, was completing successful flights into outer space and landings on the moon. With the Gemini and Apollo missions, NASA came to embody the hopes and aspirations, the future and potential, of the United States. It also provided an ironic juxtaposition with the contemporaneous domestic and international injustices that dominated the latter part of the decade. United States citizens dying in the rice paddies of Vietnam and in the streets of urban America, massive protests against the federal government, and Cold War tensions made the future look bleaker than the optimistic images of Neil Armstrong's "giant step for mankind" might otherwise suggest. NASA symbolized future hope and represented immediate contradiction.

Images and stories of civil rights and anti-war demonstrations flowed into the homes of millions of viewers from both print and electronic news sources, forcing the American people to confront a contestation over race. At issue was the racism inherent in segregation, the politics of stereotypes, and the ideals of integration. Producers, directors, writers, and network executives capitalized on this socio-political struggle. For the first time in television history, programs like East Side, West Side (1963–1964), I Spy (1965–1968), and Julia (1968–1971) employed African-Americans in major roles that were not patently stereotypical. Decision-makers responsible for the production of such series drew on domestic and international politics and experiences in the hope of selling their programs and advertisements to an audience very much sensitive to race relations.

Yet, even with the relative boom in programs that employed African- Americans, integration in late-1960s television was consistently problematic. Network programs with people of color tended to be segregated as "race" shows or hidden at the edges of prime-time. Moreover, Asian, Latino, and Native Americans were largely absent from television screens during this period, as civil rights ideals tended to be interpreted by the networks in black and white terms. When these other minority groups were represented by characters such as Hop Sing in Bonanza (1959–1973) or any of the number of white actors in red face in other westerns, it was often in the form of desexualized servants, loyal sidekicks, or unthinking savages. Even producers attempting to engage social issues felt that they must appeal to the majority—the European-American and Protestant middle-class—and not "offend." Indeed, the television programming of the period suggests that the goals, values, and ideologies of the networks were ultimately conservative, resisting change and unrestricted integration in order to maintain a stable—and dominantly white—bottom-line.

While the majority of network programming remained white, Star Trek was one of the few series that embraced and consistently spoke to the shifting meaning of race that contextualized its production and initial reception. As I suggested earlier, this effort to engage the politics and experiences of the 1960s can be traced to the efforts of a number of creative and network decision-makers involved in crafting the series. Of course, the most notable of these decision-makers was Gene Roddenberry. An avowed and outspoken "humanist" very much concerned with the "message" of his work, Roddenberry wrote many of the episodes and was involved with almost every other aspect of the show's development (casting, selecting and revising scripts, and so on).[2] In a 1991 interview with magazine editor and Roddenberry biographer David Alexander, Roddenberry acknowledges that he is both a humanist and a liberal. "I think my philosophy," he states, "is based upon the great affection I have for the human creature. I mean a tremendous affection" (30). He also explains that: "One of the underlying messages of both series [*Star Trek* and *The Next Generation*] is that human beings can, with critical thinking, solve the problems that are facing them without any outside or supernatural help" (8). This liberal-humanist philosophy is also evident in statements more contemporaneous with the original series. "Intolerance in the 23rd century?" he rhetorically asks in 1968:

> *Improbable! If man survives that long, he will have learned to take a delight in the essential differences between men and between cultures. He will learn that differences in ideas and attitudes are a delight, part of life's exciting variety, not something to fear. It's a manifestation of the greatness that God, or whatever it is, gave us. This is infinite variation and delight, this is part of the optimism we built into Star Trek (Whitfield 40)*

> *"We must learn to live together," he says with a touch of civil rights and Cold War concerns, "or most certainly we will soon all die together" (Ibid. 112).*

Roddenberry's liberal-humanist ideals are also present in the primary evidence surrounding the production of the series. In developing *Star Trek,* the creator-producer insisted that a progressive and unified earth, a one-world government, be foregrounded in the science-fiction universe. Moreover, racial harmony and tolerance were to be the norm rather than the exception in the ongoing *Star Trek* universe. In effect, he called for a multi-cultural future. For example, the original series treatment, which the creator-producer used to pitch *Star Trek* to various networks, describes a one-hour show with an integrated cast of characters that included a Latino navigator, a woman as second-in-command, and an alien science officer replete with red skin and a forked tail (a character who eventually became Spock). The treatment goes on to pitch the show as "Wagon train to the stars," an action-adventure of optimism fraught with human conflict (Whitfield 23). Unlike the science-fiction series *Lost in Space* (1965–1968), in which the characters are an all-white family and the aliens are almost always the villains—and dark—Roddenberry's vision of the future is clearly integrated.

Roddenberry's liberal-humanist vision articulated in the original treatment for *Star Trek* is not without its contradictions however. This is particularly the case in the description of the Latino navigator, José "Joe" Tyler, which is laden with stereotypical traits. The lengthy passage from the original treatment is worth quoting in full:

> *José (Joe) Tyler, Boston astronomer father and Brazilian mother, is boyishly handsome, still very much in the process of maturing. An unusual combination, he has inherited his father's mathematical ability. José Tyler, in fact, is a phenomenally brilliant mathematician and space theorist. But he has also inherited his mother's Latin temperament, fights a perpetual and highly personalized battle with his instruments and calculators, suspecting that space—and probably God, too— are engaged in a giant conspiracy to make his professional and personal life as difficult and uncomfortable as possible. Joe (or José, depending on the other party) is young enough to be painfully aware of the historical repute of Latins as lovers— and is in danger of failing this challenge on a cosmic scale. (Whitfield 29)*

José is written as a racial half-breed: one part is brilliant, a trait that comes from his Bostonian, presumably European, and paternal line; the other part is irrational, a failed Latin lover, a trait that specifically comes from his Latino and maternal line. This dichotomy is a familiar one, playing on common racial essentialisms and stereotypes about Latinos. It is also eminently entangled with naturalized gender hierarchies, with the maternal side of José characterized as emotional and the paternal side as intellectual.

With the failed Latin lover on board, Roddenberry attempted to sell *Star Trek* to a number of networks and studios. After the show was rejected by CBS, he pitched and subsequently sold it to Desilu Studios, then in its downswing after its status as a major studio when it operated shows like *I Love Lucy* (1951–1957). Desilu eventually secured interest from NBC, which was looking for the next *Lost in Space*. NBC provided Desilu and Roddenberry with capital to turn his treatment into a pilot. The eventual result was "The Cage," which featured highly evolved, giant-headed humanoids who "caged" other aliens for their material needs and intellectual pleasures. A metaphor for slavery, among other things, the pilot provided Roddenberry with an opportunity to say "something" about humanity.

NBC had problems with the pilot. Network executives at its screening—who reportedly included Grant Tinker, Vice President in Charge of West Coast Operations, and Mort Werner, Vice President in Charge of Television Programming—apparently liked the overall feel of the program, but rejected it as being "too cerebral." They also rejected a few of the characters, including Number One (Majel Barrett, listed in the credits as M. Leigh Hudec), a strong woman character who was the ship's second-in-command, and Spock, now a half-alien with pointed ears and raised eyebrows. The executives felt that neither character would be accepted by the television audience, and they made the unprecedented decision of ordering a second pilot. This decision initiated the on-going battle Roddenberry had with the network over the programming content of *Star Trek*.

Despite the network's rejection of "The Cage," Roddenberry pursued his liberal-humanist project.[3] While he cut the character of Number One, he kept the character of Spock (whom he moved to second-in-command). Moreover, he cast an even more diverse crew of characters than before, including a European-American nurse, Christine Chapel (Majel Barrett), a Communications Officer from the "United States of Africa," Uhura, a Japanese-American Helmsman, Sulu, and a Scottish Engineering Chief, Scotty (James Doohan). In the second season, a Russian "cosmonaut," Pavel Chekov (Walter Koenig), was added. Throughout *Star Trek*'s three-year run, the crew was headed by European-American Captain James T. Kirk and included a cantankerous European-American doctor, Leonard "Bones" McCoy (DeForest Kelley). Hence, one of the characters was Japanese American, one was African, two were distinctly marked as white European ethnics (mostly through their accents), one was half alien and half Euro-Human, and three were suggested to be European Americans. Though dominantly white, this was an integrated cast for 1960s network television.

Roddenberry instructed writers and directors working on *Star Trek* to utilize the multi-cultural crew in their stories. In "The Star Trek Guide," a document which explains the series to prospective writers and directors, the Enterprise crew is described as

> *International in origin, completely multi-racial. But even in this future century we will see some traditional trappings, ornaments, and styles that suggest the Asiatic, the Arabic, the Latin, etc. So far, Mister Spock has been our only crewman with blood lines from another planet. However, it is not impossible that we might discover some other aliens or part aliens working aboard our Starship. (7)*

The "Guide" goes on to advise: "We like ways of using the crewmen (extras as well as actors) to help suggest the enormous diversity of our vessel" (7).

The fact that the series is generically science fiction gave Roddenberry and the rest of the creative decision-makers space to address contemporary issues and to avoid network censorship. As John Meredyth Lucas, a writer, director, and producer of several episodes, reminisces:

> *it was great to work on Star Trek, because working in the science fiction genre gave us free rein to touch on any number of subjects. We could do anti-Vietnam stories, or civil rights stories. . . Set the story in outer space, in the future, and all of a sudden you can get away with just about anything, because you're protected by the argument that, "Hey, we're not talking about the problems of today, we're*

dealing with a mythical time and place in the future." We were lying, of course,
but that's how we got these stories by the network types. (Shatner 243)

Even Leonard Nimoy remarked in 1967 how the character of Spock enabled him "to say something about the human race" (Raddatz 25).

Despite science-fiction conventions that privilege metaphor and allegory, network decision-makers attempted to curtail and control the creative staff's liberal-humanist project. Perhaps the most famous example of this tug-of-war surrounds the production of "Plato's Stepchildren" (1968), in which a pre-shooting script calls for Kirk, manipulated by Greek-god-like aliens, to kiss Uhura. According to most speculations, this would have been network television's first interracial kiss between a black American and a white American. Apparently, NBC was concerned with the fallout of such a "first," especially among its affiliates in the South, and requested some less than subtle changes. A memorandum from Jean Messerschmidt of NBC's Broadcast Standards Department made the network's position explicit: "it must be clear there are no racial over-tones to Kirk and Uhura's dilemma" (2).[4] While many creative decision-makers resisted the network's capitulation to racism, NBC nevertheless continued with their aim of censoring the interracial "dilemma." Apparently they even requested that Spock, the racialized alien half-breed, be the one to kiss Uhura. Nichelle Nichols explains: "Somehow, I guess, they found it more acceptable for a Vulcan to kiss me, for this alien to kiss this black woman, than for two humans with different coloring to do the same thing." She continues: "It was simply and clearly racism standing in the door. . .in suits. Strange how a twenty-third century space opera could be so mired in antiquated hang-ups" (Shatner 285–86).

The scene that was aired shows Kirk paired with Uhura and Spock paired with Nurse Chapel. It begins with the telekinetic Greeks controlling the physical movements of these characters, making them walk and dance in contorted and humiliating ways for the pleasure and amusement of their captors. Soon a chorus of the powerful beings watch as their leader forces Spock to kiss Nurse Chapel several times. We actually see the Vulcan Science Officer kiss the blond nurse in three drawn out medium shots. The chorus also watch Kirk and Uhura diligently resist their forced coupling. These shots are also drawn out, dramatizing the extratextual racial tension surrounding their pairing. The Greek aliens applaud Kirk and Uhura's struggle; some even derive prurient pleasure from the anticipation of its "forbidden" outcome. Eventually the power of the aliens begins to overtake Kirk, and, in a slow dolly into a close-up, moments after Uhura gasps, the Captain pulls her closer to him. He turns her body toward the camera, the back of her head taking up most of the bottom half of the screen. Kirk is still shown diligently resisting, his eyes glaring at the omnipotent aliens, his lips pursed in anger and resentment. Their mouths are only millimeters away from each other when the camera cuts to the alien chorus in rapt attention, a seemingly self-conscious play on and reference to the imagined attention of the actual television audience. NBC's Office of Broadcast Standards and the creative decision-makers compromised: the interracial kiss was only implied.[5] Either way, of course, the coupling between black and white is coded as undesirable and even perverse—a thing to be resisted or kept repressed.

Fundamental contradictions in the liberal-humanist project are also apparent in the use of actors of color. In fact, throughout the series, the integrated supporting cast, despite Roddenberry's call to use them "to suggest the enormous diversity of our vessel," was kept at the margins of most of the stories and in the background of most of the shots. This is especially the case in the way the character of Sulu was conceived and utilized. Indeed, he is only supposed to look Asian. In "The Star Trek Guide," he is described as a white-identified Japanese American, preferring French customs over Japanese traditions. Worse yet, he is described as being confused and mystified by Asians:

Mixed oriental in ancestry, Japanese predominating, Sulu is contemporary American in speech and manner. In fact, his attitude toward Asians is that they seem to him rather "inscrutable." Sulu fancies himself more of an old-world "D'Artagnan" than anything else. (23)

Sulu's intended integration into the space of the starship comes at the expense of a recognizable identity with Japanese culture; that is, the character was conceived as having "successfully" assimilated into the Euro-American melting pot of humanity's future.

This pattern continues in the actual broadcast texts, where, despite the fact that Sulu's position as helmsman places him in the foreground of many shots, he is relegated to the background of most of the stories. Out of the seventy-nine *Star Trek* episodes, Sulu is not once the focus of a main storyline. One of the few times he does make it out of the background is in "The Naked Time" (1966), where he is shown as a rampaging swordsman on the lookout for a duel. The secondary status of Sulu is especially problematic in the second and third seasons, after Chekov joins the crew. During this period, the Russian character is given substantial roles in comparison to the Japanese helmsman. Chekov is even left in charge of the crew when Kirk, Spock, Bones, and Scotty are off the ship. Though of the same rank, Sulu is left in charge of the ship only once, in "The Omega Glory" (1968), an episode in which he has very few lines and Chekov is not featured.

The description and representation of Uhura also demonstrate the contradictory nature of Star Trek's liberal-humanist project. Like Sulu, Uhura is relegated to the spatial and narrative background for most of the episodes, making her more a token than a truly integrated character. Nichols comments on the use of her character:

> I'd get the first draft, the white pages, and see what Uhura had to do this week, and maybe it was a halfway-decent scene or two, sometimes more, and then invariably the next draft would come in on blue pages and I'd find that Uhura's presence in the show had been cut way down. The pink pages came next and she'd suffer some more cuts, then the yellow, more cuts, and it finally got to the point where I had really had it. I mean I just decided that I don't even need to read the FUCKING SCRIPT! I mean I know how to say, "hailing frequencies open."...
> (Shatner 212; author's emphasis)

The utilization of Uhura as "background color" evolved from the description of the character in "The Star Trek Guide," the first document that mentions the character:

> Uhura is also a warm, highly female female off duty. She is something of a favorite in the Recreation Room during off duty hours, too, because she sings—old ballads as well as the newer space ballads—and she can do an impersonation at the drop of a communicator. (14)

As a singing, "highly female female" African, she is written as a performance, an icon, of black beauty. In a 1967 interview for TV Guide (15 July 1967) entitled "Nichelle Nichols Complains She Hasn't Been Allowed to Leave the Spaceship," the actress commented on the dilemma: "My problem is being a black woman on top of being a woman" (10). In the episode "Mirror, Mirror" (1967), for instance, Uhura is eroticized by the camera, as several scenes show her scantily clad body in tight close-ups: her long legs, smooth stomach and large breasts—scopophilic fragments of her body— are emphasized for their womanly and exotic "beauty." It is as if her blackness is made safe and appealing when it is performed in fragmented and fetishized forms; when, in other words, it is as exoticized as it is eroticized.

The use of Spock is another site in the original series where contradictions can be seen functioning within the liberal-humanist project. The tradition of the alien in science fiction involves the foregrounding of Otherness, particularly in reference to the difficulties and conflicts stemming from physiognomic and cultural difference. Science-fiction aliens work as metaphors, as an implicit means by which human experiences and likeness are imagined and fictionalized. Spock, especially because he is a "half-breed," serves this traditional science-fiction function. Yet the character is often contained so as to be neither too literal nor too obvious about the nature of the universe and the politics of the 1960s. Even in metaphors and allegories involving aliens, the decision-makers take the racially "safe" way out.

In "City on the Edge of Forever" (1967), for example, the original script by Harlan Ellison has Kirk and Spock materialize in 1930s New York. As New Yorkers begin to notice the odd pair, Spock becomes encircled by an inflamed mob agitated by a bitter racist:

> *What kind of a country is this, where men have to stand in bread lines just to fill their bellies? I'll tell you what kind . . . a country run by the foreigners! All the scum let in to take the food from our mouths, all the alien filth that pollutes our fine country. Here we are, skilled workers and they want us to sign up for CCC camps. Civilian Conservation Corps, men—is that what we're gonna do? Work like coolies inna fields while these swine who can't even speak our language take the . . .*
> *(23-24; author's emphasis)*

Later in the script, Ellison's technical directions stipulate that in order to conceal Spock's alien features, "he has been made up to faintly resemble a Chinese" (28). Here, the writer is trying to comment on the history of racist discrimination against Chinese Americans during the Depression, using Spock as both a connotative and a denotative signifier. His goal, it seems clear, is to reveal the racist elements of class politics during this era of American history.

In the aired version of "City on the Edge of Forever," the indictment against racism was removed in favor of a comic scene in which a 1930s police officer and a few city people stare curiously at Kirk and Spock. There is no bitter racist trying to incite violence and no angry mob threatened by a "foreigner." Instead, the policeman simply looks at Kirk and Spock, as the Captain stammers out an explanation for his First Officer's physiognomic difference: "My friend is obviously Chinese. I see you've noticed the ears. They're actually easy to explain." With a slight suggestion from Spock, the Captain continues: "The unfortunate accident he had as a child. He caught his head in a mechanical rice picker." As film and television scholar Rick Worland has pointed out, the indictment against racism in this episode takes the form of a racial joke (117). The history of racism against Chinese Americans is not foregrounded but deleted. The intended reference to the history of American bigotry is not televised.

Case Study: "The Paradise Syndrome" (1968). Like "The City on the Edge of Forever," the conditions of production surrounding "The Paradise Syndrome" reveal a contradictory racial project—this time one that stereotypes Native Americans as noble savages and whites as "normal" and even divine. The basic storyline has Captain Kirk, suffering from amnesia, becoming a medicine chief for a tribe of Native Americans on a planet far from Earth. The tribe was placed there centuries ago by a "super race" who wanted to "preserve them." A story clearly susceptible to the noble savage trope, primary evidence surrounding the production of the episode reveals that responsibility for the stereotyping points directly to the liberal-humanist ideals and practices of Gene Roddenberry and other creative decision-makers. Which is to say that, irrespective of the tug-of-war between Roddenberry and the network gatekeepers, it is the creative decision-makers in this episode of *Star Trek* that participate in and facilitate racist practice.

Originally titled "Pale Face," the story outline by Margaret Armen uses explicit racialized adjectives and clichés to construct the Native-American tribe as noble savages. Kirk, Armen writes, "has found this tribe gentle, kind, and in complete attune with nature" (4). Armen has Kirk accepted into the tribe and marrying one of the women, Miramanee. This emphasizes the mythical structure of the story, that of the "paradise syndrome," which typically involves a white man escaping civilization to or lost in the wild, befriending a wise but simple tribe of natives, falling in love with a submissive—and often scantily clad—native girl, but, after saving the natives from an event or person bent on destroying them, eventually determining that living among them is not his life's mission. The white man—not the native—has evolved, and he must accept his role as a complex, civilized human. In Armen's outline, Kirk realizes that Miramanee

> *can never fit into [his] world. Simple and gentle as she is, her only place is the idyllic tribal environment of her people. Gently, he tells her that he no longer fits into her world either, that the ancient prophecy has been fulfilled and he must go on to fulfil his further duty. (8)*

The outline concludes: "He knows a part of him—the part of man that is always pagan—will always remain behind, that a poignant longing for the idyllic life of the noble savage will never leave him" (8).

The noble savage stereotype found in the development of this episode of *Star Trek* functions as a sort of fetish, much like its eighteenth-century predecessor analyzed by metahistorian Hayden White:

> *belief in the idea of a Noble Savage was magical, was extravagant and irrational in the kind of devotion it was meant to inspire, and, in the end, displayed the kind of pathological displacement of libidinal interest that we normally associate with the forms of racism that depend on the idea of a "wild humanity" for their justification. (184)*

All three aspects of White's noble savage fetish can be found lurking in Armen's outline. First, the Indians are associated with magical qualities, especially in the stereotypical representation of them as mysteriously connected to—"in complete attune with"—nature. Second, the representation of the Indians as existing in some pristine and unchanging condition—on another planet, no less—reveals an irrational devotion to a particular image of Native Americans as "noble," an image that is "fixed" in time like the fetish. This is perhaps most prominent in both the "super race's" efforts to "preserve" them and in Kirk's nostalgic longing to become one of them. Finally, the noble savage stereotype is strongly suggestive of a libidinal displacement, perhaps most clearly projected in the relationship between Kirk and the "squaw"—in which the Captain has nothing less than a "wild" time.

The use of the noble savage theme in "The Paradise Syndrome" ultimately has less to do with the lifestyle and customs of Native Americans than it does with the evolution of whiteness. In his analysis of the noble savage fetish, White goes on to argue that it ultimately "draws a distinction, in the nature of an opposition, between normal humanity (gentle, intelligent, decorous, and white) and an abnormal one (obstinate, gay, free, and red)" (188). Hence, the "abnormality" of an otherwise noble humanity cannot be understood outside the notion of a wild/savage humanity (Indians), which itself cannot be understood outside the notion of a "normal"—and, at least rhetorically, superior—humanity (whites).[6] Such an opposition thus becomes a way to define the "civility" of whiteness, which in the development of "The Paradise Syndrome" is especially evident in Roddenberry's efforts to ensure that the Indians, despite centuries of unencumbered evolution on a far-off planet, haven't really evolved:

> *if the Indians were brought here many centuries ago, it is likely that even though they retain much of their terrible custom, they would have advanced somewhat along the scale of civilization. Perhaps not to firearms, or not that fast, but perhaps added on to the Indian culture, it is a growing mastery of mechanics, which has resulted in the wheel, possibly the crossbow. . . . Not enough to deprive our tale of the wonderful simplicity of life here, but enough to stay true to the premise and to logic. (8)*

Roddenberry's insistence on representing the tribe as having advanced only far enough to invent the wheel reveals a discourse on humanity that at least implicitly includes a hierarchy of "civilizations" that has whites "naturally" on top of an evolutionary ladder.

Roddenberry's interest in representing Kirk and crew as more advanced than the Indians stems from his interest in the myth of the "paradise syndrome" (it is Roddenberry who insists that the original title of the script, "Pale Face," be changed to "The Paradise Syndrome"). In a memorandum to Fred Freiberger, the Producer of *Star Trek* during its third season, Roddenberry states his case in explicit terms:

> *Our story here, the essential and I think the most interesting and different one for our series, is whether a Herman Melville theme, i.e., modern man finding his "Tahiti," that natural and simple and happy and untroubled life all of us dream*

*about some day finding—and having found it and having held it in his hand, he
learns he's incapable of closing his hand around it and keeping it because all of
us are innocent prisoners of our own time and our own place. And, as with
Melville's "Typee," neither can our modern man (or his clerk from Boston) take
his woman from this simple life back to his land and his time, since she would be
as destroyed by it as he would be if he stayed there. This is the premise and theme,
a strong one if used properly and certainly a most powerful and enduring one in
Western Literature. (2)*

As this statement might suggest, Roddenberry's interest in a tribe of noble savages had more to do
with defining the problems of whites in a modern, civilized, and complex world, here both metaphorically and literally represented by Kirk, than it did with describing the treatment or cultures of Native-
American peoples.

The NBC censor was also concerned with the notion of the "paradise syndrome," but in the
way in which it might affect the star persona of Captain Kirk. A letter from Stanley Robertson, Manager of Film Programming, noted:

*I think that it is a major mistake to have our star, Kirk, "marry" the lovely native
girl, Miramanee, to have a child by her and then to return to "his world" with the
Enterprise when a rescue is affected. I realize that your feelings are that you can
"justify these actions" by establishing Kirk as a man engrained in the customs,
mores, and social patterns of the planet's culture. However, I think that we must
remember that even though our series takes place at a time in the future, we still
have contemporary people with contemporary views on morals, manners, etc.,
viewing our shows and, while we are able to portray others than our heroes in
opposition to these conventional points of view, we should not ever depict our
leads as having such thoughts. (2)*

The censor, aware of the logic of science fiction, was less interested in the stereotyping of Native
Americans than with maintaining the "superior" morality of the white hero.

The interest in representing whiteness as morally atop the evolutionary ladder in the making
of "The Paradise Syndrome" goes beyond the noble savage fetish. In the memorandum to Freiberger,
Roddenberry rationalizes the notion of the benevolent "super race" and, in the process, links these
aliens to Kirk. He writes:

*We are saying arbitrarily for purposes of this script that there was once, or still
may exist somewhere, a race of highly advanced and kindly humanoid aliens,
who had great love and affection for all forms of life and all levels of civilization
and hated to see the fresh and different potential of primitive cultures absorbed
and changed, such as happened on Earth with the Egyptians, Crete, American
Indians, etc. Undoubtedly, the same sort of thing happens on other planets, too—
it is a demonstrable law of progress in civilization that richly interesting primitive cultures die out and their particular values are lost when stronger cultures
absorb or destroy them. (3)*

Roddenberry's interest in the "super race," a logic clearly derivative of the social Darwinian notion
of "survival of the fittest," continues, as he tries to explain why the Indians believe Kirk is God-like:
"it is obvious that the Indians have never seen an Enterprise landing party member before and, therefore, more believable they believe Kirk is a sort of God" (7). The "demonstrable law of progress"
implicitly assumes that "white" phenotypes—which is all that separates Kirk from the Indians at
this point in the story—would be construed by "primitive cultures" as God-like, thereby linking Kirk,
not to the Indians—that is, members of his own species—but to a divine "super race."

The Kellam DeForest Research Company, hired by Roddenberry to verify facts in pre-production
stories, cites errors in "The Paradise Syndrome" script that would ultimately produce an essentialist representation of the Native Americans. The report suggests changing the tribal mixture of the

peaceful Indians, which already had been changed from simply "Mohicans" in the story outline to "A mixture of Navajo, Mohican and Mandan" in the initial script, in order to be more authentic: "The Mandans were among the most violent, intransigent of all the American Indian tribes. They made war on everyone, on any excuse. Suggest Pawnee or Cherokee." The report also notes that:

> *"Mohican" is a very bad tribal name to use for several reasons: it is not really an Indian name (Mohegan or Mahican is close). It brings to mind immediately "Last of the. . ."; and they were also very war-like. Suggest: Delaware. (The Delaware were related and sets and props would be correct for either culture.) (1)*

Finally, the research report notes that the script is not authentic in its call for Indian costuming: "feathered cloaks are associated with the natives of Polynesia and with the Aztecs. Some feathers were used by the California tribes in particular, as decorations. Use by northern and eastern tribes is not valid" (3).

Despite the Kellam report, the aired version of "The Paradise Syndrome" reproduces the noble savage stereotype with little change. The episode begins with Kirk, Spock, and McCoy beaming down to a planet that lies directly in the path of a huge asteroid which threatens an ominous collision that will ultimately kill all the planet's inhabitants—"A mixture of Navajo, Mohican, and Delaware," as Spock describes them. Upon seeing the Indians, Kirk fantasizes about their "peaceful, uncomplicated" nature, and McCoy chimes in: "Typical human reaction to an idyllic natural setting. Back in the Twentieth Century we referred to it as the Tahiti syndrome. It's particularly common to over-pressured leader-types like starship captains." Soon after the landing party finds evidence of the conscientious "super race" who wanted to "preserve" the Indians—the Noahs of the galaxy as it were—Kirk accidentally hits his head, gets amnesia, and is subsequently separated from his friends. After diligently trying but failing to rescue their Captain, Spock and McCoy return to the Enterprise to deal with diverting the impending asteroid. On the planet's surface, the Captain, unaware that he is a "more evolved" human than the Indians, befriends the tribe—eventually "rising to the top" of his "natural" ability by becoming a medicine chief and, as the Tahiti syndrome would have it, marrying, in a feathered cloak no less, one of the tribe's beautiful squaws, Miramanee (Sabrina Scharf).

Like the production documents, the noble savage stereotype in the broadcast text emphasizes the superiority of whiteness. In one scene, for example, Miramanee tries to figure out how to pull Kirk's shirt off, as she can't find any lacing. Portrayed as simpleminded, she is not that bright. Moments earlier, Kirk has saved a boy by using mouth-to-mouth resuscitation and fashioned a lamp from an old piece of pottery. Despite his amnesia, he is shown as naturally and technologically superior. The text seems to say: you can take the white man out of civilization, but you can't take civilization out of the white man. Given the impossibility of the white man's "return" to the simplicity of paradise, the ending in particular plays out the so-prescribed evolutionary sophistication of whiteness and, in the process, resolves Kirk's Tahiti syndrome. When the Indians realize Kirk is no God, they stone both him and Miramanee (it is the Indians who are violent and brutal in this version of the noble savage stereotype). Spock and McCoy eventually intervene, but only Kirk survives. In a standard Euro-Indian miscegenation narrative, the native girl dies so that Kirk, the white male hero, isn't shown unheroically and immorally leaving her and their unborn baby behind; in other words, so that Kirk can come off as a morally superior being. The starship Captain is left unencumbered in his trek towards a liberal-humanist future.

Towards a Conclusion. In its attempt to imagine "infinite diversity in infinite combinations," the network and creative decision-makers behind the production of the original *Star Trek* participated in and facilitated racist practices. First, the tension between NBC executives and the creative decision-makers transformed the more literal and bold articulations of humanism—José, a female Number One, an unprecedented kiss between a black and a white actor—onto the more metaphoric and allegorical levels. Treatments that call for an integrated cast are whitewashed; scripts that call for a radical critique of racism are diluted. The cast was still integrated, but liberally kept at the margins of narrative cause and effect. Second, the creative players themselves participated in racist practice by relying on some of the myths and ideologies of what can ultimately be described as white supremacy. In this regard, women of color are particularly brutalized, serving the scopic desires of a male-contered humanity trying to simultaneously fetishize and universalize an exotic future.

In "The Paradise Syndrome," as I have tried to show, Native Americans are systematically objectified, sites of displaced libidinal desire, metaphorically "caged" in pristine conditions on a faraway planet by a benevolent "super race" which is implicitly linked to the very white Captain James T. Kirk. In sum, despite their attempt to create a more egalitarian universe—to resist network capitulations to racism and engage and critique social issues—the creative decision-makers behind the production of *Star Trek* failed to escape the paradox of the liberal-humanist zeitgeist.

Notes

I would like to thank Vivian Sobchack for her valuable suggestions and insights.

1. For a more comprehensive analysis of the various processes informing the meaning of race in Star Trek—including narration, intertextuality, chronotopes, advertising, and reading—see my book-length study of the entire Trek phenomenon, *Star Trek* and History: Race-ing Toward a White Future (forthcoming from Rutgers UP). For a comprehensive analysis of the broadcast texts of the original *Star Trek,* see my article, "Infinite Diversity in Infinite Combinations: Diegetic Logics and Racial Articulations in Star Trek," Film & History 24:60-74, Feb-May, 1994.

2. The Gene Roddenberry Papers housed in Special Collection at the UCLA library include an extensive assortment of scripts and related production documents associated with the making of Star Trek. I would like to thank Majel Barrett for allowing me access to this collection and Brigitte Kueppers for her valuable assistance and on-going work with this collection.

3. Almost as if to rub NBC's decision to reject "The Cage" in their faces, Roddenberry incorporated the footage from the failed pilot into a two-part episode, "The Menagerie" (1966).

4. This memo also attempts to censor any material of a sexual nature: "Caution on the postures and actions of our four principles so that no impropriety can be suggested. The embraces must not be such as would embarrass a viewer, and there must be no open-mouth kissing."

5. There are several accounts of "the kiss" from the various actors involved. In her autobiography, Beyond Uhura: *Star Trek* and Other Memories (NY: Putnam's, 1994), Nichols claims that she and Shatner kissed numerous times (193–97). Nonetheless, the shot broadcast doesn't actually show a kiss (as do the shots with Spock and Chapel).

6. White also argues that the noble savage fetish in the eighteenth century transformed into a critique of nobility rather than a critique of the treatment of the Indians. The referent for the fetish, he writes, "is not the savages of the new or any other world, but humanity in general, in relation to which the very notion of 'nobility' is a contradiction" (191). In the primary evidence surrounding the making of "The Paradise Syndrome" there is no trace of concern for class differences and conflicts. Instead, the noble savage fetish and Kirk's white skin reveal an advanced humanity that resembles divinity. There is also no underlying criticism of the "nobility" of advanced human/white society in this episode. Instead, the referent most commonly articulated is the evolutionary superiority of whiteness en masse. According to Star Trek's liberal-humanist vision, humans have evolved beyond class or racial difference into what I would suggest is a white-washed future.

Works Cited

Alexander, David. "Gene Roddenberry: Writer, Producer, Philosopher, Humanist." The Humanist 51:5-30, March/April 1991.

Armen, Margaret Story Outline for "Pale Face" (March 15, 1968). Gene Roddenberry Papers, Special Collections, UCLA Library.

Barthes, Roland. "The Death of the Author." Image, Music, Text NY: Hill & Wang, 1977.

Bennett, Tony, & Janet Woollacott. Bond and Beyond: The Political Career of a Popular Hero. NY: Methuen, 1987.

Ellison, Harlan. Script for "City on the Edge of Forever" (August 12, 1966). Gene Roddenberry Papers, Special Collections, UCLA Library.

Goldberg, David Theo. Racist Culture: Philosophy and the Politics of Meaning. Oxford, UK: Blackwell, 1993.

Kellam DeForest Research Report (June 4, 1968). Gene Roddenberry Papers, Special Collections, UCLA Library.

Messerschmidt, Jean. Memorandum, NBC Broadcast Standards Department (September 4, 1968). Gene Roddenberry Papers, Special Collections, UCLA Library.

Omi, Michael & Howard Winant. Racial Formations in the United States: From the 1960s to the 1990s 2nd. ed. NY: Routledge, 1994.

Raddatz, Leslie. "Product of Two Worlds." TV Guide (March 4, 1967): 24.

Roddenberry, Gene, Memorandum to Fred Freiberger (March 31, 1968). Gene Roddenberry Papers, Special Collections, UCLA Library.

Roddenberry, Gene. "The Star Trek Guide" (April 17, 1967). Paramount TV Production/Norway Studios.

Robertson, Stanley. Letter to Gene Roddenberry (April 1, 1968). Gene Roddenberry Papers, Special Collections, UCLA Library.

Shatner, William, with Chris Kreski. Star Trek Memories. NY: HarperCollins, 1993.

White, Hayden. "The Noble Savage Theme as Fetish." Tropics of Discourse: Essays in Cultural Criticism. Johns Hopkins UP: Baltimore & London, 1978. 183–196.

Whitfield, Stephen E. The Making of Star Trek. NY: Ballantine, 1968.

Worland, Rick. "Captain Kirk: Cold Warrior." Journal of Popular Film & Television, 16:10–17, Fall 1988.

ABSTRACT. This essay uncovers and critiques the relationship between the meaning of race and the liberal-humanist project in Star Trek. While there are no doubt many factors informing this relationship, it concentrates on the activities of institutions and decision-makers responsible for the making of the series. This includes NBC, the network on which the series aired, Gene Roddenberry, the creator and executive producer, as well as various writers, directors, and actors. These "authors" were consciously and thus intentionally involved in a liberal-humanist project very much mindful of such 1960s experiences as the civil rights movement, the anti-war movement, and the Cold War. Contrary to what is commonly said about this sf series, the essay argues that Star Trek's liberal-humanist project is exceedingly inconsistent and at times disturbingly contradictory: it often participates in and facilitates racist practice in attempting to imagine what Gene Roddenberry called "infinite diversity in infinite combinations." (DB)

The Media Dramas
of Norman Lear

Michael J. Arlen

I have been trying to figure out what is so fascinating about the comedies of Norman Lear. Right now, six of Mr. Lear's shows are being broadcast every week to a prime-time audience: "All in the Family," "Maude," "Good Times," "The Jeffersons," "Sanford and Son," and "HOT L BALTIMORE." The first five programs named are currently among the dozen most popular programs in the nation, while the sixth, and newest, "HOT L BALTIMORE" (the title refers to the Hotel Baltimore, a riffraffy version of "Grand Hotel"), after just six weeks, has received a warm reception, despite a degree of wariness on the part of network-affiliate stations, several of which appear to think that in populating his run-down inn so freely with prostitutes, homosexuals, and other social misfits Mr. Lear may have been pushing his gift for jokey topicality farther than the mass audience will bear. Even so, it's probably a good bet that roughly a hundred and twenty million Americans watch Norman Lear comedies each week—which adds up to a total of roughly five billion viewers every year. Perhaps what is most fascinating about Mr. Lear's œuvre is the dimensions of its success, for he seems to be one of those ordinary but uncommon figures who come along every so often in our mass-entertainment culture and manage to achieve—more or less single-handed and with the appearance of naturalness—what tens of thousands of business geniuses and consumer theoreticians spend half the energies of the Republic vainly striving after; namely, a "feel" for what the public wants before it knows it wants it, and the ability to deliver it.

What is *not* so fascinating about Lear programs is easier to determine. Surprisingly, they are not very funny, for the most part, which is to say that the level of acting—at least, the stage presence of the actors—is generally of a higher order than the humor in each show: the jokes and joke situations. The humor is not bad, but it certainly isn't brilliant. "In my building, the roaches are so big that the crunch drowns out the television." And "Deep down, you know, he respects you." "Yes, but I don't want to dive that deep." On the whole, there are few unusual comedy routines in Lear comedies, and there has been virtually no introduction or creation of striking new comedy characters, with the possible exception of Archie Bunker, in "All in the Family," who was transplanted from the successful BBC series "Till Death Us Do Part," and, in any case, derives from a mass-entertainment cartoon that stretches back from William Bendix and Wallace Beery to Sancho Panza and Shakespeare's Pistol. And even Bunker, who has most of the best lines in his show, is given an overabundance of easy malapropisms: "Salivation Army," "Let him who is without sin be the rolling stone," " 'Pilferers will be prosecuted' means 'Queers stay out of the men's room.' " In fact, much of the aura of comedy in Lear shows (as in other television comedy programs, with the exception of Carol Burnett's) derives from television's electronic institutionalizing of the old theatrical claque: the sound track of taped audience laughter, which rises and falls, whoops, giggles, and shrieks, taking on a blurry identity of its own, like a lunatic Greek chorus, and nudging the isolated viewers into an impression of high spirits.

If the level of humor in Lear comedies is routinely professional—which in itself wouldn't be unusual, save for the enormous success of the programs—what is more visible is the level of anger.

163

For, while the sound track is laughing, the characters in Lear comedies are mainly snarling. Again, Archie Bunker stands as the prototype of the Lear angry-man character. When Bunker first appeared on American screens, in 1971, representing the politically and socially threatened silent-majority blue-collar worker, his outbursts on politics and race were taken as quaintly liberating and timely. They also had a specific quality and direction to them: blacks moving into the neighborhood, or being hired at a nearby factory. For some time now, though, Bunker's anger has become random—a random musical note that is methodically sounded by the script as it travels through each half hour. It is an accepted form of stage business. In a recent episode of "All in the Family," for example, within a space of about fifteen minutes Bunker snarled and mugged such lines as "What's the stink in the oven? What kinda animal you cookin' in there?" (It's a fish.) "So, Irene is a Catholic. That means I gotta pay for *her* mistakes?" (Irene leaves.) "Whadda I care if she leaves. She's not my guest, she's your guest." "C'mon, throw the fish on the table!" "Don't stay in there—c'm here! Move it!" "Listen to this, Commie pinko!" "Let me remind you of something, Meathead!" "Yeah, Dingbat, I'm talkin' to you in English!" "Get in, get in. Just put your keyster in the chair and shut your mouth." If Bunker's anger has settled in as a conventional shtick—like Groucho Marx's walk or Jack Benny's stinginess—it has also been picked up and incorporated into all the other Norman Lear shows, and, for the most part, with the same quality of randomness. On "Sanford and Son," which was transplanted from "Steptoe and Son," another BBC series (about two Cockney junk dealers), Fred Sanford is an irascible and bullying black man—often with only the sound track and the vaudeville mugging to tell one that the show is a comedy. In a recent episode, Sanford was waiting for the arrival of his younger sister and her new "mystery" husband. First, he wanted his truck. "Where's our truck?" he asked angrily. "Julio borrowed it," said his son, referring to a Puerto Rican neighbor. Sanford grimaced broadly and slammed his fist on a table. "Now, you gone got *Puerto Rican* all over our truck!" The taped audience erupted in laughter, the joke presumably being that it *was* a joke. Then the married sister appeared with her new husband—a white man. The audience giggled apprehensively but delightedly as the husband—a soft, droll figure—sidled warily into the room, unseen by Sanford. Time passed and Sanford still didn't notice him. Then he mistook the man for a taxi-driver. Then, finally introduced to and embraced by the new brother-in-law, he went into an elaborate and energetic sequence of grimaces and double takes, crashing about the room in a fury that was again comic mainly in the laughter of the unseen audience. "How come you're lookin' that way?" Sanford's sister said to him, feeding the line. "I just got hugged and kissed by a Snow-Whitey," replied Sanford. Afterward, he called the white husband "Mr. Intermarry," "Paleface," "Honky," "Color-Blind," and "The White Tornado," each one to bursts of applause from the tape; indeed, the only purpose or reality of the white husband's existence seemed to be as a butt for Sanford's jokey snarls.

Anger as stage business runs through nearly all Norman Lear's comedies, but it is a curious, modern, undifferentiated anger, provoking laughs from the sound track, and providing the little dramas with a kind of energizing dynamic—sometimes the only dynamic. At the beginning of an episode of "The Jeffersons," George Jefferson enters his new apartment already angry—vaguely and generally angry. Maude, in "Maude," appears to be angry at Walter, in one particular instance, for eating too much, but clearly—clearly to the audience—she is just *angry*: it is a state of being, interrupted periodically by stage-business jokes or stage-business sentiment, or sometimes stage-business problems. What is notable here is that anger in a Norman Lear comedy isn't something isolated or set apart—as with, say, Sheridan Whiteside in George Kaufman and Moss Hart's "The Man Who Came to Dinner," or in the traditional routines of "insult comedians." It has become part of the spirit of the occasion, like music in a musical comedy. Also, as with the characters themselves, who, despite their fits of problem-solving and self-awareness, return each week to the same unserial starting point, it is a rage that rarely extends much into the future, or even into the present. An individual outburst of temper may sometimes produce a concrete result, such as the disruption of a dinner, but for the most part these acts of the new anger are strangely actionless, and, in any case, are soon automatically defused and retracted. King Lear's rage has travelled, by way of Sheridan Whiteside's irritability, into the release-rhetoric of the psychotherapist's waiting room.

Modern, psychiatrically inspired or induced ambivalence may, indeed, be the key dramatic principle behind this new genre of popular entertainment. A step is taken, and then a step back. A gesture is made and then withdrawn—blurred into distracting laughter, or somehow forgotten. This seems especially true in the area of topicality—topical themes—which is supposed to be where Mr. Lear's chief contribution to new forms of comedy lies. For it is in Norman Lear comedies that the mass-entertainment public has first been persuaded to deal regularly with serious contemporary social subjects such as racism ("All in the Family"), alcoholism ("Maude"), black middle-class striving ("The Jeffersons"), and black lower-class problems ("Good Times"), and with a hodge-podge of traditionally unacceptable social and sexual situations ("HOT L BALTIMORE"). With or without the help of contemporary trends, what Mr. Lear has done in this regard is no mean achievement. He has taken a lot of the subjects that people privately talked or thought about, in between watching game shows, detective shows, and stand-up comedians, and put *those* subjects into mass-entertainment programming. His shows don't explicitly claim to be constructive or dogmatic, although the writers (and presumably Mr. Lear) are not averse to throwing in periodic doses of social democracy, but they do implicitly claim to be topical.

As things work out, though, it is a curious kind of topicality. The subject seems to be there—for instance, financial problems stemming from the recession, in a recent episode of "Maude"—but the actuality of the subject soon dissolves into the texture of the aforementioned vague anger, or else into a new type of ambivalence, which has been effected by employing fast cutting and the claque sound track. For example, in a recent episode of "HOT L BALTIMORE" the main drama concerned the breakup of a long-standing homosexual ménage involving two hotel tenants—the middle-aged George and Gordon, with George clearly the "wife" in the pair—as a result of George's decision to spend two evenings out of each week studying law. Interestingly, the roles of George and Gordon were cast with a fair amount of sympathy and contemporary realism; at least, the actors and their parts were several cuts above the traditional mass-entertainment depiction of limp-wristed effeminacy á la Billy De Wolfe. The tilt of the drama—rather more a vignette—seemed human, and even serious, but then the mood would suddenly shift, almost in mid-dialogue, into an old-timey gag or a cheap laugh played off the invisible audience. At one point—supposedly a key moment—the youthful and well-intentioned but dopey hotel manager appears on the scene to try to patch things up between the two separating roommates. The scene requires him to shake hands with George. George, quite dignified, extends his hand. The camera cuts to the hotel manager mugging his straight-arrow distaste. Then we see George, playing it seriously. Then back to the hotel manager, alternately rolling his eyes, shuffling his feet, and continuing to mug he-man embarrassment while the sound track variously giggles, sniggers, guffaws, and breathes a chorus-like sigh of relief when the handshake is finally consummated. What seemed unusual about the scene was that the other actors onstage were directed to play it seriously. In other words, the caption on the picture, so to speak, said that we were watching a human, realistic, albeit comedic treatment of a contemporary "social problem," but in fact the figures in the portrait were dissolving into images of our own (and perhaps their creator's) anxieties and ambivalences: into a caricature of the homosexual's role in our society, which the "caption" was attempting to deny. Similarly, in a recent episode of "The Jeffersons" the dramatic vignette concerned a tenants' party in the family's new apartment, in a predominantly white, upper-middle-class building, which George Jefferson had decided to give in order to show off to his neighbors and impress an important white banker with his cultivation. Predictably, the party was a social disaster. A funny "colored maid" went screaming around the room. When an effete, English-type tenant asked for "a Scotch—neat," one of the Jeffersons said, "Don't worry, you'll get a clean glass." George Jefferson had ordered, sight unseen, a grand piano, which none of the family could play, and it was delivered into the middle of the living room, so that everybody tripped over it. And so forth. But none of the people onstage batted an eye. If the real point of the story was that the Jeffersons were pushy, *arriviste*, inept, but unfortunately *there*—in fact, were uppity—it was not a point acknowledged, or even touched upon, except very slightly, by the rest of the cast. There were no haughty looks and contemptuous sneers from the other posh tenants—the way the ritzy people used to look at Charlie Chaplin when he stumbled into the wrong salon. The only way you'd know that the party was an embarrassment was from the sound track, which, with its shrieks and giggles at the awkward moments, keyed the real audience: Yes, the Jeffersons *are* uppity. We can't say it too loud, because that would be wrong. In fact, we're going to play it on the level with those other stage tenants, perhaps—Lord knows—encouraging real tenants somewhere to play it on the level with real Jeffersons. But in the meantime let's let our anxieties and ambivalences work up the real drama, and let's have a laugh.

Even so, if what could mainly be said of Norman Lear's comedies was that they were on the cheap side, playing serious topical subjects for easy laughs—with a few jokes and snarls and much professional expertise thrown in—that wouldn't be very new or very interesting, and I don't think it would account for Mr. Lear's enormous success. It may well be that Lear does more with topical humor than comedians and comedy writers before him have done, but topicality isn't his invention, nor is exploiting it a new device, recently discovered. Indeed, American mass-entertainment producers have exploited audience "seriousness" for generations, as with the *Classics*-comics pageantry of Cecil B. De Mille, or with Stanley Kramer's "message" films, or with "The Defenders" on television, or even with the slick good-think of the Smothers Brothers and the political wisecracks of Bob Hope and "Laugh-In." Topicality doesn't really seem to be what Mr. Lear does best—nor does comedy seem to be his strongest card. After watching a great many of Mr. Lear's six shows this past season, I suspect that what is most fascinating about the works of Norman Lear is that they are our first true "media" dramas.

Consider briefly how American mass-audience comedy has evolved in the past fifty years. For much of this time, comedy—both in print and onstage—was trapped within the joke: the one-liner, the two-liner, the set piece, the funny bit. From these beginnings, with the joke presented as separate or disconnected from ordinary life, came the more expansive—albeit still disconnected—narrative joke or funny story: "Nothing but the Truth"; "Bringing Up Baby"; "Abbott and Costello Meet Frankenstein." On television, the funny story survives in such now old-fashioned programs as "Hogan's Heroes" or "Gilligan's Island" (as, indeed, vaudeville one-liners still survive with Bob Hope), but, for the most part, during the last generation television—as if it had prenatally digested "The Pickwick Papers" or at least "Life with Father"—has expanded humor from the isolated joke into the so-called family comedy. In "I Love Lucy" and "The Honeymooners" and "The Beverly Hillbillies" and countless other shows, the surface emphasis was still on jokes—Lucy finds a wallet, wins a contest, loses a handbag—but the joke sector of life had been enlarged to include not merely a comedian onstage talking about farmers' daughters but much of ordinary family life, if a rather stylized version of it. Lucy at first was not a real woman, although she had many of the appurtenances of a real woman—modest house, noisy kitchen, gossipy neighbors—but she ended up actually having babies and bringing up children. More recently, Dick Van Dyke and then Mary Tyler Moore expanded the terrain of family comedy further, replacing the home family with the job family, and fashioning, as in the case of the current "Rhoda" and "The Mary Tyler Moore Show," more or less "real" people to go with the "real" problems and comedy situations. Still, "Mary" and "Rhoda" have remained by and large in the conventional mold of *families* dealing with *family* situations—either home family situations, such as boyfriends or dieting or mothers-in-law, or job family situations, such as office misadventures or employment rivalries.

The comedies of Norman Lear are probably new in that they seem to depend mainly neither on jokes nor on funny stories, nor even on family—although they often give the appearance of depending on all three—but on the new, contemporary consciousness of "media." By this I mean that the base of the Lear programs is not so much the family and its problems as it is the commonality that seems to have been created largely by television itself, with its outpouring of casual worldliness and its ability to propel—as with some giant, invisible electric-utility feeder line—vast, undifferentiated quantities of topical information, problem-discussions, psychiatric terminology, and surface political and social involvement through the national bloodstream. Thomas Jefferson, it is said, wrestled for a lifetime with the dark, felt concerns of intermarriage and miscegenation, and it is high time that Americans should be able to deal freely and rationally with such historically taboo matters. Now in the space of a single week, in two Norman Lear shows, the subject of mixed marriage twice breezes blithely by, accompanied by the usual defusing jokes and the laughter of the sound track. Have we come this far so suddenly? In which case, who are *we*? Doubtless we are the same people who, as informed adults and media children, discuss, with all the appearance of passion and involvement, events that have occurred in places we have no knowledge of and had no previous interest in, and with implications we have rarely examined, or tried to connect backward or forward to other events—but events that now sit there and *exist* in the new consciousness in the manner of found objects, tuned into by interested and uninterested parties alike.

Mr. Lear is surely not the first explorer to have stumbled on this pool of media-informed consciousness, but he is the first man, as far as I can tell, to have so formally and so successfully tapped it for the purposes of mass entertainment. It is perhaps not a step higher, but it is a step forward. Ancient drama, one might say, was concerned primarily with the act as act—as the dynamic of drama. Modern drama has gradually interposed motive and guilt as the kinetic forces. Now, maybe, we are treading dizzily into a new phase, where both act and motive have blurred or receded and what we are left with onstage (or onscreen) is the strange dynamic of a ubiquitous, unfeeling, unknowing, discursive collective consciousness. Beginning with the comedies of Norman Lear—as Aristophanes might have been the first to appreciate—we have finally been plugged in to our own Talk Show: connected to nothing except the assumption of being connected to something, which for the time being appears to be our new bond and our new family.

"Whose Barrio Is It?"
Chico and the Man *and the Integrated Ghetto Shows of the 1970s*

Greg Oguss

The popular 1970s sitcom Chico and the Man *depicted whites and Chicanos living side by side in the East L.A. barrio. As a prime-time network series,* Chico *presented a mediated fantasy space that appealed to utopian possibilities and offered multiple sorts of pleasure and displeasure to a multiracial audience, providing the opportunity to interrogate cultural signs of Otherness or Chicano-ness in comparison to whiteness, which traditionally "never has to acknowledge its role as an organizing principle," as George Lipsitz states. Although the paternalistic relationship between an older white figure and a young Chicano at the show's core invokes the racial power dynamics of other 1970s integrated ghetto shows,* Chico *offers brief disruptive moments that escape this strategy of ideological containment. These highlight the contradictory nature of the show (and TV itself), which often succeeds in quelling minoritized voices but can still be mobilized by them as an instrument for enjoyment/self-affirmation.*

Keywords: "turn to relevance"; Chicano-ness; ethnic comedy

During much of the 1970s, ghetto-centric programs were visible up and down the dial on American prime-time network television. *Sanford and Son, Good Times, Welcome Back Kotter*, and *The White Shadow* are just a few of the many shows that for the first time gave Americans lighthearted looks at historically underrepresented characters within these rarely focused on environments, at least in the context of the weekly television series. When looking to trace this remarkable shift in the networks' introduction of not only racially diverse casts but also particular economic settings seldom highlighted in a prime-time context, a number of factors should be considered. The early 1970s may seem a moment enmeshed in social upheaval, with the antiwar movement responding to America's presence in Vietnam, the concerns of the women's movement, the rising visibility of the gay rights movement, and continued racial unrest due to the failure of civil rights activism to achieve any meaningful reform.

Although these multiple upheavals may have contributed to a loosening of restrictions in popular entertainment, we might also look for an economic rationale behind this increased privileging of "the social." In this regard, perhaps the most important factor is what Todd Gitlin has labeled CBS's decision to make a "turn toward relevance," consciously pursuing a strategy to attract younger, better educated viewers with urban lifestyles at the expense of its older audience base to please advertisers interested in these demographics (Gitlin 1985, 203-11). As CBS began enjoying ratings success with shows such as *M*A*S*H* and the Norman Lear and Bud Yorkin–produced *All in the Family*—discovering that these prized urban viewers were interested in highly charged material such as racial and ethnic issues—this led to other networks copying the formula with programming that directly addressed social issues like race relations and gender conflicts (Gray 1995, 59; Watson 1998, 44). In fact, while CBS was shifting into "relevant" mode, NBC head of research Paul Klein was already making a similar argument at his network that it was precisely the makeup of those desirable individual viewers and not which "households" were watching which shows that should be among their primary concerns (Gitlin 1985, 208).[1]

This move toward socially oriented fictional programming also produced a fascinating subgenre during the same decade that has not been critically analyzed to the same extent as the larger trend: the integrated ghetto narrative, in which whites and other races live side by side within poorer urban neighborhoods. The aforementioned inner-city high school basket-ball drama *The White Shadow* falls into this category, as does the text that will be this article's primary focus: the successful and controversial East L.A.–centered *Chico and the Man*. The stories depicted on such shows clearly ignore the still extremely segregated nature of our communities in one sense, offering up a mediated fantasy space that illustrates television's need to appeal to what Fredric Jameson and others have labeled "utopian possibilities" (Gray 1995, 8). But the same programs also often provide multiple sorts of pleasure and displeasure when considered from a range of audience perspectives. And, in the case of *Chico* in particular, the contradictory representations in the text open up a space for a number of brief irruptions within the fabric of the paternalistic Euro-American ideological discourse of the program. In addition, such representations offer a chance to engage with and interrogate cultural signs of Otherness and Chicano-ness in comparison to whiteness, which traditionally "never has to acknowledge its role as an organizing principle in social and cultural relations" (Lipsitz 1998, 1).

Roots and Reactions

Ironically, the roots of *Chico and the Man*, a hit on NBC for much of its run from 1974 to 1978, grew at least partially out of the tradition of Chicano media activism, which had hit a peak a few years earlier. The show's creator, James Komack, had loosely based the character of Chico Rodriguez on an early period in the life of Ray Andrade, former leader of the by-then-defunct media activist group Justicia. Although largely dormant at the time the show premiered, some of these same activist urges were invigorated when the presentation of the show's lead character, played by Freddie Prinze, attracted the ire of many in the Mexican American community in Los Angeles. Prinze, a half–Puerto Rican and half-Hungarian standup comic hailing from a predominantly Latino section of Upper Manhattan, was a rising young star who at the age of nineteen landed a spot on *The Tonight Show*, where the appeal of his "ethnic comedy" would garner him the chance to win the role of Chico.[2] Besides Freddie Prinze, Komack had also decided to hire Ray Andrade as associate producer, mainly to "preempt any attacks from the Chicano community" (Montgomery 1989, 63). With Andrade onboard, Komack and coproducer David Wolper managed to convince NBC that protesters and advocacy groups like Justicia would not cause any trouble as they had a few years earlier when they had briefly acquired enough influence to become a remarkably vocal presence in entertainment television before the institution reasserted control over such dissent.[3]

But, nevertheless, *Chico and the Man*, which portrayed an evolving love-hate relationship that developed between a streetwise young Chicano and a disagreeable aging white bigot who owned a garage in the middle of the East L.A. barrio, aroused the outrage of the Mexican American community based on a host of issues. The press, in mainstream publications such as the *L.A. Times* and *Newsweek*, reported that the outcry focused exclusively on the casting of Freddie Prinze, rather than an "authentic" Chicano, in the role of Chico (Smith 1974; see also Waters 1974, 74–75). And some voices did exist that argued fiercely that Chico could not be a "sympathetic character when the *character* is not really a Chicano."[4] Others, however, such as Ray Andrade himself, spoke out against the show's failure to provide any writing opportunities for Chicanos, which, in turn, prompted its disparaging representation of its East L.A. setting ("Chicanos Grouchy about 'Chico'; See Ethnic Putdownby 'the Man,'" *Variety*, October 9, 1974).[5] In characterizing all of these voices as those of inconsequential extremists, the *Times'* Cecil Smith described "militant" Chicano activists "bombarding" the press with letters and articles about Prinze's maligning of the Mexican American community with his portrayal. Smith concluded that this was "blatant nonsense" that would deny an actor the ability to perform his trade, "to be what he is not," and that, in the end, the controversy mattered little to anyone outside Southern California or even "the city limits of Los Angeles" (Smith 1974).

Smith did get things right in one sense. Local concerns were one of the driving forces behind this campaign. The issue of employment opportunities within the entertainment industry for Latinos, but particularly the large Mexican American community in Southern California, had always been a central concern of the Chicano media reform movement of the late 1960s and early 1970s. In 1968, two actors, Ray Martell and Ray Andrade, ironically, had brought their grievances to the Mexican American Political Association (MAPA; see Noriega 2000, 54), a group originally founded in the early 1960s by West Coast activists and local Democratic party officials disenchanted with the party's support for the Chicano community.[6] A film and television committee of MAPA was quickly formed, marking the beginning of an organized campaign against the lack of job opportunities for Chicanos in film and TV based on Hollywood's discriminatory attitude toward Latinos in front of and behind the cameras (Noriega 2000, 55). With the entertainment industry accounting for a large share of the Southern California economy and the Latino population of the region historically denied equal access to economic opportunities within the industry, when a show about Chicano culture finally appeared on network television, it may have appeared a small but crucial step on the road away from discriminatory practices. The highly symbolic presence of a non-Chicano, half-European American performer in the coveted lead role, however, signaled to Chicanos the networks' continued disinterest in offering anything of real significance to their community. Freddie Prinze himself inadvertently encapsulated the situation rather well when he asked of the protesters, confused, "Don't these people know Wallace Beery played Pancho Villa? Or that Brando was Zapata?" (Smith 1974). The answer is, of course, that they knew all too well. And this knowledge of the history of Anglo representation of Latino images and cultures is what was fueling their anger.

Disentangling Context: Race, Comedy, Industry

Also fueling their anger was the comedic and narrative content of the show itself. With social tensions modeled on *All in the Family*, the show it ran just behind in the ratings, a good deal of the "humor" derived from the racist insults that Ed Brown, the elderly garage owner played by Jack Albertson, directed at the surrounding Chicano community. In NBC's own publicity materials touting the debut episode, Ed Brown is described as an "irascible hold-out" in East L.A., explicitly alluding to a preferred reading of the show as playing on the racially driven fear that his neighborhood and much of the country are being overrun by dark-skinned Others such as Chico Rodriguez.[7] The unintended irony here is that Los Angeles not only was founded by largely *mestizo* and mulatto settlers as a Spanish-ruled outpost in the eighteenth century (Griswold del Castillo 1979), but also was governed as a Mexican city from 1821 until the United States forcibly annexed California along with much of the Southwest at the end of the U.S.-Mexico War in 1848. And, as Raúl Homero Villa notes, it was a concerted effort in the 1920s and 1930s on the part of Anglo city planners to remove Mexican settlers from the coveted downtown spaces of Los Angeles that first pushed *mexicanos* eastward into neighborhoods like Boyle Heights, Lincoln Heights, and so on, already beginning to construct East L.A. as a "super-barrio" and rendering Ed Brown's (and the show's) sense of history nonsensical (Villa 2000, 57–61).

But in considering the kinds of discourses that the show does incorporate, we can begin to locate *Chico and the Man* within a specific context of industrial television production of the mid-1970s, as its mix of liberal-reactionary frictions and its presentation of an extremely close white/

non-white relationship were not exactly exceptional for a fictional series of its day. Under the heading of the former, for example, the very week that *Chico* debuted found John Wayne guest starring on the third-season opener of *Maude* and trading political barbs with Bea Arthur's dyed-in-the-wool liberal lead character in the service of what *Variety* termed a "highly effective" comedic entry in the often controversial series ("Television Review: *Maude*," *Daily Variety*, September 9, 1974). And, in terms of the latter, only a few days later, the premiere episode of *Get Christie Love* starring black actress Teresa Graves contained the strong suggestion that Christie had "a thing going with her white lieutenant boss," in the words of a reviewer for *Daily Variety* ("Telefilm Review: *Get Christie Love*, Market for Murder," *Daily Variety*, September, 11, 1974). Although this coupling may have been a less than obvious echo of the more combative, although still affectionate, Ed-Chico relationship, it is interesting to note that David Wolper Productions, which produced *Chico and the Man*, was also behind *Get Christie Love*.

Attempting a similar contextualization on a more modest level, *Newsweek*'s Harry Waters could easily identify *Chico* as a "brown-and-white ripoff" of the "Bunker clan" that blended *Sanford and Son*'s generational angst with ethnic enmity (Waters 1974, 74). But he failed to mention that this ethnic enmity flows only one way, with Chico bearing the brunt of it all, only deflecting Ed's slurs by telling jokes and maintaining his cheerfulness. The pilot episode of the show is particularly problematic in this regard. After Chico solves a sticky situation created by a customer's request for a new hubcap by surreptitiously taking one from the other side of the man's car, Ed castigates him as an empty-headed "enchilada yo-yo" ("The Man Meets Chico" 1974/#1). Rather than show any distress at this put-down, Chico simply replies that he's made someone "happy" and proceeds to dance around the garage, twirling an inflatable tire around his neck, indicating that ethnically personalized insults mean nothing to him. When Ed responds to his request for a permanent job with a sarcastic "drop dead," Chico does indeed "play dead" by falling to his back on the grease-covered garage floor like a dog doing a trick for a master. These opening antics would seem to support the view offered in a letter to the editor to the *L.A. Times* replying to Cecil Smith's support of the show and dismissal of its critics, in which the author characterizes the community furor as caused by a style of humor "dangerously close to the Step n' Fetchit portrayals" that continue the "traditional belittling of Mexican-Americans" in the media (John H. Brinsely, "Chico and the Man," letter to the editor, *L.A. Times*, November 18, 1974).

Interestingly, it was widely reported that the show began making "concessions" to the objections raised by the Chicano protesters, but the only example typically offered is an episode of the first season that established Chico's heritage as only half-Mexican American and half–Puerto Rican in reference to Prinze's own background (see Waters 1974, 75; see also Smith 1974; Friedman, 1978, 99), which was likely to please few Chicanos. But with the general disappearance of moments of brutal reinforcement of a racial hierarchy such as those found in the pilot episode, we might conclude that the protesters' response also scared producers into modifying the content in this regard as well.

It was, however, also the comedy of the undeniably multitalented Freddie Prinze that could appear problematic, particularly from the perspective of certain segments of the Latino audience of the period. One of the principal uses of Prinze's humor is to parry Ed's derisive remarks about the Chicano community with which he finds himself surrounded. The result is that Chico is constantly forced into the position of "defender of his race"[8] rather than one of an aggressor who might take to pointing out whites' history of discrimination against Latinos in arenas such as the job market, housing markets, and so on, which begins to explain the economically depressed condition of the barrio that Ed is always mocking. In this regard, it is useful to recall that the ghettoization of Chicanos and other peoples of color in impoverished inner-city communities like East L.A. was not simply a historical "accident." The original Chicanos—both the landowning *Californios* and the laboring *pobladores*—had been stripped of land, possessions, and political and economic power during the second half of the nineteenth century by legislative means, juridical duplicity, and overt racist violence as these new Americans were "put in their place" by the Anglo authorities (Villa 2000, 2). A century later, even with steps like the 1950 repeal of California's race-based Alien Land Law, developers continued excluding blacks, Chicanos, and Asians, allowing the growth of an exclusively white suburban population outside the L.A. city limits. If Chicanos had been subject to numerous formal and informal race-based policies and capricious treatment by the unchecked "growth machine" of American capitalism for more than a century (Sánchez 1993, 77; Villa 2000, 57), it was exclusive land-use zoning laws and barriers of incorporation erected in the postwar period that decisively separated off suburban homeowners and nonwhite populations, putting in place forms of racial, ethnic, and class segregation that still thrive (Villa 2000, 164).

Although it may sound like asking far too much of a network sitcom chasing a multiracial audience to offer up a comedic voice that incorporates a critique of whiteness that nods to these dynamics on any level, we do not need to look very far to find a highly successful example of just such a show. In a 1973 episode entitled "Fred Sanford, Legal Eagle" on NBC's *Sanford and Son*, in attempting to defend his son Lamont in court against an unjustly received traffic ticket, Fred begins questioning the cop who made the arrest as to why he never arrests any white drivers. When Fred cracks, "Look around here, there's enough niggers in here to make a Tarzan movie" to make his point, there is clearly a critical commentary evoked by the humorous interchange that is absent from the dynamics of *Chico*.[9]

In contrast, when Jack Albertson's Ed mockingly comments to Chico that "your people are always trying to steal something" after a Chicano customer mistakenly almost drives away with their only gas pump still attached to his car, the reply of the Freddie Prinze character is simply the comeback, "You're just saying that cuz I stole your heart" ("Ed Talks to God" 1977/#62). This line is accompanied by a batting of his eyelashes and a trace of a lisp, all of which begin to suggest the elements of Prinze's persona on the show that could be considered either problematic or progressive depending on the position of the viewer. With Chico adopting the traditionally "female" role to defuse Ed's ethnic prejudice, the criticisms of Chicanos of the period such as Andrade, who publicly remarked that Prinze was "too servile to Albertson" and possessed a "certain lack of machismo" (Noriega 2000, 71), become about the actor's transgression of heterosexual norms as much as his lack of narrative authority. Chico's needling of Ed with an ironic suggestion of a homoerotic relationship highlights Prinze's fusion of a comedic style incorporating a gender-bending performativity opposed to the masculine ideals of many tradition-bound Latino cultures blended with his collection of routines and affectations derived from his Puerto Rican–ness.

But Prinze's humor derived from his own Latino-specific identity could also be potentially problematic. The instantly identifiable "national catch-phrase" he came to be associated with (Waters 1974, 74), "Tha's not my job," can be seen as emblematic in this respect. Uttered smirkingly by Prinze when Albertson's character requested anything of Chico he deemed outside his explicit job description, the line certainly could be read as resistance to "the Man" in this context. And it was applauded by the studio audience (and sweetened on the laugh track) at least partially in support of such a reading whenever heard on the show.[10] But keeping in mind Todd Gitlin's (1985) explanation that these new "relevant" programs were a conscious response by the networks to pursue younger viewers with more contemporary attitudes, it is easy to see this appealing to white liberal audiences on one level and reinforcing an idea of the inherent laziness of Latino peoples on a deeper level. The genesis of the line, a joke that Prinze frequently used in his standup comedy act in his days before becoming a television star, makes this clear. He would tell audiences the story of the one Puerto Rican whom Noah took aboard his ark. Constantly complaining about everything, the Puerto Rican worried, "How many newspapers you put down for the elephant?" But when Noah asked for his help, the Puerto Rican only shrugged and responded with what was to become Prinze's catchphrase.[11] The joke is, of course, not about making the best of a bad circumstance, but simply about pointing out how shitty the situation is and removing oneself from it as completely as possible. Nor is it very easy to see this routine, in its original context, as presenting anything resembling a positive image for Latinos. It does, however, present a picture of total isolation from one's cultural heritage and allegorizes an attempt to deal with it. This is a situation that eerily prefigures Freddie Prinze's predicament as a nineteen-year-old "Nuyorican" who bids his home farewell and suddenly finds himself at the other end of the continent about to step into the unfamiliar glare of the leading role on a prime-time sitcom.

Narrative, Ideology, Containment

On a narrative level, numerous plot lines of the show did confirm Andrade's and the protesters' suspicions that issues of subjugation to a white paternalistic order revolved at the show's core in much the same way as Ed Guerrero theorizes that the black image is often in the "protective custody of a White lead or co-star, and therefore in conformity with dominant, White sensibilities" in the biracial buddy film of Hollywood cinema (Guerrero 1993, 237–46). Many of these narratives in the end depicted Ed Brown dropping his characteristically gruff exterior for a brief moment in which he would reveal a kernel of humanistic wisdom which he would then "pass on" to the uneducated cultural Other, Chico, before resuming his antagonistic pose. In "The Manuel Who Came to Dinner," the third episode of the series, it is revealed that Ed indeed once had a close friendship with a Chicano, the Manuel of the episode's title, but they had a falling-out over the question of interracial marriage when Manuel's son and Ed's daughter became romantically involved (1974/#3). Although Ed allows Chico to believe that he was against the idea of the marriage to maintain his "image," in the end, it comes out that it was actually Manuel, a Chicano, who does not believe in mixed marriages. At the episode's conclusion, Ed patches things up with Manuel regardless, demonstrating to Chico that long-term friendships are more important than grudges based on the "backward" ideas adhered to by other racial or ethnic groups. A very similarly structured episode a few weeks later depicts Ed undergoing a severe mortality crisis after reading in the obituary notices that a former friend his age has been struck down by "natural causes" ("Natural Causes" 1974/#5). Realizing that at any minute he can be snatched away to that "great barrio in the sky," Ed takes to his bed, figuring what's the use of fighting the inevitable? Bearing a grudge against the friend, who has died owing him 500 bucks, Ed also refuses to leave his bed to attend the funeral. But after being visited in his room by the grieving widow, Ed finally leaves his bed and delivers the eulogy at the funeral as has been requested of him, modeling once again for Chico the importance of casting aside petty grudges and of expressing emotions for those we care about, if only at moments when it truly matters the most. These easy moral stances taken by Ed—friendship over money, critiquing "racial purists" like Manuel—certainly may have been widely held among the show's other characters and its various audiences. But, more importantly, it was the endings of these episodes, with Ed suddenly learning his lesson or imparting a bit of wisdom, which plainly indicated his place within the narrative hierarchy in relation to Chico.[12]

In its maintenance of a paternalistic relationship between a humanistically inclined older white figure and a young Chicano, the power dynamics of *Chico* also invoke the thrust of the narratives spun by another integrated ghetto show of the 1970s, CBS's *The White Shadow* (1978–1981). Focusing on Ken Reeves, a white, ex-NBA player turned high school basketball coach in a poorer section of L.A., and a team made up of largely black kids and a couple of token whites whom he is forced to keep out of trouble, an episode entitled "Georgia on My Mind" might serve as representative of the series in this respect. Coolidge, the team's star player, begins to feel that school is an unnecessary burden on him given his considerable athletic gifts. With the cast's resident "hustler" Thorpe offering to become his personal manager, Coolidge considers dropping out and going straight to the pros or, even better, joining the Harlem Globetrotters, who just happen to be in town. With Coolidge hardly showing up for class and the black female principal's lectures on the value of an education having no effect on his mindset, it is up to Coach Reeves to turn things around. The coach cooks up a plan, telling Coolidge he will get him a tryout with the Globetrotters as long as Coolidge promises to return to school and "buckle down" if he flunks the tryout. Of course, Coach Reeves counsels his old friends in the Globetrotters to give Coolidge a phony tryout to teach him he still has a lot to learn both on the basketball court and in school before he can hope to compete on their level. But a disappointed Coolidge is still unconvinced on the ride home from the tryout that school is the place for him. And the coach is forced to give him another lecture, saying that despite his talents he's basically "spoiled." Coolidge counters that this is an easy charge for a white man to make, but Reeves dismisses this argument by informing Coolidge that he's simply someone who always looks for "the easy way out." Coolidge is then let out of the car, marking the beginning of a lengthy no-dialogue sequence. The

"TV funk" rises on the soundtrack, and he sets off on a long soul-searching trek around his neighborhood with the coach's words ringing in his ears as the scriptwriters take this time-out to show him what the "easy way out" would be for a member of a racialized minority group such as his: he passes by blacks shooting dice huddled near a building, a Latino clutching a bottle of alcohol in the shadows, and aging winos sitting on stoops, some sipping from paper bags. And, by the episode's end, Coolidge is back in Coach Reeves' office, begging for his spot back on the team.

The episode of *Chico* that makes plainest its ideological project depicts a reunion with Chico's long-lost father, Gilberto, played by Cesar Romero ("Chico's Padre" 1977/#59). Although imprisoned for car theft in Mexico when Chico was an infant and shunned by his mother's family as a result, Gilberto is now a self-made success in the fishing industry, living in Acapulco. He has determinedly tracked Chico down so that he may offer his son the opportunity to join him and gain a chance at "a better life." But Chico is resistant to this man who deserted him before. When Gilberto makes mention of the fact that Ed is "not your father," Chico stings him with the line that "he's closer to it than you are."

In the end, Chico turns his father's offer down, saying that he's got his own ideas about making it in the world. More importantly, referring to Ed, who he assumes is just down the hall, Chico stresses, "That old man in that room has helped me a lot. He's helped me get my head together, helped me finish school. Learn a trade." And, with that, the offer to connect with a crucial link to the Mexican portion of his heritage is declined. In essence, he trades a Latino father for a white father.[13] When Ed falls into the room as Chico pulls open the door, having been snooping on the conversation, he does urge "our son," as he and Gilberto are calling Chico by the episode's end, to go with his birth father, repeating that it would be a great opportunity. Even though Chico's mind will not be changed, Ed takes Gilberto's business card "just in case." Ed's brief attempt at stating Gilberto's case and apparent sympathy for his position signal that the appearance of free will is crucial and that Chico must appear to want to remain of his own volition within America's liberal paternalistic system so that the discourse of democratic choice that supports our society can proceed.

Readings and Rereadings: Text/Reception

But although a paternalistic interaction between a white "teaching" figure and the nonwhite Others in the narrative is a defining feature in all of the integrated ghetto fictions of 1970s television, *Chico and the Man* does offer scattered disruptive moments that escape this strategy of containment, often through culturally specific representations. This increased layer of complexity likely added to its popularity during the show's initial run and contributes to its enduring status as a cult phenomenon with diverse audiences. An initial example of the show offering utterly atypical images of Latino life within the space of prime-time TV is found in the montage regularly featured in the opening credit sequence. A minidocumentary of street life in East L.A., signaled by an introductory shot of the properly area-specific Boyle Heights freeway sign, the sequence displays decked-out low-riders cruising the avenues, a beaming bride in her wedding dress, a group of soccer players in a city park, Chicanos and Chicanas at work and at play, and the only noticeably interracial shot: a few white hipsters sprinkled amongst a crowd enjoying a performance by a group of Latino bongo players.

If the tone of the actual diegetic world seems far from the universe promised by this opening, one of the reasons is undoubtedly that the action all took place, like so many weekly sitcoms, "on a soundstage, where brightly lit sets guaranteed the familiarity and comfort" of an idealized middle-class world (Gray 1995, 94). Yet, through the script's incorporation of frequently untranslated Spanish lines of dialogue, a brief privileging of the Latino experience at the expense of the show's typically Anglocentric universe is allowed to occur. An angered Chicano customer may mutter, "Eso me pasa a mi por venir aquí," or "That's what I get for coming here" before storming out on a typically abrasive Ed ("Ed Talks to God"). Most of these sorts of moments in which the show moves toward a bilingual mode of interaction with its audience, briefly placing non-Spanish speakers in a relatively powerless position, however, are simple muttered oaths or curses.

A more extended example includes an episode in which Chico convinces Ed to secure a loan for the garage from a Chicano-run bank in the community ("Borrowed Trouble" 1974/#2). When Ed grows upset at the "invasive" questions of the Chicano loan officer, his rudeness threatens to end the interview. Chico steps in on Ed's behalf, and he and the Chicano loan officer exchange several heated lines in Spanish that rise in pitch until Chico turns and simply tells Ed, "We got it," regarding the loan. Although this would seem to leave many Latino audience members and other Spanish-speaking viewers with a far different perspective and a different pleasure to take away from the scene, that analysis is only half-right. The lines of Spanish uttered during the argument by Prinze and the other actor do not actually lead to any agreement being reached between their two characters, a fact that will be of no bother to the vast majority of Anglo audiences but will be duly noticed by most Latinos.

One scene that used a lengthy untranslated Spanish passage and diverged from this pattern in an ironic fashion occurs in the episode "Natural Causes." Because Ed will not leave his bed, shaken by the death of a friend into believing that his time may be up, Chico brings his family doctor by to demonstrate that Ed's fears are unfounded. Although the doctor speaks four languages, he "prefers Spanish" with his people. And, as the checkup gets underway, he begins talking in confidential tones with Chico. The commencement of this conversation gives both Chico and the show's Spanish-speaking viewers "insider" status. The conversation's subject, that the doctor wants help from Chico with his car, is also an ironic joke that the rest of the show's viewers, and Ed himself, who do not have this power of language cannot yet share. The conversation moves on, and the doctor continues to discuss how the car has been dying out little by little. Finally, the doctor reveals, it just went dead— "muerto"—making the universally recognizable sign of a slit across the throat. At this point, non-Spanish-speaking audiences are laughing because of the implication that he is possibly referring to Ed, and at Ed's expression of surprise and fear. But Spanish-speaking audiences have, of course, been reading ahead and are well aware that Ed's fear is comical precisely because it is unnecessary. The exchange is brought to a conclusion as Chico "catches everybody up" by giving Ed and the briefly disempowered segment of the audience the translation that the doctor had simply been seeking auto advice and that his car most likely has a faulty carburetor.

In addition, the conflicted and contradictory persona of Freddie Prinze himself, the series' undeniable comedic star, could occasionally produce irruptions that highlighted the fact that, as Christine Acham states, although the media have often succeeded in quelling minoritized voices, television specifically can still be mobilized by these same voices as an instrument "for enjoyment and self-affirmation" (Acham 1999, 5–6). When Prinze sheds his highly assimilated style of speech and adopts his native Puerto Rican accent to boast of his prowess as a mechanic in taking care of tricked-up Chevies or to relay a humorous anecdote about the tall tales told him by relatives as a child, the show could become something more personalized for viewers of Latin descent than simply another outlet for obtaining a few laughs. There was both the affirming imagery of seeing a Puerto Rican comic "getting over" on the strength of his Latino-specific material and the opportunity to be entertained by this same material as well. But, as protesters noted when the show first aired, Prinze's Puerto Rican–inflected Spanish, "his gesticulations, his mode of speaking, his body language," all revealed him as part of a Latino culture distinct from the Chicano tradition his character supposedly represented.[14] So, for the Latino community that was the subject of the show, such moments presented two options. A radical disengagement from the text was possible due to the alienating effect of watching a Puerto Rican actor who was "not behaving like a Chicano" properly (Ray Andrade, quoted in "Chico's Associate Producer" 1974) or, conversely, a recognition of the ties between Latin American peoples of the United States—Mexican Americans, Puerto Ricans, Cuban Americans, and so on— and the interplay of these multiple identities and selves, prompting a move away from ethnic essentialism, could also result.

There remain even rarer occasions when Prinze's character uses his fish-out-of-water status as a Chicano mechanic in a garage owned by a white man in the middle of the barrio to offer up his own take on the ridiculousness of certain elements of white society, such as bank lending practices. In "Borrowed Trouble," the episode where he convinces Ed to borrow money to invest in the garage, here is how he breaks down the way the insular lending system in America operates during the story's opening moments after he hears his boss has "never borrowed money before in my life":

> Chico: *That's un-American. Everybody borrows money. If you don't borrow money and pay it back, when you do go to borrow money, if you haven't borrowed money before and paid it back, when you do go to borrow money, they give you a funny look. Because how they know you're going to pay it back if you've never borrowed it before and paid it back?*

The convoluted illogic in this riff, which is deployed humorously to explain the insularity of the "American" bank loan system, can also be read as perhaps an implicit critique of a process that erects barriers that make it difficult or impossible for those who are stigmatized with Otherness status to ever gain enough leverage to participate. Or, as social historian George Lipsitz succinctly puts it, minorities are often told in essence, "We can't give you a loan today because we've discriminated against members of your race so effectively in the past that you have not been able to accumulate any equity" or assets to pass down or acquire loans with prior to this (Lipsitz 1998, 14).[15]

The episode does then move on with Chico and Ed visiting the Chicano bank in the neighborhood that is "looking to do things for the community," offering the archetypal American "bootstraps" philosophy and suggesting that these "outsiders" can lift themselves up by establishing their own alternative institutions to the mainstream system. Ed's own loan, obtained after the multilingual confrontation at the bank referenced earlier, does not immediately turn his business around. Although the tension grows over all of the auto parts that Chico has encouraged them to purchase with the money, Ed and the audience learn that a detour caused by a just-completed construction job has been driving the garage's customers away for several days. Chico, however, is never brought into the narrative loop regarding this information, emphasizing his place in the show's hierarchy.[16]

Throughout "Borrowed Trouble," the issue of the loan and what it potentially represents is a constant cause of friction between Ed and Chico, with each character restating or acting out a single idea again and again. For Ed, it is his racially driven mantra that there's no point in trying because "the Mexicans" have taken over and are everywhere he turns. As he tells the Chicano loan officer, "I'm presently living out of the country. . . . I live in this neighborhood." Chico, on the other hand, clutches to the motivating belief that he's got bigger goals than playing second fiddle to a washed-up white bigot in a floundering garage. Finally boiling over after Ed's bumbling and impatience chase another Chicano customer away, Chico lets loose: "I don't know what I'm doing hanging around here where I got no future." Telling Ed he needs to "repair himself," Chico decides he's quitting. Opening up the back of the beat-up van that is his home, Chico begins packing as a new customer pulls in across the garage. With the episode nearing a conclusion, Chico reconsiders his decision to quit as he watches the normally abrasive Ed make a brief attempt to demonstrate his "niceness" while serving the middle-class Chicana housewife who has pulled in to purchase a dollar's worth of gas. This rethinking of Chico's previously more uncompromising stance is an apt display of what Chicano activist Cesar Flores, at the time the show first aired, described as one of its primary weaknesses: that it serves to reinforce the prevailing white attitude toward Mexican Americans—those who are subservient and try to please "the Man" regardless of the Man's faults are those most likely to succeed ("Chicanos Grouchy" 1974). Yet, despite appropriate criticisms along these lines, we are still left with brief irruptive moments of Prinze's comedy such as the tongue-twisting riff that sets this particular plot in motion and remains a suggestive critique that the dominant financial institutions may not have any interest in including Chico's "type" regardless of how uncompromising *or* how subservient they might be.

Conclusion

Before concluding this study of the integrated ghetto fictions of 1970s TV, there remain a few broader implications to be emphasized with respect to television and media studies, particularly from a methodological standpoint. Television historiography, like much of media historiography, can often be separated into two opposing camps. Perfectly embodying the first camp, on initially encountering it, William Boddy's *Fifties Television* (1990) might appear as almost having forgotten to include his ostensible subject matter. Omitting any analysis or description of programming content and the uses that consumers might have made of these texts, Boddy writes a purely "structural history" in which industry strategies and the regulatory and critical reaction to these business practices tell the story of the transitional era of 1950s TV (Boddy 1990).[17] On the other end of the spectrum, Lynn Spigel approaches the era of 1950s television by tracing the divergent ways in which the medium was used within the home and its effect on family and gender relations. Accordingly, her culturalist historiography includes an examination of TV texts—both the programs of the 1950s and TV-related advertising narratives (Spigel 1992). In my study, the approach has arguably fallen somewhere in between these two ends of the spectrum. Operating under the assumption that structural slippages of meaning and ideological tensions exist within popular culture forms already prior to their reception contexts, this article has frequently turned to textual analysis to tell a portion of the story of 1970s television, an era of social upheaval surrounding race, class, sexuality, and identity that intensified such tensions and slippages. A direct analogue in media history is the cinema of the wartime and immediate postwar era of the 1940s. Although films of the period often inserted challenges to the "consensus" to attempt to recoup these nonmainstream ideologies and images through the workings of narrative (e.g., a brief scene of a Zoot-suiter who decides to enlist), such efforts inadvertently revealed the fundamental divisions or slippages in American life around race, class, gender, and so on.[18] With such strategies part and parcel of the "turn to relevance" programs of the early 1970s like *Chico and the Man*, this study has hopefully contributed productively to the methodological debate surrounding media historiography, especially concerning periods of intense social transformation.

Moving away from purely theoretical concerns, however, there were very tangible results linked to *Chico and the Man's* often conflicted reception. Its success in the ratings allowed the show's white creator-producer James Komack to continue to prosper in Hollywood and move on to another integrated ghetto show of the 1970s, *Welcome Back Kotter*, which also adopted the basic formula of the humanistically inclined white paternalistic figure in the middle of an integrated ghetto universe. But for Freddie Prinze, the baggage acquired along his unique and contested ride to stardom was too much to bear. At the age of twenty-two, he became a casualty of suicide. The show itself continued to run for another year after this point, testifying to its wide-ranging popularity. As a genre, the integrated weekly series set within the often hotly contested political sphere of the ghetto gradually disappeared from network screens as the onset of the Reagan-Bush era of "feel-good politics" affected a broad spectrum of cultural discourse. During this period of reenergized neoconservativism, the genre came to be supplanted by a new breed of integrated shows such as *Diff'rent Strokes*, *Webster*, and *Gimme a Break*, which surrounded the non-white characters with white middle-class families and affluence, replacing urban poverty with upward social mobility in both setting and theme (Gray 1995, 79). And other than the quickly canceled ABC sitcom *Condo* (1982–1983), which also took place in an "upwardly mobile" setting (Montgomery 1989, 236), *Chico and the Man* remained the only prime-time network series to center on *any* Latino community for more than a quarter-century after its debut.[19] But any attempt to reclaim the show as a "progressive" text—in its frequent use of untranslated bilingual dialogue, for example—is often a matter of taking one step forward and two steps back. In this sense, what can be viewed as a historic moment within mass media for Chicano culture also needs to be thought about as a historic opportunity lost.

Notes

1. Klein would become NBC's top programming executive from 1976 to 1979, overlapping the final two years of *Chico and the Man's* four-year run with the network.

2. A descriptive phrase frequently cropping up during the period. In this case, Prinze's material would play on, and heavily traded in, stereotypes attached to various ethnic groups, often mining his own inner-city Puerto Rican background. But his jokes could also add another layer,

and in a routine linking Latinos to crime, he might comment on the problem of drugs being pushed on minority groups in the ghetto by outside forces, remarking, "We live in a society that cripples people, and then punishes them for limping." This kind of social commentary did make for some strange bedfellows with the pinup idol status he achieved as *Chico and the Man* grew into a smash hit; during its successful run, Freddie was a highly visible celebrity presence, guest-hosting *The Tonight Show*, releasing a comedy album in 1975, touring regularly as a standup comedian, and being linked to several of Hollywood's most eligible females before getting married and producing the son who would become a pinup icon to a new generation of hormone-raging adolescents. On Freddie Prinze's pinup status, see "Chico's Wild Ways" (1975).

3. On Justicia's extraordinary rise and fall as a force within network TV, see Montgomery (1989, 58–63).

4. Paul Macias of T.E.N.A.Z., a national Chicano theatre group, on *Newservice*, a radio show broadcast on KNBC in Los Angeles (September 12, 1974). Transcript obtained from David L. Wolper Collection, Warner Bros. Archives, University of Southern California.

5. In his willingness to voice his opinions to the media regarding the show's shortcomings, it gradually became clear that having Ray Andrade associated with the show only exacerbated the problems that *Chico and the Man* was having regarding its image in the Mexican American community. See also *Daily Variety*'s "Chico's Associate Producer Andrade Unhappy over Show's Chicano Image," in which Andrade admits that the producers have "ignored" his suggestions regarding creative content and that he finds the show "offensive in some respects" (September 19, 1974). Not surprisingly, Andrade's association with the program was not a lengthy one. At the end of the first season, he was replaced as associate producer by Michael Manheim.

6. For an informative history of MAPA, see García (1994).

7. Press release contained in publicity kit for premiere of *Chico and the Man*, NBC Television Press Department, from David L. Wolper Collection, Warner Bros. Archives, University of Southern California.

8. In my reading of *Chico* in which Prinze's character is situated within the rubric of what the U.S. hegemonic order has variously termed the Latin, Hispanic, or Latino race, the intent is not to elide the heterogeneous cultures and crucial "mixed-race" component of the history and experience of Latino/a peoples in the Americas. Rather, it is an attempt to effectively represent the semiotic system through which the program and its racial signifiers have been understood by the great majority of its viewers in a country where the social and historical construct of race has long been a fact of life. For a concise presentation explaining race as a sociohistorical rather than biological phenomenon, see Omi and Winant (1998, 13–22). Taking California and its history of white imperialism as his case study, Tomás Algauer (1994) examines similar processes of "racialization" during the state's formative period of development. Rather than offering an implicitly binary model of racial formations, Algauer's work finds each "nonwhite" population disciplined by a distinct set of racializing discourses that helps to construct and preserve a complex social hierarchy underwritten by a logic of white supremacism (1994). Finally, Mario Barrera draws on elements of social construction theories of race, Marxism, and the anticolonialist writings of Fanon and others for his analysis of Chicano history from the end of the U.S.-Mexico War through the present (1979, see especially 196–204).

9. For further discussion of the critical mode of humor in *Sanford and Son*, see Acham (1999, 137–42).

10. The multileveled audience response is, no doubt, also based partly on a nondiegetically driven recognition of Freddie Prinze's comic star persona operating within the text, functioning here to identify Prinze more closely with his standup comedy routines than with his role as "actor."

11. For the story of the joke's incorporation into the show (among other elements of Prinze's standup act), see Smith (1974).

12. To the extent that the series purports to focus on Chico and his surroundings but only to emphasize the struggles of a white consciousness, the show calls to mind contemporary films such as *The Green Mile*, in which racism and African American martyrdom are only pretexts for a white emotional epiphany.

13. In this respect, the episode's narrative connects with Chon Noriega's argument that the show's bilingual title—which translates as "Little Boy and the Man"—signified that the producers and protesters were both contesting the same gendered terrain: "an oedipalized masculinity" (Noriega 2000, 71). As Tino Villanueva points out, however, *chico* was historically used by Anglos to refer to Chicanos of all ages as a term of condescension much the equivalent of "boy" for African Americans, widely in circulation throughout the era of legalized segregation. With the adoption of this extremely generalized and frequently patronizing term as part of its title, the show's paternalistic impulse of racial containment is visibly foreshadowed (see Villanueva 1980, 33).

14. As Paul Macias of T.E.N.A.Z. points out on the *Newservice* radio show, broadcast on KNBC in Los Angeles (September 12, 1974). Transcript obtained from David L. Wolper Collection, Warner Bros. Archives, University of Southern California.

15. Although such a reading may seem to overemphasize the significance of race in the accumulation of capital and occlude the economic barriers often imposed against working-class whites, in this particular area, there is much evidence to support the emphasis on race as a crucial factor. Lipsitz (1998) cites the creation of the Federal Housing Act (FHA) in 1934, a program to assist private lending to new home buyers, which instead quickly used racist categories in the FHA's surveys to channel nearly all loan money toward whites and away from communities of color—denying any loans to racially "subversive" areas like Boyle Heights in 1939 or giving the largely white St. Louis County, Missouri, five times as many mortgages as the racially mixed city of St. Louis from 1943 to 1960. Nor have such racebased lending policies disappeared. A recent Bank of Boston study revealed that Boston bankers made three times as many mortgage loans per 1,000 homes in neighborhoods populated by *low-income whites* as they did in low-income African American neighborhoods. See Lipsitz (1998, 5–13).

16. A point not lost on many Chicano critics of the show. See "Chicanos Grouchy" (1974) and "Chico's Associate Producer" (1974).

17. This type of approach to the study of popular culture is at least partially traceable back to Frankfurt School critics such as Horkheimer and Adorno who, in downplaying the importance of textual analysis and reception studies, were apt to take the extreme position that "the triumph of invested capital . . . is the meaningful content of every film, whatever the plot the production team may have selected" (1972, 124). Another early contribution to the "industry studies" tradition is F. D. Klingender and Stuart Legg's 1930s study on the financial intricacies of the British (and American) cinema, *Money behind the Screen* (1937).

18. For a definitive take on the American cinema of the 1940s that reveals these mechanisms in much greater clarity and finer detail, see Polan (1986).

19. In 2000, *Showtime* debuted an original series, *Resurrection Blvd.*, which depicted the contemporary Latino struggle to escape the 'hood. The show's cast also raised an issue that may sound strangely familiar. In its second season, they added a non-Latino actor, Brian Austin Green, in a heavily promoted role to reach a wider (whiter?) audience. The show ran for three seasons before being canceled by *Showtime* execs.

References

Acham, Christine. 1999. *Peace, love and soul: 70s television and black public space*. Ph.D. diss., University of Southern California.

Algauer, Tomás. 1994. *Racial faultlines: The historical origins of white supremacy in California*. Berkeley: University of California Press.

Barrera, Mario. 1979. *Race and class in the Southwest: A theory of racial inequality*. Notre Dame: University of Notre Dame Press.

Boddy, William. 1990. *Fifties television: The industry and its critics*. Urbana: University of Illinois Press.

Chico's wild ways. 1975. *16 Magazine*, March.

Davis, Mike. 1992. *City of quartz*. New York: Vintage Books.

Friedman, Norman L. 1978. Responses of blacks and other minorities to television shows of the 1970s about their groups. *Journal of Popular Film and Television* 7(1): 99.

García, Mario T. 1994. *Memories of Chicano history: The life and narrative of Bert Corona*. Berkeley: University of California Press.

Gitlin, Todd. 1985. *Inside prime time*. New York: Pantheon.

Gray, Herman. 1995. *Watching race: Television and the struggle for "blackness."* Minneapolis: University of Minnesota Press.

Griswold del Castillo, Richard. 1979. *The Los Angeles barrio, 1850–1890: A social history*. Berkeley: University of California Press.

Guerrero, Ed. 1993. The black image in protective custody. In *Black American cinema*, edited by Manthia Diawara, 237–46. New York: Routledge.

Horkheimer, Max, and Theodor W. Adorno. 1972. *Dialectic of enlightenment*. New York: Herder and Herder.

Klingender, F. D., and Stuart Legg. 1937. *Money behind the Screen*. London: Lawrence and Wishart.

Lipsitz, George. 1998. *The possessive investment in whiteness*. Philadelphia: Temple University Press.

Montgomery, Kathryn C. 1989. *Target: Prime time: Advocacy groups and the struggle over entertainment television*. New York: Oxford University Press.

Noriega, Chon A. 2000. *Shot in America: Television, the state, and the rise of Chicano cinema*. Minneapolis: University of Minnesota Press.

Omi, Michael, and Howard Winant. 1998. Racial formations. In *Race, class, gender in the United States*, edited by Paula S. Rothenberg, 13–22. New York: St. Martin's.

Polan, Dana. 1986. *Power and paranoia: History, narrative and the American cinema, 1940–1950*. New York: Columbia University Press.

Sánchez, George J. 1993. *Becoming Mexican-American: Ethnicity, culture, and identity in Chicano Los Angeles, 1900–1945*. New York: Oxford University Press.

Smith, Cecil. 1974. *Chico and the Man*: A hit in spite of the controversy. *L.A. Times*, November 10, TV Times section.

Spigel, Lynn. 1992. *Make room for TV: Television and the family ideal in postwar America*. Chicago: University of Chicago Press.

Villa, Raúl Homero. 2000. *Barrio-logos: Space and place in urban Chicano literature and culture*. Austin: University of Texas Press.

Villanueva, Tino. 1980. *Chicanos: Antología história y literaria*. Mexico: Fondo Cultura Económica.

Waters, Harry F. 1974. Hot hungarican. *Newsweek*, November 11, 74–75.

Watson, Mary Ann. 1998. *Defining visions: Television and the American experience since 1945*. Fort Worth, TX: Harcourt Brace.

Greg Oguss received his master's degree in critical studies from the University of Southern California's School of Cinema-Television. He has published articles on film, television, and new media in journals such as *Film Quarterly* and *M/C Journal*. He is currently researching a novel on hospitalnoia.

Roots: *Docudrama and the Interpretation of History*

Leslie Fishbein

*R*oots was the sleeper of the 1976–1977 television season, surprising even its makers by its phenomenal critical and commercial success. An unusual risk, ABC's production of Alex Haley's 885-page opus represented the first time that a network actually made a movie based on a major unpublished book.[1] While blacks had gained visibility on television during the 1970s, their presence had been confined largely to situation comedies and variety shows rather than drama—with the notable exception of CBS's much-touted success with *The Autobiography of Miss Jane Pittman* (1973)—and *Roots'* makers had serious reservations about whether the public would accept a historical drama about slavery as seen from the vantage point of the slave. Advance sales of commercial spots in the miniseries were sold on the prediction of a relatively modest 30 share. Shortly before its airing date, program executive Fred Silverman rescheduled the show: instead of running on twelve successive weeks, it would run for eight consecutive nights, so that if it failed the agony would not be prolonged.[2]

Silverman's decision contributed to *Roots'* phenomenal success, but that decision itself derived from an odd blend of courage and caution. Producer Stan Margulies initially suggested the concept of a *Roots* week, but an ABC executive was fearful of the consequences of a low audience share the first night, so the idea was dropped for a year. "A year later," Margulies noted, "when we had completed production, and the big decision of how to show *Roots* came up again, this was raised, and to his credit Freddie Silverman, who was then head of the network, said, 'We've done something in making this that no one has ever done before. Let's show it in a way that no one has ever shown television before!'" In order to avoid losing the week in case of *Roots'* failure, Silverman kept strong programs like *Happy Days* and *Laverne and Shirley* and parceled *Roots* out in one- and two-hour segments; his innovative use of consecutive programming made television history.[3] Brandon Stoddard, then the executive in charge of ABC's novels for television, views Silverman's decision as simultaneously bold and circumspect: "It's certain that Fred's idea of scheduling it in one week was at the time very daring and innovative and theatrical and, I think, added a tremendous amount to the success of *Roots*—there's no question about it." Stoddard noted, however, the caution implicit in scheduling the series in January rather than in the more significant sweeps week in Febraury, a rating period in which network audience share is assessed as a means of calculating the attractiveness of each network to advertisers seeking a mass audience.[4]

Roots marked a dramatic shift in the nature of television programming, even though its ultimate format may have been a product of caution as much as daring. Although *Roots* already was in production when Silverman arrived at ABC from CBS, he was primarily responsible for radically altering the format of network programming by introducing limited miniseries in lieu of open-ended weekly series, by abandoning the rigid television season in a shift to real-time programming, and by deemphasizing the situation comedy and police/adventure series in favor of the drama of the television novel.[5] ABC's previous ratings success with Leon Uris's *QB VII* in 1975 and Irwin Shaw's *Rich Man, Poor Man* in 1976 had paved the way for *Roots* by demonstrating that the miniseries form pioneered by British television had genuine appeal for American audiences.[6] The miniseries format allowed television to achieve the thematic power and narrative sweep ordinarily reserved for film; in reviewing *Roots* as a successful competitor to the movies, film critic Pauline Kael remarked: "These longer narrative forms on TV enable actors to get into their characters and take hold of a viewer's imagination."[7]

The dramatic power of *Roots* sustained audience attention for eight consecutive nights, January 23–30, 1977. According to *Newsweek*, "A.C. Nielsen reported that a record 130 million Americans—representing 85 percent of all the TV-equipped homes—watched at least part of the twelve-hour miniseries. The final episode attracted a staggering 80 million viewers, surpassing NBC's screenings of *Gone With the Wind* and the eleven Super Bowls as the highest-rated TV show of all time."[8] All eight episodes ranked among the top thirteen programs of all time in terms of estimated average audience.[9] Despite the fact that *Roots'* cast was predominantly black and its villains largely white, none of the ABC affiliates north or south rejected *Roots*. In fact, more than twenty southern cities, all formerly citadels of segregation, declared the eight-day period of the telecast *Roots* week. More than 250 colleges and universities decided to offer courses based on the television program and the book.[10]

While even during production some critics of the series had feared that *Roots* would exacerbate racial tensions, if anything it served to promote racial harmony and understanding.[11] A handful of violent incidents did follow the broadcast. After a rape episode on *Roots*, black youths clashed with white youths in a parking lot of a Hot Springs, Arkansas, high school, leaving three students injured and eighteen arrested.[12] According to Kenneth K. Hur and John P. Robinson, " 'Roots' was also blamed for racial disturbances at schools in Pennsylvania, Michigan and Mississippi, and for a siege in Cincinnati in which a man took hostages and demanded the return of his son he had abandoned 19 years previously."[13] But apart from these isolated instances of hostility, *Roots* seemed to have had a genuinely humanitarian influence on its audience. An informal survey of National Association for the Advancement of Colored People branch leaders in selected cities nation-wide revealed highly positive local response; *Roots* was credited with reviving and strengthening the black-history offerings in schools and colleges, with enlightening whites about the black heritage, and with improving the quality of television programming.[14]

Various local surveys of black as well as white viewers indicated either that *Roots* had relatively little impact upon viewers' attitudes, since those most sympathetic to the plight of slavery were most likely to watch the programs in the first place, or that its effects were largely humanitarian. A Cleveland survey found that racially liberal whites viewed the programs in disproportionate numbers and were predisposed to be sympathetic to the shows' content; the data suggested that such liberals were most influenced by *Roots'* depiction of the hardships of slavery.[15] An investigation of the response of teenagers in metropolitan Cleveland similarly revealed that the racial attitudes of the teenagers rather than degree of viewing was the most accurate predictor of perceptions of the hardships of slavery; *Roots* had most impact on already liberal youths of both races.[16] A study of the racially heterogeneous southern community of Austin, Texas, a city with substantial representation of both non-whites and Mexican-Americans, revealed a generally favorable impact of *Roots* upon its viewing audience. The white community in particular was overwhelmingly positive in its response: "They felt that the program was an accurate depiction of slavery, that the cruel and generally senseless whites depicted in the program were accurately portrayed, and they may have learned a great deal about the black culture and heritage that was previously 'missing.' "[17] A national telephone survey of 971 respondents revealed that although it was widely hypothesized that whites would react to *Roots* with increased tolerance and blacks with increased hatred or prejudice, in fact both black and white respondents overwhelmingly indicated sadness to have been their predominant reaction to the programs. *Roots* appears to have been a learning experience for both races, to have increased understanding of blacks, and to have fostered interracial communication.[18] A summary of research findings from five studies of the *Roots* phenomenon, including three mentioned above, indicates that *Roots* either reinforced audience preconceptions or that it "performed a prosocial, humanistic, and informational role for viewers."[19] At any rate, the series did nothing significant to exacerbate racial tensions and may well have eased them by fostering understanding and communication.

Roots' popular success was matched by the critical attention it received. The dramatization garnered an extraordinary thirty-seven Emmy nominations, far surpassing the record of twenty-three nominations of *Rich Man, Poor Man* the year before. The show actually received nine Emmys in fourteen categories, including that for "outstanding limited series."[20] It also was named "program of the year" at the Television Critics' Circle Awards.[21] *Roots'* author, Alex Haley, was himself deluged with honors, including a National Book Award and a special Pulitzer Prize.[22]

Roots' extraordinary popularity was the product of a combination of factors, some largely fortuitous and others the result of shrewd programming and marketing techniques. Published October 1, 1976, Alex Haley's book *Roots*, on which the series was based, became the nation's top best-seller within a month.[23] Prior to the book's appearance, its author estimated that as a result of his indefatigable lecturing during the previous six years, more than a million people had learned of his family history and of the book in which it had been reconstructed.[24] Actual publication transformed Haley into an instant public hero: "It was perhaps the first time in history a writer was so quickly elevated to this kind of 'celebrity.'"[25] But the ABC dramatization further fueled the demand for the hardcover edition, and sales hit a one-day peak of sixty-seven thousand on the third day of the TV series.[26] Haley's publisher, Doubleday, expected a favorable public response to the book, but initially the firm projected a first print run of fifty thousand copies. When Doubleday executives met with David Wolper, executive producer of the ABC series, and Brandon Stoddard, both men indicated that such a projection was ludicrously low, that Haley's material was far more powerful than the publisher realized. Nor did the Doubleday executives fully appreciate the degree to which the television version would be a twelve-hour commercial for their product.[27] Perhaps buoyed by Wolper's and Stoddard's optimism, Doubleday proved sufficiently confident of the book's success to risk a record first printing of a hard cover edition of two hundred thousand, which paid off royally once the series was televised; *Roots* remained on the best-seller list for months and sold more than a million copies at $12.50 during 1977.[28] Hence part of *Roots'* popularity as a television series was predicated upon the startling success of the book on which it was based.

Roots' success also may derive from the craftsmanship of its structure. The narrative structure of the miniseries is highly satisfying, combining the lure of end-of-episode teasers with thematic coherence within individual shows. Each show treats a single theme, an approach unique to *Roots* and to its sequel *Roots: The Next Generations*, and provides thematic resolution for the viewer by the end of the episode. While this thematic approach was employed far more blatantly in *Roots: The Next Generations* two years later, it is already present in *Roots*. For example, the first show deals with the pain and hardship slaveholding caused the whites engaged in the slave trade, a theme treated only marginally in later episodes.[29] We see the gradual corruption of a man of Puritan temperament, Captain Thomas Davies, a man of honor and steel determination, who succumbs to temptation and proves to be corruptible because he is willing to set aside his scruples to carry a cargo of slaves. Captain Davies initially merits our sympathy and respect. The script describes him as "a man who commanded by intelligence and preparation. . . . Any ship of which he's master is going to arrive on time and intact." Davies is a *naïf* regarding the means of torture employed to subdue the captured slaves; he takes refuge from the troubling world by reading the Bible, and he prefers to sail on the Sabbath to bless even this mercenary voyage—"Seems the Christian thing to do"—a decision that contrasts ironically with his distasteful inspection of the thumbscrews used to achieve compliance from the captured female slaves.

Davies regrets his decision to take command and confides his disenchantment in a letter to his wife, telling her how he rues his separation from his family, leaving unstated the moral degradation this venture has entailed, as first mate Slater enters with a terrified black girl brought to be a "belly-warmer" for the captain: "Little flesh to take the chill off them cold sheets. Didn't figure it'd be any problem to a highborn Christian man like you, sir." Although Davies insists that he does not approve of fornication, he longs for human warmth to allow him respite from his moral struggle, and he attempts to dissolve her terror, ironically introducing himself by his Christian name to the uncomprehending female and invoking heaven when he realizes that she does not understand him. Davies is ordinarily a righteous man who is corrupted by his participation in a mercenary, racist enterprise.

The gradual progress of his corruption makes it seem inevitable, and we are meant both to pity him and to identify with him as a man buffeted by forces beyond his control. It is satisfying to unmask him as human and fallible even as we condemn his lapses from Christian morality.

Moreover, the narrative structure of *Roots* is surprisingly upbeat for a drama dealing with so grim a subject as slavery. With the exception of the sixth and seventh shows, which end ominously, each evening's viewing ends with a minor triumph or on a note of promise. *Roots* never sinks into despair regarding the fate of the slaves it portrays. After its harrowing scenes of the Middle Passage, the first show concludes with the exhortation of the Wrestler, a tribal leader, for the slaves to unite as one village, to learn each other's languages, so that they may destroy their enemies, ending with Kunta's voice repeating in incantatory rhythm: "We will live! We will live!"[30]

The second show ends similarly. The overseer Ames has ordered Kunta to be beaten until be submits to his slave name Toby. Fiddler ministers to the defeated Kunta, offering him solace, reassuring him of his African identity. Fiddler fondly soothes Kunta and consoles him: "There goin' to be another day! you hear me?—There gonna be another day."[31] The verbal promise is reinforced both visually and auditorially. The camera pulls back from the scene as Fiddler rocks Kunta in his arms, sponging his wrists, a Christological image made more emphatic by the cross formed by the fencing; as we see the final image of the plantation, we hear the drumbeats of Africa, a reminder that Kunta's African identity has not been effaced. The ending of the third show reinforces this theme. Kunta has been maimed by brutal slave-catchers, who amputated his foot; he has recovered his health due to the kindly ministrations of the main-house cook, Bell, who has taunted him into walking. Her pleasure at his accomplishment dims as Kunta reasserts his African identity: "Bell—I ain't no damn Toby! I Kunta Kinte, son of Omoro and Binta Kinte . . . A Mandinka fightin' man from the village of Juffure . . . and I'm gonna do better than walk. (*beat*) *Damnit! I'm gonna learn to run!*"[32] Kunta exults in his new-found strength, and his forward movement is our last image of him.

The triumphs are proof of human will, of the persistence of identity despite the obliterating impact of slavery. At the end of the fourth show, Kunta has opted to remain with Bell and their newborn daughter rather than follow the Drummer north to freedom. To reassure Bell, whose two children had been sold away from her after her first husband tried to escape, Kunta has given their daughter the Mandinka name of Kizzy to remind her that she has come from a special people and that she has a special destiny. The scene ends with the camera tightly focused on the baby Kizzy as we hear Kunta's voice: "Your name mean 'stay put'—but it don't mean 'stay a slave'—it won't *never* mean dat!!!"[33] Although this tiny creature cannot possibly comprehend her father's meaning, his words may serve to chart her future course; in her new life is the family's hope of redemption. In the fifth show the promise of Kizzy's name is betrayed as she is sold away from her parents because she aided her young beau Noah in his futile attempt to escape. Purchased by cockfighter Tom Moore, who rapes her the first night she is on his plantation, Kizzy recovers from her wounds by vowing vengeance against her oppressor. She grimly informs Malizy: "When I has my baby. . . he's gonna be a boy. (*beat*) And when that boys grows up, I promise you one thing . . . Massa Tom Lea is gonna get what he deserve . . ."[34] Kizzy's eyes glow with a hatred that will give her the sustenance her family no longer can provide.

The sixth and seventh shows end more ominously than the others, but they too bear witness to the small triumphs possible even in slavery. The sixth show was revised significantly for telecast, its penultimate and final scenes transposed. In the August 11, 1976, script by James Lee and William Blinn, the show ends as Kizzy takes revenge on the now-ancient Missy Anne, after the latter refuses her recognition, by surreptitiously spitting into her drinking cup before she hands it to her, small revenge for a betrayal of friendship, yet a minor victory that makes life worth living.[35] As actually telecast that scene precedes another in which Mrs. Moore asks her husband how Chicken George will react when he returns from England only to learn that his family has been sold off. Moore replies cynically: "He won't come back white, my dear . . . he'll still come back a nigger. (*then*) And, really, what's a nigger to do?" He takes up his drink and continues to stare emptily out the window.[36] The televised version reduces the significance of Kizzy's minor triumph and builds suspense regarding how Chicken George will seek to reunite his family and bring it to freedom.

The seventh show also juxtaposes triumph and ominous suspense. Tom has been forced to kill Jemmy Brent, a Confederate deserter caught trying to rape Tom's wife, Irene. In killing Brent, Tom has taken up his father's mantle. When Irene turns to Tom for guidance, "he draws himself up commandingly and suddenly we see the stamp of Chicken George on him, as never before—father and leader," as he tells her they will "bury him deep . . . and forget his name!" The episode actually ends, however, with Jemmy's brother Evan Brent, suspicious about Tom's battered face, menacing Tom: "You ain't seen the last of me . . ." as he jerks on his horse's bit and rides away. The camera focuses tightly on Tom: "His gaze is burning, fierce and unconquered. As he watches Brent go, a small flicker of triumph forms in his expression as we: FADE OUT."[37]

While the note of promise or minor triumph in the earlier shows is tempered by the bitter reality of slavery, by the end of the eighth show black/white power relationships have been altered significantly, and true optimism is possible. The final show concludes with a series of major triumphs: through a ruse of Chicken George, the family escapes from peonage; it moves to its own land in Tennessee and pays tribute to its African forebear, Kunta Kinte. Chicken George intones: "Hear me Kunta . . . Hear me, ol' African . . . you who was took from your father's house in chains . . . an' made a slave in a strange land . . . you who endured because you dreamed of bein' free . . . Hear me, African . . . the flesh of your flesh has come home to freedom . . . An' you is free at last . . . and so are we . . ." By invoking Kunta Kinte, this speech provides dramatic closure for the entire series. Its rhetoric echoes the famous "I Have a Dream" speech by Martin Luther King, Jr., in its final peroration. The show then telescopes the remainder of the family history even more drastically than Haley's own book and ends with the camera revealing the narrator of that history to be Haley himself, who tells of his obsessive search to learn of his family and its history, a search that took twelve years to complete and that resulted in a book called *Roots*.[38] At this point the show's optimism is complete: not only have Haley's ancestors achieved freedom and even prosperity, but Haley has done what blacks had only dreamed to be possible, he has traced his ancestry back to Africa; he has found his roots, and those roots have made him free.

In translating Haley's epic tale of slavery and emancipation to the television screen, *Newsweek* pointed out, "ABC could not resist applying the now standard, novels for television formula: lots of softcore sex, blood, sadism, greed, big-star cameos and end-of-episode teasers."[39] *Roots* represented the first time nude scenes would be shown on prime-time network television. The frontal nudity, however, was allowed only during the first four hours to preserve the authentic look of the Mandinka women in Africa and on the slave ship.[40] And ABC exerted a bizarre form of censorship to preserve decorum as it titillated its audience: "By the fine calibration of ABC's censors, no bared female breast could be larger than a size 32 or shown within 18 feet of the camera," *Newsweek* reported.[41] The episodes with sadistic appeal included the lashing of young Kunta Kinte to force him to accept the slave name Toby and the brutal amputation of his foot by depraved slave-catchers. Yet not all of the sex portrayed was sensationalistic. Haley's ancestors exhibited remarkable sexual restraint, with Kunta and Kizzy experiencing prolonged periods of volitional celibacy. As Brandon Stoddard has noted, however, *Roots* contained "some wonderfully erotic and sexually alive scenes with some of the black families."[42] But with the exception of Genelva's attempted seduction of Kunta, Haley's ancestors are sexually expressive only in love relationships with potential or actual mates. Their marriages are uniformly blessed with sexual fulfillment, with satisfaction lasting even into old age, as in the case of Matilda and Chicken George, so *Roots*' portrayal of sexuality also constitutes a paean to familial values.

Roots debunked the myth that white Americans would reject a black dramatic series of obvious social significance.[43] But the makers of *Roots* insured this success by deliberately catering to the white middle-class sensibility. *Roots* happened to be telecast during a record cold spell at a time when many people stayed home anyway on account of the gasoline crisis, and it profited from the fact that, anticipating little serious competition, the other networks had scheduled no strong counter-programming.[44] While such extrinsic factors might account for a greater likelihood of tuning *Roots* in, they hardly explain *Roots*' ability not only to capture but to hold white attention over a period of time. The acting in *Roots* was of a higher quality than that found in much of the contemporary cinema, according to critic Pauline Kael,[45] so *Roots* provided gratis what films no longer could assure their paying public.

Since the decision was made to cast the hitherto unknown LeVar Burton as the key role of the young Kunta Kinte, ABC hedged that risk by selecting a star supporting cast for the University of Southern California drama student.[46] The choice of an unknown actor, requiring his introduction to the American audience, provided ABC with what Stoddard calls "a whole new layer of publicity and promotion." But, more important, "from a purely casting standpoint it was essential that Kunta Kinte be seen not as an actor being Kunta Kinte but this being Kunta Kinte, which is exactly what happened."[47] Since the public had no prior image of LeVar Burton, it became easier to suspend disbelief and to forget the fact that this young man was merely acting a role. To tempt whites into viewing, the rest of the cast was laden with familiar television actors. David Wolper, executive producer of the series, explicitly admitted the use of television stars to lure white viewers in particular: "You have got to remember that the audience, the TV audience, is mostly white, middle-class whites. That's why we picked Ed Asner, Sandy Duncan. Lloyd Bridges, Chuck Connors, Lorne Greene, Cicely Tyson, Ben Vercen, and Leslie Uggams, all known TV actors. This was planned like this, because again here, we were trying to reach the maximum white audience."[48]

While Haley's book had devoted more than a fifth of its text to a richly detailed account of Kunta Kinte's life in Africa, the television miniseries extracts Kunta Kinte from Africa well before the first two-hour segment is over.[49] Brandon Stoddard, then a vice-president for novels for television at ABC, explained retrospectively why his gamble on *Roots* paid off so extravagantly in terms of its appeal to the parochial interests of its audience: "What seems to interest Americans most are Americans. A miniseries about the French Revolution wouldn't do it. In *Roots*, we got out of Africa as fast as we could. I kept yelling at everyone, 'Get him to Annapolis. I don't care how. Tell the boats to go faster, put on more sails.' I knew that as soon as we got Kunta Kinte to America we would be okay."[50] The African segment of *Roots* is an exotic, Edenic interlude, an excursion into an explicitly primitive world to which we, like Kunta Kinte, can never return; hence it poses no challenge to the social assumptions of white Americans.

Just as Alex Haley had subtitled his book *The Saga of an American Family*, so too did the miniseries aim at catholicity of appeal by advertising itself as "the triumph of an American family."[51] Critic Karl E. Meyer has noted that *Roots*, in fact, is a dramatic allegory comparable to a medieval morality play, being neither fact nor fiction, but a didactic popular entertainment.[52] As such it is concerned with Everyman, a figure representing the problems and limits of the human condition. Kunta Kinte and his heirs have a universal symbolic significance that overshadows their individual histories. Alex Haley argued that the universal appeal of *Roots* derived from the average American's yearning for a sense of heritage, from the equalizing effect of thinking about family, lineage, and ancestry, concerns shared by every person on earth.[53] This longing for rootedness transcended racial divisions. As James Monaco has noted, "Black Americans are not alone in their search for ethnic roots, and it seems likely that millions of white viewers were attracted as much by the saga of immigration and assimilation as by the racial politics."[54]

Although Haley's slave family was certainly atypical—Kunta Kinte came directly from Africa to American shores, a fate reserved for fewer than 6 percent of all slaves; his family had an exceptionally precise oral tradition; and Haley's ancestors were unusually privileged, both in Africa and in America—the television version of *Roots* consistently presented Haley's family as symbolic of all blacks.[55] Interviewed in his ancestral village of Juffure, Haley claimed that his authorial purpose had been more universal than personal: "I began to realize then that the biggest challenge I had was to try and write a book which, although [*sic*] was the story of my family would symbolically be in fact the saga of Black people in this country." For Haley, the family history of any American black would differ only in detail from that of any other; the fundamental outlines of their heritage remain identical.[56] Since historical details seem irrelevant to such archetypal experience, whites, too, could respond equally well to the search for roots. Haley argued: "What *Roots* gets at, in whatever its form, is that it touches the pulse of how alike we human beings all are when you get down to the bottom, beneath these man-imposed differences we set one between the other."[57] The television miniseries echoed Haley's approach: LeVar Burton was presented as "a young man everybody could identify with" rather than as "a true African of two hundred years ago," and *Roots* was mounted as "a drama *about* black people for everybody."[58]

The telecast created burgeoning interest in genealogy and in popular searches for ethnic and familial heritage. "Following the TV-special, letters to the National Archives, where Haley did genealogical research in census manuscripts, tripled, and applications to use the research facilities increased by 40 percent," one scholarly journal reported. Genealogy was absorbed into the university curriculum and inspired books on Jewish and black ethnicity.[59] Alex Haley even donated $100,000 of his royalty money to the Kinte Foundation to provide guidance but no financial aid for those engaged in genealogical research.[60] The interest in genealogy may well have eclipsed the concern with slavery for many viewers. Significantly, when Haley himself appeared on *The Tonight Show* following the broadcast of *Roots*, he did not want to discuss slavery or its evils, but instead appeared obsessed with genealogy and with the notion that blacks could be integrated into American society because they too had families.[61]

French theorist Ernest Renan once argued that an essential factor in the making of a nation was "to get one's history wrong," that new historical research that illuminated the deeds of violence upon which all political formations must be founded may pose a danger to nationality.[62] *Roots* attempted to correct a political amnesia that had buried the horrors of slavery, but instead of threatening national self-image, *Roots* generated a search for personal heritage that transcended racial lines. In illuminating certain aspects of slavery—the victimization of blacks—it obscured others: the degree of their complicity and the degradation of character that might accompany powerlessness. ABC's promotional material for *Roots* emphasized the veracity of Haley's monumental research, explicitly billing the series as a nonfiction "ABC Novel for Television": "The epic narrative, an eloquent testimonial to the indomitability of the human spirit, involved 12 years of research and writing during a half-million miles of travel across three continents."[63] Despite their claims to essential truth, Haley's *Roots* and the television series create a new mythology to replace the older one: if slavery never robbed Kunta Kinte's heirs of their essential dignity, how oppressive could the "peculiar institution" have been? It is a myth, the epic story of the African, that sustains them during all their trials and tribulations. And Haley and the makers of the miniseries use *Roots* to conjure with, to provide a viable mythology to enable a modern audience to find rootedness in a troubled world.

In an era of mass society in which the concept of the self-made person seems of only antiquarian value, *Roots* created a compelling symbolic alternative. *Roots*, and even more blatantly *Roots: The Next Generations*, may be viewed as success stories recounting the rise of Haley's family as it achieved not only freedom but respect, prosperity, and status within the community. *Roots* differs, however, from most examples of American fictional or filmic treatment of the success theme. There are very few American success stories with happy endings, perhaps reflecting a national ambivalence toward success that allows Americans to dissipate any guilt regarding their envy of success by nothing the psychological price to be paid. Novels like Theodore Dreiser's *The Financier* and F. Scott Fitzgerald's *The Great Gatsby*, and films like *Citizen Kane* and *Mildred Pierce*, seem to imply that the acquisition of wealth and personal power precludes true happiness and fulfillment. *Roots* breaks with this pattern, since in the culminating episode the family has achieved freedom and dignity on its own land in Tennessee. In an essay on the rise of ethnic consciousness during the 1970s, James A. Hijiya has noted a significant shift in the American myth of success: "The fascination with the family and the ethnic group signals, I believe, a partial retreat from the traditional ideal of the self-made man. To an unaccustomed degree, Americans are conceiving themselves as products of groups."[64]

In *Roots* what makes the family "special" and, therefore, more worthy than its peers is its preservation of its ethnic heritage and its celebration of familial values. Chicken George returns from his triumphs as a cockfighter in England not to pursue personal success nor to achieve individual freedom but to win those accomplishments for his entire family. Because the family never forgets its roots nor its obligations to its patriarch, it remains in Alamance County after the Emancipation until Chicken George returns and sets into motion the chain of events that will lead to its genuine freedom from the debt slavery accompanying Reconstruction. That ultimate success may be acceptable to an American audience because it fulfills certain essential criteria: the blacks were tricked out of their freedom by the duplicity of Senator Justin—hence they deserved a better fate; their success came through cooperation with a good white, Ol' George—hence black success is not necessarily linked to white deprivation; they deserved some reward for their uncompensated hard labor on the former Harvey plantation; and, most important, their success was familial rather than individual so that it avoided the corruption of the sin of pride. If success is not personal, it can be enjoyed without anguish, since it is not tainted with selfishness. Many American success stories, including those listed above, are bittersweet or tragic precisely because success entails the betrayal of familial values; by effacing the dichotomy between family and success, *Roots* offers a far more tantalizing promise than most other versions of the American Gospel of Success.

Roots also mythologized the African past. For example, Haley and the makers of *Roots* recreated Haley's ancestral village of Juffure as a primal Eden.[65] The African jungle in the dramatization appeared "as manicured as a suburban golf course."[66] In fact, Juffure was no isolated bucolic haven but rather the center of an active slave trade in which the villagers were complicit. Recent historical research by Philip D. Curtin places eighteenth-century Juffure in the center of one of the region's most thriving Afro-American trading networks. But Haley preferred to ignore Juffure's complicity in the violence and brutality of the slave trade and instead celebrated it as untouched by sordid reality.[67] In the year in which Kunta Kinte was captured, 1767, a commercial war was brewing between Ndanco Sono, the powerful king of Nomi, and the English who refused to pay tribute for navigating the Gambia River in pursuit of the slave trade. In reviewing Haley's book, historian Willie Lee Rose noted: "It is inconceivable at any time, but particularly under these circumstances, that two white men should have dared to come ashore in the vicinity of Juffure to capture Kunta Kinte, even in the company of two Africans, as Haley describes it." If such whites had appeared, the king would have exacted a terrible revenge by using his fleet of war canoes, each carrying forty or fifty men armed with muskets. According to Rose, Kunta's childhood was based on a myth of tribal innocence: "In fact history seems entirely suspended in the African section. No external events disturb the peaceful roots of Kunta Kinte's childhood."[68] Although Haley's prose portrait of Juffure had been subject to substantial historical criticism, it was recreated intact in the television miniseries. Haley ultimately admitted his intentional fictionalization of Juffure, which actually had far more contacts with whites than the village he described: "Blacks long have needed a hypothetical Eden like whites have."[69]

The portrait of slavery that appears in the televised version of *Roots* is laden with inaccuracies, including many that had been criticized after the publication of Haley's book. For example, Dr. Andrew Billingsley has noted that the manhood rites of the Mandinka took three or four years, not the several days depicted in the film.[70] John Reynolds is portrayed farming cotton in Spotsylvania County in an era in which the crop would have been tobacco.[71] Chicken George's fate makes little sense after he is taken to Britain for five years by a wealthy Englishman to train his fighting cocks: "Despite Lord Mansfield's 1771 ruling in the Somersett case, announcing that once a slave set foot on British soil he became free, Haley has George remain a slave to the British lord. Sent back to America in 1860, George continues a slave, even though he stops off in New York, where the personal liberty laws would certainly have guaranteed his freedom, and he returns docilely to the South to entreat his master for liberty."[72]

Subsequent to the telecast the genealogical foundations upon which *Roots* was based were challenged on several fronts. A British reporter with a reputation for integrity, Mark Ottaway, spent a week in Gambia studying Haley's factual claims.[73] Ottaway's investigation revealed that Juffure in 1767 was hardly a "combination of third-century Athens and Club Mediterrance with peripatetic philosophers afoot!' " but rather was a "white trading post surrounded by white civilization." Its inhabitants were not victims of the slave trade but collaborators in it, aiding whites in the capture of other Africans living farther up the river, hence the improbability of one of its residents being captured in 1767. Haley seems to have chosen 1767 as the year of Kunta Kinte's capture not on the basis of information obtained in Gambia but rather because it was the only year that would coincide with Haley's American research data. Kebba Fofana, whom Haley believed to be a griot who had preserved his family's oral tradition, was in fact not a member of that hereditary caste. A reckless playboy youth, Fofana had been a drummer (*jalli*), which in Mandinka can also mean griot, but he had received no formal training in the griot's complex art and learned his stories from listening to the village elders. There is strong evidence to indicate that Fofana knew in advance the nature of Haley's quest and sought to flatter his guest by reciting a narrative pleasing to him. Shortly before his death Fofana made a deposition of the tale he had told Haley for the Gambian Archives. The names of Kunta's father and brothers do not coincide with the names used in *Roots*. It seems highly improbable that any resident of Juffure could have been captured by slavers in 1767, since the British were allowed peaceful trade by the king of Barra on the condition that none of his subjects should ever be captured as a slave. The African evidence makes it likely that Fofana's Kunta Kinte was captured after 1829. Ottaway argued, "It is undoubtedly on the assumption of accuracy that the book's commercial success is founded"; while his investigation cast doubt on that accuracy, he conceded that the symbolic truth of *Roots* remained untarnished.[74]

More recently Professor Gary B. Mills of the University of Alabama and his wife, Elizabeth Shown Mills, a certified genealogist who specializes in the ethnic minorities of the South, have demonstrated the utter unreliability of Haley's pre–Civil War genealogical research. Crucial to Haley's narrative is the linkage of the identity of the captured Kunta Kinte to that of the American slave Toby. The Millses discovered that the *"Waller slave Toby appeared in six separate documents of record over a period of four years* preceding *the arrival of the* [ship] *Lord Ligonier*. Toby Waller was not Kunta Kinte." Strong circumstantial evidence indicates that *"Toby died prior to the draft of the 1782 tax roll—which was at least eight years prior to the birth of Kizzy, according to ROOTS."* Nor is it possible to substantiate that Dr. William Waller ever owned a slave named Bell who had been callously sold away from her infants. Moreover, a "Deed of Gift" by William Waller of 1767 and additional county records indicate that the doctor's niece Ann was a fully adult married woman at the time Haley portrayed her as Kizzy's childhood playmate. A thorough study of the Waller documents filed in Spotsylvania County prior to 1810 and a continued study of family probate records filed through 1833 failed to uncover a single Waller slave by the name of Kizzy or by any of the other names Haley used to designate the Waller slaves. Nor does an analysis of country, state, and federal records substantiate Haley's portrait of the Lea family (renamed Moore for the television series). The only Thomas Lea in Caswell County, North Carolina, who was head of a household in 1806–1810 was far more affluent than the cockfighter pictured in *Roots*; Mrs. Lea was not barren and, in fact, bore at least two boys and two girls, with at least one son and one daughter surviving long enough to produce progeny of their own. The members of the Lea household do not correspond with Haley's account in *Roots*, nor could Tom Lea's economic disaster in the mid-1850s account for the dispatch of Chicken George to England in satisfaction of his debts, because Thomas Lea died between October 1844 and March 1845. In short, Haley appears to have misinterpreted or misrepresented the historical record in order to create a dramatic, stereotyped version of his family history, one with enormous popular and commercial appeal.[75]

Even the inaccuracies known at the time of the telecast were allowed to stand because the facts were far less significant than the myths *Roots* wished to generate. Haley himself conceded that *Roots* was not so much a work of history as a study in mythmaking. Haley called his methodology "faction": "All the major incidents are true, the details are as accurate as very heavy research can make them, the names and dates are real, but obviously when it comes to dialogue, and people's emotions and thoughts, I had to make things up. It's heightened history, or fiction based on real people's lives."[76] Haley's book, much like Harriet Beecher Stowe's *Uncle Tom's Cabin* (1851), is, as Meg Greenfield pointed out in *Newsweek*, "a work of historical imagination and re-creation," ultimately a powerful, provocative fiction.[77]

Subsequent events raised fundamental questions regarding Haley's authorial role in this research. In the wake of the success of the television miniseries, Alex Haley was barraged by a series of lawsuits charging him with plagiarism. While the court dismissed the charges of Dr. Margaret Walker Alexander that Haley had pilfered substantial portions of her 1966 epic novel *Jubilee*, Haley did agree to a half-million-dollar out-of-court settlement with Harold Courlander, who had charged him with plagiarizing several sizable segments of his 1967 novel *The African*. The trial illuminated the degree to which Haley had succeeded in creating an authorial persona that bore little relation to his actual experience as a writer. He denied ever having read either *Jubilee* or *The African*, an incredible omission for a writer who had spent a dozen years researching his family history. A scholarly journal asserted: "For him to have missed these books is almost akin to someone doing a book on the history of the Black church in America and knowing nothing of W. E. B. Du Bois and E. Franklin Frazier."[78] In testimony given at the trial Haley conceded that three brief passages in *Roots* had been derived from Courlander's novel. The plagiarism was depicted as inadvertent by Haley's lawyer, but his rationalization of it reveals a new side of Haley to his American audience: "Haley's counsel, George Berger of Phillips Nizer, said passages from 'The African' had probably been given to Haley during lecture tours while he was researching 'Roots,' when many of his listeners would volunteer material. The collected materials were subsequently culled by graduate students who did not identify their sources, Berger said."[79] This account contradicts Haley's repeated characterization of his twelve-year search as an arduous solitary one during which the author had to support himself with free-lance articles and lectures because any monetary return seemed so unlikely.[80] Clearly *Roots* was not simply the product of one man's quest and suffering as Haley had claimed in so many public forums, nor did it draw strictly upon his own family's authentic historical record.

The television dramatization had no more genuine respect for historical authenticity. For example, one of the most striking episodes in the televised *Roots*, the slave rebellion aboard the *Lord Ligonier*, did not occur in Haley's original version on account of seasickness and flux among the slaves.[81] There are numerous discrepancies between the miniseries and Haley's 1972 account in *The New York Times Magazine*. That account claims that the doctor, William Waller, was the one who named the African Toby after he had been maimed by slave-catchers, whereas the series has Kunta Kinte being beaten into submission less than a year after he has been acquired by the doctor's brother. In the *Times* version Kunta is captured while chopping wood to make himself a drum, whereas in the film he is making that drum, at his grandmother's request, for his younger brother Lamin. In the *Times* narrative Kunta Kinte is the eldest of four sons; perhaps to increase the pathos of his capture, he is given only one remaining brother in the film.[82] The character of Fiddler in the film has no historical basis; he is a composite of three characters in the book in order to provide continuity. David Wolper explicitly disparaged scholarly efforts to chide the film for its lack of historical accuracy: "Some critics complained because we showed a mountain peak in Henning, Tennessee, because that section of the country doesn't have mountains. Nobody cares; it is totally irrelevant. A film is not for reference, but for emotional impact to let you know how it was to live at a certain moment in time. *Roots* was supposed to let the viewing audience feel how it was to be a slave. If you're not moved by watching a film, then the film has failed."[83]

While the genealogy of *Roots* may have been flawed or even fictitious and many of the historical details inaccurate, both the book and the television miniseries provide a valuable corrective of traditional images of slavery. Certainly *Roots* effectively debunks many of the stereotypes of slave life propounded by historian Stanley M. Elkins in his seminal work *Slavery: A Problem in American Institutional and Intellectual Life* (1959). Elkins argues that the slave experience closely approximated the closed institutional framework of the Nazi concentration camp with the slaves forced to assume a strategy of accommodation via role playing in order to deal with their oppressors. Elkins claims that the role of Sambo, an infantile and utterly dependent creature, "docile but irresponsible, loyal but lazy, humble but chronically given to lying and stealing," was the most pervasive one assumed by American slaves. *Roots* argues that slaves had a remarkable ability to avoid this role, that the institution of slavery was neither coherent enough nor oppressive enough to coerce predominantly Sambo-like behavior. Kunta Kinte never becomes servile despite repeated punishments, including mutilation, for his escape attempts; nor do any of his heirs identify with their owners as "good fathers"—Chicken George has to be restrained from killing his actual father when he realizes that he is no more than valuable chattel to the man. Elkins contends that slaves brought to North America were so shocked by the effectiveness with which they were detached from their cultural background in Africa that they had no choice but to become infantile in the interests of physical and psychic survival. *Roots* shows that the African heritage was not obliterated with the first generation, that remnants of tribal culture might be transmitted even into modern times. Elkins argues that the slave child bad no other viable father-image than that of the master, since the actual male parent was divested of any effective authority over the child. *Roots* presents Kunta Kinte, Chicken George, and Tom as patriarchal figures, able to command respect and to wield authority within the familial context. The miniseries makes it clear that the slave family was a viable counterweight to the oppressive nature of the "peculiar institution."[84]

In fact, *Roots* reflected the complexities of the slave experience revealed by modern historians who objected to Elkins's monolithic view of slavery. It recognized the persistence of African culture in slave society. As Lawrence W. Levine subsequently noted in *Black Culture and Black Consciousness: Afro–American Folk Thought From Slavery to Freedom* (1977):

> *From the first African captives, through the years of slavery, and into the present century black Americans kept alive important strands of African consciousness and verbal art in their humor, songs, dance, speech, tales, games, folk beliefs, and aphorisms. They were able to do this because these areas of culture are often the most persistent, because whites tended not to interfere with many of these culture patterns which quickly became associated in the white mind with Negro inferiority or at least peculiar Negro racial traits, and because in a number of areas there were important cultural parallels and thus wide room for syncretism between Africans and Europeans.[85]*

In *Roots* Kunta Kinte and his heirs are able to preserve vestiges of African language, folk beliefs, and customs, including the ritual of naming a newborn child by lifting it upward toward a full moon, a gesture of symbolic renewal of the link to Africa.

The willingness of modern historians to do "history from the bottom up," to take seriously as evidence slave narratives and other documents illuminating, even if indirectly, the vantage point of the slave, has revealed a hitherto undisclosed pattern of quotidian slave resistance to oppression. Gilbert Osofsky takes note of numerous slave narratives that demonstrate the slaves' "perpetual war to prevent debasement": "The powerful, the self-willed, those whose spirits could not be broken and who sometimes repulsed physically all attempts to whip them, presented the ultimate challenge to the mystique of the master caste."[86] Certainly both Kunta Kinte and Tom Moore fit this rebellious image, one that modern research demonstrates to be far more common than the Elkins model of slavery would assume.

While slave narratives were written from the perspective of those who successfully escaped the toils of slavery and thus may be biased toward expressing resistance and rebellion, the Slave Narrative Collection of the Federal Writers' Project of the Works Progress Administration, compiled during the years 1936–1938 as a result of more than two thousand interviews with former slaves, similarly debanks the Elkins thesis. The interviews reveal that the "peculiar institution" left "room for maneuver, for tactics and strategies, for blacks as well as for whites." The editor of these narratives, George P. Rawick, argues that it was the slave community, rather than the more tenuous institution of the slave's nuclear family, subject to dissolution at the master's whim, that was "the major adaptive process for the black man in America." The existence of the slave community insured that slaves did not suffer total domination by the master class; it enabled its members to alleviate the worst of their oppression and at times even to dominate their masters. Built out of materials from both their African past and their American present, "with the values and memories of Africa giving meaning and direction to the new creation," the slave community provided nurture for its members, who sought dignity and identity despite their physical subjugation.[87] In *Roots* the slave community is similarly portrayed as one largely supportive of its members, whether it be Bell inspiring the injured Toby to walk again or Kunta aiding the young Noah in his plan to flee North.

In fact, *Roots* reflects the historiographical insights of Herbert G. Gutman's *The Black Family in Slavery and Freedom, 1750–1925* (1976). Relying heavily upon census manuscript materials, Gutman discovered that the prevailing stereotype of the tenuous nature of the slave family was erroneous: "Evidence of long marriages is found in all slave social settings in the decade preceding the Civil War." Despite the oppressive nature of slavery, Gutman argues, blacks were able to retain and develop familial and kinship ties that allowed them to "create and sustain a viable Afro-American culture." *Roots*, too, emphasizes the degree to which the family, based as it was on strong affectional ties and preserving remnants of the African heritage, allowed slaves to sustain dignity and identity despite generations of oppression by whites. In debunking the assertion of Daniel Patrick Moynihan that "it was by destroying the Negro family that white America broke the will of the Negro people," both Gutman's work and *Roots* have done a major service to black historiography, for they have demonstrated the essential role played by the black family in transmitting Afro-American culture across generations of enslavement.[88]

If historical details are of only peripheral interest, the series' true concern, much like Haley's, is with mythmaking. And the most potent myth that the television version has to offer is that of the family. It is ironic that Haley himself was a poor family man who had left home as a youth and subsequently was twice divorced.[89] Haley spent little time with his two children as they were growing up; he kept his family life so private that some of his oldest friends in Los Angeles did not know until Haley became a celebrity that he had grown children. Richard M. Levine has written of *Roots'* author: "Clearly, in Alex Haley, television has finally found a man whose insatiable nostalgia for the vanishing dream of the American family matches its own."[90]

The myth of the family may be a source of pride and dignity for its members, sustaining their morale despite adversity; but the family also was an institution that subverted slave efforts at escape and rebellion. The myth of the family perpetuates a nostalgic desire for self-reliance; it nourishes the belief that problems can be solved in small, decentralized units instead of preaching a wider scope for human interdependency. Historian Eric Foner has written of the constrictive effects of *Roots'* notion of the family:

> It is not simply that the narrow focus on the family inevitably precludes any attempt to portray the outside world and its institutions. To include these institutions would undermine the central theme of Roots—the ability of a family, through unity, self-reliance, and moral fortitude, to face and overcome adversity. Much like the Waltons confronting the depression, the family in Roots neither seeks nor requires outside help; individual or family effort is always sufficient.
>
> Here, I believe, lies one reason for the enormous success of Roots among whites as well as blacks. The emphasis on the virtues and self-sufficiency of family life responds to a nostalgia for a time before divorce had become widespread, women had challenged their traditional homemaker role, and children had become rebellious, when the American family existed as a stable entity. Despite the black-nationalist veneer, in other words, the values of Roots are quintessentially American.[91]

Roots was acceptable to white audiences because of its essential conservatism; it unabashedly celebrated the family. Despite its own evidence to the contrary, *Roots* upheld the notion that the revolutionary spirit of the slaves was nurtured by the family unit. One film commentator has remarked, "Not for Alex Haley the more disturbing implications of William Styron's *The Confessions of Nat Turner*—that it was only when blacks were allowed to separate themselves from that family unit that their revolt became possible."[92] While for over a century historians and sociologists have debated the ravages to the black family wrought by slavery, Alex Haley may well have been the first to suggest that slavery may have made a positive contribution to family life.

But family life, in fact, can constrain freedom. The birth of Kizzy keeps Kunta Kinte from making a final attempt to escape to freedom. Although Kizzy had vowed to avenge her rape by Tom Moore by having her firstborn manchild kill him, Kizzy ultimately dissuades Chicken George from that course by revealing that "it'd be killing your own flesh and blood. He's your papa. You're his son." And even after emancipation the family decides to remain in North Carolina despite the depredations of the night riders, because George's wife Matilda refuses to let the family leave until her husband has returned: "We is a family and we is gonna stay a family." *Roots* fails to acknowledge that family and freedom may be mutually incompatible.[93] Nor does it ever question whether the family, as a product of hostility, may not crumble once prejudice and oppression are removed. The network may have championed *Roots* as "the triumph of an American family," but that triumph may have been purchased at the expense of freedom and social consciousness.

Notes

The author would like to thank the Rutgers University Research Council for its fellowship support.

1. Harry F. Waters with Vern E. Smith, "One Man's Family," *Newsweek*, 21 June 1976, p. 73.

2. David L. Wolper with Quincy Troupe, *The Inside Story of T.V.'s "Roots"* (New York: Warner Books, 1978), pp. 50, 138; Richard M. Levine, "Roots and Branches," *New Times*, 4 September 1978, p. 54; James Monaco, "Roots and Angels: U.S. Television 1976–77," *Sight and Sound* 46 (Summer 1977):159.

3. Stan Margulies (producer), interview and discussion with Margulies and John Erman (director) in Arthur Knight's cinema class, University of Southern California, 15 February 1979. Film: *Roots: The Next Generations*, 1 reel, 7". University of Southern California Special Collections. Also see Wolper with Troupe, *Inside Story*, pp. 136–139.

4. Telephone interview with Brandon Stoddard, vice-president for ABC Entertainment, Century City, California, 20 June 1981 (hereafter referred to as Stoddard interview).

5. Monaco, "Roots and Angels," p. 159.

6. Karl E. Meyer, "Rootless Mini-series," *Saturday Review*, 20 January 1979, p. 52.

7. Pauline Kael, "Where We Are Now," *The New Yorker*, 28 February 1977, p. 90.

8. Harry F. Waters with Bureau Reports, "After Haley's Comet," *Newsweek*, 14 February 1977, p. 97.

9. "Nielsen All-Time Top 25 Programs," *Nielsen Newscast*, no. 1, 1977, p. 6. Rankings based on reports through 17 April 1977.

10. Wolper with Troupe, *Inside Story*, p. 164; Les Brown, *The New York Times Encyclopedia of Television* (New York: Times Books, 1977), p. 369.

11. Stoddard interview.

12. Waters, "After Haley's Connet," pp. 97–98.

13. Kenneth K. Hur and John P. Robinson, "The Social Impact of 'Roots,' " *Journalism Quarterly* 55 (Spring 1978):19.

14. Gloster B. Current, "Cross-Country Survey on *Roots*—The Saga of Most Black Families in America," *The Crisis* 84 (May 1977): 167–172.

15. Hur and Robinson, "Social Impact," pp. 20–24, 81.

16. K. Kyoon Hur, "The Impact of 'Roots' on Black and White Teenagers." *Journal of Broadcasting* 22 (Summer 1978):289–298.

17. Robert E. Balon, "The Impact of 'Roots' on a Racially Heterogeneous Southern Community: An Exploratory Study," *Journal of Broadcasting* 22 (Summer 1978):299–307. Quotation appears on p. 306.

18. John Howard, George Rothbart, and Lee Sloan, "The Response to 'Roots': A National Survey," *Journal of Broadcasting* 22 (Summer 1978):279–287.

19. Stuart H. Surlin, " 'Roots' Research: A Summary of Findings," *Journal of Broadcasting* 22 (Summer 1978):309–320. Quotation appears on p. 319.

20. R. Kent Rasmussen, "'Roots'—A Growing Thicket of Controversy," *Los Angeles Times*, 24 April 1977, p. 5:1; Walper with Troupe, *Inside Story*, p. 164.

21. Morna Murphy, "TV Critics Circle Picks 'Roots' as Program of Year, ABC Top Net." *Hollywood Reporter*, 13 April 1977.

22. Rasinussen, "Thicket of Controversy," p. 1; Hans J. Massaquni. "Alex Haley in Juffure," *Ebony*, July 1977, p. 42.

23. "Why Alex Haley Is Suing Doubleday: An Outline of the Complaint," *Publishers Weekly*, 4 April 1977, p. 25.

24. "PW Interviews Alex Haley," *Publishers Weekly*, 6 September 1976, p. 9.

25. Wolper with Troupe, *Inside Story*, pp. 110–111.

26. "Why 'Roots' Hit Home," *Time*. 14 February 1977, p. 69.

27. Stoddard interview.

28. David A. Gerher. "Haley's *Roots* and Our Own: An Inquiry into the Nature of a Popular Phenomenon," *Journal of Ethnic Studies 5* (Fall 1977):87.

29. Stoddard interview.

30. *Roots*, show #1, as telecast, by William Blinn and Ernest Kinoy, p. 6. Scripts of all the episodes of *Roots* were provided courtesy of David L. Wolper, David L. Wolper Productions, Warner Bothers Television, Burbank Studios, 4000 Warner Boulevard, Barbank, Calif., pp. 19, 89, 93–94. Quotation appears on p. 94.

31. *Roots*, show #2, as telecast, by William Blinn and Ernest Kinoy, p. 98.

32. *Roots*, show #3, teleplay by James Lee and William Blinn, 15 June 1976, 5th hour, p. 56.

33. *Roots*, show #4, by James Lee and William Blinn, 17 June 1976, 6th hour, p. 58.

34. *Roots*, show #5, by James Lee, second draft. 19 April 1976, 7th hour, p. 57. Note that rather than Tom Moore, in the script the name Tom Lea was actually used, as in Haley's book.

35. *Roots*, show #6, teleplay by James Lee and William Blinn. 11 August 1976, 8th hour, p. 61.

36. *Roots*, show VI. Part 2, 28 January 1977, Museum of Broadcasting, New York City. All the videotapes of *Roots, Roots One Year Later,* and *Roots: The Next Generations* were viewed courtesy of the Museum of Broadcasting.

37. *Roots*, show #7, by M. Charles Cohen, revised second draft, 30 August 1976, 10th hour, pp. 48, 50. For the last quotation the line in the actual telecast was: "You ain't seen the last of me, nigger" (*Roots*, Show VII, 29 January 1977, Museum of Broadcasting).

38. *Roots*, show #8, by M. Charles Cohen, final draft, revised final draft, 6 September 1976, pp. 100–101.

39. Harry F. Waters, "The Black Experience." *Newsweek*, 24 January 1977, p. 59.

40. Wolper with Troupe, *Inside Story*, pp. 73, 141.

41. Waters, "Black Experience," p. 59.

42. Stoddard interview.

43. Waters, "After Haley's Comet," p. 98.

44. "'Roots' Takes Hold in America," *Newsweek*, 7 February 1977, p. 26; Monaco, "Roots and Angels," p. 161.

45. Kael, "Where We Are Now," p. 90.

46. Waters, "One Man's Family." p. 98.

47. Stoddard interview.

48. Frank Rich, "A Super Sequel to Haley's Comet," *Time*, 19 February 1979. p. 87; Wolper with Troupe, *Inside Story*, pp. 62, 148.

49. Alex Haley, *Roots: The Saga of an American Family* (New York: Doubleday, 1976; reprint edition New York: Dell, 1977), pp. 11–166 out of 729 pages (all references to Haley's *Roots* will be to the mass market paperback edition, since that would be more widely available for classroom use); *Roots*, show #1, as telecast, by Williams Blinn and Ernest Kinoy, 27.

50. Wolper with Troupe, *Inside Story*, p. 44; Jean Vallely, "Brandon Stoddard Made Monster Called *Roots*," *Esquire*, 13 February 1979, p. 76.

51. Haley, *Roots*, cover; Gerber, "Haley's *Roots*." p. 94.

52. Meyer, "Rootless Mini-Series," p. 52.

53. "Haley's Rx: Talk, Write, Reunite," *Time*, 14 February 1977, p. 72.

54. Monaco, "Roots and Angels," p. 161.

55. Gerber, "Haley's *Roots*," p. 90; David Herbert Donald, "Family Chronicle," *Commentary* 62 (December 1976): 70–72; Harry F. Waters, "Back to 'Roots,'" *Newsweek*, 19 February 1979, p. 87.

56. Kalamu ya Salaam, "Alex Haley Root Man: A Black Genealogist." *Black Collegian*, November/December 1976, p. 32. Also see *Roots*, discussion between Alex Haley and Stan Marguilies, 1977, Pacifica Tape Library.

57. ya Salaam, "Root Man," p. 33.

58. Wolper with Troupe, *Inside Story*, pp. 81, 172.

59. Gerber, "Haley's *Roots*," pp. 87–88.

60. Lois Armstrong, "'Roots' Is Back with Brando and a Bumper Crop of Stars to Be," *People*, 26 February 1979, p. 59.

61. Stuart Byron, "Family Plot," *Film Comment* 13 (March-April 1977): 31.

62. Ernest Renan, *What Is a Nation?* (1882), translated by Alfred Zimmen (London: Oxford University Press, 1939 ed.), cited in Ali A. Mazrui, "The End of America's Amnesia," *Africa Reports* 22 (May-June 1977): 7–8.

63. "Roots," Gripping 12-Hour, Multi-Part Story of an American Family, Traced from Its African Origins through 100 Years of Slave Life, Will Air on ABC Starting in 1977, press release of 14 June 1976, ABC Television Network Press Relations, 1330 Ave. of the Americas, New York, N. Y. 10019. Supplied courtesy of ABC public relations department.

64. James A. Hijiya, "Roots: Family and Ethnicity in the 1970's," *American Quarterly* 30 (Fall 1978): 549.

65. Paul D. Zimmermann, "In Search of a Heritage," *Newsweek*, 27 September 1976. p. 94.

66. John J. O'Connor, "Strong 'Roots' Continues Black Odyssey," *New York Times*, 16 February 1979, p. C: 1.

67. Gerber, "Haley's *Roots*," pp. 98–99; Rasmussen, "Thicket of Controversy," p. 1.

68. Willie Lee Rose, "An American Family," review of Alex Haley's *Roots, New York Review of Books*, (11 November 1976,) pp. 1–4.

69. Kenneth L. Woodward with Anthony Collins in London, "The Limits of 'Faction,'" *Newsweek*, 25 April 1977, p. 87.

70. Research cited in *"Roots* Grows into a Winner," *Time*, 7 February 1977, p. 94.

71. "Living with the 'Peculiar Institution,'" *Time*, 14 February 1977, p. 76.

72. Donald, "Family Chronicle," p. 73.

73. Woodward with Collins, "Limits of 'Faction,'" p. 87; Robert D. McFadden, "Some Points of 'Roots' Questioned; Haley Stands by Book as a Symbol," *New York Times*, 10 April 1977, pp. 1, 29.

74. Mark Ottaway, "Tangled Roots," *Sunday Times* (London), 10 April 1977, pp. 17, 21.

75. Gary B. Mills and Elizabeth Shown Mills, *"Roots* and the New 'Faction,'" *Virgina Magazine of History and Biography* 89 (January 1981); 7–13, 16–19, 24–26. Quotations appear on pp. 8 and 10 with italics in original.

76. Lewis H. Lapham, "The Black Man's Burden," *Harper's*, June 1977, pp. 15–16. 18, "PW Interviews," pp. 9, 10.

77. Meg Greenfield, "Uncle Tom's Roots," *Newsweek*, 14 February 1977, p. 100.

78. Herb Boyd, "Plagiarism and the *Roots* Suits," *First World: An International Journal of Black Thought* 2 (1979):32.

79. "Haley Settles Plagiarism Suit, Concedes Passages," *Publishers Weekly*, 25 December 1978, p. 22.

80. Haley, *Roots*, pp. 710–729; "PW Interviews," pp. 8–9, 12; Waters, "After Haley's Comet," p. 98.

81. Haley, *Roots*, pp. 184–207.

82. Alex Haley, "My Furthest Back Person—'The African,'" *New York Times Magazine*, 16 July 1972, pp. 13, 16.

83. Wolper with Troupe, *Inside Story*, pp. 150, 178.

84. This discussion of the Elkins thesis derives from Stanley M. Elkins, *Slavery: The Problem in American Institutional and Intellectual Life* (Chicago: University of Chicago Press, 1964); see especially pp. 82, 88, 128–130.

85. Lawrence W. Levine, *Black Culture and Black Consciousness: Afro–American Folk Thought from Slavery to Freedom* (New York: Oxford University Press, 1977). While this particular formulation of Levine's thesis was published after the appearance of *Roots* as a television miniseries, Levine's basic argument was readily accessible to historians in paper and article form.

86. Gilbert Osofsky, ed., *Puttin' on Ole Massa: The Slave Narratives of Henry Bibb, William Wells Brown, and Solomon Northrup* (New York: Harper & Row, Harper Torchtanks, 1969), p. 40.

87. George P. Rawick, ed., *The American Slave*: A Composite Autobiography, vol. 1, *From Sundown to Sunup: The Making of the Black Community*; Contributions in Afro-American and African Studies, No. 11 (Westport, Conn.: Greenwood, 1972), pp. xv–xvii, 9–12.

88. Herbert G. Gutman, *The Black Family in Slavery and Freedom. 1750–1925* (New York: Pantheon, 1976), pp. xvii, 14, 327–360 *passim*. Quotations appear on pp. xvil, 14, 160.

89. Gerber, "Haley's *Roots*," p. 107; "View from the Whirlpool," *Time*, 19 February 1979, p. 88.

90. Levine, "Roots and Branches," p. 57.

91. Eric Foner, article in *Sevendays* (March 1977) reprinted in Wolper with Troupe, *Inside Story*, pp. 263–264.

92. Byron, "Family Plot," p. 31.

93. Levine, "Roots and Branches," p. 56.

The MTM Style

Jane Feuer

The MTM Image

The fact that MTM *has* a public image is significant in itself. Most TV production companies remain invisible to the public. When Norman Lear made an appearance on the last episode of the first season of *Mary Hartman, Mary Hartman*, it seemed to contradict ordinary US television practice. In fact, Lear had been unable to sell the controversial serial to any network and was syndicating it directly to local stations. But when, in 1983, Steven Bochco put in a plug for the new *Bay City Blues* ('by the producers of *Hill Street Blues*') it was on the NBC television network. Indeed it was largely through Grant Tinker's scheduling of MTM and MTM-related programming that NBC attempted to change its image from that of the 'losing' network to that of the 'quality' network, despite the network's continued low ratings. NBC's and campaign for fall 1983 was based on a notion of 'quality' for which MTM programmes provided the mode.

The image of MTM as the 'quality' production company extends to features about the company in the popular press: according to the *New York Times Magazine*, 'MTM has a reputation for fair dealing, and, by prime-time standards, high quality.'[1] Articles in the trades and in popular magazines and newspapers have demonstrated that MTM would spare no expense in the visual style of its programmes, putting 'quality' above financial considerations. Long after other sitcom producers had switched to videotape, MTM continued to seek the 'quality' look of film. And MTM hired a different breed of television actor, actors trained in the new style of improvisational comedy, such as Paul Sand, Valerie Harper, and Howard Hessemen, all of whom had their roots in improv companies such as The Second City and The Committee rather than in mainstream television acting.

Perhaps the central component in MTM's public image is its reputation for giving its creative staff an unusual amount of freedom. Article after article on MTM details the way in which Grant Tinker ran interference between his writer-producers and the network bureaucracy. According to the *Los Angeles Times*, 'sources in and out of MTM insist he gives producers the freest hand in the business.' According to the *Washington Post*, 'the consensus at MTM is that if there's a "Tinker touch", it's this harmony among Tinker and his employees.' James L. Brooks told *Time* magazine, 'Grant gave us blanket approval of anything we wanted to do, not just autonomy but support.' And Steven Bochco told the *New York Times Magazine*, 'he leaves you alone and lets you do what you can do.' Tinker himself, ever modest in interviews, has said, 'I see my prime role as being able to attract the right combinations of creative people and then staying out of their way . . . what I do mostly is try to remove distractions which might interfere with their work.[2]

To the student of cinema history, all of this sounds familiar. Much of the rhetoric of creative freedom within a system of constraints is reminiscent of *auteur* historians' claims for certain film directors. In particular, the notion of the producer as protector and organiser of creativity permeates accounts of the Freed Unit at MGM in the 1940s and 1950s.[3] In much the same manner as Tinker, Arthur Freed forged a unit of the best 'creative' talent in musical comedy. Their films are regarded as 'quality' commercial entertainment at its best. As did MTM, the Freed Unit operated under conditions of exceptional freedom in part because their concept of quality was not outside the boundaries of commercial success.

Indeed MTM might be conceptualised—as the Freed Unit has been—as a corporate 'author' in two senses and at two levels:

1. Conditions of creative freedom enabled MTM to develop an individualised 'quality' style.

2. A corporate 'signature' may be deciphered from the texts themselves.

According to Michel Foucault, 'the name of the author points to the existence of certain groups of discourse and refers to the status of this discourse within a society and culture . . .[it] accompanies only certain texts to the exclusion of others.'[4] MTM's image as the quality producer serves to differentiate its programmes from the anonymous flow of television's discourse and to classify its texts as a unified body of work, two of the functions Foucault says the author's name serves.

As a specialist 'indie prod' MTM was both an exception to the operation of American television in the 1970s and typical of that operation: exceptional in that Grant Tinker fitted his company into the cracks in the system; typical in that MTM operated under the same economic constraints as everybody else. Regardless of quality, the kitten also had to serve the devil Nielsen. The previous chapter, a narrative in the industry's own terms of absolute success (high ratings) and absolute failure (cancellation), amply demonstrates both the freedom and the constraints. But establishing such a context does not explain the structure and effectivity of the programmes themselves. The relationship between commodity production and textual production is a thorny one to theorise. The usual solution is to consider each level separately, or else to argue that one level (commodity production) determines the other (textual production) in a directly causal manner. In film theory, the 'relative' autonomy of the text from its conditions of production is now taken for granted: it has become a truism that the kind of knowledge found in the previous chapter does not explain the conditions of reception of the texts, conditions that may not correspond to a diary of profits and losses, however meticulously detailed. But in stressing the 'autonomy' part of relative autonomy, one misses the distinction between 'relative' and 'absolute'. If the corporate structure of MTM does not directly *cause* the structure of the texts or determine their reception, neither is it true that there is *no* relationship between the two levels. There exist structural correspondences (homologies) between the two levels that may be encapsulated in the terms 'quality TV' and 'quality demographics'. MTM is in the business of exchanging 'quality TV' for 'quality demographics' but we need not view this process as a functionalist correspondence without contradiction. Contradictions abound even in Tinker's dualistic image in the industry as both hard-nosed executive and 'creative genius'.

This chapter will analyse the MTM style, a style which signifies 'regular TV' and 'quality TV' simultaneously. I will argue not so much that MTM should be *considered* an author as that MTM's authorial status in industry discourse bears a relationship to its concept of 'quality'.

The Structure of the MTM Sitcom

MTM and Tandem are said to have transformed the situation comedy as a form. The MTM and Lear sitcoms, the story goes, took a mechanistic, simplistic framework for one-liners and sight gags and made it into something else: whether an instrument for social commentary (Lear) or a vehicle for 'character comedy' (MTM). In the handful of commentaries that have been written on the sitcom, this has become the orthodox view. Horace Newcomb, for example, sees the sitcom as the most elementary of TV formulas. Using *I Love Lucy* as an example, Newcomb describes the 'situation' as the funny thing that will happen this week, developing through complication and confusion without plot development or an exploration of ideas. The only movement he sees is toward the alleviation of the complication and the reduction of confusion. The audience, he says, is reassured by this problem/solution format, not challenged by choice or ambiguity or forced to examine its values. Newcomb goes so far as to put the MTM and Lear programmes outside the sitcom proper in the category of 'domestic comedy'. With domestic comedy, he says, we find a greater emphasis on persons than situations; the problems are mental and emotional; there is a deep sense of personal love among members of the family and belief in the family as a supportive group. The form may be expanded when, as in the Lear comedies, the problems encountered by families become socially or politically significant.[5]

The critical view on the MTM sitcom supports Newcomb's description of domestic comedy as a transformation of the basic sitcom structure. According to one TV critic:

> *In sitcoms, MTM's approach has always been quite specific, but its influence has also been so pervasive that it may be hard to remember what an innovation the style originally was. Before* The Mary Tyler Moore Show, *no one believed that a sitcom's foundation* had *to be in character ensembles, and humor wasn't even necessarily linked to motivation: on even the best pre-MTM sitcoms, with few exceptions, the personalities and interplay were machine-designed mostly to generate the maximum number of generic jokes—or, on family sitcoms, of generic parables . . . After MTM made likability the key, even the most mechanical sitcoms had to pay lip service to the idea of the sitcom as a set of little epiphanies.[6]*

'Character ensembles', 'motivation', 'a set of little epiphanies', have transformed the problem/solution format of the sitcom into a far more psychological and episodic formula in which—in the hand of MTM—the situation itself becomes a pretext for the revelation of character. The relative insignificance of the situation itself contrasts sharply with the Lear sitcom's significant issues. And yet one could argue that *All In The Family* actually retains the simplistic, insult-ridden, joke-machine apparatus to a far greater extent than did *The Mary Tyler Moore Show*. From the perspective of narrative and character, the MTM sitcoms are the more complex. A comparison between Tandem's *Maude* and MTM's *Rhoda*—two sitcoms from the same period and with aggressive female stars—illustrates this.

Maude is far more politically astute than Rhoda; she deals with controversial issues such as alcoholism and abortion; she is far more the 'liberated woman' than Rhoda aspires to be. Yet the show *Maude* is structurally simplistic: there is one important dilemma per week which is usually resolved at Maude's expense, the main comedy technique is the insult, and the characters are unidimensional and static. Even those episodes of *Maude* which announce their experimental quality—Maude's monologue to her therapist, Walter's bout with alcoholism—seem to thrust themselves upon the viewer. *Rhoda*, whose most controversial moment occurred when Rhoda divorced her husband, nevertheless took the sitcom in new directions, employing a variety of comic techniques, an evolving central character and, arguably, moving toward the comedy-drama blend that would become the MTM formula of the late 1970s. The MTM sitcoms inflected the form in the direction of 'quality TV', of complex characters, sophisticated dialogue, and identification. 'Character comedy' in the hands of MTM became synonymous with 'quality comedy'.

'Character' in Character Comedy

It is in its conception of character that MTM's central contribution to the sitcom form is said to have been made. If we employ the traditional literary distinction between 'round' and 'flat' characters, MTM emerges on the 'round' side of the sitcom form. Of course, the comic effect of feeling superior to a character depends upon a certain amount of stereotyping and a certain lack of depth. When, for example, Rhoda's response to her husband's departure became too serious and too psychologically 'realist' the programme departed the realm of comedy, if only for an instant, and entered into the genre referred to by the industry as 'warmedy', i.e., comedy overlaid with empathetic audience identification. When comic stereotyping occurred on *The Mary Tyler Moore Show* it was reserved for the secondary characters such as Ted and Sue Ann. Mary herself functioned as what Richard Corliss has called a 'benign identification figure', not herself the object of much comic attention or ridicule.[7] For the generation of women who came of age with Mary and Rhoda, these characters seemed 'real' in a way no other TV character ever had. Of course the 'realism' of any fictional character is an illusion of sorts. A round character seems more 'real' than a flat one simply because 'roundness' is produced by multiplying the number of traits ascribed to the character. A flat character has only a few traits, a process often referred to as 'stereotyping'. But what many in the 'quality' audience felt for Mary and Rhoda went beyond a mere quantitative depth. Their 'roundness' was also a cultural construct. The MTM women caught the cultural moment for the emerging 'new woman' in a way that provided a point of identification for the mass audience as well. The MTM women could be read as warm, lovable TV characters or as representations of a new kind of femininity. In retrospect, the fact that the early MTM sitcoms were popular successes seems astonishing, but MTM knew how to provide the right combination of warmth and sophistication.

It would appear that Brooks, Burns *et al.* arrived at the correct formula through a process of experimentation. The first episode of *The Mary Tyler Moore Show* ('Love is All Around', 1970), despite its sophisticated humour, has not advanced much beyond *The Dick Van Dyke Show* in its conception of character.[8] While Mary is already established as the nice but 'spunky' figure we will come to know and love, the secondary characters are heavily stereotyped. Rhoda is the obnoxious New York Jew who will do anything to keep Mary out of 'her' apartment. Lou is portrayed as the typical drunken newspaperman, even affecting slurred speech. ('Wanna drink?' he asks Mary.) The first episode is instructive because in its as yet undeveloped conceptions of Lou and Rhoda we can see what the MTM view of character added to the sitcom formula. From the standpoint of quality TV, the charge levelled against stereotyped characters has always been that they lack psychological realism and the potential for identification from the 'quality' audience. The sitcom remains forever on the far side of quality for this reason, since a certain amount of stereotyping is necessary to get laughs. Ted Baxter may have elicited this kind of comic laughter, but the MTM characters evoked another kind of laughter as well, which I will call 'empathetic laughter'. Empathetic laughter is what we feel for Rhoda when she takes a piece of candy and quips, 'I don't know why I'm putting this in my mouth—I should just apply it directly to my hips.' It's what we feel for middle-aged Lou Grant, bravely attempting to put on a happy face at his ex-wife's wedding.

Sometimes, we don't laugh at all. A supreme example of the ability of the MTM sitcom to skirt the boundary of melodrama occurred in an episode of *Rhoda* called 'The Separation' (written by Charlotte Brown, 1976). This unorthodox *Rhoda* episode shows us the MTM sitcom style pushed to the limits of pathos, exhibiting in extreme form MTM's conception of 'character comedy' and 'warmedy'. In typical MTM sitcom fashion, 'The Separation' follows an episodic plot structure divided into segments which are separated by commercial pauses or scene changes or both. Although the plot appears 'loose', a closer inspection reveals that it is actually tightly structured. We can divide the episode into segments and subsegments as follows:

1. *Rhoda's apartment*
   a. Rhoda and Joe bargain for a house with a real estate agent. Joe subverts the offer.
   b. Rhoda fights with Joe and locks him out on the balcony.

2. *Brenda's apartment*
   a. Brenda and Ida Morgenstern discuss Ida's camping trip and her feeling that something is amiss with a family member.
   b. Rhoda enters and fakes out Ida.
   c. Rhoda discusses her marriage with Brenda.

3. *Rhoda's apartment*
   a. Carlton the doorman hears Joe's screams and thinks it's the voice of God.
   b. After a discussion, Joe leaves Rhoda.

4. *Brenda's apartment*
   Rhoda discusses the separation with Brenda; Rhoda phones Joe.

5. *Joe's Wrecking Company*
   Ida visits Joe at work and finds out the truth.

6. *Rhoda's apartment*

Ida and Rhoda talk.

The episode is structured around three scenes of unusual seriousness (segments 1b, 3b, and 6), evenly distributed throughout. Two of these segments are preceded by light comedy 'shticks' (segments 1a and 3a) involving stereotyped characters, an insincere real estate lady and Carlton the doorman in one of his set pieces. The final segment between Rhoda and her mother, however, contains only light humour and ends on a 'warm' moment. There is no comic 'tag' at the end. Almost all US sitcoms use the tag as a opportunity for one last laugh. Even some of the serious issue-oriented Lear episodes would use the tag to lighten things up before the final credits. The standard *Mary Tyler Moore Show* and *Rhoda* episode employed the tag to end on an 'upbeat'. For example, a quite sad episode of *The Mary Tyler Moore Show* features Jerry Van Dyke as the quintessential loser—a scriptwriter for Chuckles the Clown who aspires to be a standup comic. He is humiliated in front of the WJM family when it turns out that his first standup engagement is at a bowling alley lounge. After a touching scene between Mary and Lou (discussed below), we return for the tag to find the comedian standing at the mike in the deserted lounge, finishing up his routine for an appreciative Mary.[9] In 'The Separation', the absence of the tag emphasises the melodramatic nature of the ending.

A third type of segment in the *Rhoda* episode includes scenes between Rhoda and her sister (2c and 4); and scenes between Ida and Brenda, and Ida and Joe (2a and 5), symmetrically balanced around the major scene in which Rhoda's marriage collapses. In the world of the MTM sitcom, a couple's problems become the concern of the entire family, and any disruption of the extended family relationship is treated as seriously as a divorce. A good example of this pattern is *The Mary Tyler Moore Show* episode in which a disagreement between Mary and Rhoda involves all their friends and is eventually mediated by Georgette. Marriage is never privileged above friendship. Indeed it is arguable that the true 'epiphany' of the separation episode consists not in Joe's departure but in Ida's atypical understanding response to it. Joe, an outsider to the show's family structure, could be written out, but Ida and Brenda could not be removed without the entire edifice collapsing.

As the subdivision of the episode's neatly patterned narrative reveals, 'The Separation' moves back and forth between 'warm' and 'funny' moments to the point where the two blend into 'warmedy'. For example, the opening scene with the real estate agent is a typical MTM comic reversal; she tells Joe:

> *Mr Girard, in all my years as a realtor, I have never been subjected to the shame, the humiliation, and the degradation that you put me through on that phone. Mr Girard, I have nothing but contempt for you—(cut to reverse reaction shot of Joe)—and if you're ever in the market for a house (cut back to shot of realtor) again—here's my card.*

This very funny scene is followed by the quite serious confrontation between Rhoda and Joe, ending on Rhoda's hostile but comic gesture of locking him out. The following scene between Brenda and Ida is full of snappy one-liners:

> Ida: *Your father and I are gonna just keep going until we stop having a good time.*
> Brenda: *I don't think you'll make it through the Holland tunnel.*

This exchange is set up in typical MTM three-camera fashion. There is a cut to Brenda for her joke line, a cut to Ida's reaction and a re-establishing full shot for the next routine. In addition, Brenda has her typical, self-deprecating lines, the kind of lines they used to write for Rhoda before she spun off. For example, when Rhoda tells Brenda that she and Joe haven't had sex for seven weeks, Brenda whines, 'Please, don't make seven weeks sound like a long time to me.' But there are also touching, even sentimental moments between the sisters, as when, in the same scene, Rhoda tells Brenda, 'If it were nothing, you wouldn't have your arms around me.'

The 'big' scene between Rhoda and Joe has laugh lines too, but they are echoed by the nervous laughter of the studio audience. The scene shifts from anger to humour to pathos (as when Rhoda begs, Joe, 'Don't do this to me'). It may be funny that Rhoda refuses to let Joe take his underwear, but her 'damn' at the end of the scene elicits empathy rather than laughter.

But the true 'epiphany' comes in the final scene of 'The Separation' as Ida Morgenstern confronts Rhoda with her knowledge. In her appearances on *The Mary Tyler Moore Show*, Ida functioned as a comic foil for Rhoda's neurotic behaviour. In the spin-off, however, she began to emerge as something other than a caricatured Jewish mother. In an early *Rhoda* episode, Ida went so far as to throw Rhoda out of her Bronx apartment when it became obvious that Rhoda was enjoying her reversion to dependency. This new concern for Rhoda's maturation culminates in a scene all the more touching for being many years in the making. 'Rhoda, I love you,' she says. 'Don't shut me out.' And Rhoda, herself coming of age, doesn't. In this final scene of 'The Separation', the long-time viewer is reminded of Ida's very first appearance on the parent show ('Support Your Local Mother', 1970) when Rhoda was so unable to cope with Ida's 'Bronx love' that she allowed her mother to spend three days in Mary's apartment. Now they move closer together. Ida offers to stay, then corrects herself, 'That would have been good for me, but it's not good for you.' She starts to leave. Rhoda, reduced to tears, has a reversal of her own. 'Ma,' she says, 'stick around.' They embrace, and the episode is over. There is no tag, no comic relief. The atypical poignancy of 'The Separation' stems from playing Ida against type far more than from Joe's desertion. (Indeed the pragmatic reason behind the separation was that the writers had trouble coming up with plots for the happily married couple and lines for Joe's wooden character.)

The *Rhoda* episode contradicts a commonly-held notion that the sitcom cannot allow for more than trivial character development. In fact, the MTM sitcom operates almost entirely at the level of character. It would be more accurate to say that the sitcom does not allow for complexity of *plot*. Watching MTM shows rerun, 'stripped' daily in syndication, one can view within an hour episodes from the first and last seasons of *The Mary Tyler Moore Show*. The situations are remarkably similar, even identical: Mary asks for a raise, Mary is offered a job by a competing station. But Mary herself has changed: she is more the career woman, less the daughter. This movement toward an expansion of character is arguably more an MTM than a Lear contribution to the sitcom. 'Character comedy' hinges upon the stability of the quasi-family structure, yet it permits individuals to grow within the family rather than by leaving home. Such growth should not be measured against traditional literary norms of 'recognition' and 'reversal', but rather in terms of the sitcom's internal history.

A look at MTM's approach to the opening credit sequence reveals the importance of character transformation to the MTM conception of character comedy. In the original *Rhoda* credits, a chronicle of Rhoda's life, she quips, 'I decided to move out of the house at the age of 24. My mother still refers to this as the time I ran away from home.' For the regular viewer, the change between this and Ida's incarnation in 'The Separation' is immense. Similarly, the title song of the first season of *The Mary Tyler Moore Show* begins by posing the question, 'How will you make it on your own?' In the ensuing seasons, the question has been dropped entirely. Presumably, Mary's survival on her own is no longer in question. Mary's evolution as a character represents an enormous change, not just for the static sitcom formula but for women historically as well. But critics whose conception of dramatic change can accommodate only earth-shattering moments of reversal are likely to overlook it entirely. Arguably, the viewer does not.

'Character comedy', with its emphasis on family ties (not coincidentally *Family Ties* is the title of a 1980s sitcom created by MTM alumnus Gary David Goldberg) and on identification with characters, also changed the nature of humour in the sitcom. If we accept the traditional notion that a comic effect is produced by *detachment* from character, what brand of comedy could the fetishisation of character produce?

'Comedy' in Character Comedy

> *Jim and Allan and I agree on the most important things. None of us would ever write in a gratuitous putdown just because it was funny or satirise something that was pathetic. The characters have a lot of affection for each other and we*

don't want to destroy that. (Treva Silverman, Senior Story Consultant, The Mary Tyler Moore Show)[10]

The MTM sitcom employs a range of comic devices to produce both laughter and the pathos of 'warmedy'. Although MTM might use similar comic techniques to Lear—the insult, a Lear staple, forms the basis for the interactions between Rhoda and Phyllis, Murray and Ted—they rarely have the same impact. The vast majority of laughs on the Lear sitcoms are produced by name-calling and shouting, or by the malapropisms for which Archie is famous. We laugh *at* Archie or Maude because they are self-deluded. The laugh track on Lear sitcoms is full of hoots, applause and condescending giggles, whereas the MTM audience produces little chuckles of identification more often than howls of derisive delight. Treva Silverman's remarks are clearly a slap at the Lear sitcom factory's attitude toward its characters.

In the MTM sitcom, laughter tends to be tempered by sympathy. Even the most stereotyped characters—Ted, Phyllis or Sue Ann—have their little moments of self-revelation: Ted when he meets up with the father who abandoned him as a child; Phyllis when her husband Lars has an affair with the Happy Homemaker; and Sue Ann herself when she admits to Mary that she's not attractive to men. The most ridiculous MTM characters—the group members and Howard on *The Bob Newhart Show*, for example—are rendered pathetic rather than thoroughly risible. Infantile, narcissistic characters are never expelled from the family: Ted remains on the air; Mr Carlin stays in the group; Carlton is rehired at Rhoda's request despite an astonishing lapse of 'professionalism' in his doorman duties (he has ushered in the burglars who strip Rhoda and Joe of their possessions). Yet the MTM sitcoms remain remarkably funny. This is because the comic devices employed produce the laughter of recognition, an identification that is especially acute for the 'sophisticated' audience.

Empathetic laughter transforms even the most primitive of sitcom devices: the sight gag. Every episode of *I Love Lucy* had at least one set piece of physical comedy. But they were rarely tied to character psychology. Surprisingly the sight gag turns up rather frequently on MTM sitcoms as well. Perhaps the funniest moment in 'The Separation' occurs when Ida visits Joe, unaware that he has left her daughter. After Ida insists that 'she can take it,' Joe announces, 'Rhoda and I are separated.' Ida proceeds to grab his face and pinch his cheeks with considerable force. 'Does Rhoda know?' she asks. Joe is unable to break her grip, but when he finally does, Ida claims she can behave with maturity, and then, as a parting thrust, zaps him with her handbag. This is a typical MTM situation: a character claims to be able to behave maturely, then proceeds to act childishly. A classic instance occurs on *The Mary Tyler Moore Show* when Mary, having been fired by Lou for writing with Rhoda a tongue-in-cheek obituary in the wee hours of the morning which Ted accidentally reads on the air, returns for a visit to WJM and finds another woman in her chair. In the midst of a polite visit to Lou Grant's inner sanctum, she becomes hysterical and sobs repeatedly, 'Oh Mr Grant, I want to come back.' She regains control, apologises, then lapses back into the same childish plaint. In both examples, the gag involves a set piece for the character—Mary's famous crying scenes or Ida's moments of fierce maternal protectiveness. And in each case, the motivation is familial love.

Another classic Ida Morgenstern sight gag occurs in 'Support Your Local Mother' when Ida and Mary race around Mary's sofa trying to stuff money in each other's bathrobe pocket. This hilarious scene reverberates at a number of levels. There is the obvious Bergsonian notion that humour stems from the human body being transformed into a machine. But there is also character comedy: Mary has refused to believe Rhoda's promise that Ida will drive her crazy with guilt. When Ida attempts to pay Mary hotel costs for sleeping on her sofa, she reduces Mary in the neurotic acting-out that is displayed in the physical gag.

Our response to MTM sight gags can even stem from pathos. In the Jerry Van Dyke episode, a moment of supreme embarrassment occurs when the comic is humiliated by having to deliver his standup routine to an audience of bored bowlers. In keeping with the MTM attitude toward characters, the routine is actually quite clever, which only increases our pity for the character. This reduces Mary to tears, and she flees to the ladies' room. To this point, the scene is embarrassing rather than funny. But Lou Grant, with typical paternal protectiveness, follows Mary into the ladies' room, much to the surprise of a woman who emerges from one of the stalls. As Lou attempts awkwardly to comfort Mary (herself a victim of over-identification with a friend's pain), another woman attempts twice to enter. 'Not now,' Lou growls at her. The culmination to this bizarre moment occurs as a visual joke, when Lou, trying to help Mary dry her tears, pulls out a towel from the dispenser. But it's on one of those circular rolls, and he winds up yanking the entire length of towel across the room, as the laugh track explodes with hilarity. We laugh in part at the notion of a machine not serving its proper function, in part at this bear of a man's very presence in the ladies' room, and in part at the genuine concern it takes for Lou to so abandon his macho decorum. Without the narrative context, the gag would seem only moderately funny, whereas most of Lucy's sight gags work perfectly well on their own.

But the tradition of physical comedy is not the essence of MTM character comedy; comic reversals of expectations are. Typically, an MTM script will set us up for a sentimental moment and then puncture it by reversing the predictable sentimental response. On a *Mary Tyler Moore Show* episode, Sue Ann has lured the WJM family into her studio during a November blizzard to consume the food prepared for her 'Christmas Around the World' edition of 'The Happy Housemaker'. Prior to this, Mary and Murray were reduced to stormy hostility over a disagreement as to whether Ted's new salutation should go 'news from around the corner and around the world' or 'news from around the world and around the corner'. Now they are trapped together by the blizzard. At the dinner table, Sue Ann has forced everyone to wear silly 'international' hats and sing 'A Partridge in a Pear Tree'. There is a moment of hostile silence, whereupon Georgette, ever the innocent peacemaker, begins to sing 'Silent Night' *a cappella*. This reduces Mary to sentimental guilt and she says 'Can anyone remember why we were angry with each other?', setting us up for a sentimental family reconciliation. But the reversal occurs when Murray grants 'Yeah, I can remember' and Mary replies, 'Yeah, well, me too,' and the feud continues.

The most famous MTM comic reversal occurs in 'Chuckles Bites the Dust'.[11] Chuckles the Clown, dressed up as a peanut, comes to a tragic end when he is trampled by an elephant. Mary is outraged when Lou, Murray and Sue Ann persist in making jokes about it. But at Chuckle's funeral, in an atmosphere of hushed silence, Mary bursts into peals of laughter during the eulogy. The minister consoles the mortified Mary by telling her Chuckles loved to make people laugh. Mary, of course, promptly bursts into tears. Once again we have the puncturing of potential sentimentality but also empathetic laughter, since we too laughed at the jokes about Chuckles and at the very funny eulogy.

The reversal may operate in conjunction with another kind of MTM humour, the self-deprecating 'Jewish' humour of a Rhoda, a Brenda or a Bob Hartley. Most of Rhoda's laugh lines fall into this category, but this author's favourite self-deprecating reversal occurs in the scene between Ida and Brenda in 'The Separation'. Ida tells Brenda that she 'feels in her bones' that something is amiss with a family member. Brenda takes this as an opening and muses, 'I woke up this morning feeling very alone with this fear I'd never find anybody to love me. I would just be—' We cut to a reverse shot of Ida who interrupts, 'Oh, please, I don't mean the normal stuff.' It gets a big laugh, but also sympathy for poor Brenda whose neuroses are dismissed so lightly.

'Character comedy' reinforces MTM's emphasis on the familial and the interpersonal. It frequently verges on 'warmedy'. Since 'warmedy' itself frequently verges on sentimentality, the comic reversal also has its self-mocking aspect. The same sentimental moments are often played 'straight' in the MTM dramas later in the decade. However, overt satire and self-parody are rare in the early MTM sitcoms. To be sure, local TV news operations are made fun of repeatedly in the person of Ted Baxter; and Bob Hartley's therapy group reduced psychotherapy to psycho-comedy. But because of the sympathetic attitude toward character, the satire lacks bite. This begins to change in the mid-1970s. *The Betty White Show, Phyllis, Remington Steele* and the MTM-syle *Buffalo Bill* introduce self-satire into the MTM comic repertory. Yet self-reflexivity may he interpreted as yet another mark of 'quality'.

Self-Reflexivity As Quality

'Intertextuality', a literary term, refers in its broadest sense to the ways in which texts incorporate previous texts. Sometimes this takes the form of 'self-reflexivity', when a text refers in self-conscious fashion back to itself. Both terms have been associated with 'modernist' art: T. S. Eliot's

The Wasteland operates intertextually, whereas Pirandello's *Six Characters in Search of an Author* exhibits self-reflexivity. It has been argued that these self-conscious strategies distinguish 'high-art' from the unselfconscious popular arts—such as TV series—and that even within high art, self-reflexivity distinguishes 'modernist' from 'classical' forms. Yet many popular forms are highly intertextual without being in a modernist vein.[12] In fact, the idea that within a form new works are created by recombining elements from previous texts in the same or different genres is crucial to an understanding both of Hollywood genre films and of TV series. The oft-accused lack of 'originality' of most TV series stems from this self-generating mode of construction. Intertextuality and self-reflexivity operate both as the normative way of creating new programmes *and* as a way of distinguishing the 'quality' from the everyday product. In aligning itself with the modernist self-conscious mode, the MTM style makes yet another claim to quality status. Within the MTM style, intertextual and self-reflexive references have both constructive and deconstructive purposes. When used constructively, these techniques renew and validate the style itself, as when new programmes spin off from old ones. But the same techniques may also be used so as to critique or *de*construct their own genre and style, as I will urge *Buffalo Bill* does in its commentary on *The Mary Tyler Moore Show*.

MTM's use of what Todd Gitlin calls 'recombination' places its style within the norms of textual construction in American television. As Gitlin and others have argued, even the 'innovative' *Hill Street Blues* recombines the conventions of the continuing serial melodrama with those of the cop show, adding a bit of cinéma vérité in the visual style.[13] Recombination continues from *Hill Street* with *St Elsewhere* and *Bay City Blues*. *St Elsewhere*, when it was being developed, was referred to around the shop as 'Hill Street in the hospital'. Its style is wholly derivative: the large ensemble cast, the blending of melodrama and comedy with the more or less 'realist' treatment of the medical series tradition and of controversial issues (AIDS, sex change operations), and in its use of the continuing serial narrative. *Bay City Blues* bore an even closer family resemblance to *Hill Street*, imitating even the dense image and sound track of the parent programme.

At a high enough level of abstraction, one could see the entire core of MTM programmes as a process of 'begats', with *The Mary Tyler Moore Show* as Abraham. The original programme (itself not without roots in the sitcom tradition) pioneered the ensemble cast of co-workers which would become an MTM trademark; it merged farce with forms of comedy based on empathy; it incorporated a literate style of writing in its dialogue. The sitcom spin-offs continued in this tradition with *Phyllis* and *The Betty White Show*, adding the elements of acerbic wit that would culminate in the MTM-related *Buffalo Bill*. The transition to the dramas occurred with *Lou Grant*, a programme poised midway between the sitcoms and the serial dramas. *Lou Grant* took the work-family concept from the sitcoms, added a heavier strain of drama and an emphasis on public issues, and began to expand the narrative beyond the 'series of little epiphanies' that had distinguished the sitcoms. The most issue-oriented of MTM programmes retained a focus on the personal dimension of public issues. Sometimes it seemed to stress the public dimension of personal issues as well, as when, in the final season, Billie Newman's agonised decision to remarry appeared to have cultural significance.

One can see in *Lou Grant* the beginnings of the multiple-plot line construction often claimed as one of *Hill Street*'s great innovations in prime-time drama. In an episode about child pornography, four different plots are interwoven. Already the TV convention of main plot and subplot is being deconstructed. In both the sitcom and drama, the subplot serves to 'lighten' the main plot. The Lear sitcoms would use this strategy in instances where the main plot was seen as too 'heavy'. In the *Lou Grant* episode, the two major subplots are also lighter, but they serve to reinforce the seriousness of the main plot, which concerns a young black female reporter named Sharon who gives confidentiality to a source. The conflict arises because her source is the mother of a young daughter who has allowed her child to appear in porno movies. Meanwhile, Donovan, a regular character, breaks his ankle after skydiving from a helicopter while covering a story on a mountain search and rescue team, in consequence failing to cover an important story for Lou. Both Sharon's and Donovan's commitment to getting the story at all costs alienates them from the 'Trib' family. In the end, both are accepted back into the family, with Donovan regretting his macho pride and Sharon feeling she would proceed differently in the future. In another comic subplot, a cub reporter named Lance finds out his ear problem will prevent him from achieving his goal of being the first reporter in space; this comic relief echoes the theme of risk-taking in the larger plotlines. Although the main plot/subplot division remains distinguishable, there is a thematic connection between them, and both take the form of the parable. The public issue of child pornography remains unresolved, but the familial conflicts are mediated. *Hill Street* would take the multiplication of plots one step further, reducing the sense of hierarchy to the point where the plot lines would take on nearly equal status, and rendering the sense of closure even more ambiguous.

The *Lou Grant* episode also moves toward the serial form in a discussion Sharon has with Rossi about the issue of confidentiality. Rossi refers to the time he went to jail for refusing to reveal a source. This had indeed occurred on an episode about pill pushers in a previous season. (Indeed Mary Richards had been the first MTM character to go to jail for refusing to reveal a source, so that there is a double level of historical reference operating.) Rossi recaps what had happened in the earlier episode but tells Sharon his case was different in that he wasn't protecting a criminal. The reference calls for the viewer to compare the issues involved. In this way, the series *Lou Grant* is seen as possessing a history, moving it away from the ahistorical sitcom genre and toward the continuing serial, as Rhoda's divorce had produced a series of interconnected episodes within the sitcom form. *Lou Grant*'s insistence on relating the private to the public sphere would continue in *The White Shadow* and in the serial dramas. Yet all would retain the MTM characteristic of focusing on the personal dimension of the public issue, never inverting that hierarchy as Lear had done, by using characters as stick figures in a political allegory.

In this way, intertextuality can be seen as the generator for the entire MTM output. Yet when self-referencing occurs, it tends to be constructive rather than critical of the MTM heritage. As an example of constructive reflexivity, no MTM programme is more significant than the company's excursion into musical-variety with the short-lived 1978 *Mary/The Mary Tyler Moore Hour*. The abysmal failure of Mary Tyler Moore's return to the small screen might make it appear that the programme was—like *The Texas Wheelers* or *Three for the Road*—foreign to the MTM style or aberrant in its generic uniqueness. Quite the contrary: the variety hour took the self-referencing of the MTM style to its furthest extreme in the constructive direction. A contemporary of *Lou Grant, The White Shadow, WKRP in Cincinnati* and *Taxi, Mary* faced many of the same problems as the other shows attempting to compete in the Silverman era, and in attempting to extend the MTM sitcom bloodline at a point where the blood was getting a bit tired.

Would the public accept Mary as a dancer and sketch comedienne, or would the memory of Mary Richards prevent such an acceptance? was the question the writers had to ask. Their solution was one encountered many times before in the movies and in television series: rather than ignoring Mary's past incarnation, it would become the point of reference for her present one. In the first hour of *Mary*, Mary Tyler Moore addresses the live studio audience, asking them what they've been doing on Saturday nights. The first comedy routine has Mary looking back upon Ed Asner's audition for *The Mary Tyler Moore Show*. She then introduces the 'Ed Asner' dancers, and an ensemble of fat balding middle-aged men in Lou Grant outfits emerges dancing to a disco beat. Mary then introduces the 'family' of comedy players for the new programme by showing excerpts from their audition tapes, one of which consists of imitations of Mary's lines front the old show. Although it is primarily constructive, the new programme takes an ambivalent attitude towards the old show, on the one hand wanting to capitalise on its success and the audience's affection for Mary; on the other hand wanting to go off in a newer, more 'modernist' direction, derived from the late-night improvisational comedy tradition that was then emerging. (The idea of a pure construction is of course a theoretical fiction; there can be no construction without some element of deconstruction and vice versa.) The first episode is *self*-reflexive to an extreme. In addition to the audition tapes, it features a satire on television's self-congratulatory tendencies in a recapitulation of 'historic moments from the first 25 minutes of *Mary*'. And in a segment at the end of the hour, the cast members gather at a restaurant across the street to discuss the programme we've just viewed. They decide they really like Mary, but trash David Letterman who has appeared as an obnoxious member of the ensemble.

After the ratings failure of *Mary*, the show went on hiatus and returned in a revamped version, *The Mary Tyler Moore Hour*. Far from having disappeared, the intertextual references and self-reflective moments were once again central to the show's format. Now the programme took on a backstage musical plot structure whereby Mary Tyler Moore played 'Mary McKinnon', a fictional character who just happened to have her own musical variety television show. Each week Mary McKinnon would deal with problems involving that week's guest star on the fictional programme. *The Mary Tyler Moore Hour* commenced with a re-arranged version of the old 'Love is All Around' theme song, and continued the references to Moore's previous television roles. Mary McKinnon seemed familiar; she was nice, spunky, and a pushover for manipulators. In an episode centering around Mary's fear of dancing with guest star Gene Kelly, her assistant answers the phone saying, 'She's exactly like she is on television', reinforcing our fondest desires about Mary Richards. Iris, Mary McKinnon's unglamorous female secretary, discusses Mary's weekend during which she attended a 'little' testimonial dinner in her own honour. It does not take us long to realise that Iris is a Rhoda-substitute. 'Iris, what do you want?' Mary inquires of her. 'I want your life,' Iris replies, in typical Rhoda fashion.

Not surprisingly, the new programme's only satirical comment on Mary's past involves not her sacred role of Mary Richards but her far more vulnerable stint as the feather-brained Laura Petrie on *The Dick Van Dyke Show*. Mary McKinnon's guest star is Dick Van Dyke, and the joke revolves around his never having met Mary McKinnon. The producer asks him, 'Don't you think Mary looks like the girl who played Laura Petrie?' Dick Van Dyke ponders for a moment and replies, 'No.' He goes into a flashback on the old *Dick Van Dyke Show* set, in which Laura has become a feminist, Richie a gay, etc. The skit plays the audience's recollection of their mutual video past against Van Dyke's claim never to have met 'Mary'. Finally they meet at the end of the hour. 'I auditioned for *The Dick Van Dyke Show*,' Mary McKinnon tells him. 'Rose Marie got the part.'

Although the variety hour took self-referencing to an extreme, other MTM programmes of the period also referred back to the MTM past, either directly or indirectly. A direct reference occurred on an episode of *Taxi*, the first programme produced by the MTM creative team after they left the company. In the fall 1982 première, Marcia Wallace, who had played Bob Newhart's secretary, is the guest star. In an odd play on the fictional status of a television character, Jim, one of the regular fictional characters on *Taxi*, is portrayed as idolising Marcia Wallace in her role as Carol, the secretary on *The Bob Newhart Show*. But Marcia Wallace plays 'herself'. The episode makes numerous references to Jim's memories of the older programme, culminating in a scene with all the fictional *Taxi* characters and the 'real' Marcia Wallace, in which Jim makes up a hymn of praise to the tune of the old Bob Newhart theme song. Although it is not unusual for actors to appear as 'themselves' in a fictional TV series (after all Henry Kissinger appeared as 'himself' on *Dynasty*), the complexity of the reference on *Taxi* puts it in a modernist vein, especially since the programme does not ordinarily use guest stars in this fashion. The *Taxi* episode plays on nostalgia for the earlier show, but also plays with the nature of the fictional enclosure, as does much modernist 'high art'. A similar play on the border between fiction and reality occurs in an uncharacteristic in-joke on a 1984 *St Elsewhere*. Dr Morrison goes on a tour of Boston, the locale for the hospital series, with his young son, Petey. Suddenly they pass by the 'fictional' bar, Cheers, and Dr Morrison asks Petey, 'Do you want to eat where everybody knows your name?' One expected them to go inside and chat with Sam and Diane, but the fiction of *St Elsewhere* was rapidly re-established. Nevertheless the MTM company family had asserted its intergenerational bonds, as well as acknowledging that the same 'quality' audience would watch both programmes.

Another late MTM programme which continually asserts a continuity with the modernist tradition as a claim to 'quality' is the detective show spoof, *Remington Steele*. The show displays its sophistication by having Steele solve crimes by reference to plots from old Hollywood movies. Steele's relationship to the detective genre is entirely fictional. In this way the show includes the audience in its sophisticated circle of allusions. In the pilot, Steele, an ex-jewel thief, uses for his aliases character names from old Bogart movies. In the second episode, he watches *The Thin Man* and uses its plot to solve a crime. The second season of *Remington Steele* stakes a further claim to the modernist tradition. 'Small Town Steele' alludes to the Frank Capra tradition of small town populism as Steele and Laura visit a tiny burg named 'Da Nada'. But the townspeople are inhospitable and corrupt, and Steele is disillusioned. The first year credits had featured a first-person narration by Laura Holt of how she'd become a detective and had to invent Remington Steele. But the second season credits show Laura and Steele in a cinema, watching scenes from the first season. This self-reflexive vein culminates in an episode structured around dream sequences that Laura and Steele have about each other. The final dream involves Steele looking over a balcony from which Laura has fallen in the actual plot. He screams her name, and we cut to Laura in a hospital bed, having returned to 'reality'. The source of the final dream is never revealed to the audience.

If these stylistic touches link *Remington Steele* to modern art, its many media allusions place it firmly within a television tradition. Many American and British television programmes base their jokes and parodies on media references. This in itself does not neccessarily entail a critical stance toward the television tradition, although it does reveal an awareness of television's status as 'low culture'. Most often, an appeal is made to a common media culture and a shared 'inside' knowledge among audience members. If you watch TV, you will get the joke; just as if you are an educated literary intellectual, you will 'get' the references in modernist poetry. Many MTM programmes seem to take this normative TV practice a bit further by being set in media institutions. WJM was always trying to improve its ratings, and many episodes showed these futile attempts in a humorous light. In one such episode, the WJM news team decides to broadcast from a singles bar. Mary's research goes well, but in the actual live broadcast, their sources panic in front of the cameras, and clam up, leaving Lou with egg on his face and Ted back in the studio with a lot of empty air time on his hands. MTM programmes not about media professionals often featured the media in a subsidiary way. *We've Got Each Other* had the female lead working as a photographer's assistant. Phyllis also went to work in a photography studio, allowing for jokes about advertising such as 'I backlit the sesame seeds.' This line exhibits more sophistication than the usual TV references to other programmes and stars because in order to laugh at it, you have to know what backlighting is, and you have to take an irreverent attitude towards advertising. *Remington Steele* shows its sophistication in episodes where Remington Steele and Laura Holt investigate crimes occurring in media contexts. In one such episode, they visit the set of a frozen food commercial. 'Ah, commercials, the lynchpin of the television industry,' Laura observes. Although it is not uncommon for US TV shows to mock the ads that enable them to exist, such a literate analysis is characteristic of quality TV, especially since Laura is also mocking Steele's elevated style of speech. 'Television is so disillusioning,' says Mildred Krebs in the same episode, after discovering that the romantic TV stars featured in the boeuf bourguignon commercial actually hate each other.

When media references occur on US television, they rarely take up such a deconstructive position. Yet a number of MTM series episodes have tackled the nature of their own medium in a manner verging on the critical. Since presumably it's OK for the quality audience to hate TV, this practice should not be construed as subversive in any absolute sense. It does, however, exhibit MTM's 'quality' mode of satire. Another episode of *Remington Steele* involves a sustained sendup of local TV news operations far less affectionate than *The Mary Tyler Moore Show* ever was. Various members of the news team are being murdered on the set of the evening news. After a lengthy exposé of the idiocies of producing 'happy news', it is revealed that the culprit was a formerly respectable print journalist outraged at the way the news was being corrupted into entertainment. He delivers his confession on the air in the form of a *Network*-like diatribe against broadcast news.

The Betty White Show, the most brilliant and acerbic of the MTM 'failures', also had a quite reflexive format. White's character was a toned-down version of her Sue Ann Nivens, another acid-tongued television performer. The pilot episode begins with a show-within-the-show, a TV cop show called *Undercover Woman*. The camera pulls back to reveal Betty White as Joyce, watching the female cop show on her TV. We then see the credits for *The Betty White Show* itself. This is perhaps the only recorded instance of a TV pilot within a TV pilot, setting the self-reflexive tone for the sitcom which follows. The episode revolves around whether the network (actually called 'CBS') will buy the series Joyce makes under the direction of her much-loathed ex-husband. Such a situation provides many opportunities for media-related jokes, although in typical MTM fashion another focus for humour is Joyce's relationship to her ex. The CBS liason, Doug Porterfield, figures prominently in the pilot. His title is Vice-President in Charge of Prime-time Dramatic Development, but he tells Joyce, 'Yesterday I was working in the mailroom.' (This brand of satire is repeated in a later *Taxi* episode in which the spaced-out Jim reveals an uncanny ability to predict which network programmes will 'score' in a given time slot, and becomes a consultant to a juvenile network programming executive.) At the script reading, Porterfield tries to censor a scene in which the undercover woman is disguised as a nun. 'What do you suggest,' the director says, 'that we disguise her as an atheist?' Later Joyce asks her ex-husband director, 'What is my motivation in the car chase?' Sight gags involve a burly stunt man emerging in Joyce's brief costume and a scene in which the entire set colluposes when Joyce slams the door. At a cast party celebrating the network's acceptance of the programme, Doug Porterfield reads the network's report on the show: 'Lurid, the mentality of an eight year old . . . they loved it.' The parody of the television industry combines with the show-within-a-show device to place *The Betty White Show* in the quality reflexive style. In mocking ordinary television, *The Betty White Show* exempts itself and claims quality status.

An episode of *The White Shadow* appears even more critically reflexive in that it sets up pointed parallels between a TV show within the show and *The White Shadow* itself. *The White Shadow* revolves around a white former basketball player who becomes the coach for a Los Angeles ghetto high school basketball team. Typically, the programme dealt with interpersonal conflict and social issues among the largely black, youthful cast. Unlike other MTM programmes involving media professionals, the incorporation of a parallel television programme within the programme does not evolve naturally from *The White Shadow*'s premise; the commentary in this case appears all the more overt. As did the *Betty White Show* pilot, this episode of *The White Shadow* commences directly with the internal programme. We are shown a typical TV drama series about a black kid with a drug problem, and the camera pulls back to reveal the film crew on a Los Angeles-based location accessible to the regular cast. The kids are critical of the TV show for its portrayal of blacks and for its lack of realism (all criticisms which might be levelled at *The White Shadow* itself). In the school corridors, the team members discuss this 'ridiculous' new TV show about a white principal in a black ghetto school who always gets involved in the kids' personal problems. 'Sounds like a lotta bull to me,' one of them says. At that point Reeves, the white coach, walks past and the kids do a double take, reminding us again of the parallels between the much-maligned internal show and the programme which contains it. While observing on the set, Warren Coolidge, a regular character, is invited to direct the TV episode, after he criticises its lack of realism. We then fade in to Coolidge *on* TV, in the role we saw at the beginning of the episode. He has just been cast in the lead, and the team is watching him at the coaches' home. (A third such pullback shot occurs later when it is revealed that the team is watching the internal show on a bank of TV monitors in a video shop; we always see the programme from their point of view as 'real' spectators.)

The remainder of the episode involves the problems that occur when Coolidge 'goes Hollywood', and his conflict with another team member, Hayward, who thinks the show puts black people down. The team visits Coolidge on the set and Hayward complains to the production staff that they are making blacks look like fools. Hayward's charges are corroborated in a scene in which the white director asks Coolidge to strut soulfully with a ghetto blaster. 'You don't dress like that,' Hayward tells him. 'It ain't supposed to be real,' Coolidge replies. A secondary satirical strain revolves around Coolidge's immersion in the Hollywood scene. He begins to pick up the lingo, saying that he and his girlfriend are 'on hiatus'. When they run into Ed Asner (playing himself) on the lot, Asner shakes hands with Coolidge and calls him by name. Both strains culminate when the team crashes a Hollywood party. Hayward argues with the white creative staff of 'Downtown High' who are exposed as hypocritical and more than a little racist. When Coolidge evicts them from the party, Hayward tells him he's 'developed a serious case of Oreo mentality.' Ultimately, Coolidge comes around to this point of view. He refuses to do a comic scene in which he shines a white man's shoes; the producer gives him an ultimatum and Coolidge quits, returning to the team. From this description, the episode would seem to be a scathing critique of the portrayal of blacks on American television, and possibly a self-criticism as well. Yet this latter aspect is never fully brought out. At the end, Coolidge tells the high school drama teacher that there was some good and some bad in his experience of the TV world. Moreover, the parodic exaggeration with which that world is portrayed tends to set up the team members as 'real blacks', in a sense congratulating *The White Shadow* for doing a better job than the programme portrayed within. Ultimately, the episode sets us up for a genuine self-criticism, then fails to deliver.

None of the examples discussed to this point has been wholly subversive of dominant television practices, nor have they invoked the MTM tradition in a critical manner. Indeed it could be argued that in their very 'modernism' and their satire of 'regular TV', they are further distinguishing the MTM 'quality' style. It took a non-MTM sitcom, yet one wholly within the MTM style, to take the parodic strain in this style beyond a mere 'quality' reflexivity. *Buffalo Bill* is the most subversively comic programme yet to emerge out of the MTM style. Earlier MTM sitcoms, *Phyllis* and *The Betty White Show*, had featured unpleasant lead figures and acerbic wit, but Bill Bittinger was as far as one could go from the benign identification figure that Mary Richards had epitomised. The programme received a lot of publicity, centering around the unqualified nastiness of its central character, which was seen as transgressive of television's 'likeability factor', a normative strategy central to the MTM style. The most subversive reading of *Buffalo Bill* would see it as a complete inversion of *The Mary Tyler Moore Show*. Its modernist style and use of the anti-hero makes it recuperable to the quality tradition, but it does not take a 'forced' reading to see that *Buffalo Bill* also subverts that tradition.

The inversion is accomplished by incorporating all the MTM traits and then playing them against themselves. Instead of the sympathetic Mary, we have a Ted Baxter as the main character but one without any of Ted's endearing child-like qualities nor his familial acceptance. Like Ted, Bill is wholly a television personality, a talk show host in Buffalo, New York. Unlike Ted, Bill is clever and manipulative, giving his immersion in the world of image-making a far less affectionate slant. He is a fool, but not, like Ted, an innocent fool. Instead of the gruff but kindly Lou Grant, we have Karl Schub, the ineffectual station manager whose repeated failed attempts to stand up to Bill render him a comic figure. In lieu of the naive Georgette, we have the beauteous Wendy, the show's researcher who, although a bit naive, is nevertheless committed to liberal social issues and aware of the exchange value of her good looks. The other characters are less obvious inversions of the old MTM show crew, but all lack the 'warmth' of the old characters, and lack as well much familial feeling toward Bill Bittinger. Woody, played by the same actor who had portrayed the henpecked Mr. Petersen in Bob Newhart's therapy group, is Bill's devoted and self-effacing factotum and floor manager. He would thus seem to occupy the same comic space as his previous role. Yet Woody is allowed to comment on his persona in a way Mr Petersen never could. In a moment of revelation, he tells another character that he considers Bill to he his mission in life, that Bill is so despicable that he needs Woody's faith if he is ever to be redeemed. Similarly, the two black characters, Tony, the assistant director, and the 'upp- ity' make-up man, hold Bill to account for his racism, and make scathing comments on their boss's personality. The other major character is the female director of 'The Buffalo Bill Show', JoJo, who is also Bill's sometime lover. But she is no Mary Richards, eternally respectful of 'Mr Grant'. In a con- troversial two-part episode, JoJo even has an abortion, knowing that Bill could never be a suitable father.

The *Buffalo Bill* characters thus seem to serve as a commentary on the old *Mary Tyler Moore Show* Utopian family of co-workers. They are a family, but at best a neurotic and disturbed one, headed by a father who is also a child. This twist on the warmth of the MTM family is brought out in an episode in which an unctuous correspondent for the station's 'View on Buffalo' does a spot on 'The Buffalo Bill Show' staff. We see her interviewing the various family members, trying to get the dirt on Bill. Her interviews with the cast members are intercut with scenes of Bill in his dressing room, anxiously preparing for his own interview. In each of the staff interviews, Bill is damned with faint praise. 'I don't hate Bill Bittinger,' says Karl Schub, 'occasionally he's selfish . . . he can be cruel and vicious.' To JoJo the reporter says, 'It probably helps having a personal, intimate relationship.' She proceeds to read aloud a diary of Bill's sexist comments which JoJo is forced to corroborate. Even the benevolent Wendy is led to make unfavourable comments about Bill. 'Bill can be cruel and hateful,' she says, 'but lately he hardly ever tries to get me into bed.' Meanwhile, we view Bill alone in his dressing room, trying out different charming personae for the interview. As we keep returning to these monologues, Bill's narcissistic imagination runs wild. He becomes incensed by an imaginary scene in which the reporter seduces him and he tells her, 'I'm offended by your lack of journalistic ethics.' Bill proceeds to evict the 'View on Buffalo' crew, pulling open the door and shouting 'get out' only to return from his fantasy to discover they are waiting at the door to enter. In a typical face-saving manoeuvre, Bill has nothing but praise for his staff; as he tells them afterwards, 'Liane tried to get me to knock you guys.' He traps his guilty cohorts into coming to his flat to view the broadcast.

As everyone but Bill could have predicted, all of the scenes we have watched being taped are edited into a scathing exposé of Bill Bittinger. The staff's worst comments are selected and, with heavy irony, the segment ends with Bill himself speaking of 'warmth, family and love.' (A caustic echo of Mary Richard's speech on 'The Last Show'.) After the broadcast there is a deathly silence, with everyone looking for an escape hatch. Wendy begins to cry and Karl carries her out. JoJo tells Bill, 'I said things like that to your face, but to say it on television is inexcusable.' As the deeply ashamed group gathers in the corridor. Bill, isolated as ever, drags his immense TV set onto the balcony and starts to shove it over the edge. JoJo tries to stop him, at which point Bill delivers a speech about his relationship to the family which, although pathetic in its way, is a far cry from the typical MTM attitude of sentimental familial affection:

> *Friendship happens to be a very overrated commodity . . . I believe in me . . .*
> *because I've been left too many times by too many people . . . starting with my*
> *father . . . friendship just slows me down . . . [to be and stay on TV] you'd better*
> *learn to live by yourself . . . for yourself . . . I like living alone . . . I may be the*
> *happiest person I know of . . .*

JoJo responds, 'Oh, Bill,' and as she starts to embrace him, they knock the TV set over the ledge. This undercuts any sympathy we may have felt for Bill. We return for the tag. Bill is yelling '$800 cash' while JoJo expresses concern that it might have killed someone below. 'Don't worry,' Bill tells her, 'nobody's down there . . . except Karl, Wendy, Tony, Woody . . .' and the episode ends. This is a far cry from the typical MTM pattern whereby family harmony is restored by the end of every episode. In the usual pattern, a violation of family harmony is seen as a breach that needs to be healed in order to restore the Utopian moment; in this case, the aberration is Bill's uncharacteristic moment of concern for the others, a moment which is itself rapidly undercut. As a character, Bill is compelling in his very narcissism and isolation, but he is not 'benign' and he is not an identification figure. We are more likely to identify with the other staff members and to laugh at Bill's pain, an inversion of the MTM pattern which produces a dark rather than light mode of comedy. The Buffalo Bill family is the MTM family viewed through dark glasses instead of the usual rose-coloured ones.

Even more subversive than its treatment of the work-family, is *Buffalo Bill*'s attitude toward television itself. *Buffalo Bill* directs its satire *at* television as an institution. Its critique of television does not occur on isolated episodes; it informs the very care of the programme's structure. The various broadcasts of 'The Buffalo Bill Show' take up far more time than Ted's bloopers ever did, and these on-air sequences are played off against Bill's off-camera hypocrisy. In addition, our view of the show is frequently from the inside of the control booth, so that we watch Bill's show on the various monitors and from the viewpoint of the production staff. Much of the satire is achieved through the staff's outraged reactions to Bill's on-camera antics. The 'inside' point of view is subversive as well as reflexive.

An especially blatant instance of *Buffalo Bill*'s critique of television occurs in the episode in which Bill invites an octogenerian former tap dancer on the programme. Bill coerces the old man, who has long been retired, to do a few steps on the air, during which the man has a heart attack and dies. At this point Bill goes berserk and addresses the studio audience directly. Quite like the anchorman on the *Remington Steele* episode, Bill's speech is a condemnation of television. In this case, however, the message is complicated by the fact that it was Bill himself who brought on the man's death. Bill refuses to allow JoJo to cut to a commercial. 'Television killed him,' he tells the audience, referring to it as 'the human sacrifice business.' He asks the audience to quit watching TV. Of course Bill's hypocrisy is revealed when a woman in the audience goes into labour and Bill turns it into melodrama with a 'miracle of life' speech. Then Bill runs out of steam with 51 minutes of air time left for the staff to fill. They go immediately to a pre-recorded 'Best of Bittinger'. In the tag, Bill has returned to normal, refusing to see the woman who has named her baby after him.

Buffalo Bill's critique of television is complex since the characters themselves have an ambivalent attitude toward the medium. 'The Buffalo Bill Show' is no respected Los Angeles daily; it is not even the second-rate but sincere WJM local news. The internal show is unlikely to be perceived as having any redeeming virtues, even if the programme as a whole may be read as an 'intelligent' criticism of the lowest form of television. If *The Mary Tyler Moore Show* was both regular TV and quality TV, *Buffalo Bill* was both 'quality TV' and 'radical TV'. But the programme started no trend. *Buffalo Bill* was replaced in its time slot by Allan Burns' *The Duck Factory*, a virtual re-creation of *The Mary Tyler Moore Show* set in a cartoon factory, complete with warm, likeable characters and an identification figure even more benign than Mary Richards. It also failed in the ratings, indicating that even the orthodox MTM style of sitcom may have outlived its cultural moment.

Conclusion: The Politics of MTM

Quality TV is liberal TV. Given its institutional constraints and its entertainment function, one cannot expect American television to take self-criticism to the level of a Godard film. Yet both MTM and Godard gear their discourse to an assumed audience. Godard's extreme self-reflexivity appeals to the small audience of avant-garde intellectuals who pay to see his films. The appeal of an MTM programme must be double-edged. It must appeal both to the 'quality' audience, a liberal, sophisticated group of upwardly mobile professionals; and it must capture a large segment of the mass audience as well. Thus MTM programmes must be readable at a number of levels, as is true of most US television fare. MTM shows may be interpreted as warm, human comedies or dramas; or they may be interpreted as self-aware 'quality' texts. In this sense also, the MTM style is both typical and atypical. Its politics are seldom overt, yet the very concept of 'quality' is itself ideological. In interpreting an MTM programme as a quality programme, the quality audience is permitted to enjoy a form of television which is seen as more literate, more stylistically complex, and more psychologically 'deep' than ordinary TV fare. The quality audience gets to separate itself from the mass audience and can watch TV without guilt, and without realising that the double-edged discourse they are getting is also ordinary TV. Perhaps the best example of a programme that triumphed through this process of multiple readings is *Hill Street Blues*, the programme which marked MTM's transition to the quality demographic strategy.

This does not mean that the MTM style lacks progressive elements, only that, as with all forms of artistic production under capitalism, the progressive elements may be recuperable to an ideology of 'quality'. As an illustration of the politics of quality, I will take as an extended example one of the crucial innovations that MTM gave to the sitcom and the TV drama: the idea of the family of co-workers.

Every genre of American television is based on some kind of family structure. Even the personnel of the news programmes are presented to us as a 'family'; and until MTM came along, the nuclear family was the subject of most TV genres, as it was for the Lear sitcoms. At a time when the nuclear family was under attack outside the institution of television, MTM pioneered a different kind of family, one that retained certain residual ideologies of family life while doing away with the more oppressive aspects of the nuclear family. The MTM work-family both reproduces the wholesome norms of family life on TV and presents us with a Utopian variation on the nuclear family more palatable to a new generation and to the quality audience.

Rhoda was the only successful MTM sitcom to centre on a nuclear family rather than a family bonded by work and freely chosen (even then, Rhoda didn't live at home and the Morgensterns weren't very wholesome). *The Bob Newhart Show* featured a married couple, but the family unit included Bob's co-workers and even his therapy group. Those MTM sitcoms which featured a traditional family structure—*The Texas Wheelers, Doc, The Bob Crane Show*—tended to use an extended family structure and, moreover, tended to be outside the MTM creative nucleus and outside the 'quality' style. Eventually the idea of the non-nuclear family became the television norm.

The MTM work-family is clearly a response to the breakdown of the nuclear family inside and outside of the television institution. But how are we to interpret the politics of that response? On the one hand, the work family can be seen as Utopian in a reactionary direction. It presents a view of work as a familial activity, a view far from a 'realistic' representation of the real world of work. And the work family portrayed may be seen as a conservative force, valuing stasis over change. Many episodes of *The Mary Tyler Moore Show* take for their situation an eruption of disharmony within the WJM family: Rhoda and Mary feud; Murray and Mary feud; Lou fires Mary: Mary is offered another job; Rhoda gets a chance to move back to New York (this last prior to her actual spinning-off). In every case and in traditional sitcom form, harmony is re-established by bringing the family back together at the cost of what, in another context, might be seen as change or growth. Nobody is ever permitted to leave home. As one critic has written, the MTM shows' 'standard moment of epiphany' occurs with the discovery 'that nothing ever changes and people always stay reassuringly the same'.[14] This ideology of family harmony permeates the dramas as well, the difference being that in the continuing serial format, the moments of harmony are brief. Even *Buffalo Bill* represents the unity of the work family as a positive goal; it is just that Bill's presence makes the goal an impossible one.

Many MTM programmes make explicit references to the idea of the work family. In 'The Last Show' of *The Mary Tyler Moore Show*, Mary makes a long, sentimental speech about having found a family in her friends at work. The idea of the work family as a reactionary concept is rendered explicit in an episode of *WKRP in Cincinnati*. The employees of WKRP are asked to join a union. When Travis, the 'benign identification figure' of the programme, refuses to grant a pay raise, Johnny Fever calls him 'a true crypto-fascist puppet of the managerial elite', thus exposing Travis' position seemingly on the side of the workers but really on the side of management. Yet the rest of the episode undercuts this explanation. Johnny only becomes interested in the union when he discovers he will be paid by seniority (he is the oldest living DJ). When he gets this information, he breaks into the song, 'Look for the union label', and the others join in. This song comes from an unusually proletarian advertisement widely shown on US TV in which members of the International Ladies Garment Workers Union stand in formation and sing for us to buy clothing with the union label. In invoking the advertisement, including its image of solidarity, *WKRP* mocks its message. After much discussion, the situation is resolved when Travis negotiates with the station owner. He forces her to give the employees a raise, and they "freely" vote against the union. In this way, an opposition is set up *between* the union and the family of workers (deductively, their interests might be seen as similar, but the MTM concept of the work family is an individualistic one). The owner's son, the timid Carlson, says 'We're a *family* here. I'm not going to have outsiders telling us what to do.' Andy Travis says, 'Don't let this union business split us up.' Although management is portrayed unfavourably, the message is clear: the work family does not need to organise because it is already a democratic institution; all problems can be resolved within the family structure. A union would represent an intrusion from the real world of work into an already Utopian situation. This reading of the work family would view it as a reactionary force, in that it presents an unrealistically familial view of what we know to be an alienated labour process.

Yet such a reading of MTM's own discourse about the family of co-workers is only the most obvious interpretation of the Utopian dimension of the work family. For the MTM family also represents a positive alternative to the nuclear family that had for so long dominated representations of the family on American television. If nobody ever changes (a reading we have already shown to be dubious at best), if nobody ever has to leave home, perhaps it is because the MTM family is one in which it's possible to grow up. This more positive reading depends on the assumption that American network television never represents 'realistic' solutions to 'real' problems, but that, for this very reason, it is capable of showing us ideal solutions to mythicised versions of real problems. The work family is a solution to the problems of the nuclear family. It gives us a vision of that merger of work and love that Freud said was the ideal of mental, and that many would also see as the ideal of political, health.

MTM shows us this ideal over and over again within what in reality are the most oppressive institutional contexts: the hospital, the police precinct, the TV station. Media institutions work especially well for an idealised vision of work, since we already have a mythology of 'creative' work as an ideal.

The WJM family is what Mary Richards left home for, and it fulfilled her expectations and ours. For women especially, the alternatives presented were ideal ones, not depictions of the reality of work but images of a liberated existence that could be taken as a goal to strive towards. Mary and Rhoda came to represent an ideal of female friendship, a relationship that, due to the redundancy of the sitcom form, could never be torn asunder by the marriage of either woman. Mary's romances never represented a serious threat to either her relationship with Rhoda or her family at work. If the work-family concept proved pleasureable and reproducible, perhaps it was because it provided a positive alternative for the families who watched Mary and Rhoda on their TVs.

It must be stressed that neither of these readings of the work-family concept is 'correct'. Both are possible, but only the latter can explain the pleasure the concept must have provided in order for the programmes to be popular. That pleasure can encompass both progressive longings for an alternative to the nuclear family, and 'reactionary' longings for a return to the presumed ideal family structures of the past. The liberal, quality structure of the programmes permits and encourages both kinds of pleasure.

Notes

1. 9 September 1979.

2. 16 July 1974: 2 November 1975; 13 July 1981; 9 September 1979; *Los Angeles Times*, 16 July 1974.

3. See, for example, Donald Knox. *The Magic Factory* (New York: Praeger, 1973); and Hugh Fordin. *The World of Entertainment* (Garden City, N.Y: Doubleday, 1975).

4. 'What is an Author?' *Screen*, 20 (Spring 1979), p. 19.

5. *TV: The Most Popular Art* (New York: Anchor Books, 1974).

6. Tom Carson, 'The Even Couple', *The Village Voice*, 3 May 1983, p. 59.

7. 'Happy Days are Here Again', *Film Comment*, vol, 15 no. 4 July/August 1979.

8. Described in detail in Rick Mitz. *The Great TV Sitcom Book* (New York: Richard Marek Publishers, 1980).

9. MTM also developed a 'tag' ending that would trail off in such a way that the conversation appears to continue after the programme ends; this produces a 'quality' effect by rendering the sense of closure less emphatic.

10. *New York Times Magazine*, 7 April 1974, p. 97.

11. Written by David Lloyd; described in Rick Mitz, op. cit.

12. I make this point at greater length in my book, *The Hollywood Musical* (London: Macmillan, 1982).

13. Todd Gitlin, *Inside Prime Time* (New York: Pantheon Books, 1983).

14. Tom Carson, 'Lame Duck', *The Village Voice*, 1 May 1984.

PART III

The Medium and Its Message: Television Studies & Critical Theory

The Medium Is the Message

Marshall McLuhan

In a culture like ours, long accustomed to splitting and dividing all things as a means of control, it is sometimes a bit of a shock to be reminded that, in operational and practical fact, the medium is the message. This is merely to say that the personal and social consequences of any medium—that is, of any extension of ourselves—result from the new scale that is introduced into our affairs by each extension of ourselves, or by any new technology. Thus, with automation, for example, the new patterns of human association tend to eliminate jobs, it is true. That is the negative result. Positively, automation creates roles for people, which is to say depth of involvement in their work and human association that our preceding mechanical technology had destroyed. Many people would be disposed to say that it was not the machine, but what one did with the machine, that was its meaning or message. In terms of the ways in which the machine altered our relations to one another and to ourselves, it mattered not in the least whether it turned out cornflakes or Cadillacs. The restructuring of human work and association was shaped by the technique of fragmentation that is the essence of machine technology. The essence of automation technology is the opposite. It is integral and decentralist in depth, just as the machine was fragmentary, centralist, and superficial in its patterning of human relationships.

The instance of the electric light may prove illuminating in this connection. The electric light is pure information. It is a medium without a message, as it were, unless it is used to spell out some verbal ad or name. This fact, characteristic of all media, means that the "content" of any medium is always another medium. The content of writing is speech, just as the written word is the content of print, and print is the content of the telegraph. If it is asked, "What is the content of speech?," it is necessary to say, "It is an actual process of thought, which is in itself nonverbal." An abstract painting represents direct manifestation of creative thought processes as they might appear in computer designs. What we are considering here, however, are the psychic and social consequences of the designs or patterns as they amplify or accelerate existing processes. For the "message" of any medium or technology is the change of scale or pace or pattern that it introduces into human affairs. The railway did not introduce movement or transportation or wheel or road into human society, but it accelerated and enlarged the scale of previous human functions, creating totally new kinds of cities and new kinds of work and leisure. This happened whether the railway functioned in a tropical or a northern enviornment, and is quite independent of the freight or content of the railway medium. The airplane, on the other hand, by accelerating the rate of transportation, tends to dissolve the railway form of city, politics, and association, quite independently of what the airplane is used for.

Let us return to the electric light. Whether the light is being used for brain surgery or night baseball is a matter of indifference. It could be argued that these activities are in some way the "content" of the electric light, since they could not exist without the electric light. This fact merely underlines the point that "the medium is the message" because it is the medium that shapes and controls the scale and form of human association and action. The content or uses of such media are as diverse as they are ineffectual in shaping the form of human association. Indeed, it is only too typical that the "content" of any medium blinds us to the character of the medium. It is only today that industries have become aware of the various kinds of business in which they are engaged. When IBM discovered that it was not in the business of making office equipment or business machines, but that it was in the business of processing information, then it began to navigate with clear vision. The General Electric Company makes a considerable portion of its profits from electric light bulbs and lighting systems. It has not yet discovered that, quite as much as A.T.&T., it is in the business of moving information.

The electric light escapes attention as a communication medium just because it has no "content." And this makes it an invaluable instance of how people fail to study media at all. For it is not till the electric light is used to spell out some brand name that it is noticed as a medium. Then it is not the light but the "content" (or what is really another medium) that is noticed. The message of the electric light is like the message of electric power in industry, totally radical, pervasive, and decentralized. For electric light and power are separate from their uses, yet they eliminate time and space factors in human association exactly as do radio, telegraph, telephone, and TV, creating involvement in depth.

A fairly complete handbook for studying the extensions of man could be made up from selections from Shakespeare. Some might quibble about whether or not he was referring to TV in these familiar lines from *Romeo and Juliet:*

> *But soft! what light through yonder window breaks?*
> *It speaks, and yet says nothing.*

In *Othello*, which, as much as *King Lear*, is concerned with the torment of people transformed by illusions, there are these lines that bespeak Shakespeare's intuition of the transforming powers of new media:

> *Is there not charms*
> *By which the property of youth and maidhood*
> *May be abus'd? Have you not read, Roderigo,*
> *Of some such thing?*

In Shakespeare's *Troilus and Cressida*, which is almost completely devoted to both a psychic and social study of communication, Shakespeare states his awareness that true social and political navigation depend upon anticipating the consequences of innovation:

> *The providence that's in a watchful state*
> *Knows almost every grain of Plutus' gold,*
> *Finds bottom in the uncomprehensive deeps,*
> *Keeps place with thought, and almost like the gods*
> *Does thoughts unveil in their dumb cradles.*

The increasing awareness of the action of media, quite independently of their "content" or programming, was indicated in the annoyed and anonymous stanza:

> *In modern thought, (if not in fact)*
> *Nothing is that doesn't act,*
> *So that is reckoned wisdom which*
> *Describes the scratch but not the itch.*

The same kind of total, configurational awareness that reveals why the medium is socially the message has occurred in the most recent and radical medium theories. In his *Stress of Life*, Hans Selye tells of the dismay of a research colleague on hearing of Selye's theory:

> *When he saw me thus launched on yet another enraptured description of what I*
> *had observed in animals treated with this or that impure, toxic material, he looked*
> *at me with desperately sad eyes and said in obvious despair: "But Selye, try to real-*
> *ize what you are doing before it is too late! You have now decided to spend your*
> *entire life studying the pharmacology of dirt!" (Hans Selye, The Stress of Life)*

As Selye deals with the total environmental situation in his "stress" theory of disease, so the latest approach to media study considers not only the "content" but the medium and the cultural matrix within which the particular medium operates. The older unawareness of the psychic and social effects of media can be illustrated from almost any of the conventional pronouncements.

In accepting an honorary degree from the University of Notre Dame a few years ago, General David Sarnoff made this statement: "We are too prone to make technological instruments the scapegoats for the sins of those who wield them. The products of modern science are not in themselves good or bad; it is the way they are used that determines their value." That is the voice of the current somnambulism. Suppose we were to say, "Apple pie is in itself neither good nor bad; it is the way it is used that determines its value." Or, "The small-pox virus is in itself neither good nor bad; it is the way it is used that determines its value." Again, "Firearms are in themselves neither good nor bad; it is the way they are used that determines their value." That is, if the slugs reach the right people firearms are good. If the TV tube fires the right ammunition at the right people it is good. I am not being perverse. There is simply nothing in the Sarnoff statement that will bear scrutiny, for it ignores the nature of the medium, of any and all media, in the true Narcissus style of one hypnotized by the amputation and extension of his own being in a new technical form. General Sarnoff went on to explain his attitude to the technology of print, saying that it was true that print caused much trash to circulate, but it had also disseminated the Bible and the thoughts of seers and philosophers. It has never occurred to General Sarnoff that any technology could do anything but *add* itself on to what we already are.

Such economists as Robert Theobald, W. W. Rostow, and John Kenneth Galbraith have been explaining for years how it is that "classical economics" cannot explain change or growth. And the paradox of mechanization is that although it is itself the cause of maximal growth and change, the principle of mechanization excludes the very possibility of growth or the understanding of change. For mechanization is achieved by fragmentation of any process and by putting the fragmented parts in a series. Yet, as David Hume showed in the eighteenth century, there is no principle of causality in a mere sequence. That one thing follows another accounts for nothing. Nothing follows from following, except change. So the greatest of all reversals occurred with electricity, that ended sequence by making things instant. With instant speed the causes of things began to emerge to awareness again, as they had not done with things in sequence and in concatenation accordingly. Instead of asking which came first, the chicken or the egg, it suddenly seemed that a chicken was an egg's idea for getting more eggs.

Just before an airplane breaks the sound barrier, sound waves become visible on the wings of the plane. The sudden visibility of sound just as sound ends is an apt instance of that great pattern of being that reveals new and opposite forms just as the earlier forms reach their peak performance. Mechanization was never so vividly fragmented or sequential as in the birth of the movies, the moment that translated us beyond mechanism into the world of growth and organic interrelation. The movie, by sheer speeding up the mechanical, carried us from the world of sequence and connections into the world of creative configuration and structure. The message of the movie medium is that of transition from lineal connections to configurations. It is the transition that produced the now quite correct observation: "If it works, it's obsolete." When electric speed further takes over from mechanical movie sequences, then the lines of force in structures and in media become loud and clear. We return to the inclusive form of the icon.

To a highly literate and mechanized culture the movie appeared as a world of triumphant illusions and dreams that money could buy. It was at this moment of the movie that cubism occurred, and it has been described by E. H. Gombrich (*Art and Illusion*) as "the most radical attempt to stamp out ambiguity and to enforce one reading of the picture—that of a man-made construction, a colored canvas." For cubism substitutes all facets of an object simultaneously for the "point of view" or facet of perspective illusion. Instead of the specialized illusion of the third dimension on canvas, cubism sets up an interplay of planes and contradiction or dramatic conflict of patterns, lights, textures that "drives home the message" by involvement. This is held by many to be an exercise in painting, not in illusion.

In other words, cubism, by giving the inside and outside, the top, bottom, back, and front and the rest, in two dimensions, drops the illusion of perspective in favor of instant sensory awareness of the whole. Cubism, by seizing on instant total awareness, suddenly announced that *the medium is the message*. Is it not evident that the moment that sequence yields to the simultaneous, one is in the world of the structure and of configuration? Is that not what has happened in physics as in painting, poetry, and in communication? Specialized segments of attention have shifted to total field, and we can now say, "The medium is the message" quite naturally. Before the electric speed and total field, it was not obvious that the medium is the message. The message, it seemed, was the "content," as people used to ask what a painting was *about*. Yet they never thought to ask what a melody was about, nor what a house or a dress was about. In such matters, people retained some sense of the whole pattern, of form and function as a unity. But in the electric age this integral idea of structure and configuration has become so prevalent that educational theory has taken up the matter. Instead of working with specialized "problems" in arithmetic, the structural approach now follows the linea of force in the field of number and has small children meditating about number theory and "sets."

Cardinal Newman said of Napoleon, "He understood the grammar of gunpowder." Napoleon had paid some attention to other media as well, especially the semaphore telegraph that gave him a great advantage over his enemies. He is on record for saying that "Three hostile newspapers are more to be feared than a thousand bayonets."

Alexis de Tocqueville was the first to master the grammar of print and typography. He was thus able to read off the message of coming change in France and America as if he were reading aloud from a text that had been handed to him. In fact, the nineteenth century in France and in America was just such an open book to de Tocqueville because he had learned the grammar of print. So he, also, knew when that grammar did not apply. He was asked why he did not write a book on England, since he knew and admired England. He replied:

> One would have to have an unusual degree of philosophical folly to believe oneself able to judge England in six months. A year always seemed to me too short a time in which to appreciate the United States properly, and it is much easier to acquire clear and precise notions about the American Union than about Great Britain. In America all laws derive in a sense from the same line of thought. The whole of society, so to speak, is founded upon a single fact; everything springs from a simple principle. One could compare America to a forest pierced by a multitude of straight roads all converging on the same point. One has only to find the center and everything is revealed at a glance. But in England the paths run crisscross, and it is only by travelling down each one of them that one can build up a picture of the whole.

De Tocqueville, in earlier work on the French Revolution, had explained how it was the printed word that, achieving cultural saturation in the eighteenth century, had homogenized the French nation. Frenchmen were the same kind of people from north to south. The typographic principles of uniformity, continuity, and lineality had overlaid the complexities of ancient feudal and oral society. The Revolution was carried out by the new literati and lawyers.

In England, however, such was the power of the ancient oral traditions of common law, backed by the medieval institution of Parliament, that no uniformity or continuity of the new visual print culture could take complete hold. The result was that the most important event in English history has never taken place; namely, the English Revolution on the lines of the French Revolution. The American Revolution had no medieval legal institutions to discard or to root out, apart from monarchy. And many have held that the American Presidency has become very much more personal and monarchical than any European monarch ever could be.

De Tocqueville's contrast between England and America is clearly based on the fact of typography and of print culture creating uniformity and continuity. England, he says, has rejected this principle and clung to the dynamic or oral common-law tradition. Hence the discontinuity and unpredictable quality of English culture. The grammar of print cannot help to construe the message of oral and nonwritten culture and institutions. The English aristocracy was properly classified as barbarian by Matthew Arnold because its power and status had nothing to do with literacy or with the cultural forms of typography. Said the Duke of Gloucester to Edward Gibbon upon the publication of his *Decline and Fall:* "Another damned fat book, eh, Mr. Gibbon? Scribble, scribble, scribble, eh, Mr. Gibbon?" De Tocqueville was a highly literate aristocrat who was quite able to be detached from the values and assumptions of typography. That is why he alone understood the grammar of typography. And it is only on those terms, standing aside from any structure or medium, that its principles and lines of force can be discerned. For any medium has the power of imposing its own assumption on the unwary. Prediction and control consist in avoiding this subliminal state of Narcissus trance. But the greatest aid to this end is simply in knowing that the spell can occur immediately upon contact, as in the first bars of a melody.

A Passage to India by E. M. Forster is a dramatic study of the inability of oral and intuitive oriental culture to meet with the rational, visual European patterns of experience. "Rational," of course, has for the West long meant "uniform and continuous and sequential." In other words, we have confused reason with literacy, and rationalism with a single technology. Thus in the electric age man seems to the conventional West to become irrational. In Forster's novel the moment of truth and dislocation from the typographic trance of the West comes in the Marabar Caves. Adela Quested's reasoning powers cannot cope with the total inclusive field of resonance that is India. After the Caves: "Life went on as usual, but had no consequences, that is to say, sounds did not echo nor thought develop. Everything seemed cut off at its root and therefore infected with illusion."

A Passage to India (the phrase is from Whitman, who saw America headed Eastward) is a parable of Western man in the electric age, and is only incidentally related to Europe or the Orient. The ultimate conflict between sight and sound, between written and oral kinds of perception and organization of existence is upon us. Since understanding stops action, as Nietzsche observed, we can moderate the fierceness of this conflict by understanding the media that extend us and raise these wars within and without us.

Detribalization by literacy and its traumatic effects on tribal man is the theme of a book by the psychiatrist J. C. Carothers, *The African Mind in Health and Disease* (World Health Organization, Geneva, 1953). Much of his material appeared in an article in *Psychiatry* magazine, November, 1959: "The Culture, Psychiatry, and the Written Word." Again, it is electric speed that has revealed the lines of force operating from Western technology in the remotest areas of bush, savannah, and desert. One example is the Bedouin with his battery radio on board the camel. Submerging natives with floods of concepts for which nothing has prepared them is the normal action of all of our technology. But with electric media Western man himself experiences exactly the same inundation as the remote native. We are no more prepared to encounter radio and TV in our literate milieu than the native of Ghana is able to cope with the literacy that takes him out of his collective tribal world and beaches him in individual isolation. We are as numb in our new electric world as the native involved in our literate and mechanical culture.

Electric speed mingles the cultures of prehistory with the dregs of industrial marketeers, the nonliterate with semiliterate and the postliterate. Mental breakdown of varying degrees is the very common result of uprooting and inundation with new information and endless new patterns of information. Wyndham Lewis made this a theme of his group of novels called *The Human Age.* The first of these, *The Childermass,* is concerned precisely with accelerated media change as a kind of massacre of the innocents. In our own world as we become more aware of the effects of technology on psychic formation and manifestation, we are losing all confidence in our right to assign guilt. Ancient prehistoric societies regard violent crime as pathetic. The killer is regarded as we do a cancer victim. "How terrible it must be to feel like that," they say. J. M. Synge took up this idea very effectively in his *Playboy of the Western World.*

If the criminal appears as a nonconformist who is unable to meet the demand of technology that we behave in uniform and continuous patterns, literate man is quite inclined to see others who cannot conform as somewhat pathetic. Especially the child, the cripple, the woman, and the colored person appear in a world of visual and typographic technology as victims of injustice. On the other hand, in a culture that assigns roles instead of jobs to people—the dwarf, the skew, the child create their own spaces. They are not expected to fit into some uniform and repeatable niche that is not their size anyway. Consider the phrase "It's a man's world." As a quantitative observation endlessly repeated from within a homogenized culture, this phrase refers to the men in such a culture who have to be homogenized Dagwoods in order to belong at all. It is in our I.Q. testing that we have produced the greatest flood of misbegotten standards. Unaware of our typographic cultural bias, our testers assume that uniform and continuous habits are a sign of intelligence, thus eliminating the ear man and the tactile man.

C. P. Snow, reviewing a book of A. L. Rowse (*The New York Times Book Review*, December 24, 1961) on *Appeasement* and the road to Munich, describes the top level of British brains and experience in the 1930s. "Their I.Q.'s were much higher than usual among political bosses. Why were they such a disaster?" The view of Rowse, Snow approves: "They would not listen to warnings because they did not wish to hear." Being anti-Red made it impossible for them to read the message of Hitler. But their failure was as nothing compared to our present one. The American stake in literacy as a technology or uniformity applied to every level of education, government, industry, and social life is totally threatened by the electric technology. The threat of Stalin or Hitler was external. The electric technology is within the gates, and we are numb, deaf, blind, and mute about its encounter with the Gutenberg technology, on and through which the American way of life was formed. It is, however, no time to suggest strategies when the threat has not even been acknowledged to exist. I am in the position of Louis Pasteur telling doctors that their greatest enemy was quite invisible, and quite unrecognized by them. Our conventional response to all media, namely that it is how they are used that counts, is the numb stance of the technological idiot. For the "content" of a medium is like the juicy piece of meat carried by the burglar to distract the watchdog of the mind. The effect of the medium is made strong and intense just because it is given another medium as "content." The content of a movie is a novel or a play or an opera. The effect of the movie form is not related to its program content. The "content" of writing or print is speech, but the reader is almost entirely unaware either of print or of speech.

Arnold Toynbee is innocent of any understanding of media as they have shaped history, but he is full of examples that the student of media can use. At one moment he can seriously suggest that adult education, such as the Workers' Educational Association in Britain, is a useful counterforce to the popular press. Toynbee considers that although all of the oriental societies have in our time accepted the industrial technology and its political consequences: "On the cultural plane, however, there is no uniform corresponding tendency." (Somervell, I. 267) This is like the voice of the literate man, floundering in a milieu of ads, who boasts, "Personally, I pay no attention to ads." The spiritual and cultural reservations that the oriental peoples may have toward our technology will avail them not at all. The effects of technology do not occur at the level of opinions or concepts, but alter sense ratios or patterns of perception steadily and without any resistance. The serious artist is the only person able to encounter technology with impunity, just because he is an expert aware of the changes in sense perception.

The operation of the money medium in seventeenth-century Japan had effects not unlike the operation of typography in the West. The penetration of the money economy, wrote G. B. Sansom (in *Japan*, Cresset Press, London, 1931) "caused a slow but irresistible revolution, culminating in the breakdown of feudal government and the resumption of intercourse with foreign countries after more than two hundred years of seclusion." Money has reorganized the sense life of peoples just because it is an *extension* of our sense lives. This change does not depend upon approval or disapproval of those living in the society.

Arnold Toynbee made one approach to the transforming power of media in his concept of "etherialization," which he holds to be the principle of progressive simplification and efficency in any organization or technology. Typically, he is ignoring the *effect* of the challenge of these forms upon the response of our senses. He imagines that it is the response of our opinions that is relevant to the effect of media and technology in society, a "point of view" that is plainly the result of the typographic spell. For the man in a literate and homogenized society ceases to be sensitive to the diverse and discontinuous life of forms. He acquires the illusion of the third dimension and the "private point of view" as part of his Narcissus fixation, and is quite shut off from Blake's awareness or that of the Psalmist, that we become what we behold.

Today when we want to get our bearings in our own culture, and have need to stand aside from the bias and pressure exerted by any technical form of human expression, we have only to visit a society where that particular form has not been felt, or a historical period in which it was unknown. Professor Wilbur Schramm made such a tactical move in studying *Television in the Lives of Our Children*. He found areas where TV had not penetrated at all and ran some tests. Since he had made no study of the peculiar nature of the TV image, his tests were of "content" preferences, viewing time, and vocabulary counts. In a word, his approach to the problem was a literary one, albeit unconsciously so. Consequently, he had nothing to report. Had his methods been employed in 1500 A.D. to discover the effects of the printed book in the lives of children or adults, he could have found out nothing of the changes in human and social psychology resulting from typography. Print created individualism and nationalism in the sixteenth century. Program and "content" analysis offer no clues to the magic of these media or to their subliminal charge.

Leonard Doob, in his report *Communication in Africa*, tells of one African who took great pains to listen each evening to the BBC news, even though he could understand nothing of it. Just to be in the presence of those sounds at 7 p.m. each day was important for him. His attitude to speech was like ours to melody—the resonant intonation was meaning enough. In the seventeenth century our ancestors still shared this native's attitude to the forms of media, as is plain in the following sentiment of the Frenchman Bernard Lam expressed in *The Art of Speaking* (London, 1696):

> 'Tis an effect of the Wisdom of God, who created Man to be happy, that whatever is useful to his conversation (way of life) is agreeable to him ... because all victual that conduces to nourishment is relishable, whereas other things that cannot be assimilated and be turned into our substance are insipid. A Discourse cannot be pleasant to the Hearer that is not easie to the Speaker; nor can it be easily pronounced unless it be heard with delight.

Here is an equilibrium theory of human diet and expression such as even now we are only striving to work out again for media after centuries of fragmentation and specialism.

Pope Pius XII was deeply concerned that there be serious study of the media today. On February 17, 1950, he said:

> It is not an exaggeration to say that the future of modern society and the stability of its inner life depend in large part on the maintenance of an equilibrium between the strength of the techniques of communication and the capacity of the individual's own reaction.

Failure in this respect has for centuries been typical and total for mankind. Subliminal and docile acceptance of media impact has made them prisons without walls for their human users. As A. J. Liebling remarked in his book *The Press*, a man is not free if he cannot see where he is going, even if he has a gun to help him get there. For each of the media is also a powerful weapon with which to clobber other media and other groups. The result is that the present age has been one of multiple civil wars that are not limited to the world of art and entertainment. In *War and Human Progress*, Professor J. U. Nef declared: "The total wars of our time have been the result of a series of intellectual mistakes . . ."

If the formative power in the media are the media themselves, that raises a host of large matters that can only be mentioned here, although they deserve volumes. Namely, that technological media are staples or natural resources, exactly as are coal and cotton and oil. Anybody will concede that society whose economy is dependent upon one or two major staples like cotton, or grain, or lumber, or fish, or cattle is going to have some obvious social patterns of organization as a result. Stress on a few major staples creates extreme instability in the economy but great endurance in the population. The pathos and humor of the American South are embedded in such an economy of limited staples. For a society configured by reliance on a few commodities accepts them as a social bond quite as much as the metropolis does the press. Cotton and oil, like radio and TV, become "fixed charges" on the entire psychic life of the community. And this pervasive fact creates the unique cultural flavor of any society. It pays through the nose and all its other senses for each staple that shapes its life.

That our human senses, of which all media are extensions, are also fixed charges on our personal energies, and that they also configure the awareness and experience of each one of us, may be perceived in another connection mentioned by the psychologist C. G. Jung:

> *Every Roman was surrounded by slaves. The slave and his psychology flooded ancient Italy, and every Roman became inwardly, and of course unwittingly, a slave. Because living constantly in the atmosphere of slaves, he became infected through the unconscious with their psychology. No one can shield himself from such an influence.*

(Contributions to Analytical Psychology, *London, 1928*)

Programming As Sequence or Flow

Raymond Williams

[. . .]

In all developed broadcasting systems the characteristic organisation, and therefore the characteristic experience, is one of sequence or flow. This phenomenon, of planned flow, is then perhaps the defining characteristic of broadcasting, simultaneously as a technology and as a cultural form.

In all communications systems before broadcasting the essential items were discrete. A book or a pamphlet was taken and read as a specific item. A meeting occurred at a particular date and place. A play was performed in a particular theatre at a set hour. The difference in broadcasting is not only that these events, or events resembling them, are available inside the home, by the operation of a switch. It is that the real programme that is offered is a *sequence* or set of alternative sequences of these and other similar events, which are then available in a single dimension and in a single operation.

Yet we have become so used to this that in a way we do not see it. Most of our habitual vocabulary of response and description has been shaped by the experience of discrete events. We have developed ways of responding to a particular book or a particular play, drawing on our experience of other books and plays. When we go out to a meeting or a concert or a game we take other experience with us and we return to other experience, but the specific event is ordinarily an occasion, setting up its own internal conditions and responses. Our most general modes of comprehension and judgment are then closely linked to these kinds of specific and isolated, temporary forms of attention.

Some earlier kinds of communication contained, it is true, internal variation and at times miscellaneity. Dramatic performances included musical interludes, or the main play was preceded by a curtain-raiser. In print there are such characteristic forms as the almanac and the chapbook, which include items relating to very different kinds of interest and involving quite different kinds of response. The magazine, invented as a specific form in the early eighteenth century, was designed as a miscellany, mainly for a new and expanding and culturally inexperienced middle-class audience. The modern newspaper, from the eighteenth century but very much more markedly from the nineteenth century, became a miscellany, not only of news items that were often essentially unrelated, but of features, anecdotes, drawings, photographs and advertisements. From the late nineteenth century this came to be reflected in formal layout, culminating in the characteristic jigsaw effect of the modern newspaper page. Meanwhile, sporting events, especially football matches, as they became increasingly important public occasions, included entertainment such as music or marching in their intervals.

This general trend, towards an increasing variability and miscellaneity of public communications, is evidently part of a whole social experience. It has profound connections with the growth and development of greater physical and social mobility, in conditions both of cultural expansion and of consumer rather than community cultural organisation. Yet until the coming of broadcasting the normal expectation was still of a discrete event or of a succession of discrete events. People took a book or a pamphlet or a newspaper, went out to a play or a concert or a meeting or a match, with a single predominant expectation and attitude. The social relationships set up in these various cultural events were specific and in some degree temporary.

Broadcasting, in its earliest stages, inherited this tradition and worked mainly within it. Broadcasters discovered the kinds of thing they could do or, as some of them would still normally say, transmit. The musical concert could be broadcast or arranged for broadcasting. The public address—the lecture or the sermon, the speech at a meeting—could be broadcast as a talk. The sports match could be described and shown. The play could be performed, in this new theatre of the air. Then as the service extended, these items, still considered as discrete units, were assembled into programmes. The word 'programme' is characteristic, with its traditional bases in theatre and music-hall. With increasing organisation, as the service extended, this 'programme' became a series of timed units. Each unit could be thought of discretely, and the work of programming was a serial assembly of these units. Problems of mix and proportion became predominant in broadcasting policy. Characteristically, as most clearly in the development of British sound broadcasting, there was a steady evolution from a general service, with its internal criteria of mix and proportion and what was called 'balance', to contrasting types of service, alternative programmes. 'Home', 'Light' and 'Third', in British radio, were the eventual names for what were privately described and indeed generally understood as 'general', 'popular' and 'educated' broadcasting. Problems of mix and proportion, formerly considered within a single service, were then basically transferred to a range of alternative programmes, corresponding to assumed social and educational levels. This tendency was taken further in later forms of reorganisation, as in the present specialised British radio services One to Four. In an American radio programme listing, which is before me as I write, there is a further specialisation: the predominantly musical programmes are briefly characterised, by wavelength, as 'rock', 'country', 'classical', 'nostalgic' and so on. In one sense this can be traced as a development of programming: extensions of the service have brought further degrees of rationalisation and specialisation.

But the development can also be seen, and in my view needs to be seen, in quite other ways. There has been a significant shift from the concept of sequence as *programming* to the concept of sequence as *flow*. Yet this is difficult to see because the older concept of programming—the temporal sequence within which mix and proportion and balance operate—is still active and still to some extent real.

What is it then that has been decisively altered? A broadcasting programme, on sound or television, is still formally a series of timed units. What is published as information about the broadcasting services is still of this kind; we can look up the time of a particular 'show' or 'programme'; we can turn on for that item; we can select and respond to it discretely.

Yet for all the familiarity of this model, the normal experience of broadcasting, when we really consider it, is different. And indeed this is recognised in the ways we speak of 'watching television', 'listening to the radio', picking on the general rather than the specific experience. This has been true of all broadcasting, but some significant internal developments have greatly reinforced it. These developments can be indicated in one simple way. In earlier phases of the broadcasting service, both in sound and television, there were *intervals* between programme units: true intervals, usually marked by some conventional sound or picture to show that the general service was still active. There was the sound of bells or the sight of waves breaking, and these marked the intervals between discrete programme units. There is still a residual example of this type in the turning globe which functions as an interval signal in BBC television.

But in most television services, as they are currently operated, the concept of the interval—though still, for certain purposes, retained as a concept—has been fundamentally revalued. This change came about in two ways, which are still unevenly represented in different services. The decisive innovation was in services financed by commercial television. There was a specific and formal undertaking that 'programmes' should not be interrupted by advertising; this could take place only in 'natural breaks': between the movements of a symphony, or between the acts in *Hamlet*, as the Government spokesman said in the House of Lords! In practice, of course, this was never complied with, nor was it ever intended that it should be. A 'natural break' became any moment of convenient insertion. News programmes, plays, even films that had been shown in cinemas as specific whole performances, began to be interrupted for commercials. On American television this development was different; the sponsored programmes incorporated the advertising from the outset, from the initial conception, as part of the whole package. But it is now obvious, in both British and American commercial television, that the notion of 'interruption', while it has still some residual force from an older model, has become inadequate. What is being offered is not, in older terms, a programme of discrete units with particular insertions, but a planned flow, in which the true series is not the published sequence of programme items but this sequence transformed by the inclusion of another kind of sequence, so that these sequences together compose the real flow, the real 'broadcasting'. Increasingly, in both commercial and public-service television, a further sequence was added: trailers of programmes to be shown at some later time or on some later day, or more itemised programme news. This was intensified in conditions of competition, when it became important to broadcasting planners to retain viewers—or as they put it, to 'capture' them—for a whole evening's sequence. And with the eventual unification of these two or three sequences, a new kind of communication phenomenon has to be recognised.

Of course many people who watch television still register some of these items as 'interruptions'. I remember first noticing the problem while watching films on British commercial television. For even in an institution as wholeheartedly commercial in production and distribution as the cinema, it had been possible, and indeed remains normal, to watch a film as a whole, in an undisturbed sequence. All films were originally made and distributed in this way, though the inclusion of supporting 'B' films and short features in a package, with appropriate intervals for advertising and for the planned selling of refreshments, began to develop the cinema towards the new kind of planned flow. Watching the same films on commercial television made the new situation quite evident. We are normally given some twenty or twenty-five minutes of the film, to get us interested in it; then four minutes of commercials, then about fifteen more minutes of the film; some commercials again; and so on to steadily decreasing lengths of the film, with commercials between them, or them between the commercials, since by this time it is assumed that we are interested and will watch the film to the end. Yet even this had not prepared me for the characteristic American sequence. One night in Miami, still dazed from a week on an Atlantic liner, I began watching a film and at first had some difficulty in adjusting to a much greater frequency of commercial 'breaks'. Yet this was a minor problem compared to what eventually happened. Two other films, which were due to be shown on the same channel on other nights, began to be inserted as trailers. A crime in San Francisco (the subject of the original film) began to operate in an extraordinary counterpoint not only with the deodorant and cereal commercials but with a romance in Paris and the eruption of a prehistoric monster who laid waste New York. Moreover, this was sequence in a new sense. Even in commercial British television there is a visual signal—the residual sign of an interval—before and after the commercial sequences, and 'programme' trailers only occur between 'programmes'. Here there was something quite different, since the transitions from film to commercial and from film A to films B and C were in effect unmarked. There is in any case enough similarity between certain kinds of films, and between several kinds of film and the 'situation' commercials which often consciously imitate them, to make a sequence of this kind a very difficult experience to interpret. I can still not be sure what I took from that whole flow. I believe I registered some incidents as happening in the wrong film, and some characters in the commercials as involved in the film episodes, in what came to seem—for all the occasional bizarre disparities—a single irresponsible flow of images and feelings.

Of course the films were not made to be 'interrupted' in this way. But this flow is planned: not only in itself, but at an early stage in all original television production for commercial systems. Indeed most commercial television 'programmes' are made, from the planning stage, with this real sequence in mind. In quite short plays there is a rationalised division into 'acts'. In features there is a similar rationalised division into 'parts'. But the effect goes deeper. There is a characteristic kind of opening sequence, meant to excite interest, which is in effect a kind of trailer for itself. In American television, after two or three minutes, this is succeeded by commercials. The technique has an early precedent in the dumbshows which preceded plays or scenes in early Elizabethan theatre. But there what followed the dumbshow was the play or the scene. Here what follows is apparently quite unconnected material. It is then not surprising that so many of these opening moments are violent or bizarre: the interest aroused must be strong enough to initiate the expectation of (interrupted but sustainable) sequence. Thus a quality of the external sequence becomes a mode of definition of an internal method.

At whatever stage of development this process has reached—and it is still highly variable between different broadcasting systems—it can still be residually seen as 'interruption' of a 'programme'. Indeed it is often important to see it as this, both for one's own true sense of place and event, and as a matter of reasonable concern in broadcasting policy. Yet it may be even more important to see the true process as flow: the replacement of a programme series of timed sequential units by a flow series of differently related units in which the timing, though real, is undeclared, and in which the real internal organisation is something other than the declared organisation.

For the 'interruptions' are in one way only the most visible characteristic of a process which at some levels has come to define the television experience. Even when, as on the BBC, there are no interruptions of specific 'programme units', there is a quality of flow which our received vocabulary of discrete response and description cannot easily acknowledge. It is evident that what is now called 'an evening's viewing' is in some ways planned, by providers and then by viewers, *as a whole*; that it is in any event planned in discernible sequences which in this sense override particular programme units. Whenever there is competition between television channels, this becomes a matter of conscious concern: to get viewers in at the beginning of a flow. Thus in Britain there is intense competition between BBC and IBA in the early evening programmes, in the belief—which some statistics support—that viewers will stay with whatever channel they begin watching. There are of course many cases in which this does not happen: people can consciously select another channel or another programme, or switch off altogether. But the flow effect is sufficiently widespread to be a major element in programming policy. And this is the immediate reason for the increasing frequency of programming trailers: to sustain that evening flow. In conditions of more intense competition, as between the American channels, there is even more frequent trailing, and the process is specifically referred to as 'moving along', to sustain what is thought of as a kind of brand-loyalty to the channel being watched. Some part of the flow offered is then directly traceable to conditions of controlled competition, just as some of its specific original elements are traceable to the financing of television by commercial advertising.

Yet this is clearly not the whole explanation. The flow offered can also, and perhaps more fundamentally, be related to the television experience itself. Two common observations bear on this. As has already been noted, most of us say, in describing the experience, that we have been 'watching television', rather than that we have watched 'the news' or 'a play' or 'the football' 'on television'. Certainly we sometimes say both, but the fact that we say the former at all is already significant. Then again it is a widely if often ruefully admitted experience that many of us find television very difficult to switch off; that again and again, even when we have switched on for a particular 'programme', we find ourselves watching the one after it and the one after that. The way in which the flow is now organised, without definite intervals, in any case encourages this. We can be 'into' something else before we have summoned the energy to get out of the chair, and many programmes are made with this situation in mind: the grabbing of attention in the early moments; the reiterated promise of exciting things to come, if we stay.

But the impulse to go on watching seems more widespread than this kind of organisation would alone explain. It is significant that there has been steady pressure, not only from the television providers but from many viewers, for an extension of viewing hours. In Britain, until recently, television was basically an evening experience, with some brief offerings in the middle of the day, and with morning and afternoon hours, except at weekends, used for schools and similar broadcasting. There is now a rapid development of morning and afternoon 'programmes' of a general kind. In the United States it is already possible to begin watching at six o'clock in the morning, see one's first movie at eight-thirty, and so on in a continuous flow, with the screen never blank, until the late movie begins at one o'clock the following morning. It is scarcely possible that many people watch a flow of that length, over more than twenty hours of the day. But the flow is always accessible, in several alternative sequences, at the flick of a switch. Thus, both internally, in its immediate organisation, and as a generally available experience, this characteristic of flow seems central.

Yet it is a characteristic for which hardly any of our received modes of observation and description prepare us. The reviewing of television programmes is of course of uneven quality, but in most even of the best reviews there is a conventional persistence from earlier models. Reviewers pick out this play or that feature, this discussion programme or that documentary. I reviewed television once a month over four years, and I know how much more settling, more straightforward, it is to do that. For most of the items there are some received procedures, and the method, the vocabulary, for a specific kind of description and response exists or can be adapted. Yet while that kind of reviewing can be useful, it is always at some distance from what seems to me the central television experience: the fact of flow. It is not only that many particular items—given our ordinary organisation of response, memory and persistence of attitude and mood—are affected by those preceding and those following them, unless we watch in an artificially timed way which seems to be quite rare (though it exists in the special viewings put on for regular Reviewers). It is also that though useful things may be said about all the separable items (though often with conscious exclusion of the commercials which 'interrupt' at least half of them) hardly anything is ever said about the characteristic experience of the flow sequence itself. It is indeed very difficult to say anything about this. It would be like trying to describe having read two plays, three newspapers, three or four magazines, on the same day that one has been to a variety show and a lecture and a football match. And yet in another way it is not like that at all, for though the items may be various the television experience has in some important ways unified them. To break this experience back into units, and to write about the units for which there are readily available procedures, is understandable but often misleading, even when we defend it by the gesture that we are discriminating and experienced viewers and don't just sit there hour after hour goggling at the box.

For the fact is that many of us do sit there, and much of the critical significance of television must be related to this fact. I know that whenever I tried, in reviewing, to describe the experience of flow, on a particular evening or more generally, what I could say was unfinished and tentative, yet I learned from correspondence that I was engaging with an experience which many viewers were aware of and were trying to understand. There can be 'classical' kinds of response, at many different levels, to some though not all of the discrete units. But we are only just beginning to recognise, let alone solve, the problems of description and response to the facts of flow.

Encoding/Decoding

Stuart Hall

Traditionally, mass-communications research has conceptualized the process of communication in terms of a circulation circuit or loop. This model has been criticized for its linearity—sender/message/receiver—for its concentration on the level of message exchange and for the absence of a structured conception of the different moments as a complex structure of relations. But it is also possible (and useful) to think of this process in terms of a structure produced and sustained through the articulation of linked but distinctive moments—production, circulation, distribution/consumption, reproduction. This would be to think of the process as a 'complex structure in dominance', sustained through the articulation of connected practices, each of which, however, retains its distinctiveness and has its own specific modality, its own forms and conditions of existence. This second approach, homologous to that which forms the skeleton of commodity production offered in Marx's *Grundrisse* and in *Capital*, has the added advantage of bringing out more sharply how a continuous circuit production–distribution–production—can be sustained through a 'passage of forms'.[1] It also highlights the specificity of the forms in which the product of the process 'appears' in each moment, and thus what distinguishes discursive 'production' from other types of production in our society and in modern media systems.

The 'object' of these practices is meanings and messages in the form of sign-vehicles of a specific kind organized, like any form of communication or language, through the operation of codes within the syntagmatic chain of a discourse. The apparatuses, relations and practices of production thus issue, at a certain moment (the moment of 'production/circulation') in the form of symbolic vehicles constituted within the rules of 'language'. It is in this discursive form that the circulation of the 'product' takes place. The process thus requires, at the production end, its material instruments—its 'means'—as well as its own sets of social (production) relations—the organization and combination of practices within media apparatuses. But it is in the *discursive* form that the circulation of the product takes place, as well as its distribution to different audiences. Once accomplished, the discourse must then be translated—transformed, again—into social practices if the circuit is to be both completed and effective. If no 'meaning' is taken, there can be no 'consumption'. If the meaning is not articulated in practice, it has no effect. The value of this approach is that while each of the moments, in articulation, is necessary to the circuit as a whole, no one moment can fully guarantee the next moment with which it is articulated. Since each has its specific modality and conditions of existence, each can constitute its own break or interruption of the 'passage of forms' on whose continuity the flow of effective production (that is, 'reproduction') depends.

Thus while in no way wanting to limit research to 'following only those leads which emerge from content analysis'[2] we must recognize that the discursive form of the message has a privileged position in the communicative exchange (from the viewpoint of circulation), and that the moments of 'encoding' and 'decoding', though only 'relatively autonomous' in relation to the communicative process as a whole, are *determinate* moments. A 'raw' historical event cannot, *in that form*, be transmitted by, say, a television newscast. Events can only be signified within the aural–visual forms of the televisual discourse. In the moment when a historical event passes under the sign of discourse, it is subject to all the complex formal 'rules' by which language signifies. To put it paradoxically, the event must become a 'story' before it can become a *communicative event*. In that moment the formal sub-rules of discourse are 'in dominance', without, of course, subordinating out of existence the historical event so signified, the social relations in which the rules are set to work or the social and political consequences of the event having been signified in this way. The 'message form' is the necessary 'form of appearance' of the event in its passage from source to receiver. Thus the transposition into and out of the 'message form' (or the mode of symbolic exchange) is not a random 'moment', which we can take up or ignore at our convenience. The 'message form' is a determinate moment; though, at another level, it comprises the surface movements of the communications system only and requires, at another stage, to be integrated into the social relations of the communication process as a whole, of which it forms only a part.

From this general perspective, we may crudely characterize the television communicative process as follows. The institutional structures of broadcasting, with their practices and networks of production, their organized relations and technical infrastructures, are required to produce a programme. Using the analogy of *Capital*, this is the 'labour process' in the discursive mode. Production, here, constructs the message. In one sense, then, the circuit begins here. Of course, the production process is not without its 'discursive' aspect: it, too, is framed throughout by meanings and ideas: knowledge-in-use concerning the routines of production, historically defined technical skills, professional ideologies, institutional knowledge, definitions and assumptions, assumptions about the audience and so on frame the constitution of the programme through this production structure. Further, though the production structures of television originate the television discourse, they do not constitute a closed system. They draw topics, treatments, agendas, events, personnel, images of the audience, 'definitions of the situation' from other sources and other discursive formations within the wider socio-cultural and political structure of which they are a differentiated part. Philip Elliott has expressed this point succinctly, within a more traditional framework, in his discussion of the way in which the audience is both the 'source' and the 'receiver' of the television message. Thus—to borrow Marx's terms—circulation and reception are, indeed, 'moments' of the production process in television and are reincorporated, via a number of skewed and structured 'feedbacks', into the production process itself. The consumption or reception of the television message is thus also itself a 'moment' of the production process in its larger sense, though the latter is 'predominant' because it is the 'point of departure for the realization' of the message. Production and reception of the television message are not, therefore, identical, but they are related: they are differentiated moments within the totality formed by the social relations of the communicative process as a whole.

At a certain point, however, the broadcasting structures must yield encoded messages in the form of a meaningful discourse. The institution-societal relations of production must pass under the discursive rules of language for its product to be 'realized'. This initiates a further differentiated moment,

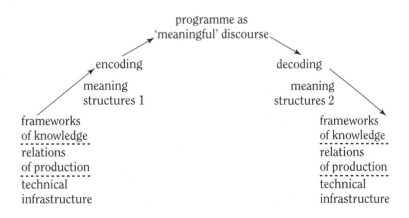

in which the formal rules of discourse and language are in dominance. Before this message can have an 'effect' (however defined), satisfy a 'need' or be put to a 'use', it must first be appropriated as a meaningful discourse and be meaningfully decoded. It is this set of decoded meanings which 'have an effect', influence, entertain, instruct or persuade, with very complex perceptual, cognitive, emotional, ideological or behavioural consequences. In a 'determinate' moment the structure employs a code and yields a 'message': at another determinate moment the 'message', via its decodings, issues into the structure of social practices. We are now fully aware that this re-entry into the practices of audience reception and 'use' cannot be understood in simple behavioural terms. The typical processes identified in positivistic research on isolated elements—effects, uses, 'gratifications'—are themselves framed by structures of understanding, as well as being produced by social and economic relations, which shape their 'realization' at the reception end of the chain and which permit the meanings signified in the discourse to be transposed into practice or consciousness (to acquire social use value or political effectivity).

Clearly, what we have labelled in the diagram 'meaning structures 1' and 'meaning structures 2' may not be the same. They do not constitute an 'immediate identity'. The codes of encoding and decoding may not be perfectly symmetrical. The degrees of symmetry—that is, the degrees of 'understanding' and 'misunderstanding' in the communicative exchange—depend on the degrees of symmetry/asymmetry (relations of equivalence) established between the positions of the 'personifications', encoder–producer and decoder–receiver. But this in turn depends on the degrees of identity/non-identity between the codes which perfectly or imperfectly transmit, interrupt or systematically distort what has been transmitted. The lack of fit between the codes has a great deal to do with the structural differences of relation and position between broadcasters and audiences, but it also has something to do with the asymmetry between the codes of 'source' and 'receiver' at the moment of transformation into and out of the discursive form. What are called 'distortions' or 'misunderstandings' arise precisely from the *lack of equivalence* between the two sides in the communicative exchange. Once again, this defines the 'relative autonomy', but 'determinateness', of the entry and exit of the message in its discursive moments.

The application of this rudimentary paradigm has already begun to transform our understanding of the older term, television 'content'. We are just beginning to see how it might also transform our understanding of audience reception, 'reading' and response as well. Beginnings and endings have been announced in communications research before, so we must be cautious. But there seems some ground for thinking that a new and exciting phase in so-called audience research, of a quite new kind, may be opening up. At either end of the communicative chain the use of the semiotic paradigm promises to dispel the lingering behaviourism which has dogged mass-media research for so long, especially in its approach to content. Though we know the television programme is not a behavioural input, like a tap on the knee cap, it seems to have been almost impossible for traditional researchers to conceptualize the communicative process without lapsing into one or other variant of low-flying behaviourism. We know, as Gerbner has remarked, that representations of violence on the TV screen 'are not violence but messages about violence':[3] but we have continued to research the question of violence, for example, as if we were unable to comprehend this epistemological distinction.

The television sign is a complex one. It is itself constituted by the combination of two types of discourse, visual and aural. Moreover, it is an iconic sign, in Peirce's terminology, because 'it possesses some of the properties of the thing represented'.[4] This is a point which has led to a great deal of confusion and has provided the site of intense controversy in the study of visual language. Since the visual discourse translates a three-dimensional world into two-dimensional planes, it cannot, of course, *be* the referent or concept it signifies. The dog in the film can bark but it cannot bite! Reality exists outside language, but it is constantly mediated by and through language: and what we can know and say has to be produced in and through discourse. Discursive 'knowledge' is the product not of the transparent representation of the 'real' in language but of the articulation of language on real relations and conditions. Thus there is no intelligible discourse without the operation of a code. Iconic signs are therefore coded signs too—even if the codes here work differently from those of other signs. There is no degree zero in language. Naturalism and 'realism'—the apparent fidelity of the representation to the thing or concept represented—is the result, the effect, of a certain specific articulation of language on the 'real'. It is the result of a discursive practice.

Certain codes may, of course, be so widely distributed in a specific language community or culture, and be learned at so early an age, that they appear not to be constructed—the effect of an articulation between sign and referent—but to be 'naturally' given. Simple visual signs appear to have achieved a 'near-universality' in this sense: though evidence remains that even apparently 'natural' visual codes are culture-specific. However, this does not mean that no codes have intervened; rather, that the codes have been profoundly *naturalized*. The operation of naturalized codes reveals not the transparency and 'naturalness' of language but the depth, the habituation and the near-universality of the codes in use. They produce apparently 'natural' recognitions. This has the (ideological) effect of concealing the practices of coding which are present. But we must not be fooled by appearances. Actually, what naturalized codes demonstrate is the degree of habituation produced when there is a fundamental alignment and reciprocity—an achieved equivalence—between the encoding and decoding sides of an exchange of meanings. The functioning of the codes on the decoding side will frequently assume the status of naturalized perceptions. This leads us to think that the visual sign for 'cow' actually is (rather than *represents*) the animal, cow. But if we think of the visual representation of a cow in a manual on animal husbandry—and, even more, of the linguistic sign 'cow'—we can see that both, in different degrees, are *arbitrary* with respect to the concept of the animal they represent. The articulation of an arbitrary sign—whether visual or verbal—with the concept of a referent is the product not of nature but of convention, and the conventionalism of discourses requires the intervention, the support, of codes. Thus Eco has argued that iconic signs 'look like objects in the real world because they reproduce the conditions (that is, the codes) of perception in the viewer'.[5] These 'conditions of perception' are, however, the result of a highly coded, even if virtually unconscious, set of operations—decodings. This is as true of the photographic or televisual image as it is of any other sign. Iconic signs are, however, particularly vulnerable to being 'read' as natural because visual codes of perception are very widely distributed and because this type of sign is less arbitrary than a linguistic sign: the linguistic sign, 'cow' possesses *none* of the properties of the thing represented, whereas the visual sign appears to possess *some* of those properties.

[. . .]

The level of connotation of the visual sign, of its contextual reference and positioning in different discussive fields of meaning and association, is the point where *already coded* signs intersect with the deep semantic codes of a culture and take on additional, more active ideological dimensions. We might take an example from advertising discourse. Here, too, there is no 'purely denotative', and certainly no 'natural', representation. Every visual sign in advertising connotes a quality, situation, value or inference, which is present as an implication or implied meaning, depending on the connotational positioning. In Barthes's example, the sweater always signifies a 'warm garment' (denotation) and thus the activity/value of 'keeping warm'. But it is also possible, at its more connotative levels, to signify 'the coming of winter' or 'a cold day'. And, in the specialized sub-codes of fashion, sweater may also connote a fashionable style of *haute couture* or, alternatively, an informal style of dress. But set against the right visual background and positioned by the romantic sub-code, it may connote 'long autumn walk in the woods'.[6] Codes of this order clearly contract relations for the sign with the wider universe of ideologies in a society. These codes are the means by which power and ideology are made to signify in particular discourses. They refer signs to the 'maps of meaning' into which any culture is classified; and those 'maps of social reality' have the whole range of social meanings, practices, and usages, power and interest 'written in' to them. The connotative levels of signifiers, Barthes remarked, 'have a close communication with culture, knowledge, history, and it is through them, so to speak, that the environmental world invades the linguistic and semantic system. They are, if you like, the fragments of ideology'.[7]

The so-called denotative *level* of the televisual sign is fixed by certain, very complex (but limited or 'closed') codes. But its connotative *level*, though also bounded, is more open, subject to more active *transformations*, which exploit its polysemic values. Any such already constituted sign is potentially transformable into more than one connotative configuration. Polysemy must not, however, be confused with pluralism. Connotative codes are *not* equal among themselves. Any society/culture tends, with varying degrees of closure, to impose its classifications of the social and cultural and political world. These constitute a *dominant cultural order*, though it is neither univocal nor uncontested. This question of the 'structure of discourses in dominance' is a crucial point. The different areas of social life appear to be mapped out into discursive domains, hierarchically organized into *dominant or preferred meanings*. New, problematic or troubling events, which breach our expectancies and run counter to our 'common-sense constructs', to our 'taken-for-granted' knowledge of social structures, must be assigned to their discursive domains before they can be said to 'make sense'. The most common way of 'mapping' them is to assign the new to some domain or other of the existing 'maps of problematic social reality'. We say *dominant*, not 'determined', because it is always possible to order, classify, assign and decode an event within more than one 'mapping'. But we say 'dominant' because there exists a pattern of 'preferred readings'; and these both have the institutional/political/ideological order imprinted in them and have themselves become institutionalized.[8] The domains of 'preferred meanings' have the whole social order embedded in them as a set of meanings, practices and beliefs: the everyday knowledge of social structures, of 'how things work for all practical purposes in this culture', the rank order of power and interest and the structure of legitimations, limits and sanctions. Thus to clarify a 'misunderstanding' at the connotative level, we must refer, *through* the codes, to the orders of social life, of economic and political power and of ideology. Further, since these mappings are 'structured in dominance' but not closed, the communicative process consists not in the unproblematic assignment of every visual item to its given position within a set of prearranged codes, but of *performative rules*—rules of competence and use, of logics-in-use—which seek actively to *enforce* or *pre-fer* one semantic domain over another and rule items into and out of their appropriate meaning-sets. Formal semiology has too often neglected this practice of *interpretative work*, though this constitutes, in fact, the real relations of broadcast practices in television.

In speaking of *dominant meanings*, then, we are not talking about a one-sided process which governs how all events will be signified. It consists of the 'work' required to enforce, win plausibility for and command as legitimate a *decoding* of the event within the limit of dominant definitions in which it has been connotatively signified. Terni has remarked;

> *By the word* reading *we mean not only the capacity to identify and decode a certain number of signs, but also the subjective capacity to put them into a creative relation between themselves and with other signs: a capacity which is, by itself, the condition for a complete awareness of one's total environment.*[9]

Our quarrel here is with the notion of 'subjective capacity', as if the referent of a televisional discourse were an objective fact but the interpretative level were an individualized and private matter. Quite the opposite seems to be the case. The televisual practice takes 'objective' (that is, systemic) responsibility precisely for the relations which disparate signs contract with one another in any discursive instance, and thus continually rearranges, delimits and prescribes into what 'awareness of one's total environment' these items are arranged.

This brings us to the question of misunderstandings. Television producers who find their message 'failing to get across' are frequently concerned to straighten out the kinks in the communication chain, thus facilitating the 'effectiveness' of their communication. Much research which claims the objectivity of 'policy-oriented analysis' reproduces this administrative goal by attempting to discover how much of a message the audience recalls and to improve the extent of understanding. No doubt misunderstandings of a literal kind do exist. The viewer does not know the terms employed, cannot follow the complex logic of argument or exposition, is unfamiliar with the language, finds the concepts too alien or difficult or is foxed by the expository narrative. But more often broadcasters are concerned that the audience has failed to take the meaning as they—the broadcasters—intended. What they really mean to say is that viewers are not operating within the 'dominant' or 'preferred' code. Their ideal is 'perfectly transparent communication'. Instead, what they have to confront is 'systematically distorted communication'.[10]

In recent years discrepancies of this kind have usually been explained by reference to 'selective perception'. This is the door via which a residual pluralism evades the compulsions of a highly structured, asymmetrical and non-equivalent process. Of course, there will always be private, individual, variant readings. But 'selective perception' is almost never as selective, random or privatized as the concept suggests. The patterns exhibit, across individual variants, significant clusterings. Any new approach to audience studies will therefore have to begin with a critique of 'selective perception' theory.

It was argued earlier that since there is no necessary correspondence between encoding and decoding, the former can attempt to 'pre-fer' but cannot prescribe or guarantee the latter, which has its own conditions of existence. Unless they are wildly aberrant, encoding will have the effect of constructing some of the limits and parameters within which decodings will operate. If there were no limits, audiences could simply read whatever they liked into any message. No doubt some total misunderstandings of this kind do exist. But the vast range must contain *some* degree of reciprocity between encoding and decoding moments, otherwise we could not speak of an effective communicative exchange at all. Nevertheless, this 'correspondence' is not given but constructed. It is not 'natural' but the product of an articulation between two distinct moments. And the former cannot determine or guarantee, in a simple sense, which decoding codes will be employed. Otherwise communication would be a perfectly equivalent circuit, and every message would be an instance of 'perfectly transparent communication'. We must think, then, of the variant articulations in which encoding/decoding can be combined. To elaborate on this, we offer a hypothetical analysis of some possible decoding positions, in order to reinforce the point of 'no necessary correspondence'.[11]

We identify *three* hypothetical positions from which decodings of a televisual discourse may be constructed. These need to be empirically tested and refined. But the argument that decodings do not follow inevitably from encodings, that they are not identical, reinforces the argument of 'no necessary correspondence'. It also helps to deconstruct the commonsense meaning of 'misunderstanding' in terms of a theory of 'systematically distorted communication'.

The first hypothetical position is that of the *dominant-hegemonic position*. When the viewer takes the connoted meaning from, say, a television newscast or current affairs programme full and straight, and decodes the message in terms of the reference code in which it has been encoded, we might say that the viewer *is operating inside the dominant code*. This is the ideal-typical case of 'perfectly transparent communication'—or as close as we are likely to come to it 'for all practical purposes'. Within this we can distinguish the positions produced by the *professional code*. This is the position (produced by what we perhaps ought to identify as the operation of a 'metacode') which the professional broadcasters assume when encoding a message which has *already* been signified in a hegemonic manner. The professional code is 'relatively independent' of the dominant code, in that it applies criteria and transformational operations of its own, especially those of a technico-practical nature. The professional code, however, operates *within* the 'hegemony' of the dominant code. Indeed, it serves to reproduce the dominant definitions precisely by bracketing their hegemonic quality and operating instead with displaced professional codings which foreground such apparently neutral-technical questions as visual quality, news and presentational values, televisual quality, 'professionalism' and so on. The hegemonic interpretations of, say, the politics of Northern Ireland, or the Chilean *coup* or the Industrial Relations Bill are principally generated by political and military elites: the particular choice of presentational occasions and formats, the selection of personnel, the choice of images, the staging of debates are selected and combined through the operation of the professional code. How the broadcasting professionals are able *both* to operate with 'relatively autonomous' codes of their own *and* to act in such a way as to reproduce (not without contradiction) the hegemonic signification of events is a complex matter which cannot be further spelled out here. It must suffice to say that the professionals are linked with the defining elites not only by the institutional position of broadcasting itself as an 'ideological apparatus',[12] but also by the structure of *access* (that is, the systematic 'over-accessing' of selective elite personnel and their 'definition of the situation' in television). It may even be said that the professional codes serve to reproduce hegemonic definitions specifically by *not overtly* biasing their operations in a dominant direction: ideological reproduction therefore takes place here inadvertently, unconsciously, 'behind men's backs'.[13] Of course, conflicts, contradictions and even misunderstandings regularly arise between the dominant and the professional significations and their signifying agencies.

The second position we would identify is that of the *negotiated code* or position. Majority audiences probably understand quite adequately what has been dominantly defined and professionally signified. The dominant definitions, however, are hegemonic precisely because they represent definitions of situations and events which are 'in dominance', (*global*). Dominant definitions connect events, implicitly or explicitly, to grand totalizations, to the great syntagmatic views-of-the-world: they take 'large views' of issues: they relate events to the 'national interest' or to the level of geo-politics, even if they make these connections in truncated, inverted or mystified ways. The definition of a hegemonic viewpoint is (a) that it defines within its terms the mental horizon, the universe, of possible meanings, of a whole sector of relations in a society or culture; and (b) that it carries with it the stamp of legitimacy—it appears coterminous with what is 'natural', 'inevitable', 'taken for granted' about the social order. Decoding within the *negotiated version* contains a mixture of adaptive and oppositional elements: it acknowledges the legitimacy of the hegemonic definitions to make the grand significations (abstract), while, at a more restricted, situational (situated) level, it makes its own ground rules—it operates with exceptions to the rule. It accords the privileged position to the dominant definitions of events while reserving the right to make a more negotiated application to 'local conditions', to its own more *corporate* positions. This negotiated version of the dominant ideology is thus shot through with contradictions, though these are only on certain occasions brought to full visibility. Negotiated codes operate through what we might call particular or situated logics: and these logics are sustained by their differential and unequal relation to the discourses and logics of power. The simplest example of a negotiated code is that which governs the response of a worker to the notion of an Industrial Relations Bill limiting the right to strike or to arguments for a wages freeze. At the level of the 'national interest' economic debate the decoder may adopt the hegemonic definition, agreeing that 'we must all pay ourselves less in order to combat inflation'. This, however, may have little or no relation to his/her willingness to go on strike for better pay and conditions or to oppose the Industrial Relations Bill at the level of shop-floor or union organization. We suspect that the great majority of so-called 'misunderstandings' arise from the contradictions and disjunctures between hegemonic–dominant encodings and negotiated–corporate decodings. It is just these mismatches in the levels which most provoke defining elites and professionals to identify a 'failure in communications'.

Finally, it is possible for a viewer perfectly to understand both the literal and the connotative inflection given by a discourse but to decode the message in a *globally* contrary way. He/she detotalizes the message in the preferred code in order to retotalize the message within some alternative framework of reference. This is the case of the viewer who listens to a debate on the need to limit wages but 'reads' every mention of the 'national interest' as 'class interest'. He/she is operating with what we must call an *oppositional code*. One of the most significant political moments (they also coincide with crisis points within the broadcasting organizations themselves, for obvious reasons) is the point when events which are normally signified and decoded in a negotiated way begin to be given an oppositional reading. Here the 'politics of signification'—the struggle in discourse—is joined.

Notes

1. For an explication and commentary on the methodological implications of Marx's argument, see S. Hall, 'A reading of Marx's 1857 *Introduction to the Grundrisse*' (1974).

2. J. D. Halloran, 'Understanding television', Paper for the Council of Europe Colloquy on 'Understanding Television' (University of Leicester 1973).

3. G. Gerbner *et al, Violence is TV Drama: A Study of Trends and Symbolic Functions* (The Annenberg School, University of Pennsylvania 1970).

4. Charles Peirce, *Speculative Grammar,* in *Collected Papers* (Cambridge, Mass.: Harvard University Press 1931–58).

5. Umberto Eco, 'Articulations of the cinematic code', in *Cinemaists,* no. 1.

6. Roland Barthes, 'Rhetoric of the image', in *Image-Music-Text* (1971).

7. Roland Barthes, *Elements of Semiology* (Cape 1967).

8. For an extended critique of 'preferred reading', see Alan O'Shea, 'Preferred reading' (unpublished paper, CCCS, University of Birmingham).

9. P. Terni, 'Memorandom', Council of Europe Colloquy on 'Understanding Television' (University of Leicester 1973).

10. The phrase is Habermas's, in 'Systematically distorted communications', in P. Dretzel (ed.), *Recent Sociology 2* (Collier-Macmillan 1970). It is used here, however, in a different way.

11. For a sociological formulation which is close, in some ways, to the positions outlined here but which does not parallel the argument about the theory of discourse, see Frank Parkin, *Class Inequality and Political Order* (Macgibbon and Kee 1971).

12. See Louis Althusser, 'Ideology and ideological state apparatuses' in *Lenin and Philosophy and Other Essays* (New Left Books 1971).

13. For an expansion of this argument, see Stuart Hall, 'The external/internal dialectic in broadcasting', *Fourth Symposium on Broadcasting Policy* (University of Manchester 1972), and 'Broadcasting and the state; the independence/impartiality couplet', *MCR Symposium,* University of Leicester 1976 (CCCS unpublished paper).

Prime Time Ideology:
The Hegemonic Process
in Television Entertainment

Todd Gitlin

Many of the formal conventions of American television entertainment are supports of a larger hegemonic structure. After proposing the concept of ideological hegemony as a useful approach to questions of ideology and control, I indicate inter-related ways in which television messages are integrated into the dominant system of discourse and the prevailing structures of labor, consumption, and politics, in particular through these formal features of prime-time network programs: (1) format and formula (including the rigidity of program length and the narrative curve of action); (2) genre; (3) setting and character type; (4) topical slant; and (5) the solution imposed on the fictional problem. Within certain definite limits—related both to the core of dominant values and to market tolerances—these formal structures are flexible: for example, some of Norman Lear's comedies have disrupted stereotypical conventions of static character and imposed solution. The hegemonic commercial cultural system routinely incorporates some aspects of alternative ideology and rejects the unassimilable. I trace this process to the self-contradictory nature of the dominant ideology.

Every society works to reproduce itself—and its internal conflicts—within its cultural order, the structure of practices and meanings around which the society takes shape. So much is tautology. In this paper I look at contemporary mass media in the United States as one cultural system promoting that reproduction. I try to show how ideology is relayed through various features of American television, and how television programs register larger ideological structures and changes. The question here is not, What is the impact of these programs? but rather a prior one, What do these programs mean? For only after thinking through their possible meanings as cultural objects and as signs of cultural interactions among producers and audiences may we begin intelligibly to ask about their "effects."

The attempt to understand the sources and transformations of ideology in American society has been leading social theorists not only to social-psychological investigations, but to a long overdue interest in Antonio Gramsci's (1971) notion of ideological hegemony. It was Gramsci who, in the late Twenties and Thirties, with the rise of Fascism and the failure of the Western European working-class movements, began to consider why the working class was not necessarily revolutionary; why it could, in fact, yield to Fascism. Condemned to a Fascist prison precisely because the insurrectionary workers' movement in Northern Italy just after World War I failed, Gramsci spent years trying to account for the defeat, resorting in large measure to the concept of hegemony: bourgeois domination of the thought, the common sense, the life-ways and everyday assumptions of the working class. Gramsci counterposed "hegemony" to "coercion"; these were two analytically distinct processes through which ruling classes secure the consent of the dominated. Gramsci did not always make plain where to draw the line between hegemony and coercion; or rather, as Perry Anderson shows convincingly (1976)[1], he drew the line differently at different times. Nonetheless, ambiguities aside, Gramsci's distinction was a great advance for radical thought, for it called attention to the routine structures of everyday thought—down to "common sense" itself—which worked to sustain class domination and tyranny. That is to say, paradoxically, it took the working class seriously enough as a potential agent of revolution to hold it accountable for its failures.

Because Leninism failed abysmally throughout the West, Western Marxists and non-Marxist radicals have both been drawn back to Gramsci, hoping to address the evident fact that the Western working classes are not predestined toward socialist revolution.[2] In Europe this fact could be taken as strategic rather than normative wisdom on the part of the working class; but in America the working class is not only hostile to revolutionary *strategy*, it seems to disdain the socialist *goal* as well. At the very least, although a recent Peter Hart opinion poll showed that Americans abstractly "favor" workers' control, Americans do not seem to care enough about it to organize very widely in its behalf. While there are abundant "contradictions" throughout American society, they are played out substantially in the realm of "culture" or "ideology," which orthodox Marxism had consigned to the secondary category of "superstructure." Meanwhile, critical theory—especially in the work of T. W. Adorno and Max Horkheimer—had argued with great force that the dominant forms of commercial ("mass") culture were crystallizations of authoritarian ideology; yet despite the ingenuity and brilliance of particular feats of critical exegesis (Adorno, 1954, 1974; Adorno and Horkheimer, 1972), they seemed to be arguing that the "culture industry" was not only meretricious but wholly and statically complete. In the Seventies, some of their approaches along with Gramsci's have been elaborated and furthered by Alvin W. Gouldner (1976; see also Kellner, 1978) and Raymond Williams (1973), in distinctly provocative ways.

In this paper I wish to contribute to the process of bringing the discussion of cultural hegemony down to earth. For much of the discussion so far remains abstract, almost as if cultural hegemony were a substance with a life of its own, a sort of immutable fog that has settled over the whole public life of capitalist societies to confound the truth of the proletarian telos. Thus to the questions, "Why are radical ideas suppressed in the schools?", "Why do workers oppose socialism?" and so on, comes the single Delphic answer: hegemony. "Hegemony" becomes the magical explanation of last resort. And as such it is useful neither as explanation nor as guide to action. If "hegemony" explains everything in the sphere of culture, it explains nothing.

Concurrent with the theoretical discussion, but on a different plane, looms an entire subindustry criticizing and explicating specific mass-cultural products and straining to find "emancipatory" if not "revolutionary" meanings in them. Thus in 1977 there was cacophony about the TV version of *Roots*; this year the trend-setter seems to be TV's handling of violence. Mass media criticism becomes mass-mediated, an auxiliary sideshow serving cultural producers as well as the wider public of the cultural spectacle. Piece by piece we see fast and furious analysis of this movie, that TV show, that book, that spectator sport. Many of these pieces have merit one by one, but as a whole they do not accumulate toward a more general theory of how the cultural forms are managed and reproduced—and how they change. Without analytic point, item-by-item analyses of the standard fare of mass culture run the risk of degenerating into high-toned gossip, even a kind of critical groupie-ism. Unaware of the ambiguity of their own motives and strategies, the partial critics may be yielding to a displaced envy, where criticism covertly asks to be taken into the spotlight along with the celebrity culture ostensibly under criticism. Yet another trouble is that partial critiques in the mass-culture tradition don't help us understand the *hold* and the *limits* of cultural products, the degree to which people do and do not incorporate mass-cultural forms, sing the jingles, wear the corporate T-shirts, and most important, permit their life-worlds to be demarcated by them.

My task in what follows is to propose some features of a lexicon for discussing the forms of hegemony in the concrete. Elsewhere I have described some of the operations of cultural hegemony in the sphere of television news, especially in the news's framing procedures for opposition movements

(Gitlin, 1977a,b)[3]. Here I wish to speak of the realm of entertainment: about television entertainment in particular—as the most pervasive and (in the living room sense) *familiar* of our cultural sites—and about movies secondarily. How do the *formal* devices of TV prime-time programs encourage viewers to experience themselves as anti-political, privately accumulating individuals (also see Gitlin, 1977c)? And how do these forms express social conflict, containing and diverting the images of contrary social possibilities? I want to isolate a few of the routine devices, though of course in reality they do not operate in isolation; rather, they work in combination, where their force is often enough magnified (though they can also work in contradictory ways). And, crucially, it must be borne in mind throughout this discussion that the forms of mass-cultural production do not either spring up or operate independently of the rest of social life. Commercial culture does not *manufacture* ideology; it *relays* and *reproduces* and *processes* and *packages* and *focuses* ideology that is constantly arising both from social elites and from active social groups and movements throughout the society (as well as within media organizations and practices).

A more complete analysis of ideological process in a commercial society would look both above and below, to elites and to audiences. Above, it would take a long look at the economics and politics of broadcasting, at its relation to the FCC, the Congress, the President, the courts; in case studies and with a developing theory of ideology it would study media's peculiar combination and refraction of corporate, political, bureaucratic and professional interests, giving the media a sort of limited independence— or what Marxists are calling "relative autonomy"— in the upper reaches of the political-economic system. Below, as Raymond Williams has insisted, cultural hegemony operates within a whole social life-pattern; the people who consume mass-mediated products are also the people who work, reside, compete, go to school, live in families. And there are a good many traditional and material interests at stake for audiences: the political inertia of the American population now, for example, certainly has something to do with the continuing productivity of the goods-producing and -distributing industries, not simply with the force of mass culture. Let me try to avoid misunderstanding at the outset by insisting that *I will not be arguing that the forms of hegemonic entertainment superimpose themselves automatically and finally onto the consciousness or behavior of all audiences at all times:* it remains for sociologists to generate what Dave Morley (1974)[4] has called "an ethnography of audiences," and to study what Ronald Abramson (1978) calls "the phenomenology of audiences" if we are to have anything like a satisfactory account of how audiences consciously and unconsciously process, transform, and are transformed by the contents of television. For many years the subject of media effects was severely narrowed by a behaviorist definition of the problem (see Gitlin, 1978a); more recently, the "agenda-setting function" of mass media has been usefully studied in news media, but not in entertainment. (On the other hand, the very pervasiveness of TV entertainment makes laboratory study of its "effects" almost inconceivable.) It remains to incorporate occasional sociological insights into the actual behavior of TV audiences[5] into a more general theory of the interaction—a theory which avoids both the mechanical assumptions of behaviorism and the trivialities of the "uses and gratifications" approach.

But alas, that more general theory of the interaction is not on the horizon. My more modest attempt in this extremely preliminary essay is to sketch an approach to the hegemonic thrust of some TV forms, not to address the deflection, resistance, and reinterpretation achieved by audiences. I will show that hegemonic ideology is systematically preferred by certain features of TV programs, and that at the same time alternative and oppositional values are brought into the cultural system, and domesticated into hegemonic forms at times, by the routine workings of the market. Hegemony is reasserted in different ways at different times, even by different logics; if this variety is analytically messy, the messiness corresponds to a disordered ideological order, a contradictory society. This said, I proceed to some of the forms in which ideological hegemony is embedded: *format and formula; genre; setting and character type; slant;* and *solution.* Then these particulars will suggest a somewhat more fully developed theory of hegemony.

Format and Formula

Until recently at least, the TV schedule has been dominated by standard lengths and cadences, standardized packages of TV entertainment appearing, as the announcers used to say, "same time, same station." This week-to-weekness—or, in the case of soap operas, day-to-dayness—obstructed the development of characters; at least the primary characters had to be preserved intact for next week's show. Perry Mason was Perry Mason, once and for all; if you watched the reruns, you couldn't know from character or set whether you were watching the first or the last in the series. For commercial and production reasons which are in practice inseparable—and this is why ideological hegemony is not reducible to the economic interests of elites—the regular schedule prefers the repeatable formula: it is far easier for production companies to hire writers to write for standardized, static characters than for characters who develop. Assembly-line production works through regularity of time slot, of duration, and of character to convey images of social steadiness: come what may, *Gunsmoke* or *Kojak* will check in to your mind at a certain time on a certain evening. Should they lose ratings (at least at the "upscale" reaches of the "demographics," where ratings translate into disposable dollars),[6] their replacements would be—for a time, at least!—equally reliable. Moreover, the standard curve of narrative action—stock characters encounter new version of stock situation; the plot thickens, allowing stock characters to show their standard stuff; the plot resolves—over twenty-two or fifty minutes is itself a source of rigidity and forced regularity.

In these ways, the usual programs are performances that rehearse social fixity: they express and cement the obduracy of a social world impervious to substantial change. Yet at the same time there are signs of routine obsolescence, as hunks of last year's regular schedule drop from sight only to be supplanted by this season's attractions. Standardization and the threat of evanescence are curiously linked: they match the intertwined processes of commodity production, predictability and obsolescence, in a high-consumption society. I speculate that they help instruct audiences in the rightness and naturalness of a world that, in only apparent paradox, regularly requires an irregularity, an unreliability which it calls progress. In this way, the regular changes in TV programs, like the regular elections of public officials, seem to affirm the sovereignty of the audience while keeping deep alternatives off the agenda. Elite authority and consumer choice are affirmed at once—this is one of the central operations of the hegemonic liberal capitalist ideology.

Then too, by organizing the "free time" of persons into end-to-end interchangeable units, broadcasting extends, and harmonizes with, the industrialization of time. Media time and school time, with their equivalent units and curves of action, mirror the time of clocked labor and reinforce the seeming naturalness of clock time. Anyone who reads Harry Braverman's *Labor and Monopoly Capital* can trace the steady degradation of the work process, both white and blue collar, through the twentieth century, even if Braverman has exaggerated the extent of the process by focusing on managerial *strategies* more than on actual work *processes*. Something similar has happened in other life-sectors.[7] Leisure is industrialized, duration is homogenized, even excitement is routinized, and the standard repeated TV format is an important component of the process. And typically, too, capitalism provides relief from these confines for its more favored citizens, those who can afford to buy their way out of the standardized social reality which capitalism produces. Thus Sony and RCA now sell home video recorders, enabling consumers to tape programs they'd otherwise miss. The widely felt need to overcome assembly-line "leisure" time becomes the source of a new market—to sell the means for private, commoditized solutions to the time-jam.

Commercials, of course, are also major features of the regular TV format. There can be no question but that commercials have a good deal to do with shaping and maintaining markets—no advertiser dreams of cutting advertising costs as long as the competition is still on the air. But commercials also have important *indirect* consequences on the contours of consciousness overall: they get us accustomed to thinking of ourselves and behaving as a *market* rather than a *public*, as consumers rather than citizens. Public problems (like air pollution) are propounded as susceptible to private commodity solutions (like eyedrops). In the process, commercials acculturate us to interruption through the rest of our lives. Time and attention are not one's own; the established social powers have the capacity to colonize consciousness, and unconsciousness, as they see fit. By watching, the audience one by one consents. Regardless of the commercial's "effect" on our behavior, we are consenting to its domination of the public space. Yet we should note that this colonizing process does not actually require commercials, as long as it can form discrete packages of ideological content that call forth discontinuous responses in the audience. Even public broadcasting's children's shows take over the commercial forms to their own educational ends—and supplant narrative forms by herky-jerky bustle. The producers of *Sesame Street*, in likening knowledge to commercial products ("and now a message from the letter B"), may well be legitimizing the commercial form in its discontinuity and in its invasiveness. Again, regularity and discontinuity, superficially discrepant, may be linked at a deep level of meaning. And perhaps the deepest privatizing function of television, its most powerful impact on public life, may lie in the most obvious thing about it: we receive the images in the privacy of our living rooms, making public discourse and response difficult. At the same time, the paradox is that at any given time many viewers are receiving images discrepant with many of their beliefs, challenging their received opinions.

TV routines have been built into the broadcast schedule since its inception. But arguably their regularity has been waning since Norman Lear's first comedy, *All in the Family*, made its network debut in 1971. Lear's contribution to TV content was obvious: where previous shows might have made passing reference to social conflicts, Lear brought wrenching social issues into the very mainspring of his series, uniting his characters, as Michael Arlen once pointed out, in a harshly funny *ressentiment* peculiarly appealing to audiences of the Nixon era and its cynical, disabused sequel.[8] As I'll argue below, the hegemonic ideology is maintained in the Seventies by *domesticating* divisive issues where in the Fifties it would have simply *ignored* them.

Lear also let his characters develop. Edith Bunker grew less sappy and more feminist and commonsensical; Gloria and Mike moved next door, and finally to California. On the threshold of this generational rupture, Mike broke through his stereotype by expressing affection for Archie, and Archie, oh-so-reluctantly but definitely for all that, hugged back and broke through his own. And of course other Lear characters, the Jeffersons and Maude, had earlier been spun off into their own shows, as *The Mary Tyler Moore Show* had spawned *Rhoda* and *Phyllis*. These changes resulted from commercial decisions; they were built on intelligent business perceptions that an audience existed for situation comedies directly addressing racism, sexism, and the decomposition of conventional families. But there is no such thing as a strictly economic "explanation" for production choice, since the success of a show—despite market research—is not foreordained. In the context of my argument, the importance of such developments lies in their partial break with the established, static formulae of prime time television.

Evidently daytime soap operas have also been sliding into character development and a direct exploitation of divisive social issues, rather than going on constructing a race-free, class-free, feminism-free world. And more conspicuously, the "mini-series" has now disrupted the taken-for-granted repetitiveness of the prime time format. Both content and form mattered to the commercial success of *Roots;* certainly the industry, speaking through trade journals, was convinced that the phenomenon was rooted in the series' break with the week-to-week format. When the programming wizards at ABC decided to put the show on for eight straight nights, they were also, inadvertently, making it possible for characters to *develop* within the bounds of a single show. And of course they were rendering the whole sequence immensely more powerful than if it had been diffused over eight weeks. The very format was testimony to the fact that history takes place as a continuing process in which people grow up, have children, die; that people experience their lives within the domain of social institutions. This is no small achievement in a country that routinely denies the rich texture of history.

In any event, the first thing the industry seems to have learned from its success with *Roots* is that they had a new hot formula, the night-after-night series with some claim to historical verisimilitude. So, according to *Broadcasting*, they began preparing a number of "docu-drama" series, of which 1977's products included NBC's three-part series *Loose Change* and *King*, and its four-part *Holocaust*, this latter evidently planned before the *Roots* broadcast. How many of those first announced as in progress will actually be broadcast is something else again—one awaits the networks' domestication and trivializing of the radicalism of *All God's Children: The Life of Nate Shaw*, announced in early 1977. *Roots'* financial success—ABC sold its commercial minutes for $120,000, compared to that season's usual $85,000 to $90,000—might not be repeatable. Perhaps the network could not expect audiences to tune in more than once every few years to a series that began one night at eight o'clock, the next night at nine, and the next at eight again. In summary it is hard to say to what extent these format changes signify an acceleration of the networks' competition for advertising dollars, and to what extent they reveal the networks' responses to the restiveness and boredom of the mass audience, or the emergence of new potential audiences. But in any case the shifts are there, and constitute a fruitful territory for any thinking about the course of popular culture.

Genre[9]

The networks try to finance and choose programs that will likely attract the largest conceivable audiences of spenders; this imperative requires that the broadcasting elites have in mind some notion of popular taste from moment to moment. Genre, in other words, is necessarily somewhat sensitive; in its rough outlines, if not in detail, it tells us something about popular moods. Indeed, since there are only three networks, there is something of an oversensitivity to a given success; the pendulum tends to swing hard to replicate a winner. Thus *Charlie's Angels* engenders *Flying High* and *American Girls*, about stewardesses and female reporters respectively, each on a long leash under male authority.

Here I suggest only a few signs of this sensitivity to shifting moods and group identities in the audience. The adult western of the middle and late Fifties, with its drama of solitary righteousness and suppressed libidinousness, for example, can be seen in retrospect to have played on the quiet malaise under the surface of the complacency of the Eisenhower years, even in contradictory ways. Some lone heroes were identified with traditionally frontier-American informal and individualistic relations to authority (Paladin in *Have Gun, Will Travel*, Bart Maverick in *Maverick*), standing for sturdy individualism struggling for hedonistic values and taking law-and-order wryly. Meanwhile, other heroes were decent officials like *Gunsmoke's* Matt Dillon, affirming the decency of paternalistic law and order against the temptations of worldly pleasure. With the rise of the Camelot mystique, and the vigorous "long twilight struggle" that John F. Kennedy personified, spy stories like *Mission: Impossible* and *The Man From Uncle* were well suited to capitalize on the macho CIA aura. More recently, police stories, with cops surmounting humanist illusions to draw thin blue lines against anarcho-criminal barbarism, afford a variety of official ways of coping with "the social issue," ranging from *Starsky and Hutch's* muted homoeroticism to *Barney Miller's* team pluralism. The single-women shows following from *Mary Tyler Moore* acknowledge in their privatized ways that some sort of feminism is here to stay, and work to contain it with hilarious versions of "new life styles" for single career women. Such shows probably appeal to the market of "upscale" singles with relatively large disposable incomes, women who are disaffected from the traditional imagery of housewife and helpmeet. In the current wave of "jiggle" or "T&A" shows patterned on *Charlie's Angels* (the terms are widely used in the industry), the attempt is to appeal to the prurience of the male audience by keeping the "girls" free of romance, thus catering to male (and female?) backlash against feminism. The black sitcoms probably reflect the rise of a black middle class with the purchasing power to bring forth advertisers, while also appealing *as comedies*—for conflicting reasons, perhaps—to important parts of the white audience. (Serious black drama would be far more threatening to the majority audience.)

Whenever possible it is illuminating to trace the transformations in a genre over a longer period of time. For example, the shows of technological prowess have metamorphosed over four decades as hegemonic ideology has been contested by alternative cultural forms. In work not yet published, Tom Andrae of the Political Science Department at the University of California, Berkeley, shows how the Superman archetype began in 1933 as a menace to society; then became something of a New Dealing, anti-Establishmentarian individualist casting his lot with the oppressed and, at times, against the State; and only in the Forties metamorphosed into the current incarnation who prosecutes criminals in the name of "the American way." Then the straight-arrow Superman of the Forties and Fifties was supplemented by the whimsical, self-satirical Batman and the Marvel Comics series of the Sixties and Seventies, symbols of power gone silly, no longer prepossessing. In playing against the conventions, their producers seem to have been exhibiting the self-consciousness of genre so popular among "high arts" too, as with Pop and minimal art. Thus shifts in genre presuppose the changing mentality of critical masses of writers and cultural producers; yet these changes would not take root commercially without corresponding changes in the dispositions (even the self-consciousness) of large audiences. In other words, changes in cultural ideals and in audience sensibilities must be harmonized to make for shifts in genre or formula.

Finally, the latest form of technological hero corresponds to an authoritarian turn in hegemonic ideology, as well as to a shift in popular (at least children's) mentality. The Seventies generation of physically augmented, obedient, patriotic super-heroes (*The Six Million Dollar Man* and *The Bionic Woman*) differ from the earlier waves in being organizational products through and through; these team players have no private lives from which they are recruited task by task, as in *Mission: Impossible*, but they are actually *invented* by the State, to whom they owe their lives.

Televised sports too is best understood as an entertainment genre, one of the most powerful.[10] What we know as professional sports today is inseparably intertwined with the networks' development of the sports market. TV sports is rather consistently framed to reproduce dominant American values. First, although TV is ostensibly a medium for the eyes, the sound is often decisive in taking the action off the field. The audience is not trusted to come to its own conclusions. The announcers are not simply describing events ("Reggie Jackson hits a ground ball to shortstop"), but interpreting them ("World Series 1978! It's great to be here"). One may see here a process equivalent to advertising's project of taking human qualities out of the consumer and removing them to the product: sexy perfume, zesty beer.

In televised sports, the hegemonic impositions have, if anything, probably became more intense over the last twenty years. One technique for interpreting the event is to regale the audience with bits of information in the form of "stats." "A lot of people forget they won eleven out of their last twelve games. . . ." "There was an extraordinary game in last years World Series. . . ." "Rick Barry hasn't missed two free throws in a row for 72 games. . . ." "The last time the Warriors were in Milwaukee Clifford Ray *also* blocked two shots in the second quarter." How *about* that? The announcers can't shut up; they're constantly chattering. And the stat flashed on the screen further removes the action from the field. What is one to make of all this? Why would anyone want to know a player's free throw percentage not only during the regular season but during the playoffs?

But the trivialities have their reason: they amount to an interpretation that flatters and disdains the audience at the same time. It flatters in small ways, giving you the chance to be the one person on the block who already possessed this tidbit of fact. At the same time, symbolically, it treats you as someone who really knows what's going on in the world. Out of control of social reality, you may flatter yourself that the substitute world of sports is a corner of the world you can really grasp. Indeed, throughout modern society, the availability of statistics is often mistaken for the availability of knowledge and deep meaning. To know the number of megatons in the nuclear arsenal is not to grasp its horror; but we are tempted to bury our fear in the possession of comforting fact. To have made "body counts" in Vietnam was not to be in control of the countryside, but the U.S. Army flattered itself that the stats looked good. TV sports shows, encouraging the audience to value stats, harmonize with a stat-happy society. Not that TV operates independently of the sports event itself; in fact, the event is increasingly organized to fit the structure of the broadcast. There are extra time-outs to permit the network to sell more commercial time. Michael Real of the University of California, San Diego, used a stopwatch to calculate that during the 1974 Super Bowl, the football was actually moving for—seven minutes (Real, 1977). Meanwhile, electronic billboards transplant the stats into the stadium itself.

Another framing practice is the reduction of the sports experience to a sequence of individual achievements. In a fusion of populist and capitalist dogma, everyone is somehow the best. This one has "great hands," this one has "a great slam dunk," that one's "great on defense." This indiscriminate commendation raises the premium on personal competition, and at the same time undermines the meaning of personal achievement; everyone is excellent at something, as at a child's birthday party. I was most struck by the force of this sort of framing during the NBA basketball playoffs of 1975, when, after a season of hearing Bill King announce the games over local KTVU, I found myself watching and hearing the network version. King's Warriors were not CBS's. A fine irony: King with his weird mustache and San Francisco panache was talking about team relations and team strategy; CBS, with its organization-man team of announcers, could talk of little besides the personal records of the players. Again, at one point during the 1977 basketball playoffs, CBS's Brent Musburger gushed: "I've got one of the greatest players of all time [Rick Barry] and one of the greatest referees of all time [Mendy Rudolph] sitting next to me! . . . I'm surrounded by experts!" All in all, the network exalts statistics, personal competition, expertise. The message is: The way to understand things is by storing up statistics and tracing their trajectories. This is training in observation without comprehension.

Everything is technique and know-how; nothing is purpose. Likewise, the instant replay generates the thrill of recreating the play, even second-guessing the referee. The appeal is to the American tradition of exalting means over ends: this is the same spirit that animates popular science magazines and do-it-yourself. It's a complicated and contradictory spirit, one that lends itself to the preservation of craft values in a time of assembly-line production, and at the same time distracts interest from any desire to control the goals of the central work process.

The significance of this fetishism of means is hard to decipher. Though the network version appeals to technical thinking, the announcers are not only small-minded but incompetent to boot. No sooner have they dutifully complimented a new acquisition as "a fine addition to the club" than often enough he flubs a play. But still they function as cheerleaders, revving up the razzle-dazzle rhetoric and reminding us how uniquely favored we are by the spectacle. By staying tuned in, somehow we're "participating" in sports history—indeed, by proxy, in history itself. The pulsing theme music and electronic logo reinforce this sense of hot-shot glamor. The breathlessness never lets up, and it has its pecuniary motives: if we can be convinced that the game really is fascinating (even if it's a dog), we're more likely to stay tuned for the commercials for which Miller Lite and Goodyear have paid $100,000 a minute to rent our attention.

On the other hand, the network version does not inevitably succeed in forcing itself upon our consciousness and defining our reception of the event. TV audiences don't necessarily succumb to the announcers' hype. In semi-public situations like barrooms, audiences are more likely to see through the trivialization and ignorance and—in "para-social interaction"—to tell the announcers off. But in the privacy of living rooms, the announcers' framing probably penetrates farther into the collective definition of the event. It should not be surprising that one fairly common counter-hegemonic practice is to watch the broadcast picture without the network sound, listening to the local announcer on the radio.

Setting and Character Type

Closely related to genre and its changes are setting and character type. And here again we see shifting market tolerances making for certain changes in content, while the core of hegemonic values remains virtually impervious.

In the Fifties, when the TV forms were first devised, the standard TV series presented—in Herbert Gold's phrase—happy people with happy problems. In the Seventies it is more complicated: there are unhappy people with happy ways of coping. But the set itself propounds a vision of consumer happiness. Living rooms and kitchens usually display the standard package of consumer goods. Even where the set is ratty, as in *Sanford and Son*, or working-class, as in *All in the Family*, the bright color of the TV tube almost always glamorizes the surroundings so that there will be no sharp break between the glorious color of the program and the glorious color of the commercial. In the more primitive Fifties, by contrast, it was still possible for a series like *The Honeymooners* or *The Phil Silvers Show* (Sergeant Bilko) to get by with one or two simple sets per show: the life of a good skit was in its accomplished *acting*. But that series, in its sympathetic treatment of working-class mores, was exceptional. Color broadcasting accomplishes the glamorous ideal willy-nilly.

Permissible character types have evolved, partly because of changes in the structure of broadcasting power. In the Fifties, before the quiz show scandal, advertising agencies contracted directly with production companies to produce TV series (Barnouw, 1970). They ordered up exactly what they wanted, as if by the yard; and with some important but occasional exceptions—I'll mention some in a moment—what they wanted was glamor and fun, a showcase for commercials. In 1954, for example, one agency wrote to the playwright Elmer Rice explaining why his *Street Scene*, with its "lower class social level," would be unsuitable for telecasting:

> We know of no advertiser or advertising agency of any importance in this country who would knowingly allow the products which he is trying to advertise to the public to become associated with the squalor . . . and general 'down' character . . . of Street Scene. . . .
>
> On the contrary it is the general policy of advertisers to glamorize their products, the people who buy them, and the whole American social and economic scene. . . . The American consuming public as presented by the advertising industry today is middle class, not lower class; happy in general, not miserable and frustrated. . . . (Barnouw, 1970:33).

Later in the Fifties, comedies were able to represent discrepant settings, permitting viewers both to identify and to indulge their sense of superiority through comic distance: *The Honeymooners* and *Bilko*, which capitalized on Jackie Gleason's and Phil Silvers' enormous personal popularity (a personality cult can always perform wonders and break rules), were able to extend dignity to working-class characters in anti-glamorous situations (see Czitrom, 1977).

Beginning in 1960, the networks took direct control of production away from advertisers. And since the networks are less provincial than particular advertisers, since they are more closely attuned to general tolerances in the population, and since they are firmly in charge of a buyers' market for advertising (as long as they produce shows that *some* corporation will sponsor), it now became possible—if by no means easy—for independent production companies to get somewhat distinct cultural forms, like Norman Lear's comedies, on the air. The near-universality of television set ownership, at the same time, creates the possibility of a wider range of audiences, including minority-group, working-class and age-segmented audiences, than existed in the Fifties, and thus makes possible a wider range of fictional characters. Thus changes in the organization of TV production, as well as new market pressures, have helped to change the prevalent settings and character types on television.

But the power of corporate ideology over character types remains very strong, and sets limits on the permissible; the changes from the Fifties through the Sixties and Seventies should be understood in the context of essential cultural features that have *not* changed. To show the quality of deliberate choice that is often operating, consider a book called *The Youth Market*, by two admen, published in 1970, counseling companies on ways to pick "the right character for your product":

> But in our opinion, if you want to create your own hard-hitting spokesman to children, the most effective route is the superhero-miracle worker. He certainly can demonstrate food products, drug items, many kinds of toys, and innumerable household items. . . . The character should be adventurous. And he should be on the right side of the law. A child must be able to mimic his hero, whether he is James Bond, Superman or Dick Tracy; to be able to fight and shoot to kill without punishment or guilt feelings (Helitzer and Heyel, 1970).

If this sort of thinking is resisted within the industry itself, it's not so much because of commitments to artistry in television as such, but more because there are other markets that are not "penetrated" by these hard-hitting heroes. The industry is noticing, for example, that *Roots* brought to the tube an audience who don't normally watch TV. The homes-using-television levels during the week of *Roots* were up between six and twelve percent over the programs of the previous year (*Broadcasting*, Jan. 31, 1977). Untapped markets—often composed of people who have, or wish to have, somewhat alternative views of the world—can only be brought in by unusual sorts of programming. There is room in the schedule for rebellious human slaves just as there is room for hard-hitting patriotic-technological heroes. In other words—and contrary to a simplistic argument against television manipulation by network elites—the receptivity of enormous parts of the population is an important limiting factor affecting what gets on television. On the other hand, network elites do not risk investing in *regular* heroes who will challenge the core values of corporate capitalist society: who are, say, explicit socialists, or union organizers, or for that matter born-again evangelists. But like the dramatic series *Playhouse 90* in the Fifties, TV movies permit a somewhat wider range of choice than weekly series. It is apparently easier for producers to sell exceptional material for one-shot showings—whether sympathetic to lesbian mothers, critical of the 1950s blacklist or of Senator Joseph McCarthy. Most likely these important exceptions have prestige value for the networks.

Slant

Within the formula of a program, a specific slant often pushes through, registering a certain position on a particular public issue. When issues are politically charged, when there is overt social conflict, programs capitalize on the currency. ("Capitalize" is an interesting word, referring both to use and to profit.) In the program's brief compass, only the most stereotyped characters are deemed to "register" on the audience, and therefore slant, embedded in character, is almost always simplistic and thin. The specific slant is sometimes mistaken for the whole of ideological tilt or "bias," as if the bias dissolves when no position is taken on a topical issue. But the week-after-week angle of the show is more basic, a hardened definition of a routine situation *within which* the specific topical slant emerges. The occasional topical slant then seems to anchor the program's general meanings. For instance, a 1977 show of *The Six Million Dollar Man* told the story of a Russian-East German plot to stop the testing of the new B-1 bomber; by implication, it linked the domestic movement against the B-1 to the foreign Red menace. Likewise, in the last Sixties and Seventies, police and spy dramas have commonly clucked over violent terrorists and heavily-armed "anarchist" maniacs, labeled as "radicals" or "revolutionaries," giving the cops a chance to justify their heavy armament and crude machismo. But the other common variety of slant is sympathetic to forms of deviance which are either private (the lesbian mother shown to be a good mother to her children) or quietly reformist (the brief vogue for *Storefront Lawyers* and the like in the early Seventies). The usual slants, then, fall into two categories: either (a) a legitimation of depoliticized forms of deviance, usually ethnic or sexual; or (b) a delegitimation of the dangerous, the violent, the out-of-bounds.

The slants that find their way into network programs, in short, are not uniform. Can we say anything systematic about them? Whereas in the Fifties family dramas and sit-coms usually ignored—or indirectly sublimated—the existence of deep social problems in the world outside the set, programs of the Seventies much more often domesticate them. From *Ozzie and Harriet* or *Father Knows Best* to *All in the Family* or *The Jeffersons* marks a distinct shift for formula, character, and slant: a shift, among other things, in the image of how a family copes with the world outside. Again, changes in content have in large part to be referred back to changes in social values and sensibilities, particularly the values of writers, actors, and other practitioners: there is a large audience now that prefers acknowledging and domesticating social problems directly rather than ignoring them or treating them only indirectly and in a sublimated way; there are also media practitioners who have some roots in the rebellions of the Sixties. Whether hegemonic style will operate more by exclusion (Fifties) than by domestication (Seventies) will depend on the level of public dissensus as well as on internal factors of media organization (the Fifties blacklist of TV writers probably exercised a chilling effect on subject matter and slant; so did the fact that sponsors directly developed their own shows).

Solution

Finally, cultural hegemony operates through the solutions proposed to difficult problems. However grave the problems posed, however rich the imbroglio, the episodes regularly end with the click of a solution: an arrest, a defiant smile, an I-told-you-so explanation. The characters we have been asked to care about are alive and well, ready for next week. Such a world is not so much fictional as fake. However deeply the problem is located within society, it will be solved among a few persons: the heroes must attain a solution that leaves the rest of the society untouched. The self-enclosed world of the TV drama justifies itself, and its exclusions, by "wrapping it all up." Occasional exceptions are either short-lived, like *East Side, West Side*, or independently syndicated outside the networks, like Lear's *Mary Hartman, Mary Hartman*. On the networks, *All in the Family* has been unusual in sometimes ending obliquely, softly or ironically, refusing to pretend to solve a social problem that cannot, in fact, be solved by the actions of the Bunkers alone. The Lou Grant show is also partial to downbeat, alienating endings.

Likewise, in mid-Seventies mass-market films like *Chinatown, Rollerball, Network* and *King Kong*, we see an interesting form of closure: as befits the common cynicism and helplessness, society owns the victory. Reluctant heroes go up against vast impersonal forces, often multinational corporations like the same Gulf & Western (sent up as "Engulf & Devour" in Mel Brooks's *Silent Movie*) that, through its Paramount subsidiary, produces some of these films. Driven to anger or bitterness by the evident corruption, the rebels break loose—only to bring the whole structure crashing down on them. (In the case of *King Kong*, the great ape falls of his own weight—from the World Trade Center roof, no less—after the helicopter gunships "zap" him.) These popular films appeal to a kind of populism and rebelliousness, usually of a routine and vapid sort, but then close off the possibilities of effective opposition. The rich get richer and the incoherent rebels get bought or killed.

Often the sense of frustration funneled through these films is diffuse and ambiguous enough to encourage a variety of political responses. While many left-wing cultural critics raved about *Network*, for example, right-wing politicians in Southern California campaigned for Proposition 13 using the film's slogan, "I'm mad as hell and I'm not going to take it any more." Indeed, *the fact that the same film is subject to a variety of conflicting yet plausible interpretations may suggest a crisis in hegemonic ideology*. The economic system is demonstrably troubled, but the traditional liberal recourse, the State, is no longer widely enough trusted to provide reassurance. Articulate social groups do not know whom to blame; public opinion is fluid and volatile, and people at all levels in the society withdraw from public participation.[11] In this situation, commercial culture succeeds with diverse interest groups, as well as with the baffled and ambivalent, precisely by propounding ambiguous or even self-contradictory situations and solutions.

The Hegemonic Process in Liberal Capitalism

Again it bears emphasizing that, for all these tricks of the entertainment trade, the mass-cultural system is not one-dimensional. High-consumption corporate capitalism implies a certain sensitivity to audience taste, taste which is never wholly manufactured. Shows are made by guessing at audience desires and tolerances, and finding ways to speak to them that perpetuate the going system.[12] (Addressing one set of needs entails scanting and distorting others, ordinarily the less mean, less invidious, less aggressive, less reducible to commodity forms.) The cultural hegemony system that results is not a closed system. It leaks. Its very structure leaks, at the least because it remains to some extent competitive. Networks sell the audience's attention to advertisers who want what they think will be a suitably big, suitably rich audience for their products; since the show is bait, advertisers will put up with—or rather buy into—a great many possible baits, as long as they seem likely to attract a buying audience. In the news, there are also traditions of real though limited journalistic independence, traditions whose modern extension causes businessmen, indeed, to loathe the press. In their 1976 book *Ethics and Profits*, Leonard Silk and David Vogel quote a number of big businessmen complaining about the raw deal they get from the press. A typical comment: "Even though the press is a business, it doesn't reflect business values." That is, it has a certain real interest in truth—partial, superficial, occasion- and celebrity-centered truth, but truth nevertheless.

Outside the news, the networks have no particular interest in truth as such, but they remain sensitive to currents of interest in the population, including the yank and haul and insistence of popular movements. With few ethical or strategic reasons not to absorb trends, they are adept at perpetuating them with new formats, new styles, tie-in commodities (dolls, posters, T-shirts, fan magazines) that fans love. In any case, it is in no small measure because of the economic drives themselves that *the hegemonic system itself amplifies legitimated forms of opposition*. In liberal capitalism, hegemonic ideology develops by domesticating opposition, absorbing it into forms compatible with the core ideological structure. Consent is managed by absorption as well as by exclusion. The hegemonic ideology changes in order to remain hegemonic; that is the peculiar nature of the dominant ideology of liberal capitalism.

Raymond Williams (1977) has insisted rightly on the difference between two types of non-hegemonic ideology: *alternative* forms, presenting a distinct but supplementary and containable view of the world, and *oppositional* forms, rarer and more tenuous within commercial culture, intimating an authentically different social order. Williams makes the useful distinction between *residual* forms, descending from declining social formations, and *emergent* forms, reflecting formations on the rise. Although it is easier to speak of these possibilities in the abstract than in the concrete, and although it is not clear what the emergent formations are (this is one of the major questions for social analysis now), these concepts may help organize an agenda for thought and research on popular culture. I would add to Williams' own carefully modulated remarks on the subject only that there is no reason *a priori* to expect that emergent forms will be expressed as the ideologies of rising *classes*, or as "proletarian ideology" in particular; currently in the United States the emergent forms have to do with racial minorities and other ethnic groups, with women, with singles, with homosexuals, with old-age subcultures, as well as with technocrats and with political interest groups (loosely but not inflexibly linked to corporate interests) with particular strategic goals (like the new militarists of the Committee on the Present Danger). Analysis of the hegemonic ideology and its rivals should not be allowed to lapse into some form of what C. Wright Mills (1948) called the "labor metaphysic."

One point should be clear: the hegemonic system is not cut-and-dried, not definitive. It has continually to be reproduced, continually superimposed, continually to be negotiated and managed, in order to override the alternative and, occasionally, the oppositional forms. To put it another way: major social conflicts are transported *into* the cultural system, where the hegemonic process frames them, form and content both, into compatibility with dominant systems of meaning. Alternative material is routinely *incorporated*: brought into the body of cultural production. Occasionally oppositional material may succeed in being indigestible; that material is excluded from the media discourse and returned to the cultural margins from which it came, while *elements* of it are incorporated into the dominant forms.

In these terms, *Roots* was an alternative form, representing slaves as unblinkable facts of American history, blacks as victimized humans and humans nonetheless. In the end, perhaps, the story is dominated by the chance for upward mobility; the upshot of travail is freedom. Where Alex Haley's book is subtitled "The Saga of an American Family," ABC's version carries the label—and the self-congratulation—"The *Triumph* of an American Family." It is hard to say categorically which story prevails; in any case there is a tension, a struggle, between the collective agony and the triumph of a single family. That struggle is the friction in the works of the hegemonic system.

And all the evident friction within television entertainment—as well as within the schools, the family, religion, sexuality, and the State—points back to a deeper truth about bourgeois culture. In the United States, at least, hegemonic ideology is extremely complex and absorptive; it is only by absorbing and domesticating conflicting definitions of reality and demands on it, in fact, that it remains hegemonic. In this way, the hegemonic ideology of liberal capitalism is dramatically different from the ideologies of pre-capitalist societies, and from the dominant ideology of authoritarian socialist or Fascist regimes. What permits it to absorb and domesticate critique is not something accidental to capitalist ideology, but rather its core. *The hegemonic ideology of liberal capitalist society is deeply and essentially conflicted in a number of ways.* As Daniel Bell (1976) has argued, it urges people to work hard, but proposes that real satisfaction is to be found in leisure, which ostensibly embodies values opposed to work.[13] More profoundly, at the center of liberal capitalist ideology there is a tension between the affirmation of patriarchal authority—currently enshrined in the national security state—and the affirmation of individual worth and self-determination. Bourgeois ideology in all its incarnations has been from the first a contradiction in terms, affirming "life, liberty and the pursuit of happiness," or "liberty, equality, fraternity," as if these ideals are compatible, even mutually dependent, at all times in all places, as they were for one revolutionary group at one time in one place. But all anti-bourgeois movements wage their battles precisely in terms of liberty, equality or fraternity (or, recently, sorority); they press on liberal capitalist ideology *in its own name*.

Thus we can understand something of the vulnerability of bourgeois ideology, as well as its persistence. In the twentieth century, the dominant ideology has shifted toward sanctifying consumer satisfaction as the premium definition of "the pursuit of happiness," in this way justifying corporate domination of the economy. What is hegemonic in consumer capitalist ideology is precisely the notion that happiness, or liberty, or equality, or fraternity can be affirmed through the existing private commodity forms, under the benign, protective eye of the national security state. This ideological core is what remains essentially unchanged and unchallenged in television entertainment, at the same time the inner tensions persist and are even magnified.

References

Abramson, Ronald

1978   Unpublished manuscript, notes on critical theory distributed at the West Coast Critical Communications Conference, Stanford University.

Adorno, Theodor W.

1954   "How to look at television." Hollywood Quarterly of Film, Radio and Television. (Spring.) Reprinted 1975: 474–488 in Bernard Rosenberg and David Manning White, (eds.), Mass Culture. New York: The Free Press.

1974   "The stars down to earth. The Los Angeles Times Astrology Column." Telos 19 (Spring 1974): (1957) 13–90.

Adorno, Theodor W. and Max Horkheimer

1972   "The culture industry: Enlightenment as mass deception." Pp. 120–167 in Adorno and (1944) Horkheimer, Dialectic of Enlightenment. New York: Seabury.

Altick, Richard

1978   The Shows of London. Cambridge, Massachusetts: Harvard University Press.

Anderson, Perry

1976   "The antinomies of Antonio Gramsci." New Left Review 100 (November 1976–January 1977): 5–78.

Barnouw, Erik

1970   The Image Empire: New York, Oxford University Press.

Bell, Daniel

1976   The Cultural Contradictions of Capitalism. New York: Basic Books.

Blum, Alan F.

1964   "Lower-class Negro television spectators: The concept of pseudo-jovial scepticism." Pp. 429–435 in Arthur B. Shostak and William Gomberg (eds.), Blue-Collar World. Englewood Cliffs: Prentice-Hall.

Braverman, Harry

  1974   Labor and Monopoly Capital: The Degradation of Work in the Twentieth Century. New York: Monthly Review Press.

Czitrom, Danny

  1977   "Bilko: A sitcom for all seasons." Cultural Correspondence 4: 16–19.

Dickstein, Morris

  1977   Gates of Eden. New York: Basic Books.

Ewen, Stuart

  1976   Captains of Consciousness. New York: McGraw-Hill.

Gitlin, Todd

  1977a   "Spotlights and shadows: Television and the culture of politics." College English April: 789–801.

  1977b   " 'The whole world is watching': Mass media and the new left, 1965–70." Doctoral dissertation, University of California, Berkeley.

  1977c   "The televised professional." Social Policy (November/December):94–99.

  1978a   "Media sociology: The dominant paradigm." Theory and Society 6:205–253.

  1978b   "Life as instant replay." East Bay Voice (November-December):14.

Gouldner, Alvin W.

  1976   The Dialectic of Idology and Technology. New York: Seabury.

Gramsci, Antonio

  1971   Selections From the Prison Notebooks. Quintin Hoare and Geoffrey Nowell Smith (eds.), New York: International Publishers.

Helitzer, Melvin and Carl Heyel

  1970   The Youth Market: Its Dimensions, Influence and Opportunities for You. Quoted pp. (1973) 62–3 in William Melody, Children's Television. New Haven: Yale University Press.

Kellner, Douglas

  1978   "Ideology, Marxism, and advanced capitalism." Socialist Review 42 (November–December): 37–66.

Leiss, William

  1976   The Limits to Satisfaction. Toronto: University of Toronto Press.

Mann, Michael

  1973   Consciousness and Action Among the Western Working Class. London: Macmillan.

Mills, C. Wright

  1948   The New Men of Power. New York: Harcourt, Brace.

Morley, Dave

  1974   "Reconceptualising the media audience: Towards an ethnography of audiences." Mimeograph, Centre for Contemporary Cultural Studies, University of Birmingham.

Real, Michael R.

  1977   Mass-Mediated Culture. Englewood Cliffs: Prentice-Hall.

Silk, Leonard and David Vogel

  1976   Ethics and Profits. New York: Simon and Schuster.

Williams, Raymond

  1973   "Base and superstructure in Marxist cultural theory." New Left Review 82.

  1977   Marxism and Literature. New York: Oxford University Press.

Willis, Paul

    n.d.   "Symbolism and practice: A theory for the social meaning of pop music." Mimeograph, Centre for Contemporary Cultural Studies, University of Birmingham.

Notes

1. Anderson has read Gramsci closely to tease out this and other ambiguities in Gramsci's diffuse and at times Aesopian texts. (Gramsci was writing in a Fascist prison, he was concerned about passing censorship, and he was at times gravely ill.)

2. In my reading, the most thoughtful specific approach to this question since Gramsci, using comparative structural categories to explain the emergence or absence of socialist class consciousness, is Mann (1973). Mann's analysis takes us to structural features of American society that detract from revolutionary consciousness and organization. Although my paper does not discuss social-structural and historical features, I do not wish their absence to be interpreted as a belief that culture is all-determining. This paper discusses aspects of the hegemonic culture, and makes no claims to a more sweeping theory of American society.

3. In Part III of the latter, I discuss the theory of hegemony more extensively. This will be published in book form by the University of California Press in 1980.

4. See also, Willis (n.d.) for an excellent discussion of the limits of both ideological analysis of cultural artifacts and the social meaning system of audiences, when each is taken by itself and isolated from the other.

5. Most strikingly, see Blum's (1964) findings on black viewers putting down TV shows while watching them. See also Willis' (n.d.) program for studying the substantive meanings of particular pop music records for distinct youth subcultures; but note that it is easier to study the active uses of music than TV, since music is more often heard publicly and because, there being so many choices, the preference for a particular set of songs or singers or beats expresses more about the mentality of the audience than is true for TV.

6. A few years ago, *Gunsmoke* was cancelled although it was still among the top ten shows in Nielsen ratings. The audience was primarily older and disproportionately rural, thus an audience less well sold to advertisers. So much for the networks' democratic rationale.

7. Borrowing "on time," over commensurable, arithmetically calculated lengths of time, is part of the same process: production, consumption and acculturation made compatible.

8. The time of the show is important to its success or failure. Lear's *All in the Family* was rejected by ABC before CBS bought it. An earlier attempt to bring problems of class, race and poverty into the heart of television series was *East Side, West Side* of 1964, in which George C. Scott played a caring social worker consistently unable to accomplish much for his clients. As time went on, the Scott character came to the conclusion that politics might accomplish what social work could not, and changed jobs, going to work as the assistant to a liberal Congressman. It was rumored about that the hero was going to discover there, too, the limits of reformism—but the show was cancelled, presumably for low ratings. Perhaps Lear's shows, by contrast, have lasted in part *because they are comedies:* audiences will let their defenses down for some good laughs, even on themselves, at least when the characters are, like Archie Bunker himself, ambiguous normative symbols. At the same time, the comedy form allows white racists to indulge themselves in Archie's rationalizations without seeing that the joke is on them.

9. I use the term *loosely* to refer to general categories of TV entertainment, like "adult western," "cops and robbers," "black shows." Genre is not an objective feature of the cultural universe, but a conventional name for a convention, and should not be reified—as both cultural analysis and practice often do—into a cultural essence.

10. This discussion of televised sports was published in similar form (Gitlin, 1978b).

11. In another essay I will be arguing that forms of pseudo-participation (including cult movies like *Rocky Horror Picture Show* and *Animal House*, along with religious sects) are developing simultaneously to fill the vacuum left by the declining of credible radical politics, and to provide ritual forms of expression that alienated groups cannot find within the political culture.

12. See the careful, important and unfairly neglected discussion of the tricky needs issue in Leiss, 1976. Leiss cuts through the Frankfurt premise that commodity culture addresses false needs by arguing that audience needs for happiness, diversion, self-assertion and so on are ontologically real; what commercial culture does is not to invent needs (how could it do that?) but to insist upon the possibility of meeting them through the purchase of commodities. For Leiss, all specifically human needs are social; they develop within one social form or another. From this argument—and, less rigorously but more daringly from Ewen (1976)—flow powerful political implications I cannot develop here. On the early popularity of entertainment forms which cannot possibly be laid at the door of a modern "culture industry" and media-produced needs, see Altick (1978).

13. There is considerable truth in Bell's thesis. Then why do I say "ostensibly?" Bell exaggerates his case against "adversary culture" by emphasizing changes in avant-garde culture above all (Pop Art, happenings, John Cage, etc.); if he looked at *popular* culture, he would more likely find ways in which aspects of the culture of consumption *support* key aspects of the culture of production. I offer my discussion of sports as one instance. Morris Dickstein's (1977) affirmation of the critical culture of the Sixties commits the counter-part error of overemphasizing the importance of *other* selected domains of literary and avant-garde culture.

PART IV

In Search of "Quality": The Struggle for Representation and Relevance

Excessive Style
The Crisis of Network Television

John Thorton Caldwell

Television is to communication what the chainsaw is to logging.
—Director David Lynch[1]

There isn't much out there that looks real.
—Director/cameraman Ron Dexter[2]

Disruptive Practice

On the Friday September 8, 1989, edition of ABC's nightly news, erudite anchor Peter Jennings bemoaned the advent of what he termed "trash television." Prefacing his remarks by reference to a previous report by ABC on the subject, Jennings described the phenomenon with a forewarning. Norms of quality, restraint, and decorum notwithstanding, the new and ugly genre would in fact shortly premiere. Citing H. L. Mencken's adage about not overestimating the intelligence of the American people, Jennings signed off that evening with an obvious air of resignation. The class struggle, one sensed, might soon be lost.

Within two evenings, Jennings's warning was fulfilled. The highly evolved intertextuality that characterized television of the late 1980s was about to witness one of its most extreme manifestations to date. On Saturday, September 9, independent station KHJ-Channel 9 of Los Angeles uncorked the one-hour premiere of *American Gladiators* in syndication to stations throughout the country. Two nights later superstation KTLA-Channel 5 of Los Angeles aired its own nationwide trash spectacular—a two-hour premiere version of a show named *Rock-and-Rollergames*. Later that fall, pay-per-view television made available to cable viewers nationwide a special called *Thunder and Mud*. This latter trash hybrid featured various low-culture luminaries, and included Jessica Hahn of the recent PTL–Jim Bakker sex scandal, female mud wrestlers, wild-man comedian Sam Kinison, and the all-woman heavy-metal rock group She-Rok. The *Los Angeles Times* labeled the spectacle "Sex, Mud, and Rock-and-Roll." The producers, however, preferred the derivative punch of *Thud* to the official program title *Thunder and Mud*. To the show's makers, *Thud* was a "combination female mud-wrestling act–heavy-metal rock concert–game show with some comedy bits thrown in."[3] If any doubts remained about mass culture's reigning aesthetic in 1989, it was certainly clear that stylistic and generic restraint were not among its properties.

Rock-and-Rollergames was slated, interestingly, to air against the widely popular and front-running network sitcom *Roseanne*. Such competition was formidable given the vertically scheduled and heavily promoted sequence of shows that followed *Roseanne* Tuesday nights on ABC. Given trash television's excessive and low-culture pretense, such competition was significant, since *Roseanne* was being celebrated as television's premier "low-culture" hit; a status it had achieved with both viewers and tabloids during the previous season. By late fall, KHJ-TV had shifted *Rock-and-Rollergames* to Saturday mornings, and had renamed (and reduced) the spectacle to *Rollergames*, still in wide syndication in 1993. *American Gladiators* found itself shifted later in the year to the weekend schedule, and in subsequent years to late weekday afternoon strips. Together with its prime-time airings, *Gladiators* found a lucrative niche by actively extending its competition out into the audience. Open trials were held throughout the country in highly publicized gladiator competitions at places like the Los Angeles Coliseum. Although trash television did not turn out to be an overwhelmingly dominant genre in primetime, *Gladiators* and other shows continued successfully in production with much success through the next four seasons. Musclebound, steroid-pumped women gladiators like Zap continued to grace the pages of *TV Guide* and the sets of celebrity talk shows through 1993.[4] A medieval variant of the trash spectacular, called *Knights and Warriors*, entered the trash programming fray in 1992–1993. Nickelodeon hyped and cablecast its hyperactive trash-gladiatorial clones, *Guts* and *Guts: All Stars*, for the younger set throughout the 1993–1994 season.

Although the genre was defined from the start by its distinctive no-holds barred look, trash spectaculars were also symptomatic of a broader and more persistent stylistic tendency in contemporary television—one that was not always castigated as trash nor limited to low-culture content. That is, trash-spectaculars can be seen as a stylistic bridge between lower trash shows—like professional wrestling or *The Morton Downey, Jr.* shock-talk show (series that exploited very low production values to blankly document hyperactive onstage performances for the fan situated squarely in the stands or on the sofa)—and higher televisual forms that more extensively *choreograph* visual design, movement, and editing *specifically for the camera*. Even mid-1980s shows with higher cultural pretension or prestige, like *Max Headroom* or *Moonlighting* on ABC or MTV's manic game show *Remote Control*, frequently stoked their presentational engines with excesses not unlike those that characterized trash spectaculars. Although broadcast manifestations of the televisual tendency took many shapes, stylistic excess has continued to rear its ostensibly ugly head—even in the ethically pure confines of Peter Jennings's network news division.

Bells and Whistles and Business as (Un)Usual

> *We don't shy away from the aesthetic nature of the business. We have one foot on the edge, and we have to keep it there.*
>
> —*Local station executive, WSVN-TV, Miami*

Starting in the 1980s, American mass-market television underwent an uneven shift in the conceptual and ideological paradigms that governed its look and presentational demeanor.[5] In several important programming and institutional areas, television moved from a framework that approached broadcasting primarily as a form of word-based rhetoric and transmission, with all the issues that such terms suggest, to a visually based mythology, framework, and aesthetic based on an extreme self-consciousness of style. This is not just to say that television simply became more visual, as if improved production values allowed for increasing formal sophistication. Such a view falls prey to the problematic notion that developments in technology cause formal changes and that image and sound sophistication are merely by-products of technical evolution. Rather, in many ways television by 1990 had retheorized its aesthetic and presentational task.[6] With increasing frequency, style itself became the subject, the signified, if you will, of television. In fact, this self-consciousness of style became so great that it can more accurately be described as an activity—as a performance of style—rather than as a particular look.[7] Television has come to flaunt and display style. Programs battle for identifiable style-markers and distinct looks in order to gain audience share within the competitive broadcast flow. Because of the sheer scope of the broadcast flow, however—a context that simultaneously works to make televised material anonymous—television tends to counteract the process of stylistic individuation.[8] In short, style, long seen as a mere signifier and vessel for content, issues, and ideas, has now itself become one of television's most privileged and showcased signifieds. Why television changed in this way is, of course, a broader and important question. Any credible answer to the question is only possible after systematically and patiently analyzing representative program texts. By closely examining style and ideology in a range of shows and series that celebrate the visual, the decorative, or the extravagant a more fundamental reconsideration of the status of the image in television becomes possible.

Televisuality was a historical phenomenon with clear ideological implications. It was not simply an isolated period of formalism or escapism in American television or a new golden age. Although quality was being consciously celebrated in the industry during this period, the celebration had as much to do with business conditions as it did with the presence of sensitive or serious television artists.[9] Nor was televisuality merely an end-product of postmodernism.[10] The growing value of excessive style on primetime network and cable television during the 1980s cannot simply be explained solely by reference to an aesthetic point of view. Rather, the stylistic emphasis that emerged during this period resulted from a number of interrelated tendencies and changes: in the industry's mode of production, in programming practice, in the audience and its expectations, and in an economic crisis in network television. This confluence of material practices and institutional pressures suggests that televisual style was the symptom of a much broader period of transition in the mass media and American culture. Yet historical changes are seldom total. Six principles—ranging from formal and generic concerns to economic and programming functions—further define and de-limit the extent of televisuality. These qualifications will be more fully examined through close analysis in the chapters that follow.

1. Televisuality was a stylizing *performance*—an exhibitionism that utilized many different looks. The presentational manner of televisuality was not singularly tied to either low- or high-culture pretense. With many variant guises—from opulent cinematic spectacles to graphics-crunching workaday visual effects—televisuality cut across generic categories and affected some narrative forms more than others. For example, the miniseries proved to be a quintessential televisual form, while the video-originated sitcom—at least with a few notable exceptions—resisted radical stylistic change. Conceived of as a *presentational attitude*, a display of knowing *exhibitionism*, any one of many specific visual looks and stylizations could be marshaled for the spectacle. The process of stylization rather than style—an activity rather than a static look—was the factor that defined televisual exhibitionism.

Consider *Entertainment Tonight*, for example, a hallmark televisual show that influenced a spate of tabloid, reality, and magazine shows during the 1980s. *Variety* hailed *ET*, a forerunner of tabloid horses *A Current Affair* and *Inside Edition*, as "the granddaddy of all magazine strips" for its "brighter look and provocative stories."[11] Having survived over three thousand individual episodes and having prospered nationally in syndication for over a decade by 1993, the show's executive producer explained the show's secret to success: "We continued to update our graphics and other elements of production, the bells and whistles. If you look at our show, let's say once a month for the last seven years, the only constants are the title, the theme, and John and Mary hosting the weekday show. Everything else continues to change. So we go through a continual process of reinventing the wheel."[12] *ET*, then, airing five days a week, year-round, defines itself not by its magazine-style discourse or host-centered happy talk, but by the fact that the viewer can always expect the show's style—its visual and graphic "bells and whistles"—to change. Televisuality, then, is about constantly reinventing the stylistic wheel.

2. Televisuality represented a *structural inversion*. Televisual practice also challenged television's existing formal and presentational hierarchies. Many shows evidenced a structural inversion between narrative and discourse, form and content, subject and style. What had always been relegated to the background now frequently became the foreground. Stylistic flourishes had typically been contained through narrative motivation in classical Hollywood film and television. In many shows by the mid-1980s however, style was no longer a bracketed flourish, but was the text of the show. The *presentational status* of style changed—and it changed in markets and contexts far from the prestige programming produced by Hollywood's primetime producers.

Broadcasting magazine, for instance, described the dramatic financial reversal of the Fox television affiliate in Miami's highly competitive market. The ratings success of WSVN-TV was seen as a result of the station "pumping out" seven hours of news "that mirrors the music video in its unabashed appeal to younger viewers—flashy graphics, rapid-fire images, and an emphasis on style." While the trades saw the economic wisdom of stylistic overhauls like this one, television critics marveled at the station's able use of an aggressive, wall-to-wall visual style to revive a dead station.[13] Even the vice presidents at WSVN theorized the journalistic success of the station in artistic terms, as a precarious but necessary form of aesthetic risk taking.[14] By marketing cutting-edge news as constructivist plays of image and text, even affiliate station M.B.A-types now posed as the avant-garde.

3. Televisuality was an *industrial product*. Frequently ignored or underestimated by scholars, television's mode of production has had a dramatic impact on the presentational guises, the narrative forms, and the politics of mainstream television. More than just blank infrastructure, television's technological and production base is smart—it theorizes, orchestrates, and interprets televisual meanings—and is partisan. The mode of production is also anything but static; it changes. The production base, then, is both a product of shifting cultural and economic needs and a factor that affects how we receive and utilize television and video. In order to talk adequately about television style or narrative, one needs at least to recognize that *television is manufactured*.

Technology, geographical issues, and labor practices were all important components in the formation of a televisual mode of production. There was, for example, a direct relationship between certain production tools—the video-assist, the Rank-Cintel, digital video effects—and popular program styles in the 1980s. Yet these tools did not cause television's penchant for style. Rather, they helped comprise an array of conditions, and a context, that allowed for exhibitionism.

Digital video technology, for instance, has had an enormous effect on the look of mass-market television, yet it has not infiltrated all of television's dominant genres. Primetime workhorse Universal Television, for example, justified digital technology only in terms of specific narrative needs: "We're getting more and more into digital. There's no standard formula that's applied to every single show, and every show doesn't get the same services in the same way from the same facility. With sitcoms, we're not into the digital domain yet—not to say that it won't be happening soon."[15] Digital imaging, then, once thought to be a futurist preoccupation now shadows even conservative television genres in Hollywood. Yet far from the sitcoms and genres of Studio City and Burbank, the same effects became defining factors and prized properties. At a very different level in broadcasting during this period even local stations began to manufacture alternative identities around a technologically driven aesthetic. In "personnel upgrades" regional broadcasters like WRAL-Channel 5 in Raleigh, North Carolina expected key production personnel to have visual arts degrees and electronic imaging technologies skills. News and promotional producers as well were now expected to "be able to write and produce promos that sell and touch emotion, (and) *must be proficient in all aspects of production with an eye for visuals that cut through the clutter*."[16] Even outside of primetime's prestige television, then, market competition was defined as clutter, and striking visuals and high-tech graphics as obligatory corporate strategies. New televisual tools had arisen to meet the dense onslaught of programming alternatives.

4. Televisuality was a *programming phenomenon:* Showcase television in itself was nothing new, but the degree to which broadcasters showcased to counterprogram was distinctive. Television history offers important and influential precedents for quality television: the Weaver years at NBC in the 1950s; the MTM/Tinker years at CBS in the 1970s; the Lear era at CBS in the 1970s. Programming designed around special-event status was also not entirely new, although the kind of prestige and programming spin that special events offered threatened to dominate television by the late 1980s. Everything on television now seems to be pitched at the viewer as a special event—from nondescript movies of the week to the live coverage of some local catastrophe on the eleven o'clock news—so much so in fact, that the term *special* is now almost meaningless. Showcase and event strategies that used to be limited to sweeps now pervade the entire year. No programming confesses to being commonplace.

While event-status television offered programmers one way to schedule nightly strips, "narrowcasting"—a result of demographic and ratings changes starting in the late 1970s—allowed for a different kind of aesthetic sensitivity in primetime programming. Broadcasters began to value smaller audiences if the income-earning potential and purchasing power of those audiences were high enough to offset their limited numbers. Narrowcast shows that averaged ratings and shares in the low- and mid-teens in the late 1980s—like ABC's *thirtysomething* and CBS's *Tour of Duty*—would never have survived a decade earlier, given the higher ratings expectations in broadcasting at that time.[17] The audience numbers needed for primetime success continued to fall in the 1980s. Although the Nielsens were slow to change from their ideal of an average viewing family, advertisers, cable, and direct broadcast satellite systems (DBS) executives were obsessed with clarifying ever narrower niches tied to economic, racial, age, and regional differences.[18] This industrial reconfiguration of the audience, in the name of cultural diversification, helped spawn the need for cultural- and ethnic-specific styles and looks. Fox, Black Entertainment Television, TNT, and Lifetime each developed distinctive and highly coded looks that reflected their narrowcast niches and network personalities. Gender- and ethnic-specific groups do not, apparently, coalesce around content-specific narration alone. Stylistic ghettos continue to be manufactured by cable and broadcast networks according to maps of their supposed niche potential.

5. Televisuality was a *function of audience*: While the audience was being redefined and retheorized from the outside by broadcast and cable programmers, the cultural abilities of audiences had also apparently changed by the 1980s. While trash spectaculars betrayed new stylistic appetites in what have traditionally been deemed lower-taste cultures, the networks during this period learned to cash in on yuppie demographics as well. Many viewers expected and watched programs that made additional aesthetic and conceptual demands not evident in earlier programming. Even if such demands came in the form of irony or pastiche, shows like *Late Night with David Letterman* on NBC and *The Gary Shandling Show* on HBO presupposed a certain minimal level of educational, financial, and cultural capital. Such a background provided viewers both with an air of distinction—as viewers in the know—and presupposed enough free time to actually watch late-night programming, terrain once written off as fringe.

The fact that television was no longer anonymous, also presupposed fundamental changes in the audience. While many British directors in Hollywood—Ridley Scott (*Thelma and Louise*), Tony Scott (*Top Gun*), and Alan Parker (*Mississippl Burning*)—had started as highly respected television commercial directors before breaking into features, American film directors before the 1980s had typically been segregated away from television agency work. There was, and to some degree still is, an ego problem and an institutional wall between the advertising and feature-film worlds. This segregation, however, began to change in the mid-1980s. Heavyweight film directors now were self-consciously hyped as producers of TV commercials.[19] David Lynch (*Blue Velvet*) designed pretentious primetime Obsession ads; Martin Scorsese (*Mean Streets*) produced an opulent Georgio Armani cologne spot for a mere $750,000; Rob Reiner (*A Few Good Men*) and Richard Donner (*Lethal Weapon*) both directed big-production-value Coca-Cola spots; Francis Ford Coppola (*Apocalypse Now*) directed a sensitive and familial thirty-second road-movie for GM that was never aired; Woody Allen (*Annie Hall*) spun out a commercial supermarket farce; Jean-Luc Godard (*Tout Va Bien*) did an avant-garde and overblown European Nike ad; and the venerable Michelangelo Antonioni (*Blow-up*)—the closest thing that serious Western cinema has to an aesthetic patriarch—choreographed a psychedelic spot for Renault.

The clients of these figures were inevitably impressed with their auteurist entourage, at least before the spots were produced and aired. Agency directors who had dominated the field outside of Hollywood, however, were less than happy with this opportunistic invasion of showcased aesthetics on television. Clio Award-winning director Joe Pytka grumbled that such auteurs underestimated the difficulty of the fifteen- and thirty-second short-forms.[20] Nevertheless, the auteur-importing mode—popularized by Ridley Scott, Spike Lee, and David Lynch in the mid-1980s—remained a viable fashion well into the 1990s with CAA's strong-armed invasion of the ad world from Hollywood in 1993.[21] The auteur-import business raises important questions about television practice: who is patronizing whom? CAA now acts more like televisual Medicis—with directors Donner and Reiner their kept artists—than traditional point-of-sale admen. Aesthetic promotion now flows both ways in commercial television—to the client and the patron—in a corporate ritual seldom kept from the audience. Audience consciousness and facility makes this commerce of authorial intent possible. Marketing aesthetic prestige presupposes and strokes audience distinction and self-consciousness.

6. Televisuality was a product of *economic crisis*. Televisuality cannot be theorized apart from the crisis that network television underwent after 1980. Stylistic excess can be seen as one way that mainstream television attempted to deal with the growing threat and eventual success of cable. Stylistic showcases, high-production value programming, and Hollywood stylishness can all be seen as tactics by which the networks and their primetime producers tried to protect market share in the face of an increasingly competitive national market. No longer could CBS, NBC, and ABC—protected by the government as near monopolies since the late 1940s and early 1950s—assume the level of cash flow that they had enjoyed up to the late 1970s. Although the networks faced the first cable players in 1980 and 1981 with a smug and self-confident public face, this facade began to crack as each year took its toll on corporate profits. CNN and MTV were merely the first in a line of very profitable challengers to sign on to cable for the long haul. The trades gave blow-by-blow accounts of the precipitous decline in network primetime viewing. The networks had enjoyed complete dominance—an incredible 90 share—during the 1979–1980 season, but saw this figure plummet to a mere 64/65 share by 1989–1990.[22]

Complicating things further still, the new fourth network, Fox, was profitable by 1989 and was eating directly into shares of the big three. Financial analysts reported that 40–45 percent of Fox's additional revenues in 1993 would come at the expense of ABC, directly reducing the network's yearly revenues by $50 million.[23] Fox's growing appetite was a network problem, not just because there were fewer pieces of market pie to share with Fox, but because of the demographic stratification within those pieces. Fox gained its market toehold and survived by specializing in the hip 18–34 demographic, but now was expanding into ABC's 18–49 year old range. Escalating and unrealistic production budgets were also part of the network diagnosis. The trades explained the collapse of quality network shows like *thirtysomething, I'll Fly Away*, and *The Wonder Years* as a result of inflated budgets. Even half-hour shows could now regularly cost $1.2 million per episode—an unheard-of level even for hour-long series two decades earlier.[24] By the late 1980s front-page stories in the national press were loudly trumpeting the demise of the networks, who were "under attack"—besieged by an array of new video delivery technologies.[25] By the early 1990s, the networks were publicly wringing their hands, as victims of cable, of unfair regulatory policies, and of syndication rules. Government regulators characterized the market as driven by "ferocious competition that was unimagined ten years ago."[26]

In one decade, network viewership declined by a corporation-wrecking 25 percent. This hemorrhaging of viewership may seem ironic, given the fact that high-style *televisuality also emerged during the very same years*. I will argue in the pages that follow, however, that televisuality addressed the very same economic problem that hostile takeovers would tackle in 1986 and 1987. Stylistic exhibitionism and downsizing were obviously very different organizational tactics. One came from programming and encouraged budget-busting expenditures of capital; the other came from corporate management and brought with it widespread layoffs and fiscal austerity. Yet both, paradoxically, attempted to solve the same corporate crisis: the declining market share of the networks. In some ways, this was payback time for network television. The market incursion of network broadcasters in the 1950s had itself created an economic crisis in Hollywood that sent the film studios scrambling for excessively styled forms: cinemascope, technicolor and 3-D. Depending on how one looked at it, televisuality in the 1980s was either a self-fulfilling deathwish by extravagant producers, or a calculated business tactic that increased market share.

The Terrain

Televisuality can be mapped out along several axes: formal, authorial, generic, and historical. From a formal perspective, televisual programs gained notoriety by exploiting one of two general, and production-based, stylistic worlds: the cinematic and the videographic. The cinematic refers, obviously, to a film look in television. Exhibitionist television in the 1980s meant more than shooting on film, however, since many nondescript shows have been shot on film since the early 1950s. Rather, cinematic values brought to television spectacle, high-production values, and feature-style cinematography. Series that utilized this mode typically promised broadcasters and audiences alike television's big picture. Situated at the top of the programming hierarchy, shows like *Moonlighting, Crime Stories, Wiseguy,* and *Beauty and the Beast* fit well with the financial expectations of network primetime programming. They also inevitably drew critical attention by their very programming presence and cinematic air of distinction. It was as if the televisual producers packaged labels with their cinematic shows that read: *"Panavision Shows That We Care."*

Televisual programs that exploited the videographic guise, on the other hand, were more pervasive and perhaps more anonymous than cinematic ones, but were certainly no less extravagant in terms of stylistic permutation. In fact, for technological reasons, videographic shows made available to producers, at any given time, more stylistic options. That is, such shows had more embellishment potential given their origins in electronic manipulation. Far different from the bland and neutral look that characterized video-origination studio productions in earlier decades, videographic televisuality since the 1980s has been marked by acute hyperactivity and an obsession with effects. If MTV helped encourage the stampede to film origination in primetime, then CNN demonstrated the pervasive possibilities of videographic presentation. Starting in 1980—and without any apparent or overt aesthetic agenda—CNN created and celebrated a consciousness of the televisual apparatus: an appreciation for multiple electronic feeds, image-text combinations, videographics, and studios with banks of monitors that evoked video installations. Ted Turner had coauthored the kind of cyberspace that video-freaks and visionaries had only fantasized about in the late 1960s.

The "give 'em hell" look of MTV, on the other hand, popularized a mode of production that changed the very way television was produced beginning in 1981. By shooting on various film formats and then posting electronically on tape, indie producers were no longer rigidly locked into a single production medium. Earlier telefilm producers, by contrast, were required to produce a single conformed negative for broadcast and a positive print made from source material that was uniform in format and stock. With the MTV prototype, however, it no longer mattered where the material came from (stock, live, graphic material), what format it was shot on (super-8mm, 16mm, 35mm), or whether it was black and white or color. Once transferred in post-production to electronically recorded tape, almost any element could be combined or composited, mixed and matched, in useable configurations. Not only were labor and business structured differently in the new videographic worlds—CNN was a nonunion shop and MTV utilized an eclectic mix of production personnel (from studio technicians to independent producers to animators to video artists)—but the very technologies that gave MTV national audiences allowed for and encouraged a different kind of look and stylistic expectation.

By the time of its network airing in 1986, then, *Max Headroom* was merely a self-conscious and premeditated reference and homage to an existing industry-proven, videographic prototype. Like two other pervasive forms, primetime commercial spots and music videos, *Max Headroom* operated between the two stylistic modes by mixing and matching elements from both cinema and digital imaging. Purer forms of videographic televisuality were actually more common in cost-effective and low-end programming, like *Entertainment Tonight, Hard Copy, America's Most Wanted,* and *Rescue 911.* Live coverage—especially of crises like the Gulf War, the L.A. rebellion, and the yearly spectacle of the Super Bowl—has had an especially ravenous appetite for videographic exhibitionism. Although videographic series typically evoke less critical attention than prestige cinematic programming, they frequently undergo more tortured attempts to crank-out aesthetic embellishment. A fetish for effects rules the videographic domain. This emerging formal axis between the cinematic and the videographic can also be sketched out in historical terms (Table 1). While *Moonlighting, Crime Stories, The Equalizer,* and *thirtysomething* continued to push film-based primetime into more excessive directions, *Max Headroom, Pee-Wee's Playhouse,* and *Remote Control* synthesized the electronic and videographic lessons of MTV and CNN for new national audiences.

A second way to understand televisual programming is to consider it along an axis formed by relative degrees of authorial intent and manufactured notoriety. Commercial spots were certainly not unique in flaunting directorial auras to the mass audience. Part of the emergence of the quality myth in 1980s television was that television was no longer simply anonymous as many theorists had suggested. Names of producers and directors assumed an ever more important role in popular discourses about television. While Aaron Spelling and Norman Lear were already household names, other producer-creators like Michael Mann and Stephen Bochco began to be discussed alongside their actors and series in popular magazines and newspapers. As with American film in the 1960s, authorial intent played an important role as an indicator and guarantor of aesthetic quality in primetime programming of the 1980s.

The centrality of this process can be demonstrated by considering televisual authorship within three organizing systems: marquee/signature television, mainstream conversions, and auteurist imports. Not only do the corporate and cooperative origins of television complicate singular attributions of authorship, but the various degrees of authorial deference within the industry show that televisual authorship is also part of calculated programming strategy. While many shows merit no authorial attribution by broadcasters, some demanding shows exploit it as a lifejacket, as a prop for survival, as a device used to weather programming clutter and to find loyal audiences. When *Brooklyn Bridge* suffered threats of network cancelation in 1992 and 1993 due to poor ratings, the show's producer took stage before the press on a regular basis—proof positive that there was indeed a series of substance hidden under the very nose of the American people. Such showcase producers are manufactured by production companies and networks as banner-carriers, much in the way that Stephen Bochco and Michael Mann were showcased in 1981 and 1984. Other signature producer types, like

TABLE I The Historical Field Televisual Events

1980	1981	1982	1983	1984	1985	1986

The Cinematic

					• Moonlighting	
				• Miami Vice		• thirtysomething
	• Hill Street Blues		• St. Elsewhere			• The Equalizer
	• Dynasty		• Winds of War		• Amazing Stories	
	• MTV			• Nike spots		• Crime Story
• CNN		• Marco Polo		• Chiat/Day Macintosh spots		
	• Entertainment Tonight					• Pee-Wee's Playhouse
		• Late Night with David Letterman				• SNL Opening
			• Nickelodeon		• Live Aid	
				• West 57th Street		

The Videographic

NOTE: The *general* position of the titles laid out along the vertical axis suggests the *degree* to which the series utilized one of the two most privileged televisual modes plotted: the cinematic or the videographic mode. Although many of the positions are only approximations (since some shows might emphasize one trait in one episode and the other in another installment), some clear and direct lineages are evident: from CNN to *Live Aid* to the coverage of the L.A. rebellion and *Zoo TV* on the electronic, videographic axis; and from MTV to *Miami Vice* to *Quantum Leap* and *Cop Rick* on the cinematic axis. Note as well that

Marshall Herskovitz, Diane English, David Letterman, and Joshua Brand, continue this showcasing tradition. As signature producers, each has functioned as a promotional marquee; a spotlit entré for programming seasons on their respective networks: ABC, CBS, NBC, and Fox (Table 2).

While these marquee producer-creators are television insiders—honed, disciplined, and groomed through the ranks of the primetime industry—a second group of televisual authors come from the outside. Auteur imports from Hollywood and feature filmmaking typically elicit even more press than the Bochcos and Manns, but usually garner much poorer ratings. Among the great ironies of programming in the past decade has been, first, that television now attracts a wide range of film directors, and second, that most of these directors "fail" when brought on board to produce shows for networks. The list of auteur imports in primetime television since 1980 reads like a who's who list at Cannes: Spike Lee, Francis Ford Coppola, Steven Spielberg, George Lucas, David Lynch, Ridley Scott, Robert DeNiro, Barry Levinson, and Oliver Stone have all "done" TV. If the insider showcase producers are signature banner-carriers who give a network's seasonal offerings personality, then the auteur imports are aesthetic badges and trophies of distinction pure and simple. To the networks, any financial risk that comes with Lucas, Spielberg, and Stone is, apparently, worth it. What the networks get in return is a visionary aura of artistry and aesthetic challenge—an attitude they can toy with, at least until cancelation inevitably comes. Never mind the fact that much of the rest of programming is by comparison authorially mundane. Even if for a fleeting season, this imported class and visionary flash promises to work wonders for network programming—at least when aired and hyped in the right way; as when Levinson's *Homicide* was slated after the Super Bowl telecast or when Oliver Stone's *Wild Palms* barraged the viewer on multiple May sweeps nights in 1993.

1987	1988	1989	1990	1991	1992	1993
						• Wild Palms
			• Cop Rock	• Northern Exposure		• seaQuest dsv
• Max Headroom		•Quantum Leap		• Homefront		• Tribeca
• Beauty and the Beast			• Twin Peaks	• I'll FlyAway	• Picket Fences	
	• China Beach			• Brooklyn Bridge		
		• Midnight Caller		• Seinfeld	• Young Indiana Jones	
	• War and Remembrance		• Camarena		• Hat Squad	• Homicide
	• Lonesome Dove					
• AT&T Spots		• Men	• Herman's Head		• Phillips' Clear Sound spots	
			• The Simpsons			•X-Files
	• Obsession spots		• In Living Color			• Animaniacs
• Tracey Ullman Show		• American Gladiators			•Mighty Morphin Power Rangers	
• Remote Control		• The Julie Brown Show			• P.D.I. Morphing spots	
• Max Headroom			• Hard Copy		• Roundhouse	
• A Current Affair		• Rock-and-Rollergames			• 1992 Olympics	
	• Unsolved Mysteries		• America's Funniest Home Videos			
	• America's Most Wanted				• Honda VR spots	
				• I-Witness Video		
			• Gulf War		• Zoo TV/Fox	
				• L.A. rebellion		• Bradymania

other shows, like *Max Headroom* in 1987, was influential on both ends of the stylistic spectrum: it flaunted the postmodern, dystopic cinematic looks of Ridley Scott's feature *Blade Runner*, but collaged them with endlessly dense videographic and cybernetic configurations, surveillance, etc. Whenever possible, the series listed correspond to the years cited above them in the table, although space limitations mean that these are only approximations. Many of the shows and series laid out on this chart will be discussed in the pages and chapters that follow.

TABLE 2 The Players Primetime Televisuality

I. Showcase producers	II. Mainstream Conversions	III. Auteur-Imports
Marquee signatures	Acquired Mannerisms	Cinematic Spectacle
Network Banner Carriers	Embellished Genres	Visionary Emigres

Bochco, Steven Hill Street Blues, 1981–1987 L.A. Law, 1986–1993 Cop Rock, 1990–1991 NYPD Blue, 1993–	*Bellasario, Donald* Magnum P.I., 1980–1988 Tales of the Gold Monkey, 1982 Airwolf, 1984–1988 Quantum Leap, 1989–1993	*Spielberg, Steven* Amazing Stories, 1985–1987 seaQuest dsv, 1993–1994
Mann, Michael Miami Vice, 1984–1989 Crime Story, 1986–1988 Drug Wars: Camarena Story, 1990	*Cannell, Stephen J.* The A-Team, 1983–1987 Riptide, 1984–1986 Stingray, 1986–1987 Wiseguy, 1987–1990 Silk Stalkings, 1991–	*Coppola, Francis* The Outsiders, 1989–1990 Faerie Tale Theater, 1986 The Conversation, 1995–
English, Diane Murphy Brown, 1988– Double Rush, 1995–	*Spelling, Aaron* Love Boat, 1977–1986 Fantasy Island, 1978–1984 Dynasty, 1981–1989 Hotel, 1983–1988 Twin Peaks, 1990–1991 And the Band Played On, 1994	*Lynch, David* Obsession spots, 1990 Twin Peaks, 1990–1991 American Chronicles, 1990–1991 Hotel Room, HBO, 1993
Letterman, David Late Night With, NBC, 1982–1993 David Letterman Show, 1993–		*Scott, Ridley* Chiat/Day Mac spots, 1984
Kelly, David Picket Fences, 1992– Chicago Hope, 1994–	*Brooks, James L.* Mary Tyler Moore, 1970–1977 Tracey Ullman Show, 1987–1990 The Simpsons, 1990–	*Townsend, Robert* Townsend Television, 1993–1994 Parent 'Hood, 1995– McDonalds Spots, 1995–
Hewrskovitz and Zwick thirtysomething, 1987–1992 My So Called Life, 1994–		*Spheeris, Penelope* Thunder and Mud, 1989 Prison Stories HBO, 1991
Brand and Falsey St. Elsewhere, 1983–1984 Northern Exposure, 1990– I'll Fly Away, 1991–1994		*McBride, Jim* The Wonder Years, 1990
		Lee, Spike MTV Spots, 1986 Saturday Night Live, 1986 Air Jordan/Nike spots, 1990
		Lucas, George The Young Indiana Jones, 1992–1994, 1994–
		DeNiro, Robert Tribeca, 1993
		Zemeckis, Robert Tales from the Crypt, 1992
		Levinson, Barry Homicide, 1993–1995
		Stone, Oliver Wild Palms, 1993

So what, you say, Lynch, Levinson, and Stone were no more than bright but very curious flashes in the programming pan. This kind of import business in itself is no proof that televisuality dominated broadcasting during the 1980s. Yet, the auteurist import business is really just the tip of an iceberg. A third category of television producer-directors shows that authorship and excessive televisual style are linked in lower forms of television as well. The last fifteen years or so have also seen a marked stylistic change in successful but middle-of-the-road primetime producing figures. If stylistic exhibitionism was substantive and pervasive it should have affected these types of figures as well. Consider the marked stylistic differences between early and late works by Stephen J. Cannell, Donald Bellasario, Aaron Spelling, and James L. Brooks. In *Magnum P.I., The A-Team*, and *Love Boat*, Bellasario, Cannell, and Spelling all succeeded by exploiting flesh and chrome rather than a stylized look. Such extra-cinematic objects were typically displayed in front of a neutral camera. The production apparatus was designed to show off and allow physical action and anatomy rather than pictorial or narrative embellishment. Later series by the same producers, however, show something very different. By the end of the decade Bellasario authored the quintessential televisual show *Quantum Leap*; Cannell choreographed *Sting-Ray*, a *Miami-Vice* clone; and Spelling banked on cinematic opulence in *Dynasty*. Other producers, like James L. Brooks—considered a quality producer by industry types and critics alike—actually gained their fame by making shows that were *visually uninteresting*. Brooks's early accomplishment in the rather bland-looking 1970s sitcom *Mary Tyler Moore* seems sedate by comparison to the presentational volatility and niche mentality of his *Tracey Ullman* show at Fox in the late 1980s. Even very competent, but middle-of-the-road producers, then, learned to value and exploit style for its own sake during this period. Who says television can't teach old dogs new tricks?

A third way of delineating the forms and functions of televisuality is to examine them within the framework of genre, since stylistic exhibitionism has not equally influenced all program formats. The extent of the trend can be better understood by comparing genres that favored televisual performance and those that did not. Television's bread-and-butter genres—where stylistic excess is an exception—include daytime talk shows, soap operas, video-origination sitcoms, nonprimetime public affairs shows, some public access cable shows, nonprofit public service announcement spots (PSAS), and late-night off-air lest patterns. While PSAS and infomercials function as cheap but lucrative filler, the sitcom may have resisted televisuality for ideological reasons; that is, because of its inherently conservative cultural function.[27] In an ideological sense the sitcom, in almost every decade, always manages to reconfigure and update the nuclear family. In 1980s shows like *Full House* this meant awkwardly linking multiple parents of the same sex together as surrogate parental figures.[28] With the very myth, viability, and survival of the nuclear family as its chief creative task, primetime sitcoms had little need for the presentational possibilities—and the air of distinction—offered by stylistic exhibitionism. For a number of reasons, then, some genres simply do not care about style.

Many others, however, continue to share a marked penchant for stylistic exhibition. Although I have referred already to prestige film-origination genres—the miniseries, primetime soaps, and quality hour-long dramatic series—many other film-based shows market visual excess in broadcast and cable delivery systems: hyperactive children's television, archival syndicated programs, sitcoms and their parodies on Nickelodeon, feature film presentations on pay-cable channels, and a boundless number of commercial spots shot on film and aired across the channel spectrum. While many televisual program forms survived the industry's economic crash of 1989–1992, several flagship televisual genres from the 1980s—the miniseries, primetime soaps, and primetime dramas—were prematurely, and with some self-serving eulogies, declared dead by industry executives at the start of the 1990s. (The reasons for this eclipse and the ways that televisuality survived in hybrid forms are discussed in the final section of the book.)

Video-origination genres, by contrast, have continued to share a penchant for exhibitionism and include: network television sports shows, cable news, music television, magazine shows, most reality programming, home shopping networks, local commercials for cars and personal injury lawyers, and a veritable ton of interstitial and nonprogram material airing around the clock on almost all non-pay channels. Supermodel Cindy Crawford's videographic showcase, *House of Style* on MTV, provides but one explicit example of the exhibitionism that pervades television outside of primetime. Fashion- or anatomy-conscious thirteen-year-old white suburban girls or boys who watch her show are enticed by a type of performance that differs little from other televisual appeals made during off-primetime programming ghettos. Super-discount, high-volume auto-malls bankroll thirty- and sixty-second spot frenzies on the weekends; while ex-Fox CEO Barry Diller's QVC network teases home-shoppers with graphics-dense consumer bait, When down-home, regionally owned, right-to-work corporations like Wal-Mart produce national ads that look like a cinematographer's showreel, the implications are clear: mass retailing has made televisuality not just a passing production fashion, but a national consumer buying trend.

Modes and Guises

Popular TV critics have been accused by academics of wrongly isolating important and deserving shows out of the continual, redundant, and monotonous broadcast flow.[29] David Marc, for example, has argued against the critical and textual isolation of episodes, because: "The salient impact of television comes not from 'special events,' . . . but from day-to-day exposure. The power of television resides in its normalcy."[30] According to this perspective, individual episodes are rarely memorable, although series and their cosmologies are. Most academic theorists have followed this lead by attempting to elaborate fundamental structural and ideological conditions that comprise television's flow, the super-text, and the audience. I am arguing something very different here: that special television is a concern not just of critics, but of the industry and the audience alike. A great deal of television in the last fifteen years is significant precisely because it self-consciously rejects the monotonous implications of the flow and the conservatism of a slowly changing series cosmology. Whether or not televisual shows actually succeed in providing alternatives to this kind of stasis is not the issue. What is important is that they promote special status and pretend to both difference and change. Apart from a few important scholarly works, the very idea of special television has been undertheorized as an industry strategy and stylistic preoccupation.[31] Special television has historically played an important role in programming, and continues to do so today.

I have already indicated that many forms of televisuality have a difficult time raising their stylistic heads above the broadcast clutter, yet the obsession with distinction and with special status pervades both high and low forms of televisuality. *Whether deserving or not*, production technologies and writer-directors alike now continually angle for attributions of distinction. Many primetime televisual shows, for example, can be viewed as "loss leaders."[32] From this merchandising perspective, it does not totally matter if distinctive televisual shows—like *Homefront, Brooklyn Bridge*, and *Wild Palms*—score low ratings, return poor advertising revenues, and face cancelation. After all, most shows have low ratings and are canceled. The cancelation rate for new series is in fact overwhelmingly high and has been for some time. That is the very nature of television. This condition of turnover, an inherent part of program development, makes the critical emphasis on lauding select survivors a shortsighted fallacy. Since the 1970s, when shows like *All in the Family, Mary Tyler Moore*, and *M.A.S.H.* were designated and artificially isolated as distinctive, critics have ignored the vast majority of shows that come and go. Many shows that disappeared, ironically, made even more earnest formal and narrative claims to distinction than those critically privileged Emmy and ratings winners. Given the fact that most of the shows on television are ultimately ratings losers, which type of series should be deemed more symptomatic of a period, the few with high ratings and prestige, or the greater number with high prestige-claims but predictably low numbers? The ratings dominance in the mid-1980s of the conservatively styled *Cosby Show*, for example, does little to conceal the fact that almost everyone else up and down the ratings ladder was struggling to keep their signature looks above water. Distinction is an obligatory and pervasive programming tactic, not just a retrospective and limited critical atribution.

This kind of perspective—the cultural logic of distinction, of televisual loss leaders and special events—cannot be explained, however, without recognizing the fundamental role that style plays in facilitating distinction. More than just case-by-case formal taxonomies of televisual modes, then, the studies that follow aim to describe the favored guises of televisuality as part of a broader aesthetic economy. Coexistent with American mall culture, stylistic designations foreground television's obsession with merchandising and consumerism. The guises—boutique, loss leader, digital franchising, tabloid, trash, and ontological strip-mall—suggest both the programming logic of televisual forms and the types of presentational appeals and relationships televisual forms establish with viewers. Couching the performance of style in economic terms does more than just remove the discussion from the airless confines of formalism, it also demonstrates the fundamental industrial and cultural import of stylistic representations in television. Although my construal of an aesthetic economy may be open to criticism, the concept does not necessarily constrain or ignore the force of economic and political realities in the world at large. Television is part of the world at large and cannot be viewed apart from business conditions. This framework enables us to see televisuality as the industrial instrument and socially motivated ritual that it is. Unlike the fine arts, television aesthetics have never been locked into an intellectual netherworld of pure discourse.[33]

Those arrays of videographic signals and codes that are used pervasively in mass market television make up what might be called, in another context, its televisual language.[34] This language, furthermore, has emerged as part of a broader ideology of stylistic excess, one that pervades contemporary American television and mass culture alike.[35] Yet it is important to note from the start that even in the mass-produced industrial West, there is surely no singular ideology at work in mass culture.[36] For this reason, any paradigms that I refer to must be seen as part of a broader bundle of privileged views, some of which contradict each other. Paradigms can *compete, contradict*, and *coexist*.[37] Also, by "emergence," I hope to suggest that ideology, here taken to include even the way we think about art and imagery, involves an *uneven development*. Mythologizing takes place over time and so is inevitably partial or irregular in its presence.[38] A gloss of Thomas Kuhn's "paradigm shifts" in the history of science might suggest that revolutions in worldviews are drastic, comprehensive, and complete.[39] Last epoch's paradigms are, as it were, cleanly banished by new worldviews to the outdated ash heap of history. But this oversimplification of Kuhn in no way describes cultural change in the late twentieth century. Because there is no cultural pope to centrally organize and determine aesthetic culture, today's mass-media Copernicus must instead ply his or her paradigmatic wares on an open market—on a multinational electronic bazaar, only loosely regulated by the Federal Communications Commission (FCC).

For these reasons competing ideologies continue to coexist in broadcast and cable television. The visually and cinematically sophisticated *thirtysomething*, for example, was merchandized in book form even after its cancelation—a unique compendium of great and "sensitive" writing—as a way of "reliving moments with our favorite family."[40] Other shows, like Rush Limbaugh's syndicated right-wing shock-talk show, still invoke and use reductive studio production modes more typical of the 1970s than the 1980s. The question of which aesthetic paradigm governs television, in fact, depends as much on who you ask as on anything else. Robert S. Alley and Horace Newcomb, for example, claim that television is a "producer's medium"—but do so only after interviewing numerous television producers.[41] Jack Kuney argues that television is a director's medium—that the director "sets both the tone of the program and determines a show's impact on its audience"—after interviewing numerous television directors.[42] Whose medium do you think television would be if, instead, one interviewed editors, lighting designers, art directors or camera people; that is, any one of the hundreds of other people involved in primetime program production? The tension between aesthetic paradigms is not, then, limited to academic debates. Such conflict is an inevitable part of the television industry, as any one who has left a production "due to creative differences" can tell you. Given this context, then, the occasional presence of low-resolution or amorphous imagery within the present broadcast or cable spectrum does not disprove that a new aesthetic sensibility has emerged.[43] The trends and practices that I am theorizing are part of a *trajectory* of influences; notions that are bought and sold, aired and syndicated, cloned and spun-off. Even the ways that style is performed changes from season to season. Yet the widespread sensibility and urge to aestheticize and stylize suggests that televisuality is more than a passing fashion.

Nagging Theoretical Suspicions

Because so many recent trends in critical theory set themselves up in stark opposition to the aesthetic, the project outlined here may seem on shaky ground at best. John Fiske defines cultural studies, for instance, as a "political" framework in polar opposition to a study of culture's "aesthetic" products.[44] Why erase the aesthetic, in this way, as a theoretical and analytical category? What can be gained by this analytical retreat? Several important tactical assumptions, championed in high theory, work to hobble effective analyses of televisual style. Before examining, at the conclusion of this book, how a number of fundamental and strategic intellectual commitments have worked to conspiratorialize the image, it is important to consider how several more tactical schools in contemporary theory have impacted televisual analysis. Less antagonists of the image than heuristic complications, postmodernism, "deindustrialized" cultural studies, "glance theory," and the "ideology of liveness" myth all merit reexamination in light of television's penchant for exhibitionism.

Postmodernism. Given the traits of televisuality that I've already sketched out, one might ask, "Why not simply go to the postmodern theory as a basis for interpretation?" After all, the disembodied signifiers and textual extravagance that I describe here are central components in the postmodernist paradigm as well. This may be so. But stated simply, apart from textual description, postmodernism has little to offer broader explanations of American television. This is not because postmodern theory is wrong, only because the theory cannot be used easily to distinguish between what is postmodern and what is not postmodern in American television. Any systematic look at the history of television soon shows that all of those formal and narrative traits once thought to be unique and defining properties of postmodernism—intertextuality, pastiche, multiple and collaged presentational forms—have also been defining properties of television from its inception. Television history, unlike Hollywood film history, cannot be as neatly periodized into sequential stylistic categories: primitive, classical, baroque, modern, and postmodern. The hip gratifications that result from discovering loaded intertexts in *The Simpsons*, for example, are not necessarily unique to television in the 1990s, and tend to overshadow the fact that intertextuality was a central component in television from the start. Comedy-variety shows in the late 1940s and early 1950s—and not just Ernie Kovacs—repeatedly parodied and pastiched cultural conventions. Many other shows on both the local and national level combined intertextual fragments taken from various traditions—newsfilm, vaudeville, photography, radio comedy and drama—into single thirty- and sixty-minute program blocks. From a postmodernist point-of-view, 1940s and 1950s television had it all: self-reflexivity in *Burns and Allen*, intertextuality in *Texaco Star Theater*, direct address in *The Continental*, pastiche in *Your Show of Shows*; and social topicality—modernism's nemesis—in *I Love Lucy* and *The Loretta Young Show* (both made allusions to the Korean War for example).[45] Unlike classical Hollywood cinema, television had no centered gaze from the very start, and seldom had any seamless or overarching narrative. Multiple narrational modes issued from the same works, and audiences were constantly made aware of television's artifice and embellishment. In these ways, then, television has always been postmodern. Television has always been *textually messy*—that is, textural rather than transparent.

Consider, for example, two recent cable programs that gained critical notoriety in 1993: *Mystery Science Theater 3000* on Comedy Central and *Beavis and Butt-head* on MTV. Both bear all of the celebrated hallmarks of postmodernism and both utilize the same basic structuring motif: the series' "stars" sit and watch the same thing the audience watches, but make off-handed, on-camera comments that are either ironic, banal, hip, sexually loaded, or simply gross. Although *Beavis and Butt-head* is intended for a teen and preteen crowd that can appreciate a world numbed by too much glue-sniffing and *Mystery Science Theater 3000* is intended for jaded yuppies, both make an on-screen mockery of "found footage": *Mystery Science* deconstructs old low-budget trash and horror films; *Beavis and Butt-head* deconstructs heavy metal, music videos, and phantom video artifacts. Both are hip, ironic, and somewhat smart as well. Distinctively postmodern? Well, not quite. In the late 1940s Dumont Network's *Window on the World* used the same device. Dumont's host takes a breather from the show's on-stage action to mock and free-associate about bizarre turn-of-the-century archival footage unspooling in the studio's film chain. As beauty contestants in Atlantic City parade before the viewer, the announcer ironically mocks both their bizarre bodies and their ridiculous fashions. Like *Mystery* and *Beavis*, there is no laugh track. Like *Mystery* and *Beavis*, *Window* ironically deconstructs the newsreel for a knowing and hip *1949* audience. Like the audience for *The Simpsons* and for *Beavis and Butt-head*, Dumont is playing its intertexts for those "in the know." Television has either always been postmodern, or its postmodern tactics are a part of a much different and less celebrated dynamic.

Apart from its descriptive capabilities however, postmodernism also speculates on the big picture behind such devices and attitudes. Fredric Jameson sees in such tactics late capitalism's logic and obsessive reenforcement of consumption. Jean Baudrillard is more fatalistic, and depoliticizes the universe even as he hallucinates about global spectacle. Jean-François Lyotard finds in postmodern practices evidence of the disappearance of distinctions between subject and object. But how do these explanations account for industrial and historical changes in American television? The descriptive tools of postmodern theory are powerful, but the theoretical grounding is frequently tautological. That is, once an account has committed itself to Jameson, Baudrillard, or Lyolard's logic, it tends to end up back at that logic even after exhaustive analysis. Postmodern theory can tell cultural analysis little more than the theory has already confessed to up front. Postmodern theory determines analysis, determines theory, determines analysis in an endless loop. I hope, in some small way not to prejudge this period in American television history by imposing tautological postmodern explanations. Such haste not only depreciates history, it also requires an analytical act of faith.

Deindustrialized cultural studies. Because of its underlying interest in popular culture and audience, this book shares in many of the tenets and objectives of cultural studies. Yet cultural studies, at least as it is sometimes marketed in academia and when it focuses on media, tends to gloss over one of the most important components of televisuality—the industry. This evasion is ironic given cultural studies current fascination with "technologies"—of gender, of cybernetics, of surveillance, of the body, of medical discourses. Even as television studies disappear into cultural studies, the field tends to ignore the extensive technological base of the subject itself: TV technology. It is perhaps easier to traverse multiple pop culture fields, than to account for workhorse technologies that comprise the dominant institution through which mainstream America consumes culture. The television industry may not be as flashy as VR and cyberpunk (tell that to Cindy Crawford, Billy Idol, and the folks over at *Liquid Television*), but it is, depending on one's perspective, surely no less problematic or ideologically complex.

As the academic turf called culture is taken on by humanities and arts colleges, media theorists now range freely and easily over the discursive and problematic turf once owned by sociologists, anthropologists, and political scientists. This recent and important intellectual overhaul, the leap to the culturally macroscopic as an antidole to disciplinary Balkanization, risks ignoring the need for more preliminary and extensive groundwork studies on questions of cultural and institutional *stylistics*. Even the development of a stylistic poetics of television is an important project.[46] It has become an academic fashion in recent years for intellectuals to go native, and so wed high critical theory with thoroughly vernacular forms from low culture. Recent anthologies suggest an institutional desire for validation at the hands of the everyday and the banal.[47] I am less interested in wielding the weapons of high theory to stake intellectual claim to the lowly than in explicating and questioning the ways that low culture itself performs and theorizes. All programming forms are complicated and mediated by style and technology even though "scientific" approaches, and many cultural studies approaches, tend to avoid or downplay this fact.[48] My call here, then, is not simply "back to the text," but back to the "televisual apparatus."[49] For after recognizing and accounting for the centrality and complexities of style, it is important to move beyond mere formal taxonomies. Describing how televisual technologies allow for, but also cut off and delimit, engagement with viewers, is surely an important concern for critical and cultural studies alike.

Glance theory: the myth of distraction. Glance theory, perhaps more than any other academic model, sidetracked television studies from a fuller understanding of the extreme stylization emergent in television in the 1980s. The myth's most cherished assumption? That television viewers are, by nature distracted and inattentive. Although its roots lie in the earlier work of Marshall McLuhan and Raymond Williams, John Ellis was the most forceful proponent of this definitive view. He argued that TV viewers not only lacked "intensity," but that they also gave up looking at all, by "delegating" their sight to the TV set.[50] This view—what I would call a "surrendered gaze theory"—while very influential, could not be a less accurate or useful description of emergent televisuality. Variations of the glance theory are however, commonplace: "We turn on the set casually; we rarely attend to it with full concentration. It is generally permissible to talk or to carry out other activities in its presence . . . (activities that) preclude absorption."[51] Ellis's position is an elaboration of Williams's earlier concept of the television "flow."[52] Within Williams's elaboration of the flow and McLuhan's rich speculations on media are keys to glance theory's flaws: *The mode of the TV image has nothing in common with film* or photo."[53]

This extreme dualism between film and television—this mythology of "essential media differences" espoused by McLuhan—forms the categorical basis for many future speculations on television, including the glance theory. Once one assumes that there are innate experiential differences between the two media, then critical theorists are merely left to explain, post facto, the cultural and political reasons for those differences. Strangely enough however, Ellis and Williams deduced from this premise conclusions that were diametrically opposed to those of McLuhan. Whereas McLuhan argued that the low-resolution phenomenon fostered a highly active viewer response, one necessitated by the need to give conceptual closure to video's mosaiclike imagery, Ellis and Williams deduce just the opposite.[54] For them, the mosaiclike crudeness fosters inattentiveness and distraction, an inherent phenomenon that programmers try to overcome with the flow. Most contemporary critical works on television have followed the rationalizations of the later Williams-Ellis model of glance theory as an ideology, rather than the phenomenologically based and ostensibly naive futurism of McLuhan.[55] Ironically, the very same dualism—of essential media differences—gave one tradition an *active* viewer, and the other a viewer that *acquiesced*.

This distracted surrender gaze theory seems so far from an accurate portrayal of contemporary television consumption that one wonders whether glance theorists base their explanations of TV only on primitive shows produced in the early, formative years of the medium. When Ellis describes the "ignorance" and inability of TV viewers to know about the obscure and "inconsequential details" of television personalities, he seems to have mistaken TV viewers for what he describes as entranced and uniquely committed "cinephiles." Any cursory survey of the massive popular literature on television—including *Soap Opera Digest, TV Guide, People Magazine*, and others—will show a *extreme consciousness* by viewers of personality, marketing, and star promotion. Such literature also replicates on a mass scale a great amount of narrative detail in television, by summarizing a wide range of plot and character details in soaps and other genres.[56] The videophile—an impossibility according to Ellis—by the 1990s is actually a very informed and motivated viewer.[57] Contrary to glance theory, the committed TV viewer is overtly addressed and "asked to start watching" important televised events. The morasslike flow of television may be more difficult for the TV viewer to wade through than film, but television rewards discrimination, style consciousness, and viewer loyalty in ways that counteract the clutter. Whereas viewership for film is a one-shot experience that comes and goes, spectatorship in television can be quite intense and ingrained over time. Any definition of television based on the viewer's "fundamental inattentiveness" is shortsighted.[58]

The credence given glance theory in subsequent applications was due as much to television's inherent domestic context as to anything else. The notion of inattentiveness fit well the new emphasis on the home and on the "social use" and "object use" of the television set itself—an object that had to compete with other pieces of furniture "in a lighted room."[59] Again, the chief principles of glance theory are invoked: a distracted viewing context, a weak display, and a *very* unmotivated viewer.[60] Although some critics questioned the characterization of television's "regime of vision" as one where the viewer "lacks concentration," others extended the distraction model by shifting and overemphasizing the use of television sound rather than sight.[61] Even recent updates of the glance theory are based on the very problematic notion that television viewers are not actually *viewing* television but that the television is in the background while viewers are actually doing something else.[62] In an otherwise insightful analysis of video replay and video rental movies, one recent theorist attacks theory's aversion to low-culture viewing pleasures, while at the same time, continuing the orthodoxy that "there is a specific way" that television is watched. But if this particular TV viewer is *actually doing something else*, as the author says—while television is merely issuing-forth in the background—why extrapolate that this preoccupation with something else is symptomatic of the way television is *always* watched? Why not use an engaged and entranced viewer as the example upon which to build a theory of viewership?

Once the phenomenological basis for glance theory was academically sanctioned, however, more complicated ideological and psychoanalytic explanations were rushed to the fore. Since cinema spectatorship was commonly construed as psychologically regressive and hallucinatory—as a "totalizing, womblike, dreamstate"—television, forever cinema's antithesis, was couched as just the opposite.[63] Following Freud, Jacques Lacan, and Christian Metz, film's viewing hallucination, like the dream, was described as an "artificially psycho(tic)" state that focused on the *pleasure of the Image*.[64] Television's "more casual" forms of looking, by contrast, "substituted liveness and directness for the dream-state, immediacy and presentness for regression."[65] Because repeated television viewing presupposes *some kind* of pleasure however, psychoanalytic theorists sought the source of this pleasure and unity in places *other* than cinema's womblike state. From this point of view, television viewers, despite distractions and interruptions, achieve "an exhilarating sense" of power when they range across and "control" a wide variety of flow material. The ability to choose visually rather than to hallucinate visually is seen as a key to the pleasures of televisual distraction.

The fact that *some* TV viewers *are* deeply engaged in specific programs—and do find *pleasure* in entranced isolation while watching a show, star, or favorite performer—puts the validity of the psychoanalytic account into question. Since the conditions presupposed by the psychoanalytic glance theory are neither necessary or sufficient prerequisites for viewing, the applicability of the theory is severely compromised. Further problematizing psychologistic extensions of the glance are attempts to solidify the gaze versus glance, film versus video dichotomies into a model that explains male versus female gendering. It has become popular to see televisual distraction as a feminizing process and to extrapolate to polar conclusions that cast cinematic spectatorship as male and televisual spectatorship as female. The centrality of the housewife in the early decades of television does lend credence to this theory. There are, however, many pervasive and hyperactive forms of televisuality that can in no way be construed as feminine.[66] In fact, a number of hypermasculinist televisual tendencies have been an important part of television from the start.

Four correctives then, are in order: first, the viewer is not always, nor inherently, distracted. Second, if theorists would consider the similarities between television and film—rather than base universalizing assumptions on their "inevitable" differences—glance and surrender theories would fall from their privileged theoretical pedestals. Third, psychoanalytic and feminizing extensions of glance theory tend to put critical analysis into essential and rigidly gendered straitjackets. Fourth, and finally, even if viewers are inattentive, television works hard visually, not just through aural appeals, to attract the attention of the audience; after all, it is still very much in television's best narrative and economic interests to engage the viewer. Theorists should not jump to theoretical conclusions just because there is an ironing board in the room.

The ideology of liveness myth. Any effective analysis of televisual style must also shake itself of one other theoretical obsession: liveness. In recent American television, liveness is frequently packaged as an artifact. As often as not, pictorialism rather than realism, rules the context in which liveness is flaunted and seen. This practice of live embellishment flies in the face of some of the most cherished mythologies of television, ones that presuppose immediacy and nowness as the basis for television. Whereas glance theory focuses specifically on the nature of reception, the liveness mythology implicates production and cultural issues as well. The notion surely has its origins in the history of television production. In the pre-tape 1950s, television *was* live and broadcasters celebrated this distinctive fact. Yet, definitions of television and liveness emerged in phenomenological studies in the 1960s, in prescriptive aesthetics and manifestos in the 1970s, and in sophisticated poststructuralist analyses of the 1980s. Never mind that the technical medium itself has changed dramatically, and that it has done so several times. In high theory, the liveness paradigm simply will not die.

Although hardly ever cited by critical theorists, McLuhan laid the foundation for the academic myth of liveness, when he defined the medium as an "all-at-onceness" created by global television's erasure of time and space.[67] Other theorists expanded on the notion of television's innate liveness and nowness by examining the medium's broader appetite for currency and presentness even in non-live genres. Peter Wood argued from psychoanalysis that television's similarity to dreams caused it to evoke a "great wealth of familiar and often current material stored in the viewer's mind."[68] Horace Newcomb proposed a television aesthetic that was based in part on a commitment to the present, although he used the designation "history" to describe this form of currency. Newcomb alluded to the power of the present in television by arguing that "the television formula requires that we use our contemporary historical concerns as subject matter."[69] That is, sitcoms and historical programs alike elaborate contemporary cultural issues and current events. Within this tradition, then, everything in programming, *fiction as well as news and live coverage*, is a cultural and psychological operation defined by the present. Presentness and the past are inextricably related.

The myth of nowness also fed back into alternative production practice starting in the late 1960s. Video artists and electronic politicos alike embraced the liveness myth as a key to radical video production. Techno apologists argued that the instantaneous electronic medium altered "habitual ways of seeing" and transformed human experience. The technology-determined revolution was at hand.[70] Artists found in the "real-time" experience of live video, a fundamental force that could alter both personal experience and social practice.[71] Temporality was construed as magic; simultaneity as shamanism; and video art as altered consciousness. Video installations, environments, and small format tapes were designed and hyped around the concept.[72] Poet and modernist aesthetician David Antin, in a prescriptive treatise for media art, pursued what he termed the "*distinctive* features of the medium." Like Harold Rosenberg's advocacy of abstract expressionism before him (arguments that reduced painting to existential action), and Clement Greenberg's rationales for minimalism (ideas that reduced visual art to flatness and reflexivity), Antin attempted to reduce the phenomenon of television to its essence and its industrial obligation. Antin described video's fundamental and defining components as time and immediacy.[73] Postformalist critics and theorists like Rosalind Krauss later used simultaneity and liveness to demonstrate the centrality of psychosexual narcissism in the work of important video artists.[74] Works by Vito Acconci, Elizabeth Holt, and others exploited the medium's liveness through feedback loops and lengthy and indulgent performances, all as ways of exposing the human subject's "unchanging condition of perpetual frustration."[75] In an art world disciplined by rituals of specificity, video's immediacy myth was the perfect weapon for critical exclusion.

Even outside the limited institutions of video art, criticism, and theory, however, the liveness myth was snowballing. Basic production texts praised television's unique ontological burden for "realism and *authenticity*."[76] Others contrasted the event-bound time of television to the innately sequential and objective time of film. Television's "most distinctive function [is] the live transmission of events. . . . The now of the television event is equal to the now of the actual event."[77] Mimicking the rhetoric of network television, then, production theorists argued that good television exploits the sense of nowness, since it is inextricably linked to an external event. Liveness, then, came to have completely different ideological effects, depending on the theorist who invoked it. For prescriptive modernist critics and video visionaries, on the one hand, liveness was a key to disruptive and *radical* artistic practice. Conventional production people like Alan Wurtzel and Herbert Zettl, on the other hand, argued that liveness was a fundamental quality of any good *mainstream* production work. The myth still held center stage, although the political implications of liveness clearly remained in the eye of the beholder.

During the 1980s television theorists who immigrated from film studies—a field that had spent nearly two decades deconstructing the ontology and ideology of realism—provided convincing explanations for the popularity of a related concept in television: the liveness ideology.[78] That is, liveness was seen to cover over the excessive heterogeneity and confusion of the broadcast flow by giving the medium a sense of abiding presentness.[79] Unlike many earlier critical theories, this view correctly noted that liveness in television is neither neutral, simple, nor unproblematic.[80] Other examinations also exposed liveness as a construction, but were even more explicit in *overstating the notion that liveness "pervades every moment of broadcast."*[81] As long as high theory continues to overestimate the centrality of liveness in television—even as it critiques liveness—it will also underestimate or ignore other modes of practice and production: the performance of the visual and stylistic exhibitionism.

More recent studies suggest that the industry has deontologized its own focus. Television now defines itself less by its inherent temporality and presentness than by pleasure, style, and commodity. Todd Gitlin's anthology of television criticism shows a renewed interest in "a common attention to the implications of form and style."[82] His own analysis is a highly visual account of the mood and tone of imagery and style in high-tech car commercials and the blank sleekness of *Miami Vice.*[83] David Marc takes as his analytical object a genre in television historically related to, and defined by, liveness. The comedy-variety show is linked to stand-up comedy and other overtly presentational forms of comedy that unfold in real-time. Presentational comedy, then, involves the traits one associates with liveness: improvisation, snafus, and spontaneity. Marc, however, describes the genre not around the notion of liveness, but as a spectacle of excess, a "framed" artform that "accepts the badge of artifice."[84] Margaret Morse's recent work analyzes television within an American culture that invests heavily in rituals of distraction.[85] Television is linked to the ontology of the freeway, the shopping mall, and theme parks. These three recent approaches. Gillin's *iconographic* view of television, Marc's explication of *artifice* in liveness, and Morse's *architectonic* analysis and critique, are all indicators of the importance *style and materiality, rather than temporality*, have come to play in contemporary television.

Yet, the ideology of liveness myth lives on, even if in modified form. A sophisticated analysis of catastrophe programming on television describes the ideology of time, and the sense of continuity that drives it on, as both a target and victim of broadcast catastrophes.[86] Liveness, at least when linked to death and disaster, is textually disruptive but ultimately pleasurable since its coverage works to assure domestic viewers that the catastrophe is not happening to them.[87] Television is again defined, even in this catastrophe theory, by its temporality and not by its image.[88] Yet, if catastrophic liveness *is* marginal and disruptive, then it is also an exception that proves the rule; it is an exception that indicates the dominance on a day-to-day basis of more conventional image and sound pleasures. If traumatic liveness induces extreme anxiety in the viewer, then hypostatized time and massive regularity comfort the viewer by providing a rich but contained televisual spectacle, an endless play of image and sound. The degree to which liveness and simultaneity still govern even recent theorizations is suggested by catastrophe theory's account of the new telecommunications technology: "The more rapid internationalization of television via the *immediacy* of satellites . . . replicates the *emphasis on transmission.*[89] Such an account suggests that liveness and immediacy will be even more important in global television than they are today.

This view ignores the fact that even satellite system broadcasts in Asia and Africa today seldom emphasize either immediacy or liveness. Star Network out of Hong Kong, for example, has become a quintessential packager of aged entertainment products—music videos, dramas, reruns—rather than a conduit for liveness, immediacy, or catastrophe. Very little, in fact, looks live or transmitted in international broadcasting. Even the domestic broadcasting of live and unscripted media events— like ABC's *Monday Night Football*, or major league baseball—are comprehensively planned, scripted, and rehearsed; are in fact highly regulated and rigidly controlled performances, fabricated to fit a restricted block of viewing time.[90] Now, as in McLuhan's 1960s, the resilience of the liveness myth still has as much to do with a vague notion (and hope?) of technological determinism as it does with anything else. As long as theorists look to the new technologies of television to prove the centrality of presence, simultaneity, nowness, or transmission, they perpetuate one of broadcasting's most self-serving and historical mythologies. Television has always boasted liveness as its claim to fame and mark of distinction, even though the programming that floods from its channels seldom supports this air of distinction and pretense of liveness.

In the spring of 1993, Mike Myers and Dana Carvey, stars of the recent hit film *Wayne's World*, hosted *Short Attention-Span Theater* on Comedy Central.[91] In the new world of cable, apparently, even *Saturday Night Live* alums could parody television's glance theory. Yet the trades discussed their appearance not as an indication of television's inherent distraction, but as just the opposite: the episode aimed to break the limitations of niche advertising by attracting a different audience. Niche economics on cable, after all, preclude the kind of inattentiveness that theorists celebrate as one of television's defining qualities.

Television and its performers have been no less conscious of the *stylistic* possibilities of liveness. David Koresh, founder of the Branch Davidian sect, proved that he understood the quintessential nature of televisual production when he forewarned: "The riots in Los Angeles would pale in comparison to what was going to happen in Waco. Texas."[92] Unlike his apocalyptic predecessor Jim Jones in Guyana—who suicidally fled to the afterlife rather than face NBC's approaching electronic news gathering (ENG) cameras—Koresh betrayed neither ontological subtlety nor televisual stage fright. The fires that raged when Los Angeles burned in 1992 provided not a sense of simultaneity or realism, but rather a powerful and codified template for stylized and horrific spectacle. The alienated televisuality of the L.A. rebellion could be appropriated and choreographed for the benefit of the mass audience, even by those in other places and with very different apocalyptic ends. Unfortunately for David Koresh and his followers, the ATF assault troops in Waco proved that the televisual spectacle, once unleashed, had an unforgiving mind of its own.

Notes

1. Quoted in Laurence Jarvik and Nancy Strickland, "Cinema Very TV" *California* (July 1989), 198.

2. Quoted in Christina Bunish, "The Search for Realism: Directors David Steinberg, Ron Dexter and Bob Eggers Face the Challenges of Capturing Reality," *Film and Video* (September 1990), 66.

3. Jeff Kaye, "Sex, Mud and Rock and Roll," *Los Angeles Times,* November 9, 1989, F1.

4. Kedvin Cosgrove, "Regis' Recipe for a Healthy Life," *TV Guide,* March 6, 1993, 8–11.

5. I choose the term "mass-market" television rather than the more traditional concept of "network" television, since broadcasting had clearly been overhauled and pluralized by 1990. "Mass-market" expresses a kind of programming and economic scale that is not limited to a few privileged broadcast corporations, but rather encompasses other institutions that work over national media markets with high-production value programming. This term, then, would include Fox (the fourth network), superstations, large-scale syndication companies, CNN, MTV, and other media corporations that produce and program on a national level.

6. Retheorization refers to how changes in practice and production discourse evidence shifts in working assumptions and orienting perspectives, not to the intentional and conscious formulation of theoretical premises and principles as ends in themselves.

7. Performative aspects of media have traditionally been associated with dramatic and theatrical elements, whereas style is typically postured as a static and fixed formal property owned by works of art. Here, with the concept "performance of style," I hope to indicate a shift away from an assumption of style as static property toward style as a hyperactive presentational process.

8. "Individuation" is a popular psychological term referring to a person's development of distinct ego boundaries and distinguishable personal behaviors. Stylistic individuation could, however, be as easily described in economic terms as a kind of product differentiation. Looking at the overt discourse of practitioners in the media industry suggests, however, the importance and degree of investment given to construing creative personas behind program looks and production accomplishments. The psychologizing of the media discourse by practitioners should not be taken as a refutation of broader economic interests, however, for the two strata are probably intricately tied to each other.

9. Still one of the most engaging and detailed accounts of the golden age of live anthology drama in the 1950s is Eric Barnouw's *Tube of Plenty: The Evolution of American Television* (New

York: Oxford University Press, 1975, 1992), a book that isolates skilled and serious artists at the center of broadcasting's live and dramatic showcases during that period.

10. The extent to which this type of production practice challenges privileged academic theories—like postmodernism and cultural studies—is discussed more fully at the end of the this introduction, and in the chapters that follow.

11. John Dempsey, "More Mags Will Fly in the Fall: Too Much of a Good Thing?" *Variety,* April 12, 1989, reprinted in Marilyn Matelski and David Thomas, *Variety: Broadcast-Video Sourcebook I* (Boston, Focal Press, 1990), 27. *Entertainment Tonight* is produced by Paramount Television; *A Current Affair* is a production of 20th Century Fox Television; and *Inside Edition* is produced and syndicated by King World.

12. Jim Van Messel, executive producer, *Entertainment Tonight* as quoted in Mike Freeman, "*Entertainment Tonight* Turns 3,000," *Broadcasting and Cable,* May 8, 1993, 30.

13. Said the critics: "What they've done is close to a miracle. They were dead and found the fountain of youth." TV Critic Tom Jicha, quoted in Harry A. Jessell, "New Wave Newscasts, Anchor WSVN Makeover: Ex-Affiliate Finds a New Niche," *Broadcasting,* October 12, 1992, 24.

14. Joel Cheatwood, vice-president of news, and Bob Leider, executive vice-president, WSVN-TV, quoted in ibid.

15. Bruce Sandzimier, vice-president of editorial, Universal Television. Katherine Stalter, "Working in the New Post Environment," *Film and Video* (April 1993), 100.

16. "Help Wanted, Program Production and Others," *Broadcasting,* November 30, 1992, 57. In mundane station management activities like hiring, WRAL-TV5 in North Carolina, in personnel upgrades, now expected its graphic designers to have visual arts design degrees and to be proficient in Paintbox, animation, and still-store technologies. Even verbal- and text-oriented broadcast positions, like that of the news promotion producer at WRAL, were advertised and keyed to essential visual communications skills.

17. David Poltrack, CBS's senior vice-president of planning and research. Richard Zoglin, "The Big Boy's Blues," *Time,* October 17, 1988, 59.

18. This diversification trend mirrors, of course, developments over the last century in advertising.

19. These examples are described in Jeffrey Wells, "Is It the Reel Thing: Big Name Directors Try to Bring Film Magic to Coke Ads," *Los Angeles Times,* February 17, 1993, F1, F6.

20. Ibid., F7.

21. See discussion in chapter 10 of this book, "Televisual Economy," of the changes in business structure that CAA's appearance as a major agency player in 1993 caused.

22. *Variety,* September 30, 1987. *Variety,* September 13, 1989, reprinted in Matelski and Thomas, 73.

23. By 1994 the network's growth was predicted "to cost ABC at least $75 million per year in lost revenue." Tom Wolzien, as quoted in Geoffrey Foisie, "Fox Hounds ABC-TV, *Broadcasting and Cable,* June 14, 1993, 65.

24. "The real killer" of *Wonder Years* "was economics not prudishness." Coupled with escalating cast salaries, "the budget soared to $1.2 million per half-hour episode. Many hour-long dramas are shot for less." Steve Weinstein, "Reeling in the Bittersweet 'Wonder Years'," Los Angeles Times, May 12, 1993, F1, F6.

25. "Zapped: The Networks Under Attack," Time, October 17, 1988, 56–61.

26. *Broadcasting,* July 4, 1989. Cited also in J. Fred MacDonald, *One Nation Under Television* (New York: Pantheon, 1990), 253.

27. Two recent books underscore the recurrent academic view that the sitcom works to reinforce status quo values. Ella Taylor, *Primetime Families* (Berkeley: University of California Press, 1980), demonstrates the resilience of the myth of the nuclear family on network television up to its conservative reconstitution in 1980s sitcoms. Darrel Hamamoto, *Nervous Laughter:*

Television Situation Comedy and Liberal Democratic Ideology (New York: Praeger Publishers, 1990), makes a compelling case that the sitcom—even in its liberal manifestations—has systematically worked to elide racial and ethnic issues and threats to the mainstream, white, status quo.

28. *Full House* (ABC, 1987–1993).

29. Raymond Williams, *Television, Technology, and Cultural Form* (New York: Schocken, 1975).

30. David Marc, *Demographic Vistas: Television in American Culture* (Philadelphia: University of Pennsylvania Press, 1983), 5.

31. These exceptions include, of course, Jane Feuer et al. *MTM: Quality Television* (London: British Film Institute, 1985), and Horace Newcomb and Robert S. Alley, *The Producer's Medium* (New York: Oxford University Press, 1983).

32. The mercantile analogy of the "loss leader" is applied in the analysis of epic forms of televisuality, like the miniseries, in chapter 6.

33. This criticism holds true for fine art up to and including the period of high modernism. Although the intellectual-theoretical crutch that I speak of has always been more important to the art world than to Hollywood, various conceptual, video, and performance artists since 1968 have attempted to break through the art world's ideological props by engaging and critiquing the institution's support systems and economic industry.

34. If one were to view the research of this book within the tradition of film theory, the idea of a media-specific "language" certainly has ample precedent. Here, however—in a project that seeks to explicate the nature of *nonverbal* semiosis in television—the linguistic term creates problems of its own for analysis. Given my focus then, the analysis that follows will target: (1) visual modes of presentation distinctive to television; (2) aesthetic modes that are borrowed and redefined by television; and (3) cultural practices that impinge upon and inform these modes. The presentational modes that I refer to are generally and predominantly nonverbal and differ from orthodox film language. Media language models tend to focus on and privilege editing, narrative structure, and syntax. Televisuality, by contrast, privileges images—with *simultaneous* components typically displayed within a shared frame. In general, the televisual modes that I am theorizing represent a divergence from classical narrative cinema and television.

35. Having summarized my project in this way, a few additional words about terminology and definitions are in order. In television programming's shift toward visuality—both as a formal trait and as program content—stylistic signifiers are regularly stripped from their traditional signifieds and made open to continual redefinition and reuse. Given the centrality of what postmodernism terms disembodied signifiers, however, televisuality can also be profitably seen as an *industrial process* of assigning and bestowing value, not just as a look. But televisuality should be seen as more than just an industrial shift to, and preoccupation with, visual imagery. In a less macroscopic but no less important sense, televisuality also refers to that trait now common in television whereby programs intentionally engage the viewer with *multiple* and *simultaneous* layers of perceptual and discursive information, many times overwhelming him or her by combining visual, spatial, gestural, and iconic signals. Televisuality is, in this sense, a phenomenon of communicative and *semiotic overabundance*. Although isolated examples of the phenomenon existed in earlier periods in television history, and frequented feature film history, television popularized and cashed-in on this semiotic process and display of overabundance in the 1980s. Finally, televisuality implicates more than just industrial and aesthetic issues, and the final chapters will attempt to address the trend's historical and ideological significance.

36. I am utilizing "ideology" in the way that E. Ann Kaplan defines the Althusserian variant of the term. in *Rocking Around the Clock* (New York: Methuen, 1987), 188, she describes ideology as a "series of representations and images, reflecting conceptions of "reality" that any society assumes. Ideology thus no longer refers to beliefs people consciously hold but to myths that a

society lives by, as if these myths referred to some natural, unproblematic reality." In this sense image and style-practice can be seen as part of any ideology and cultural mythology.

37. One key to understanding the ideology of style can be found in the contradictory and competing aspects at work within an emerging paradigm or myth. Structural anthropology has taken the narrative process (by which contradictions are covered over and resolved) to be a key to a culture's mythology. See Claude Lévi-Strauss, "The Structural Study of Myth," *Structural Anthropology,* trans. Claire Jacobson and Brooke Grundfest Schoepf (New York: Basic Books, 1963), 206–231. Mimi White in her essay "Ideological Analysis and Television," *Channels of Discourse*, ed. Robert Allen (Chapel Hill: University of North Carolina Press, 1987), 134–171, has argued that it is precisely television's textual contradictions that expose the workings of ideology.

38. In describing the emergence of visuality as "uneven, partial, and irregular," I do not aim to lessen its importance as a distinct and identifiable phenomena. Rather, I hope to show its presence and power as an historical phenomenon—in the same way that Nick Browne's analysis of post–May 1968 French film theory demonstrated that "history assumes the aspect of an ensemble of unevenly developed, stratified and shifting relations enacted in a new social setting. Old connections are broken and displaced; new structures and commitments are in the process of emerging. The sense of uneven, fragmented movement of diverse but associated themes makes the ensemble of these texts an unfinished work site." Nick Browne, ed., *Cahiers du Cinéma: 1969–1972, The Politics of Representation* (Cambridge: Harvard University Press, 1990), 1. I will argue that the same scale of contentious shifting has occurred in recent television, but for very different reasons.

39. I hope when analyzing media to synthesize Kuhn's influential concept of epochal paradigm shifts, with the less cognitive perspectives of cultural-ideology studies and social mythology. Thomas Kuhn, *The Structure of Scientific Revolutions* (Chicago: University of Chicago Press, 1962).

40. The "writers of *thirtysomething," thirtysomething stories* (New York: Pocket Books, 1992).

41. Newcomb and Alley, *The Producer's Medium.*

42. Jack Kuney, *Television Directors on Directing* (New York: Praeger Publishers, 1990).

43. And surely with the proliferation of infomercials and talk shows, more of these low-resolution forms of TV are on the way.

44. John Fiske states that "the term 'culture,' used in the phrase 'culture studies,' is neither aesthetic and humanist, but political.... Culture is not, then, the aesthetic product... but rather a way of living in an industrial society." "British Cultural Studies and Television," in *Channels of Discourse*, 254. A good collection of more recent cultural studies works is Tony Bennett, Susan Boyd-Bowman, Colin Mercer, and Janet Woollacott, eds., *Popular Television and Film: A Reader* (London: British Film Institute, 1981).

45. A number of these shows will be discussed in more detail in chapter 2. Pastiche and mocking parody were a requisite part of *Your Show of Shows* ("Ten From *Your Show of Shows,"* n.d., (PVA-1906t). The textual fold-in of the military took place in *I Love Lucy,* "Lucy Gets Drafted," December 24, 1951 (PVA-81t), and the *Loretta Young Show,* "Dateline Korea," March 13, 1955, (PVA-8890t).

46. In current media theory, poetics has become a problematic concept. David Bordwell, in *Making Meaning* (Cambridge: Harvard University Press, 1989), 263ff., makes a case for poetics as a substitute for the excesses and shortcomings of most current interpretive-based film study. While the notion of poetics is caught up in this current debate, it is worth noting that its earlier usage by the Russian formalists assumed that the framework included a cultural and politial dimension. More current theorists like Michael Renov, in a keynote address at the Thirteenth Annual Ohio University Film Conference on Documentary, called for a new project to develop a systematic "poetics of documentary" (Athens, Ohio, November 1990). Certainly the focus of poetics on stylistic formation, materiality, perceptability, and function are worth

addressing and applying to contemporary television practice. Such a strategy is not incompatible with ideological analysis.

47. Colin MacCabe, ed., *High Theory/Low Culture: Analyzing Popular Television and Film* (New York: St. Martin's Press, 1986).

48. Given this semiotic density and the abundance of channels involved in perception, it is likely that if one has not accurately defined the stylistically complicated object of investigation, then one is not even accounting for or controlling the constants and variables involved in the process. In short, a lot of close textual and aesthetic work needs to be done even before the broadcasting scholar can do good science. Academic broadcasting could have tended to overlook the extreme complexity of the actual viewing situation and of the televisual text itself, in lieu of a dominant concern with master interpretive allegories, verbal content or social meanings and effects. Much work remains to be done in terms of accurately describing the texts and intertexts that present and perform such contents and effects.

49. The history of film theory clearly demonstrates the limitations of formal taxonomies, which tend to reify description and overvalue aesthetic norms. It is worth noting in this regard that perhaps the two most influential media taxonomists, Christian Metz and Sergei Eisenstein, at least eventually changed course by correctly seeing and describing taxonomies within and as a part of an ideological and psychological dynamic. Eisenstein's writings clearly demonstrated a tension between syntactical taxonomies and constructivist inclinations on the one hand (tendencies he shared with other montage theorists like Lev Kuleshov and V. I. Pudovkin), and his overarching sense or obligation, on the other hand, to account for film's formal taxonomies as social and politial weapons. *Film Form: Essays in Film Theory,* ed. and trans. by Jay Leyda (New York: Harcourt Brace, 1949) and *Film Sense,* ed. and trans. by Jay Leyda (New York: Harcourt Brace, 1942). Christian Metz first emerged in the 1960s as a theorist whose work promised scientific and endless noninterpretive cross-sections of film form and film structure in works like *Film Language,* trans. by Michael Taylor (New York: Oxford University Press, 1974). By 1976, Metz's *The Imaginary Signifier* (Bloomington: Indiana University Press, 1976) seemed to turn its back on the dead syntactical categorization of his earlier work by leaping to complicated conjectures about the spectator's social and psychological self. The scope of analysis is limited, once this impulse in theory has categorized, or promised to categorize, all of its formal options and taxonomies.

50. "It is TV that looks at the world; the TV viewer glances across TV as it looks. This delegation of the look to TV and *consequent loss of intensity in the viewer's own activity of viewing* has several consequences." John Ellis, *Visible Fictions: Cinema, Television, Video* (London: Routledge and Kegan Paul, 1982), 164.

51. Richard Adler continues: "The inevitable commercial interruptions virtually preclude prolonged absorption." "Introduction: A Context for Criticism," *Television as a Cultural Force,* ed. Richard Adler (New York: Praeger, 1976), 6.

52. Both Ellis and Williams sought to describe the fundamental components of the medium and experience of television. But glance theory also partakes of and elaborates an earlier academic schema, that is, the globalizing polar dichotomies that Marshall McLuhan described when comparing television to film. Raymond Williams, *Television, Technology and Cultural Form* (New York: Schocken, 1975).

53. "The mode of the TV image has nothing in common with film or photo, except that it offers also a nonverbal gestalt or posture of forms. With TV the viewer is the screen.... The TV image is visually low in data.... The film image offers many more millions of data per second, and the viewer does not have to make the same drastic reduction of items to form his impression. He tends instead to accept the full image as a package deal." Marshall McLuhan, *Understanding Media: The Extensions of Man* (New York: McGraw-Hill, 1964), 272.

54. McLuhan comments that "the viewer of the TV image, with technical control over the image, unconsciously reconfigures the dots into an abstract work of art, on the pattern of Seurat or

Rouault.... The TV image is now a mosaic mesh of white and dark spots." *Understanding Media*, 273.

55. Ellis, in fact, makes the incredible generalization that: "The broadcast TV viewer is not engaged by TV representation to any great degree: broadcast TV has not so far produced a group of telephiles to match the cinephiles who have seen everything and know the least inconsequential detail about the most obscure actor and directors. Broadcast TV does not habitually offer any great incentives to start watching TV." (*Visible Fictions,* 162). Williams argued that since television does not exist in discrete and isolated programs, but rather is constantly interrupted and linked to other programming in the evening, analysts should study the expanded programming sequence rather than individual units. Because of this basic understanding, later theorists would conclude that such a fragmented and cluttered aesthetic object would not logically entice viewers to the kind of intense engagement that cinephiles experience at the cinema.

56. In addition to the substantial popular publishing industry that focuses on television, television programming itself encourages style and detail consciousness on the part of viewers. Shows like *Entertainment Tonight* and *Arsenio,* and many other clones on cable, constantly spotlight the content and style of television.

57. In all fairness to Ellis, and others, glance theory may have accounted more credibly for television in the 1970s or early 1980s. Regardless of its origins, however, glance theory is made suspect by current television practice. The primetime television industry especially fashions programs and nonprogram materials with increasing style- and fashion-consciousness. Even when Ellis was writing, *MTV* and *Miami Vice* and miniseries like *Shogun* had established highly *visual* arenas for narrative, music, and drama. In the decade that followed a growing concern with stylishness evolved out of these forms. Some shows mimicked MTV and *Vice.* Others made their own claims for unique visual style (*Crime Story, Max Headroom, Hill Street Blues, L.A. Law*). By 1989, shows like CBS's *Beauty and the Beast* were mise-en-scène–strong and narrative-weak. Writers for such shows were faced with script assignments requiring many viewer pages and having long nonverbal scenes displaying auspicious and expressionist lighting effects. Directional lighting, colored gels, smoke, and synth music permeated primetime programming. The artistic reference in look was closer to Rembrandt than it was to the "ideology of inattentiveness" that glance theorists promoted. *TV Guide* promoted the special nature of such shows: these were not shows to be glanced at. Television by 1990 was in many cases self-consciously hip and excessively styled. There was no longer a zero-degree formal syntax and style at work here. The idea of a neutral and colorless writing, in short, a de-aestheticized style in the work of Alain Robbe-Grillet was promoted by Roland Barthes in *Writing Degree Zero* (New York: Hill and Wang, 1953), xvi, 76. The zero-degree style of TV in the 1950s and early 1960s was a dominant and rather than radical or modernist tendency. Glance theory simply missed the opportunity to elucidate and explain the newer and important televisual forms—a refusal that helped reinforce television theory's denigration of the image.

58. In a critique of Ellis's book, "Television at a Glance," by Brian Winston (*Quarterly Review of Film Studies* 9, no. 3 [Summer 1984], 256–261), the British theoretical tradition from which Ellis's work comes is interrogated and rejected. Winston attacks almost all of Ellis's central assumptions: his ideas about television and enigma, the medium's essential temporal regularity, the importance of the nuclear family, the emphasis on the glance as a defining factor, and his underlying attitude and valuation of popular culture in general. Strangely enough, few have followed through on Winston's suggestions. Among my goals here are: (1) to show that glance theory and the related mythology of liveness predated the work of Ellis in American media studies by many years; (2) to demonstrate that glance theory continues to be widespread and popular in more contemporary critical work and cultural studies; and finally, (3) to suggest how the assumption and misperception of inattentiveness may actually be a key to television's underlying logic and appetite for embellishment, ornamentation, and stylishness.

59. In his explanation of the symbolic social use of television in the home Dennis Giles states: "But given the distractions of home viewing, given the fact that the TV image rarely dominates a room by its size alone and that it competes against other possible objects of vision in a lighted room, TV pictures are less forceful than theatrical movie images in holding the viewer's attention." Dennis Giles, "Television Reception," *Journal of Film and Video* 37, no. 3, (Summer 1985): 12–25.

60. Since Giles is concerned with the symbolic function of television set as furniture and icon, his remarks are suggestive. They tend, however, to devalue the aural-visual spectacle that television increasingly tries to heighten.

61. "[Television] emphasizes another invocatory drive: hearing; *sound dominates* [and] ensures continuity of attention," says Robert Deming, in "The Television Spectator-Subject," *Journal of Film and Video* 37, no. 3 (Summer 1985): 49.

62. A recent analysis by Valerie Walkerdine shows the extent of this TV-as-background assumption: "There is a specific way in which television is watched. This differs from the fascinated concentration of the spectator in the darkened cinema, and also from the way that television is often *used as a backdrop to domestic*??????? Replay," in Manuel Alverado and John O. Thomson, eds., *The Media Reader* (London: British Film Institute, 1990), 349.

63. "The *totalizing, womblike effects of the film-viewing situation represent* [for Baudry], the activation of an unconscious desire to return to an earlier state of psychic development, one before the formation of the ego, in which the divisions between the self and other, internal and external, have not yet taken shape." Sandy Flitterman-Lewis, "Psychoanalysis, Film, and Television," in Robert Allen, ed., *Channels of Discourse,* 182.

64. This "womblike," "artificially psycho[tic]" state of the film viewer as a dreamer is for Flitterman-Lewis tied directly to the visual emphasis of cinema. What links this process to the cinema is the fact that it occurs in terms of visual images—what the child sees at this point (a unified image that is distanced and objectified) forms how he or she will interact with others at later stages in life. Ibid., 183.

65. Flitterman-Lewis contrasts television to this process in several important ways. Thus television substitutes liveness and directness for the dream state, immediacy and presentness for regression. It also modifies primary identification in ways that support its *more casual forms of looking.* The television viewer is a distracted viewer.

66. See especially the discussion of the live-remote mode in chapter 9, and the militarist guises of crisis coverage in chapter 11.

67. "It is the total involvement in all-inclusive *nowness* that occurs in young lives via TV's mosaic image." McLuhan, *Understanding Media,* 292. "Ours is a brand new world of *allatonceness.* 'Time' has ceased, 'space' has vanished. We now live in a global village…a *simultaneous* happening" (italics mine). Marshall McLuhan and Quentin Fiore, *The Medium Is the Message: An Inventory of Effects* (New York: Bantam Books, 1967), 63.

68. Peter H. Wood, "Television as Dream," in *Television as a Cultural Force,* Richard Adler, ed. (New York: Praeger, 1976), 23.

69. Horace Newcomb, *Television: The Most Popular Art* (New York: Anchor Books, 1974), 258.

70. "What is video then? Video is a process of expression that is *instantaneous,* electronic, and playable on one or more screens, through images and sound *transforming time into experience* and altering the habitual way the audience has of seeing. The soul of video is change, not permanence." Jonathan Price, *Video Visions: A Medium Discovers Itself* (New York: New American Library, 1972), 4.

71. What started in part as a countercultural and social movement to appropriate the tools of television production became within this aesthetic a way to alter personal consciousness. A focus on liveness, real time, and simultaneity could be wielded, in short, for both social and political ends.

72. Since video is a medium of *real time,* that is, because it transmits the temporal quality of the process being recorded, it alters our experience of our own memory, of history, and of daily life. Frank Gillette, "Masque in Real Time," in Ira Schneider and Beryl Korot, eds., *Video Art* (New York: Harcourt, Brace, Jovanovich, 1976), 219.

73. The industry wishes, or feels obligated, to maintain the illusion of *immediacy*, which it defines rather precisely as "the *feeling* that what one sees on the TV screen is living and actual reality, *at that very moment taking place*" (italics mine). David Antin, "Video: The Distinctive Features of the Medium," in *Video Art,* 177. It followed from this aesthetic that important video art (video art worthy to be curated, collected, and funded) was videowork that exploited the property of liveness and real time.

74. "These are the two features of the everyday use of medium that are suggestive for a discussion of video: the simultaneous reception and projection of an image, and the human psyche as a conduit." Rosalind Krauss, "Video: The Aesthetics of Narcissism," in *New Artists Video,* Gregory Battcock, ed. (New York: Dutton, 1978), 45.

75. The popularity among critics of real time and narcissistic video was due in part to the fact that such work overtly illustrated Lacan's "mirror stage"—a heuristic and psychoanalytic paradigm that became increasingly fashionable in intellectual circles during the decade. Yet, such work, legitimized only by prescriptive theory in the 1970s, ultimately had little impact on television production in general. Krauss, "Video: The Aesthetics of Narcissism," 55.

76. "Television viewers have come to expect a higher degree of *realism and authenticity* in every aspect of television, from news and documentaries to entertainment and sports programming. Shooting on location is one way to enhance a production" (italics mine). Alan Wurtzel, *Television Production* (New York: McGraw-Hill, 1979), 510.

77. "You should think of television performing *its most distinctive function, the live transmission of events*.... Contrary to film, the basic unit of television, the television frame, consists of an ever-changing picture mosaic.... Each television frame is in a continual state of becoming.... As such, the sequence of the actual event, cannot be reversed when shown on television.... *The now of the television event is equal to the now of the actual event* in terms of objective time, that is, the instantaneous perception by the observer of the actual event and by the television viewer" (italics mine). Herbert Zettl, *Sight, Sound, Motion: Applied Media Aesthetics* (Belmont, Calif.: Wadsworth, 1973), 263.

78. "In terms of mode of address, I have argued that notions of 'liveness' lend a sense of flow which overcomes extreme fragmentation of space." Jane Feuer, "The Concept of Live Television: Ontology as Ideology," in *Regarding Television,* E. Ann Kaplan, ed. (Los Angeles: The American Film Institute, 1983), 19.

79. Feuer's explanation is so good because it ties the liveness ideology to one of the most influential concepts in television critical theory, the flow. Yet, assertions about the centrality of liveness made from the analysis of one talk show raise other problems. Williams, *Television,* 86–118.

80. "Television's self-referential discourse plays upon the connotative richness of the term 'live,' confounding its simple or technical denotation with a wealth of allusiveness. Even the simplest meaning of 'live'—that the time of the event corresponds to the transmission and viewing times—reverberates with suggestions of 'being there'... 'bringing it to you as it really is.' The contradictory television coinage 'live on tape' captures the slippage involved." Feuer, "The Concept of Live Television," 14. This view is important in correcting earlier glosses and essentialisms of liveness *theory,* but wrong, as a I hope to show later, if it implies that liveness is a dominant myth in television *practice.* Other important myths are also at work; myths that suggest neither simultaneity, presentness, or "being there." With the emergence of pictorialism and the preoccupation with individuated program looks as common objectives in recent television, there is no reason to position liveness as *the* determining ideology. Rather liveness has become one stylistic item on the larger menu of visuality. This view, then, is an inversion of Feuer's. Whereas Feuer argues that stylistic codes produce realism and liveness, I am

suggesting that liveness is a visual code and component of a broader stylististic operation. It is a look that can be marshaled at will, feigned and knowingly exchanged with ontologically aware viewers.

81. Robert Vianello critiques the conflation of the live and the real by showing that liveness is a complicated and political construct in "The Power Politics of 'Live' Television" (*Journal of Film and Video* 37, 3 [Summer 1985], 39), yet overvalues liveness by claiming that its promise "pervades every moment" of broadcast: "It is on these instantaneous and spontaneous transmissions that television truly establishes itself as a social institution of the real.... Television becomes the perpetual possibility of making contact with the real; it is this possibility which pervades every moment of broadcast."

82. Todd Gitlin, "Introduction: Looking Through The Screen," in Todd Gitlin, ed., *Watching Television* (New York: Pantheon, 1986), 6.

83. Gitlin, "Car Commercials and Miami Vice: 'We Build Excitement," in *Watching*, 136–161.

84. Marc, *Demographic Vistas*, 21.

85. Margaret Morse, "The Ontology of Everyday Distraction," in *Logics of Television: Essays in Cultural Criticism*, Patricia Mellencamp, ed. (Bloomington: Indiana University Press, 1990), 193–221.

86. "Successive, simultaneous time, measured by regular, on-the-half-hour progamming...indefinitely multiplied by cable and satellite transmission, hypostasized by familiar formats and aging stars in reruns and remakes, trivialized by scandal and gossip, is disrupted by the discontinuity of catastrophe coverage. So-called heterogeneity or diversity ceases as do commercials and TV continuity time as we focus on a single event.... TV time of regularity and repetition, continuity and 'normalcy,' contains the potential of interruption, the thrill of live coverage of death events." Patricia Mellencamp ?????? Catastrophe: Or Beyond the Pleasure Principle of Television," *Logics*, 243–244. Mellencamp has reversed the logic of the liveness myth, while at the same time acknowledging and presuming its centrality. Unlike earlier liveness theorists, for her "simultaneity" does not stand for liveness but for a massively and artificiality constructed temporality. That is, television is no longer seen as simultaneous with *live events*, but as simultaneous with itself and with *other programs* that happen at the same time. In Mellencamp's reversal, "liveness" stands not for the dominant norm in television, but as the potentially disruptive agent that can attack and expose conventional programming pleasures.

87. Ibid., 261–262.

88. This view of catastrophic temporality seems to devalue the fact that even catastrophes are immediately stylized and constrained as pictures and endless loops, with encrusted graphics, in a process of almost immediate representation that can make even the Kennedy assassination or fires caused by arson in Malibu in some sense pleasurable. Certainly stylized catastrophe loops are more pleasurable to most than coverage of the same events on the radio.

89. The full quote reads: "The more rapid internationalization of television via the *immediacy* of satellites on a *global* allocation of an electromagnetic spectrum never imagined as nationally determined, replicates the *emphasis on transmission*." Patricia Mellencamp, "Prologue," in *Logics of Television*, 3. (italics mine).

90. Probably the most forceful indication of the continuing centrality of liveness in contemporary media theory is Daniel Dayan and Elihu Katz's *Media Events* (Cambridge: Harvard University Press, 1992), pubished after this chapter was written. A very good critique of Dayan and Katz, and a reconsideration of ontological aspects of liveness, is James Friedman, "Live Television: Ceremony, (Re)presentation, Unstructured and Unscripted Events," presented at the Screen Studies Conference, Glasgow, Scotland, June 1993.

91. Sharon D. Moshavi, "Niche Cable Networks Attract Advertisers of Same Genre," *Broadcasting and Cable* (March 8, 1993). 47.

92. Louis Sahagun and Michael Kennedy, "FBI Puts Blame on Koresh for Cultists' Death," *Los Angeles Times*, April 21, 1993, A13.

There's No Place Like Home: The American Dream, African-American Identity, and the Situation Comedy

Bambi L. Haggins

Few would argue with the assertion that the American Dream doesn't pack the ideological punch it once did. From the pages of national newspapers to *Frontline*, from books detailing the "fall from grace" of the American Middle Class to those who claim the Dream was stolen, a multiplicity of voices, on the right and on the left, have, more or less, sounded the death knell for the relevance of the American Dream.[1] Yet everyone who lives in the United States is exposed to this national myth. Within the mythology of the Dream there is something tantamount to a promise that with ingenuity, perseverance, and "faith," anyone can succeed in America. It seems that regardless of whether or not one believes "the myth," we are exposed to it daily: in institutions within our communities, in American history courses, in the pages of local newspapers, and, of course, in the constructions and fictions of the large and small screens. Notions of home in the United States are inextricably tied to constructions of family, nation, and the myth of the American Dream. No medium is more responsible for reflecting and refracting these notions than the electronic hearth: television.

The televisual reifications of suburban bliss produced in the medium's early years spoke to the post-war iteration of the American Dream, and no television genre accomplished this more effectively than the situation comedy. While the contemporary sitcom certainly still represents a fable of the American Dream, it does so within the context of a social milieu that has changed since the days of "Wally and the Beaver" televisual homogeneity.

As the most widely accessible American medium, television is the loom upon which the thread of Dream mythology is woven—often imperceptibly—into the fabric of American culture. For the purposes of this essay, the texts and their times as well as the mythology of the Dream will be examined as strands in a televisual tapestry that can only be unraveled through a sort of threefold intertextual analysis. First, by examining the American Dream in its historical and contemporary iterations, one can discern how the mythos reacts to, refigures, and reflects the ideologies imbedded in American political thought. Second, by analyzing texts of the situation comedy, not only is the disparity between the social milieu of the series' televisual world and that of the given era revealed, one is also able to determine what aspects of American life are idealized and propagandized. Finally, by exploring the interplay between notions of home and the American Dream (as televisually made myth and ambiguous ideological "given"), this essay endeavors to examine how the mythos impacts how we are seen, how we see ourselves, and how we view the promises implied in the Dream.

The tracing of the mythos of the American Dream—a "site" mapped by emotion and intellect—becomes a sort of philosophical inquiry as well as an ideological one; finding home adds a spiritual dimension.[2] The myth is one thread in an ever-changing hue in televisual tapestries: it is as amorphous as it is pervasive. The myth is refurbished for the contemporary spectator due to the fact that fragments of televisual tapestries are recycled: as generic conventions are borrowed, scenarios are rewritten and narratives, by virtue of repetition (read: reruns), become codified. However, this ideological recycling is more than simply a matter of "buying into the Dream." It is a far reaching process that has an undeniable impact on the formation of national identity.

The Dream mythology is by definition (or, dare I say, by lack of it) a myth based upon *faith*—faith in the promises of democratic ideals and social mobility. If one assumes that the Dream is always political, then it would follow that its mythology, in whatever form, serves the propagation of a particular ideology. Yet despite the fact that many might view "The American Dream" as a sort of ideological "given." I believe, particularly as it relates to African-Americans, that there is an ambiguity or, perhaps more aptly, a duality in the mythos. For African-Americans, as for most people in the United States, their relationship with the American Dream is far more complex than one of either uncritical acceptance or rejection: we are continually coming to terms with the tenets of the Dream just as we are always in the process of negotiating national and cultural identity.

Interpretation of the Dream: Finding Home

Although the inception of the actual term "The American Dream" can be assigned to a period in the latter part of the nineteenth century (somewhere between the 1867 publication of Horatio Alger's *Ragged Dick* and the 1886 dedication of the Statue of Liberty, with the promise of Emma Lazarus's "The New Colossus"), tenets of Dream mythology also flow from intellectual and spiritual impulses that predate the national rationalizations of the late nineteenth century.[3]

The interrogation of the Dream and national identity seems particularly timely and is taking place across many registers as historians like Arthur Schlesinger bemoan the "disuniting of America," cultural theorists like Audre Lorde reflect upon the "mythic norms" of American popular culture, and journalists like Russell Baker question the academic soundness of theoretical inquiries into popular culture (namely, television).[4] In terms of contemporary discourse, particularly in television studies, the concept of the Dream has often been connected with postwar suburbanization: the bedtime story for a consumerist culture where the happily-ever-after transpires in a sort of middle-class Nirvana.[5] Clearly, these constructions of the American Dream play a significant part in contemporary iterations of the mythos. Nonetheless, as we approach the end of the millennium, myths of American national identity—including the televisually realized versions—can no longer easily be swallowed whole by a progressively jaded and diverse populace.

In a country where globalization, technological innovations, and the destabilization of the nuclear family are reshaping our senses of time, space, and identity, the desire for a timely definition of "home" is being expressed with even greater fervor. Simultaneously, the process of "coming to terms" with the notion of home and with national/cultural identity has been decidedly problematized as the metaphors of the melting pot or the benign pluralism of the "salad bowl" no longer suffice.[6] Simone Weil asserted, "To be rooted is perhaps the most important and least recognized need of the human soul" (qtd. in Said 364). The desire for a safe, secure place where we can belong is, undoubtedly, universal. Yet two significant questions remain unanswered and, perhaps, are unanswerable: what is the price paid for belonging, and what does it mean to be safe?

The positive connotation of the construction of home has, for instance, been aptly explored by bell hooks: "it was about the construction of a safe place where Black people could affirm one another and by so doing heal the wounds inflicted by racist domination" (42). However, home as a safe haven loses its liberatory luster when examined as corollary to the Dream mythos. There is a duality built into this construction of home that reveals both "the dangers and the pleasures" inherent in the process of defining national identity: the limitations of exclusivity and the possibilities of inclusivity present an ideological conundrum which could be seen as a contributing factor to a sort of national identity crisis.

A national identity crisis is not a new phenomenon for the African-American community—for many Blacks, the internalization of an American identity has always been a conflicted and conflictual process. W. E. B. Du Bois asserted almost a century ago that Blacks experience an internal division, a *double consciousness*: "One ever feels his twoness—an American, a Negro; two souls, two thoughts, two unreconciled strivings, two warring ideals in one dark body whose dogged strength alone keeps it from being torn asunder" (Du Bois 615). The double consciousness of the African-American seems to intersect with the duality of the promises of the Dream—with the "unreconciled strivings" speaking to the unkept promises of the Dream. Yet the mythos, as idealized and inexorable covenant, continues to inform what it means to be an American for Blacks and Whites.

When viewed as a complex, everyday myth, the Dream appears to feed into an often contentious form of "national" affinity, one that might be seen not solely as forced but also as a willed affinity. Benedict Anderson's notion of the "imaginary linkage" created by print capitalism, which credits the "simultaneous consumption ('imagining') of the newspaper-as-fiction" (35–36) along with the linkage's construction, can quite logically be extended to the readily and widely accessible medium of television.[7] It also seems more than coincidental that, within an American context, the birth of print capitalism took place in the latter part of the nineteenth century as the Reconstruction forced legislative recognition and, later, legal denial of the rights of Blacks as Americans, as the social ills of Industrialization forced (albeit, limited) attention to the swelling underclass, and, of course, when the mythos of the Dream became an explicit part of national consciousness.

While it does not require an intellectual leap of faith to link Horatio Alger's most famous rags-to-riches immigrant hero. Ragged Dick, to Norman Lear's George Jefferson, the Black, self-made dry-cleaning magnate, other more arcane correlations reveal the significant role played by television in fostering a process of intellectual assimilation so subtle that it is, more often than not, discounted.

For example, it is possible for one to make the argument that John Winthrop's "City upon the Hill" can be seen as an early "directive" of the Dream which continues to influence American political discourse.[8] The ethos of Winthrop's de facto sermon is reconstructed in the description of America as an exemplar of "democratic" ideals. The mythos of the Dream can be viewed as a site of convergence for a multiplicity of philosophical, political, and spiritual ethics, stretching back into the maxims of the Enlightenment project and forward into the discourse of "public intellectuals" (from Alexis de Tocqueville to Cornell West), the rhetoric of politicians (from Thomas Jefferson to Bill Clinton), and the narratives of the electronic hearth (from *The Adventures of Ozzie and Harriet* to *Living Single*). The mythos is inflected by the political philosophy and American political code, a de facto canon of democracy (i.e., John Locke's *Two Treatises on Government*, Jean Jacques Rousseau's *The Social Contract*, the writings of Jefferson, including the Declaration of Independence) which plays as significant a role in the formation of the American Dream as the Algeresque rales of valorous assimilation. Yet, intriguingly, there is a duality imbedded in even these idyllic constructions of democratic ideals: the enlightened self-interest of the "social contract" was far from inclusive in terms of who established the parameters of the contract itself, and the conflictual nature of Jeffersonian democracy embodied the separation between the pragmatic implementation of ideology and the Nirvana of a country where "all men are created equal."

The exploration of these interpretations of the Dream provides a point of departure for discerning how the mythos, like identity, is constantly in flux—a concept that impacts and inflects popular culture as it is impacted and inflected by shifts in the social and political milieu. This trajectory hints at the fact that the always political nature of the Dream mythology is also endowed with an often unacknowledged subtext of spirituality in which the new "City upon the Hill"—the televisual community—reinforces the notion of America as political and moral exemplar. And, as Sut Jhally and Justin Lewis state, "Although the American Dream wasn't invented for television, television appears to nourish and sustain it" (73).

In addition, on some level there is a "profound emotional legitimacy" to the imagined and utopian notion of America as democratic state that can only be understood by interrogating what it means to possess a nationality, what it means to be American.[9] In *The Disuniting of America*, Arthur Schlesinger cites Alexis de Tocqueville in valorizing the process of *Americanization*: "'Imagine, my dear friend, if you can . . . a society formed of all nations of the world . . . people having different languages, beliefs and opinions: in a world [that is] a society without roots, without memories, without prejudices, without common ideas . . . yet a hundred times happier than our own." Schlesinger adds, "What alchemy could make this miscellany into a single society?"

What Schlesinger implies but fails to state specifically is that the "alchemy" is the homogenization process (200). This position assumes that if the price of the Dream is cultural specificity, then the promised "equality of condition"—the equal footing from which, ideally, each American embarks and the promise at the core of Tocqueville's praise of the then-fledgling democracy—will naturally occur. Cornell West in *Race Matters* offers a differing reading of the fragile experiment:

> *the much heralded stability and continuity of American democracy was predicated on Black oppression and degradation. Without the presence of black people in America, European-Americans would not be white . . . What made America distinctly American to them was not simply the presence of unprecedented opportunities but the struggle for seizing these opportunities in a new land in which black slavery and racial caste served as the floor upon which white class, ethnic and gender struggles could be diffused and diverted. (156)*

In other words, the price could not (cannot) always be paid nor the promise fulfilled—for certain Americans, access to the Dream and to democracy has always been limited. In fact, in his often-cited treatise on the "great experiment," *Democracy in America*, Tocqueville's prediction for the next cause of revolution seems, by implication, to recognize this reality: "If ever America undergoes great revolutions, they will be brought about by the presence of the black race on the soil of the United States; that is to say they will owe their origin, not to equality, but to the inequality of condition" (268).

Two centuries later, most African-Americans are still plagued by the inequality of condition. From the "three-fifths" clause to the Fourteenth Amendment, from *Plessy* to *Brown*, from *Bakke* to California's Proposition 209, their legal status as Americans has been and remains a point of contention—as does their access to the Dream. In 1998, the economic good times, when the "need" for affirmative action has passed (as "proven" by the passage of Proposition 209), one third of African-Americans are no closer to the promise of the Dream than they were thirty years ago.[10] Yet the promise of the Dream still has its hold on the souls of Black folks.

The African-American's position as a "national subject" is problematized not only by institutional marginalization but by rifts within the community that run along lines of class, ethnicity, and color. In the history of African-American thought, two differing approaches for assuring (eventual) Black access to the Dream can be seen in W.E.B. Du Bois's "Talented Tenth" and Booker T. Washington's "so slow stand."[11] Even with his acceptance of double consciousness, Du Bois proposed that a few of the best and brightest could forge inroads into mainstream America that the rest could follow, which seems to echo Dream mythology in the proposed march forward. Washington's conciliatory premise that Blacks, as a group, must ease into equality and liberty, proving themselves worthy of liberty as exemplary Americans, constructs the image of a separate but equal "City upon the Hill."

The directives encompassed in Washington's *Up from Slavery* and Du Bois's *Souls of Black Folks* are both predicated upon the notion that African-Americans, as individuals and as members of communities, will act for the collective good. However, this notion of collective good, which is akin to "enlightened self-interest," is not guaranteed in America, whether in a black or white social milieu. Yet the Dream for African-Americans appears to be encased in a sort of ethos of deferred gratification. "a politics of fulfillment: the notion that a future society will be able to realize the social and political promise that present society left unaccomplished" (Gilroy 97).

The duality of the Dream also materializes when the idealized, ideological imperatives of the mythos come into conflict with more pragmatic (and less altruistic) pursuits (the commitment of a consumerist ideology: read "moving on up"). In fact, even Tocqueville was aware of the problems inherent in a country so fond of property, always in danger of complacency and of losing and/or abandoning enlightened self-interest:

> *I must confess that I apprehend much less for democratic society from the boldness than from the mediocrity of desires. What appears to me most to be dreaded*

is that in the midst of the small, incessant occupations of private life, ambition should lose its vigor and its greatness; that the passions of man should abate, but at the same time be lowered; so that the march of society should every day be more tranquil and less aspiring. (268)

In other words, becoming comfortably middle class is a threat to the possibilities of democracy. The American Dream is the promise of the "possibility" and also its denial. The central question, which alludes to the duality and duplicity in the promises of the Dream, has been expressed throughout American history (whether in the musings of Tocqueville or the nineties controversy that rages over Affirmative Action): "Can equality of opportunity be achieved without equality of condition?" The mythos of the Dream, particularly in its televisual iterations, elides this question almost entirely.

The Dream Will Be Colorized

The television situation comedy—the most popular American artform—is a virtual textbook that can be "read" to help lay bare the mores, images, ideals, prejudices and ideologies shared—whether by fiat or default—by the majority of the American public.

—*Darrell Hamamoto, Nervous Laughter*

Since the moment of television, which coincided with the gestation of ranch house suburbia, the medium has played a vital role in reestablishing the myth of the American Dream. Historically, the medium has given social instruction to the masses warming themselves by the electronic hearth. During the "Installation Period" (1945–50), the image of the electronic hearth itself was tied to the American Colonial Revival notions of home, giving a *founding fathers* sort of authority to the burgeoning new medium, rich with the symbolism of patriotism, domestic tranquillity, and, most importantly, security.

The situation comedy of the postwar period offered social instruction that supported the redefinition of home and family, not as a reversion to the prewar ethos but, rather, offering the embodiment of the dream of nuclear familialism in which father, mother, and child lived in harmony within a mythic televisual suburban neighborhood. The realities of postwar America—the Red Scare, the growing awareness of racial inequity, the burgeoning youth culture and the rebellion that accompanied it—necessitated an illusion of safety and security. In this era, the home of the situation comedy was a site of instruction as well as one of reassurance.[12] As Lynn Spigel concludes, this instruction, even in the face of blatant racial inequities, seemed to find an audience on the margin as well: "Even families that were not welcomed into the middle-class melting pot of postwar suburbia [African-Americans and other ethnic/racial minorities] were promised the dream of domestic bliss would come true through the purchase of a television set" (44). While the dearth of representations of African-Americans (as anything other than "mammies" or "sambos")[13] would have seemed to support a different conclusion, for many African-Americans, entrée into the world of televisual spectatorship offered the promise of entrée into the American middle class that the medium depicted. Television, then as now, propagates idealized images less intended for our edification than for our entertainment—in the glow of the electronic hearth, things seem less complicated, less problematic: "the TV hearth is still functioning as a time trip out of the tumult of history into the placid wealth of American myth. No matter what discordant images may flash across the screen—wars, racial hatred, disease, family violence, abject poverty, natural catastrophe—they are all neutralized, in fact denied, in the TV Hearth" (Ticci 62).

The sitcom's shift from suburb to city, from nuclear family to extended and alternative families (even from central character to ensemble cast) speaks to changes in the American cultural landscape. However, the situation comedy has not become the "poster genre" for diversity. The fictive world of the sitcom remains, for the most part, the last bastion of the hermetically scaled social milieu. Parallel constructions of American life are created—often in Black and White—in "mirror sitcoms" like

The Cosby Show/Family Ties and *Living Single/Friends*. Through the examination of these televisual texts, one can begin to trace the ways in which the mythology of the Dream is perpetuated and how the desire for the Dream is fulfilled with an ease rarely actualized in American society during the waning years of the twentieth century. Ingrained within the narratives of the contemporary sitcom is an ideological center as tightly tied as ever to notions of the American Dream. There are necessarily variations in the televisual constructions of Dream mythology due, in part, to the fact that, as Todd Gitlin states, "hegemonic ideology changes in order to remain hegemonic" (531).

The "mirror sitcoms" are informed by the variation Herman Gray refers to as "separate but equal discourses." Their narratives "situate Black characters in domestically centered Black worlds and circumstances that essentially parallel those of whites. Like their white counterparts, these shows . . . maintain a commitment to the universal acceptance into the transparent 'normative' middle class" (87). Gray's term is exemplified in two eighties domestic comedies par excellence, *Family Ties* and *The Cosby Show*. However, an examination of these series reveals color coding in the allegedly colorblind Dream mythology. While both series depict the travails of upper-middle-class family life inside carefully constructed social milieus, within the fabric of their fables of bourgeois domesticity *Family Ties* and *The Cosby Show* present "loose" and "strict" interpretations, respectively, of what it takes to achieve the American Dream.

The premise for *Family Ties*, which ran from 1982 to 1989, was generation gap comedy: what happens when two liberal children of the sixties. Steven and Elyse Keaton, have three children of the eighties. The series, created by "self-proclaimed hippie" Gary David Goldberg and set in suburban Ohio, often found its comedic payoff in the disparity between the "enlightened" social consciousness and laid-back style of the parents and the "me generation" ethos of the children, particularly Alex, who slept under a poster of Wilham F. Buckley and had one of Nixon at his bedside. Despite the series' self-conscious parodying of Reagan-era values, the character that emerged as its star was Michael J. Fox, who, as Alex P. Keaton, became a teen heartthrob pin-up for the Right; in fact, "President Reagan revealed, in a speech to the Boy Scouts of America, that *Family Ties* was his favorite television program" (Hamamoto 9).

The sensation raised by *The Cosby Show* came from a markedly different direction. The series depiction of the Huxtable family continued the "movin' on up" trend of Blacks in sitcoms of the late seventies and early eighties (*The Jeffersons, Different Strokes, Benson*). However, unlike its predecessors, for whom "movin' on up" meant moving into a fundamentally White world, the world of the Huxtables was primarily Black, and the series began with the family as long-standing members of the upper middle class. From their brownstone in Brooklyn Heights, lawyer-mother Clair and obstetrician-father Cliff, along with their children, constructed a new vision of the American Dream. Herman Gray states, "In *The Cosby Show*, Blackness, although an element of the show's theme, character and sensibility, was mediated and explicitly figured through home life, family and middle-classness" (80). This African-American nuclear family's experience was embraced by the viewing public because "it is a middle class family that happens to be Black" (Gray 80).

The interrogation of yuppie Zeitgeist, a continual theme in *Family Ties*, is illustrated in the show's final episode, "Alex Doesn't Live Here Anymore." The Keaton nuclear family finally disbands as Alex heads for a job at a top Wall Street firm. Alex sees the $70K position as the culmination of his life's work, while Elyse, seemingly manifesting the "emptying nest" syndrome, questions the values that Alex is taking with him to New York:

> Elyse: You need to ask yourself, will this [job] bring me fulfillment.
> Alex: It will bring it, clean it and have it pressed for me in the morning.

A temporary estrangement between Elyse and Alex develops as both grapple with the impending reconstitution of home. In the end, mother and son are reconciled, each accepting the inevitability of change and still affirming the significance of home and family:

> Elyse: I love being Alex Keaton's mother.
> Alex: I love being Elyse Keaton's son.

Given that the struggle between Boomer liberalism and the "me" generation ethos of the eighties was a narrative staple of the series oeuvre, as embodied in clashes between the parents (the public broadcaster dad and folksinging architect mom) and their offspring (the captain of finance wannabe son, quintessential material girl, and future Gen-Xer daughter, respectively), it seemed appropriate that the show would end with an ideological equivalent of agreeing to disagree. The series finale underscores the message that the family ties that bind are stronger than the belief systems that threaten to sever them, which, in and of itself, is a telling reflection of an ambivalent relationship with the value system of the Reagan era.

The Cosby Show offered a rare case where the premiere show of a series clearly projected its entire trajectory. From the first episode in 1984, it was clear that the traditional values embedded in the American Dream would be fervently espoused: the Keaton style of parenting would not play in the Huxtable home. The central story line of the episode is the parental reaction to son Theo's abysmal report card. Clair is too angry to speak rationally to her son; the task falls to Cliff, the patriarch, to explain the importance of academic achievement. After Cliff points out the impossibility of getting into college with D-filled report cards. Theo replies that he doesn't plan to go to college but rather to be like "regular people." Using Monopoly money, Cliff illustrates the fiscal plight of "regular people": the stack of money given to Theo, as "regular people's" monthly salary, disappears as Cliff subtracts the costs of living. Cliff remarks, nodding to the now penniless Theo, "Regular people." Although the situation is handled with pragmatic humor, the class-based expectations built into the Huxtable world (and the fictive world of the sitcom, in general) are clearly revealed here and differentiate this middle-class milieu from the world of "regular people."

Theo then makes a speech that one might expect to be the "moment" of the show. In the sitcom, the moment is the point in the narrative that supplies a sentimental or otherwise emotional payoff for the conflict built into the episode, eliciting the "aw, isn't that sweet" or "aw, isn't that too bad" response from the viewer.

> Theo: You're a doctor; Mom's a lawyer—you're successful. Maybe I was born to be regular people. If you weren't a doctor, I wouldn't love you any less. I love you because you're my dad. And so maybe instead of acting disappointed because I'm not like you, maybe you can just accept me for who I am and love me anyway because I'm your son.

After a beat, Cliff replies, "Theo, that is the dumbest thing I've ever heard in my entire life." Although the discussion closes with kinder, gentler reasoning (Cliff to Theo: "I just want you to do the best you can, that's all"), instead of a moment when Theo asserts his individuality and his rejection of a middle-class work ethic, it becomes one of humorous, patriarchal correction in which Father (Cliff) knows best and directly communicates the values imbedded in the American Dream.

Although not the story of a blue-collar family that Cosby had initially proposed, he retained creative control of the series throughout its run and had a very specific notion of where the series should and should not go. His control over the construction of *The Cosby Show* included having a psychiatrist on board for the series: "[He] called on [Alvin F.] Poussaint, a long-time friend, to be the show's consultant because he 'wanted the show to be real, the psychological interactions of the family to be real. And he wanted the issues to be real issues, universal to families'" (qtd. in Fuller 69).

However, many "real" issues did not make their way into the series' narratives. Issues of class were not directly confronted on the series: in one episode, Vanessa gets into a fight with a girl who calls her *rich*; Cliff explains. "Your mother and I are rich, you have nothing." Probably in response to the criticism over the fiscal insulation of the Huxtable clan, Clair's cousin from Bedford-Stuyvesant came to live with the family in 1990. Furthermore, Cosby, as creative producer of the series as well as its star, remained adamant that the crisis in race relations need not be a part of the narrative: "It may seem that I'm an authority because my skin color gives me a mark of a victim. But that's not a true label. I won't deal with the foolishness of racial overtones on the show. I base an awful lot of what I've done simply on what people will enjoy" (Gray 80).

Ironically, the final episode, Theo's graduation from NYU. "And So We Commence," aired on April 30, 1992, while images of rage in the news coverage of the L.A. uprising acted as a lead-in to the series that night. *The Cosby Show's* depiction of African-American access to the American Dream, contrasted with the explosion of racial tensions and L.A. burning, made one question how much the "positive imagined" of the Huxtable world had to do with the actual state of race relations in the United States.

As more sophisticated adult viewers, many of us watched with qualified joy as *The Cosby Show* "transformed" the electronic hearth into a cozy space for the valorous fables of the Black upper middle class. The series and its literal and virtual spin-offs, *A Different World* and *The Fresh Prince of Bel-Air*, acted as testaments to the "new accessibility" of the American Dream. Yet once again the gap between the "hoped for" status of these televisual texts and the actual lived experiences of African-Americans could not be ignored.[14] The "positive imagined" of *The Cosby Show* and its spin-offs could be seen as serving dual functions in terms of social instruction: depicting the African-American family as a colorized incarnation of the "mythic norm" and then reiterating the promise of the American Dream. Yet both functions are as disturbing as they are reassuring.

In Sut Jhally and Justin Lewis's *Enlightened Racism*, a study funded by Bill Cosby, the authors persuasively denounce the dual function of the series: "*The Cosby Show*, by incorporating a black family into the American Dream plays an important part in this ideological process . . . their [the Huxtables'] success assures us that in the United States everyone, regardless of race or creed, can enjoy material success" (73). Jhally and Lewis state unequivocally that the Huxtable version of the American Dream "is built on the cracks in an otherwise fairly solid class system . . . [in which] these happy few are seen as confirming the American Dream, whose strange logic transforms them from the exception to the rule, creating the idea that there are, in fact, no rules" (73).

The indictment of the colorized Dream of *The Cosby Show* made in *Enlightened Racism* undoubtedly raises valid questions about how the series, this televisual construction of an ostensibly egalitarian, post civil rights, "post-racial" world, assuaged mainstream (read: White) fears about issues of race and class in American society. However, as Herman Gray observed: "The show labored to construct a different view of American racial order. In the process, 'The Cosby Show' positioned blacks and whites within that order differently. And it is upon the social and cultural ground of that difference that the cracks, fissures, celebrations and suspicions were mobilized" ("Response" 120).

The Cosby Show reconfigured race and, in so doing, threw the issue of racial representations in the faces of audience, televisual consumer and critic alike. The Huxtables' easy access to the American Dream and the series' dual functions created, and perhaps demanded, further discussion on what is (and is not) the "Black Experience" in post—civil rights America.

In both *The Cosby Show* and *Family Ties*, the act of passing on a particular value system—the familial guidelines for access to the Dream—is intertwined within the trials and tribulations of the televisual families. In addition, great pains are taken to make sure that the next generation (particularly the eldest male) learns these lessons and lives by them. While it would be unfair to assert that the narratives privileged the sons over the daughters, it seems clear that the ideological educations of Theo and Alex were a priority for the televisual parents: assuring that the boys knew what was expected of them and what was desired for them was the dominant theme. Though it is true that the two series differ in terms of the offsprings' acceptance of the familial ethic, these domestic comedies were clearly Dream mythology morality plays, with the version in black giving a more idealized depiction of the whole family getting (and keeping) their piece of the Dream.[15]

While the Keatons and the Huxtables offered social instruction on Dream mythology to baby boomers and their progeny, the next televisual iterations of the mythos reflected a nineties reconfiguration of family and a (slightly) retooled version of the Dream.

Fast forwarding to the postbacklash, postmodern, post–L.A. uprising nineties, picture a small group of friends, connected by either familial or long-standing ties of friendship. Gen-Xers all, living in style in New York City, struggling with career, commitment, and identity. This pitch describes both Fox's *Living Single* and NBC's *Friends*.

The goal of Yvette Lee Bowser, the creator/ executive producer of *Living Single*, was "to depict African-Americans in television in a realistic, humorous way. . . . The beauty of the *Living Single* characters is that they are honest with each other, as my friends and I are. Maybe not all people interact the same way, but the [show] is about my life. It's about my friends" (42). The show, created as a vehicle for rap star Queen Latifah (Khadejah). was the first to showcase four upwardly mobile Black women on a prime-time situation comedy. The pragmatic wisdom of Khadejah, the founder and editor of the indie magazine *Flavor* and den mother to the troop, perpetually acts as a guiding force for Synclaire, Khadejah's ditsy, struggling actress-cousin; Max, the bright and brassy lawyer who was Khadejah's college roomie; and Regine, the social-climbing siren who changes male targets as often as she changes hairstyles.

Like the Fox series, which preceded its NBC counterpart by one season, *Friends* is a sitcom that focuses on the relationships between a tight-knit group of singles in New York City. "According to executive producers Kevin Bright, Marta Kauffman and David Crane: 'Friends' is a show about love, sex, careers and a time in life when everything is possible. It's about searching for commitment and security—and a fear of commitment and security. And, most of all, it's a show about friendship—because when a person is young and single in the city, friends and family are synonymous." As the lead-off show of NBC's "Must See TV" Thursday night line-up, *Friends* has had a place in the Nielsen top 10 since its sophomore season. The series depicts the tribulations of the Geller siblings. Ross and Monica, the perennial "nice guy" and the perfectionist "little sister," and their troupe of eccentric, yet archetypal, twenty-something friends: Chandler, the adult version of the class clown: Phoebe, a New Age masseuse and budding songstress; Joey, the less-than-rocket-scientist wannabe actor; and Rachel, the princess who traded in her credit cards (and fiancé) for a chance at independence.

These series unashamedly speak to the lucrative eighteen to thirty-five demographic, although their humor, the vernacular, and the gags are, to a great extent, culturally specific. In addition, the social milieu that they present is almost entirely homogeneous.[17] There is a sameness in the construction of these essentially "racially pure" worlds that speaks directly to the "safe haven" notion of home, which, some may argue, accurately reflects the greater population's experience of friendship in the home place.

Bowser cites the commercial success and critical acclaim of Terry McMillan's novel *Waiting to Exhale* as contributing to getting *Living Single* on the air; however, the complex gender and class issues that are the core of the novel seldom, if ever, surface in the narrative of the series. The absence of these relevant social issues from the *Living Single* narratives (as well as those of *Friends*, for that matter) is disappointing but not surprising. "Even as the situation comedy has stressed the affirmative aspects of liberal democracy, it has done so within the framework of a system of commercial television that limits the emancipatory potential of American popular culture" (Hamamoto 154).

Elayne Rapping bemoans other questionable trends in the new situation comedy:

> *These new sitcoms. . . seem to be functioning as a cheering squad for the end of work and family life as we, and the media heretofore, have known it . . . what I see as I watch them is a scary commercial message on behalf of the new economic system, in which most of us will have little if any paid (never mind meaningful) work to do, and the family ties (remember that old show?) that used to bind us . . . have become untenable. (23.3)*

Rappings's assertion that these televisual texts mark a departure from the days when "we learned to watch sitcoms and commercials—the classic genres—to find out how to adapt" (23.4) fails to entertain the notion that this "new" (and perhaps not improved) paradigm of the sitcom might also be viewed as social instruction. What I believe Rapping sees as a slacker ethos ingrained in some characterizations must be examined on two levels: in terms of both the literal construction of the characters within the text and the manner in which the shows, on the narrative level, depict the characters' theoretical and/or practical acceptance (rather than the rejection) of commitment, consumerism, and the goals attached to achieving the American Dream.

On a literal level, several characters on *Living Single* and *Friends* have found their career niche: Ross seems enthralled with his job as a paleontologist at the American Museum of Natural History, Joey is unsuccessful but committed to acting. Khadejah is the publisher/editor of a hip, slick, and cool magazine, and Max is an aggressive and successful public defender. Perhaps what Rapping reads as a lack of morivation has more to do with an ambivalent acknowledgment of the fact that a college education (which most of these characters possess) is no longer a guarantee of a career, or even a job, to which one can commit one's life.[18]

Notions of familial loyalty are present in both of these sitcoms: Monica and Ross and Synclaire and Khadejah are relatives who are also close friends. The other relationships depicted are, for the most part, long-standing—since high school or at least since college. In the case of *Friends*, levels of dysfunction in the nuclear families of the central characters (parental bias, divorce, desertion) privilege the community of friends as family. *Living Single* reflects a corrective impulse in which the long-standing tradition of extended African-American familial ties is preeminent.[19] While not nuclear, these constructions still invoke the same ties of "traditional values" typical of the situation comedy milieu.

On a narrative level, each show has addressed issues of family traditions, like the reinstatement of the gridiron quest for the Geller Cup in *Friends* (the trophy for a Thanksgiving Day football game) and the pursuit of great Aunt Ida's blessing required for Overton and Synclaire's engagement in *Living Single* (a faux Gullah ritual). The sense of "social responsibility" is engaged in Max's role as corrupt then redeemed politician and Ross's as the surrogate "father of the bride" at the wedding of his ex-wife and her lesbian lover. Unlike the seventies Lear comedies, these are not "issue of the week" shows; the social instruction is usually given in a more subtle and softer tone. However, it seems that the tone is often shaded by the color of the social milieu it depicts.

The work ethic is central both to Rappings's criticism of these new series and to the notion of the Dream. The positive image constructions of the characters on *Living Single* speak directly to this ethic. While the GenXers of *Friends* wander slowly toward the American Dream, for those of *Living Single* it is a much more directed process. Despite criticism about the "unrealistic" nature of the social milieu depicted in each of these series, the underlying ideological tone addresses the ways in which the groups represented in each text must go about finding their entrée into the myth. The milieu of *Living Single* depicts an imagined space for African-Americans to actively pursue their "share" in the Dream, whether through a niche in the print media (Khadejah and her magazine) or through success with "good old American ingenuity" (inventor and handyman Overton). In *Friends*, emotional rather than professional growth is foregrounded: the struggle for "happily ever after" is consistently privileged over the pursuit of success.

This point can be illustrated by selecting family history "moments" from the 1997 season. While the narrative content may vary, each speaks to the essence of its series and, accordingly, to its construction of home and the Dream. The first (from *Friends*) records the visual answer to the question about which of the friends had "hooked up" with whom. In a flashback, the origins of individual character traits are explored, group dynamics are configured, and the almost-affairs are revealed: Monica and Chandler are seen as hapless singles intrigued by the not-so-bright bad boy, Joey; newly dumped Ross almost finds solace in the arms of the flower child hold-over, Phoebe. Only Rachel has changed from her freshly coifed, Bloomingdale-bag-carrying, "princesslike" glory to an ex-princess struggling to become an individual. This flashback episode functions more as an eccentric character study than a *Friends* history lesson; it reflects more about how little most of them have changed rather than how much they have grown. The second moment (from *Living Single*) records the night of Khadejah's awards ceremony where she is named "Most Promising Young Journalist." Over the course of the night, during the aborted limo ride and subsequent subway ride, the gang reflects on their time together. Most of the characters have changed significantly: former law student Max has become an attorney and an elected official; editing a magazine has replaced delivering pizza for Khadejah; Synclaire has gone from country bumpkin struggling actress to a (sometimes) gainfully employed actress; and Regine finally has a millionaire in her marital sights. For each of the characters, it is a "rags to riches" story: by virtue of their hard work, they are achieving their dreams.

These "moments" are significant because they encapsulate the different relationships the two series have with the mythos of the Dream. Like *The Cosby Show* and *Family Ties*, the nineties' mirror sitcoms reflect differing degrees of acceptance and adherence to the guidelines for accessing the Dream. The *Friends* moment remains anecdotal—a story of the not-so-distant "old days" told over a latte—while Khadejah's final thank you to her friends speaks to a collective effort of those moving forward as a group, as family, striving together to seize a piece of the Dream.

In many ways, the ideological core of *Living Single* is more traditional than its NBC counterpart (it espouses the ethic of work and commitment in a way that *Friends* does not), because, in a very real sense, *Friends* doesn't have to. The perpetual angst, which is fodder for much of the witty repartee that fills the narrative of *Friends*, is almost entirely absent in *Living Single*. There appears to be little tolerance for unending egocentric ruminations on the individual human condition in the Fox sitcom. Whereas in the world of *Friends*, characters operate on the assumption that the Dream can eventually be accessed, those of *Living Single* know that there is no such guarantee. The "corrective impulses"—designed to counter the "negative" televisual stereotypes of African-Americans—that inflected the construction of the upper-middle-class milieu of *The Cosby Show* play a significant role in character construction and narrative trajectory in *Living Single*. In other words, in these colorized fables of social instruction, the repeated object lesson calls for commitment to a decidedly middle-class pursuit of happiness: a steadfast adherence to a work ethic is required to earn a piece of the Dream.

The narratives of both dyads of mirror sitcoms, *The Cosby Show/Family Ties* and *Living Single/Friends*, are inflected by the mythos of the American Dream. In each sitcom, the "families" have found a "home" that allows them to move, whether purposefully and directly or hesitantly and circuitously toward their American Dreams. They supply a level of reassurance that access to the Dream is both feasible and attainable. But, as is true with most mediated reassurance, the promise often remains unfulfilled. In the process, the blame falls not upon the inaccessibility of the Dream but, rather, upon those who could not gain access. The "corrective impulses" that fostered "positive" representations can inadvertently become rhetorical tools used to assert that lack of access to the Dream to equality of condition—is tied not to issues of opportunity but to issues of volition. Henry Louis Gates Jr. aptly states:

> As long as all blacks were represented in demeaning or peripheral roles, it was possible to believe that American racism was, as it were, indiscriminate. The social vision of "Cosby" [and, I would argue, that of "Living Single"], however, reflecting the minuscule integration of blacks into the upper middle class . . . reassuringly throws the blame for black poverty back onto the impoverished. (Qtd. in Fuller 138)

Finding home—in the American middle class, in the electronic hearth, and in the American political mainstream—remains for all but the most privileged "grandchildren" of the Talented Tenth an impossible homecoming.[20]

Conclusion: American Dreaming—A Personal Reflection

"Ideology" to Americans usually smacks of a foreign disease: something that afflicts other people. But ideology means nothing more or less than a set of assumptions that become second nature; even rebels have to deal with it. Television can no more speak without ideology than we can speak without prose. We swim in its world even if we don't believe in it.

—*Todd Gitlin,* Inside Prime Time

As the fourth of six women raised by parents who, as children, had experienced the realities of the Depression era South and who came of age in wartime and postwar California, I was raised to have an unwavering belief in the "possibility" of achieving the American Dream. But even though my parents "bought into" the populist American ideology of commitment, consumerism, and social mobility, they did so with an acknowledgement of the duality imbedded in the promise of the "possibility." Television supplied an ongoing ideological tutorial.

"You can't be as good as they are, you-have-to-be-better," my mother would say. On numerous occasions, at the height of my liberal naïveté, I would dismiss that warning as the vestiges of her having come of age in the segregated South. Yet I grew up watching televisual iterations of the "super Negroes"—Alexander Scott (*l-Spy*), Julia Baker (*Julia*), Mr. Dixon (*Room 222*)—who taught me that we had to be better in order to "get our piece" of the Dream. On some subterranean level, this object lesson has been imprinted on my psyche and continues to be reified by my life experience. For better or for worse, this lesson is part of the "home" that I carry with me. And even as my siblings and I gain the trappings of the Dream (the careers, the diplomas, the fiscal security), we are always already learning that lesson. When we watched *The Cosby Show*, we knew: that is us and yet not us.

The American Dream, an amorphous ideological entity, a national mythos, remains perpetually within my field of vision and perpetually out of focus. The mythos continues to resonate in varying registers: a rhizomatic trope that interweaves ideologies that are both conflicting and complementary. The adages of the Puritan Work Ethic are nestled beside the familial wisdom imparted by my mother and father. As LeAnita McLain stated over a decade ago: "I have fulfilled the entry requirement of the American Middle Class, yet I am left, at times, feeling unwelcome and stereotyped. I have overcome the problems of food, clothing and shelter, but I have not overcome my old nemesis, prejudice. Life is easier being Black is not" (14). Having been raised in a nuclear family where the primacy of education as a means of advancement was an unquestioned ethic and having benefited from the spirit of Affirmative Action. I know that mine cannot be seen as the embodiment of the African-American experience. Indeed, there is no place like the Dream. However, the ongoing influence of the mythos cannot be dismissed. The glow of the "possibility" shines in the sitcom morality plays of the electronic hearth, where the televisual home fires still burn but the warmth—the promises of the Dream—remains deferred.

Notes

1. See Paul Taylor's six-part *Washington Post* series on "Fading American Dream" (first article, 1 February 1996). *Frontline's* "Does America Still Work" (first aired 21 May 1996), Katherine S. Newman's *Falling from Grace: The Experience of Downward Mobility in the American Middle Class*, and Donald L. Barlett and James B. Steele's *America: Who Stole the Dream*.

2. My use of the term "mythos" rather than myth is deliberate. The definition of mythos given by Northrup Frye, in reference to "narrative pre-generic elements of literature," refers to the conflation of narrative impulses—the tragic with the romantic, the comedic with the satiric—encompassing multiple permutations: variations on themes where the mixture of impulses retain their color (or essence) while the hue (the mood or tone) is transformed. Given that I see the American Dream as a site of convergence for a multiplicity of political, ideological, and spiritual impulses, I believe the term "mythos" allows a more inclusive and more provocative construction of Dream mythology.

3. In *Ragged Dick* the eponymous hero's transformation from "rags to riches" takes place as the result of saving a rich man's son from drowning, not from the slow, steady rise associated with perseverance and hard work.

4. See Russell Baker's "Idea for a Sitcom," *New York Times*, op-ed section, 21 October 1997.

5. Lynn Spigel, Elaine Tyler May, and Mary Beth Haralovich are a few of the many television theorists/historians whose discussions of the Dream interrogate its postwar iteration in consumerist culture.

6. As Teshome Gabriel and Hamid Naficy note, "The metaphors of the 'melting pot' with its implication of homogenization of differences and otherness or the 'salad bowl' and the

'unmeltable ethics' with their connotations of benign pluralism and coexistence of differences, [which] evoke ideologies of conformity and affirmation . . . have [been proven] untenable" (xi).

7. Just as the newspaper reader is "continually reassured that the imagined reality is visibly rooted in everyday life" by viewing "exact replicas" of his text being "consumed" by those around him, the televisual reader's anxiety is assuaged by the assurance (through Nielsen ratings, water cooler conferences and the sight of others in the glow of the electronic hearth) that they are linked to a larger televisual community that shares in these televisual depictions of the national imagination.

8. Delivered in 1630, the future colonial governor and active Calvinist John Winthrop's "sermon." "A Model of Christian Charity," pronounced the Massachusetts Bay Colony and the people of New England as the new Chosen, destined to guide the rest of the world: "For we must consider that we shall be as a city upon the hill: the eyes of all people are upon us."

9. In *Imagined Communities: Reflections on the Origin and Spread of Nationalism*, Benedict Anderson proposes that "nationalism has to be understood by aligning it not with self-consciously held political ideologies, but with the large cultural systems that preceded it out of which—as well as against which—it came into being"(12). However, Anderson's assertion, while valid, exposes "the chicken or the egg" conundrum with discourse on the formation of national identity: how can there be a sense of national affinity or identity without a national ideology? And what national institutions or "large cultural systems" can exist outside the reach of the national ethos?

10. In *The Future of the Race*, Cornell West and Henry Louis Gates Jr. state, "Economists have shown that fully one-third of the members of the African American Community are worse off economically today than they were the day that King was killed" (xii).

11. See Booker T. Washington's "Chapter XIV: The Atlanta Exposition Address," in *Up from Slavery*, and W. E. B. Du Bois's "Talented Tenth: Memorial Address," *H. E. B. Du Bois: A Reader*, 317–53.

12. While gender issues are not the focus of this study, it would be censurable not to acknowledge that home must obviously be considered a gendered space. Both Lynn Spigel's *Make Room for Television* and Nina Liebman's *Living Room Lectures* offer insight into the relationship between women and home during the postwar era.

13. The "mammies" like the protagonist of *Beulah* and the "sambos" like "Andy" and "Kingfish" (*Amos 'n' Andy*) were the representational norm for Blacks in the early years of the electronic hearth.

14. While my family may have shared the values espoused by the Huxtables, which in some ways was simply a modern Anderson family ethic (aka *Father Knows Best*), we certainly did not share either their bank account or their lifestyle.

15. Theo became the responsible college graduate Clair and Cliff wanted, while Alex remained virtually unchanged. Alex's politics and sense of social responsibility were still diametrically opposed to those of his parents.

16. This statement was excerpted from the *Friends* fact sheet on the NBC Website.

17. In the case of the extremely high profile *Friends*, the lack of color has become fodder for jokes on late night and even on other situation comedies. On the 13 November 1997 episode of NBC's *News Radio*, the story line detailed the heat-induced daydreams of the station staff. The daydream of the only woman of color on staff takes place in the lunch room, where she fantasizes about being in a multiple people of color workplace. In the daydream she is joined by her multicultural hallucinatory coworkers, and they discuss how it makes you wonder about equal opportunity when there is "only one of us." She is jarred back into reality as an all-Anglo group of coworkers joins her. The group conversation takes a route very different from that of her daydream. The first coworker says, "So did everybody see *Friends* last night? I never mass it." Along the same lines, when David Schwimmer (Ross) hosted *Saturday Night Live*, the commercial advertising his appearance showed Schwimmer standing next to Tim Meadows,

the African American member of the SNL troupe; Schwimmer tells viewers to be ready to see him do some things you'll never see on "Must See TV," Nettles adds, "You'll see Ross talking to a black man." (It is also significant to note that there is a minimal Anglo presence in *Living Single* as well.)

18. To a certain extent, the examination of sitcom history (in terms of the construction of the ensemble show) reveals a trajectory from the family home to the workplace as home to an alternative construction of home in a space of leisure like the bar in *Cheers*, the coffee shop in *Seinfeld*, and Central Perk in *Friends*. The workplace, which was so integral to shows like *The Mary Tyler Moore Show* and *Barney Miller*, had been progressively replaced by places of leisure long before the term "slacker" even emerged. After all, we know that Cliff and Norm had jobs (as mailman and sometime CPA, respectively), but their identity was clearly defined by their place at the bar in *Cheers*. For further discussion of the ensemble sitcom, see Ella Taylor's *Prime Time Families* and *MTM "Quality Television,"* ed. Jane Feuer, et al.

19. The African-American family ties depicted in *Living Single* seem to counter both the notion of disconnected Black families (without history or family tradition—an echo of families ripped apart by slavery) and to warn against the individualist pursuits of the American Dream, which threaten the familial ties that bind in Black communities

20. In the preface to *The Future of the Race*, while explaining the motivation behind their "analysis" in which they "think through—and critique Du Bois's challenge of commitment to service." Gates and West refer to themselves as "we, two grandchildren" of the group of intellectuals Du Bois dubbed the "Talented Tenth" (vii).

Works Cited

Brown, Malaika, "Sisterhood Televised: Yvette Bowser and the Voices She Listens To." American Visions (April–May 1995): 42–43.

Du Bois, W. E. B. The Souls of Black Folks (1903). Norton Anthology of African American Fiction. Ed. Henry Louis Gates Jr. and Nellie Y. McKay. New York: W. W. Norton & Co., 1998.

——. "Talented Tenth: Memorial Address." W. E. B. Du Bois: A Reader, Ed. David Levering Lewis. New York: Henry Holt & Co., 1995.

Fuller, Linda K. The Cosby Show; Audience, Impact, Implications. Westport, CT: Greenwood Press, 1992.

Gabtiel, Teshome H., and Hamid Naticy. "Preface." Otherness and the Media: The Ethnography of the Imagined. Ed. Naficy and Gabriel, Langhorne, PA: Harwood Academic Publishers, 1993.

Gates, Henry Louis, Jr., and Cornell West. The Future of the Race. New York: Vintage Press, 1996.

Gilroy, Paul. The Black Atlantic: Modernity and Double Consciousness. Cambridge, MA: Harvard UP, 1993

Gitlin, Todd. Inside Prime Time. New York: Pantheon Books, 1985.

——. "Prime Time Ideology: The Hegemonic Process in Television Entertainment." Television: The Critical View. 5th ed. Ed. Horace Newcomb New York: Oxford UP, 1994.

Gray, Herman. "Response to Justin Lewis and Sut Jbally." American Quarterly 46 (March 1994).

——. Watching Race: Television and the Struggle for Blackness. Minnepolis: U of Minnesota P. 1995.

Hamamoto, Darrell. Nervous Laughter: Television Situation Comedies and Liberal Democratic Ideology. New York: Praeger, 1989.

hooks, bell. Yearning: race, gender and cultural politics. Boston: South End Press, 1990.

Jhally, Sut, and Justin Lewis. Enlightened Racism: The Cosby Show, Audiences and the Myth of the American Dream. Boulder, CO: Westview Press, 1992.

McClain, LeAmta. A Foot in Each World. Evanston, IL: Northwestern UP, 1987.

Rapping, Elayne "The Seinfeld Syndrome." Progressive (September 1995): 23.1–23.12.

Said, Edward. "Reflections on Exile." Out There: Marginalization and Contemporary Cultures. Ed. Russell Ferguson, Martha Gever. Trinh T. Min-ha, and Cornell West. New York and Cambridge: Museum of Contemporary Art and MIT Press, 1992.

Schlesinger, Arthur, Jr. The Disuniting of America. New York: W. W. Norton & Co., 1992.

Spigel, Lynn. Make Room for Television: Television and the Family Ideal in Postwar America. Chicago: U of Chicago P. 1992.

Ticci, Cecelia. Electronic Hearth. New York: Oxford UP. 1991.

Tocqueville, Alexis de. Democracy in America Ed. Richard D. Heffner, New York: Mentor/New American Library, 1956.

Washington, Booker T. Up from Slavery. New York: Doubleday. Page & Co., 1901.

West, Cornell. Race Matters, New York: Vintage Press, 1994.

Black Representation in the Post Network, Post Civil Rights World of Global Media

Herman Gray

Introduction

Much about the world of American network television has changed in the years since I completed *Watching Race* (Gray 1995). I ended *Watching Race* with the 1992 television season. Although I was disappointed with the cancellation of several of my favourite programmes, I remained hopeful about the prospect of black representations on American network television. Black-oriented shows like *The Cosby Show* and *It's a Different World* moved from premiere network schedules to the financially lucrative world of returns and syndication. Although a perceptible shift from a focus on the middle class to urban youth appeared for a while, they were replaced in the network schedule with black shows preoccupied with domestic families, parenting, and social relationships. Fox Television continued its quest for legitimacy and financial profitability with black shows like *New York Under Cover* and a staple of hip-hop youth oriented comedies.

Two new networks—Warner Brothers (WB) and Paramount (UPN)—joined Fox in challenging the dominance of the three major networks. To do so the new networks used black-oriented programming to anchor their evening schedule. This use of black-oriented comedies to get a scheduling toehold in a network's formative years continues the programming strategy that the Fox News Corporation used in its formative years. With the least to lose financially and reputationally, Fox Television took greater (aesthetic and marketing) risks by pursuing urban and youth audiences interested in black-oriented programming (Zook 1994; Gray 1995; Watkins 1998). Today new networks like Warner Brothers and Paramount operate in an environment transformed by cable and satellite delivery systems and niche marketing (Burrough and Master 1997; Sterngold 1998b).

By 1997 black cast and black theme oriented shows were still confined largely to the genre of situation comedy and entertainment variety. The major networks scheduled a mixture of night-time drama featuring black lead characters. These included NYPD *Blue, ER, Law and Order, Chicago Hope, Homicide: Life on the Street, Touched By an Angel, 413 Hope Street* and *Players*. The network also scheduled the usual fare of black-oriented situation comedies with identifiable black actors like Bill Cosby, Gregory Hines, LL Cool J and Jaleel White.

There is little news here. These developments are quite unremarkable. The network strategy of offering programmes that feature all black casts and themes accompanied by a smaller number of shows with a sprinkling of black cast members continue a pattern that began in the early 1970s following the urban rebellions of the previous decades. But I do remain curious, even intrigued by the excessive and persistent dwelling by journalists and some scholars on the ebb and flow of black television representations from season to season.

For instance, according to a 1998 *New York Times* piece, the prospect for black television representations seemed considerably more dismal than prior seasons (Sterngold 1998a). Indeed, it seems that the hour-long drama has finally delivered the goods by staging programmes with multiracial casts, devoting story-lines to complex depictions of black life, and locating such programmes in integrated workplace settings. Apparently this has not been the case for television's construction and representation of the intimate domestic spaces of home and family. For not only does the representations of blacks remain largely confined to the genre of situation comedy, but also there seems to be a general apprehension (if not outright fear) on the business side about the financial risks involved in pursing racial crossover dreams. As interesting to me is the discursive frame through which journalists, critics, industry observers, network executives and television makers talk about television representations and race. The conventional wisdom seems to be that black and white television viewers like and watch different programmes. The financially risky and culturally pressing question is whether or not white viewers will watch shows about black life that feature predominately black casts?

The structural and financial circumstance of the US television industry continue to evolve including the fact that audiences are migrating in record numbers to other forms and sites of service delivery (Burrough and Masters 1997; *The Economist* 1997b). In such a context, the racial politics of audience composition, viewing preferences and financial risks articulated by the stability of data on the racial basis of audience preferences may well be the cultural expression of a crisis. In this instance television is the pre-eminent space of the public sphere. I want to suggest that this crisis is cultural and structural. That is, that the structural transformations in the global media industry are articulated culturally and that the racialization that structures audience preferences in US network television are expressive of the developments. Moreover I want to ponder what this circumstance means for black television programming and black media representations, both in terms of possibilities and limitations.

Black television representations are shaped by shifting conditions of possibility that include new global markets, larger and more powerful interlocking structures of ownership, newer and more complex relations between products and means of distribution and circulation, and less and less regulation by local, national and international governments. Among the most far-reaching and consequential transformations affecting American television are passage of the 1996 Telecommunications Act, the changes in corporate ownership of media conglomerates, the emerging structure and global reach of entertainment/media/information companies, and rapid advances in new technologies and programme delivery (Andrews 1996).

In the years since the close of the 1992 network television season (where the concluding episode of the year's most popular programme, *The Cosby Show*, was broadcast opposite news coverage of the flames of the Los Angeles rebellion), a new industrial logic has emerged. Within this logic, larger and often more nimble corporate entities have formed ensuring access to larger and larger capital resources that afford bigger and bigger shares of the global entertainment/information/communications market. Through joint ventures, buy-outs, mergers, and new investments, global companies like Fox, Warner, TCI and Microsoft have solidified their positions as global players. These companies acquired television stations, film studios, cable operations, satellites, publishing houses, record companies, theme parks and communications infrastructure. While remaining large complex bureaucratic organizations, these global media corporations are organized into smaller and more efficient administrative (and creative) units, designed to strategically and efficiently deploy precise methods to identify markets, generate products, control distribution, and move them anywhere on the globe. Larger and larger, yet nimble and more flexible administrative and financial units are structured to generate and distribute a diverse range of entertainment and information products. The goal is to establish greater access to and control of global markets.

In this new mediascape, distinctive creative, technological and financial entities and activities—computers, cinema, telephony, broadcasting, publishing, satellite, theme parks, cable, music and electronics—are organized to form giant global media firms like TCI, Time Warner, Fox News Corporations, Disney and Seagram. While this kind of reconfiguration was anticipated in the late 1970s and early 1980s, one of the immediate political and legal factors that facilitated its realization was, of course, the passage of the 1996 Telecommunications Act (United States Government 1996). The Act restructured major aspects of the telecommunications industry. These included the scope of federal regulation and oversight, the size and composition of firms, the assignment of broadcast frequencies for television, radio, and cellular telephones, the upper limit on the operation and ownership of broadcast stations, the control of delivery systems and the complementarity between various media technologies.

The 1996 Telecommunications Act sharply deregulated the telecommunications industry. This gave major US corporations like Time Warner, General Electric, Fox News Corporation, TCI, Microsoft, Seagram and Disney the green light to pursue mergers, joint ventures, new research and development, and worldwide expansion with the blessings (and supposed oversight) of the US Congress. So profound and far reaching was the 1996 Telecommunications Act that no aspect of American (and to a lesser extent global) telecommunications was left unaffected.

As the major corporate players acquire new properties, enter joint ventures, and otherwise pursue the globe as one giant market for media, information and entertainment newer more powerful and diverse corporate entities appear. Microsoft the computer software giant is suddenly in the television business, Fox News Corporation is in the sports and satellite business, General Electric is in the sports arena business and Time Warner owns news, cable, film, publishing and music entities (Auletta 1997). Television production companies, television stations, television networks and cable operations all represent components of these global media giants.

In the new environments of global media, companies must maintain consistent sources of content or software that can be moved efficiently through multiple delivery systems (such as computers, television sets, CD players or movie screens) aimed at markets across the globe. The technological distinctions, organizational partitions and cultural meanings that once defined technologies, delivery systems or media are no longer meaningful in any productive sense. Media content moves just as easily from novel to cinema screen to television to video to theme park and programming (Davis 1997). With such a voracious demand for content to fill markets worldwide, telecommunications companies must contend with increasing production costs, greater consumer choices, and more varied delivery systems all of which are intended to exert control over production, distribution, and markets.

Through joint ventures, multiple ownership (TCI for instance owns controlling interests in the black cable network operation Black Entertainment Television) and cooperative development agreements covering hardware and software, the major corporations extended their control (Auletta 1997). As consumers we experience these forms of control at the point of our most familiar and mundane encounters with the telephone receiver, the cable box, the computer screen and the television set.

Where have all the black shows gone?

The 1997 autumn season of American network television indicates a pattern with regard to black television representation. In the autumn television schedule, black television shows are still present, however they are concentrated largely among the programme offerings of the newest television networks. They were also mainly situation comedies. Of the six commercial television networks, Warner Brothers (WB), Paramount (UPN) and Fox News Corporation (Fox) have a combined total of sixteen shows that can be identified as black or black oriented prime time programmes. Of the traditional majors, CBS programmed three and NBC one. ABC did not schedule a single black show for the 1997 season. Fox scheduled three (including the only night-time drama), WB scheduled four and UPN placed a total of five shows on its autumn schedule. Most of the scheduled programmes are returning from the previous several seasons; of these the most popular and well known black show on Fox is *Living Single* starring Queen Latifah. *Living Single* was initially cancelled, but quickly revived by Fox after a successful letter writing compaign by the show's fans. The often-controversial *Martin* and the popular *New York Undercover* were not renewed for the 1997 Fox line-up.

In addition to Queen Latifah, familiar stars like Bill Cosby, the members of the Wayans family, Jamie Fox, Brandy (Moesha), Steve Harvey, Jaleel White and Malcolm Jamaal Warner all returned to the prime time television schedule. It should come as no surprise that situation comedy is the dominant genre and households and workplaces are the dominant setting for shows this season. Stories about adolescent maturation, relationships, friendships and room-mates provide continuing storylines and narrative action. This season's televisual black Americans are drawn largely from the middle and working classes and it includes both students and retirees who range in ages from small children to elders. Characters live in various domestic arrangements including extended families, shared living spaces, marriages and nuclear families. All of the situation comedies fall within the predictable conventions of the genre—medium shots, light-hearted dramas, everyday difficulties and relationship tensions. These genre conventions move characters through predictable experiences and situations that provide momentary transformation. The action and emotional cues are pumped up and pushed along with laughter provided by enthusiastic studio audiences and laugh tracks. Contemporary music, fashion, language and information give the shows the feel of being steeped in contemporary urban black popular culture and style that is made explicit with regular guest appearances by entertainers and athletes. Recognizable figures—mostly athletes and musicians—regularly find their way to the small screen. Similarly former television personalities like Will Smith (*Fresh Prince of Bel Air*) and Martin Lawrence (*Martin*) have moved from the weekly grind of sustaining a weekly series to the more lucrative world of film.

While not particularly remarkable aesthetically, the fact is that these shows help blacks to sustain a presence, albeit separate, in the media-scape of American network television. This stubborn separate (and not always equal) racial representation on American commercial network television remains the source of continuing frustration and concern, especially on the part of media activists, journalists and scholars. Upon closer inspection it is apparent that the most integrated casts and story-lines take place on hour-long dramatic programmes like *ER, Homicide* and *NYPD Blue*. These shows are often set in the public spaces of work. However, the genre of situation comedy—long associated with intimacy, family, romance and domesticity—is a site of some of the most benign but persistent segregation in American public culture.

Furthermore, while the television industry continue to maintain what many see as a minimal commitment to black presence on commercial network television, the shows that do survive are located, least structurally anyway, in the least risky part of the network schedule (and the low investment sector of corporation). WB, UPN and Fox—all among the newest networks—use the principle of narrow-casting and the strategy of niche marketing to target their start-up markets: youth. Even though ABC, NBC, and CBS still enjoy a considerable share of the commercial television market, when cable and the new networks are factored in the traditional network share is below 50 percent. Traditional networks like NBC have also adopted niche marketing strategies by positioning their operations as name brands that appeal to white middle-class professionals with shows like *Friends, Seinfeld, Frasier, Cybil, Suddenly Susan, Third Rock from the Sun, ER* and *NYPD Blue*. As with cable, the newest networks have made the greatest inroads into the traditional network share by targeting youth and urban markets. That is, these new networks pursue such programming strategies until they establish a logo or product identity with advertisers and key sectors of their market.

From the culture of the television business and financial interests of media corporations, what appears on the social and political radar as segregation and containment of black shows, may, be the articulation of the new industry logic. Since the television environment is no longer dominated by three major networks, the force of various new delivery systems, global media operations and marketing clutter is felt ever more immediately and directly. This means that in order to remain competitive, television programmers must be more focused, efficient and explicit about their audiences, their programmes, and their so-called product identity. Despite their claims to the contrary, to remain competitive networks long ago abandoned the strategy of alming the least objectionable programmes at the widest possible audiences. Cable operators, upstart networks and some majors have made explicit marketing decisions to use programming to target and reach various demographics. Black shows may not be contained so much as they are developed and deployed by networks to gain a specific market advantage in an increasingly cluttered schedule.

This segmented programming strategy suggests that Fox, UPN and WB are modelled explicitly after cable (Carter 1998; New York Times Magazine 1998). Together with cable the modest success of the new networks in such a short period is helping to reshape the scheduling, marketing and programming of the US television industry. These operations are after smaller, more sharply defined demographics. They schedule relatively inexpensive shows (including reruns, films, game shows and reality programmes) with identifiable stars and personalities. They combine various forms of programming and service delivery including cable wire, the traditional broadcast signal and satellite service.

The cultural politics of black representation

These powerful structuring conditions are constitutive and productive. They are structuring forces expressed culturally. But social choices and cultural frames saturate these structuring conditions. Cultural meanings shape the organization and use of media products and representations. Where black representations are concerned, therefore, the very conception of a black show or black programming (even as an expression of local, regional and national sensibilities and identities) must be theorized in relationship to these structuring conditions and cultural meanings. Given these circumstances, black television makers and programmers face the very real prospect that the circuits, meaning(s) and uses of blackness are accelerated and more dispersed than ever before. (The sign of blackness as always circulated discursively, historically and geographically.) Moreover black American intellectuals and cultural workers have always exercised, to the extent possible, a measure of control over how and what blackness signified. In light of the new technologies, sophisticated means of circulation and reconfigured systems of production, the contemporary challenge is not just to consider the narrative of assimilation versus separation of black Americans in network television, but how blackness means, what it means and where.

Just what exactly is a black programme and what does it signify? Discursively the emphasis on the local conditions of production, the specific social circumstances in which they are received and the particular cultural meaning that they express will continue to shape what such representations mean in the US. Its encounter with and circulation in the new global media environment will mediate the cultural meanings of blackness. I still want to insist on the cultural significance and historical specificity of black television programming that emanates from the US. The cultural significance of black images generated from the US rests with how they function as cultural sites for the articulation of specific meanings, relations, histories and struggles. At the same time the significance of this programming can no longer just be limited to local and specific meanings and politics in the US. Programming constraints (especially American commercial networks) shapes these very local and particular meanings and cultural encounters that are neither local nor specific to the US. It is very clear that American network executives remain deeply ambivalent and suspicious of black shows to do any more than generate short-term profits in US television markets. But new technologies or exhibition, circulation, and delivery make it possible to broaden the field of vision and play for the first time.

Now (black) programme makers and buyers can ask, for perhaps the first time, how will black television programming play in the distant reaches of the vast corporate marketplace made possible by satellite, cable, the Internet and other forms of global delivery? Will the demands of distant markets rob locally based black programming of its specificity and historicity? Is the prerequisite for black television shows (and cinemas) that they travel well? That they speak in a universal language? And if so, what is that language(s) and what is the embodied representation(s) through which it is expressed? Is it the naturalized (racialized) athletic and dancing black body? Perhaps it is the body endowed with musical prowess? Is it the black corporal body of liberal civil rights? Perhaps it is the neo-nationalist subject of hip-hop discourse? As the American television experience seems to suggest, the desire for blackness articulated in the public spaces of integrated workplaces is preferable to that which threatens the intimate spaces of the family and domesticity. This narrative is, of course, a very old story in the American racial imagination.

Shows that finally make it to a network schedule (or a cine-plex screen) now more than ever are required by the structure of new corporate owners, delivery systems and global markets to speak in a universal language recognizable across (or perhaps through) the particularities of history, circumstance, experience and geography. Black shows now mean in relation to a rapidly changing political and cultural field of finance, production, exhibition and circulation of media software that includes sports, film, music, games, fashion and style. The travels of media representations of blackness also provides an occasion to grapple directly with the role of media and television in the cultural production of the US as a structured racial and national formation. The meanings, pleasures and identifications we generate from black television representations, no matter where and how it travels, still bear the perceptible traces of the specifically American circumstance in which blackness is constructed and operates.

Black representation and the post-civil rights public sphere

While liberal journalistic discourses about segregation and integration, crossover and separation persist in the US, the shifting global media environment may well provide the occasion for asking a different kind of question about the racial politics of American network television and its programming practices. They may present the opportunity for making sense of television's representations and audience reception patterns as the expression of the breakdown even irrelevance of a conception of (a mass mediated) public sphere organized by the discourse of civil rights. The persistence of racialized programming patterns and viewing preference may well suggest the presence of a post-civil rights public sphere (Lipsitz 1994).

The new logic of television broadcasting in the US may well have two seemingly contradictory social implications for television representations of blackness. In purely economic and marketing terms television shows about blacks will continue to appeal to (network) programmers to the extent that they can compliment and heighten the product identification of their programmer (networks). This means that as traditional network identities—expressed through their logos and stable of programmes on a given evening, across the schedule and throughout the season—become more focused and explicit the defining market characteristics and aesthetic parameters of a network will drive the demand for programmes. The genre, star power, programme conventions and scheduling strategies cannot help but remain constraining as they continue to guide programme suppliers. While it may well fulfill demand within identifiable genres designed to attract a particular market niche, this strategy, developed to reduce market uncertainty, will mean that the programme offerings that do manage to find their way to a networks programme schedule will remain safe and conventional. As buyers and schedulers of programmes, network executives continue, indirectly at least, to shape the range, look, content and style of a show that it seeks to programme. All of this is with the explicit aim of matching advertisers with the ears and eyes of those guaranteed by the networks.

A broader range of service delivery options and the rising importance of television programmes as sources of product identity for global media companies may well mean greater possibilities for black and minority representations to circulate more widely within and across various market niches. Indeed, a stable and persistent finding in the US indicates that blacks and whites like and view different programmes (Sterngold 1998a). Black oriented programming that enjoys wide reception in black households, seldom if ever register with white viewers. As I have already noted, rather than see or read this finding as a failure of the ideal of integration in the post-civil rights public sphere, perhaps the finding can be read as an opportunity to register black tastes, interests and pleasures. The real question is whether or not programme makers and buyers will respond to these expressions of tastes and preferences. Though the range of difference within a given market niche will perhaps be reduced, the proliferation of niches—the 500 channel model touted for digital television—could mean more programming outlets for black film, video and television makers. (The hegemony of corporate control of television means that even with the proliferation of channels and new delivery systems, this proliferation may well mean that these 500 plus channels will look more alike than different.)

If this is true, then the most immediate implication is the appearance of programming that is driven less by the demand for intelligibility and relevance by broad audiences who may speak a given language or know the intimacies of a particular cultural experience. Though relatively small, the success of ethnic programming on low cable stations and low power operations is but one example. Story-lines, cultural assumptions and social context may be more directly assumed and thus easily negotiated under such conditions than those that presently exist. Politically this situation makes for some interesting possibilities for engaging memories, histories and stories that are particular and specific at the same time as they have global implications. Directed at specific audiences in particular places, such stories also require information and understandings rooted in identifications, loyalties and interests that transcend such specificity and particularity.

Of course imagining such possibilities for the new broadcast environment assumes that the global corporate entities remain open to identifying and serving such niches (and that they are profitable). Make no mistake about it, at this point American television broadcasting is a buyer's market. Giant entertainment/information/media companies control the libraries, film holdings, book lists and software around the world. With their vast financial resources and through their control of telephone lines, satellites, broadcast stations, publishing houses and software, there is little doubt but that they are the major purchasers and schedulers of programming content around the world.

Nonetheless, in the changing climate of global broadcasting, the logic that drives this global structure still must respond to and organize the uncertainty that still exists at the local level. Even as it continues to structure identifications and alliances that can be realized through the new technologies of communication, it can never completely discipline nor absolutely control such possibilities. Thus it would appear that blacks, Asians, Latinos, gays and lesbians can get a small toehold into an industry whose hallmark is packaging our desires and identifications. While it is true that the control which these global entities exercise over the programming options available to us all is increasingly hegemonic, in the end they must still be able to reach the eyes and ears of real people if they are to survive.

Conclusion

The immediate problem for black programme makers is no longer the challenge of making black programmes, they are available perhaps as never before. The problem of making a greater variety of programmes—and getting them to desirable audiences—may well be the more urgent challenge. In addition, negotiating the logic of the market as a terrain on which forms of community, identification and association are constructed and structured is as tricky as it is potentially productive. Programme makers will face the competing demands of generating programmes that speak to the specific concerns of particular and local markets. By the same token these programmes must travel to distant markets and audiences with different histories, traditions, languages and experiences. The meanings (and politics) of blackness will have to be negotiated with the terms of these competing aesthetic and economic demands.

How does one speak with confidence about what such shows mean and how, when the audiences and the markets they organize do not always share particular histories, identifications and experiences? To be sure, in a global media world such as ours, neither immediate experience nor shared identification is required for a given programme to produce meaning and pleasure. (Indeed, I suppose one might argue that our modern global media-scape itself—whether the Internet, cinema, music or satellite—constructs identifications and shared histories through its very existence.) However, representations, no matter where they circulate or how they are generated, are more than free floating signifiers cut loose from the social and historical mooring that make them intelligible in the first place. Though media representations do obviously mean at multiple levels and in different times and places, they continue to bear the traces of their conditions of production and the historicity of their time and place.

Further reading

Davis, S.G. (1997) *Spectacular Nature: Corporate Culture and the Sea World Experience*. Berkeley, CA: University of California Press.

Gray, H. (1995) *Watching Race: Television and the Struggle for 'Blackness'*. Minneapolis, MN: University of Minnesota Press.

Herman, E. and McChesney, R. (1997) *The Global Media: The New Missionaries of Corporate Capitalism*. London: Cassell.

Lipsitz, G. (1994) *Dangerous Cross Roads*. London: Verso.

Sreberny-Mohammadi, A., Winseck, D., McKenna, J. and Boyd-Burrett, O. (eds) (1998) *Media in Global Context*. London: Edward Arnold.

Why "Beulah" and "Andy" Still Play Today: Minstrelsy in the New Millennium

Bambi L. Haggins

Introduction

This essay was inspired by the reaction of many of my students to seeing episodes of *Beulah* and *Amos 'n' Andy* in a course on the history of American television. While they clearly understood why *Amos 'n' Andy* had been deemed offensive, they couldn't understand why *Beulah*, which most found cringingly unwatchable, had not been questioned. Given that I basically shared their views, I began to consider how this sort of *hierarchy of objectionability* played out in attitudes towards representations of Blackness in the contemporary Black sitcom and the way we, as scholars and spectators, analyze them. Although some might be tempted to argue that clearly times have changed since Beulah hi-de-ho'd around the kitchen for the pleasure and edification of her young White charge—that 'cooning'[1] for the camera is a thing of days gone by—events of the past few years underscore how far we *haven't* come.

In July of 1999, the National Association for the Advancement of Colored People (NAACP)[2] made its first formal assault on network programming since the campaign that resulted in *Amos 'n' Andy* being pulled from network play. When NAACP president Kweisi Mfume blasted the networks for offering a fall lineup that was 'a virtual whitewash of programming' in the organization's memo on diversity, it began the process of putting televisual representations of race on the agenda for networks execs, political pundits and the viewing audience at large.[3] Threatened blackouts (and brownouts)—boycotts of network programming by people of color coalitions—National Council for La Raza, National Asian American Telecommunications Association and the NAACP—as well as public forums on issues of diversity within the institutions of the industry (like the National Association of Broadcasters) have yielded pledges to increase diversity from the Big Four (ABC, CBS, Fox, NBC). However, the actual results have been mixed.

As a result of new network 'consciousness,' Black television dramas have come—and gone—from network primetime.[4] The situation comedy remains the staple of Black representation in television fiction. According to the 'African American Television Report,' over half of the African-American characters seen on network television as series regulars are in sitcoms with a majority on upstart netlets, UPN and the WB ('Screen Actor Guild . . .', 2000, par. 6).

Upon examining representations of Blacks in the earliest examples of African-American centered comedies, *Beulah* and *Amos 'n' Andy*, those found in post-*Cosby Show* sitcoms that premiered before the threatened 'blackout'—*The PJ's* on Fox (later on the WB), UPN's *The Secret Diary of Desmond Pfeiffer*, and *The Hughleys* on ABC (transplanted to UPN)—as well as two series born in the age of 'new consciousness,' UPN's *The Parkers* and *Girlfriends*, a disconcerting tendency becomes clear: 'Beulah' and 'Andy' still play today. In other words, over 40 years after television's happy darky domestic served 'her' family for the last time, the character constructions and stock comic 'bits' of minstrelsy[5] continue to inflect the narratives of Black sitcoms. However, before venturing into the analysis

308

of the contemporary televisual texts, it is vital to understand the context in which Beulah and Andy originally played as well as the climate for and content of the conflicted and conflictual discourses currently circulating around comedic constructions of Blackness.

Back in the Day: Unquestioned (?) Minstrelsy And Beyond

Arguably, the situation comedy can be viewed as an over-determined cultural artifact—each series simultaneously producing and reflecting trends in American society. The televisual iterations of suburban bliss, the 1950's domestic comedies, had only one acceptable place for Black Americans—in the kitchen. As Gray asserts: 'In the televisual world of the early fifties, the social and cultural rules of race relations were explicit; black otherness was required for white subjectivity; blacks and whites occupied separate and unequal worlds; black labor was always in the service of white domesticity . . . black humor was necessary for the amusement of whites' (Gray, 1995, p. 75).

Beulah supplied all the ingredients for a good old-fashioned minstrel show. Beulah served as the personification of the happy darky domestic, her child-like idiot friend, Oriole, as a queen-sized pickaninny and her beau, Bill, as a conflation of the Coon and the Tom, the Black working man who avoided work and responsibility but did a good Uncle Remus when the White folks were around. It seems mind-boggling that this series did not inspire the same ire in the Black middle class (in the form of the NAACP) that was directed at *Amos 'n' Andy*.

Three actors played Beulah, each of whom had to varying degrees been relegated to 'mammy' roles: veteran performer Ethel Waters, who originated the role (1950–52); and was briefly replaced by Scarlet O'Hara's mammy, Hattie MacDaniel (six episodes), and finally by Louise Beavers, a classically trained actor, who left the show in 1953, while it was still highly rated. The image of the 'mammy' seems crafted to both undermine and underscore the role played by African-American women. The fact that Black women, either by default (as single parents) or by design (as a familial tradition), have been the very foundation of reassurance and stability in Black lives and struggles has been co-opted. In *Beulah*, the needs and desires of Black women are erased (as is the existence of their homes and families). But, for the most part, the same folks in the Black bourgeoisie who bitterly condemned *Amos 'n' Andy* just didn't have *as much* of a problem with *Beulah*.

The problem with *Amos 'n' Andy* was, in reality, Kingfish and Andy. The conniving and ridiculous Kingfish with his butchering of the English language (misspeaking) and his constant embellishing (whether for profit or self-aggrandizement) and the good-hearted but essentially shiftless Andy (whose shortcuts to the good life are always unsuccessful) dominated the series' episodes. The shrewish behavior of the most central female character, Sapphire, Kingfish's wife, acted as narrative garnish. Middle-class values are embodied in level-headed Amos, who, along with his rarely seen wife, Ruby, get little airtime—and are no closer to getting their piece of the American Dream than are Kingfish or Andy.

The NAACP campaign to remove the show was eventually successful in 1953, when longtime sponsors Blatz Beer pulled out. Despite the racist and stereotypical representations of African-Americans that appeared in *Amos 'n' Andy*, 'many poor, working class and even middle-class blacks still managed to read against the dominant discourse of whiteness and find humor in the show . . . [but] . . . tastes pleasures and voices in support of the show were drowned out by the moral outrage of middle-class blacks' (Gray, 1995, p. 75). In addition, *Amos 'n' Andy* played into the 'separate but equal' discourse that showed a hermetically sealed community of color where Blacks were sampling the 'good life'—even if they were not the central characters. Alvin Childress who played 'Amos' defended the series, 'I didn't feel it harmed Negroes at all . . . Actually the series had many episodes that showed the Negro with many professions and businesses like attorneys, store owners and so on, which they had never had in TV or movies before' ('Alvin Childress . . .', 1986).

The utilization of the minstrel archetypes in the early years of the electronic hearth is not surprising. Both *Amos 'n' Andy* and *Beulah* were carryovers from radio—the former being the colorized version of the radio show that had been performed by Charles Correll and Freeman Gosden, the

White creators of the series, and the latter as a spin-off of Fibber McGee and Molly. Neither of these series were going after a Black audience share—the minstrel archetypes were deliberate and designed to amuse and comfort the new medium's predominantly White audience. One might contend that *Amos 'n' Andy* upset the sensibilities of the Black middle class not only because it put Black faces in narrative blackface but also because this televisual minstrel show was set in Harlem—which, even in the early 1950s, retained the veneer of a golden age of the Black intelligentsia. The same Black middle-class voices that railed against *Amos 'n' Andy* were relatively silent on the *Beulah* front[6]: the White middle class gained comfort from the happy darky, and the Black middle class ignored her—after all, none of them did day work.

In the intervening decades between *Beulah* and *The Parkers*, representations of Blackness evolved to include: the Super Negroes of the 1960s showing the Great Society dream of integration with good Blacks like the young war widow of *Julia* or *I Spy's* international man of mystery and former Rhodes scholar, Alexander Scott; the ghetto comedies of the 1970s that made poverty look oddly pastoral with *Good Times'* incredibly shrinking Evans family of the South side of Chicago projects, which started out as close-knit and nuclear and ended with J.J. (the Sambo, as the head of the household); and the Super African-Americans with Phylicia Rashad and Bill Cosby as the JD/MD parental embodiment of the colorized American Dream. If one assumes that *The Cosby Show*, the 1980s domestic sitcom *par excellence*, marks the most complete assimilation of an African-American series into the network mainstream, then it would follow that, in the 1990s, an era of niche programming and the proliferation of cable, the legacy of minstrelsy would have faded from the electronic hearth. But, of course, you would be wrong—a point confirmed by the Fox sitcom developed for the former host of HBO's *Def Comedy Jam*, Martin Lawrence. The progeny of 'Andy' and 'Beulah' still play on network television—whether on Fox, the newest member of the Network big boys, or on UPN. The motivations behind these programming choices are both suspect and many.

Televisual (Dis)Comfort: Race and the Situation Comedy

One takes a certain risk when tackling contemporary televisual constructions of Blackness. The easy part is calling attention to the reincarnation of Sapphire in *Martin's* Sheneneh or the Stepin' Fetchit buffoonery of Marlon on *The Wayans Brothers*; the hard part is to avoid forcing characters into historical defined racist archetypes—like the 'pure' mammy, sambo and, of course, the coon—while still acknowledging the minstrel lineage of these characters. The lack of awareness on the part of the critic can lead to the simple binaryism of positive and negative representations. As Robert Stam and Ella Shohat aptly note in *Unthinking Eurocentrism*, a scholar can fall into an analytical trap: 'Behind every Black child performer the critic discerns a "pickaninny" . . . behind every corpulent or nurturing Black female a "mammy" . . . [thereby running] the risk of reproducing the very racial essentialism they were designed to combat' (Shohat and Stam, 1995, p. 199).

On the other hand, when one looks at televisual representations of Blackness as cultural products, which as Herman Gray notes, are 'part of an ongoing dialogue within and across social locations and positions within and outside black communities,' there is the urge to find empowerment in the surge of images of African-Americans. In Gray's seminal text, *Watching Race*, he pointed to the proliferation of images of Blackness in the early 1990s—exemplified by shows like *Frank's Place*, *A Different World* and *In Living Color*—as 'television representations [that] explode and reveal the deeply rooted terms of [racial] hierarchy' (1995, p. 10). While there is a clear case for the liberatory potential of these series (none of which made it through the 1990s)—as social spaces of contestation— I am not certain the same can be said for most Black sitcom texts today. In addition, I find it disconcerting that, as a result of many postmodern, poststructuralist readings of programs (and the representations within them), which maintain that progressive and regressive forces can be discerned in the performances of identity within televisual texts, we seem to have lost the facility for outrage. All texts can be redeemed in the re-reading.

It seems somehow appropriate that two of the most provocative interventions on the newest iterations of minstrelsy were provided in the form of cinematic texts for the big and small screens, respectively: Spike Lee's feature, *Bamboozled* (2000), and Reggie Rock Bythewood's HBO drama, *Dancing in September* (2000). Although it is not my intention to debate the merits of either film (a detailed discussion of these very different texts goes beyond the boundaries of this essay), the specific questions that these cinematic works raise are infinitely pertinent to this study: What is the insidious nature of minstrelsy in televisual representations of Blackness? And, just as significantly, how do these texts spread the blame for keeping 'cooning' on television alive?

One might argue that Lee's satire, which traces the rise and fall of both Pierre Delacroix, the hip, Harvard-educated and sole person of color working for an upstart netlet (played in high theatricality by Damon Wayans) and his black-faced Frankenstein of programming, *Mantan: The New Millennium Minstrel Show*, strains the bounds of credulity. After all, literal blackface couldn't play with today's 'racially enlightened' audiences, right? Nonetheless, particular sequences in the films directly relate to commentaries made by those in the business of putting Black shows on the air. In the sequence in which Delacroix's boss, Dunwitty (Michael Rappaport), the poster boy for misappropriation of Black culture, gives him an ultimatum about the kind of programming the network needs, a clear message is given about what Black shows will not work in the post-*Cosby* era:

> Dunwitty: *The material you've been writing is too white bread. It's white people with Black faces. The Huxtables, Cosby—a genius, revolutionary, Theo, Lisa Bonet—dope. But we can't go down that road again. (Taking a stack of scripts in hand) A black family moves into a white, middleclass suburban enclave . . . shit . . . Garbage, too clean. It's too antiseptic.*

Delacroix's creation of just what Dunwitty wants 'a coon show' that 'is so negative, so offensive and racist' proves to be a runaway hit. The power of success seduces Dela (as he is later called), Mantan/Manray, the homeless tap dancer nee minstrel show star (played by Savion Glover) and Sloan (Jada Pinkett Smith), Dela's assistant (who puts her social consciousness on temporary hold because of a combination of ambition and loyalty)—and this seduction is a prominent part of the film's narrative. What is perhaps most disturbing is what the image of blackface minstrelsy does and does not mean to today's viewing public. As Stephen Holden notes, 'In one of the funniest and most disturbing scenes, members of the show's live audiences, all of whom put on blackface, pop up from their seats to explain enthusiastically why they are niggers' (Holden, 2000).

I do not mean to suggest that the *exact* same thing could happen on network television today but, as Todd Boyd stated, 'When you look at the last five years of Black representation on television, the shows that tend to be the most outrageous also draw the most audiences' (Braxton, 2000a). While the search for the holy grail of a 20-share[7] motivates everyone involved in producing television programs (Black or White, comedy or drama), in the current programming climate, a television comedy is given very little time to find an audience—and it has to be funny. Often 'being funny' translates into falling back into long held stereotype staples.

Dancing in September, chronicles the intersecting paths of two young African-American rising stars in the television industry, a comedy writer, Tommy Crawford (Nicole Ari Parker) and a network exec, George Washington (Isaiah Washington). Almost immediately, the film depicts a clash over whether to take the low (stereotypical) road. In the sequence, Tommy is one of a dozen of a fairly diverse group of writers (there are at least five other people of color); however, she is the only writer who questions any part of the script written by Mel, the Anglo head writer (Peter Onorati). Her desire to humanize the dialogue is met with complete incredulity:

> Tommy: Do we need to button this with a joke? Shelly says, 'Of course, I forgive you. I love you.' Then we have Winston like a jerk saying, 'Baby, not only do you have a big behind, you have a big heart.' Why can't we go out with him saying, 'I love you, too.'
> Mel: For one, we're a sitcom and maybe you haven't noticed but sitcoms tend to look for the humor.
> (A chorus of affirmations for Mel follows.)
> Tommy: We'd get more mileage if we made him sound like a human being . . .

311

Mel: I think he does sound like a human being.

Later, Tommy presides over *Just Us*, the story of a tough African-American juvenile court judge who adopts the charming Maurice, a young Black orphan, after he faces her in court for the third time. It is also the first bona fide hit for the new network. The small initial changes that she is asked to make have become more substantive. In the sequence preceding the replicated scene, the end of a *Just Us* episode is shown filmed three different ways and intercut with the suggestions from network brass that it 'needs to be funnier.' The first version includes the gentle, well-spoken delivery of a woman revealing that she is the orphan's birth mother and a 'spit-take' follows; in the final version, the revelation is made with an almost sexualized stroke of the cheek (I'm yo' mama) and the havoc that ensues includes an Electric Slide dancing robber being foiled by the projectile chicken bone that his 'mama' has 'humorously' Heimliched out of Maurice. Interestingly, the earlier writers' meeting sequence is replicated. Tommy defends her definition of 'funny' to Malik, another young African-American writer. Given that the conflict between Tommy and Malik revolves around the 'evolution' of the Judge's character (who, within the narrative, is played by a two-time Tony award winning actress), the choice of who was acceptable to push into stereotypical caricature echoes discussions of *Beulah* versus *Amos 'n' Andy* and the troubling notion of a hierarchy of objectionability:

> Malik: Maurice tells the judge that his date was his birth mom and she goes on and on about how she doesn't believe him and she says, 'If you do the crime, you do the time, pay the fine or have my foot in your behind.'
> (The folks at the table explode in laughter)
> Tommy: So what's your problem?
> Malik: She's an educated woman but she sounds ignorant. The only thing missing is her rolling her eyes and bobbing her head. I'm sorry but why does the sister have to talk like that?
> Tommy: Because it's funny and shows that are funny stay on the air.
> Malik: Yeah, I agree with you . . . it's funny. Coming from a hoochie mama on E. 47th Street. Tommy, why can't we be funny and honest? I don't know any sister— especially a judge—that would talk like that in this situation.

While this can be seen as an illustration of the jading of an idealist (Tommy), it also begs the question, 'Of what price laughter?' In *Dancing*, Tommy's show, *Just Us*, is transformed by network pressure and the creator's capitulation from a series that 'isn't three jokes a page but sounds like real people' to a showcase for the series' orphaned Black kid, Maurice. Played James (Vicellous Reon Shannon), a street kid who is a naturally gifted actor (and bipolar), the character of Maurice with his catchphrase/choreography (James Brownesque spin), 'You got to keep it real' becomes the Jimmie 'Dy-no-mite' Walker of the season. However, even with this transformation, it is not the character of Maurice but rather the character of Judge Warner that is completely transformed. Judge Warner begins as a tough-as-nails but elegant matriarch and evolves into someone who sounds (and gesticulates) like the stereotypical sexualized and lower-class Black woman—a head-bobbing 'hoochie mama.' Tommy's willful blindness regarding this integration of the mammy/mama bits of minstrelsy is worth noting particularly in relationship to the sitcoms that survived the 'outrage' over Black representation.

Perhaps, in part, the problems in representations of race are the fault of a genre that derives its comedy from the way that 'characters' act and react in a certain situation—and there are only so many situations that 'work.' It was probably for that very reason that the April 16th *Entertainment Weekly* heralded the 'death of the programming genre that has most shaped American popular culture: the sitcom' (p. 27). In his *de facto* eulogy of the genre, Steve Lopez states: 'with the exception of a scant few comedies . . . the current generation of sitcoms has two fundamental problems: the situation, which is mind-numbingly familiar, from one show to the next. And the comedy, which not only is a threat to national intelligence but often carries the unfortunate burden of not being funny' (Lopez, 1999, p. 27).

In this light, we have to consider the almost schizophrenic nature of the pitch mentality in network programming today—which seems to be producing mongrel textual hybrids through a sort of mix and match aesthetic that is both stylistically unstable and narratively unsatisfying. How else can we explain *Homeboys from Outer Space*? If sitcoms, in general, are no longer dwelling in the realm of 'quality television'—exemplified by the MTM series of the 1970s (*The Mary Tyler Moore Show, Rhoda, The Bob Newhart Show*)—Black comedies are, for the most part, residing in the sixth circle of the Inferno, reserved for comic mediocrity. But whose fault is that?

WCWB: Writing Comedy While Black

> *My writers wanted to understand the Black experience—so I fired them. (Chris Rock,* The Chris Rock Show; *visually quoted in* Bamboozled*)*

Some would blame the writers, particularly the African-American writers, who construct the narratives of the Black sitcom. Sharon Johnson, as a Black woman over 30, is hardly the sitcom writer norm (i.e. White, male and under 30); she expressed frustration over being required to recycle stereotypes during her stint on a Black oriented sitcom: 'The attitude is let's just put anything with black faces up there because we know that black people will watch' (Lopez, 1999, p. 30). Black television writer producer, Thad Mumford, whose credits include *M*A*S*H* and *A Different World*, described Black sitcoms as 'just horrible' but he maintains that he doesn't 'Blame the writers . . . I blame the networks for their limited view of how they see blacks on television. On every black show there is a lingering patina of stereotypes' (Braxton, 1999).

Others would blame the creator/producers. But as Ralph Farquhar, producer of the positivist teen sitcom *Moesha* and the highly acclaimed and quickly cancelled *South Central*, notes 'The networks assume that white America is much more racist than they've been proven to be in other areas . . . There's crossover if there's an effort to create the exposure. It's a marketing problem, but they don't want to do that. So there's the chitlin' circuit on TV' (Sterngold, 1998). Thad Wilmore, executive producer of *The PJ's* (along with Eddie Murphy), takes a more conciliatory route: 'It's just the way Hollywood thinks, it's not a racist thing. It's just the nature of the beast. They're concerned with the bottom line . . . they go with what they are most comfortable with.' (Hall, 1999).

Yet, even as these instances of sitcom minstrelsy are critiqued, it is vital to remember that television first and foremost is a commercial medium. The institutional practices of the industry—from counter-programming strategies to who can write for what show—is rationalized in terms that are always economic rather than ideological. The survival of the Black sitcom, as a genre, is dependent upon the ever-changing perceptions that inform these institutional policies.

Taking the Black Block: A Netlet Strategy

> *Obviously, if you are going to launch a new network, the most important thing is getting good ratings in the top thirty urban markets. If other networks want to ignore the Black audience . . . hey . . . all the better for the WPX by offering counter-programming . . . and the CPAA (Colored People's Advancement Association: read NAACP) will point to you as an example. (George Washington in* Dancing in September*)*

Washington's take on the 'obvious' direction for the fictional network clearly articulates the counter-programming strategy that has become common practice in the netlet world. The Black Block comedy programming strategies were used first by Fox, which has considerably lightened its programming since establishing itself as the fourth network. They have been adopted by both the WB and UPN. In 1999, the WB Thursday night line up (*The Wayans Bros., The Jamie Foxx Show, The Steve Harvey Show* and *For Your Love*) mirrored the counter-programming strategy used by the then fledgling Fox netlet through the mid-1990s with its Thursday night lineup of *Martin, Living Single* and *New York*

Undercover. The logic was: we'll lose the White 18–34 demo to NBC's Must See TV, let's go after the non-White audience in the same age bracket. So *Living Single* played against *Friends* (the same show in Black and White). By 2000, UPN had solidified Monday night as its Black Block of comedy programming with *Moesha, The Hughleys, Grown-Ups* and *Malcolm & Eddie* (the latter two series have since been replaced by *The Parkers* and *Girlfriends* the following season). However, as Keenan Ivory Wayans, creator of Fox's most celebrated and controversial comedy series of that era, *In Living Color*, notes, 'Fox changed the course of Black television unintentionally. They didn't go out to make Black shows, they went out to make alternative programming' (Zook, 1999, p. 105).

As the two rivals for the title of fifth network, the practices of the WB and UPN are very similar but their programming ethos differ. In 1998, the then UPN President Dean maintained that any 'network following a narrowcast is ultimately doomed to failure' and that broadcasters have a 'social responsibility to court a wider audience . . . that there has to be something that brings America together and unites it' (Lowry, 1998). In sharp contrast, WB chief executive Jamie Kellner stated bluntly, 'If you don't focus on a certain group of people, I think you become unimportant to any group of people' (Lowry, 1998). In the past, the WB has used this philosophy to expand its viewer base—with teen centered programming like *Buffy the Vampire Slayer, Dawson's Creek* and *Felicity* (thereby moving ahead of UPN towards fifth network status). And, despite UPN's espoused position, both of the upstarts have looked toward comedy programming to open up the 'urban' (read: non-White) audience. Both broadcasting entities have catered to Black viewers—seeking to fill a niche not adequately served by the major networks—at least in terms of the sitcom. A.J. Jacobs' prediction in his 1996 *Entertainment Weekly* article that 'the bigger UPN and the WB get, the whiter they become' has certainly proven true for Fox: nearly three-fourths of their programming has no Black series regulars (Braxton, 2000b). The programming tides are shifting at the WB and UPN: the WB's teen wave appears to have peaked and it has lost one of its only critically praised programs (*Buffy*) to UPN, where *WWF Smackdown* has become its cash cow. While one may wonder about the fate of the Black sitcom once all the netlets 'come of age,' the question of minstrelsy in the texts that *do* exist—the shows of the present and recent past—have even greater significance. As Robin Means-Coleman states:

> Black situation comedy, as a more bigoted contribution to the racialized regime of representations, has a clear and definable history, from its theater minstrel roots to the most recent Neo-minstrelsy series, that reveals racial ridicule and buffoonery to be typical and representative . . . African Americans have much at stake as they encounter hyper-racial representations. *(2000, p. 139)*

The Class of 1999: Before Race Was a 'Problem' on TV

Two contemporary Black comedies, *The PJ's* and *The Diary of Desmond Pfeiffer*, were members of the sitcom class of 1999—although *Desmond Pfeiffer*'s run would fall well short of season one graduation. Each series came under some degree of media scrutiny and each presents constructions of Blackness that keep the specters of Beulah and Andy floating through their narratives. *The PJ's*, Eddie Murphy's animated—actually, foamation (think California Raisins)—series depicted life in the projects. The first volley against *The PJ's* came from Spike Lee, who called the series 'incredibly demeaning . . . I kind of scratch my head why Eddie Murphy's doing this . . . I'm not saying that we're above being made fun of and stuff but it's really hateful, I think, towards Black people, plain and simple.' Lee is not alone here—when it first aired, *The PJ's* was the hot button series for debates about Black on Black representations.

In the series, Thurgood Stubbs is a master of his domain as the super of the Hilton Jacobs project; a mixture of Fred Sanford and Kingfish, he is also perpetually seeking shortcuts and schemes to enhance or solidify his position. Life with Super makes poverty perversely pastoral. There are roaches, forties of malt liquor, gunshots played for laughs in ambient sound—in other words, *The PJ's* makes *Good Times* look like a documentary on housing project life but, apparently, realism isn't the point here. In response to the criticism of the series, *LA Times* critic Howard Rosenberg (1999) states that *The PJ's* is as much of a 'slap in the face against blacks as *The Simpsons* is as against whites . . . In the matter of *The PJ's* are some Black skins really that thin?' Larry Wilmore, the series executive producer, expresses with some exasperation: 'I thought we would have gotten to the point now that we can make fun of ourselves, but people say the images are so offensive they don't even want to hear the point you're trying to make.' However, despite the controversy fueled by Lee's comments and limited negative press from Black journalists like Denene Miller, *The PJ's*, which scored the network's second most watched series premiere with almost 22 million viewers, had found a temporary home at Fox. However, by the end of the following season, *The PJ's*, which had been moved, preempted and put on hiatus by Fox several times over the course of the 2000 season, was cancelled and promptly relocated to the WB as an unsuccessful midseason replacement (Spring, 2001).

The Secret Diary of Desmond Pfeiffer had an even shorter life. The series was doomed from the start—if not from a premise that reflects a schizophrenic pitch mentality (yeah, let's put *Benson*, except kind of proper and British, in the White House . . . just before the Civil War) then from the rabid protests from a plethora of folk including Jesse Jackson, NAACP and the Brotherhood Crusade. The first thing that strikes me about *Desmond Pfeiffer* is the fact that it is simply not funny—painfully unfunny: a libidinous (and unfulfilled) Mary Lincoln, a blusteringly helpless and hapless, Abe, Pfeiffer's White manservant (whom he treats like a . . . you guessed it . . . slave) and Desmond himself (Chi McBride), whose demeanor fluctuated between proper British and proper Bed-Sty. And, while I understand that the analysis of racial representations in a comedy has to go beyond a 'thumbs up, thumbs down' critique, I think that it is pertinent here. *Desmond Pfeiffer* was an easy target. I cannot imagine that by the end of week three it would not have gone the way of *Homeboys from Outer Space*.

The picketing, the news conferences, the countless op-ed like the *LA Times* Counterpunch articles—Christopher Coles' (1998) piece that compared the campaign against *Desmond Pfeiffer* with the religious right's campaign against Terence McNally's controversial play retelling of the life of Christ, 'Corpus Christi,' and angrily questioned why 'there had been hardly a peep from the anti-censorship crowd' over Pfeiffer's impending demise—or Earl Ofari Hutchinson's (1998) claim that *Desmond Pfeiffer* was 'the latest and most absurd addition to a long list of network assassinations on the Black Image.' I think viewing *Desmond Pfeiffer* as either striking a blow against either Black representation or the first amendment overstates the importance of this particular series—which even without the negative press probably wouldn't have made it through the season. It supplied an easy source of righteous indignation without the risk of taking on a company like Disney (the producers of *The PJ's*) or a Black star (Eddie Murphy, one of the few African-American actors who can 'open' a movie). However, the comparative analysis of these series, and other Black sitcoms, forces the scholar and/or spectator to interrogate how far one can go into the realm of the objectionable for the sake of humor—again, what price laughter? So we know slavery isn't funny, but urban poverty can be played for laughs. There's not clear consensus in the industry nor in the audience. Issues of representation are further problematized when positivist impulses are conflated with Beulahesque 'bits.' Such is the case with ABC's *The Hughleys*.

In an episode from the first season, 'Why Can't We Be Friends?,' the burden of perception placed upon Blackness is addressed quite overtly. In this instance, the tolerant White neighbor must come to terms with the existence of racism in his social sphere just as the protagonist, the self-made businessman, Hughley, must come to terms with the fact that middle classness is not insulation against racism. After Dave (Eric Allan Kramer) takes Darryl and Milsap (John Henton) to his favorite local bar, an altercation ensues in his absence when another 'local' questions the 'source' of Darryl's ability to live in this tony suburb:

> Local: Who do you play for?
> Darryl: Don't you recognize me? I'm Mark McGuire.
> Local: You must be one of those rappers.
> Darryl: Sap, I can't rap and I can't run. What am gonna do for money?
> Local: (to his friends) It must be pharmaceuticals.

Dave returns to intervene and the Local departs as he offers to buy drinks for Milsap and Darryl because he didn't know that they were with Dave.

> Milsap (angrily): What difference does that make?
> Darryl: No, I promised my wife I'd rob a liquor store on the way home.
> Milsap: I'll go with you. Maybe I'll get my third strike so I can go see my daddy.

Despite the biting critique in that particular sequence, co-creator and star D.L. Hughley asserted that just because 'You're black [doesn't mean] you always have to be making a political statement.' In keeping, one might argue that the series can be seen as an updating of *The Jeffersons*—with Darryl as George, the neighbors as the Willises, and Milsap cast in Florence's role of 'keeping it real'— a reminder of the family's ties to the Black community. However, issues of race inflect the narrative in ways that reflect and refract the process of identity formation in the contemporary American social milieu. In another episode, Hughley is concerned when his son begins to take the role of 'class clown' to win acceptance in his new school:

> Hughley: For many of your friends, you're the first one of us they've gotten to
> know. They don't get BET out here. . . You've got a great opportunity and you have
> to take advantage of it.

Again, the burden of perception regarding Blackness is addressed and placed squarely on the shoulders of the individual who is gaining access to the mainstream—in this case, upper middle-class suburbia. One might even hear the strains of DuBois' Talented Tenth ethos echoed in the charge given from one generation to the next—passed from father to son.

The fact that *The Hughleys* struggles with the notion of 'staying Black' in suburbia is also intriguing. Darryl's continued friendship with Milsap, an old neighborhood buddy who he is coaxing towards suburban life, establishes his (albeit loose) ties with the Black community. However, there are also instances when the 'performance' of Blackness—proving authenticity—means reverting to stereotypes:

In the Thanksgiving episode of the series, Yvonne (Elise Neal), the central female protagonist, the wife and mother of *The Hughleys*, must 'prove' herself to Darryl's mother and several older Black ladies, by making a 'soul food accented' holiday meal. She is finally able to win them over by adopting their 'Beulah-speak': 'Chile, I been up since 4 am and I'm so tired I got grocery bags under my eyes, my knees are calling me names y'all don't wanna and I think I done popped an ear bone or something from sneezing up this paprika.' This performance mirrors the stereotypical construction of Black domestic; it could just as easily have been transcribed from Beulah—as she and Oriole swapped stories at the end of their work day—as from this series attempt to have Yvonne prove her authenticity as a mother and as a 'sistah.' It seems troubling that in this positivist construction of Black life, Yvonne can do 'Beulah' but it would be unthinkable for Darryl to do 'Andy.'

Furthermore, the controversy over the cancellation of *The Hughleys* on ABC (and its jump to its current home at UPN) was exacerbated by the appearance of the new ABC sitcom, *My Wife & Kids* (midseason, 2001), which stars Damon Wayans in the travails of a self-made businessman, his wife and their cute kids in suburbia. In many ways, it appeared that this series had been created to replicate and replace the other. Hughley expressed outrage over what he perceived as a programming bait and switch: sell the audience on the premise of a show the network didn't own (*The Hughleys* produced by Greenblatt Janollari Studios, an independent) replace it with one that they did (*My Wife & Kids* is produced by Disney-owned Touchstone Television—a corporate step-brother of ABC). 'You're doing my show all over again,' said Hughley. 'The only difference [is] that I'm not on it. . . I'm insulted because we did that show that was based on my life. . . if you take my life and shoot it with another set of Black folks, I've got a problem with that' (Braxton, 2001).

It is too early to tell what effect the controversy will have on either show—whether *My Wife & Kids* will become the *Cosby Show* for the new millennium as the folks at Touchstone and ABC hope or whether *The Hughleys* will regain its first season ratings success. What is clear, however, is that, in making the jump to UPN, *The Hughleys* has gotten a bit broader and a bit rougher. In an episode from the 2000–2001 season, in which Darryl trades quips with guest Rose Marie in a manner reminiscent of George and Florence on *The Jeffersons*, the familial ethos seems a bit askew: Darryl and Yvonne's greatest motivation for their White neighbors reconciliation is a game of 'slut on the couch' that Dave's arrival postponed. While the relationship between the couple was never Ward and June Cleaver sterile, the prevalence of sexual innuendo seemed less about being sexy than about being *sensational*. After all, Cliff never commented on Claire's 'great ass.' While *The Hughleys* is the only survivor of this sitcom class of 1999, the direction the series has taken seems to be an indication of the 'big and broad' road more traveled.

The New Millennium Black Sitcom: Let's Hear It for the Girls

In the wake of the NAACP memo on diversity (as well as the cinematic critique offered by *Bamboozled* and *Dancing in September*), some critics would contend that times had already changed for the better. As *USA Today* scribe Robert Bianco claimed in chiding Lee's criticism of network racial representations: 'The worst of TV's shucking and jiving minstrel comedies—shows such as the WB's *The Wayans Bros.* or UPN's *Malcolm & Eddie* and the infamous *Homeboys from Outer Space* are gone replaced in a large part by tamer, middle-class sitcoms.' But one must consider whether a 'middle-class' milieu guarantees 'tamer' content or does it simply mean the 'bits' of minstrelsy are not as clearly discernible through socially tinted spectatorial lenses—those of class and gender.

In 2000, UPN introduced two new situation comedies post NAACP memo on diversity, *The Parkers* and *Girlfriends*. *The Parkers*, a spin-off of the positivist teen sitcom *Moesha*, took a different comedic direction from its parent show. Whereas *Moesha* only sprinkled broad comedy in its narrative fare, over-the-top comedy was the roux for *The Parkers'* gumbo. Nikki (Mo'Nique) and Kim (Countess Vaughn), formerly the comic relief on *Moesha*, are mother and daughter and best friends— they are even attending Santa Monica College together. The closeness of the mother/daughter relationship is central to all of the series' episodes, even if the writing, in general, tends towards an 'easy' laugh. For example, Kim enters in a leopard mini and a revealing top, Nikki, who is dressed conservatively (as if for church), immediately comments on her daughter's attire:

> Nikki: Kim, I know you don't plan to meet the Reverend in that hoochie outfit. . . ooh, cute shoes.
> Kim: Why you trippin,' Mama? He's just a man.
> Nikki: Uh-uh. . . He's a man of the cloth.
> Kim: Well, I should hope so. I don't want to see him naked.

The series' star, stand-up comedian, Mo'Nique, says the series 'is about a mother who raised that baby [and] did not give up, fought the struggle and now has gone back to college. . . It's about a 30-something brother, who is a college professor. It is very positive.' As one of the series' producers, Sara Finney, notes, 'A lot of people find these character very relatable, they feel comfortable with them. . . and a lot of women have said it's great to have a big, beautiful role model like Mo'Nique.' Arguably, the nature of that 'comfort' is problematic ('The Parkers Win. . .', 2000). Furthermore, some would contend that the claims of positivity—the praise of Professor Oglevee (Dorien Wilson) as someone who can 'keep The Cosby legacy alive'—are undermined by other stereotypical character constructions. As *New York Times* critic Robert F. Moss (2001) notes:

> *It's a losing effort, what with Nikki grabbing at his rear-end, and serves to remind us that the urbane owlish Cosby persona has been all but buried in the Eddie Murphy revolution, an upheaval that has brought dozens of boisterous inner city voices to the contemporary chitlin' circuit, and to some movies and television.*

While I'm not sure that Moss' comparison of Professor Oglevee and Cliff Huxtable (Cosby) is particularly apt, his mention of Nikki's ass grabbing speaks to bits of minstrelsy in the Black sitcom to which audiences have become accustomed. The construction of the hyper-sexualized Black female is nothing new on either the big or small screen. Nikki's unrelenting pursuit of the professor is on hiatus only during other sexual flights of fancy and the assertion of physical power by a big Black woman (Nikki's intimidation of those who disagree with her) may not hearken back to Beulah but they certainly seem very Sapphire. These are images found in the history of the Black sitcom—it's Jackeé's Sandra Clark of *227* or LaWanda Page's Aunt Esther of *Sanford and Son*.[8]

Television critics like Matthew Gilbert assert that *The Parkers* wastes its potential: 'Nikki and Kim are creatures with bite, and they would be a lot funnier with material that didn't rely on sentimentality and nitwit sex gags' (Gilbert, 1999). Nonetheless, *The Parkers* is the highest rated series in African-American households (on broadcast, cable and in syndication) and apparently, there is some truth to Countess Vaughn's assessment of the shows appeal: 'We want to make people laugh and we stretch it a bit. . . It's good to get in front of the TV and laugh *at* two crazy women' (Gilbert, 1999, p. 25, my emphasis).

Girlfriends is a series about four thin, beautiful girlfriends who talk about love, life and sex in ways so familiar that it has earned the nickname of '*Sex and the City* in Black.' However, because the series is on network television and a primetime sitcom on UPN, the comedy, while not quite as bawdy, is definitely broader than its HBO counterpart—as are the constructions of the individual characters. With *Girlfriends*' creator Mara Brock Akil 'wanted to show African-American women, who are dynamic and multi-layered' with the second goal of broaching racial issues '[i]n a funny way that can create water cooler discussion or debate.' Like *Sex and the City*, the series centers on one woman, Joan (Traci Ellis Ross), the successful lawyer/'good girl' of the quartet and her relationship with her girlfriends: her legal assistant and protégée, Maya (Golden Brooks), the slightly trampy but designer savvy, Toni (Jill Marie Jones), and the free-spirited, 'hippie chick' Lynn (Persia White).

Both the social commentary and the sexual frankness of the series lack subtlety and also feed into some troubling issues of representation. In one episode, Lynn states that being bi-racial makes her a 'complex woman' only to be told by Toni, whose speech is normally 'crisp', Standard English: 'I hate to break it to you, complex woman, but, in America, you black.' This kind of strategic lapse into 'sistah-friend'—my term for a sort of non-standard, 'keeping it real' (often affected) Black dialect—occurs with other characters in the narratives from the girlfriends themselves to miscellaneous guest stars (like Phil Morris' Dr. Spenser, who slips into 'brother-man' to tell his cable-loving, patient Maya, 'Girl, suck it up and get some cable'). While one could argue that this exemplifies how Black people are sometimes compelled to speak in multiple voices to negotiated variant communities, one still wonders why such a reassertion of Blackness is necessary on a Black sitcom.

In 'One Night Stand,' Joan, whose year long period of celibacy is beginning to take a toll, acts as the central theme of the episode which focuses on condom talk, the 'oversized myth of the Black male penis' and fantasies of various African-American male's clutching their 'gifts.' While this episode does embody some of the unabashed sexuality that makes its HBO twin so successful, others found the construction troubling. In an interview with *Newsweek*, Spike Lee commented on this very episode:

> I was watching the show Girlfriends *last week, and I mean, is that the only thing Black women can talk about is getting f**ked? And then the show had Black men holding their johnsons and looking into the camera smiling. What white show has white men grabbing their nuts and smiling into the camera? And why do all the Black people have to sing and dance in the opening sequence? The subtext is 'Lord, we're so happy we on TV.'* (Samuels, 2000, p. 75)

Conclusion

To argue that *The Parkers* or *Girlfriends*. . . or even *The PJ's*. . . has the same racist resonance as *Mantan: The New Millennium Minstrel Show* would be ludicrous. It would be an argument that one could refute without much effort and then congratulate oneself on being a part of a society that is moving towards a post racial age. So that is not the argument I intend to make. There is a multitude of ways to coon without breaking out the burnt cork. While the overt blackface may be gone, there is a patina of minstrelsy underneath many of the existing Black sitcom texts of the new millennium. There are ways in which I might argue that the new millennium Black sitcoms simply recirculate comic bits of minstrelsy in which the female characters—like Nikki in *The Parkers* or Judge Warner in *Dancing in September*'s sitcom *Just Us*—in ways that are disconcerting but somehow not despicable. I had originally intended to assert that these series were, in actuality examples of a sort of 'coon'-lite programming, which cut ideological blackface—the rearticulations and reinventions of mammies and coons—with just enough positivist rhetoric to make it difficult to be sure if that had genuinely been the case. However, even this complex notion of duplicitous representations is too simplistic.

In the process of writing this essay, I spoke to a friend and colleague (who is also a television scholar) about my interpretation of the 'hoochie outfit' exchange between Nikki and Kim in the episode of *The Parkers* described in the previous section. Without hesitation, I launched into a scathing critique of the series—which ended with the claim that 'no mother would say that to her daughter.' My friend, who is also an African-American woman, replied, 'She might say it—if you were wearing a hoochie mama outfit.' As the writer/director of *Dancing in September* succinctly stated:

> *I think it's OK for there to be some very broad, negative shows on the air. What I*
> *may see as negative, other people may not. I mean, there are dumb white shows*
> *on the air, too. I think the dilemma with Black TV is 'Where are other shows?*
> *Where are the thought provoking African American shows? (Hill, 2001, par. 5)*

Here Bythewood addresses the notion of taste in this discussion of minstrelsy—because the process of reading a televisual text is inflected and impacted by the cultural and ideological baggage that one brings with him/her to small screen.

I can't help wondering whether the conflicted and conflictual reactions to televisual representations of African-Americans in sitcoms are deeply rooted in the same impulses that made 'Beulah' okay and 'Andy' objectionable; that made the 'ghetto' experience synonymous with the 'Black' experience; that made forms of spoken language controversial long before African-American verbal English (commonly known as 'ebonics') was a curricular issue; and that continue to define what is positive and what is Black enough and who makes that determination.

Yet, within all the ambivalence and inconsistencies built into the discussion of racial representations, one thing seems clear—the blame for regressive representations always resides outside of the group to which the *de facto* critic belongs. There are times when discourse degenerates into a simple blame game with the critic/scholar, the audience and the industry each finding fault in the others' actions or inactions. In reality, all of us—whether spectator or actor, writer or producer, network exec or television scholar—unequally share the credit and the culpability for the evolution and intransigence of televisual representations of race.

As J. Fred MacDonald stated in *Blacks In White TV*, his history of televisual representations of African-Americans from the moment of television to the rise of cable: 'Because there is comparatively little minority representation in radio, and television, and because each performance by an African-American is regarded as a chance to make a statement about realities, each appearance takes on additional weight' (MacDonald, 1992, p. 123). His statement expresses the points upon which the industry, the critic and the audience agree—the pool of televisual constructions of African-American life is limited and the representations within it are, more often than not, problematic. As of the beginning of 1999, there are 11 million African-American households, yet out of more than 115 shows airing on six broadcast networks, only 18 shows feature an African-American cast or lead character, with 10 of those shows airing on UPN and the WB (Hall, 1999). Even with 'increase' in the numbers of representations, as the number of Black sitcoms shrink—from 15 Black sitcoms in 1997 to six in 2001—so do the number of characters who have a recurring space on the televisual landscape (Moss, 2001). Ultimately, the numbers still drive both public and private discourses surrounding racial representations—whether share points or numbers of Black shows currently on the air.

Sadly, one thing is certain. When next I channel surf the airwaves for comedic representations of Blackness, I will still have to look hard to find them. Once I do, I will see many of the characters doing an all-too-familiar shuffle—it's a new millennium shuffle but a shuffle nonetheless.

Notes

1. This term, which refers to the adoption of any vestige of the racist stereotypes of the minstrel show into the popular entertainments that followed the genre's timely demise, is derived from perhaps the most patently offensive minstrel archetype: the 'coon.' As Donald Bogle notes, the coon was 'the most blatantly degrading of all black stereotypes. The pure coons emerged as no-account niggers, those unreliable, crazy, lazy, subhuman creatures good for nothing more than eating watermelons, stealing chickens, shooting crap, or butchering the English language.' Bogle, Donald (1973/1974) *Toms, Coons, Mulattoes, Mammies, & Bucks: An Interpretive History of Blacks in American Films*, New York: Continuum, p. 8.

2. Since its inception in 1909, the NAACP has been fighting for the political, economic and social advancement of the African-American community as well as other communities of color.

3. The widely circulate NAACP memo on diversity outlined sweeping demands for increased diversity behind the camera as well as in front.

4. CBS's *City of Angels* and ABC's *Gideon's Crossing*, once hailed as shining examples of the Black presence in primetime drama, have been cancelled.

5. During the 19th century, the minstrel show was popular entertainment in the northern cities among immigrants, the unskilled, as well as some in the middle and upper classes. These earliest minstrels were White performers who blackened their faces with makeup made from burnt cork and 'mimicked' Blacks. While the minstrel show was a pre-Vaudevillian variety show brand of entertainment, arguably, its attraction for White audiences was its assertion of White superiority as it depicted White entertainers as caricatures of slaves in the South and ex-slaves in the North. This original brand of minstrelsy and the assumption by White audiences that was an essentially faithful imitation of African-American speech, singing and dancing established racist archetypes regarding Blackness that have yet to be erased from popular culture. Following the Civil War, Black performers began to perform in minstrel shows: they, too, performed in blackface—literally and figuratively—as they pretended to be someone pretending to be Black. This notion of an externally defined notion of Blackness—of minstrelsy—continues to be a problematic aspect of contemporary representation of African-American culture and identity.

6. *Beulah* was mentioned in the 1951 NAACP resolution critical of current television season. However, the most virulent attacks against the 'resurgence' of minstrelsy—whether in the courtroom (the suit against CBS) or in the popular Black press—were directed at *Amos 'n' Andy*.

7. According to Nielsen Media Research, 'The terms rating and share are basic to the television industry. Both are percentages. A rating is a percent of the universe that is being measured, most commonly discussed as a percent of all television households. As such, a rating is always quantifiable, assuming you know the size of the universe (TV households, persons, women 18–34, and so forth). A share is the percent of households or persons using television at the time the program is airing and who are watching a particular program. Thus, a share does not immediately tie back to an actual number, because it is a percent of a constantly changing number—TV sets in use. Shares can be useful as a gauge of competitive standing. A 20-share would represent a phenomenally high rating.' See Nielsen Media Research FAQ for more information on the flawed American ratings system: <http://www.nielsonmedia.com/FAQ/indexhtml>.

8. As the supporting character in what was a hybrid domestic/ensemble comedy set in a Black neighborhood in Washington, DC, Sandra (Jackeé Harry) vamps around like an African-

American Mae West of the 1980s' sitcom set in an apartment building No. 227. As a supporting character on *Sanford & Son*, Aunt Esther (LaWanda Page) is the shrewish and holier-than-thou sister-in-law of widowed junkman, Fred Sanford (Redd Foxx), in a remake of the British series, *Steptoe & Son* set in the 'ghetto' (Watts, California).

References

'Alvin Childress Dies; Played Amos in TV's "Amos 'N' Andy"' (1986) Obituary, *Washington Post*, April 22: Metro C6.

Braxton, Greg (1999) 'Prime Time for a Show of Diversity . . .' *Los Angeles Times*, February 14: Calendar 3.

Braxton, Greg (2000a) 'Outlandish? Yes, and a Hit; Television 'The Parkers' Is Big, Over-the-Top and Very Successful with Black Viewers . . .' *Los Angeles Times*, April 28: Calendar F1.

Braxton, Greg (2000b) 'Study Finds Blacks Seen Most on Comedies, New Networks . . .' *Los Angeles Times*, February 25: Calendar F24.

Braxton, Greg (2001) 'Family Feud: Was One ABC Sitcom About an African American Family Used to Replace Another,' *Newsday*, April 8: D21.

Coles, Christopher (1998) 'First Amendment Means Pfeiffer, Too,' *Los Angeles Times*, October 12: Opinion F3.

Gilbert, Matthew (1999) 'The Parkers Misses the Funny Bone,' *The Boston Globe*, August 30: C6.

Gray, Herman (1995) *Watching Race: Television and The Struggle for Blackness*, Minneapolis: University of Minnesota Press.

Hall, Lee. (1999) 'African American Watch More TV Yet Are Often Ignored,' *Electronic Media*, February 1: 12.

Hill, James (2001) 'Reggie Rock Bythewood Talks about the Powers of TV,' *BET.com* 2, February. Available online at: <http://www.bet.com/LIFESTYLES/o.c-2.38-188978.00.html>.

Holden, Stephen (2000) 'Trying on Blackface in a Flirtation with Fire,' *New York Times*, October 6: E1:27.

Hutchinson, Earl Ofari (1998) 'History Falsified Not Satirized,' *Los Angeles Times*, October 12: Opinion F3.

Jacobs, A.J. (1996) 'Black to the Future . . .' *Entertainment Weekly*, June 14: 15–16.

Lopez, Steve (1999) 'The Death of the Sitcom,' *Entertainment Weekly*, April 16: 27–31.

Lowry, Brian (1998) 'For Rival UPN and WB: The Future Is a Matter of Focus,' *Los Angeles Times*, July 27: Calendar 2.

MacDonald, J. Fred. (1992) *Blacks in White TV: African Americans in Television Since 1948*, Chicago: Prentice–Hall.

Means-Coleman, Robin R. (2000) *African American Viewers and the Black Situation Comedy: Situating Racial Humor*, New York: Garland.

Moss, Robert F. (2001) 'The Shrinking Life Span of the Black Sitcom,' *New York Times*, February 25: Section 2, 19.

'The Parkers Win Big Laughs As No. 1 Show in Black Households' (2000) *Jet*, April 10: 25.

Rosenburg, Howard (1999) 'The PJs': Equal Opportunity Satire; Much Like Animated Spoof Series Before It, This Spin on an African American Family is Irreverent and Endearing,' *Los Angeles Times*, January 9: Calendar F1.

Samuels, Allison (2000) 'Spike's Minstrel Show,' *Newsweek*, October 2: 75.

'Screen Actor Guild Presents Final Results of Comprehensive Look at African American Characters in Prime Time Television' (2000) SAG Press Release, 7 June. Available online at: <http://www.sag.org/pressreleases/pr-b0006J2html>.

Shohat, Ella and Robert Stam (1995) *Unthinking Eurocentrism: Multiculturalism and the Media*, London and New York: Routledge.

Sterngold, James (1998) 'A Racial Divide Widens on Network TV,' *New York Times*, December 28: Section 6, 14.

Zook, Kristen Brent (1999) *Color by Fox: The Fox Network and the Revolution in Black Television*, New York: Oxford University Press.

Be The One That You Want
Asian Americans in Television Culture, Onscreen and Beyond

L.S. Kim

To be invisible in visual culture is to not have power in society.[1] Asian Americans have not been completely invisible in the history of American popular culture, but what visibility they possess has taken delimiting and disempowered forms: in derogatory political cartoons during the building of the transcontinental railroad, in divisive newspaper and magazine articles during World War II, in a smattering though consistent set of appearances in Hollywood films (as servile, sinister, or even by white performers in yellowface), in explicit dehumanizing news images of defeated or victimized bodies during the Vietnam conflict, and "oh, yeah . . . in *M*A*S*H*." This line belongs to Margaret Cho, Korean American comedienne. Through her work, Cho has mapped out a road of rejection and invisibility and has illustrated, demonstrated, and demanded respect for herself, Korean Americans, and others who have been marginalized.

The struggle for "fair representation" of racial minorities in American television is a long and continuing one. Herman Gray has written about the significance of "blackness" in its discursive forms, particularly during the Reagan era in which "blackness" was codified as menacing and criminal, and when the vastly popular *The Cosby Show* was received as a televisual panacea and ideological counterpoint. Darrell Hamamoto has researched (and searched for) television programs about Asians and Asian Americans and reveals that though there have been yellow faces, the portrayals have been limiting. Chon Noriega has written a book on Chicanos in the media who have forged a politicized and perhaps alternative media amidst an industrial and sociological backdrop.[2] The study and representation of Native Americans in television is almost nil. What can increase the representation of characters of color in television, and what is the role that viewers play in the process?

One realm of inquiry is finding out what enables television producers and network executives to develop new programs with minority characters. A "liberal" industry, Hollywood is still a business— but is this really the bottom-line, that "green is the color that matters?" The major questions this article will address are: How does the relationship between media makers and media consumers work to shift the status quo in television programming? Where does tracing the historical representation of Asian Americans lead us? What exactly are spectators buying with their "viewer dollars"? People who watch television are not only "viewer-consumers" but they are "viewer-citizens." Individuals need to recognize their role in not only consuming but in producing media culture. Rather than passive spectators, television viewers function as the linchpin to programming decision-making, whether or not they accept this politicized cultural role.

What is at stake is how to get more complex, Asian American characters on television. Media culture consists of the creators—the television industry, and the consumers—the viewers or spectators. Asian Americans are also viewers-consumers-citizens who have potential to transform racial representation in television.

Is Change Possible?

Who must make the first move—Hollywood, the general (mostly white) public, or perhaps Asian American viewers-consumers, along with other activist allies? It seems a tautology to believe that viewers are not interested in seeing African American characters in an hour-long drama or Asian American men as romantic leads, and therefore, this is why television programs like these are not made. Despite what ratings may (or may not) show, there is a projected "mass audience" that television executives and advertisers use to dictate their work; this status quo community prevents a conscious innovation of television programming in terms of racial representation.

In fall 1999, the National Association for the Advancement of Colored People (NAACP) protested just before the new television season began. The concern was that in the line-up of twenty-six new shows, none had any major characters of color. How could not a single show be offered with a lead who was not white? From whence did this come—unimaginative and racist writers, producers, and networks, or from dull and complacent audiences? It took the tenacity and organization of the coalition of ethnic media watch groups who joined the NAACP—American Indians in Film and Television, the National Asian Pacific American Legal Consortium, and the National Latino Media Council—to threaten boycotting television networks in order to bring about some changes. In some cases, the changes were last minute, and in others they were superficial (an industry term, "coloring up," emerged). A glance at today's prime-time television (including and particularly in commercials) will catch faces of different racial and ethnic backgrounds, albeit in the background of many scenes; the face of television is gazing back at us in new and subtle ways.

Network executives and producers depend on viewers to watch their programs. They measure viewing practices to determine what kinds of programs to develop and schedule. Here lies the potential for innovation and negotiation, but this potential remains mostly dormant. Television executives create programs based on what they *anticipate* viewers will like, based on what they perceive has *already* been popular. The status quo—idealized stories of white middle-class families—has worked in the past and therefore executives bank on similar programming to work in the future. Still, changes and improvements do get eked out because the system cannot entirely avoid what is happening in the larger society. Moreover, the television industry relies on feedback from individual viewers and from different categories of viewers.

Taking into consideration the foundational theories of how television functions, there are two mechanisms that allow for change in television. First, the televisual text is polysemic, allowing for multiple readings and meanings; this results in viewers' ability to contest or rewrite the presentation of characters of color. An image or a performance can be understood by Asian Americans in a different way than by non-Asian Americans, and in a way that is empowering rather than embarrassing or disgraced (the reverse is true, too).[3] Moreover, racial discourse by definition involves the negotiation of diverse racial meanings. Second, narrative structure is unique in television; programming involves "open narratives," meaning that although each episode starts and finishes, the story never ends. There is an ongoing series of episodes (for example, situational comedies), and a successful series is one that does not end. Thus, television must adapt according to changing societal tastes and values in order to keep its audience. Television as an interactive, polysemic medium with an open narrative structure is a formation that can sustain the status quo, contain counter-hegemonic stories and images, and yet also facilitate advancements and absorb changes in the representations of race and race relations.

The Nielsen ratings show who and when selected groups of people watch which television programs. In addition to weekly ratings, the Nielsen Organization releases bi-annual "Reports on Television" and has recently begun compiling special reports on viewing patterns of African Americans and Hispanic Americans. (There is no such study of Asian Pacific American viewing practices.) The attention paid to racial minority groups has come after long criticism that the surveys were inaccurate and biased; like television programming, television program ratings methods have been modified in response to public concern. As Todd Gitlin describes, network executives, television producers, and writers care deeply about ratings, and yet also have an ambivalent relationship to them in practice: "they distrust them and rely on them at the same time."[4] Poor ratings will bring about the cancellation of a program, but there is a whole life cycle of a television show (i.e., the concept and development stages) before it even airs and gets rated. Producers use ratings of past programs to rule over future ones. The actual ratings of a specific show are not what influences whether that show gets made in the first place but rather, if it will continue to be made.[5] The catch-22 with programs about Asian Americans is that high ratings in favor of such programming do not exist yet because the programs have not existed yet. Nevertheless, it is within the serendipity of ratings and network programming decision-making that there is space for Asian American viewers, including students and activists, to intervene.

Analyzing the Representation of Asian Americans

This discussion is not focused on racism in Hollywood, but rather on how Asian Americans are positioned in relation to racial formation on television. Michael Omi and Howard Winant have defined racial formation as the sociohistorical process by which racial categories are created, inhabited, transformed, and destroyed.[6] From a racial formation point of view, race involves both social structure and cultural representation. Thus, racialization is structural and ideological.

Visual text and social or cultural context have a symbiotic relationship. Television and "the real world" interact mutually and are dependent upon one another. In television, there is regularly a displacement of context onto/into text and then further, of text into subtext. Social and cultural discourses often become subtextual discourses in television. For example, the constraints of patriarchy are seen but not really heard in early television (think of Lucy Ricardo's desperate attempts to "get into show business" and get out of the house in the classic, *I Love Lucy*), or the fear of the working/independent woman dealt with in later programs (as in *Murphy Brown* and her perceived threat to "family values" by having a baby without a husband). Nonetheless, this connection between displaced subtext and real social issue can be interpreted, interrupted, disrupted by viewers—whether they support a program, whether they write letters of protest, whether they successfully agitate or simply vote-with-their-remote.

Within television programming, the visibility of specific racial groups varies under different conditions of societal change. For example, with the Civil Rights Movement, African Americans were no longer seen as domestics or handymen (as characters such as Beulah or Eddie Rochester); instead, Asian Americans displaced them as servants in white households. Asian Americans occupied the role of the servant in programs such as *Bonanza, Bachelor Father*, and *The Courtship of Eddie's Father* in the 1960s. Images of contented, passive, and "good" Asian servants supplemented images of alien Vietnamese and enemy Vietcong in the news.

In television, the figure of the racialized character represents not just individual racial identity but stands for a broader pattern of socialized racial relations, together with gender and class relations. What appears on the surface to be simply structured family situation comedy with its banal plots and thinly drawn characters (think of *Happy Days* featuring "the Fonz" on one hand and "Ah-nold" on the other) contains complex racial, economic and gendered dimensions that when unpacked, tell us about the myths that American viewers found, and continue to find, reassuring.

The 1960s: Asians as Foreigners. . .and Servants

The genre of the western in both film and television has served a purpose of romanticizing America's past (particularly in terms of race relations and in establishing whiteness). Of the top ten shows according to the Nielsen ratings for the 1960–1961 season, the first six were westerns or western/rural-themed (*Gunsmoke, Wagon Train, Have Gun Will Travel* which had two Asian characters called, "Hey Boy" and "Hey Girl," *The Andy Griffith Show, The Real McCoys*, and *Rawhide*). By 1965, comedy emerged as the favorite genre with *Gomer Pyle, U.S.M.C., The Andy Griffith Show, The Beverly Hillbillies, Hogan's Heroes, Green Acres, Get Smart, My Three Sons, The Dick Van Dyke Show*,

Petticoat Junction, Gilligan's Island, and including comedy/variety shows *The Red Skelton Hour, The Ed Sullivan Show*, and *The Jackie Gleason Show* in the top twenty-five. *Star Trek* was a space western, albeit a multicultural one. Among its cast is cult favorite George Takei.

By the last season of the decade, some color was added (literally, television was broadcast in color for the first time in 1968) to the top of prime time television in such programs as *The Bill Cosby Show* (#11), *Hawaii Five-O* (#19), and *The Mod Squad* (#23), with *Julia* at #7 the previous year; *Walt Disney's Wonderful World of Color* (#9) was a successful series as was *Bonanza* (#3) which featured the character of Chinese houseboy, Hop Sing. One significant show that premiered in 1968 which was not ever in the top twenty-five but remained popular in syndication after its three-year run is *The Courtship of Eddie's Father*.

The Courtship of Eddie's Father is about a widowed father, his precocious and sweet son, and their housekeeper, who form a kind of family in the midst of racial and gender politics (i.e., questions about national identity and the role of women). Oscar Award-winning film actress, Miyoshi Umeki, plays Mrs. Livingston, not surprisingly, as a quiet-but-wise figure in the bachelor household. She is portrayed as humorous and quirky because of her malapropisms and the Oriental (sounding) flute music that accompanies her when she enters a room, yet she is efficient and unassuming. She is also loved by Eddie and presumably, by "Mr. Eddie's Father," as Mrs. Livingston calls him. The series is about a bachelor father whose son is searching for a new wife/mother when they already have someone to do the "woman's work" in their home. In negotiates this role of the wife/mother, bringing in a bevy of beauties (including professional women) for Eddie's father to consider, while the watchful Mrs. Livingston is there cooking for his dates. Simultaneously, there is the undeniable racial and cultural barrier that prevents these two from becoming a legitimate couple, at least not in the 1960s, when the last few anti-miscegenation laws were being declared unconstitutional. Produced by James Komack, a liberal producer/writer and fan of Umeki, the narratives in the series consistently attempt to work through difference of race/ nationality and gender without being able to come to a resolution. Television is, after all, a form of "endless deferment."[7]

Despite ethnic pride and political and artistic activism of the 1960s, "yellow power" was not exhibited or expressed in any significant way on television. Asians were not understood or seen as American. Two other prime time programs which featured Asian faces in the 1960s besides *The Courtship of Eddie's Father* were *Bachelor Father* and *Bonanza*, in which Sammee Tong and Victor Sen Yung, respectively, both played Chinese house servants. Although one program is set in the American West of the previous century and the other is situated in modern-day west L.A., the representation of the Asian man is the same, despite the passage of one hundred years. Whether it is Hop Sing with his long shirt and queue (braid), or Peter wearing a white waiter's jacket and black bow tie, their race is feminized, and the Asian man is dressed to serve. What all three shows have in common is twofold: that the Asian characters were not only servants, literally subservient, but also, that they were conceived of as Asian rather than Asian American. These characters are in a subordinated position by race, class, gender, and nationality. Even Bruce Lee portrayed Kato, the Green Hornet's very able assistant and valet!

The Civil Rights Movement, the anti-Vietnam War Movement, and the ethnic activism of Chicanos, Native Americans, as well as Asian Americans surged in the 1960s. In contrast to the nightly news reports of urban uprisings and of war abroad, prime time offered the opposite (the "magic-com" was created in this period: *My Favorite Martian, Bewitched, I Dream of Jeannie*). The industry (with some courageous producers like Hal Kanter) was able to push through a few new shows with racial and social content: *Julia, East Side West Side, I Spy*, and *The Bill Cosby Show*. All were more urban and more cosmopolitan; *The Courtship of Eddie's Father* was also a "liberal show." This liberalism was born out of the momentum of the times generally, but it was specifically linked to "the vast wasteland" speech delivered by President Kennedy's FCC Chairman, Newton Minow and to the vigilant and demonstrative NAACP who also made a call for better programming.

The 1970s: Asians and Asian Americans as Absent . . . or Foreigners

Asians and Asian Americans were seen about as much (or about as little) in the 1970s as in the 1960s. Television in the 1970s can be divided into two distinct eras, marked by two auteurs: Norman Lear in the early part of the decade, and Garry Marshall in the late 1970s.[8] Norman Lear is famous for his groundbreaking programs, starting with *All in the Family* in 1971. He continued with the creation of shows with political content, specifically in terms of race, for example, the economic status of racial minorities, as well as race relations. *All in the Family, Good Times, The Jeffersons, Chico and the Man*, and *Sanford and Son* were top ten shows. *Maude*, also in the top ten and also a progeny (spin-off) of *All in the Family*, was part of another television trend of the early 1970s of presenting independent, feminist women including *The Mary Tyler Moore Show* with spin-offs *Rhoda* and *Phyllis*, and *One Day at a Time*, which was about a divorced single mother.

But prime time in the latter half of the 1970s was dominated by the light comedy fare of Garry Marshall: *Happy Days, Laverne & Shirley*, and *Mork & Mindy* each, or in combination, occupied the top three spots from 1975–1979. Marshall has said that he wanted to bring a feeling of "no worries" to American audiences. He was helped by hour-long series belonging to the oeuvre of the prolific and successful Aaron Spelling, who not only brought us *Charlie's Angels*, but also *The Love Boat* and *Fantasy Island*. The shows that were hits by the end of the decade are markedly less directly political (*Three's Company, Eight Is Enough*, and *The Dukes of Hazzard* carried viewers into the 1980s).

The one program that endured and spanned the entire decade was *M*A*S*H*. It was in the top ten for ten years, from its second year on. This "anti-war comedy" had quite a list of ingredients: politics, race, non-American setting, serious topics but also serious comedy. It is also the only show that presented Asian characters (set in Asia) on a regular basis, besides television news images of the Vietnam War. It was, in essence, a displaced metaphor of the Vietnam War, transposed onto Korean soil but with the same enduring battle between Communism and so-called democracy. It was a subtle, if not contradictory, criticism of war. Furthermore, its political bite, already degraded from the original film, seemed to become weaker and weaker as the seasons wore on. In her bold stand-up show, Margaret Cho jokes that the only Asians she saw on TV growing up were on *M*A*S*H* and *Kung Fu*, which she says should have been called, "Hey, That Guy's Not Chinese" because a white actor played the title role (though Bruce Lee originally developed the script along with its producer).

The most visible Asian face during this period was that of actor Pat Morita, though what kind of visibility he had is questionable. In *Happy Days*, the third-generation Japanese American actor played the character of Arnold, a spewing, spatula-waving cook who could not even pronounce his own name. Before this role, he took a short stint playing a character named "Ah Chew" on Lear's *Sanford and Son*. Briefly after his first year on *Happy Days* (to which he would return), Morita starred in his own show, *Mr. Takahashi and Tina* (also known as *Mr. T. and Tina*).[9] The program employed several Asian characters/actors, but it was very quickly cancelled. It was perhaps picking up on the ethnic sitcom trend of similarly titled, *Chico and the Man* and *Sanford and Son*. Morita would go on to become famous in his role as "Mr. Miyagi" in the four *Karate Kid* films, and he also combined film and TV personas by selling the "wisdom" of using Colgate Toothpaste in the 1980s.

The 1980s: Asian Americans as Model Minority . . . and Token

Asian Americans on television (even when portraying Asians) were still few in number by the 1980s. In the meanwhile, Asian immigration had been steadily increasing after the McCarran-Walter Immigration and Nationality Act of 1965, which removed the ban on Asian immigrants to the United States (but it still kept count by extending the national origins quota system set up by the Johnson-Reed Act of 1924). New immigrants came to the U.S., including Korean immigrants and Southeast Asian refugees. In the 1970s, the industry had pushed to the colloquial "left" in bringing out many programs with characters of color, mostly African Americans, which was a stark contrast to television in the 1960s. Inevitably, there was a move from social awareness with some risk-taking and experimenting to the neo-conservative era that began in the 1980s. At one extreme Vincent Chin's murder literally embodied the Japan-bashing propagated through the media; at the other, the ideological (and thereby representational) concept/image of the model minority was also being generated in media and culture.

The relationship between television programming and political context is at once real, and at the same time elusive. In his book on what makes prime time tick, Gitlin discusses the specter of conservatism that haunted producers and executives in the 1980s and the ways in which decisions were made out of fear. He writes, "An industry devoted to satisfying abstract audiences does not usually attract individuals with firm moral positions in the first place."[10]

During this period, there were virtually no Asians or Asian Americans on prime time television. One program can be noted, though not for being good, was called *Gung Ho*. The program ran in 1986 and starred Gedde Watanabe, infamous for his role as Long Duk Dong in the wildly popular teen film, *Sixteen Candles* (1984). The program, based on the film by the same name in which Watanabe also starred, is about Japanese autoworkers who move to the U.S. to operate an American plant, "Japanese-style." While seemingly representing a gesture of outreach, there was an underlying tension concerning competition with Japan in a strained and even failing American economy. The program failed; viewers did not find it—either the script or the theme—funny. Instead, the programs that shot up the ratings charts were *The Cosby Show* and *Dynasty*. Both programs were Reagan-era texts that reproduced the myths of meritocracy and upward mobility. Achieving the American Dream, however, was not seen as belonging to Asian Americans. There was one Asian character in a top program in the 1980s: Chau-Li Chi who played "Chau-Li," a butler, in the nighttime soap opera, *Falcon Crest*.

The 1990s: Asian Americans as Either/Or

In 1990, the cult hit *Twin Peaks* premiered. Joan Chen played a Chinese gang mistress, prostitute, and all-around dragon lady who marries/is saved by a wealthy older white man. When he dies, she then ends up with the town sheriff (a white man) whom she cannot ultimately be with because she is "bad." Despite her seductive, whispering demeanor, or perhaps because of it, her character is punished in the end. Josie Packard's final fate is that she gets turned into a maid forced to serve her former sister-in-law, and then, her fate is literally sealed by her being turned into a doorknob.

When Josie no longer has men to manipulate, she thereby loses control of the mill, which was a great source of income, because she does not have men to "do business with." She no longer wields any power and is radically reduced from a rich widower and beautiful owner of the mill to a desexualized, humbled servant.[11]

In studying Asian Americans in television, there is one program that stands above all the rest: *All-American Girl* starring Margaret Cho. Premiering in 1994, this was the first American television program about an Asian American family. Its star was the young stand-up comic and a favorite on the college-circuit, Margaret Cho. Cho's stand-up material included stories, impressions, and jokes about growing up Asian American, about her Korean grandparents, and about her Korean immigrant parents, especially her mother. She was talented enough to earn a chance at her own television show much like other comics who began working on television around that time: Roseanne Barr, Jerry Seinfeld, Ellen DeGeneres, and Brett Butler. However, unlike some of her older, more experienced and powerful counterparts, Cho did not have creative control, and her stand-up material was "loosely translated" into sitcom bunk. Furthermore, Cho's power of self-identity was lost, and both she and her character, Margaret, came across as awkward and unfortunately unfunny.

With a program as unprecedented and closely watched as this, particularly by Asian Americans, there were many criticisms. Asian American audiences had a mixed reaction: elation and shock that the show was even on, and disappointment to the point of embarrassment that the show was bad. Cho felt great pressure from scrutinizing Asian American viewers; their dissatisfaction had some influence on the producers and writers of the show, as Cho describes in her book, *I'm The One That I Want*:

Since there had been such a backlash from the Asian-American community, an effort was made to make the show more "authentic." An Asian consultant was hired, mostly to help actors with their accents and to determine the Feng Shui on the set. It was all the more insulting because the actors didn't need any help, and "authenticity" was never the problem. . . . The idea that there is one defining, "authentic" Asian-American experience ignores the vast diversity of which we are capable. It discounts the fact that there can be many truths, and holds us in a racial spiderweb. We were accused of being racist because we did not ring true as an "authentic" Asian-American family, when the real racism lies in the expectation of one.[12]

Although the creators of the show (which did not include Cho) hired an "Asian consultant" as well as an Asian American writer (though not Korean American), the network's main concern was for the general, i.e., white, audience; it was not meant to cater to Asian Americans, who only make up about 2 percent of the viewing public. The faltering of the new program was compounded by the fact that the scripts were simply poor.

The major problems with the representation of Asian American family and culture pivot on the intersection of gender and race. The character of older brother Stuart portrayed Asian American men as perfectionist, no fun, and effeminate. Though accomplished professionally and academically, the Asian American man is still being portrayed as physically meek in popular American culture; further, this meekness is naturalized as (passed off as) an "Asian" trait. At the same time while not represented as "masculine" in the western sense—muscular, deep-voiced, heterosexual—Stuart is shown to be "more traditional" than Margaret, which translated into him being chauvinist. Either way, it was an unsexy, unflattering representation of an Asian American man.

In one specific episode, Margaret's mother asks her to become better friends with her future sister-in-law, Amy (played by Ming Na Wen). Amy is portrayed as a "more traditional" Asian American, meaning she falls into all the preconceived trappings of what it means to be an Asian female—studious, polite, cooks well, does what Stuart instructs, and dresses conservatively in floral dresses. This is the "lotus blossom" trope as opposed to the "dragon lady" character-type. She is pitted against Margaret's position as being clearly more "American" than "Asian." The problem is not only that "American" is equated with freedom, independence, and fun while "Asian" is represented as repressed and backward in comparison, but that these two are conceived of as mutually exclusive. In other words, Asian *and* American is not a comprehendible identity, and the idea expressed is that women of Asian descent can be either a "good" Asian female, or a liberated "all-American girl," but not both. The first prominent role of an Asian American on prime time television was thus schizophrenic about her identity.

The Millennium: Asian Americans Trickle in . . . as Females, Children, and Cartoons

A discussion of the current status of Asian Americans on television reveals three key configurations: first, Asian American females are in vast majority—Asian American men basically do not exist in visual culture; second, Asian Americans are seen in programs that air on the non-big three network channels—Fox, WB, HBO, UPN, and MTV—aside from one show on NBC; and third, Asian American characters are seen in highest occurrence in children's programming, that is, as children and as cartoons.

In the first four years of the millennium, there have been just three successfully running prime time (i.e., not syndicated) network programs that have Asian American characters in recurring roles. In 2000, there were only three Asian American characters of the hundreds of characters on television, up one from the previous year. The most prominent character in the 2000 season was Ling Woo on *Ally McBeal*, played by Lucy Liu. Before her blockbuster appearances in the *Charlie's Angels* films, this actress was often confused with Lisa Ling, who starred as one of the co-hosts on the

Barbara Walters morning talk show, *The View*. Icy, sexy, wealthy, snobby, and over-accomplished, she owns several businesses including an escort service, designs fashions, cuts hair, knows secret (Asian) sex tricks, and has a law degree. Ling is a dragon lady of sorts.

A second successful and recurring role involves experienced actress, Ming Na. (She has dropped her surname.) Ming Na has recently returned to *E.R.*, reviving a role she had a few years earlier (1994–1995). No longer the competitive, hard-working, insecure (and, as it turns out, wealthy) Asian American medical student, she now is a working physician. Upon her return, she is pregnant, unmarried, and the father of her unborn baby is African American; she has quite a situation to explain to her parents, which she actually does not do. The seemingly perfect, model daughter from earlier in the series came back with a myriad of problems—and patients—to attend to.

The third prime time program with an Asian American character is the WB's *Gilmore Girls*. The bespectacled young friend of main character Rory Gilmore, Lane Kim is played by Keiko Agena. (Agena also had a small guest role as a college student activist for women's rights on the popular *Felicity* before joining the cast of *Gilmore Girls*.) Through her friendship with Rory, viewers see Lane's struggles for independence not simply as a teenager, but as a Korean American teenager. Since *All-American Girl*, there has not been such cultural specificity surrounding an Asian American character. Though unlike Margaret in *All-American Girl*, Lane in *Gilmore Girls* is allowed to negotiate her Koreanness along with her Americanness.[13]

Just four years ago, these were the only three Asian American characters in a recurring role in network television. Other mentionables include: Sammo Hung on *Martial Law* on CBS, however, is Asian, not Asian American, and though capable and charming, he fulfills an expected martial arts trope. This series also included American actress Kelly Hu, as well as Arsenio Hall, making it a rare show with an all-minority lead cast; it is no longer on the air. Russell Wong starred in the short-lived *Vanishing Son* as a Chinese man who flees to the U.S. after participating in a protest for freedom; he too, is shown performing martial arts as his key attribute. Garrett Wang played Harry Kim on *Star Trek: Voyager* on the UPN network, though this is a science fiction universe, and he is in a more typical role as an unemotional scientist. The series ended in 2001.

On the other end of the gender and coolness spectrum is sassy Janet, the pretty Korean American on MTV's wildly popular reality series, *The Real World: Seattle*. Like Lane Kim on *Gilmore Girls*, Janet is given cultural specificity that provides a different context to her struggles and choices; her mother, aunt, and sister even visit her at the communal house, revealing a whole other world that Janet is from. Janet also marked the trend of including an Asian American (or part-Asian American) female for programs made for the MTV demographic, e.g., other seasons of *The Real World* and *Road Rules* among the plethora of reality television formatted shows now airing on MTV. Another (young) Korean American woman offered to a young adult demographic is MTV veejay/reporter, SuChin Pak. She deftly delivers music news and has been given higher profile assignments like MTV's coverage of award shows. Her look is edgy, New York, but feminine; she is a hipper Connie Chung.

Finally, there have been three Asian American men who materialized on prime time television very recently: John Cho (perhaps best known for his role in the film, *Better Luck Tomorrow*) in *Off Centre*, Eddie Shin in the very short-lived *That 80s Show*, and Bobby Lee who joined the cast of Fox's late night comedy show, *Mad TV*, in 2001. Only Bobby Lee has survived, but like Steve Park on *In Living Color* before him, his "face time" is limited in comparison to the rest of the comedy sketch players. He plays "strange" characters like Communist leader Kim Jong Il, or often silent or lurking characters like "Jai" in Mad TV's spoof of *Queer Eye for the Straight Guy*. (Jai is the one of the "fabulous five" who is least recognized and least liked.)

Korean Canadian Sandra Oh currently plays Rita on the non-network HBO half-hour comedy *Arli$$*, one of the few examples of comedies which feature Asian American characters. Oh plays an artsy, slightly wacky but smart character with chutzpah. Her racial identity is acknowledged and on occasion, it is featured as a storyline. She has received strong notice for the diverse and different characters she has portrayed in films such as *Double Happiness, Barrier Device, Last Night, Dancing at the Blue Iguana*, and most recently in *Under the Tuscan Sun* with Diane Lane. Oh portrays characters whose Asianness emerges or does not emerge in varying degrees, while maintaining the integrity of a character in a way that is nuanced, engaging, and unique for an Asian American/Asian Canadian performer.

Rosalind Chao is an actress who has worked steadily in both television and film portraying Asian characters and later, Asian American characters. She played Keiko O'Brien on *Star Trek: The Next Generation* and *Deep Space Nine* and has made numerous guest appearances on many top-rated television programs such as *Falcon Crest, E.R., The West Wing* (which also had a minor role of a Japanese American intern in its first season), *Monk*, and in two new programs this 2003-2004 season: *10-8* as Lt. Maggie Chen and *The O.C.* as Dr. Kim, the president of an elite private high school.

B.D. Wong, who played Margaret Cho's brother in *All-American Girl*, is another performer (and a Tony-award winning actor) who deserves attention. He held a guest-starring role as psychologist Dr. George Huang at the end of the 2000 season of *Law & Order: Special Victims Unit* and has since joined the cast as a regular. He also held a recurring role on the controversial, innovative HBO series about prison life, race, sex, and violence, *Oz*. He played the role of Father Ray Mukada, a priest who counseled the incarcerated men. Both Wong and Chao play straight-laced, serious asexual professionals, i.e., numerous times as "Dr.s."[14]

Subsets of Asian Americans on Television . . . as Females and as for Children's Consumption

Of this female characterization, there are two specific "roles" that Asian Americans take in/on television. The first example, which has been apparent for many years, is that of the Asian female news reporter. Though she speaks "like an American" in that she speaks English with no accent, she looks "very Asian"—shiny, straight, bobbed hair, and elaborate, exaggerated eye makeup. Darrell Hamamoto calls it "the Connie Chung Syndrome."[15] Another key element in this portrayal is the pairing of an Asian American woman with a white male co-anchor.[16] This particular combination of Asian American female and white male became a ratings winner and was replicated on station after station, local and national, from California to Iowa.[17] Asian American women newscasters are "aesthetically pleasing" and deliver the news with a projection of intelligence and yet also with deference (to her co-anchor). This role has become a widespread profession for young Asian American women, and it has also become a character type.

A second high visibility image of Asian Americans on television is in the particularly feminine role of the figure skater. Olympic medalists Michelle Kwan and Kristi Yamaguchi are among the most well known Asian American faces for young people today. Kwan is still competing and has appeared in a television special in which she skated in the role of Disney's Mulan, a Chinese, not a Chinese American, character.[18] Both Kwan and Yamaguchi are "classic" figure skaters, elegant and lovely, pretty and feminine. Commentary on their skating extends to their character and upbringing: disciplined, hardworking, with self-sacrificing parents. Femininity and studiousness are attributes easily associated as "Asian"—it is this "type" of Asian American that is promoted and accepted in American culture and that is given air time on American television.

Another genre in which Asian Americans are presented, and particularly for increasingly younger viewers, is that of children or cartoons, or children in cartoons. On Saturday morning, from 7 a.m. to 12 noon, there are numerous programs with Asian American characters (both leads and supporting), plus the anime-adapted series, *Pokemon*, *Digimon*, and *Card Captors*. Out of the six major channels (ABC, CBS, NBC, Fox, WB, and PBS), this averaged out to two programs out of six every hour, a whopping 33 percent, which is outstanding in comparison to prime time television. According to the "Fall Colors 2000–2001: Prime Time Diversity Report," 75 percent or 1,688 characters are white on television from 8 p.m. to 11 p.m., which is when most Americans watch television. African Americans have a visible presence of 17 percent, and Asian Pacific Americans are represented at 3 percent.[19] For primary recurring characters who are Asian Pacific American, the number goes down to 2 percent. Moreover, there is an overall pattern consistent with last year's study that diversity decreases when focusing on main/lead characters: "In both the 1999–2000 and 2000–2001 seasons, prime time diversity diminished when non-recurring and secondary characters were not included in the analysis."[20] It is in children's programming where the most Asian Americans are seen.

Change is Possible

Lois Salisbury, president of Children Now, states, "while the industry to one degree or another has responded to the criticisms about the lack of diversity, there clearly is still a problem. Any way you carve it, the more central a character is to a program, the more likely he or she is white."[21] The study titled, "Fall Colors: How Diverse Is the 1999–2000 TV Season's Prime Time Line-Up?," was conducted by the non-profit social policy organization as part of its Children & the Media Program; it looked at all primary, recurring, and non-recurring characters on 274 episodes of ninety-two prime time programs on the six major broadcast networks. The study found that UPN featured the largest representation of minority characters, 35 percent, while ABC offered the fewest, 13 percent, of all characters; NBC had 16 percent, Fox 19 percent, CBS 20 percent, and the WB featured 23 percent minority characters. Of characters in high school or younger, African American youths constituted 7.9 percent, Latino / as 3.7 percent, Asian Pacific Americans 1.2 percent, and Native Americans 0.6 percent. Although the representation of race among teenagers is lacking, the percentage of Asian American teens is still higher than the percentage of Asian American adults seen on television.

The main approach taken in television programming decision-making is that "ratings are what matter." Yet ratings are variable, an unknown factor, created by the viewers, not by the producers. The relationship between media makers and media viewers-consumers is one in which the audience wields the ultimate power: television executives will make whatever they perceive viewers want. Asian Americans need to communicate to networks the specific kinds of representations they desire. Ratings are not the sole factor contributing to programming decisions; media activism together with media research also contribute to change.

Of around 3,000 ideas, about 100 will be scripted, of which perhaps twenty-five will go to pilot; at each network, five to ten pilots will get on the air; at each network, one or two shows will stay on long enough to be renewed for a second season.[22] Critical intervention takes place between the developmental stages of a concept to a pilot getting on the television schedule. Although viewers normally have no direct access to that process, it is their continuing societal presence, however abstract, which is influential. We viewers have the right to make known what we want: a more racially and culturally diverse picture that "reflects" back to us the multicultural society that we are. The flip side of the protest/boycott coin is fandom. Fans can forge a more direct relationship with the producers of a television show, demonstrating that viewers' actions make a difference in programming: ". . . fans are more aware of the power of coordinated action, and the television industry is more aware of the fan sites" as producers of the cancelled program, *Roswell*, realized this through a Tabasco sauce mail-in campaign.[23]

Asian Americans need to recognize their active role in the ways television programs are made and to take up a more pro-active role in our own representation. Asian Americans need to take advantage of the contradictions, vagary, and serendipity in television programming, to know that it is a space for contestation and dissent, and to know that spectatorship is more than merely "watching" culture, it is participating in creating culture.

One joke that Cho offers in her stand-up act about her experience starring in a network television series is that the producers tossed around other possible titles for the show—*East Meets West, Wok on the Wild Side*—to which Cho joked, "Hey! It's my show, let's call it Chinkies." Cho's realization of the power she has not only as a performer, but as an individual should resonate for Asian American television viewers-consumers-citizens. The following passage from her book expresses her shocked realization of the power she harnesses (my emphasis added):

> *It never occurred to me that I was the star.*

> *It never occurred to me that I could have told the network that I didn't want to lose weight.*

It never occurred to me that the only reason anybody was there was because of me.

The show was called All-American Girl *and I was the* All-American Asshole *because I never realized it.*[24]

Margaret Cho is part of a new generation of Asian American children of immigrants coming of age. There is a surging of pride and power within a newly emerging Asian American youth culture. Furthermore, martial arts action films from Hong Kong, anime from Japan, and other "Asian imports" are growing fast in popularity, along with what I call New Orientalist "Asianish" texts like *The Matrix* and *Kill Bill*. This is happening among Asian Americans and non-Asian Americans alike. It is in this new media universe that the representation of Asian Americans can, possibly, finally come into being. More Asian Americans need to become writers, directors, producers, and performers in Hollywood even if this is "against type" according to Hollywood's as well as our own varying traditions. Asian Americans must harness their technological skill, economic power, and political focus to influence the television industry so that Asian Americans will have a stronger presence on and beyond television.

Notes

1. As stated by Professor George Gerbner, who has been conducting research on television representations of gender roles, racial characters, class and occupational categories for over three decades. In *The Electronic Storyteller* (1998), produced by Media Educational Foundation.

2. See Herman Gray, *Watching Race: Television and the Struggle for "Blackness"* (Minneapolis: University of Minnesota Press, 1997); Darrell Hamamoto, *Monitored Peril: Asian Americans and the Politics of TV Representation* (Minneapolis: University of Minnesota Press, 1994); Chon Noriega, *Shot in America: Television, the State, and the Rise of Chicano Cinema* (Minneapolis: University of Minesota Press, 2000).

3. A recent example of this is the whirlwind popularity of William Hung, a contestant on *American Idol 3* (2004). After a failed and certainly unique audition that involved the Taiwan immigrant and Berkeley engineering student punching out the Ricky Martin tune, "She Bangs," fans (many Asian American) rallied around Hung on the Internet. He has a fan site at http://www.williamhung.org, and several women have declared that they want to marry him. The original spectacle of the "chinky" guy was re-appropriated and reclaimed, and Hung was made into a hero for his courage and earnestness. Hung, indeed, took up and embraced with abandon visual space, and he says, "I already gave my best. I have no regrets at all."

4. As Todd Gitlin quotes Scott Siegler, former CBS vice-president for drama development in *Inside Prime Time* (Berkeley: University of California Press, 2000 edition), 23.

5. Networks also conduct audience research through such methods as preview audience testing of new pilots.

6. Michael Omi and Howard Winant, *Racial Formation in the United States: From the 1960s to the 1980s* (New York: Routledge, 1994), 55.

7. A full analysis and discussion of *The Courtship of Eddie's Father* is available in L.S. Kim, "'Serving' American Orientalism: Negotiating Identities in *The Courtship of Eddie's Father*," *Journal of Film and Video* 55:4.

8. See Horace Newcomb's *The Producer's Medium: Conversations with Creators of American TV* (New York: Oxford University Press, 1983).

9. Interestingly, "Takahashi" was Arnold's last name too. But it is not the same character; Taro Takahashi in this series is a "brilliant Japanese inventor," transferred from Tokyo to Chicago who has to deal with the "Americanization of his household by a nutty, effervescent, Nebraska-born housekeeper named Tina." See Tim Brooks and Earle Marsh, *The Complete Directory To Prime Time Network TV Shows, 1946–Present* (New York: Ballantine Books, 1992).

10. Gitlin, 225.

11. Lahn Sung Kim, "Maid in Color: The Figure of the Racialized Domestic in American Television," (Ph.D. diss., University of California, Los Angeles, 1997), 191.

12. Margaret Cho, *I'm the One That I Want* (New York: Ballantine Books, 2001), 140.

13. The significance of opening credits is that they express what and whom the show is about. The 1999 Children Now study included an analysis of opening sequences finding: "Only 17% of the shows examined have a cast of diverse characters in the opening credits. The credits were deemed a critical component to look at, since the device is used to frame and remind viewers about the show, its characters and its premise." I would like to add one character to the list of current Asian Americans on television, even though she does not appear in the opening sequence: in the animated series, *King of the Hill*, there is a Laotian American girl, Kahn Junior, who is Bobby's neighbor, school friend, and potential girlfriend. While having a spot on prime time, she follows the pattern of being female and a child (and a good student as well).

14. There are a few additional examples I would like to raise: a Japanese American character, Janet, was on the last two seasons of *Beverly Hills 90210* (1998–2000), played by hapa Korean American actress Lindsay Price; she was involved in an interracial relationship and eventual marriage with a baby, and the program showed occasional visits/conflicts with her disapproving parents. Price was one of six main characters on the much-hyped *Coupling*, which was to follow in the footsteps of *Friends* in *Friends'* last season; it failed miserably. In the 1980s, there was a show called *Sidekicks* (1986–1987) that included a young Asian American boy played by Ernie Reyes, Jr. as a martial arts "kicking" pal to a detective played by Gil Gerard. Ming Na Wen played Trudie in *The Single Guy* (1996–1997); what was progressive is that she was "blindcast" for the role, and consequently, her being Chinese American was acknowledged on occasion, as with Janet in *Beverly Hills 90210*, when her disapproving parents came to visit.

15. Hamamoto, 244.

16. Related to this racial politic/racial hierarchy is the fact that it is rare to see a lead anchor who is a Black male. The preferred presentation is of a white male authority figure (as in the national news broadcasts of all three major networks), with women and then men of color at secondary and tertiary rank.

17. The point is not that Iowa lacks sophistication to sponsor such images, but that it lacks a large Asian American viewing audience, which, in turn, means that producers and programmers employ Asian American women newscasters not to attract Asian American viewers, but rather, they have the general (white) audience in mind in creating and offering such an "aesthetic."

18. For further analysis of Yamaguchi and Kwan, and Asian American ice skaters as model minorities, please see my forthcoming article, "American Orientalism and the Political Aesthetics of National Identity," available upon request.

19. Children Now, "Fall Colors 2000–2001: Prime Time Diversity Report," 9.

20. *Ibid.*, 25.

21. Greg Braxton, "Study Finds that While Diversity Exists, Primary Casts Remain Mostly White and Male," *Los Angeles Times*, January 12, 2000.

22. Gitlin, 21.

23. Sophia Hollander, "The 'Roswell' Army Fights for Its Show on the Web," *New York Times*, June 10, 2001.

24. Cho, 141.

In Ms. McBeal's Defense: Assessing Ally McBeal as a Feminist Text

Amanda D. Lotz

At the time of its 1997 debut *Ally McBeal* inspired uncommon popular and academic debate. Few other shows at the time came close to equaling the column space devoted to Ms. McBeal and her colleagues, and the lack of unanimity of critical opinion made it a particularly compelling phenomenon. *Ally McBeal* served as a catalyst for discussions of feminism and femininity in addition to the more conventional reviews commonly written by television critics. The character of Ally, embodied in the gamine frame of actress Calista Flockhart, debuted to a society unprepared for the divergence she provided from the female characters who preceded her. The disjuncture of her character relative to those in series who most recently had been hailed as feminist, such as *Murphy Brown, Roseanne,* and *Designing Women,* led to speculation and pontification over what McBeal's presence and popularity indicated about women's gains and feminism's status.

Debut reviews of *Ally McBeal* were generally laudatory and emphasized the series' play with fantasy through digital graphic insertions, although critics were notably ambivalent about the title character. James Collins summed up many critics' uncertainty by acknowledging that their concern resulted from her predicaments seeming false because she had not yet earned the audience's sympathy (Collins, 117). Six months into the first season, reviews shifted to address the emerging debate in opinions about the series, a split that seemed a function of naysayers who sought a continuation of the role model trajectory of working women characters and proponents who either identified with the characters or were entranced by the series' whimsy.[1]

It is impossible to know whether viewers would have recognized *Ally McBeal*'s contribution to contemporary deliberations about dominant social scripts related to gender norms if the press had not explicitly identified her as the "new face of feminism." Television critics writing in newspapers and magazines acknowledged Ally as the latest in a series of remarkable female characters such as Ann Marie of *That Girl*, Mary Richards of *The Mary Tyler Moore Show*, and Murphy Brown (Chambers, "*Ally McBeal*;" Stark; Grossberger; Jefferson; Dowd). Despite the series' drama-comedy blend and ensemble emphasis, critics connected Ally to the trajectory of "new woman" stories that had built narratives around single working women in situation comedies. Curiously, only one mentioned the series and character that offered the greatest similarity, the title character of *The Days and Nights of Molly Dodd* (NBC, 1987–1988; Lifetime, 1989–1991) (Svetkey, 22). Molly Dodd's likeness was so distinct that popular criticism of Ally McBeal virtually repeated what had been written about Dodd ten years earlier (see Wilson, 110–114).

The mainstream press framed the popular discussion about the show and determined the primary analytical lens for considering the series in its initial reviews. The question of feminism in relation to *Ally McBeal* would arguably become over-determined during the summer between its first and second seasons when a poorly researched and arbitrarily informed article on the state of contemporary feminism by Gina Bellafante appeared in *Time* and used Ally's head as the current embodiment of feminism (a legacy that also included Susan B. Anthony, Betty Friedan, and Gloria Steinem) (Bellafante, 54–60). From that point on, the character, the series, and even Flockhart became central to questions about the emergence of a new generation of women and the status of feminism in U.S. society. In many accounts, invoking *Ally McBeal* became a shorthand for the coterminous rise of female-centered although ambiguously feminist content emerging in various media, including the novel *Bridget Jones's Diary*, music acts ranging from the Lilith Fair tour to the Spice Girls, as well as television series *Sex and the City* and *Buffy the Vampire Slayer* (Parker, Williamson, Stack).

The arbitrary and undefined use of prefixes before the term feminist in reviews and commentary exacerbated uncertainly about *Ally McBeal*'s relationship to feminism.

> *I'm not ready for the post-post-post feminist [Katz, 36].*

> *Ally McBeal has become an icon of New Feminism [Scruggs, 1B].*

> *Ally is the quintessential postfeminist. She has all the professional advantages Mary [Richards, of* The Mary Tyler Moore Show*] never had, but unlike her more traditionally feminist sitcom sister, she doesn't want to make it on her own [Chambers, "How," 58].*

> *[Ally McBeal is] a poster girl for postmodern feminism [Schneider, 92].*

> *A groundbreaking postfeminist television anthem for the New Woman of the '90s. [Svetkey, 22].*

> *Ally is a heady, seductive brew of feminist and anti-feminist ideals [Heywood, B9].*

> *[Ally McBeal is] savvy yet vulnerable, fallible yet likable, feminist yet not. . . . These feminine virtues are accompanied by feminine weaknesses—by the painstaking vulnerability that has become the trademark of television's post-feminists [Shalit, 30].*

Alternately, commentators discussed the cultural impact or significance of the show in terms of these variously labeled feminisms.

> *The most remarkable postfeminist trend is not about women. It's about men. The idea that women should mimic men is now dead. Now men mimic women [Dowd, C5].*

> *Ally has struck a nerve with twentysomething women who feel both excited and confused by the choices bestowed upon them by the feminist movement [Chambers, 58].*

> *The show is important not so much for what its lead character says or does, but for what the program itself attempts and symbolizes. This is a drama about a woman, and such excursions have been surprisingly rare in the history of prime-time television [Stark, 13].*

The use of jargon rather than clearly defined articulations of feminism by these articles also obscured the adjustments in social attitudes toward the term "feminist" and what have traditionally been considered feminist ideals.

One of the greatest challenges facing feminism is the frequent misrepresentation of its goals and foundations by mainstream media outlets that provide the forum through which most people encounter descriptions of or commentary about feminism. Articles such as Bellafante's become authoritative to the general populace, despite the fact that few if any feminists would agree that feminism is any of the things Bellafante proposes (see NOW). Judy Mann notes of the *Time* article, "A hefty fifty percent of those from the ages eighteen to thirty-four told the pollsters in the *Time*/CNN survey that they share 'feminist' values, by which they generally mean they want a world in which they can choose to be anything—the President or a mother, or both" (E03). Yet these same respondents do not consider themselves feminists. This inconsistency makes clear that the ideals of feminism are alive and thriving, but that considerable uncertainty surrounds the label, even as just plain "feminism."

The frequent use of the term feminism with various prefixes may have left readers confused about the precise argument commentators were making, but certainly buoyed viewers' recognition that the series was dealing with gender issues in a significant way. *Ally McBeal* conformed to the various "new woman" codes that had become dominant in representing women since *The Mary Tyler Moore Show*. Its female characters are uniformly single, possess upwardly mobile, highly professionalized careers, and live without connection to family in a major city.[2] Perhaps it was this adherence to the "new woman" symbolic code that prevented many from recognizing the series' departure. Ally and her female colleagues inaugurate characters that might be named "new, new women" as a result of their divergence from the contexts that defined their predecessors.

In this article I address the finite text of five full seasons of *Ally McBeal* and the contribution the series made to the circulation of feminist discourses and ideas. Ultimately, I argue that the series did offer significant feminist innovation and may be the prototypic example of a postfeminist series—at least as in evidence by 2005. I do not use postfeminist as synonymous with anti-feminist or after feminism, although these uses are suggested by some journalistic and academic criticism of the series (Kim; Vavrus; Shalit). Rather, I find postfeminist the best descriptor of this series because of the theoretical innovation postfeminism provides and because it draws attention to the contextual breaks that series such as *Ally McBeal* typify.

Despite the copious attention to the series and its feminist or antifeminist attributes, many assessments neglected the series' significance by failing to consider a triumvirate of contextual variances that made *Ally McBeal* fundamentally unlike the predecessors with which critics commonly compared it. Reviews of the series indicate that many believed *Ally McBeal* signified changes in social formations and gender norms, although assessments rarely attended to the complexity with which the series was enmeshed with other socio-historical changes. The series introduced a considerable break from previous female-centered series as a result of its late 1990s historical context, its characters' post–Baby Boom, post-second-wave generational context, and its representational context as one of many coterminous female-centered dramas on U.S. television. Even though many critics immediately connected Ally and her colleagues with a legacy of other female characters, few acknowledged the fundamental difference in the context of this series and many others emerging in subsequent seasons. Additionally, many reviews considered only the series' first few seasons, which provides a significant limitation because of the radical variation of the show from season to season during its five-year run.

The divergence of the series' historical, generational, and representational contexts necessitates a different critical and analytical frame for evaluating the series relative to those of previous eras. In some ways the features interrelate in a manner making them seem indistinct, yet three discrete phenomena exist. First, the socio-cultural context of life in America in the late 1990s provided clear differentiation from the early 1970s in which audiences greeted previous "new woman" series such as *The Mary Tyler Moore Show* and even the late 1980s and early 1990s of series such as *Murphy Brown*. *The Mary Tyler Moore Show* could not have explored sexual harassment law in the same manner available to *Ally McBeal* (particularly because it had not yet been named), and the significance of a single woman with a career varies vastly because of changes in cultural norms. Some of the concerns critics had of the series resulted from their expectation that a feminist character of the 1990s would embody the same form as a feminist character of the 1970s, but that this historical difference would require the 1990s character to be a hyper-embodiment of the 1970s character. Mary Richards personified 1970s feminism and Murphy Brown then earned her feminist distinction by enhancing Mary's professionalism. By this logic, a 1990s feminist character would then need to embody professionalism even more than Murphy, and clearly, this was not the case with Ally. This expectation is an outcome of logic rooted in the role model framework that was common in media criticism during second-wave feminism and provided valuable tools in that context. If career women were "feminist" representations in the 1970s, then the default critical mode suggested that the more career-oriented the character, the more feminist she is. But the cultural meaning of a woman with a career varies significantly in 2000 from its meaning in the early 1970s.

The variation in generational context is likely even more significant to delimiting the range of stories available to *Ally McBeal*. All of the female television characters that drew feminist accolades as new women prior to *Ally McBeal*'s arrival belonged to the Baby Boom generation and were consequently in their teens and twenties during the era in which second-wave feminism advocated social change.[3] Baby Boom characters would have grown up experiencing sexism that seems unimaginable now and fought to gain access to the male-dominated professional workforce. The characters of *Ally McBeal* and other contemporary series such as *Sex and the City* belong to another generation, whose identity (both fictional and in reality) is very much defined by experiencing the gains of second-wave activists' efforts. Sexism certainly has not been eradicated for these women, but the emphasis second-wave activists placed on opening the public sphere to women meant that access to education and professional careers were far less contested.

The narrative of *Ally McBeal* consequently exists in a cultural milieu modified from that of its second-wave precursors, and its characters possess a worldview variant from those who preceded them. Cultural events and experiences bind writers to contexts that become inscribed in the series' stories. Ally's generation was raised with both Disney fairy tales and second-wave feminism without much mainstream attention to their incompatibility. The varied generational context of the characters in *Ally McBeal* does not explain away the flightiness and apolitical tendencies many feminist critics have emphasized, but it is an important feature in understanding the series and likely why it captivated such sizable audiences of Ally's generational cohort.

Finally, the representational context in which *Ally McBeal* circulates, particularly by its third season, requires an analytical frame unlike those used previously. The late 1990s and early years of the twenty-first century provided an unprecedented proliferation of female characters in central dramatic roles. Where one or two series became feminist touchstones in previous eras (and they were most often situation comedies), *Ally McBeal* shared television schedules with more than twenty dramatic series featuring a central female protagonist. Before this era, a paucity of fully developed female characters bore the burden of representing all working women and circulated in a socio-historical context more hostile to women choosing professional careers. In an environment in which a comparatively vast plurality of single, professional female characters exists, each one need not appear as a role model for all women, nor must she conform to the limited possibilities afforded previous characters.

These contextual features become critical to developing a sophisticated analysis of the series and its contribution to gender scripts and feminist discourses. Indeed, a very different understanding of the show can be advanced if its context is not considered. Many acknowledged that the series included a spark of something truly significant, but the conventional frame of analysis failed those who sought to identify the variation the series provided.

Explaining Postfeminism

It is impossible to know what journalists such as Katz, Chambers, Schneider, and Shalit meant in referencing *Ally McBeal* as a post-post-post feminist, postfeminist, or postmodern feminist show. Articles such as these never explain their terms or their prefixes, and explanation is vital because feminist media scholars have used postfeminist to describe contradictory ideological positions (See Lotz, "Postfeminist," 111–115). Most academic scholarship prior to the mid–1990s (and by contextual clues, likely the journalists quoted here) used postfeminist as equivalent to anti-feminist, or as a descriptor indicating an era when feminism is no longer needed: a literal after feminism (Faludi; Press; Dow; Modleski; Kim; Vavrus). In national contexts outside of the U.S., some feminist scholars have used postfeminism to demarcate expansion and adjustments in theory since the height of the second wave. This use is as "feminist" and equally as activist as previous versions of feminism, but takes into account postmodern and post-structuralist deconstruction of women as a singular cate-gory in an attempt to address the varied relations to power women experience based on other aspects of their subjectivity. This theorization of postfeminism also incorporates activist structures charac-teristic of new social movements (see Lotz, "Communicating"; Brooks; McRobbie; Gamble; Moseley and Read; Arthurs).

Elsewhere, I extrapolated from postfeminist theory to delimit four attributes of postfeminist media content, including narratives that explore the diverse relations to power women inhabit, depic-tions of varied feminist solutions and loose organizations of activism, texts that deconstruct binary categories of gender and sexuality, and the depiction of situations illustrating the contemporary struggles faced by women and feminists (Lotz, "Postfeminist," 116–117). Postfeminist theory remains in the process of development, so that these may not be the only attributes to characterize postfem-inist media forms. This understanding of postfeminism relies on a more sophisticated theoretical framework than its anti-feminist denotation and is useful for explaining a period of ideological trans-formation. Such a perspective also aids in demarcating the contextual breaks that distinguish a show such as *Ally McBeal* from many of its predecessors.

The attributes of postfeminist media forms listed above are best explained through example, requiring a closer look at the text of *Ally McBeal*. The series exhibits characteristics of postfeminism in various ways: through its ensemble of female characters with diverse perspectives, by exploring contemporary legal issues affecting women—such as sexual harassment—as complex sites for the expression of cultural expectations of gender roles and power, by raising the possibility of non-binary understandings of categories such as gender and sexuality, and by depicting a postfeminist perspec-tive on the contemporary dilemmas women experience. *Ally McBeal*'s success in drawing the desired audience and its instigation of cultural discussion about its representations of characters and issues further illustrate the importance of critically assessing the series in relation to postfeminist ideas. I am not arguing that the series stands as some ideal embodiment of feminism or postfeminism that indicates women's gains or an equitable society. *Ally McBeal* is a complex and contradictory text of great richness and depth. Limitations and moments of conservative ideology most certainly exist in *Ally McBeal*, but a text without such features is unnecessary nor even ideal.

Ally McBeal as a Postfeminist Text

In May of 2002 David E. Kelley completed Ally's journey, making it possible to review a finite story and consider the series in a comprehensive manner. A complete narrative enables analysis that can assess the validity of various arguments about the character and the series as indicative of a fem-inist evolution or a retrograde containment of second-wave activism. Perhaps early critics were too quick in their evaluation or maybe Kelley preordained the series' conclusion by the end of the first season. Many critics sought for Kelley to offer more evidence of a feminist evolution in seasons two and three, rather than Ally's downward spiral of near hysteria. But critics must not forget the delayed gratification necessary in serialized television; audiences likely would have bored quickly had Ally ear-lier exhibited the certainty she found in the series' last season.

Even with the closure a series finale provides, *Ally McBeal* remains a complicated text to con-sider. The tone and constant variation of the series account for much of the extreme disparity in evaluations. *Ally McBeal* may have had the unusual attribute of being fairly single-authored—with creator and executive producer Kelley writing most episodes—but the uncertain tone Kelley gave the series undermined the uniformity such authorship might suggest. Narratives often slipped unpre-dictably from realistic melodrama to comedy and fantasy sequences, which made varied interpreta-tions freely possible—including the possibility that the dramatic and comedic depictions of characters were parodic and critical of the very concepts they explored. Although television theorists generally acknowledge the polysemic possibilities of television texts, *Ally McBeal* took this potential further and seemed to *encourage* multiple readings. The nagging uncertainty of whether various characters and situations were being posed as parody or with literal seriousness did the most to advance this ambiguous tone and inspire bipolar critical reactions.

The lack of a dependable central character through which the audience could gauge the series' message and ideology exacerbated uncertainty. Martha Nochimson argues, "Structurally, each *Ally* episode began as if it were going to be a conventionally plot-driven show, only to be derailed when the humor on the show, with its intensity of radical and abrupt slippages, refused to resolve conflict to the expected single perspective point of view . . . words and situations turned representation wrong side out and back again so that it was impossible to attain any kind of seamless view" (27). Despite affording McBeal title character status, the narrative positioned John Cage as the moral center of the story for the first four seasons, but the character's eccentricities and oddities served to discredit him as well. In the final season, Kelley reintroduced McBeal with a certain maturity that she had previously lacked; although she had always been, as Cage remarked in the finale, "the soul of this place" (5–22, "Bygones").[4]

In addition to the complex tone of the series, the season-to-season variation makes it difficult to speak of *Ally McBeal* in generalities. Substantial cast changes altered the dynamics of this character-driven series and even episodic organization varied in each of the five seasons. Season one featured episodes organized with two primary plots (one court case, one personal dilemma) and characters Ally, Billy, Georgia, Elaine, Renee, Richard, Whipper and John. Nelle and Ling were added in the second season, while Whipper became a secondary character. The dual plot structure continued initially, but courtroom stories began to dwindle as the romance between Ally and Billy rekindled. The series changed considerably in season four as a result of the departure of Billy, Georgia, Whipper, and Renee, and new romances between Ally and Larry Paul, John and Melanie West, and the triangle of attraction among Richard, Ling, and Jackson Duper became central serial narratives. In its final season the series returned to a more balanced court-personal split, however, the constantly changing cast made the season highly variable. The point of this summary is to acknowledge from the outset the impossibility of clearly demarcating a singular entity of what the series *Ally McBeal* ever was.

Negotiation of Different Perspectives Among a Female Ensemble

Ally McBeal features an uncommon majority of women, with as many as six regular and one recurring female characters who exhibit varied and divergent identities. The prevalence of female characters and narrative focus on them creates an atmosphere ripe for the exploration of the diverse perspectives among women. Notably, despite the range of ethnic subjectivities evident at a visual level, the series does not differentiate among its female characters by socio-economic status, ethnicity, or sexuality, but through variant opinions and political outlooks.

In addition to its sizable female cast, the series' frequent use of topic material emphasizing gender issues makes it a nearly exemplary series for examining heterogeneous constructs of women and their concerns. Almost without exception, the firm accepts cases affecting women or cases specifically salient to the private sphere: a space often occupied by women. These stories deal with prostitution, sex-based discrimination, sexual harassment, and questions of family or relationships, which led Brenda Cooper to argue that the series consequently "privileges women and their ways of experiencing a patriarchal world, thus creating a feminine spectatorship for viewers" (420). The legal storyline in each episode allows the series to match the examination of an issue inflected by gender politics with character-driven personal plots, which further makes the episodic text a combination of strategies and genres. Issue-oriented legal plots are significant because of how they twist and recast common feminist issues. Through the development of often-exaggerated circumstances, the series reveals women to be positioned discrepantly in relation to power and laws, despite legal presumptions that define women uniformly.

When an episode places these female characters in the context of an event or issue, they react distinctively, which illustrates the diverse perspectives among them. The range of viewpoints on issues or events provided by the female ensemble is just one way that *Ally McBeal* explores differences among women and thus produces an implicit postfeminist discourse. An example of disparate female and feminist perspectives in the negotiation of personal issues appeared in an early episode following the arrest of partner John Cage for soliciting a prostitute (1–02, "Compromising Positions"). This episode presents the characters debating the ethics of dating behavior and whether it is more honest for John to solicit a prostitute than to buy a woman a few drinks to convince her to come home with him if all he seeks is a sexual partner. John tries to present his action as less exploitative and consequently female-friendly if not feminist. Ally, however, views the gender power dynamics differently and reprimands him. John's reasoning clearly dismays Georgia, but does not move her to action, and Elaine and many of the other female support staff indicate approval. The series revisits this issue and offers yet another lens through which the audience can consider the power dynamics and implications of prostitution in the third season when Nelle, who is dating John, learns of the past arrest (3–09, "Out in the Cold"). Nelle offers a feminist examination of the issue and tries to rectify her personal politics in favor of legalizing prostitution with the feelings of disappointment she experiences when learning of John's past. The episodes provide competing views on prostitution, each presenting itself as endeavoring to be feminist, yet the series never gives sex workers a voice. The complex construction of prostitution reflects the divergent feminist positions for and against its legalization, a plurality indicative of the diversity of feminist perspectives.

Ally McBeal depicts female characters responding in diverse and discrepant ways to both legal and personal dilemmas. By featuring so many women in primary roles, the series can regularly depict women as a group composed of varied outlooks in a manner unavailable in series with just one or two female characters whose primary narrative function is as contrast to the perspective of male characters. The varied perspectives the female characters exhibit and their participation in issue debate represent women as complexly configured, which is characteristic of postfeminist approaches. The series foregrounds the diversity and complexity among women rather than portraying the women as similar in belief, yet in contradiction to their male co-workers. Importantly, despite their contradictory outlooks, deep bonds underlie the relationships among the women. Nochimson argues that, "Looking at Ally as a role model was inappropriate in a show in which the feminism was located not in Ally, but between characters, in new relational paradigms" (29). Some critical debate exists on this point as others have made much of "cat fight" scenes in which the women squabble with digital graphics of feline heads superimposed on their bodies (Vavrus, 420; Shugart, Waggoner, and O'Brien Hallstein, 205). Such scenes require close and contextualized analyses. Kelley has a history of explicitly responding to critics in his series' texts, and the "cat fight" scenes also might be seen as a reflexive awareness of the criticism of women's depictions in a parodic way, rather than the literal interpretation others have taken.[5]

A more persuasive criticism of the limitation of the series in this area can be made of the series' inattention to how ethnicity, class, and sexual identity contribute to the characters' varying subjectivities. Although the series was cast with atypical inclusion of African Americans and even an Asian American actor, Kelley intentionally chose a "colorblind" approach that never commented on the experiences of racism the characters would likely encounter, particularly when Ally dated a black man in much of the second season (Braxton, Fl). The series' discussion of gay rights and inclusion of gay characters was also limited. The show represented lesbians and gay men in occasional episodes, but offered an ambiguous ideological position. An exceptionally stereotypical lesbian character, Margaret Camero, appears in two different episodes, first as an opponent's witness and later in search of representation (2–19, "Let's Dance;" 2–23, "I Know Him by Heart"). Camero's portrayal might be best understood as parodic, with the text criticizing stereotypes of lesbians, particularly as articulated in text by homophobe Richard. Admittedly, the depiction easily can be interpreted without recognizing the parody, in which case, the text reinforces some lesbian stereotypes. Ideally, a postfeminist text would engage critique of identity difference more fully (perhaps this was most evident in the Lifetime series *Any Day Now*, 1998–2002), but *Ally McBeal* does move toward a postfeminist standard through its multivocality.[6]

Critiquing Legal Solutions and Liberal Feminist Answers

Ally McBeal exhibits the second attribute of postfeminist discourse, depicting varied feminist solutions and loose organizations of activism, through its interrogation of gender issues in a way that illustrates the inadequacy of legal standards that uniformly apply laws to all women when their relation to power varies greatly. The series' critique of legal solutions that are the outcome of second-wave liberal feminist perspectives also evinces the second postfeminist attribute. The courtroom forum creates an environment for political discussion that might otherwise appear out of context in a fictional television series and provides the characters with a space for speeches about contemporary issues. Kelley consistently focuses on gender-inflected topics in the *Ally McBeal* courtroom, unlike other series—even his own—that interrogate a broader range of politics. The legal situations in *Ally McBeal* offer characteristics of postfeminism through their challenging of traditional liberal feminist positions and solutions to inequality, examination of the legal effects of sexual harassment laws, and illustration of discrepancies among women despite uniform legal definitions of women.

Cases related to sexual harassment provide numerous examples of the series' engagement with and negotiation of feminist politics. In most all cases, the firm wins either the case or its attempt not to have a case dismissed and is on the side that arguably possesses the most feminist credibility (although some situations appear deliberately convoluted and complex). The series' pilot begins with Ally as a victim of unwanted groping by a fellow attorney, which leads her to join Cage, Fish & Associates (1–01, "Pilot"). In another episode, the secretarial staff files a sexual harassment suit against the firm because male ogling of a female mail clerk creates a sexually charged workplace (1–08, "Drawing the Lines"). Although the staff organizes and plans a walkout, the collective action is undercut when the narrative reveals the suit is an attempt by Elaine to get the lawyers' attention because she feels excluded from their social relationships. Another case involves a woman suing her employer, whom she has never met, for harassment. She argues that not sleeping with him prevented her promotion, despite the fact this employer never made such a requirement evident (1–18, "The Playing Field").

Throughout the series, the legal cases became increasingly outrageous, as when Ling attempts to sue a Howard Stern-esque "shock jock" because of the environment created in her workplace by the broadcast of his show (2–02, "They Eat Horses, Don't They"). She also tries to sue an employee for harassment because she believes he had sexual thoughts about her, a case she loses (2–06, "You Never Can Tell"). The program also examines the merits of corporate attempts to avoid harassment claims, as the firm represents a couple fired for violating their company's "date and tell" office policy by not disclosing their relationship (2–14, "Pyramids on the Nile"). In the final harassment case of season two, the firm represents an employer sued by a female worker who claims the employer's "Beach Day" policy of allowing workers to wear bathing suits to work is a form of sexual harassment (2–20, "Only the Lonely").

The law governing sexual harassment continued to be tested in season three, first with a case in which the firm represents a woman and her employer who are sued by other female employees because the defendant contributes to the creation of a sexually charged environment by wearing suggestive clothing and flirting with male co-workers (3–02, "Buried Pleasures"). The firm next represents a magazine editor who sues her employees for sexual harassment after they circulate pamphlets calling her "the nymph" and organize a "blue flu" that results in late publication of the magazine and her consequent firing (3–06, "Changes"). In a rare situation, the firm does not win its case.

In season four the series continued to enact the sexual harassment debate, but with stories that ultimately took a feminist stance despite contradictory and complicated rhetoric. This season emphasized women accused of sexual harassment, in which Cage, Fish took a radical feminist approach in many defenses and argued women as different from men (4–02, "Girls' Night Out"; 4–07, "Love on Holiday"; and 4–21, "Queen Bee"). In season five, new firm member Jenny Shaw represents Raymond Milbury, who is sued by an opposing counsel for sexual harassment and features much of the chauvinism of Richard without the incompetence to undercut it (5–04, "Fear of Flirting"). The jury finds against Raymond, affirming his behavior as that of a sexist boor, but orders only $.75 be paid in damages in recognition that it was asked to apply sexual harassment law beyond its boundaries.

The continuing and often extreme reworking of potential sexual harassment litigation chronicled above illustrates how behavior leading to the creation of sexual harassment laws can become trivialized, but the dialogue in these episodes offers additional political engagement with the issue. Analysis of this aspect of the representation of sexual harassment is challenging because of the conflicted and contradictory positions presented and the text's refusal to support a single coherent perspective. For instance, although Richard and Billy present chauvinist polemics in defending clients, they often do so either in the process of arguing for a clearly aggrieved woman or in a way that can be interpreted as illustrating their incompetence as lawyers. In the first situation, the text often reaches what can be argued as a feminist end, but does so by a questionably feminist means. For example, Richard succeeds in winning an evidentiary hearing for a woman filing a sexual harassment suit with the following speech:

> *Women are victims. They need special help. When you look at the evolution of the sexual harassment laws, what we're really saying is that women should qualify under the Federal Disabilities Act. They are less able. They cannot cope with romance in the workplace. They cannot contend with having to do a job and have a man smile at them [1–18, "The Playing Field"].*

Billy makes a similar speech in a firm conference meeting, arguing:

> *We're talking about sexual harassment law, Ally; let's not expect it to make sense. We just have to assume that if any woman anywhere at anytime feels the slightest twinge of hypersensitivity, and she can link it to anything remotely sexual, she has a cause of action. The courts will protect her, which is good, because as a matter of law, women need protection [3–02, "Buried Pleasures"].*

In another episode he tells the client he represents, who is suing for sexual harassment, that sexual harassment is a "stupid law that works as an equalizer for weak women" (3–06, "Changes").

Leslie Heywood argues that this sort of dialogue "neutralizes the feminist critique of larger issues by making the ideas behind that critique sound silly" (Heywood, B9). Arguably this does occur. At the same time, however, the series repeatedly examines an important feminist issue and opens for cultural debate the myriad ways sexism circulates within society. Ally, Georgia, and Nelle obviously disdain the above speeches; and because the series lacks a reliable central character, the text does not make a preferred position evident. In these scenes and the earlier situation noted with John Cage, a feminist perspective develops through what Cooper terms "the comic spectacle of maleness." She contends, "Many of the series' plots are developed through exaggerated and humorous depictions of chauvinist attitudes and behaviors, and through scenes that overtly question male sexuality," and notes that, "Men's justification for sexually objectifying women is a frequent target of ridicule" (425–6). Very different interpretations of the series are possible depending on the complexity with which critics approach rhetorical, ideological, and narrative analysis. Consequently, I do not suggest that my interpretation is the only one available, but it is as practicable as the anti-feminist interpretations others have suggested (Kim; Vavrus; Shalit).

Although the series' exploration of sexual harassment law was highly varied, episodes such as the one involving the shock jock illustrate the feminist potential of the series. Some of the extreme situations that the text raised implicitly query the boundaries of sexual harassment and do not criticize the existence of sexual harassment codes so much as illustrate the difficulty of defining their boundaries. A conservative analysis of the series' representation of sexual harassment reads the difficulty in determining parameters as arguing that because a line cannot be drawn, no sexual harassment laws should exist. Yet, the text does not support this position above others, especially since the series depicts both Ally and Georgia benefiting from laws that help women combat workplace power inequities displayed through harassment and discrimination. Feminist interpretations use the series' representation of the difficulty in determining the extent of sexual harassment code application as evidence of how widespread and culturally ingrained many sexist practices are in a way that illustrates the need for continued feminist activism. Criticism of the ambiguity of sexual harassment laws, then, is not necessarily an anti-feminist position. In many cases *Ally McBeal* illustrates the inadequacy of current law and the constraints of using a legal system that attempts uniform application. Such an interpretation exposes the limited utility of legal solutions and identifies a need for continued cultural and social examination to understand the formation and transmission of inequity and bias.

The construction of sex-based legal issues and solutions in *Ally McBeal* is characteristic of postfeminism in various ways. First, it expands from individualistic liberal feminist approaches to combating sex oppression. In some cases, second-wave feminists encouraged women to use self-help strategies or consciousness-raising to help them overcome experiences of harassment or discrimination by learning to feel better about themselves, but *Ally McBeal* does not impose individualistic solutions on victims of sex-based injustice. In other situations, liberal feminists believed that enacting legal protection would eliminate problems such as harassment and discrimination. The series' critique of sexual harassment laws illustrates the limitations of legal remedies and the depths of sex-based prejudice. The variety of situations the series poses for examining sexual harassment also depicts how workplace power can result from factors other than gender and the very different relations to power women can inhabit.

Deconstructing Gender

The third attribute of postfeminist discourse, the deconstruction of distinct binary categories of gender and sexuality, plays a central role in postfeminist theories, but is much less discernable in contemporary television series. Likewise, it is less evident than other attributes in *Ally McBeal*, but arguably the occasional utterances the series provides are more substantial than in any other series airing on U.S. broadcast networks at the time. In *Ally McBeal*, the deconstruction of binaries appears in episodes exploring transvestite, transsexual, and bisexual characters.

The series offers little critique of gender classifications, such as male and female, and even tends to reinforce essentialist understandings, as when Ally differentiates behavior as distinctly "male" or Richard and Billy criticize how "women" act. However, the wide range of circumstances through which the series examines sexual harassment law can be seen as a deconstruction of gender in the determination of workplace power. Cases exploring the type of femininity displayed by a female employer who either harasses or is harassed by a male employee illustrate the complex ways individuals embody their gender classification and power.

The series also featured two plotlines dealing with transvestite or transsextual characters. In the first, Ally represents a transvestite prostitute and comes to understand the complexity of his perception of gender identity and the reason he does not wish her to use a psychiatric defense (1–10, "Boy to the World"). The characters establish a connection in an unusually melodramatic episode that concludes with the firm hiring Stephanie/Steven as support staff. In its final scene, however, the episode takes Ally to the location of his murder, which suggests the series could not sustain its initial support of gender play. In a more extended series of episodes in the fourth season, firm member Mark Albert begins dating and falling in love with a woman who reveals herself as a pre-op transsexual (4–02, "Girls' Night Out;" 4–03, "Two's a Crowd;" 4–04, "Without a Net;" 4–07, "Love on Holiday;" 4–12, "Hats Off to Larry"). The episodes depict Mark's struggle with his emotional attachment to the woman, but culturally ingrained revulsion of her transsexuality, which Richard and Nelle exacerbate by making homophobic comments. In a depiction similar to Ally's dealing with her bisexual suitor (discussed below), Mark ultimately rejects Cindy, but the text wavers in its support for his decision. Cindy returns to the firm for representation a few episodes after the breakup because she has found a man who accepts her difference and wishes to marry her. The firm fights against the prohibition of same-sex marriage but fails out of judicial limitations. Richard then marries the couple in a legally insignificant but symbolically meaningful gesture.

Ally McBeal is slightly more flexible in its depiction of categories of sexuality, although not nearly enough to present an organized deconstruction of sexual identity. The series raises the existence of bisexuality—a possibility rarely addressed by U.S. television, but does so in a way as multivalent as the depiction of the Margaret Camero character. When Ally learns that a suitor who otherwise seems perfect is bisexual, she is overwhelmed by homophobic images and dismisses him, although the text suggests she is wrong to do so (3–13, "Pursuit of Happiness"). Additionally, in an episode in which Ally and Ling kiss, both admit enjoying the experience, but also contend that they do not find it as satisfying as kissing a man (3–02, "Buried Pleasures"). Here, the exploration and curiosity the characters experience is never acknowledged as bisexual behavior and the characters repeatedly affirm that they are heterosexual and want to be so, but also admit they are curious and even have an urge to kiss each other. The characters are confused about the implications of their desires on their sexuality, so they over-determine their heterosexuality in dialogue, while their actions (kissing each other, pretending to be a lesbian couple) illustrate the mutability of sexual identity and how it can be performed on a continuum.[7] Despite these few narrative moments, the series' construction of gender and sexuality categories remains less deconstructed than might be expected of a postfeminist text, but suggests a loosening of binary norms.

Ally's Search for Mr. Right

The representation of career women struggling with their expectations of and options for romantic partnership and their consequent anxiety are important to consider in relation to feminism because feminists have worked to give women the option of a career. Additionally, feminists have fought cultural myths suggesting that finding a husband is the most defining accomplishment of a woman's life. *Ally McBeal*'s female characters are part of the generation first receiving the benefits secured by second-wave feminist activism throughout their lives. The new career possibilities afforded them consequently force many of the characters to reconcile the independence provided by their career success with their desire for romantic relationships. For many, the challenge comes not in finding a relationship, but in finding the right one.

The depiction of women struggling to have both career and family can be viewed as an example of the fourth attribute of postfeminist discourse because this depiction raises and examines struggles faced by women within the contemporary cultural milieu in which some feminist gains have been achieved but most relations of power remain structured by patriarchy. Popular media often give voice to such concerns as well as to contradictions in cultural expectations. Anxiety about finding the right partner appears in a preponderant manner in *Ally McBeal* and several other series airing coterminously. Ally's unsuccessful attempts to find a suitable mate structure the series' initial seasons (although both John and Richard pursue a similar goal with less narrative emphasis) and her expressions of the lack of fulfillment she finds in her professional success and work-dominated life drew considerable feminist ire and suggestion of the anti-feminist ideology of the series (Kim; Vavrus; Shugart, Waggoner, and O'Brien Hallstein).

In the past, some feminists may have categorically criticized the expression of such personal concerns as anti-feminist or as a reactionary attempt to contain feminist gains. Admittedly, one can interpret this depiction of anxiety to suggest that successful professional women cannot find the relationships they desire because of their careers—and this interpretation is evident in many of the journalistic criticisms of *Ally McBeal*. In contrast, the text constructs this issue with more complexity than this interpretation recognizes and Ally's career is by no means clearly the cause of her uncertainties about her personal life. Additionally, aspects of postfeminism make the expression of such personal anxieties acceptable and open up personal aspects of women's lives for consideration. It is also important to consider how the ongoing narrative of serial television prevents a conclusion or an answer to the characters' concerns and instead depicts the characters in a continuous process of negotiating contradictory personal desires until the series' conclusion. Importantly, *Ally McBeal* did not end with Ally's wedding, but with a character who had grown comfortable inside her own skin, who no longer pined for her life to match a culturally imposed social script, and the character's recognition that the journey is as important as the destination and that hindsight revealed the times that challenged her as highly satisfying.

Ally McBeal's main contribution to a cultural negotiation of career and family is its ambivalence: it recognizes the career gains the character achieves as an advance, but simultaneously depicts uncertainly about how to evaluate this success compared with other desires. In this ambivalence the series accepts the multiple plans, choices, and goals women may have in a way that corresponds to developments evident in postfeminism as a feminist theory that specifically embraces differences among women and that provides for discrepancy among equally feminist perspectives on issues.

Feminists of all kinds have placed the importance for women to have choices at the center of their theoretical and activist concerns and the multiplicity of characters in the late 1990s enable the depiction of characters making varied choices without suggesting containment. If a female character chooses to emphasize her personal life and is consequently categorically denounced as anti-feminist—even when many other representations exist—feminism has provided her very little choice at all. Significant anxiety and frustration result from the continued adherence to binaries of femininity and feminism established during the second-wave battle against the limited gender roles available to women at that time. These stories in *Ally McBeal* indicate an organic emergence of unspoken cultural undercurrents and it remains possible that its texts and the characters' dilemmas have connected with viewers in such a way to help initiate such organization-based change. At the minimum, the series initiated a dialogue that encouraged a reconsideration of the status of feminism on various personal and political fronts.

Conclusion

Finding the feminist (or even postfeminist in my terms) potential of *Ally McBeal* unquestionably requires considering the series through a different frame than has traditionally been used to gauge feminist, "new women," or empowered female television characters and their texts. The various discrepancies in context operating in the case of *Ally McBeal* justify the need for an adjusted frame, and the developing terrain of postfeminist theory lends itself to understanding the variation of this series. Further, the exceptional degree to which the series resonated with the female audiences who viewed *Ally McBeal* in nearly record numbers—particularly in early seasons—requires consideration that moves beyond assumptions of false consciousness. This series unquestionably touched a cultural nerve that was clearly exposed yet uncommented upon by the late 1990s.

The uncertain questions that remain relate to what the legacy of *Ally McBeal* will be. Will the cultural debate that embroiled the series force other character innovations with postfeminist attributes into ignominy because of analysis lacking context? Can we develop critical tools that acknowledge the complicated status of female characters in the twenty-first century? Will the journalistic debates and anti-feminist co-optation of weak analyses such as Bellafante's scare Hollywood's creative minds from offering other contestable and innovative images or encourage them to expand the trail Kelley initiated? Can we develop more sophisticated analyses and understandings of female characters that deviate from "role model" standards and yet reach audience members? And now that such a range of post–Baby Boom characters exist, how will they continue to redefine the issues facing women?

In the nearly ten years since *Ally McBeal*'s debut, few series have offered the consistent and sophisticated storytelling about women's lives after the intervention of second-wave activism and the related challenges. Most series do not comment on the challenges that result for women who live in a culture in which some feminist gains have been achieved but much of patriarchy remains firmly entrenched. Stories depicting the new options available to women may now circulate in series featuring tough career women and women involved in more equitable romantic relationships, but most assume these gains without dealing with the complexity of residual sexism and patriarchal power. The engagement, uncertainty, and ambivalence of *Ally McBeal* with a society in change allowed the innovation and novelty of the series that has yet to be replicated or extended. Although new series tell stories about women that draw critics and viewers (for example *Desperate Housewives* and *Grey's Anatomy* of late), no subsequent series has utilized postfeminist strategies to engage and interrogate gender relations in contemporary society in the way endeavored and achieved by *Ally McBeal*.

Notes

1. Throughout the series' run, a substantial number of negative reviews were based on the series deviation from "reality" (real lawyers don't wear short skirts, have so much time to talk, act that way in court). While such arguments make fine special interest pieces, most television critics realize that adherence to "reality" is not an imperative in evaluating fictional storytelling. Additionally, because of my focus on feminism and gender, I am not able to devote space to assessing Kelley's "colorblind" approach to the series. Critique of the series' implicit and explicit racism is important and complicated, but beyond the scope of this article.

2. Georgia initially provides an exception, but she later separates from Billy and then becomes a widow.

3. A similar divergence can be argued of *Xena: Warrior Princess*, which began in 1995, and *Buffy the Vampire Slayer*, which began five months before *Ally McBeal*. Discussion of generation is irrelevant in *Xena's* case because of its fantastic mythical setting, but I would argue *Buffy the Vampire Slayer* faces challenges similar to *Ally McBeal* in deviating from the Baby Boom generation setting.

4. In the final season Ally displayed considerable new maturity as a mentor to youthful doppelganger Jenny, was promoted to firm partner in John's absence, purchased a house, became the mother of a 10-year-old girl conceived from an egg Ally had donated during law school, and spent much less time pining for love.

5. For example, Kelley responded explicitly to critics such as Bellafante with a storyline in which McBeal is asked to be a role model—but only if she makes some changes in her appearance.

6. Like nearly all U.S. television series, socio-economic class does not emerge as a factor in characters' subjectivity, although it is likely to have considerable effect in contributing to varied outlooks among women.

7. For a more thorough assessment of how television depicts bisexuality and its appeals of lesbian chic characters see Clark.

Works Cited

Arthurs, Jane. "*Sex and the City* and Consumer Culture: Remediating Postfeminist Drama." *Feminist Media Studies* 3.1 (2003): 83–98.

Bellafante, Gina. "Feminism: It's All About Me!" *Time*, 29 June 1998: 54–60.

Braxton, Greg. "Colorblind or Just Plain Blind? 'Race Not Being an Issue Makes It an Issue,' Says David E. Kelley of an Unspoken Topic on *Ally McBeal*. But Others Say He's Being Irresponsible." *Los Angeles Times*, 9 February 1991: FI.

Brooks, Ann. *Postfeminisms: Feminism, Cultural Theory, and Cultural Forms*. New York: Routledge, 1997.

Chambers, Veronica. "*Ally McBeal*." *Newsweek*, 13 October 1997: 71.

_____. "How Would Ally Do It?" *Newsweek*, 2 March 1998: 58–61.

Clark, Danae. "Commodity Lesbianism." *Camera Obscura* 25 (1991).

Collins, James, "Ally McBeal." *Time*, 10 November 1997: 117.

Cooper, Brenda. "Unapologetic Women, 'Comic Men' and Feminine Spectatorship in David E. Kelley's *Ally McBeal*." *Critical Studies in Media Communication* 18.4 (2001): 416–435.

Dow, Bonnie. *Prime-Time Feminism: Television, Media Culture, and the Women's Movement Since 1970*. Philadelphia: University of Pennsylvania Press, 1996.

Dowd, Maureen. "Ally McBeal Is a Unisex Role Model." *The New York Times*, 15 April 1998: C5.

Faludi, Susan. *Backlash: The Undeclared War Against American Women*. New York: Crown, 1991.

Gamble, Sarah, ed. *The Routledge Critical Dictionary of Feminism and Postfeminism*. New York: Routledge, 2000.

Grossberger, Lewis. "Ally's No. 1 Ally." *MEDIAWEEK*, 16 February 1998: 38.

Heywood, Leslie. "Hitting a Cultural Nerve: Another Season of *Ally McBeal*." *Chronicle of Higher Education*, 4 September 1998: B9.

Jefferson, Margo. "You Want to Slap Ally McBeal, But Do You Like Her?" *The New York Times*, 18 March 1998: E2.

Katz, Alyssa. "*Ally McBeal*." *The Nation*, 15 December 1997: 36–39.

Kim, L. S. "*Sex and the Single Girl* in Postfeminism: The F Word on Television." *Television & New Media* 2.4 (2001): 319–334.

Lotz, Amanda D. "Postfeminist Television Criticism: Rehabilitating Critical Terms and Identifying Postfeminist Attributes." *Feminist Media Studies* 1.1 (2001): 105–121.

_____. "Communicating Third-Wave Feminism and New Social Movements: Challenges for the Next Century of Feminist Endeavor." *Women and Language* 26.1 (2003): 2–9.

_____. *Redesigning Women: Television After the Network Era*. Urbana-Champaign: University of Illinois Press, 2006.

McRobbie, Angela. *Postmodernism and Popular Culture*. New York: Routledge, 1994.

Mann, Judy. "An Unfair Assessment of Feminism." *The Washington Post*, 26 June 1998: E03.

Modleski, Tania. *Feminism Without Women: Culture and Criticism in a "Postfeminist" Age*. New York: Routledge, 1991.

Moseley, Rachael, and Jacinda Read. " 'Having it *Ally*': Popular Television (Post-) Feminism." *Feminist Media Studies* 2.2 (2002): 231–249.

Nochimson, Martha P. "*Ally McBeal*: Brightness Falls from the Air." *Film Quarterly* 53.3 (2000): 25–32.

NOW. "NOW Issues Friendly Advice for *Time* Magazine." National Organization for Women, June 1998. 3 July 2002. *http://www.now.org/press/06–98/time.html*.

Parker, Kathleen. "Feminism Isn't Dead, Just Bored and Confused." *Orlando Sentinel*, 27 June 1998: 15A.

Press, Andrea L. *Women Watching Television: Gender, Class and Generation in the American Television Experience*. Philadelphia: University of Pennsylvania Press, 1991.

Schneider, Karen S. "Everybody's Picking on Calista Flockhart's Weight." *People Weekly*, 9 November 1998: 92.

Scruggs, Afi-Odella E. "Miniskirt Feminism Baffles Veterans." *The Plain Dealer*, 21 October 1998: 1B.

Shalit, Ruth. "Canny and Lacy." *The New Republic*, 6 April 1998: 27–33.

Shugart, Helene A., Catherine Egley Waggoner, and D. Lynn O'Brien Hallstein. "Mediating Third-Wave Feminism: Appropriation as Postmodern Media Practice." *Critical Studies in Media Communication* 18.2 (2001): 194–210.

Stack, Teresa. "Fiction Is Not a Feminist Issue." *Pittsburgh Post-Gazette*, 18 July 1998: A13.

Stark, Steven D. "Ally McBeal." *The New Republic*, 29 December 1997: 13–15.

Svetkey, Benjamin. "Everything You Love or Hate About *Ally McBeal*." *Entertainment Weekly* 30 January 1998: 20–26.

Vavrus, Mary Douglas. "Putting Ally on Trial: Contesting Postfeminism in Popular Culture." *Women's Studies in Communication* 23.3 (2000): 413–428.

Williamson, Linda. "Let's Get Real on *Ally McBeal*." *Toronto Sun*, 2 July 1998: 15.

Wilson, Pamela. "Upscale Feminine Angst: *Molly Dodd*, the Lifetime Cable Network and Gender Marketing." *Camera Obscura* [special volume on "Lifetime: A Cable Network for Women," edited by Julie D'Accil 33–34 (1994): 102–131.

Gay-Themed Television and the Slumpy Class
The Affordable, Multicultural Politics of the Gay Nineties

Ron Becker

This article links the success of gay-themed programming in the 1990s to the sensibility of an emerging class of Socially Liberal, Urban-Minded Professionals (the "Slumpy" class). In the era's neoliberal climate where multicultural celebrations of diversity mixed with calls for fiscal responsibility, being socially liberal and fiscally conservative became the political position of choice for a growing number of well-educated and upwardly mobile baby boomers and Generation Xers. As it came to be articulated in the '90s, homosexuality fit conveniently into this delicate balance. Highly visible political battles over gay rights gave homosexuality a cutting-edge allure dulled just enough by its assimilationist goals. Meanwhile gays and lesbians, reported to be well educated with a disproportionate amount of disposable income, seemed to be economically self-sufficient. For those looking for an affordable politics of social liberalism, supporting gays and lesbians fit the bill, and consuming gay-inclusive television offered members of the Slumpy class a convenient way to affirm their open-mindedness.

Keywords: gay; multiculturalism; *Seinfeld*

We're not gay! Not that there's anything wrong with that. Jerry Seinfeld and George Costanza were anxious to set the record straight on the February 11, 1993, episode of the hit NBC sitcom *Seinfeld*. Entitled "The Outing," the episode places sexuality—both homo and hetero—front and center in a plot structured around a decidedly 1990s twist on an age-old comedy convention: mistaken (sexual) identity. The trouble for Jerry and George starts when they sit down for lunch with gal pal Elaine Benes. As the gang blathers on about nothing, Elaine spies a woman at the next table eavesdropping on their conversation. Looking to spice up her day, she decides to give the woman an earful and motions to the guys to play along. "Just because you two are homosexual, so what?" she exhorts loudly. "I mean, you should just come out of the closet and be openly gay already." So the plot is set in motion. In typical sitcom fashion, coincidence and confusion ensue when the eavesdropper later shows up at Jerry's apartment to interview him for a newspaper profile. When her subsequent article reports that Jerry is gay and George is his longtime companion, the news spreads like wildfire.

Author's Note: The author would like to thank Julie D'Acci. The Gay & Lesbian Alliance Against Defamation provided financial support for the larger project from which this article originates.

For the rest of the episode, the pair frantically attempt to reclaim their heterosexuality, all the while trying not to appear homophobic. After all, Jerry explains, although he may not be gay, he definitely has "many gay friends" and firmly believes that being gay "is fine, if that's who you are." In fact, by the end of the episode, everyone from Kramer to Jerry's mom makes sure to temper their obvious shock and distress about the gay thing with a "not-that-there's-anything-wrong-with-that" tag line, which comes to serve as the episode's mantra of straight, gay-friendly political correctness.

I open with this now-famous episode of the quintessential 1990s sitcom *Seinfeld* because its preoccupation with homosexuality—its obsession with the categorical difference between straight and gay—would surface repeatedly in so many of the era's sitcoms and dramas. Before *Queer as Folk* (2000-current), *Will & Grace* (1998-current) and an openly lesbian Ellen Morgan (1997–1998) helped draw so much attention to the visibility of gays and lesbians on U.S. television, gay material had already become one of the most remarkable programming trends of the decade. Between 1994 and 1997, well over 40 percent of all prime-time network series produced at least one gay-themed episode, nineteen network shows debuted with recurring gay characters, and hit shows like *Roseanne, Friends, Frasier,* and *NYPD Blue* (to name but a few) seemed to include gay jokes and references to homosexuality every week. And while *Seinfeld*'s satiric and ostensibly nihilistic digs at political correctness may have been unique for American television, "The Outing"'s narrative about (sexual) identity and the politics of straight tolerance were actually quite typical of both 1990s U.S. television and the wider culture out of which it emerged.

Elsewhere, I have argued that this striking increase of gay material on '90s television was driven, in part, by shifting network conceptions of and intensified competition for the so-called quality audience—those upscale eighteen- to forty-nine-year-olds assumed to be the most active consumers with the most disposable income (Becker 1998). Although this "quality" audience had been the underlying target demographic of all three networks for decades, the continued erosion of network audience shares as well as the growing currency of niche marketing principles among advertisers forced the Big Three to target this most lucrative demographic far more aggressively, with programming tailored more narrowly to their perceived interests. In an era of psychographic profiling, however, the networks did not simply target upscale eighteen to forty-nine-year-olds. Instead, as trade press discourse and prime-time lineups indicate, they assumed that the affluent and upwardly mobile adults they sought were sophisticated cosmopolitans who wanted edgy, risqué programming with an ironic sensibility. Competition to attract those kinds of viewers was fierce. By the mid-'90s, programs designed to appeal to a broad audience (family sitcoms like *Home Improvement*) or that tended to skew older (*Murder, She Wrote; Matlock*) were out of fashion. Edgy, ironic shows geared to perceived adult sensibilities—shows that pushed the envelope of TV content and style—got all the buzz, dominated the networks' development seasons, and won plumb schedule positions. As Matt Williams, cocreator of ABC's *Home Improvement* observed, "Everything's a scramble for demographics now. . . . Now its 'kids don't sell,' so you've got to be young, hip, urban, professional" (Du Brow 1995). With all three networks battling to reach this audience, finding a way to distinguish their programming in an increasingly saturated market of *Friends* and *Seinfeld* clones became important. The dramatic increase of gay material in this period indicates that network executives believed that including gay characters and gay-themed episodes was just such an effective strategy.

In this article, I augment this industry-focused explanation by situating the rise of gay-themed programming and industry conceptions of its quality audience in their wider social context—specifically in relation to the emergence of what I call the Socially Liberal, Urban-Minded Professional (Slumpy) class and the neoliberal political climate within which it evolved. Gay material was useful for network executives, in part, I argue, because it was useful to certain viewers for whom watching prime-time TV with a gay twist was a convenient way to establish a "hip" identity. It is certainly important not to conflate the industry's conception of its audience with the lived experiences of viewers; such conceptions are (in the case of U.S. network television) shaped by the economic imperatives of an advertising-based medium and an imprecise ratings system (Ang 1991). Nevertheless, such notions do change in response to social change, and network executives' imprecise notions of a "hip" eighteen to forty-nine target demographic did, if in distorted ways, reflect the shifting attitudes and identities of many Americans. More precisely, it reflected a vague awareness of what might best be described as a new social class—one that has come into its own over the last two decades. The Slumpy class is broadly composed of the upscale and upwardly mobile baby boomers and Generation Xers whose centrist politics built Clinton's moderate middle, whose unprecedented levels of college education drove the postindustrial information economy, and whose incomes helped fuel everything from the bull market to the popularity of L.A. Eye Works. Throughout much of the 1990s, then, network executives were interested in creating programs that would appeal to such viewers. Like Julie D'Acci's (1994) analysis of the working women's audience and Jane Feuer's (1995) work on the yuppie audience, this article explores the relationship between programming strategies and target audiences. But more specifically, in examining the Slumpy class, particularly its social values and political attitudes, I describe what might be called a Slumpy sensibility—an analytic construct that can help us theorize the ways in which some viewers, positioned by specific discourses and social experiences, may have made meanings and found pleasure in television programs like *Seinfeld*.[1]

While network interest in such viewers had a significant effect on much of the decade's television, this article will focus more narrowly, examining the Slumpy class and its sensibility to better understand why gay-themed programming was such a viable narrowcasting tool in the 1990s. My interest in and conceptualization of the Slumpy class arose in the mid-'90s as I tried to understand the sudden increase of gay material on network television (Becker 1998). More recently, cultural satirist David Brooks and regional planner Richard Florida, each working from different perspectives and toward different ends, have studied the emergence of essentially the same class I had identified. A brief summary of Brooks's and Florida's arguments will provide a helpful overview of this new social class, its demographic profile, and its social mores. I then augment that broad portrait by examining how multiculturalism and the political correctness debates of the early '90s dovetailed smoothly with the decade's strengthening neoliberalism and, in doing so, laid the groundwork for what I argue is a hallmark of the Slumpy sensibility—a socially liberal, fiscally conservative political position. As multiculturalist discourses gained wider circulation in corporate boardrooms, on college campuses, and across popular culture, maintaining at least an appearance of celebrating social differences became *de rigeur* for those who wanted to be "hip" and "sophisticated." For many, however, this newfound multicultural tolerance seemed comfortable only when accompanied by the security of a fiscal conservatism that demanded a status quo economic policy. As it came to be articulated in the 1990s, homosexuality fit conveniently into this delicate balance. Highly visible political battles over gay rights and Christian conservative invasions into gay bedrooms gave homosexuality a cutting-edge allure dulled just enough by its assimilationist goals to appeal to a relatively broad base of straight neoliberals. Although victims of political discrimination, gays and lesbians, it seems, were also economically self-sufficient. Reported to be affluent and well educated with a disproportionate amount of disposable income, gays and lesbians were something of a model minority. For those looking for an affordable politics of social liberalism, I argue, supporting gays and lesbians fit the bill, and consuming gay-inclusive cultural representations offered straight Slumpies a painlessly passive way to affirm their open-mindedness.

Slumpies, Bobos, and the Creative Class

Cultural observer David Brooks satirizes the social codes and lifestyle trends of what he calls Bobos—short for bourgeois bohemians. According to Brooks (2000), Bobos constitute a new and expanding educated class for the information age and are distinguished by their unprecedented fusion of a bohemian antiestablishment spirit with a bourgeois pursuit of material security through a solid work ethic. Brooks links the rise of the Bobo class to the dramatic democratization of the nation's colleges and universities between 1960 and 1975 and to the millions of working- and middle-class baby boomers who streamed out of them. By the 1990s, upwardly mobile boomers had apparently matured, not only supplanting their elders as the nation's business leaders and cultural trendsetters but also reconciling their hippie idealism with their yuppie self-absorption "into one social ethos"

(p. 10). The old cultural lines that had separated black-clad, Kafka-reading, cappuccino-drinking, urbane intellectuals from gray-clad, *Wall-Street-Journal*-reading, scotch-drinking, suburban stock-brokers had all but disappeared.

At the core of the bourgeois-bohemian ethos lie the seemingly inevitable tensions that result from the attempt to wed incongruous value systems. "Those who want to win educated-class approval," Brooks asserts, "must confront the anxieties of abundance: how to show—not least to themselves—that even while climbing toward the top of the ladder they have not become all the things they still profess to hold in contempt, . . . how to reconcile . . . their elite status with their egalitarian ideals" (p. 40). Bobos constantly try to find ways to resolve these contradictions. Casual Fridays, for example, help make workaholism seem less Dickensian, while eco-adventure vacations make time-off seem productive. Paying outrageous prices for needless luxuries like French antiques would be vulgar, but paying outrageous prices for staples ("water at $5 a bottle, . . . a bar of soap at $12") is conspicuous in a down-to-earth sort of way (p. 97). Buying overpriced soap from socially conscious retailers like The Body Shop is even better, and buying corporate-made Nikes is not so bad as long as the ad features a gritty rendition of the Beatles' "Revolution" or some Nick Drake song. "It's not that we're hypocrites," Brooks points out. "It's just that we're seeking balance. Affluent, we're trying not to become materialistic" (p. 96).

Economist Richard Florida's analysis traces the rise of what he calls the "creative class." Unlike Brooks, Florida grounds his discussion in labor statistics and census data. Amid the decades-long shift toward a postindustrial economy, Florida and others have identified the increasingly central role of information and creativity as the basic drivers of economic growth. Typified by the high-tech sector, America's new economy is "explicitly designed to foster and harness human creativity" and "has given rise to a new dominant class" (Florida 2002, 66). Rooted in such structural economic changes, the creative class is defined by occupational function. Relying on U.S. Bureau of Labor Statistics and occupational classification systems, Florida argues that the creative class includes roughly thirty-eight million Americans (30 percent of all employed people). This includes a super-creative core of 15 million Americans—scientists, engineers, writers, artists, educators—whose "economic function is to create new ideas, new technology, and/or new creative content" (p. 8). Around this core, Florida identifies twenty-three million "creative professionals"—problem-solving workers in knowledge-intensive industries like hightech, health care, financial services, and business management where education and creative thinking are important.[2]

Although the creative class grew steadily since the 1950s, its ranks swelled during the '80s and '90s in conjunction with the rise of the postindustrial economy, leading to what Florida calls a "tectonic shift in the U.S. class structure" (p. 76). The creative class has doubled in size since 1980 when it numbered less than nineteen million and constituted only 20 percent of the workforce. Such gains coincided with the decline of the industrial economy and the once dominant working class, which accounted for roughly 40 percent of the workforce in the 1950s but constituted only 26 percent by 1990. Conversely, the same period saw a dramatic expansion of the service class, which by 1999 included fifty-five million workers (43 percent of the workforce)—a growth rate partially attributable to an expanding creative class increasingly outsourcing work once done by the family. While the creative class grew in sheer numbers, its cultural and economic power grew even more dramatically. Relative to the increasingly deunionized working class and the ununionized Service Class, members of the creative class saw their incomes soar, resulting in a growing gap in terms of both economic and social capital.[3]

Like Brooks, Florida describes the shared sensibility that helps unite this new social group. Members of the creative class, he claims, tend to hold what political scientists call "postmaterialist" values; their economic security often translates into progressive attitudes toward sex, gender equality, and the environment as well as an overall interest in lifestyle issues. Relying on interviews and focus groups, Florida argues that members of the creative class tend to value merit, individuality, creativity, and diversity. Unlike their educated-elite predecessors of the '50s and '60s who built an aristocratic, Ivy League world of WASPy exclusion, this new social class value brains over breeding. They imagine themselves as nonconformists and seek out environments where ability and effort (not conformity to the norm) are rewarded. Seeing themselves as outsiders, they want to live in communities and work in companies where difference is appreciated. Several of the creative class members Florida interviewed, for example, told him that at job interviews they often ask if the company offers same-sex partner benefits, even when they themselves were straight, because gay-friendly policies signaled an unusually tolerant climate (p. 79). In fact, Florida notes that the creative class has segregated itself into those cities they find compatible with their lifestyles and values.[4] Cities with reputations for being tolerant, diverse, and open to new ideas (e.g., San Francisco, Austin, Madison) became magnets for the well-educated, creative professionals. Analyzing U.S. Census data, Florida discovered a positive and statistically significant correlation between cities with high concentrations of the creative class and those with high concentrations of gay households, foreign-born residents, and artistically creative people, such as singers, actors, sculptors, and dancers.[5]

Bobos, the creative class, and my concept of the Slumpy class provide a historical context that helps us better understand network executives' nebulous notion of a "hip" quality audience. I retain my original term *Slumpy* because I feel it productively evokes industry discourse about its target audiences while highlighting the political sensibility that is central to my conceptualization of this social class. I deliberately use the term *social class* to indicate that Slumpies not only share a similar position within a specific economic structure but also share many of the same values and cultural preferences.[6] As Florida's analysis demonstrates, a social class is rooted in unequal and changeable economic conditions, and the postindustrial economy's privileged creative workers certainly constitute the core of the Slumpy class. In the complex processes behind the formation of social identities, however, nothing is cut and dried, and our position in the economic structure is but one of many interrelated factors shaping our sense of self. Although I would argue that the attitudes of most creative professionals would likely correspond well with a Slumpy sensibility, not all will. Conversely, many whose incomes, occupations, or geographic locations put them outside narrowly drawn boundaries of the educated elite could still hold the political positions and cultural identity I outline below.

In fact, I would argue that the emergence of the Slumpy class and the contours of its sensibility are symptomatic of a larger, decades-long change in social identities—a shift away from class identities and politics based primarily on shared positions vis-à-vis relations of production and toward a proliferation of identities shaped by consumption patterns and categories such as race, gender, and sexuality[7] (Aronowitz 1992; Clark and Inglehart 1998). The 1990s, then, not only saw a "tectonic shift in U.S. class structure" but also a transformation of social class identities. In a post–civil rights, Post-Fordist American culture influenced by identity politics and market segmentation, a unified American identity likely lost its efficacy among many of the well-educated, upscale professionals Brooks, Florida, and I describe. The Slumpy class's sensibility described below, I argue, reveals one response of a social elite forced to confront its own privilege. In fleshing out the Slumpy sensibility and how it helps explain the success of gay-inclusive television, I start by examining the prominence of multiculturalist discourses in the early 1990s.

Multiculturalism, Political Correctness, and the Slumpy Sensibility

In the early '90s, American culture seemed unusually preoccupied with difference, specifically cultural difference. No longer something to be ignored or eradicated, difference was confronted and celebrated, marketed and consumed, managed and leveraged. Multiculturalism, tolerance, and diversity gained a new currency among a growing number of Americans fixated on the changing dynamics of a seemingly fragmenting society. The intensity of the debates around multiculturalism and its pop culture offspring, political correctness, foregrounded issues of cultural diversity in unprecedented ways, transforming yuppies into Slumpies by rekindling the youthful bohemian ideals many boomers had seemed to outgrow in the '80s.

American colleges and universities served as one important springboard from which discourses of multiculturalism and the affirmation of difference entered wider circulation in the early '90s. Speech codes, inclusionary reading lists and admissions policies, and ethnic studies requirements became increasingly common as educators and administrators tried to sensitize their students and colleagues to the ways in which notions of a unified American identity privileged the values of a firmly entrenched white, Eurocentric, patriarchal, and heterosexist culture. Such changes certainly did not go unchallenged, and the subsequent debate propelled issues of multiculturalism from college campuses to national headlines. As Ellin Willis (1999) points out, conservatives "knew that it mattered what went on in universities, especially the elite kind. Decisions about what went on there—what counted as bona fide knowledge—resonated through the educational system as well as the culture as a whole" (p. 22). Although conservatives within academia had resisted multiculturalism's growing influence throughout the '80s, the battle was not joined in earnest and on a national scale until the end of 1990. In a barrage of articles, cultural conservatives viciously decried so-called political correctness. With mass-market books like Roger Kimball's *Tenured Radicals* (1990) and Dinesha D'Souza's *Illiberal Education* (1991), the Right took their anti-PC battle to the mainstream and helped make the diversity agenda a national issue. By the spring of 1991, millions of Americans had read countless op-ed pieces and feature stories in relatively high brow magazines like *Atlantic Monthly, Forbes*, and *New Republic* as well as in *The New York Times, Newsweek*, and *Time*.[8] Pundits from both sides appeared everywhere from *Good Morning America* to *Nightline*. As one observer commented, "Within the span of a few months, PC went from an obscure phrase spoken by campus conservatives to a nationally recognized sound bite" (Wilson 1995, 14).

While heated debates over academic agendas raged on, multiculturalism had quietly made significant inroads into the human resource divisions of many multinational corporations. Although the business sector had grappled with diversity issues for years, there was a growing sense of urgency around the topic in the late 1980s.[9] In 1987, for example, W. B. Johnston and A. H. Packard's influential *Workforce 2000* stressed how demographic trends and increased globalization were creating an increasingly diverse and fragmented society. In this new context, one expert claimed, a successful organization would be one that tried to "capitalize on the advantages of its diversity—rather than attempting to stifle or ignore the diversity—and to minimize the barriers that can develop as a result of people's having different backgrounds, attitudes, values, behavior styles, and concerns" (Bowens et al. 1993, 36).[10] In the early '90s, many corporations rushed to update their human resource divisions. Policies developed and implemented in the '60s and '70s to foster corporate cultures in which everyone was treated the same were abandoned in favor of management techniques designed to tap into the differences that existed among employees (Allen 1991, 14). To that end, corporations like Digital Equipment, Kellogg, and MCI spent millions developing diversity training programs. Many brought in outside consultants to conduct "culture audits," and both employees and managers were increasingly required to attend diversity awareness training. Workshops, seminars, role-playing games, instructional videos, and discussion groups exposed participants to the diverse values and experiences of various cultural backgrounds and encouraged them to appreciate the ways those differences could enhance the workplace.[11]

By the early '90s, multicultural rhetoric about inclusion and the affirmation of difference echoed across the political and cultural landscape. During the 1992 presidential campaign, for example, Bill Clinton frequently tapped into the diversity agenda, vowing in one widely reported campaign promise, "If you vote for me, I will give you an administration that looks like America." Press coverage of Clinton's initial appointments overtly connected his selection process to contemporary debates over quotas and the value of diversity.[12] Meanwhile, in the realm of cable TV programming, the producers of MTV's *The Real World* (which debuted in the summer of 1992) carefully cast their show with a similar strategy of inclusion in mind. For participants and viewers, the show functioned much like a four-month-long diversity-training seminar. In reflecting on her relationship with her white housemate John, for example, African American Los Angeles cast member Tami Akbar admitted, "[At first] I said 'OK, he's from Kentucky. He's wearing a cowboy hat, he yells heehaw at the top of his lungs—he's a racist. . . . Over time, [though,] I learned he's not anything like I envisioned him to be, and he learned the same about me" (Elber 1993). Disney even hopped on the multicultural bandwagon with films like *Pocahontas* (1995). Its hit song "Colors of the Wind" provided a critique of Eurocentrism and lyrics that could serve as a fitting slogan for any diversity training workshop: "You think the only people who are people / Are the people who look and think like you/But if you walk the footsteps of a stranger/You'll learn things you never knew you never knew" (Schwartz 1995). From Latino History Month programs in public libraries to Kwanzaa displays at city halls, from debates over New World colonization and the 500th anniversary of Columbus's arrival in the Americas to battles over racist high school mascots, exhortations to acknowledge and celebrate cultural difference pervaded American society.

In this environment, "politically correct," or PC for short, was a ubiquitous adjective—a convenient buzzword used to identify someone or something perceived to be sensitive (sometimes overly sensitive) to multicultural sensitivity and specific positions on issues like abortion, environmentalism, and gun control. In the syndicated cartoons of Jeff Shosel, for example, Politically Correct Person, a new superhero for the 1990s, fought the dangerous influence of his archenemy Insensitive Man. Meanwhile, *New York* magazine asked its readers, "Are You Politically Correct? . . . [Are you] Misogynistic, Patriarchal, Gynophobic, Phallocentric, Logocentric? [Are you] guilty of racism, sexism, classism? Do [you] say 'Indian' instead of 'Native American'? 'Pet' instead of 'Animal Companion'?" (Taylor 1991, 32). In the realm of popular opinion, political correctness and, by extension, multicultural notions of tolerance seemed to take it on the chin. By 1993, *Time* identified a "pop-culture backlash against p.c." (Zoglin 1993, 71). Best selling books like *Politically Correct Bedtime Stories* lampooned PC jargon and revisionism. Television shows like *Murphy Brown* and *Seinfeld* satirized earnest PC zealots. And comics like Bill Maher found success being "politically incorrect." The backlash against political correctness indicated a frustration with some diversity advocates' perceived stridency and channeled a conservative, white male voice. However, it also indicated that multicultural notions of cultural sensitivity had become the status quo.

The fact that in the parlance of the early '90s, one could *be* politically correct makes clear just what was at stake in the battle over multiculturalism—namely, people's political values and social identities. The political correctness debates were so intense in part because the Right believed that the ultimate goal of many college administrators was to change the way students thought. "There is an experiment of sorts taking place in American colleges," *Newsweek* reported. "Or more accurately, hundreds of experiments at different campuses, directed at changing the consciousness of this entire generation of university students" (Adler et al. 1990, 48). While discounting conservatives' incendiary attempts to characterize such "experiments" as a nefarious plot to brainwash America's impressionable youth, I would argue that one of multiculturalism's objectives was to transform students' attitudes and behavior. On this, college administrators were not alone; by requiring employees to attend diversity workshops, human resource mangers had similar goals. As Pushkala Prasad and Albert J. Mills (1997) point out, "Diversity programs consequently attempt to facilitate transformations by altering organization members' beliefs, values, and ideologies in dealing with difference at the workplace" (p. 8).

Such consciousness-raising efforts, I argue, influenced the emerging ethos of America's newly expanding educated class of Slumpies. Even though multicultural discourses seemed to be everywhere in the early '90s, they circulated most intensely and carried the greatest weight at major colleges and multinational corporations. As a result, celebrate-diversity rhetoric likely shaped the sensibilities of creative professionals more significantly than (or at least in ways distinct from) those of other demographic segments.[13] For many well-educated and upwardly mobile Americans, then, being politically correct helped forge an identity as a hip cosmopolitan (both in their own eyes and the eyes of others). Voting for the Latina city-council candidate over the white man; using phrases like African American instead of black; and expressing one's moral indignation over the ban against gays and lesbians in the military were marks of distinction—signals that helped identify one's educational level, class standing, and cultural identity.

Looking to reconcile their bohemian ideals with their bourgeois materialism, as Brooks would say, Slumpies also found that careful shopping could do the job as well. In the early '90s, marketers quickly realized that multicultural difference could be profitably commodified, packaged, and sold. "Commercial correctness," "cause-related marketing," and "point-of-purchase politics" became new buzzwords in an ad industry looking to target the growing number of upscale consumers seemingly attuned to political correctness. For the first time, major corporations like Benetton, Ben & Jerry's, and The Body Shop advocated specific social issues in ads that consciously blurred the line between product promotion and public service announcement (Amos 1993; Elliott 1993). It is not entirely clear whether the following copy from a 1993 Timberland ad, for example, was trying to sell footwear or promote PC activism: "Give the boot to racism. This message is from Timberland, but when it comes to racism and hatred it doesn't matter to us who makes your boots. Just put them on, join hands with City Year and stand up to racial intolerance" (McCarthy 1993). By buying a Native American dream catcher for a colleague's baby shower or taking friends to the most authentic Indian restaurant in town, by getting your child an African American Barbie or shopping at stores like Benetton, by attending a drag show or watching gay-inclusive television, yuppies transformed themselves into Slumpies.

This compatibility should not be surprising; after all, with shared roots in the fragmentation of an increasingly diverse, identitarian, and global U.S. society, multiculturalism, post-Fordism, and the Slumpy class were ontologically connected. Multiculturalism's refutation of the American melting pot model can be seen as the ideological counterpart to the economic logic of market segmentation and the practice of niche marketing. Multiculturalism's celebrations of difference, however, not only legitimize social fragmentation (and by extension market fragmentation) through encouraging people to acknowledge and celebrate the differences that separated them, they also (as we will see below) helped to make the differences of the Other, especially the marginalized Other, appealing commodities to consume. In his comment about the commodification of cultural differences in Britain's new post-Fordist global marketplace of products/identities, Jonathan Rutherford (1990) makes the link: "It's no longer about keeping up with the Jones, it's about being different from them. From World Music to exotic holidays in Third World locations, ethnic TV diners to Peruvian knitted hats, cultural difference *sells*. . . . Otherness is sought after for its exchange value" (p. 11).[14]

Consuming cultural difference commodified for one's convenience and being repeatedly encouraged to celebrate diversity did not guarantee that one's consciousness was thoroughly transformed. Responding to multicultural education initiatives was likely a complicated process of negotiation for most Slumpies—one marked by mixed motivations and a deep ambivalence. Diversity rhetoric, after all, urged people to acknowledge and celebrate the same social differences that had long been socially disavowed or vilified—a difficult task even for the most sincere. And although multiculturalism, with its emphasis on equality, appealed to people's sense of moral righteousness, institutions that championed diversity also tried to legislate it. Ethnic studies courses and sensitivity training were frequently compulsory, derogatory speech was prohibited, and other rules (both spoken and not) created environments where valuing difference was rewarded. For some, certainly, multiculturalism corresponded with deeply held commitments to social equality, and for others, being—or at least appearing to be—politically correct was a matter of expediency, not moral principle. For most, however, self-interest and moral rectitude were surely intricately intertwined. Adopting the right attitude made it easier not only to fit in at work, in school, and with friends but also to feel good about one's moral character. Celebrating the difference of the marginal was valued as a marker of one's open-minded nature as well as one's social position as a highly educated, upscale (or at least upwardly mobile) cosmopolitan who was not about to be mistaken for an old-fashioned moralist, right-wing bigot or even a member of the reluctantly tolerant middle.[15] Assuming any social position involves negotiating an odd fit, being politically correct could be a highly ambivalent activity. Aspirations to embrace difference often existed side by side with persistent fears and prejudices, and a sincere desire to "do the right thing" could often chafe under institutional mandates requiring compliance. As a result, within even the most well intentioned, a dissonance remained—a dissonance between the illiberal attitudes reinforced by a social order still structured by classism, racism, sexism, homophobia, and so on, and the politically correct sensibility they professed to hold. Not surprisingly, then, the Slumpy sensibility was tremendously ambivalent, and its affirmation of diversity could be highly circumscribed.[16]

For the Slumpy surrounded by multicultural rhetoric, consuming cultural difference held out a closely related promise—namely, the allure of marginality. Postcolonial and critical race scholars have long pointed out that encountering the socially marginal is often seen as a transformative experience, what bell hooks calls "eating the other." For hooks, contemporary culture capitalizes on the promise of encountering difference: "Commodity culture in the United States exploits conventional thinking about race, gender, and sexual desire by 'working' both the idea that racial difference marks one as Other and the assumption that sexual agency expressed within the context of racialized sexual encounter is a conversion experience that alters one's place and participation in contemporary cultural politics" (hooks 1992, 22). Although hooks focuses on racial difference and sexual desire, her point can be extended. At a time when multicultural discourses valued, commodified, politicized, and perhaps even fetishized difference and identity, being marginalized on almost any axis enjoyed a cultural cache with certain socially enlightened members of the educated class; from a politically correct perspective, being black, Latino, gay, or disabled seemed to offer one an inherent edginess forged from social oppression. On the other hand, within the economy of political correctness (although certainly not the economy of social power), being white, straight, middleclass, or male was, at the very least, dull and, at times, condemnable.[17] Like Brooks's Bobos confronted by the "anxieties of abundance," Slumpies confronted the anxieties produced by their white, straight, and/or patriarchal privilege. Consuming cultural difference seemed to offer the possibility of being transformed—or at least of reconciling their privilege with their ideals of social equality.

Neoliberalism and the Socially Liberal, Fiscally Conservative Slumpy

If members of an expanding educated elite were surrounded by celebrate-diversity rhetoric in the early '90s, they were also inundated by neoliberal discourses valorizing personal responsibility and the therapeutic power of the free market. Despite Clinton's victory in 1992, Reaganist policies aimed at dismantling the liberal welfare state and their legitimating discourses continued, becoming, according to one critic, "the new hegemonic ideology" (Gamble 2001, 127). The decade's booming economy, market globalization, the collapse of the Eastern bloc, deregulation, free trade agreements, and the high-tech revolution helped bolster a resurgent belief in the unquestionable superiority of free market capitalism. This "market triumphalism," as Judith Goode and Jeff Maskovsky (2001) have called it, was particularly conspicuous in the welfare reform movement. With the passage of the Personal Responsibility and Work Opportunity Reconciliation Act in 1996, Contract-with-America Republicans and New Democrats "ended welfare as we knew it" by gutting AFDC. Public support was fueled by media coverage, social science research, and conservative rhetoric that racialized and pathologized the poor by articulating "government handouts" to reports of inner-city drug use, black female promiscuity, welfare queens, school drop outs, and crime (Piven 2001; Abramovitz and Withorn 1999; Brown 1999). Originally conceived as a corrective to the inequities of a profit-driven market economy, welfare was now to blame for fostering a culture of poverty that failed to instill a sense of personal responsibility. The market was now the solution; its competitive environment would improve the moral fiber of the underclass, nurturing a "responsibilization of the self" (Peters 2001, 19).[18] In a decade marked by Clinton's "New Covenant," the Million Man March, dotcom entrepreneurship, and *Oprah*, being self-reliant was an increasingly hegemonic virtue.

This neoliberal logic resonated well with the sensibilities of an expanding and upwardly mobile educated elite. Slumpies' ostensibly counter-cultural fondness for being maverick outsiders dovetailed well with the economic individualism at the heart of the neoliberal enterprise, and their meritocratic belief that skill and effort should lead to success revealed a liberal blindness to structuring inequalities and echoed calls for personal responsibility. As they tracked the miraculous growth of their mutual funds, 401K plans, and stock options, many socially liberal, urban-minded professionals found their boats lifted by the rising tide of the "new economy." Surrounded by such neoliberal discourses and with more to lose than ever, many members of the expanding educated elite were drawn to economic policies that promoted fiscal constraint, targeted tax cuts, and welfare reform.

By the mid-'90s, this new social class had established a new political position—one that reconciled their bohemian ideals of social equality and their bourgeois materialism. In being socially liberal and fiscally conservative, Slumpies found a way to synthesize multicultural discourses that celebrated diversity and neoliberal discourses that celebrated the free market. The emergence of this political position, what Clinton called the "vital center," is symptomatic of what political scientists call the postmaterialist politics of a New Political Culture. With roots in the '70s but a noticeably growing role in the political dynamics of postindustrial countries in the '90s, this New Political Culture has undermined the traditional class politics and left-right ideologies that had structured debated and social identities for much of the 20th century. According to Terry Nicholas Clark and Ronald Inglehart (1998), New Political Culture revived neoliberal faith in market individualism, distinguished social issues from fiscal issues, reassessed the welfare state, emphasized consumption and lifestyle issues more than workplace and job issues, and was supported by younger, more educated, affluent citizens. The growing currency of multicultural discourses among well-educated boomers and Generation Xers following in their wake also fostered their socially liberal, fiscally conservative politics. Multiculturalism, if not in academic theory then most certainly in its corporate and popular incarnations, focused on the inequity of cultural representations without drawing the connections to economic and institutional structures of power or to the unequal distribution of wealth. As such, multiculturalism made it easier for a fiscal conservatism to exist side by side with socially (or perhaps we should more accurately say culturally) liberal ideas.[19]

The Slumpy class's socially liberal, fiscally conservative ethos reconfigured the political landscape in the 1990s.[20] On one hand, this new elite class was turned off by the Republican Party's close ties to Christian conservatives and its increasingly moralistic tone. Culture warrior Pat Buchanan (1992), for example, laid bare the far right's socially conservative values in his infamous speech at the 1992 Republican convention: "There is a religious war going on in this country for the soul of America. It is a cultural war as critical to the kind of nation we shall be as the Cold War itself, for this war is for the soul of America" (p. 714). To voters predisposed to socially liberal attitudes and increasingly surrounded by multicultural discourses, the Right's antiabortion, antigay, family-values agenda was far too blatantly intolerant. "After more than 12 years of significant influence in the Republican Party," one pundit observed after Bush's decisive loss in 1992, "they [the Religious Right] finally scared the bejeezus out of suburban America" (Postrel 1993, 4). Democrats, on the other hand, suffered from their association with New Deal-styled tax-and-spend policies that seemed to care more for pork belly projects and welfare mothers than the supposedly hard-working middle class. Neither party's traditional platform satisfied this moderate middle. As one self-identified socially liberal, fiscally conservative poll respondent put it, "Religious groups are trying to ruin this country from the right, and the other side is intent on spending everyone else's money" ("This Is What You Thought," 1996, 141). A Gen X spokesperson put it even more succinctly: "We're not fond of deficits or bigots" (Gardner 2000). In this political climate, members in both parties rushed to adapt. "New Republican" Governors like New Jersey's Christine Todd Whitman and Massachusetts' Bill Weld had enormous success among suburbanites in 1994 by running on the two Ts: tax cuts and tolerance. Meanwhile, 1996 GOP presidential candidate Arlen Specter linked his New Republican platform to old-fashioned Republican libertarianism: "I agree with former Arizona Sen. Barry Goldwater when he said we need to keep government out of our pocketbooks, off our backs and out of our bedrooms" ("'Liberal' Specter Joins GOP Race" 1995). Meanwhile, "New Democrats" like Paul Tsongas, Bill Bradley, and, of course, Bill Clinton abandoned the traditional New Deal coalition, called for fiscal responsibility in the face of the mounting national deficit, and fought for environmental issues, campaign finance reform, anticrime measures, abortion rights, free trade, and gay rights. While Clinton appointed African Americans, Lations, women, and gays and lesbians to key administration positions and attended a black church, he also declared that the era of big government was over and vowed to "end welfare as we know it."

Slumpies and the Affordable Politics of Gay Chic

> Sometimes I just gotta have my gays around me.
> —Openly straight comedienne Kathy Griffin
> on an HBO Comedy Special, 1996.

> It's the '90s, and it's hip to be queer.
> —Openly lesbian comedienne Lea Delaria on *Arsenio*, 1993.

The Slumpy sensibility, then, which emerged as a newly expanded educated elite, looked to balance their socially liberal, bohemian identities as hip cosmopolitans with their fiscally conservative, bourgeois values as America's newest upwardly mobile elite class. As it came to be constructed in the 1990s, homosexuality was a particularly pragmatic fit for Slumpies looking to find an affordable politics of affirmative multiculturalism. Gay issues, for example, were often included in multicultural educational discourse. Terms like "fag" and "dyke" were added to campus speech codes and residence hall diversity programs sensitized undergraduates to the problem of homophobia. Gay and lesbian studies programs and gay-themed courses appeared more frequently, and queer theory became fashionable in certain academic circles. Meanwhile, a growing number of major corporations like Apple, Boeing, and Coors added sexual orientation to their nondiscrimination policies, sponsored gay and lesbian employee groups, or offered same-sex health benefits. A prominent 1991 *Fortune* article titled "Gay in Corporate America" informed its readers: "Odds are that there are almost as many gay employees in the workforce as there are blacks, but most of them will be invisible." By the early '90s, more than 3,000 AT&T employees had attended homophobia workshops where they received "accurate information to replace myths they may have swallowed, such as that homosexuality is 'curable' or that gay men are sexual predators" (Stewart 1991, 50).

Despite such multicultural discourses, supporting gays and lesbians was still a relatively exceptional marker of just how open-minded one was. In a post-PC environment, expressing public platitudes about the importance of antiracist attitudes, for example, had become obligatory in most social circles. Homosexuality, on the other hand, was still publicly condemnable for many. In the early '90s, gay rights battles over "don't ask, don't tell," the Defense of Marriage Act, and antigay initiatives like Colorado Amendment 2 and Oregon's Measure 9 generated viciously homophobic discourses that circulated widely as the media rushed to cover the hot-button issue. In an effort to "balance" their coverage of gay rights stories, mainstream media legitimized overtly antigay rhetoric in ways they no longer did in their coverage of most other civil rights movements. As such heated debates and the numerous polls conducted to measure Americans' attitudes about homosexuality made perfectly clear, many people still found gays and lesbians immoral. In fact, a 1993 Gallup Poll found that almost 50 percent of Americans did not favor the decriminalization of same-sex behavior (Vaid 1995, 20). In this context, expressing one's support for gays and lesbians still held out the allure of marginalizing oneself; if postmaterialist politics and multicultural discourses made being intolerant in general déclassé among the Slumpy class, being gay-friendly was particularly hip.

Although victims of social intolerance, gays and lesbians were also increasingly affluent, or so it was reported. In the 1990s, marketers (anxious to uncover untapped market niches); glossy gay magazines like *The Advocate, Out*, and *Deneuve* (anxious to attract national advertising dollars); and gay-oriented ad agencies and market research firms like Mulryan/ Nash and Overlooked Opinions (anxious to sell their services) helped construct the gay community as an ideal consumer demographic. Profiles of gay and lesbian consumers popped up in both the trade and popular press throughout the early '90s, and their statistics were almost always compared to data for so-called average Americans. One report, for example, claimed that 40 percent of lesbians and 47 percent of gay men held managerial jobs compared with 15 percent and 31 percent nationwide. 27 percent of gay people were frequent fliers compared to a national average of 2 percent (Kalafut 1992, 32). According to a 1995 report by Mulryan/Nash, "61 percent of gay people have a four-year college degree, as opposed to 18 percent of average Americans. . . . 43 percent of gay people work out in a gym as opposed to 8 percent of average Americans. . . . 64 percent of gay people drink sparkling water as opposed to 17 percent of Americans" (Schulman 1995, 28). Other surveys claim that a typical gay male couple earned $51,600 a year, while the average straight couple earned only $37,900. The average lesbian couple reportedly earns $42,800 (Streitmatter 1995, 314). According to Aka Communications, a marketing research firm that focuses on gay consumers, 18 percent of gay households have incomes over $100,000 (Carson 1992, 6). Explaining why his company targeted gay consumers, Chris Auburn, marketing representative for Miller Brewing, put it succinctly: "The gay community has a lot of money" (Chura 1999, 3).[21] Imbricated within the self-interest of the marketing industry and produced by highly questionable research methods, such statistics grossly distorted the economic status of many gays and lesbians. Nevertheless, this discursive construction circulated widely in the 1990s, helping to paint an image of the gay community as being economically well off.

As it came to be articulated in the '90s, then, homosexuality fit conveniently into the delicate (and ambivalent) balance of the Slumpy's socially liberal, fiscally conservative agenda. Careful analysis of mainstream press coverage of gay rights throughout the decade reveals a consistent focus on the ways homosexuality was linked to America's moral, not economic, struggles.[22] Although clearly marking gays and lesbians as the victims of bigotry, coverage of the era's most visible gay rights issues—namely, access to military service, adoption rights, hate crime laws—framed gays and lesbians as a minority ostensibly asking only for social acceptance not downwardly redistributive social welfare policies. Amid widely circulating reports of gay affluence, homophobia was largely regarded as a cultural issue, not an economic one. Despite the importance of federal funding for research, for example, the AIDS battle was framed less as a struggle for tax dollars than a battle against ignorance and fear. Even mainstream coverage of an economic-equity issue like domestic partnership benefits seemed to reinforce stereotypes of gay economic prosperity by drawing attention to white-collar corporate policies rather than issues facing the working poor. Moreover, marketers' interest in and repeated reports about gay and lesbian consumers seemed to confirm the emancipatory power of free market capitalism and the validity of market liberalism. When defined as an issue of personal freedom in the face of an intrusive government trying to legislate values and private behavior, gay rights also suited the era's casual libertarianism.[23] The moralistic rhetoric of Christian conservatives like Pat Buchanan, Jerry Falwell, and Pat Robertson made gay rights an issue many social liberals could get behind. In the cultural logic of the 1990s, gays and lesbians were something of a model minority for the socially liberal, fiscally conservative minded. They were victims of political discrimination and antiquated mores but were apparently economically self-sufficient. Being gay-friendly, then, seemed to simply require celebrating cultural differences and offered an affordable politics of social liberality.

Certainly, Slumpy attitudes towards homosexuality were far from consistent, but I argue that an underlying ambivalence actually helped fuel their support for gays and lesbians. While Slumpies were proud of having gay friends and firmly believed that there was nothing wrong with homosexuality, for example, we can imagine that few ever thought about raising their children free of presumptive heterosexuality. More importantly, for most, attitudes about gay men and lesbians continued to develop in the context of, and thus be shaped by, prescribed definitions of masculinity and femininity and by long-standing discourses linking homosexuality to deviancy, illegality, and sin. After all, being gay-friendly could give Slumpies the thrill of edginess precisely because it involves transgressing social norms; accepting homosexuality implied that there was something that needed to be accepted.

In the early '90s, then, homosexuality crossed the often-fine line between being scorned and being chic as gays and lesbians suddenly acquired just the right kind of marginal allure for America's newest educated elite. According to a 1993 issue of the upscale, urban-targeted men's fashion magazine *Gentleman's Quarterly*, "Gay chic has emerged from the underground and floated to the surface—it's not just for club goers anymore. Anyone, even your dad, can pick up a newspaper or turn on the television and see unvarnished gay product" (Kamp 1993, 95). Movies like *Priscilla, Queen of the Desert, Jeffrey,* and *Philadelphia* brought gay themes from the art house to the urban multiplex. RuPaul took drag-queen divatude from Saturday nights at the local gay club to prime-time on VH1, while *The New Republic* editor Andrew Sullivan and *Angeles in America* scribe Tony Kushner were tapped to star in Gap ads. Calvin Klein underwear model Marky Mark stated publicly that it was cool "to suck dick" (even if he didn't do it). And red AIDS-awareness ribbons became a required black-tie accessory at Hollywood awards ceremonies. Lesbians were not left out of the trend either. In fact, lesbian chic became a genuine pop-culture phenomenon all its own. From Madonna's much-discussed "Justify My Love" video to Banana Republic's "My Chosen Family" print ads, attractive women who had sex with attractive women were all the craze. Lesbianism made it onto *Rolling Stone*'s hot list, while out comedian Lea DeLaria made it onto *Arsenio*. The trend reached its peak in the summer of 1993. ABC's newsmagazine show 20/20 aired a story on Northhampton, Massachusetts—"Lesbianville, USA." Mainstream magazines like *Newsweek, New York*, and *Vogue* ran prominent articles that translated lesbian lingo like "femme," "butch," and "lipstick lesbian" into terms their hip, straight readers could understand.[24] And, of course, gay material became commonplace on network television.

If consuming "unvarnished gay product" was one increasingly convenient way to get a bit of the Other in the early '90s, actually defecting from the banality of a straight identity became another. In 1993, the *Village Voice* identified the emergence "the Queer Straight, that testy love child of identity politics and shifting sexual norms" (Powers 1993, 30). Out of the mix of multiculturalism, a rejuvenated gay and lesbian activism, and poststructural theory, straight academic and bohemian twenty-somethings looking to renounce their oppressive heterosexuality forged a new category of sexual identity for themselves. These new "Queer Straights" continued to have heterosexual sex in the bedroom but cultivated a public image of gender and sexual ambiguity—"queer in the streets, straight in the sheets" is the lingo of the time. Although the Queer-Straight sensibility may have been a relatively small subcultural phenomenon, figures such as Madonna, Sandra Bernhard, Sharon Stone, and Kurt Cobain created a relatively mainstream counterpart. Stone, for example, seemed proud to admit that she had gone on a date with a woman, while grunge guru Kurt Cobain claimed he "was gay in spirit" and "an advocate for fagdom." Even those less willing to flirt with the idea of being gay found a caveat to a straight identity in the pithy bumper-sticker slogan: STRAIGHT BUT NOT NARROW. Whether it was a self-identified queer-straight New York University undergraduate who cultivated the image of transgressive sexuality or a heterosexual couple in Kearny, Nebraska, that organized a party for the coming-out episode of *Ellen*, embracing gay culture in and of itself seemed to save one from the unhip suburbs of straightsville.

In sharp contrast and as a point of comparison, the economic position and social construction of African Americans would most likely have been particularly disquieting to the socially liberal, fiscally conservative Slumpy sensibility.[25] In the economic reality of the early '90s, America's long history of racialized economic inequality intensified (Masey and Denton 1993; Williams 1993; Oliver, Johnson, and Farrell 1993). Meanwhile, in the national imagination, black poverty was not just unfortunate but threatening. In 1992, the interconnected problems of inner-city poverty and racial injustice exploded on the streets of Los Angeles and were brought into white America's living rooms via 24-hour news coverage of burning buildings, unchecked looting, and a police force seemingly rendered ineffectual in the face of black rage. Such economic realities and social discourses that linked blackness to criminality and violence made it difficult to ignore the fact that race relations in the United States were intricately linked to the unequal distribution of wealth. As one young black man told Oprah Winfrey and her TV audience on an episode that aired shortly after the uprising, "Brothers and sisters don't have it like the so-called people who go out and work everyday and get in their nice cars and get in their nice houses; we come from the streets, we live in hell, we go through the trials and tribulations of all types of things, and when a situation happens like this, and people want to get theirs, and when they work hard and they still can't get groceries, and they see the place burning up, what you gonna do" (Fiske 1994, 172).

For an expanding class of Slumpies looking for an affordable politics of social liberality, I would argue that the politics of race were less expedient than those of sexual identity. Slumpies certainly professed to hold antiracist attitudes, but gays and lesbians represented a more easily digestible Other.[26] Supporting affirmative action, reparations for slavery, or progressive welfare reform—all significant black civil rights issues in the '90s—would not have dovetailed neatly with a Slumpy-styled neoliberalism. In fact, if white Slumpies' fiscal conservatism (epitomized by quiet support of welfare reform) masked deep frustration with the intractability of race relations, their support of gays could be seen as a compensating move—a way to shore up their identities as social liberals in the face of their fiscal conservatism. Studies, for example, claim that while baby boomers and Generation Xers were noticeably more tolerant of newer lifestyles and supportive of the idea of equality, they shared virtually the same intolerant attitudes toward blacks as older generations (Hill 1997, 122). Similarly, while Florida's (2002) creative class would often judge the appeal of a corporation by asking about its policy on same-sex partnership benefits, Florida found a negative correlation between high concentrations of Black residents in a city and high concentrations of the kind of high-tech industries to which educated elites flocked (p. 263). In the realm of cultural consumption, the rise of gay material on prime-time network television coincided with the growing invisibility of black characters—a development so striking that it led the NAACP to threaten to boycott the industry in 1999. The few black characters that made it on to prime-time were increasingly segregated into black-oriented programming blocks that attracted virtually all-black audiences. This segregation was often explained as the inevitable result of narrowcasting or the racist politics of TV production, and both certainly played a role. Yet the fact that white Slumpies looking for hip and edgy programming seemed to find gay-inclusive TV appealing (while, for all practical purposes, ignoring black-inclusive TV) tells us something, I think, about this new social class's politics of cultural consumption.[27]

Gay-Themed Television, *Seinfeld*, and the Ambivalent Slumpy

On '90s television, gay characters, jokes, and references to homosexuality served as textual selling points to Slumpy viewers for whom gayness held a particular appeal. Gay characters became as much a requisite element of many series' mise-en-scéne as a big-city apartment and a coffee shop. In fact, they seemed to pop up as fast as Starbucks franchises; they tended to be equally clean and upscale—frequently mirroring the marketer's profile of the affluent, trendy, gay consumer. Much of the era's gay material also reflected the Slumpy sensibilities' ambivalence about both homosexuality and heterosexual privilege. Whereas most gay-themed episodes in the 1980s featured coming-out narratives in which the drama or comedy centered on the moment of revealed homosexuality and the shocked responses of straight family and friends, in the 1990s, gay-themed narratives often focused on situations in which straight characters confronted and negotiated their heterosexuality. Episodes involving mistaken sexual identity, for example, expose society's presumption of heterosexuality. When Frasier tries to set up his new boss with Daphne, for example, the gay boss assumes he's out on a date with Frasier; in the end, both men have to come out. Such episodes also blur the line between straight and gay, queering heterosexuality, if only momentarily. In other episodes, gay characters frequently serve as props that establish the sophistication of straight characters (or expose their lack of it). The heroic doctors on *ER* never bat an eye when their patients' same-sex partners enter the room, and *Beverly Hill 90210*'s Brandon Walsh uses the bully pulpit of his newspaper to denounce the homophobia of antigay adoption laws. More problematically, Roseanne revels in her ability to nonchalantly go to a lesbian bar, but when Nancy's girlfriend kisses her, she freaks out.[28]

Certainly more analysis is required to flesh out the ways gay-themed programming in the 1990s spoke to the Slumpy sensibility. Although such in-depth textual analysis is beyond the scope of this article, I want to conclude by briefly returning to the "not-that-there's-anything-wrong-with-that" episode of *Seinfeld*, for it exposed the Slumpy's anxieties and internal conflicts as overtly as any program of the era. Satirizing politically correct straight affirmations of difference, "The Outing" plays the Slumpy sensibility's public homofriendly facade off against its inner homophobic anxieties. The turning point in the episode's narrative comes when Jerry and George finally realize that the reporter interviewing them assumes they are gay.

Jerry:	Oh God! You're that girl from the coffee shop that was eavesdropping on us. I knew you looked familiar!
George:	Oh no! Oh no!
Reporter:	I'd better get going.
Jerry:	There's been a big mistake here.
George:	Yeah, Yeah.
Jerry:	We did all that for your benefit. We knew you were eavesdropping. That's why my friend said all that. It was on purpose. We're not gay! Not that's there's anything wrong with that.
George:	No, of course not.
Jerry:	I mean its fine if that's who you are.
George:	Absolutely!
Jerry:	I mean I have many gay friends.
George:	My father's gay.

Exposed in this scene are the coexisting fears of homosexuality and homophobia. On one hand, Jerry and George's panicked response and insistent denial reveals a profound unease with homosexuality. Before the reporter leaves, in fact, George insists they have sex right then so he can prove his heterosexuality to her. On the other hand, they are equally anxious to convince her that they are not bigots, that their disavowal does not come from homophobia. They are desperate to prove that they do not have any problem with "that." Their excessive effort, however, only underscores their anxiety. This complex performance of anxious gay affirmation is repeated throughout the episode, not only by Jerry and George but also by Kramer, Jerry's mom, and George's mom.

Most simply, of course, watching a program that acknowledged homosexuality with a plot structured around mistaken (homo)sexuality (as opposed to the episode of *Home Improvement* that originally aired opposite and that acknowledged only the heterosexual nuclear family with a plot structured around the husband's wacky anniversary present) helped certain viewers demonstrate their hipness level. The genius of "The Outing" and its allure to the Slumpy sensibility, however, was that it allowed Slumpies to have their cake and eat it too—to feel self-satisfied about their edgy support of gays and lesbians while laughing at jokes that tap into their residual anxieties about the Other's homosexuality, their own heterosexuality, and the indeterminate boundary between the two. Wrapped in *Seinfeld's* typical cloak of ironic distance, the episode can claim to be slyly critiquing Jerry and George's heterosexual insecurities, exposing their unreflective PC lip service to gay tolerance as simply a thin veneer covering their unresolved prejudices. On one hand, then, socially liberal viewers can laugh at Jerry and George's heterosexual panic and, in doing so, feel multiculturally superior. On the other hand, the episode's humor repeatedly taps into the viewer's unresolved prejudices. Proving that it is a fine line between celebrating gayness and celebrating gay stereotypes, for example, much of the episode's humor centers on an ironic acknowledgement of cultural assumptions about gay men and gay male culture. But more importantly, I would argue that Jerry and George's panicked reaction is funny, even to Slumpy viewers, because, on some level, they identify with their anxiety. The viewer's ambivalence toward homosexuality and the imperatives of both political correctness and heterosexuality fuel their nervous laughter.

Notes

1. In her analysis of yuppie television in the '80s, Feuer (1995) offers the category of the yuppie spectator, which she defines as "a construct of the analyst, i.e., anyone who can even momentarily be placed in a yuppie subject position" (p.44). Although the term's theoretical baggage makes it somewhat problematic, the Slumpy sensibility might usefully be thought of as something of a spectator position. Although I would argue that the well-educated, upscale, creative professionals I profile below would more easily and perhaps more likely adopt that position, anyone could theoretically approach and interpret television texts through a Slumpy sensibil-

ity. Alluding to spectator theory also raises the possibility of Slumpy texts—that is, programs whose narratives position all viewers as Slumpies and encourage them to read the text from a Slumpy subject position. The extent to which the cultural tastes and political common sense of the Slumpy class had become hegemonic in the 1990s would suggest that one could make such an ideologically inflected argument.

2. While similar, Florida's "creative class," defined as it is by specific types of creativity activity, differs significantly from popular concepts of white-collar workers or the professional-managerial class. This does not mean that there are not important connections between them. Early studies of the professional-managerial class likely identified many of the roots of this new social class, and many creative professionals would conform to most people's definition of white-collar workers. The categories, however, are not synonymous.

3. Average annual salaries by class for 1999 were as follows: creative class ($48,751), working class ($27,799), service class ($22,059), entire United States ($31,571) (Florida 2002, 77).

4. The creative class has not been alone in this development. In analyzing U.S. Census data, Florida (2002) argues that the "U.S. working population is re-sorting itself geographically along class lines." Old migration patterns from rust belt to sun belt became more complex in the 1990s as creative class workers moved to cities like San Francisco, Austin, Madison, and Burlington. Meanwhile, the working class dominates manufacturing centers like Detroit, Decatur, Alabama, Hickory, North Carolina; and the service class dominates resort towns like Las Vegas, Honolulu, and Cape Cod, as well as Sioux Falls, Rapid City, and Bismarck. In many locations, the creative class, especially the super-creative core have virtually no presence. This segregation is "disturbing" to Florida because, he argues, that in a postindustrial economy, a high concentration of creative class workers is essential to a region's economic growth, income levels, and high-tech development. Cities dominated by the service and working classes (and the people living there) face being shut out of the information economy. The growing income gap between the creative class and other social groups may be an indicator of this trend (pp. 236–43).

5. Florida's primary goal is to help local leaders improve their city's economic health. He asserts that the presence of high concentrations of members of the creative class is a key predictor of economic vitality. Cities looking for rising population figures, higher incomes, and strong high-tech industry, he argues, need to be focused on the three T's: technology, talent, and tolerance. Attracting the creative class (or more specifically its talent) by fostering a tolerant environment will bring around the kind of technological innovation that fuels economic growth in the information economy. In fact, Florida maintains that in analyzing data for the 1990s, tools that measure openness to tolerance and creativity (like the Gay index, Melting Pot index, and Bohemian index) were actually better predictors of a region's growth than conventional tools that measured human capital, high-tech industry, and corporate presence (Florida 2002, 249–66).

6. Admittedly, the Slumpy Class does not yet have a clear sense of itself as a distinct class nor has it been nominated in popular or niche-marketing discourse like the working class had been in the '30s and yuppies were in the '80s. However, as Florida (2002) says of his creative class, "It has an emerging coherence" (p. 68).

7. According to scholars, this development has been fueled by the increase in higher education and the related rise in the knowledge economy, the credit system and the growing prominence of consumption as a sign of social distinction, the cultural effect of identity politics including multiculturalism, and the demise of regulated capitalism in the face of globalization and market liberalism (Aronowitz 1992; Clark and Inglehart 1998). The correspondence between these forces and those Brooks, Florida, and I identify at play behind the rise of the Slumpy class indicates just how imbricated the Slumpy class is with these large-scale social shifts. Note that acknowledging the growing importance of race, gender, and sexuality to people's identities is not to say that relations of production play a less determinate role in shaping people's experiences, opportunities, or access to power than they had before. Economic forces are utterly

salient. However, as people form self-conscious identities, economic forces are increasingly mediated by other categories of experience that serve as the bases for self-understanding.

8. For a selection of prominent mainstream coverage of the issues, see Adler (1990), Berenstein (1990), "He Wants to Pull the Plug on the PC" (1990), Prescott (1990), D'Souza (1991a, 1991b, 1991c), "Academic in Opposition" (1991), and Will (1991a, 1991b).

9. By the early '90s, the American Assembly of Collegiate Schools of Business had endorsed diversity issues as a necessary element of business school curricula. The 1992 theme for the Annual Academy of Management Meeting was "The Management of Diversity." (Cavanaugh 1997; Gentile 1994).

10. Such sentiments were echoed by the Harvard Business School's Nathaniel Thompkins: "Many companies are making a thrust toward quality and productivity to become more competitive in a global market. This means more and better products from each employee. But you can't do that unless you understand the differences each employee brings to the table. You can't have successful quality or productivity programs unless you value, recognize and appreciate the differences that individuals bring to your program." Thompkins claimed that by 1991, 80 percent of U.S. companies were aware of the new dynamics of diversity in a tightening global labor market, but that only 30 percent had taken action (Allen 1991, 17).

11. A popular, seven-part video series titled *Valuing Diversity*, for example, included interviews with senior executives who explained why they championed diversity, tips for managers looking to better motivate minority employees, a discussion of how stereotypes limit employee productivity, and dramatized workplace scenarios where cultural differences lead to miscommunication (MacDonald 1993, 24; Allen 1991, 16; Sims and Sims 1993, 76).

12. In fact, direct links were made to the specific battle over multiculturalism on college campuses by conservative critics who lambasted the appointment of University of Wisconsin Chancellor Donna Shalala to head the Department of Health and Human Services. According to several reports, Shalala was known for turning her university into an "epicenter of multiculturalism" and informed readers that she was known in academic circles as the "queen of PC" (Evan 1993).

13. I would not argue that multicultural discourses did not reach members of the working or service class or rural residents, the elderly, and the working poor. Instead, I argue that the educated elite working in occupations enumerated by Florida (2002) were more likely to be exposed to certain kinds of multicultural discourses repeatedly and that a certain brand of politically correct affirmation of difference gained a currency among that social class in ways different than among other social groups. Members of the working or service classes participating in union organizing or inner city residents dealing with local coalition politics likely interacted with multiculturalism in different ways than their Slumpy counterparts.

14. I certainly do not ascribe to a simplistic economic reductionism, however. The relationship between multiculturalism and post-Fordism is certainly not a simply base/superstructure one.

15. The result of opinion polls measuring Americans' attitudes regarding homosexuality and gay rights became a de facto genre convention for feature articles in mainstream newsmagazines throughout the 1990s. Such polls consistently indicated that while between 70 percent and 80 percent of respondents believed gays and lesbians should not be discriminated against in such areas as employment and housing, 57 percent said that homosexuality was unacceptable and 62 percent opposed same-sex marriage. Although only impressionistic, such consistent poll data suggests a fuzzy but significant line between the roughly 40 percent of respondents who demonstrate what *Rolling Stone* called "a sort of distasteful tolerance" and the 30 percent who not only tolerate but, as evidenced by their belief in the moral acceptability of homosexuality and support for more affirmative policies like same-sex marriage, embrace gay and lesbian difference (Dreyfuss 1999).

16. Of course tolerance itself is a highly complicated notion. Critics argue that multicultural tolerance is a disguised way to reproduce structures of power while making things appear equal. As

Ghassan Hage (1994) argues, "It is a form of symbolic violence in which a mode of domination is presented as a form of egalitarianism" (pp. 28-9). After all, only those in power are asked to be tolerant, and asking people to be tolerant does nothing to change his/her capability of being intolerant. The structures of power that privilege them in the first place are not altered.

17. Exnomination has been a powerful strategy of the dominant, allowing whiteness, patriarchy, heterosexuality, and so forth, to serve as the naturalized norm against which all subordinated others are judged. This strategy has some limitations, however, in a social context where markers of difference are valued, at least culturally. Talking specifically about whiteness, George Yudice (1995) argues, "Multiculturalism and identity politics have not constructed an imaginary for whites who want to participate in the extension of citizenship to all" (p. 258). I would argue that the same could be said for heterosexuality.

18. Also see Smith 1999.

19. Since both multiculturalism and the New Political Culture (NPC) emerge out of the same shifting terrain of postindustrial capitalism and economic globalization, their compatibility should not be surprising.

20. In an unscientific but highly telling *Glamour* magazine reader poll, 75 percent of respondents agreed that the United States needed a third party, and of those, 52 percent said that their "ideal third party candidate" would be "fiscally conservative but at the same time socially liberal." ("This Is What You Thought" 1996, 141). The 1990s saw a reformulation of political identities and voting blocks. By the mid-'90s, political pundits repeatedly referred to the emergence of a new block of intensely disgruntled voters who were dissatisfied with the political platforms of both the Democrats and the Republicans. These voters were frequently described as a some-what undifferentiated group of centrists calling for a third party candidate to represent its unified interests. In a *New York Times Magazine* article, however, Michael Lund (1995) problematized this simplistic approach, and his analysis helps get a slightly more focused picture of the shifting political landscape and the Slumpy ethos. He argued that these alienated voters (approximately 33 percent of the electorate) are actually strongly divided into two distinct camps. The first, which he calls the moderate middle, were highly suburban managers and professionals with advanced degrees who were socially liberal, fiscally conservative, progay, proenvironmentalist—essentially, the Slumpy class. Many of them, he claims, were Rockefeller-styled Republicans alienated by the increasing influence of the religious right on the GOP. The second block he calls the radical center, using a term coined by sociologist Donald Warren in the 1970s. These voters had often been Reagan Democrats (white, blue-collar, high school–educated workers from the Midwest, South, and West) who were alienated by New Deal welfare programs. They tended to be "liberal, even radical in matters of economics, but conservative in morals and mores" (p. 72). Such voters were drawn to the charismatic populism of Ross Perot and Pat Buchanan. Although these two blocks had formulations specific to the '90s, Lund sees them linked to longer trends in American political history: "The difference is reminiscent of the class and cultural divide between upper-middle-class metropolitan Progressives and the rural and small-town Populists at the turn of the century, who viewed each other with suspicion even though they shared many criticisms of the existing order" (p. 72).

21. For more on the construction of the affluent gay market, see Becker (1998, 40-3), Chasin (2000), and Gluckman and Reed (1997).

22. The following assertions were based on careful examination of all articles focused on gay issues (as listed in the Readers Guide to Periodical Literature) and a more limited analysis of major newspaper articles on gay rights from *The New York Times, The Washington Post*, and *Los Angeles Times* between 1990 and 1998. An analysis of gay-rights coverage in such mainstream press sources as *Time, Newsweek, U.S. News & World Report* as well as more highbrow lifestyle, political, and culture magazines like *The New Yorker, The New Republic, Esquire, GQ, Glamour, National Review, Rolling Stone*, and *The Nation*, I argue, offers a glimpse at mainstream and elite discourses on gay rights.

23. Of course, this attitude cut both ways. While voters in Oregon rejected Measure 9, which would have amended the state constitution to state that homosexuality was "abnormal, wrong, unnatural, and perverse," voters in Colorado passed a proposition to overturn existing antidiscrimination laws when antigay forces successfully framed the issue as a case of special rights and excessive legislation.

24. For the most prominent coverage, see Kasindorf (1993); Swisher (1993); Jetter (1993); Salholtz et al. (1993); Kantrowitz and Senna (1993); Beck, Glick, and Annin (1993); Rubin (1993); and Snead (1993).

25. The economic realities and cultural discourses of American race relations do not exist separately from the emergence of '90s-styled neoliberalism. Racist discourses about black poverty, laziness, and criminality were likely key factors behind the growing popularity of fiscal conservatism and antiwelfare policies that came along with it.

26. It is important to note how this cultural dynamic ignores the existence of black gays and lesbians—an erasure that demonstrates the ways American culture works to deny the intersectionality of racial and sexual politics. My argument here reflects less a theoretical blindness to the multiple ways race and sexuality intersect than it reflects the extent to which gays and lesbians were constructed as white in the American imagination and the extent to which both the gay and black civil rights movements were dominated by single-issue politics.

27. As a point of contrast, disaffected white teenagers seemed to be drawn to specific (often commodified and sanitized) elements of urban black culture in the 1990s. The entertainment industries discovered/cultivated a market among white suburbanites enthusiastic for certain Rap music, black clothing styles, and urban vocabulary.

28. *Frasier* (NBC), "The Matchmaker," April 10, 1994; *ER* (NBC), "Long Day's Journey," January 1, 1995; *ER* (NBC), "It's Not Easy Being Green," February 1, 1996; *Beverly Hills, 90210* (FOX), "The Nature of Nurture," March 18, 1998; *Roseanne* (ABC), Don't Ask, Don't Tell," March 1, 1994.

References

Abramovitz, Mimi, and Ann Withorn. 1999. Playing by the Rules: Welfare Reform and the New Authoritarian States. In *Without Justice for All: The New Liberalism and Our Retreat from Racial Equality*, edited by Adolph Reed, Jr. Boulder, CO: Westview.

Academic in Opposition. 1991. *Time*, April 1, 66–9.

Adler, Jerry, Mark Starr, Farai Chideya, Lynda Wright, Pat Wingert, and Linda Haac. 1990. Taking Offense. *Newsweek*, December 24, 48–54.

Allen, Gray. 1991. Valuing Cultural Diversity; Industry Woos a New Work Force. *IABC Communications World*, May, 14.

Amos, Denise Smith. 1993. Companies Crusading for a Cause. *Publisher's Weekly*, July 18, 12.

Ang, Ien. 1991. *Desperately Seeking the Audience*. London: Routledge.

Aronowitz, Stanley. 1992. *The Politics of Identity: Class, Culture, Social Movements*. New York: Routledge.

Beck, Melinda, Daniel Glick, and Peter Annin. 1993. A (Quiet) Uprising in the Ranks. *Newsweek*, June 21, 60.

Becker, Ron. 1998. Prime-Time Television in the Gay Nineties: Network Television, Quality Audiences, and Gay Politics. *The Velvet Light Trap*, no. 42:36–47.

Berenstein, Richard. 1990. The Rising Hegemony of the Politically Correct. *The New York Times*, October 28, 1.

Bowens, Howard, Jarrow Merenivitch, L. Patricia Johnson, Anthony R. James, and Debra J. McFadden-Bryant. 1993. Managing Cultural Diversity towards True Multiculturalism: Some

Knowledge from the Black Perspective. In *Diversity and Differences in Organizations: An Agenda for Answers and Questions*, edited by Ronald R. Sims and Robert F. Dennehy. Westport, CT: Quorum.

Brooks, David. 2000. *Bobos in Paradise: The New Upper Class and How They Got There.* New York: Simon & Schuster.

Brown, Michael K. 1999. Race in the American Welfare State: The Ambiguities of "Universalistic" Social Policy since the New Deal. In *Without Justice for All: The New Liberalism and Our Retreat from Racial equality*, edited by Adolph Reed, Jr. Boulder, CO: Westview.

Buchanan, Pat. 1992. The Election Is about Who We Are. *Vital Speeches of the Day* 58 (23): 712–5.

Carson, Teresa. 1992. Agencies Push Gay Market Ads to Banks. *The American Banker*, May 21, 6.

Cavanaugh, J. Michael. 1997. (In)corporating the Other? Managing the Politics of Workplace Difference. In *Managing the Organizational Melting Pot: Dilemmas of Workplace Diversity*, edited by Pushkala Prasda, Albert J. Mills, Michael Elmes, and Anshuman Prasad. Thousand Oaks, CA: Sage.

Chasin, Alexandra. 2000. *Selling Out: The Gay & Lesbian Movement Goes to Market.* New York: St. Martin's.

Chura, Hillary. 1999. Miller Reconsiders Gay-Themed TV Spot. *Advertising Age*, July 12, 3.

Clark, Terry Nichols, and Ronald Inglehart. 1998. The New Political Culture: Changing Dynamics of Support for the Welfare State and Other Policies in Postindustrial Societies. In *The New Political Culture*, edited by Terry Nichols Clark and Ronald Inglehart, 9–72. Boulder, CO: Westview.

D'Acci, Julie. 1994. *Defining Women: Television and the Case of* Cagney & Lacy. Chapel Hill: University of North Carolina Press.

Dreyfuss, Robert. 1999. The Holy War on Gays. *Rolling Stone*, March 18.

D'Souza, Dinesh. 1991a. Illiberal Education. *Atlantic Monthly*, March, 51.

_____. 1991b. Sins of Admission. *New Republic*, February 18, 30–3.

_____. 1991c. The Visogoths in Tweeds. *Forbes*, April 1, 81–6.

Du Brow, Rick. 1995. Television; Networking '90s Style. *Los Angeles Times*, April 9.

Elliott, Stuart. 1993. A Survey Says that Cause-Oriented Campaigns Don't Just Make People Feel Good, They Work, Too. *The New York Times*, December 6. Retrieved from http://www.lexis-nexis.com.

Elber, Lynn. 1993. MTV's Reality Based Soap Opera, "Real World" Returns. *Associated Press*, June 22. Retrieved from http://www.lexis-nexis.com.

Evan, Roland. 1993. Shalala Belies Clinton's Centrist Image. *Chicago Sun-Times*, January 8.

Feuer, Jane. 1995. *Seeing through the Eighties: Television and Reaganism.* Durham, NC: Duke University Press.

Fiske, John. 1994. *Media Matters: Everyday Culture and Political Change*. Minneapolis: University of Minnesota Press.

Florida, Richard. 2002. *The Rise of the Creative Class: And How It's Transforming Work, Leisure, Community and Everyday Life*. New York: Basic Books.

Gamble, Andrew. 2001. Neo-Liberalism. *Capital & Class* 75 (Autumn): 127–34.

Gardner, Dan. 2000. Gen X at UA. *The Ottawa Citizen*, January 29.

Gentile, Mary C. 1994. Introduction. In *Differences that Work: Organizational Excellence through Diversity*, edited by Mary C. Gentile. Boston: Harvard Business Review Book.

Gluckman, Amy, and Betsy Reed, eds. 1997. *Homo Economics: Capitalism, Community, and Lesbian and Gay Life*. New York: Routledge.

Goode, Judith, and Jeff Maskovsky. 2001. Introduction to *The New Poverty Studies: The Ethnography of Power, Politics, and Impoverished People in the United States*. New York: New York University Press, 4.

Hage, Ghassan. 1994. Locating Multiculturalism's Other: A Critique of Practical Tolerance. *New Formations* 24 (Winter): 19–34.

He Wants to Pull the Plug on the PC. 1990. *Newsweek*, December 24, 52–3.

Hill, Kevin A. 1997. Generations and Tolerance: Is Youth Really a Liberalizing Factor? In *After the Boom: The Politics of Generation X*, edited by Stephan C. Craig and Stephan Earl Bennett. Lanham, MD: Rowman & Littfield.

hooks, bell. 1992. *Black Looks*. Boston: South End Press.

Jetter, Alexis. 1993. Goodbye to the Last Taboo. *Vogue*, July, 86–8.

Johnston, W. B., and A. H. Packard. 1987. *Workforce 2000: Work and Workers for the 21st Century*. Indianapolis, IN: Hudson.

Kalafut, Kathy. 1992. Alternative Demos; Profile on Aka Communications, Inc. *Mediaweek*, September 14, 32.

Kamp, David. 1993. The Straight A Queer. *Gentleman's Quarterly*, July, 95.

Kantrowitz, Barbara, and Danzy Senna. 1993. A Town Like No Other. *Newsweek*, June 21, 56–7.

Kasindorf, Russell. 1993. Lesbian Chic: The Brave, New World of Gay Women. *New York*, May 10, 30–7.

"Liberal" Specter Joins GOP Race. 1995. *St. Petersburg Times*. March 31.

Lund, Michael. 1995. The Radical Center or the Moderate Middle. *New York Times Magazine*, December 3, 72.

MacDonald, Heather. 1993. The Diversity Industry. *The New Republic*, July 5, 24.

Masey, Douglas S., and Nancy A. Denton. 1993. *American Apartheid: Segregation and the Making of the Underclass*. Cambridge, MA: Harvard University Press.

McCarthy, Colman. 1993. Here Comes Santa Cause. *Washington Post*, December 14.

Oliver, Melvin L., James H. Johnson, Jr., and Walter C. Farrell, Jr. 1993. Anatomy of a Rebellion: A Political-Economic Analysis. In *Reading Rodney King, Reading Urban Uprising*, edited by Robert Gooding-Williams. New York: Routledge.

Peters, Michael, A. 2001. *Poststructuralism, Marxism, and Neoliberalism: Between Theory and Politics*. Lanham, MD: Rowman & Littlefield.

Piven, Frances Fox. 2001. Welfare Reform and the Economic and Cultural Reconstruction of Low Wage Labor Markets. In *The New Poverty Studies: The Ethnography of Power, Politics, and Impoverished People in the United States*, edited by Judith Goode and Jeff Mushovsky. New York: New York University Press.

Postrel, Virginia I. 1993. Lost Causes. *Reason*, January, 4.

Powers, Ann. 1993. Queer in the Streets, Straight in the Sheets. *Village Voice*, June 29, 30.

Prasad, Pushkala, and Albert J. Mills. 1997. From Showcase to shadow: Understanding the Dilemma of Workplace Diversity. In *Managing the Organizational Melting Pot: Dilemmas of Workplace Diversity*, edited by Pushkala Prasda, Albert J. Mills, Michael Elmes, and Anshuman Prasad. Thousand Oaks, CA: Sage.

Prescott, Peter S. 1990. Learning to Love the PC Canon. *Newsweek*, December 24, 50–51.

Rubin, Sylvia. 1993. The New Lesbian Chic. *San Francisco Chronicle*, June 22.

Rutherford, Jonathan. 1990. A Place Called Home: Identity and the Cultural Politics of Difference. In *Identity, Community, Culture, Difference*, edited by Jonathan Rutherford. London: Lawrence & Wishart.

Salholtz, Eloise, Daniel Glick, Lucille Beachy, Carey Monerrate, Patricia King, Jeanne Gordon, and Todd Barrett. 1993. The Power and the Pride. *Newsweek*, June 21, 54–60.

Schulman, Sarah. 1995. Gay Marketeers. *The Progressive*, July, 28.

Schwartz, Stephan. 1995. Colors of the wind. On original soundtrack recording for *Pocahontas*. Burbank, California: Wonderland Music Company, Inc. (BMI)/Walt Disney Music Company (ASCAP).

Sims, Serbrenia J., and Ronald R. Sims. 1993. Diversity and Difference Training in the United States. In *Diversity and Differences in Organizations: An Agenda for Answers and Questions*, edited by Ronald R. Sims and Robert F Dennehy. Westport, CT: Quorum.

Smith, Preston, H. 1999. Self-Help, Black Conservatives, and the Reemergence of Black Privatism. In *Without Justice for All: The New Liberalism and Our Retreat from Racial Equality*, edited by Adolph Reed, Jr. Boulder, CO: Westview.

Snead, Elizabeth. 1993. Lesbians in the Limelight. *USA Today*, July 13.

Stewart, Thomas A. 1991. Gay in Corporate America. *Fortune*, December 16, 50.

Streitmatter, Roger. 1995. *Unspeakable: The Rise of the Gay and Lesbian Press in America*. Boston: Faber and Faber.

Swisher, Kara. 1993. We Love Lesbians! Or Do We? *Washington Post*, July 18.

Taylor, John. 1991. Are You Politically Correct? *New York*, January 21, 32–40.

This Is What You Thought. 1996. *Glamour*, June, 141.

Vaid, Urvashi. 1995. *Virtual Equality: The Mainstreaming of Gay & Lesbian Liberation*. New York: Anchor.

Will, George. 1991a. Curdled Politics on Campus. *Newsweek*, May 6, 72.

———. 1991b. Literary Politics. *Newsweek*, April 22, 72.

Williams, Rhonda M. 1993. Accumulation as Evisceration: Urban Rebellion and the New Growth Dynamics. In *Reading Rodney King, Reading Urban Uprising*, edited by Robert Gooding-Williams. New York: Routledge.

Willis, Ellin. 1999. *Don't Think, Smile!: Notes on a Decade of Denial*. Boston: Beacon.

Wilson, John K. 1995. *The Myth of Political Correctness: The Conservative Attack on Higher Education*. Durham, NC: Duke University Press.

Yudice, George. 1995. Neither Impugning nor Disavowing Whiteness Does a Viable Politics Make: The Limits of Identity Politics. In *After Political Correctness: The Humanities and Society in the 1990s*, edited by Christopher Newfield and Ronald Strickland. Boulder, CO: Westview.

Zoglin, Richard. 1993. The Shock of the Blue: Beavis and Butthead, Ted and Whoopi, Howard Stern and his "Private Parts": Whatever Happened to Political Correctness—and Good Manners? *Time*, October 25, 71.

HBO and the Concept of Quality TV

Jane Feuer

In his foreword to *Reading Six Feet Under*, British television journalist Mark Lawson writes: 'So what is most notable about *Six Feet Under* is not only that it is bold and original within the context of television schedules but also that it has no clear ancestry in any area of culture' (2005: xix).

The goal of this paper is to refute this statement utterly. I believe that *Six Feet Under* not only has a clear ancestry within art cinema but also that the series bears a significant debt to a tradition that I am going to call 'quality television.' Like Alan Ball's *American Beauty* (1999), surely the most art-cinema derivative film ever to win an Academy Award, *Six Feet Under* reeks of a European art cinema heritage in combination with a more televisual tradition of quality lifted from the miniseries of Dennis Potter and also from the more serialised tradition of American quality television that I will outline below.

The judgement of quality is always situated. That is to say, somebody makes the judgement from some aesthetic or political or moral position. If I had had the language of reception aesthetics at my command in the early 1980s when I first used the term quality TV, I could have said that the decision as to which TV shows, if any, to name as *quality* TV comes from within what Stanley Fish calls an *interpretive community*, that is, a professional community whose norms, ideals and methods determine an interpretation's validity (2005). Tony Bennett politicises this concept when he calls the interpretive community a *reading formation* (2003). (That is, situating readers within institutional structures determining what counts as a text or a context, and what distinguishes literary from non-literary concerns.) Reception theory teaches us that there can never be a judgement of quality in an absolute sense but that there are always judgements of quality relative to one's interpretive community or reading formation. That is why the term quality TV has to be used *descriptively* if one wants to understand how it operates discursively. Politically, of course, one always has an agenda and mine has been and will be to deflate some of the more pretentious claims by which intellectuals and the *culturati* use cinema and theatre to denigrate TV. I will not have time here to trace the total history of an opposition between quality TV and 'trash' TV (Feuer 2003: 98). Let me just say that such an opposition goes back to the very beginning of US television programming, when a sharp contrast existed between live anthology drama and the emerging forms of series TV.

Even before a normative notion of 'everyday television' had solidified, the idea of 'quality drama' existed in the form of the live 'anthology' teleplays of the 1950s. Written by New York playwrights, appealing to an élite audience and financed by individual corporate sponsors as prestige productions, these live TV dramas carried the cachet of the 'legitimate' theatre. In their minimal use of film techniques as well as the excitement of their live broadcasts these 'single play' dramas exhibited a pattern that would remain important to future generations of quality drama. On the one hand, they defined themselves as quality because they exploited an essential characteristic of their medium: the ability of television to broadcast live in a way films could not. On the other hand, their prestige came from an association with a 'higher' form of art: theatre, a form that at this time was widely acknowledged by intellectuals as superior to the film medium as well. Thus when, as sometimes happened, one of these anthology dramas was adapted into a movie (for example, *Marty* in 1955; and *Days of Wine and Roses* and *Requiem for a Heavyweight* in 1962), it underwent an odd transformation in cultural prestige. No matter how prestigious the film version, the television version has come to be seen as of lasting quality, because of its exploitation of the essence of the medium (liveness) and because it was thus closer to the theatrical. The film adaptations of these teleplays remain obscure, but the live dramas are still admired and studied even in the technically crude kinescope versions of them that remain. The Golden Age of Live TV achieves its aura in both directions: technologically it was experimental, and structurally it was 'theatre' and (like the future HBO) 'Not TV'.

To the US television industry—defined as a community of profit-minded capitalists interested in 'delivering' audiences and not texts—the term quality describes the demographics of the audience. Delivering a quality audience means delivering whatever demographic advertisers seek, or in the case of premium cable, attracting an audience with enough disposable income to pay extra for TV. Although excellent articles on the political economy of the shift to cable have already been written (Jaramillo 2002: 59–75), I would like to stress here the continuity in audience quality between the networks and cable services. The shift of 'quality drama' from the networks to pay cable does not alter this; in fact it intensifies it. Although a cable service such as HBO has a very small audience of subscribers, much smaller than the equivalent audience for network quality drama, they happen to be the very upscale demographic willing to pay extra for more specialised and more highbrow fare. Pay cable services value Nielsen ratings as well as subscriber numbers. Compare these judgements of value made in 2002 for *Six Feet Under* and *The West Wing*, respectively:

> *[From* Variety*] . . . the hoped-for audience bounce for the final hour of* Six Feet Under *on June 3 at 9pm never materialized, but the episode still delivered a 10.7 rating in cable homes. That's almost exactly on par with the 11.0 that the series averaged over the previous 12 weeks of original episodes (Dempsey 2002).*

and

> *[from* USA Today *discussing a decline in ratings for* The West Wing*] . . . yet NBC argues that* West Wing *is still extremely valuable because it reaches a high concentration of wealthy viewers—it's the only primetime series whose viewers ages 18–49 have a median income of more than $75,000 a year . . . it remains the series that attracts the most upscale demo on television, and it's arguably in the most competitive time slot [against* The Bachelor*] according to Warner Bros. TV president Peter Roth (Levin 2002).*

But most other interpretive communities do not define quality by economic criteria alone. The Christian right defines it by adherence to their own sense of religious values. Others such as the now-defunct activist group Viewers for Quality Television tend to value programmes that convey a morally and politically positive message from a more liberal perspective. For most journalistic reviewers, quality is an aesthetic choice of a particular kind defined by a consensus among programme creators and liberal intellectuals (more about this later). And for academic television studies, 'quality' is a descriptive term that identifies a television genre called quality drama. By the 1990s, Robert J. Thompson was able to argue that, 'quality [drama] has become a genre in itself, complete with its own set of formulaic characteristics' (1996: 16).

Thus there can be a serious conflict of interest among interpretive communities making judgements of quality regarding the same television programme. In order to illustrate the rhetoric of what appear to be primarily aesthetic judgements of quality, I would like to present an extended comparison between two more or less contemporary examples of shows I have already identified as possessing a quality audience: NBC's *The West Wing* and HBO's *Six Feet Under*. Contemporaneous with each other and often in close competition for the prestigious Emmy Awards (in 2003, for example, *Six Feet Under* received 16 nominations; *The West Wing* had 15), these programmes lay claim to defining quality drama today. As always with claims to 'quality', the discourse surrounding these shows contradicts an analysis of their structure. *The West Wing* almost perfectly conforms to Thompson's model for quality TV defined as a genre of television. Yet the discourse surrounding it works to separate it out from the rest of television. *Six Feet Under*, by contrast, conforms to the HBO model of being 'not TV'. It does this in the same way as other HBO dramas and in a way similar to the most famous network yuppie demographic 1980s show, *thirtysomething*. The claim to being 'not TV' is made by claiming to be something else: namely, art cinema or modernist theatre.

The West Wing adheres so closely to television's mainstream of quality drama from the 1980s and 1990s that I consider it almost a textbook case. The fact that the show claims to be totally unique and original only reinforces my point; quality drama always claims to be original in relation to the regular TV norms of its era. Yet generically speaking, an analysis of the first four episodes of the show reveals just about every 'formulaic characteristic' developed by quality drama in the 1980s and 1990s.

First of all, it is serialised (this always links quality drama to a potentially negative comparison to soap opera, as we shall see when we look at the reception context). Like all quality TV drama, *The West Wing* is a soap opera in terms of narrative structure although not in terms of melodramatic style. Like other quality dramas (and as sometimes happens on daytime and primetime soaps), it does not simply break down each segment into a standard number of separate storylines, but rather it attempts to juxtapose, interweave and orchestrate the plot threads together in a quasi-musical fashion. Aaron Sorkin has been praised for his ability to juxtapose storylines and vary levels of seriousness, sometimes through a startling juxtaposition, other times by a theme and variations rhythmic mingling of the different threads. For example, 'In Proportional Response' (1: 3) begins by picking up two major storylines from the end of 'Post Hoc, Ergo Propter Hoc' (1: 2), the death of Morris Tolliver (Ruben Santiago-Hudson) and the Sam Seaborn (Rob Lowe) call-girl incident, both of which have to be 'managed' by the White House. After the credits, a new thread, the hiring of Charlie Young (Dulé Hill) to be personal aide to the president is woven into a scene about the military response to Syria's downing of a military plane on which Tolliver was a passenger. However, *West Wing* executive producer John Wells had already employed these techniques on *China Beach* 10 years previously, even though he never gets mentioned as a *creative* contributor to *The West Wing*.

The West Wing uses a large ensemble cast who function as a family of co-workers, indeed—as was true of *Hill Street Blues* and *St. Elsewhere*—it is a supremely patriarchal family. The emphasis on bringing domesticity into the workplace does not distinguish this show from quality medical or cop shows; it is the type of work they do that differs, a distinction of subject matter rather than genre or structure.

In the quality tradition, *The West Wing* juxtaposes moments of comedy with scenes of high seriousness, often ending on an elegiac note. The first three episodes conclude with a 'presidential moment' in the oval office. Like *Hill Street Blues* and *thirtysomething*, the scripts employ elevated language and overlapping dialogue with many quick clever exchanges of wit. Certain recurring 'stock' scenes punctuate the episodes and give them regularity: for example, C.J. Cregg's (played by Alison Janney) press briefings echo the roll call scenes in *Hill Street Blues*.

The HBO 'not TV' series take a different stance towards the US network quality drama tradition. Following a less well-trodden path, these dramas want to avoid being associated with the quality drama genre. Tracking a minority tradition within quality drama but one identifiable from *Twin Peaks* and *thirtysomething*, *The Sopranos* and *Six Feet Under* rely on media other than television for their structure, even though both contain obvious elements of serialised narrative. David Chase originally wanted *The Sopranos* to be sold as a film and he considers each episode to be 'a little movie' (Longworth 2000). *Six Feet Under* is highly serialised, uses multiple storylines and an ensemble cast, but it too identifies stylistically with the non-televisual genre of European art cinema. This greater structural reliance on cinema is obvious from the opening credits. The imagistic *Six Feet Under* title sequence (by Digital Kitchen) is like a little art movie in itself and even merits a featurette on the US DVD release. The musical theme by second-generation Hollywood film composer Thomas Newman bears no resemblance to classic TV drama theme music. According to an internet source, 'Newman often utilizes a set of unusual and rare instruments alongside a standard symphony orchestra to create an enigmatic and highly unique sound that is both lush and pastoral, but infused with the rhythms and textures of world music' (Newman 2003). The sound of the *Six Feet Under* title theme is primarily comprised of a combination of piano and synthesised strings. The pizzicato-style strings come from a live orchestra. Viola and violin weave throughout and the melodic theme is performed by an 'evi' (electronic valve instrument), which sounds like a soprano clarinet. The instrumentation is said to sound 'African' (Newman 2005). *The West Wing*, on the other hand, follows in a tradition of television quality drama theme music, composed by W.G. 'Snuffy' Walden, known for his themes for such TV series as *thirtysomething, I'll Fly Away* and *My So-Called Life*, and *Once and Again* (i.e. the Zwick-Herskovitz franchise but also *Roseanne*). The featurette on the first season DVD describes how Walden composed the theme on guitar and then synthesised it for full orchestra to give it a more 'presidential' sound.

Six Feet Under's ancestry in television drama could not be clearer than in the little homage to television auteur Dennis Potter in 'The Foot' (1: 3).[1] In this sequence, Claire Fisher (Lauren Ambrose) walks into a realistic scene in the family kitchen and immediately goes into a musical number that might have been a direct quotation from *Pennies from Heaven*. In 'The New Person' (1: 10), David Fisher (Michael C. Hall) does the little Bob Fosse number, 'Got a Lot of Living To Do', like a number from *All That Jazz*, a film that tried to blend the dream sequences of a Fellini movie with a more native American show-business tradition—in form if not in content not unlike *American Beauty*. Not surprisingly, the actors who play Claire and David are accomplished musical comedy performers.

The use of paradigmatic narrative derived from TV soap opera, as opposed to the more linear narrative of the typical 'classical Hollywood film', structures *Six Feet Under* in a tradition of American television drama. The show's reliance on alternating storylines portrayed by a large ensemble cast was never clearer than in 'That's My Dog' (4: 5), when the writers attempted a more cinematic and linear mode of narration. David's abduction by a hitchhiker turns the multiple storyline format into a suspense thriller as the single narrative thread takes over the episode. Subsequent episodes detail the aftermath of David's attack and his post-traumatic stress, isolating his storyline from others in the ongoing family saga. Without the paradigmatic structure, David's storyline descends into a second-rate Hollywood thriller, but the writers must have felt that rendering the narrative more linear would make it more 'cinematic' and thus 'not TV', forgetting that quality drama was always 'not TV' but rather a peculiar elevation of soap opera narrative structure.

Beyond its avant-garde music, *Six Feet Under* reaches out to an entire tradition in modernist cinema that thematises life and death, dream and reality: the cinema of Federico Fellini, Ingmar Bergman and Alain Resnais, to name a few of its godfathers. In the second season premiere, Nate Fisher (Peter Krause) enters into a fantasy that his father is playing Chinese checkers with a man and a woman, who turn out to be Death (Stanley Kamel) and Life (Cleo King). This thinly veiled allusion to Antonius Block (Max von Sydow) playing chess with Death (Bengt Ekerot) in Bergman's *The Seventh Seal* (1955) serves to remind us that *Six Feet Under* shares the thematic materials of films that have been certified as serious art. But now the strained seriousness of the original film text is subject to postmodern parody as Life and Death attempt to hump each other. This use of dream diegesis has become a staple of art cinema. In *Seeing through the Eighties*, I traced the curious evolution by which the dream sequence—a staple of popular entertainment forms such as Hollywood musicals and soap operas—evolves via *thirtysomething* into the *dream diegesis*, a much more art cinematic confusion of levels between dream and reality (Feuer 1995: 86–92). Dream diegesis becomes a structural lynchpin of *Six Feet Under* in which the issue of dream or reality can be easily linked to the issue of dead or alive. Ghosts populate this show, with the father (Richard Jenkins) who died in the first episode appearing constantly in a nether status between dream and symbolism. The dead bodies that populate the show reappear as ghosts, most notably when the apparition of a dead gay boy (Marc Foster, played by Brian Poth) appears to David at the end of the first season in 'A Private Life' (1: 12) and spurs him to action in his coming-out dispute with the Episcopal Church.

Throughout its first season, *Six Feet Under* frequently relies upon a fantasy trope often used by Potter and also common to a long tradition of US quality drama. In these subjective wish-fulfilment point-of-view shots, characters see not reality but rather their desires. In 'An Open Book' (1: 5) and 'Knock, Knock' (1: 13), David's discomfort with his gayness in his role as a church deacon is expressed first by a point-of-view shot from the pulpit in which he imagines a congregation full of naked men, and later by a fantasy that the actual congregation applauds when he comes out to them. But David is not the only character to undergo subjectively portrayed wishes. Claire expresses her dissatisfaction with high school by making her math teacher's head explode and by imagining the popular girls reciting narratives about their futures ('Brotherhood', 1: 7). When Ruth Fisher (Frances Conroy) accidentally takes Ecstasy, she enters a desaturated, blue-filtered dream world complete with an appearance by the late Nate Sr ('Life's Too Short', 1: 9). Even without drug enhancement, Ruth fantasises that her Russian florist boyfriend (Ed O'Ross) appears in a military uniform when she is supposed to be on a date with Hiram Gunderson (Ed Begley Jr). In 'The Trip' (1: 11), her consciously avowed tolerance of David's homosexuality is belied by an image of her son having sadomasochistic sex with another man; in the fantasy she responds by squirting them with a very phallic garden hose.

In yet another manifestation of dream diegesis, dead characters or characters' past selves appear and interact in the present with live characters in a manner reminiscent of modernist theatre. Most notably, Nate Sr appears frequently throughout the show as a subjective memory image for other family members. Claire, for example, dreams that she is watching TV with him, she converses with her dad at Federico Diaz's (played by Freddy Rodriguez) son's christening party and imagines that her father is taking home movies of her ('Knock, Knock', 1: 13). Throughout season one Mark Foster haunts David, aiding him in his coming-out process, and Brenda repeatedly has flashes to scenes from the book her therapist wrote about her as a child, *Charlotte Light and Dark*.

Surely, though, the most extended use of dream diegesis occurs in the third season premiere ('Perfect Circles', 3: 1) in the form of Nate's 'dream' while undergoing brain surgery. Both this sequence and the less extensive Chinese checkers match that opens season two were directed by Rodrigo García, who is the son of Nobel Prize winner for Literature Gabriel García Márquez, a writer associated with the 'magical realist' style of twentieth-century fiction that David Lavery argues exerts a powerful influence on both *American Beauty* and *Six Feet Under* (2005a: 27–32). Some of the series' most surrealistic moments were his. Although, as Rodrigo García puts it in his DVD commentary for the season two premiere, Alan Ball 'moves in and out of reality and fantasy seamlessly', this effect is just as easily attributed to García's own direction of the show's most 'magical' dream diegeses. As Lavery puts it, 'When critics identified *American Beauty* as "magic realism", the plastic bag scene being key to the designation, and when *Six Feet Under* is similarly identified, is it not because of its comparable recognition—sometimes grotesque, sometimes fantastic—of "this entire life behind things"?' (27). He continues that 'Latin American authors such as Gabriel García Márquez, Julio Cortazar, Isabel Allende and Jorge Luis Borges have made "magic realism" a literary household phrase' (ibid), yet I would argue that it is a phrase that, to the American television viewing public, would still be considered a manifestation of high culture.

I am not going to analyse this sequence (as Lavery offers an extensive account as cited above) in the sense of trying to interpret what it means because structured ambiguity is always built into such sequences in art cinema. Suffice it to say that it used a *miseen-abyme* structure, at first implying to the audience that Nate has died but then revealing the dream diegesis to have its origins in Nate's unconscious state. I would identify this sequence as the most drastic example of *Six Feet Under*'s self-identification with modernist art cinema. Not only does *Six Feet Under* reference art cinema, the show also interprets itself as art cinema. It does this through self-promotion on HBO, through supplementary materials included on the DVD release and by encouraging critics such as Lavery to offer readings of it.

HBO has for a while used the clever technique of interdiegetically connecting its Sunday night shows in its promotions into a single, unified world. In its promotions, HBO shows us how savvy it is and how postmodern in that it interprets its own texts. Realising the pretentiousness of its claim to being 'Not TV', HBO has already parodied itself in the form of the water-cooler promos that claim that 'It's Not TV. It's H2O'. Allow me to quote from the self-promotional materials put out by the company that made the water-cooler ad:

HBO recently called upon Wonderland Productions' editorial, music, sound design and audio post services to help them create the critically acclaimed promo, 'Water-cooler'. This deadpan, mockumentary-style campaign credits the cable network's stellar line up of shows with bringing back banter around the office water cooler, and saving the US water cooler industry from oblivion.

Since producer/editor/composer Bill McCullough launched Wonderland in 2001, HBO has called upon him to execute the creative vision of promo campaigns through the post production process for a prestigious line up of shows, including Six Feet Under, Def Poetry *and* Angels in America. *'Watercooler' is the most recent HBO project to take advantage of the Soho-based boutique's collaborative, full-service approach to post production (*New York, NY, 25 March 2004*).*

As a savvy postmodern cable service, HBO is always one step ahead of critics who think that HBO doesn't know how obvious its 'not TV' campaign really was.

Moreover, just in case you miss the promos, creator Alan Ball's commentary on the DVD interprets the show for you as you watch it. It's like getting a little critic/auteur in the handsomely packaged DVD box. In his commentary on the first season finale, Ball points out some of his favourite symbolic shots. He informs us that a shot looking down a road echoes another 'tunnel' shot in the pilot and that this was a 'conscious choice' to symbolise the journey to death. He explains that the ghosts are not ghosts per se but rather 'a dramatic technique we use to portray the internal dialogue of the character'. For instance, Mark Foster's ghost 'articulates David's internal homophobia and self-loathing'.

So, HBO is a full-service cable service. It gives us texts that are not TV. It interprets them for us. It promotes them as art cinema. It punctures its own promotions to show how postmodern it is. It praises its promo spots as art cinema. It completely eliminates the need for this book. What is left for us critics to write about?

We might want to ask: how can a show so obviously making use of serialisation be 'not TV'? HBO might answer: because it uses serial form so clumsily and takes pride and brand recognition from its status as art cinema. That is exactly what *thirtysomething* did for the 1980s and exactly what placed that show outside the conventions of the quality television genre. What places *The West Wing* firmly in the centre of the quality TV genre is its smooth orchestration of storylines.

Yet interviews in the trade and popular press given by the creators of HBO drama make every attempt to reinforce the claim that their shows are *theatre* not TV. An August 2002 article in *Variety* quotes Alan Ball saying that writers like him, who come out of the theatre 'tend to have a more grounded understanding of structure and storytelling that's outside the standard TV paradigm' (Hofler 2002). Craig Wright, story editor for HBO, who had a new play *Water Flower Water* at the summer 2003 Contemporary American Theater Festival says that 'unlike other TV shows, which might be more explicitly plot-driven, a huge focus of *Six Feet Under* is to show the complexity of the people. That's what feels theatrical about the show to me' (quoted in Hofler 2002). Jill Soloway continues: 'As opposed to quick TV moments, the human conflicts are played out over time. We have those slower moments that you often see in a play' (ibid).

In case you were thinking of a few examples of those slower, more character-driven moments from quality dramas of the last 20 or so years, I should like to point out that the claim to theatricality is achieved through the erasure of a long tradition of quality TV drama that *is* TV. My point is borne out by an astonishing story in *USA Today* right after Sorkin left *The West Wing* (Bianco 2003). The article claims that 'the thrill is gone' for having allowed hack TV people like John Wells and John Sacret Young to take over from Sorkin. I am not going to cast my vote as to whether the thrill was gone before or after Sorkin left. I just want to point out that two of the prime architects of quality drama responsible for the last season of *China Beach* and the first season of *ER* have been relegated to the status of game-show producers, while Sorkin replaces them rhetorically as a unique authorial voice.

Although *The West Wing* follows the tradition of a serialised orchestration of quality drama perhaps to the same level as had *China Beach* and *ER*, rhetorically—in competition with *The Bachelor*—it still gets to be 'not TV'. If reality TV is said to be 'unscripted', *The West Wing* achieves its reputation by being perhaps the most 'scripted' text to appear on turn of the century network television. This comes from the stature given to Aaron Sorkin as a TV-outsider auteur. For instance, when *The West Wing* was taking its lumps from the press for losing its prized 18–34-year-old female viewers to *The Bachelor* in the fall of 2002, Aaron Sorkin gave a tongue-in-cheek interview to *Newsweek* saying he TiVos his own show but he *watches The Bachelor*. Sorkin then confesses, of course, that he's never really seen the reality show but 'we understand that some of the younger women have gone to *The Bachelor* so instead of starting our episodes with a recap, what we'll be doing is having Janel Moloney marry a millionaire celebrity boxer. There's gonna be a quick ceremony Then they're gonna eat worms' (Anon 2002). Obviously he has never watched *The Bachelor* because he has confused it with stereotypes from other reality shows. But then there is no cultural capital for Sorkin in knowing the nuances of reality TV. In fact he knows that his cultural capital lies in not knowing anything about reality TV.

Reality TV is the great other to quality drama. Yet discursively, reality TV can also be authored, as proven by the well-known branding of producer Mark Burnett's franchise on *Survivor* and now on *The Apprentice*. Read this from Burnett's bio on the NBC website:

> *One of the driving forces behind reality television and a true visionary, Mark Burnett has a long history of executive producing Emmy Award-winning television in international locations. Burnett's entrepreneurial spirit pioneered the success of the reality 'unscripted' drama series, garnered skyrocketing ratings and introduced millions of Americans to an entirely new television genre (NBC website).*

Since reality TV is arguably no more or less 'original' than HBO drama and since both genres have their authors and geniuses, why should one form have so much more artistic status than the other? Both are what Todd Gitlin (2000) called 'recombined' forms of television. The reality show merges certain forms of documentary with the game show and the soap opera. Quality drama merged soap opera with an established genre such as the cop show or the medical series. HBO drama merges series or serialised TV with postmodern theatre or art cinema. And there's the rub. To the interpretive community that *writes* about TV, and who share a field of reference with those who create quality TV but not reality TV, only certain re-combinations matter.

I believe I have demonstrated that there is nothing 'new' or 'original' generically between HBO drama and the television tradition of quality drama that cannot be ascribed to an equally generic tradition of art cinema. Thus we can locate a gap—I am even tempted to call it a contradiction—between the textual analysis of quality drama and its discursive context.

Index